Honkers and
Shouters

other works by arnold shaw

AUTHOR:

Belafonte, An Unauthorized Biography
The Rock Revolution
The Rockin' 50s
Sinatra: Twentieth Century Romantic
52nd St.: The Street of Jazz (originally published as
    The Street That Never Slept: N.Y.'s Fabled 52d St.)
The World of Soul

COMPOSER:

The Bubble-Gum Waltzes
Mobiles, 10 Graphic Impressions for Piano
The Mod Moppet, 7 Nursery Rip-Offs for Piano
Plabiles, 12 Songs Without Words for Piano
Sing A Song of Americans. Lyrics by Rosemary & Stephen Vincent Benet
Stabiles, 12 Images for Piano
A Whirl of Waltzes

Honkers and Shouters

arnold shaw

THE GOLDEN YEARS OF RHYTHM AND BLUES

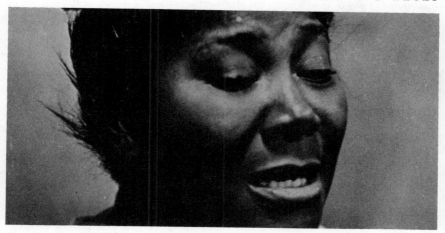

Macmillan Publishing Co., Inc.   *new york*

To the memory of DINAH WASHINGTON, T-BONE WALKER, and LOUIS JORDAN, and to all the great blues singers who helped give depth and height to American popular music.

Macmillan Publishing Co., Inc.
866 Third Avenue, New York, N.Y.   10022
Collier Macmillan Canada, Ltd.

Library of Congress Cataloging in Publication Data
Shaw, Arnold.
    Honkers & shouters.
    Bibliography: p.
    Includes index.
    1. Blues (Songs, etc.)—United States—History
and criticism. I. Title.
ML3561.B63S53   784   77-18511
ISBN 0-02-610000-2

First Printing 1978

Designed by Jack Meserole

Printed in the United States of America

contents

acknowledgments   xi

introduction: **Anatomy of Rhythm and Blues**   xv

Rhythm and Blues Under Fire   xxiii

1. The Roots

Leroy Carr and Tampa Red   3

Mamie Smith · Leroy Carr · Tampa Red · Thomas A. Dorsey (Georgia Tom) · Blind Boy Fuller

Spats and a Washboard—and Hokum   11

Lonnie Johnson · Roosevelt Sykes · John Lee (Sonny Boy) Williamson · Jazz Gillum · Washboard Sam

Big Bill Broonzy   19

Memphis Minnie · Kansas Joe · Lester Melrose

Uprights in the Turpentine, Lumber, and Levee Camps   27

Speckled Red · Little Brother Montgomery · Sunnyland Slim · Big Boy Crudup

The Ballin' Towns   36

St. Louis Jimmy · Robert Johnson · Champion Jack Dupree · Memphis Slim · Joe Turner · Pete Johnson · Jimmy Rushing

The Boogie Woogie Craze, and 1938   51

Pine Top Smith · Jimmy Yancey · Meade Lux Lewis · Albert Ammons · Count Basie · Billie Holiday · Slim & Slam

Blues Bands—and Louis Jordan   57

Lionel Hampton Band · Lucky Millinder · Erskine Hawkins · Cab Calloway · Louis Jordan

groove 1   **LOUIS JORDAN** / 65

groove 2   **BERLE ADAMS** / 76

2. The Components

Pvt. Cecil Gant and the "Sepia Sinatras"   89
Cecil Gant · Charles Brown · Lowell Fulson · Ivory Joe Hunter · Amos Milburn · Charles Brown · Roy Brown · Roy Milton

groove 3   **LOWELL FULSON** / 104

T-Bone Walker and the Electric Guitar   113
T-Bone Walker · Lester Sill · Eddie Durham · Charlie Christian · Les Hite · Freddie Slack

groove 4   **AARON "T-BONE" WALKER** / 117

Black Is Green: Preconditions for the Rise of R & B   123

Pioneer R & B Labels and Groups   129
Leon and Otis René · Joe Liggins · Eli Oberstein · The Mississippi Sheiks · Joe Davis · Una Mae Carlisle · The Five Red Caps · Savannah Churchill · The Four Tunes · Pete Johnson · Joe Turner · Herb Abramson · The Ravens · Sonny Til & the Orioles · The Five Royales · Bobby Freeman · The Larks · Mahalia Jackson · Wynonie Harris

groove 5   **BOBBY SHAD** / 140

Gospel Song, and Dinah Washington   144
Sallie Martin · Dinah Washington · Clyde Otis · Fred Norman · Thomas A. Dorsey · Gatemouth Moore

groove 6   **LEON RENÉ** / 150

groove 7   **JOHNNY OTIS** / 158

The Honkers   168
Paul Williams · Big Jay McNeely · Illinois Jacquet · Earl Bostic · Bill Doggett · Clifford Scott · Maxwell Davis · Rudi Pompanelli · Sam "The Man" Taylor · Sam Butera · King Curtis

3. The California Cataclysm

Record Company in a Cigar Box 179

Art Rupe · The Sepia Tones · Roy Milton · Jimmy Beard · Greg Lee · Jack Gutshall · Jimmy Liggins · Camille Howard · The Soul Stirrers · Lloyd Price · Larry Williams · Little Richard · Joe Liggins · Percy Mayfield · Sam Cooke

Record Company on a Railroad Track 194

Bihari Brothers · Hadda Brooks · Lester Sill · Johnny Dolphin · Hunter Hancock · Smokey Hogg · Pee Wee Crayton · Roy Hawkins · John Lee Hooker · Elmore James · Ike Turner · Jimmy Witherspoon · B. B. King · Shirley Gunter & The Queens · The Teen Queens · The Cadets · The Jacks · Etta James · Jesse Belvin

groove 8 **JIMMY WITHERSPOON** / 211

groove 9 **B. B. KING** / 216

Two Other Family-Owned Record "Indies" 226

Jack McVea · Paul Reiner · Ralph Bass · Mesner Brothers · Helen Humes · Amos Milburn · Charles Brown · Lightnin' Hopkins · Floyd Dixon · Peppermint Harris · Thurston Harris · The Five Keys · Shirley & Lee · Gene & Eunice

groove 10 **RALPH BASS** / 235

Bay Area Blues 247

Bob Geddins · Lowell Fulson · Jimmy McCracklin · Roy Hawkins · Lafayette Thomas · Johnny Fuller · Jimmy Wilson · Chris Strachwitz · Mance Lipscomb · Big Joe Williams · Big Jay McNeely · Clifton Chenier

From Fats Domino to Sam Cooke 261

Lew Chudd · Antoine "Fats" Domino · Dave Bartholomew · Ricky Nelson · Smiley Lewis · The Spiders · Dootsie Williams · The Penguins · The Medallions · The Meadowlarks · Randy Wood · The Del-Vikings · The Soul Stirrers · Sam Cooke

4. The Midwest Mavericks

Record Company in an Icehouse   275

Syd Nathan · Lucky Millinder · Bull Moose Jackson · Henry Glover · Tiny Bradshaw · Bill Doggett · Lonnie Johnson · Ivory Joe Hunter · Wynonie "Mr. Blues" Harris · Ralph Bass · Billy Ward and the Dominoes · The Charms · The Five Royales · Lowman Pauling · The Midnighters · Hank Ballard · Little Willie John · James Brown

Storefront Record Company   289

Chess Brothers · Gene Ammons · Willie Mabon · Willie Dixon · Etta James · Muddy Waters · Howlin' Wolf · Bo Diddley · Little Walter · The Moonglows · The Flamingos · Otis Rush

Chicago's Black-Owned Record Company   315

James Bracken · Vivian Carter Bracken · Calvin Carter · The Spaniels · The El Dorados · The Dells · Gladys Knight & the Pips · Jimmy Reed · John Lee Hooker · The Diablos · Jerry Butler · Curtis Mayfield · Dee Clark · Betty Everett · Gene Chandler · Joseph Brown · Eddie Boyd

groove 11   **RANDY WOOD** / 327

5. East Coast R & B

Savoy Records of Newark, New Jersey   343

Herman Lubinsky · Teddy Reig · Lee Magid · Ralph Bass · Little Esther (Phillips) · Mel Walker · Johnny Otis · Big Maybelle · Varetta Dillard · Nappy Brown

groove 12   **FRED MENDELSOHN** / 353

groove 13   **LEE MAGID** / 358

Lenox Avenue and Broadway R & B   370

Ahmet Ertegun · Herb Abramson · Joe Morris · Stick McGee · Jerry Wexler · Ruth Brown · La Vern Baker · Joe Turner · Nugetre · Ray Charles · Clyde McPhatter · The Drifters · Ben E. King · Chuck Willis · The Clovers · The Coasters · Leiber and Stoller · Phil Spector · Tommy Dowd

groove 14 AHMET ERTEGUN / 395

groove 15 RUTH BROWN / 398

groove 16 JERRY WEXLER / 410

groove 17 LESTER SILL / 415

groove 18 OSCAR COHEN / 419

The Street-Corner Groups and the NY "Indies" 422

The Cadillacs · The Majors · The Four Fellows · The Harptones · George Goldner · The Crows · Frankie Lymon & the Teenagers · The Valentines · Richard Barrett · The Cleftones · The Chantels · The Flamingos · Little Anthony & the Imperials · Bobby Robinson · The Vocaleers · Wilbert Harrison · Buster Brown · Bobby Marchan · Lee Dorsey · Gladys Knight & the Pips · King Curtis · Screamin' Jay Hawkins · Jackie Wilson

groove 19 JACKIE WILSON / 441

groove 20 DANNY KESSLER AND OKeh RECORDS / 445

groove 21 AL SILVER AND HERALD RECORDS / 450

groove 22 BOB ROLONTZ AND GROOVE RECORDS / 460

groove 23 SAM WEISS AND OLD TOWN RECORDS / 466

groove 24 SOL RABINOWITZ AND BATON RECORDS / 470

The Philadelphia Scene 472

Dick Clark · Charlie Gracie · The Rays · Chubby Checker · Billie & Lillie · Freddy Cannon · Duane Eddy

6. Down-South R & B

The Black-Owned Texas Company 479

Don Robey · Gatemouth Brown · The Five Blind Boys · The Bells of Joy · Marie Adams · Johnny Ace · Big Mama Thornton · Bobby "Blue" Bland · Little Junior Parker · Jimmy Clanton

From Nashville to New Orleans 489

Ernie Young · Arthur Gunter · Louis Brooks & His Hi-Toppers · The Marigolds · The Gladiolas · The Crescendos · Lonesome Sundown · Lightnin' Slim · Slim Harpo · Earl King · Frankie Ford · Professor Longhair

Sun Records 496

Sam Phillips · Col. Tom Parker · Elvis Presley · Rufus Thomas

7. The Disk Jockey Scene

"King of the Moon Doggers"   507
Alan Freed · Huggie Boy · Hunter Hancock · Al Benson

groove 25   **HUNTER HANCOCK** / 518

Coda. The End of an Era

The R & B Revival   523

discography   529

select bibliography   542

index   543

acknowledgments

In 1945, when I joined Leeds Music Corporation, now MCA Music, as director of publicity and advertising, the company was dedicated to promoting a Cecil Gant recording of "I Wonder." Except for some of Louis Jordan's records—and he recorded a number of Leeds publications, including "Is You Is, or Is You Ain't (Ma' Baby)?"—the Gant disk was crucial in igniting the rhythm and blues explosion of the mid-40s. Thus, I had the good fortune to begin my career in the music business with a firm whose office was frequented by such blues notables as J. Mayo Williams, pioneer black recording manager of Paramount Records and later of Decca; singer-songwriter Alberta Hunter, author of "Down-Hearted Blues"; songwriter Perry Bradford, who helped launch the blues craze of the 1920s with "Crazy Blues," as recorded by Mamie Smith; and many others. I am indebted to all of them, as well as to Lou Levy, founder and president of Leeds, for arousing my interest in and initiating my understanding of black music.

In the 1950s I became part of the R & B scene as a music executive and as a producer of R & B records. I owe a debt to the late Steve Sholes of RCA Victor and the late Syd Nathan of King Records, both of whom released masters I produced and, in the case of Sholes, arranged for me to produce records in the RCA Victor studios.

This book had its beginnings in the 1960s when I wrote articles for special editions of *Billboard*'s "World of Soul" on assignment by Paul Ackerman, editor emeritus of the publication. I remember Paul, not only for these assignments, but because he was a most stimulating luncheon companion who shared my interest in English literature as well as contemporary music. Let me also mention with gratitude Hal Cook, publisher emeritus of *Billboard,* who made it possible for me to Xerox several thousand pages of the magazine, saving me countless hours of research time.

My indebtedness to various R & B record company owners, producers, songwriters, managers, and artists is quite apparent in the titles of the twenty-five grooves (taped interviews) appearing in this book. I was particularly fortunate in being able to talk and tape with T-Bone Walker and Louis Jordan, both of whom died while this book was being written. During my years in the music business, I also had the good fortune to gather insights and information from Jerry Blaine of

Jubilee Records, Syd Nathan of King Records, Herman Lubinsky of Savoy, critic Ralph J. Gleason (later of *Rolling Stone*), Leonard Chess of Chess Records, Saul Bihari of Modern Records, disk jockey Alan Freed, singer Dinah Washington, and Joe Glaser of Associated Booking Corporation, all of whom, I regret, are no longer with us.

Among others whose help I would like to acknowledge—help given through taped interviews, conversations, or correspondence—are Herb Abramson, A & R director of National Records and co-founder of Atlantic Records; Al Berman, managing director of the Harry Fox Agency; Ruth Bowen, president of Queen Booking Corporation; Bob Braun of Cincinnati's 50-50 Club; singer James Brown; Oscar Cohen, president, and Art Engler, both of Associated Booking Corporation; Lewis Chudd, founder of Imperial Records; arranger Morty Craft of Melba Records; Joe Delaney, formerly of Decca and London Records and now a well-known Las Vegas newspaper, radio, and TV commentator; author Dave Dexter, formerly of Capitol Records and now a *Billboard* staffer; singer-songwriter Bo Diddley; engineer and record producer Tom Dowd of Atlantic Records; producer Milt Gabler, formerly of Decca Records; Bob Geddins, record producer and songwriter of the San Francisco Bay Area; Henry Glover, songwriter and A & R chieftain of King and Roulette Records; John Hammond, celebrated talent scout of Columbia Records; David Kapp, former A & R chief of Decca, RCA Victor, and Kapp Records, the last of which he founded; Paul Kapp, former manager of the Delta Rhythm Boys; Larry Newton of Derby Records and now director of the Ray Charles record complex; Sam Phillips of Sun Records; singer Della Reese; Phil Rose, formerly of Glory Records; Art Rupe, founder and president of Specialty Records; Russ Sanjek, vice-president of BMI; Herm Schoenfeld of *Variety*; publicist Jim Seagrave, an avid R & B fan; Joel Selvin of the San Francisco *Chronicle*, who was most instrumental in broadening my knowledge of Bay Area blues; Bobby Shad, formerly of Mercury Records and now owner of Time/Mainstream Records; Johnny Sippell of *Billboard*; Chris Strachwitz, founder of Arhoolie Records and blues connoisseur; Art Talmadge, formerly of Mercury Records and now of Musicor Records; Hy Weiss of Old Town Records; and Bill Willard of *Daily Variety*.

Since the blues grew as a folk art, a treasure trove of material existed before records and publication gave the songs a more permanent form than that emerging from oral transmission. I have followed the procedure of other historians and scholars in associating a given song with the performer who created an appealing recording or performed it constantly. I can only hope that I have not slighted one creative artist as against another in the credits. I have also sedulously tried to identify copyright material and am pleased to present the following list of songs, brief excerpts of which I have used to illumine the text.

"Blues Before Sunrise." Words and music by Leroy Carr. Copyright 1950, 1963 by Leeds Music Corporation.

"It's Too Short." Words and music by W. R. Calaway and C. Williams. Copyright 1934 by Pickwick Music Corporation.

"Chicago Blues." Words and music by Lonnie Johnson. Copyright 1962 by Leeds Music Corporation.

"The Dirty Dozens." Words and music by Rufus Perryman. Copyright 1929 by MCA Music. Also words and music by J. Mayo Williams and Rufus Perryman. Copyright 1929, 1930 by Leeds Music Corporation. Copyright renewed 1956, 1957 and assigned to Leeds Music Corporation.

"Mean Old Frisco Blues." Words and music by Arthur Crudup. Copyright 1947, 1963 by Duchess Music Corporation.

"Heavy Heart Blues." Words and music by Champion Jack Dupree. Copyright 1941 by Wabash Music, Inc.

"Roll 'Em Pete." Words and music by Pete Johnson and Joe Turner. Copyright 1941, 1963 by Leeds Music Corporation.

"Low Down Dog." Words and music by Joe Turner. Copyright 1948 by St. Louis Music.

"Nobody in Mind." Words and music by Joe Turner. Copyright 1960 by Unichappell Music.

"I Wonder." Words and music by Cecil Gant and Raymond Leveen. Copyright 1944 by Leeds Music Corporation.

"Sixty Minute Man." Words and music by William Ward and Rose Marks. Copyright 1951 by Armo Music Corporation.

"The Huckle Buck." Words by Roy Alfred. Music by Andy Gibson. Copyright 1948 by United Music Corporation.

"Home Is Where the Hatred Is." Words and music by Gil Scott-Heron. Copyright 1971 by Bob Thiele Music, Ltd.

"Yakety Yak." Words and music by Jerry Leiber and Mike Stoller. Copyright 1958 by Tiger Music, Inc.

I would feel remiss if I did not acknowledge Bruce Carrick, whose enthusiasm nurtured the book in its early stages; Ken Stuart, whose sensitive and dedicated reading of the manuscript influenced its present shape and content; and Beth Rashbaum, who brought the project to fruition. I wish also to thank my young daughter Mindy Sura for keeping the dial of my car radio tuned to local rock stations (even when I wanted to hear the news) so that my ear for R & B was sharpened by daily contact with contrasting, current black styles.

ARNOLD SHAW

Las Vegas
June 1974

introduction

Anatomy of Rhythm and Blues

Young people of today sometimes think of their music as if it were an original creation of the Elvis Presley/Pat Boone generation of the 1950s. But Presley would have been the first to acknowledge that he was the musical son of a cotton-picking, Mississippi, rhythm-and-bluesman, Arthur "Big Boy" Crudup, and that his musical progenitors included such R & B singers as Little Richard and Big Mama Thornton, whose raucous styles he imitated and whose songs he recorded. The fact is that in its beginnings rock 'n' roll was derivative rhythm and blues—and today's mainstream, like the color of my true love's hair, is preponderantly black. Yet the relation of R & B to the past and its contribution to the future have been slighted, and until now there has been no comprehensive history of its rise and development.

The term *Rhythm and Blues* came into use in the late '40s after *Billboard* magazine substituted it for *race*. The trade magazine made the change in its issue of June 25, 1949, in a chart headed until then "Top 15 Best Selling Race Records." The term *race records* had been in use since 1920 when a best-selling OKeh record of "Crazy Blues" by Mamie Smith stirred the disk companies of the day to record the black female vaudeville artists, later known as the classic blues singers. In time the term became a catchall for any type of recording by a black artist—jazz, folk, pop, big band. When World War II sensitized people to the pejorative overtones of the term, *rhythm and blues* came into being—and it, too, came to be used as a convenient catchall.

In this book I am concerned with R & B as an indigenous black art form and style—not with its rock derivatives, nor with its revival in the late '60s, nor with soul music. The focus is on the era, post-swing to pre-Beatles (1945–60), when the style flowered and established itself as an identifiable sound. The emphasis is on the artists, writers, and singing groups that created it and on the record producers and companies that nurtured it. Not too long ago, a *Rolling Stone* reviewer wrote: "The term R & B first came into general usage as a postwar euphemism for what had been known as 'race records.' " By the time it came into general use, R & B was not a euphemism for something else. It *was* something else: a different quantity, esthetically, chronologically, and sociologically, and it is the unique differences with which I am concerned.

If the blues was trouble music and urban blues adjustment song, then R & B was good-time dance music. If the blues was rural song and urban blues city music, R & B was black ghetto music. If the blues was loneliness and self-expression song, and urban blues nostalgia and growing music, then R & B was group and joy music. If the country bluesman wailed and the urban bluesman sang, the rhythm and bluesman shouted—and soulmen howled and screamed. Country and delta blues were a man and his guitar (sometimes with harmonica added); urban bluesmen were backed by guitar and/or piano, bass, and drums; rhythm and bluesmen sang to combo accompaniment and electrified instruments. These are brittle metaphors. They illuminate, but they also blind. Offering sharp, provocative distinctions, they blur similarities, transitional qualities, variants, and shadings that are necessary to a full understanding, which is what I hope the text will provide.

R & B came roaring out of the churches of black America, the black bands of the swing era, and the segregated ghettos of big cities. Gospel song, heard in storefront, Sanctified, and shouting Baptist churches, gave it intensity and excitement. The black bands contributed the beat and the boogie, and nurtured the singers who became solo artists. The ghettos created the climate and provided the incentive for poor, young blacks.

Economically, R & B was a product of the jukebox, the shortage of disks in black locations, and the rising purchasing power of black people during and after World War II. Technologically, R & B was made possible by the development of tape recording, a process that brought the cost of making masters within the reach of small entrepreneurs. Psychologically, it was an expression of a people enjoying a new sense of freedom, hemmed in though that freedom was by ghettos. R & B disks helped blacks establish a new identity—the kind that led a little old black lady to refuse to yield her seat to a white in an Alabama bus; that led to the rise of Martin Luther King, Jr.; and that resulted in the 1954 Supreme Court ruling on school desegregation.

The explosion came in Los Angeles as we were nearing the end of World War II. "Now, R & B started here in LA," Johnny Otis has said. "Roy Milton was here, Joe Liggins was here, T-Bone Walker was here, Charles Brown was here, I was here, and others, too. By forty-eight or forty-nine it was set—we had an art form, though we didn't know it then."

The word *started* poses a problem, for truth to speak, R & B was germinating in New York in the early '40s. Pioneer record labels like Beacon, Savoy, Keynote, Varsity, DeLuxe, and National were aiming their product at Harlem, Newark, and the black ghettos of neighboring cities. The peak of the development came in the early '50s with the emergence of labels like Chess in Chicago, King in Cincinnati, Peacock in Houston, Modern, Imperial, and Specialty in LA, and Atlantic in New York.

As Mamie Smith's disk of "Crazy Blues" ignited the blues explosion of the 1920s, so Pvt. Cecil Gant's best-selling record of "I Wonder" gave impetus to the rise of independent record labels in 1945. A year later, Louis Jordan, the "Father of R & B," scored a million-seller in "Choo Choo Ch'Boogie" and R & B found in his Tympany Five its meter (boogie/shuffle) and its sound (horns *cum* rhythm). Each of these records was a crossover, just as R & B, written by blacks, played and sung by blacks, and directed at a black audience, was to strive for white acceptance. But—and this is the vital fact about R & B —groups like the Orioles, the Crows, the Moonglows, and the Drifters, to name just a few, achieved that acceptance on their own terms, unlike the Ink Spots and the Mills Brothers, who had sugared their style for white palates.

R & B was liberated music, which in its pristine form represented a break with white, mainstream pop. Developing from black sources, it embodied the fervor of gospel music, the throbbing vigor of boogie woogie, the jump beat of swing, and the gutsiness and sexuality of life in the black ghetto.

The roots of R & B (Part I) run deep in the black earth of slavery, during which religion gave Negroes a sense of their identity and worth and the spirituals vibrated with the hope of deliverance. But the most immediate antecedents of R & B were the country bluesmen who migrated from the South in the '20s and, having worked the battered uprights in turpentine, lumber, and levee camps, settled in ballin' towns like St. Louis, Kansas City, Memphis, and especially Chicago, where flourishing recording studios gave circulation to their creations. Reacting to their new environment, they reshaped their material, converting the melancholy blues of Blind Lemon Jefferson, the prison blues of Bukka White, and the cry-for-a-handout blues of all itinerant country bluesmen into the more sophisticated urban blues of Big Bill Broonzy, Joe Turner, and Roosevelt Sykes.

The most important source of R & B was gospel music, whose repertoire, form, and style left an indelible imprint. There are no 12-bar blues in R & B, but the 8-bar form of pop and gospel, as well as its 16-bar form, are a commonplace. As Ben E. King, assisted by Leiber and Stoller, secularized the gospel hymn "Stand By Me" and produced an R & B standard; so Hank Ballard, Etta James, Ray Charles, and scores of other black writers substituted the flesh for the spirit in gospel songs to create R & B hits. But they maintained the fervor of the originals and thereby gave R & B an exuberance and driving energy that captured young white ears in the '50s and powered the revolution that turned pop music upside down. The spiritual jubilation of gospel song erupted into Louis Jordan's pagan "Let the Good Times Roll," and "My Jesus Is All the World to Me" became Ray Charles' "I Got a Woman."

By the end of World War II, all the components of the new style (Part 2) were available for synthesis. When a bluesman shouted to the accompaniment of a honking tenor sax and oscillating electric guitar, energized by a boogie beat or a hopping shuffle, that was R & B. The style had its soulful ballad strain, with a drifting Charles Brown and other "sepia Sinatras" preparing the way for the intense romanticism of Dinah Washington and Sam Cooke. Johnny Otis, performer and impresario, and producers Ralph Bass, Bobby Shad, Randy Wood, Art Rupe, Lee Magid, and Lester Sill all tell it like it happened in interviews I taped with them.

Once the restrictions on shellac (used to surface records) were lifted after World War II, independent record companies sprang up to meet the demands of blacks, still unwelcome in white theaters and clubs, for home and jukebox entertainment. Art Rupe started Specialty Records in a cigar box—literally. Syd Nathan set up King Records in a defunct Cincinnati icehouse. The Chess brothers began making records in the back of a Chicago storefront office, using their toilet as an echo chamber. Ahmet Ertegun and Jerry Wexler converted their fourth-floor Manhattan office into a studio by pushing aside and stacking their desks. Like Modern and Chess, many started as family enterprises, and a handful like Atlantic and Savoy, as well as the Bihari and Chess labels, developed into million-dollar corporations. The rise of small R & B record companies during the '40s and '50s constitutes one of the most remarkable and fascinating chapters in the history, not only of American music, but of small business in this country.

Equally amazing was the growth of the so-called "doo-wop" sing-ing groups whose sounds dominated R & B in the '50s. To call them street-corner groups is no misnomer; indeed, that was where The Drifters, The Harptones, and The Penguins congregated, thereafter using school yards, subway stations, park benches, and tenement hallways and stoops as free rehearsal halls. Other than sports and crime, singing was the major route by which underprivileged blacks could escape the degradation of second-class citizenship. There were literally thousands of these groups so that the streets of Harlem, Watts, and other ghetto areas became one huge arena of black song. Prowled by record producers, the ghettos, along with amateur night at New York's Apollo Theatre, became hunting grounds for new talent.

So long as R & B remained a black ghetto music, it was disregarded by the white establishment—parental, religious, and radio. But when white youngsters began buying R & B disks and attending black bashes like those disk jockey Alan Freed sponsored in the Cleveland area and later in New York, all phalanxes of the white world mounted an attack. Criticism, censorship, bans, and outright destruction of records reached a peak in the payola investigations of 1959–60. Alan Freed, who revolutionized the announcing style of disk jockeys and who was responsible for naming the bastard child of rhythm and blues "rock 'n' roll," became a major target and victim. R & B suffered a temporary decline until the Beatles, Rolling Stones, and other English groups appeared on the American scene to acknowledge their musical debt to the great rhythm-and-bluesmen, to record their songs, and to sponsor appearances by them. The R & B revival of the late sixties followed. But during 1964 *Billboard* eliminated R & B charts to avoid duplication, as R & B records, sweetened by the use of strings and polished arrangements, became regular crossovers into pop.

R & B has been criticized as vulgar. Partisans of the style prefer to call it "earthy," "funky," and "down-home." LeRoi Jones has maintained that its vulgarity assured its "meaningful and emotional connection with people's lives." But Jones regards R & B as less per-sonal than the older forms of the blues because the pounding rhythm subverts the lyric content, it is more easily faked, and performance tends to monotony.

Valid as these criticisms are, they should be weighed against R & B's tremendous assets. It stemmed from a rich, indigenous folk tradition, whereas pop music was a mishmash of European influences. For Tin Pan Alley's June/moon romanticism and saccharine sentimentality, it substituted a harsh, if earthy, realism. Its artlessness, a product of fumbling amateurs, introduced an experimental freshness. Body music rather than head or heart music, R & B achieved social commentary in comic playlets like The Coasters' "Yakety-Yak" and "Charlie Brown."

More than anything else, R & B brought vitality into pop music—such vitality that it overwhelmed a generation of teenagers, white as well as black, European as well as American. Nor should we underrate the communication and rapport it promoted between young whites and blacks, a musical rapprochement still to be realized in other walks of American life.

A word about the grooves, as I call the twenty-five taped interviews that appear in this book. There are really many more, but as in the case of Joe Bihari of Modern Records and Art Rupe of Specialty Records, they sometimes appear in chapters. It was singer Bonnie Raitt, "Daughter of the Blues," as she was called in a *Rolling Stone* headline, who crystallized something I had been feeling but could not find words for. "There's something awkward," she said, "about getting close to old people, you're just asking for so much heartache. You know they're gonna die, and you watch them not get appreciated and you know the time's coming."

That was the way I felt when I talked with T-Bone Walker and Louis Jordan in what are, I believe, the last interviews they gave before they died. T-Bone, who didn't look ill, just said: "I havin' the dizzy spells." And Louis Jordan, who was quite effervescent, sat sunning himself in his backyard, copper bracelets on his wrists and ankles in a struggle against arthritis. And there was Saul Bihari, whom I could not see because he lay dying in a hospital, made a vegetable by a crippling stroke; instead, his brother Joe described to me the birth and growth of Modern Records. And Herman Lubinsky, with whom I corresponded, having dealt with him during the R & B years, but who died before I went to New York to interview him and other record makers.

All of these men were part of that vigorous upsurge of black music that occurred during and after World War II. It was a devastating experience for me to see them in their declining days. Or, as I worked on this book, to read of their deaths: Ivory Joe Hunter, who had submitted songs to me: Don Robey of Peacock Records; tenorman Gene "Jug" Ammons; Arthur "Big Boy" Crudup; the great Howlin' Wolf; swamp bluesman Lightnin' Slim, and others. In a way, the most disturbing "death" was that of Harlem's Apollo Theatre. It did not shutter its doors, but sometime in 1976 the shrine of black music stopped presenting live talent and discontinued the Wednesday evening amateur nights, the springboard for decades of some of the greatest artists in American pop music.

By the same token, it was a stirring experience to talk and tape with Jimmy Witherspoon, who had his biggest record in 1949, "Ain't Nobody's Business," and who is still a vigorous performer; Lowell Fulson, whose biggest seller, "Blue Shadows," came out in 1950 and who has just recorded a new album, which I had the joy of annotating; B. B. King, who first made the charts in '51 with "Three O'Clock Blues" and who continues to tour and perform in major showrooms eleven months of the year; Johnny Otis, that extraordinary man and artist, who had a flock of hits in 1950 and who continues to produce R & B records as well as perform; and Jackie Wilson, a dynamo of energy the night I saw and interviewed him, but who has since suffered a near-fatal heart attack.

Further to document the development of the art, I taped interviews with as many record producers as would cooperate—creative men like Ahmet Ertegun and Jerry Wexler of Atlantic Records, pioneer Leon René of Exclusive Records, Al Silver of Herald Records, Sol Rabinowitz of Baton Records, and others. The inside view of record-making that emerges from these grooves offers, I hope, an unusual, in-depth picture of the search for talent and material; the travail of cutting a record; the complexities of dealing with artists, writers, and disk jockeys; the difficulties of promoting a new disk; and the business side of being a small independent and trying to build a record company with black artists in a white world.

.

I have used the word *black* throughout the book, except for the early section, which deals with developments of the '20s and '30s. As the reader may know, *Negro* was then the customary term and, as one of the artists I interviewed noted, *black* was then a term of opprobrium. In short, I use *Negro* only for historical reasons. By the same token, I know that LeRoi Jones has adopted the name Imamu Amiri Baraka and prefers to be known by it. Unfortunately, the book to which I refer is still in print under his old name and I have used it, without meaning any disrespect, simply for that reason.

.

Writing this book has been a journey backward in time, not only in terms of the subject matter but also of my own working career in the pop music field from 1944 to 1966. Two years after I joined Leeds Music Corporation in the spring of 1945, *The New York Times Magazine* printed my first article on pop music. It concerned "Open the Door, Richard," a novelty R & B smash that involved a large cast of black artists, including tenor saxist Jack McVea, vaudevillians Dusty Fletcher and John Mason, Count Basie, and Louis Jordan, and that crossed over into the mainstream to become a pop hit.

"Sh-Boom" has been singled out by several historians as the first national rock 'n' roll hit. It became that as a result of a white cover record by The Crew Cuts. But I paid $6,000 for a 50 percent share of the copyright on the basis of a recording by The Chords, a black group on the unknown Cat label. I purchased the share for Hill & Range, which I then served as general professional manager, from Jerry Wexler, who had just joined Atlantic Records and was to become one of the most successful producers of black recordings.

By the time I became the creative head of Edward B. Marks Music Corporation in 1955, publishers as well as the big record companies were avidly scanning releases by black artists in the hope of latching onto an R & B song that could cross over and go pop. The very first song on which I expended the company's finances and my energies was "Piddily Patter Patter," a tune I purchased from Herman Lubinsky of Savoy Records, who had recorded it with Nappy Brown. I regret to say that it did not make it, despite a cover by Patti Page on Mercury. Not long after, I bought the rights to "Soldier Boy" on the basis of a Glory Record by The Four Fellows.

As the years progressed, I cut a number of R & B disks for Syd Nathan of King Records. Capitol Records released sides I made with Zabethe Wild. RCA Victor released the original disk of "Lollipop," which I produced with a mixed duo, Ronald & Ruby and which became a pop best-seller in 1958 as the result of a cover by The Chordettes on Cadence Records.

I guess that the fondest memory of those years is of my association with Dinah Washington, who made a hit of E. B. Marks' "What a Diff'rence a Day Makes" and then recorded "I Didn't Know I Was Crying," a song on which I collaborated with a gifted and prolific black writer, Rose Marie McCoy.

These personal experiences and others contribute, I hope, a measure of insight which this comprehensive study of R & B might not have had if I had approached the subject completely from the outside.

I got a jazz-playin' piano and a great
   big rockin' chair (repeat)
You can rock in rhythm by the music
   that you hear.
                    —BUMBLE BEE SLIM

Rhythm and Blues Under Fire

IN 1954, Barry Hansen, later to be a San Francisco disk jockey but then a seventh-grader in an exclusive Minneapolis prep school, was suffering through a dancing class. He was dying to get home to his V-M record player and particularly to a record of "Shake, Rattle, and Roll" by Bill Haley & The Comets. To accompany the lesson in the Lindy Hop, the dancing master put on a record of that very song, but not by Haley.

"I simultaneously forgot my unfortunate partner," Hansen recalls in a liner note to a Joe Turner album, "the Lindy Hop and Bill Haley, and dashed to the phonograph goggle-eyed over the red-and-black label of the spinning 78 and goggle-eared over the music. It was 'Shake, Rattle, and Roll,' but it sure wasn't Bill Haley. It was something far more sinister."

It was, in fact, Joe Turner's original Atlantic recording of the song, selected by the dancing master because of its propulsive beat. "I liked the beat and a lot more," Hansen adds. "It was several years before I could understand all the words, the ones that were too earthy for Haley [who bowdlerized the Charles Calhoun lyrics]. . . . And there in the snowbound Upper Midwest, an R & B fan was born."

In 1954 R & B fans were being born, not only among Midwestern white teen-agers, but among Southern whites. In '54, Elvis Presley was a nineteen-year-old kid with long sideburns and a sneer, living with his parents in a Memphis housing project. Driving a truck by day, he was studying to be an electrician at night. But he was also trying to persuade Sam Phillips of Sun Records to cut some sides with him. He had come initially to the Memphis Recording Service, as Phillips called his studio, to cut an Ink Spots ballad, "My Happiness," as a birthday present for his mother. When he finally made an audition tape for Phillips, he sang several country songs in a heavy *vibrato* style imitative of Dean Martin and Billy Eckstein, two of the day's most popular vocalists. It was, however, another singer, one he did not imitate on that occasion but who deeply influenced him, who led to his first Sun Records.

"I dug the real low-down Mississippi singers," Presley has said, "mostly Big Bill Broonzy and Big Boy Crudup, although they would scold me at home for listening to them."

xxiii

It was a song by bluesman Big Boy Crudup, "That's All Right (Mama)," recorded by Crudup in 1946 on Victor, that became Presley's first release. Two months later, in October 1954, Sun brought out a second disk by Presley, "Good Rockin' Tonight," written by bluesman Roy Brown and an R & B hit in 1948 for Wynonie "Blues" Harris on King Records.

But even before 1954, white youngsters were turning their radio dials to the small wattage stations that played R & B disks for black ghetto listeners. Indicative of their response to these segregated recordings is a Holiday Ball run in the Cleveland area in December 1953. The featured performers at Alan Freed's ball were Billy Ward & The Dominoes, Little Walter & His Jukes, Ralph William's jump band, and other R & B acts. The ball was promoted exclusively through announcements by Freed on his WJW programs. At two dollars a head, more than 5,000 youngsters appeared at the Akron Armory. Of greater significance than the numbers was the makeup of the audience: A large percentage were white teen-agers.

By 1953–54 R & B had been a form of black-ghetto expression for over a decade. Recordings were made and released mostly by small "indie" labels that sprang up in cities with large black populations, like LA, Chicago, and New York. The white establishment—music, broadcasting and social—was as aware of these records as it was of the black ghettos, but from World War II to the Supreme Court's ruling on school desegregation in May 1954, they were neither interested nor concerned. When white teen-agers began responding strongly to R & B, however, the situation changed drastically. "NOTICE! STOP! Help Save the Youth of America," read a circular distributed in the South.

DON'T BUY NEGRO RECORDS

If you don't want to serve negroes [sic] in your place of business, then do not have negro records in your juke box or listen to negro records on the radio.

The screaming idiotic words, and savage music of these records are undermining the morals of our white youth in America.

Call the advertisers of radio stations that play this type of music and complain to them!

In Houston, the Juvenile Delinquency and Crime Commission, a semiofficial body, issued a list of objectionable disks and urged radio stations to ban them. Included were such titles as "Honey Love," by The Drifters; "Too much Lovin'," by The Five Royales; "Work with Me, Annie," by The Midnighters; "I Got a Woman," by Ray Charles; and the classic "Every Day I Have the Blues," by Lowell Fulson. Spanning the years from 1951 through 1954, the thirty "objectionable" disks did not include a single record that was not by a black artist or on an R & B label. What ostensibly made them objectionable was off-color lyrics.

"Leer-ics," as he typed them, also became the focus of an attack by editor Abel Green of *Variety*. "The most casual look at the current crop of 'lyrics,' " Green wrote in an editorial, "must tell even the most naive that dirty postcards have been translated into songs. Compared to some of the language that loosely passes for 'lyrics' today, the 'peel-table papa' and 'jellyroll' terminology of yesteryear is polite palaver. Only difference is that this sort of lyric was off in a corner by itself. It was the music underworld—not the main stream."

In short, if R & B had just stayed in its place in the black ghettos, who would give a damn about the words?

The *Variety* blast quickly drew a response from an unexpected source: an established, white, ASCAP songwriter who took the position that white pop songs were hardly less "leer-ical" than black R & B tunes.

"As far as I can remember," wrote Al Stillman, whose numerous hits include Johnny Mathis perennials like "Chances Are" and "It's Not for Me to Say," "practically all lyrics, except *Barney Google*, have been dirty—with the carriage trade practitioners, Cole Porter, Larry Hart, etc., contributing their share. What, unless you are innocent-minded, could be dirtier than *You Took Advantage of Me, Heat Wave, All of You, The Night Is Young and You're So Beautiful* (as open a proposition as I ever heard), *Small Hotel* (it says Bridal Suite but the presumption is merely that he intends to register as Mr. and Mrs.). . . . Even as ethereal an ode as Oscar Hammerstein's *All the Things You Are* ('that moment divine, when all the things you are are mine') is a refined *All of You* ('the north and south of you'). . . .

"Actually, the object of all leericists, outside of W. S. Gilbert [Gilbert & Sullivan], has always been to get as close to the Main Subject as possible without stating it and/or 'cleaning it up' by marrying 'em in the last line. The current rock 'n' rollers are not beating around the bush. But without condoning 'em, it's at least a less hypocritical approach."

•

The burgeoning popularity of "Sh-Boom," a hit of summer '54, which I helped promote and publish, brought an attack from a strange quarter. Stan Freberg, who had made a name for himself by satirizing hits like the theme music of "Dragnet," rushed out a takeoff on "Sh-Boom." When he appeared on CBS' "Juke Box Jury," emcee'd by disk jockey Peter Potter, to premiere his disk, he said, "All R & B records are dirty and as bad for kids as dope."

If Freberg was joking, Potter was not. The attack prompted Hunter Hancock, another Los Angeles dj who programmed black records, to comment, "It'll take more than Stan Freberg to kill rhythm and blues. . . ."

That R & B survived its birth is surprising in view of the opposition that came from even one segment of blacks. E. Franklin Frazier, the distinguished black sociologist, has observed that the black middle class, having failed to gain acceptance in white society by aping the white middle class, developed deep feelings of inferiority. These found expression in a slavish adherence to convention, expensively vulgar status symbols, and a hypocritical set of high-flown moral standards. Having castigated the blues because of its association with or reminder of slavery, the black bourgeoisie shunned R & B as low-brow and vulgar.

"The very vulgarity of Rhythm & Blues," LeRoi Jones writes in *Blues People*, "assures its meaningful emotional connection with people's lives." And bluesman Aaron "T-Bone" Walker has said, "I guess that obscenity was built up with commercial playing of the blues. Usually, I don't think it's bad because a good blues singer is so sincere . . . that he has a feeling and meaning beyond the dirty words. . . ."

Early opposition to R & B came also from devotees of the "true" blues, as they liked to term country blues. Paul Oliver, Samuel Charters and, to a degree, Pete Welding—all dedicated and probing students of the blues—are among those unwilling (perhaps unable) to view post–World War II development in the blues as anything but dilution and diminution. Approached by a scholar who seemed to equate purity with age, pioneer bluesman Lonnie Johnson asked, "Are you another one of these guys who wants to put crutches under my ass?"

As for jazz aficionados and musicians, R & B was anathema to them, even though some of its practitioners came from jazz backgrounds and an improvising tenor sax was a feature of R & B disks. R & B was damned, despite its sheer rhythmic vitality, because it was ostensibly entertainment, not self-expression, and because it was simplistic dance music—a curious condemnation since jazz had originally been that, and entertainment, too. It was only when jazzmen began invading concert halls that R & B moved into the clubs, bars, and cabarets deserted by them. How great the snobbery was becomes apparent in *The Sound of Soul*, where Phyl Garland notes that the great Ray Charles was dismissed at first "by jazz-loving, middle class blacks . . . as merely another hoarsely-shouting R & B man."

So R & B was rejected, ridiculed, and renounced by the avant garde as well as the "moldy figs," by scholars as well as social snobs, by white liberals as well as white Southern racists.

Despite the formidable attacks, R & B expanded so much that between the early '40s and mid-'50s more than 100 small record companies sprang up to fill a swelling demand. By the early '50s, the sound was bursting out of America's ghettos. By the time school desegregation was decreed in 1954, white recording artists like Bill Haley, The Crew Cuts, and even Red Foley and Perry Como were beginning to garner hits by covering black artists. The emergence of R & B as rock 'n' roll in 1955 and its eventual domination of the mainstream of pop was just a matter of time.

What did R & B have that gave it this impact and appeal? To find the answer, we have to go back . . .

I. The Roots

Blues is sad music and it's happy music. Also secret language music. It has two things. By the fact that it's a lament, it has the dignified beauty of black people expressed in it. And because of its obvious innocence and sincerity, it captivated the world. It isn't because it's got a drum that came from Africa but because it has a soul that came from suffering.

—AHMET ERTEGUN

I'm goin' up north where they say,
money grows on trees,
I don't give a doggone if ma black
soul leaves.
—COW COW DAVENPORT

Leroy Carr and Tampa Red

BACK to the sun-drenched cotton fields where slaves communicated with each other or vented their feelings in formless and sometimes wordless *cries, calls, field hollers,* and *arhoolies. . . .* Back to the railroad gangs, roustabouts, turpentine camps, and prison chain gangs where the call-and-response of *worksongs* and the percussive rhythms of hammers, axes, and tampers energized and "lightened" work. . . . Back to churches where *spirituals* served as overt expressions of religious fervor and covert songs of protest and freedom. . . . Back to the medicine and tent shows where *washboard, jug, and string bands* entertained the gullible purchasers of surefire nostrums. . . . Back to the *marching bands* that respectfully accompanied a deceased brother to the cemetery and then jazzed the dirge on the trot back home. . . . Back to the plush Storyville bordellos and the Kansas City buffet flats where a "professor" provided a bubbly *ragtime* background on a tinny piano. . . . Back to the plantations of the Mississippi Delta and the streets of Texas tenderloins where the *blues* took shape. . . . Back to the storefront churches where tamborines, handclapping, and an out-of-tune upright helped raise the emotive level of *gospel* songs to the frenzy of "talking in tongues." . . . Back to the *minstrel shows* and the Negro vaudeville circuit of TOBA (Theatre Owners Booking Association, also known as "Tough on Black Artists"), where Ma Rainey, Bessie Smith, Bertha "Chippie" Hill, and the so-called *classic blues* singers sang 12-bar blues to the accompaniment of a jangling *barrelhouse* piano or *two-beat jazz* band. . . . Back to the Chicago and Harlem rent parties where *boogie woogie* and *stride piano* players provided a honky-tonk background for gin and chitlins.

All of these sounds and rhythms figure in the development of R & B, some more remotely than others. For the most immediate antecedents of the style, we must turn to a group of bluesmen who migrated to Chicago from the South in the late '20s and early '30s and who helped transform country blues into urban blues.

They came to Chicago in part because of a movement generated by a Harlem vaudeville singer named Mamie Smith, who came from Cincinnati. In 1920, at the urging of a persistent Negro songwriter

3

named Perry Bradford, OKeh cut several of his songs with Mamie, including "Crazy Blues." Although no great return was anticipated from these first recordings by a Negro, "Crazy Blues" sold in such quantities that in January 1922, *Metronome* reported, "Every phonograph company has a colored girl recording blues."

The three major companies of the day actually had more than one female blues singer. OKeh's roster included buxom and eye-glassed Sippie Wallace, attractive teen-ager Victoria Spivey, and Sara Martin, remembered for sides she made with King Oliver. Paramount prided itself on having the "Mother of the Blues," Ma Rainey; the "Uncrowned Queen of the Blues," Ida Cox; and writer-singer Alberta Hunter, whose songs included the unforgettable "Down-Hearted Blues." Columbia Records boasted the "Empress of the Blues," Bessie Smith and the "World's Champion Moaner," Clara Smith (no relation).

These female Negro singers came trooping onto disk from the country's vaudeville theaters and minstrel shows. Singing 12-bar blues, they became known as the classic blues singers. Unlike country bluesmen who accompanied themselves on acoustic guitar and harmonica—"harp" in their lingo—the classic blues singers worked with jazz pianists like Clarence Williams, Fletcher Henderson, and James P. Johnson, or with 5- and 6-piece New Orleans-style jazz bands like Lovie Austin & Her Blues Serenaders. Their blues had a beat. It was blues wedded to jazz.

OKeh's recording director, Ralph J. Peer, is supposed to have fixed on the term *race* to describe its 8000 series of blues recordings. To counter OKeh's claim as the makers of "The Original Race Records," Paramount recording director J. Mayo Williams called their 12,000 series "The Popular Race Record." (Williams was black and later became the founder of one of the first black-owned labels; his Black Patti Records was, alas, short lived, as was Black Swan, another early black-owned label.) When Vocalion Records, then owned by the Brunswick-Balke-Collender Company of Chicago, emerged as the fourth major "race" label in 1926, Jack Kapp, the head of its "race" division and later founder of Decca, adopted the slogan, "Better and Cleaner Race Records."

With the market for blues records booming along with the American economy of the Great Bull Market, Victor Records moved aggressively into the rapidly-expanding Negro field in 1927 by luring Ralph Peer away from OKeh. By then, the market had seemingly veered from classic to country blues, due in large part to the tremendous appeal of Blind Lemon Jefferson, Paramount Records' remarkable find in Texas.

Now, recording men began roving around the country, seeking rural bluesmen and trundling portable equipment into Southern cities. Ralph Peer, who had done field recording as early as 1923 in Atlanta, concentrated on the Memphis area, where he found important white as well as black blues singers: hillbilly Jimmie Rodgers as well as Frank Stokes (who made a famous two-sided version of " 'Taint Nobody's Business").

Credit for field recording the first of the Mississippi blues pioneers, Cryin' Sam Collins, goes to Gennett Records, a subsidiary of the Starr Piano Company of Richmond, Indiana, that contributed greatly to documenting the blues. Paramount Records did no field recording, but relied on music stores (whose role has been inexcusably neglected) to unearth talent and steer it to their studios in Chicago and, later, Grafton, Wisconsin. A Jackson, Mississippi, storekeeper brought to Paramount's attention such great pioneers as Son House, Skip James, and Charles Patton, just as a Dallas music clerk accounted for the acquisition of Blind Lemon. In the peak years of blues recording, 1927–29, according to Dixon and Godrich in *Recording the Blues*, Paramount led "both in the number of records released and in the range of singers recorded."

Although records were cut in cities other than Chicago, it was the Windy City that was the fulcrum of blues recording, and country bluesmen became part of a broad migration of Negroes to it.

•

"Chi—ca—go . . . Chi—ca—go . . . that toddling town," they sang in 1922, and Southern Negroes came toddling in droves. For years, the Chicago *Defender*, read by Negroes all over the country, had urged: "If you can freeze to death in the North and be free, why freeze to death in the South and be a slave?" In the booming '20s, they came to State Street, "that great street," finding a welcome only in its southerly reaches. Here, a huge black ghetto mushroomed and pre–World War II urban blues evolved.

"The Illinois Central Railroad brought the blues to Chicago," said George Leaner, who began selling blues records in the late '30s in his Groove Record Shop at Forty-seventh and South Park streets. "With the thousands of laborers who came to work in the meat-packing plants and steel mills, came Peetie Wheatstraw, Ollie Shepard, Blind Boy Fuller, Washboard Sam, Little Brother Montgomery, Blind Lemon, Memphis Minnie, and Rosetta Howard."

In 1920, Big Bill Broonzy came from Arkansas, assured of a job as a redcap. Tampa Red migrated from Florida in 1925. Lonnie Jackson arrived in 1927, coming from New Orleans by way of St. Louis, springboard of Roosevelt Sykes of Arkansas, who hit Chicago in 1929. By the early '30s, Memphis Minnie was in the Windy City, along with Washboard Sam.

These were the influentials of the 1930s. They shaped a new blues sound, a sound first heard in the recordings of short-lived Leroy Carr and long-careered Tampa Red. Both gave impetus to a type of blues, set in motion by the classic blueswomen, that was pop inflected or jazz inflected, danceable, and presented as entertainment, not necessarily self-expression or catharsis.

•

Leroy Carr, who was born in Nashville in 1905 and grew up in the black section of Indianapolis, became an overnight sensation in 1928 when he entrained for Chicago and made his famous Vocalion recording of "How Long, How Long Blues," a song for which he wrote the music. Most of Carr's songs were sad tales of mean mamas, women gone wrong, and the love of booze, the last a real-life problem that contributed to his premature death at thirty. But even if his material was traditional, his style was not. And that's what gives him his singular place in the metamorphosis of the blues.

His diction was crystal clear, and he accompanied himself at the piano—he was possibly the first impressive blues pianist—aided and abetted by the jazzy guitar work of Scrapper Blackwell, who did not merely chord, but acted as a responsorial voice on single strings. Unlike the rural bluesmen, Carr was not an involved vocalist. Singing in a thin, high-pitched, Hoosier-inflected voice, with a slight *rubato* but few sustained notes, he talked rather than shouted, mused rather than worried, complained rather than cried. But his great forte was in creating a mood, especially of longing and loneliness, as in "How Long, How Long Blues" and his other outstanding disk, "In the Evening (When the Sun Goes Down)," a song he wrote. "Today has been such a long and lonesome day,/ I've been sitting here thinking/ With my mind a million miles away. . . ." Mood-making was a quality he shared with pop singers.

And there was something plaintively appealing in his laments, even in slyly humorous lines like: "She likes my music but my tool's too short. . . ." "I can't help it if I can't play it long/ I'm just a little skinny fellow and I ain't very strong."

Carr was hardly a little fellow, as a photograph of him at a baby grand piano proves. Light-complexioned, he had enormous hands, was obviously tall since he sits hunched over, and he wore a toothy, confident grin and had a solid jawline. Among Chicago bluesmen of the '30s he was held in such high repute that, as Big Bill Broonzy tells it in a rare, five-volume spoken-and-sung Verve recording, a group of them drove from Chicago to Indianapolis just to hear him sing. When they arrived, Carr was in bed. They roused him, but he had no desire for fellowship or song. But they told him that if he wanted to go back to sleep he had to sing "In the Evening When the Sun Goes Down." Says Big Bill: "He was one of the greatest blues writers I've ever known, and he'll never die because a song like this don't die."

Carr's acceptance after the release of "How Long Blues" was so instantaneous that Vocalion recorded him and Scrapper Blackwell six times more within a period of months. Despite the depression, Carr continued recording steadily through the early '30s, attaining a peak of releases in 1934. Although he is best remembered for moody, semipoetic blues like "Hurry Down Sunshine," "Midnight Hour Blues," and "Blues Before Sunrise," he ventured into autobiography in "Naptown Blues" and "Carried Water for the Elephant," a recollection of the early days when he worked with a traveling circus. His last Vocalion session, the year before his death, included the ironically prophetic "Six Cold Feet in the Ground."

Carr's death in 1935 is shrouded in mystery. Carr had been persuaded that year by Tampa Red to leave Vocalion Records. But when he and Scrapper Blackwell were signing contracts at the studios of Bluebird Records, an argument developed that carried over into the recording session. Furious because he felt that he was not receiving the credit he deserved, Blackwell became so obstreperous that he was ousted from the studio and Carr did the date (not too successfully) by himself. It was the last time Blackwell saw Carr alive for Leroy did not attend an after-recording party held that night at the club where Tampa Red was appearing.

According to Tampa, Carr died of TB shortly afterward in Memphis. But this disputed rumor soon gave rise to another: that he had died of pneumonia. Still another, reported by Samuel Charters in his pioneer study *The Country Blues*, was that during a drinking spree at the Memphis brothel-dancehall where he was living, "somebody put a spider in his whiskey." Many historians now believe that he died of nephritis aggravated by acute alcoholism, but the month of his death still varies from April to June to July, depending on which source you consult.

Upon Carr's death, several artists and record companies tried to trade on his popularity. Amos Easton, who recorded as Bumble Bee Slim, cut "The Death of Leroy Carr" on Decca, and Bill Gaither, another friend, recorded "The Life of Leroy Carr" on OKeh. A radio-store proprietor in Louisville, Kentucky, Gaither and his pianist, Honey Hill, could sound like Carr—and Decca issued a series of disks, billing Gaither as "Leroy's buddy."

Carr's partnership with guitarist Blackwell contributed mightily to his popularity and sales. They were the Bing Crosby and Eddie Lang of the blues. The combination of light, blues-tinted piano and jazzy, melodic guitar produced a new sound that found a waiting audience among urban Negroes. Despite squabbles, originating seemingly in Scrapper's resentment of Carr's greater renown, their success was such that many blues singers were moved to seek permanent partners. Big Bill Broonzy found Joshua Altheimer, Lonnie Johnson joined with Blind John Davis, and Tampa Red collaborated with Georgia Tom and, later, with Big Maceo.

As Carr moved blues singing in a sophisticated, urban direction, formulating a style that was widely imitated by bluesmen into the early '40s, so his collaboration with Scrapper helped establish piano-guitar as the new distinctive accompaniment for the blues.

•

Tampa Red's partnership with Georgia Tom was not as long lived as many of the others, but it led to one of the biggest and most-recorded blues of the day. "It's Tight Like That" was erotic in its words, its suggestiveness further emphasized by Tampa's sly-eyed delivery. In later years, the song proved an embarrassment to Georgia Tom, who as Thomas A. Dorsey became a leading gospel composer. He reportedly maintained that he wrote the music with great reluctance. But Tampa insists that Tom helped with the suggestive lyrics and that they "stole" the melody from a blues by Papa Charley Jackson.

Although Georgia Tom's first royalty check in 1929 was over $2,400, there is no truth to the claim that it delayed his turn to gospel music. In fact, Thomas A. Dorsey composed his first gospel song, "If You See My Savior, Tell Him You Saw Me" as early as 1926. The son of an Atlanta preacher, he grew up listening to the hymns of the famous Dr. Isaac Watts, as well as blues and jazz. Although Dr. C.

H. Tindley, founder of the Tindley Methodist Church in Philadelphia and a celebrated hymn writer, was his inspiration, Dorsey also said, "Blues is a part of me, the way I play the piano, the way I write." According to gospel scholar Tony Heilbut, "From 1929 on, Dorsey committed himself exclusively to gospel," and became, let it be added, the seminal figure in the spread of gospel music. As the sacred and secular were combined in Dorsey's work, so R & B developed as a secularization of gospel themes and style.

To turn back to "It's Tight Like That," Lonnie Johnson (collaborating with Spencer Williams) tried to latch onto its popularity by hurriedly recording a version with the title "It Feels So Good." The Mississippi Sheiks recorded "Loose Like That" on OKeh. As other record companies rushed to cash in, J. Mayo Williams prompted Tampa to cut another version with his Hokum Jug Band. After Tampa and Tom cut versions three and four, Jimmie Noone recorded it with his Apex Club Orchestra. By early 1929 Vocalion was advertising "5 Red Hot Records" of the erotic novelty. Columbia tried to carve a slice of the market with a disk by Clara Smith, employing a provocative accompaniment of trombone and piano. Although the original version by Tampa and Tom reportedly sold a resounding three-quarters of a million disks, it had competition in a jazzy version by McKinney's Cotton Pickers on Victor.

"Party Blues," a type of blues into which "It's Tight Like That" fits snugly, were prevalent during the '20s and '30s. After Tampa Red, Blind Boy Fuller, whose locus was the tobacco mill towns of North Carolina, was probably the best-known singer of "dirty" blues. Of the more than 100 blues he recorded for American Recording Corporation's various labels (Vocalion and Perfect among them), a large number were party blues. Fuller, incidentally, was indirectly responsible for one of the most durable performing partnerships in the blues field. Harmonica player Saunders Terrell, better known as Sonny Terry, lived with him for some years and met his future partner, guitarist Brownie McGhee, at Fuller's home in Durham, North Carolina. (Despite their farm and mill town backgrounds, Brownie and Sonny were not country bluesmen. Neither were they rhythm-and-bluesmen. Call them folk singers—like Leadbelly, with whom they worked for a time.)

"It's Tight Like That . . . beedle-um-bum" started Tampa Red on a career that spanned two decades. A light-complexioned Negro with a moon-shaped face and a receding hairline, "The Guitar Wizard" (an early billing) was born in Smithville, Georgia, between

1900 and 1906. On the early death of his parents, Hudson Wood-bridge, as he was christened, went to live with his grandmother in Tampa, Florida, and assumed the name of Hudson Whittaker. Although he grew up in Florida, he mastered the Mississippi bottle-neck style—fretting the guitar with the broken-off head of a Coke bottle placed on his pinky. "Instead of all that finger doublin' and crossin'," he told liner-note writer Jim O'Neal, "I got me a bottleneck. I couldn't play as many strings as a fella playin' a regular Hawaiian guitar but I got the same effect. I was the champ of that style."

Tampa's big break came when he teamed with Georgia Tom, formerly Barrel House Tom of Atlanta, who was Gertrude "Ma" Rainey's accompanist and bandleader. Photos of Tom in this period reveal a man in a heavy, tailored coat and elegant cap, looking seduc-tively through heavy-lidded, half-closed eyes. A year after Ma Rainey's last record session in '28—Tampa participated—Tom set off in the direction that made Thomas A. Dorsey the foremost writer of gospel songs of our time. Soon, he partnered with Sallie Martin, a raucous-voiced gospeler, and was touring the country's black churches. In 1932, he convened the first Gospel Singers' Convention.

By 1929 Tampa's record releases ran ahead of Leroy Carr's and popular Blind Blake's one-a-month releases, and numbered twice as many as Blind Lemon and Lonnie Johnson. In the '30s he recorded for Bluebird with his Chicago Five, a so-called jazz group that cut hokum songs and pop tunes written by him. His impact derived largely from a penchant for suggestive lyrics like "Somebody's Been Using That Thing" and "It's All Worn Out." Only Big Bill Broonzy approached his mark of 100 recordings made between 1920 and 1942, the year when wartime restrictions on shellac (used in the manufacture of records) forced all companies to curtail new releases. Although Tampa continued making records for Victor, Bluebird's parent company, after the war and although he had a small chartmaker ("When Things Go Wrong") as late as 1949, he lacked the personality to make it on the concert stage as Big Bill did. Moreover, public taste veered in the postwar years toward the tough, electric style of bar bluesmen like Muddy Waters.

The death of his wife led Tampa to become a heavy drinker. But his friends helped him, as friends helped Charley Christian, to destroy himself. "I had to get away from them," he observed later. "They was always at you. It's nice to be sociable but, brother, you can be too sociable. I drank myself into a nervous breakdown." The death of Tampa's wife and child in an auto accident led Thomas Dorsey to write "Precious Lord," regarded as his greatest gospel song and the song that Martin Luther King, Jr., reportedly requested for the evening service on the day he was shot to death in Memphis. After recovering in a mental hospital, Tampa made two LP's for Prestige/Bluesville Records. He performed in public for the last time in San Francisco in 1961.

Despite Tampa's enormous popularity throughout the '30s, Leroy Carr, in a brief seven-year career, was more influential in moving the blues in an urban and urbane direction.

I'm tired of this Jim Crow, gonna leave
*   this Jim Crow town,*
Doggone my black soul, I'm sweet
*   Chicago bound.*
                    —COW COW DAVENPORT

Spats and a Washboard —and Hokum

IN December 1928 in Chicago, Paramount Records formed and recorded a group it called The Hokum Boys. Tampa Red played guitar, Georgia Tom manned the piano, and both vocalized with Bob Robinson, a lesser-known bluesman. Their first two sides, "Selling That Stuff" and "Beedle Um Bum," were so well received that Paramount recorded the group again in January and February. The personnel varied; the concept did not. Eventually, there were the Famous Hokum Boys, with Big Bill Broonzy on guitar; Hokum Jug Band; Hokum Trio; Harlem Hamfats; and Tampa Red & His Hokum Jug Band.

Nothing is so revelatory of the migrant state of mind in the period between the depression and World War II as the hokum band craze. What listeners heard was a reminiscence of their rural past combined with a sense of being above it. The performers gave expression to ambivalent feelings, ribbing and reverencing their backgrounds, mixing derision and nostalgia.

Many of the bluesmen who came to the "Hog Butcher of the World" wanted it known that they were not hicks. They called themselves by names like St. Louis Jimmy (James Oden), Kansas City Bill (William Weldon), Kansas Joe (Wilber "Joe" McCoy), Memphis Slim (Peter Chatman), Memphis Minnie (Minnie Douglas McCoy), Tampa Red (Hudson Whittaker) and Georgia Tom (Thomas A. Dorsey).

Not long after they arrived, the worldwide depression, ushered in by the cataclysmic Stock Market Crash of October 1929, dealt the record industry a devastating blow. Industry sales toppled from $104 million in '27 to $6 million in '32. Paramount shuttered its doors in 1931. The same year Columbia discontinued its 14000 "Race" series, and Brunswick its 7000 series. Vocalion discontinued its 1000 series in '32 and OKeh withdrew its 8000 "Race" series in '34. It was a tough time for the exiles, as it was for blacks generally, and it added a raw topical edge to the blues. But Bluebird took wing in 1932 and helped some black artists weather the economic holocaust, and Decca, opening its doors in '34, launched its 7000 "Race" series under the capable direction of J. Mayo Williams, formerly of Paramount and Vocalion.

Of the migrants, seven set the pace in developing the new-sounding urban blues that emerged in these years. In addition to Leroy Carr and Tampa Red, whom we have already met, they include Lonnie Johnson from New Orleans, Roosevelt Sykes from Arkansas, Sonny Boy Williamson from Tennessee, Washboard Sam from Arkansas, and Big Bill Broonzy from Mississippi. Except for Carr, all were Bluebird artists in the years when the label was central to the changeover.

•

Lonnie Johnson was one of the bluesmen whose recording career came to a standstill during the depression. Although he had been making records since 1925, when he sang and fiddled on an OKeh disk by Charles Creath's Jazz-O-Maniacs, he left OKeh's New York studio on August 13, 1932, and made no records for five years. It was an anomalous situation since he was unquestionably the most versatile of the exiles. An accomplished blues singer who was also an outstanding jazz guitarist, he played several instruments well and was the only one of the migrants who later scored an R & B hit. That was in 1948 when "Tomorrow Night" was a King Records best-seller.

With his career at a standstill, Johnson supported himself by working on the railroads and in the steel mills of Chicago. Inevitably, this experience developed in him a new toughness and a brashness of outlook, reflected in the blues of the postdepression years.

"My first night in Chicago," he sang in "Chicago Blues," "my friends really treated me fine./ Then overnight they all changed like Daylight Saving Time,/ And everything I wanted, I had to lay my money down on the line. . . ."

Except for 1927, when he cut in Chicago, Johnson did his early recording in St. Louis or New York. But after the five-year hiatus, he recorded in Chicago constantly. By then he used drums on some of his dates, string bass on others, and he cut nonbluesy titles like "I'm Nuts Over You" and "Man Killing Broad."

The longest-lived of the migrants, Lonnie was born in New Orleans on February 2, 1889, and died in Toronto, Canada, on June 16, 1970, after an auto accident. He came from a large family that was wiped out, except for him and his brother, by the deadly Spanish flu epidemic of World War I. While his father, who played fiddle, was alive, Lonnie worked on street corners with him. Jazz bassist Pops Foster recalls hearing the two and remembers Lonnie "as the only guy we had around New Orleans who could play jazz guitar."

During the World War I years, he traveled with a theatrical stock company entertaining American troops, after which he rambled through Texas and up to St. Louis. While working in a St. Louis steel foundry, he won a singing contest at the Booker T. Washington Theatre, owned by ragtime pianist Charles Turpin. Jesse Stone, then a local music-store proprietor who acted as a talent scout, brought him to the notice of OKeh Records.

The most jazz-oriented of the bluesmen of the '30s, Lonnie was versatile enough to accompany Texas Alexander, a country shouter who sang songs in the arhythmic style of field hollers. But he also made recordings—rare for a bluesman of those days—with Duke Ellington, Louis Armstrong's Hot Five, and with his own Harlem Footwarmers. His most surprising collaboration was with a Philadelphia jazz guitarist, Salvatore Massarro, who played with The Mound City Blue Blowers and later with Paul Whiteman. It was a unique collaboration, because of the mixing not only of styles but of skin pigmentation. Of Eddie Lang, as Massarro became known, Johnson has said: "We got together in the old OKeh studios in New York. . . . We'd sit down and get to jiving." Eddie Lang's name never appeared on the disks, ostensibly because he was under contract to another diskery, but more likely because of the racial situation. Lang was billed as Blind Willie Dunn.

Johnson's versatility extended to other things besides music. In 1929 he went on tour with the great Bessie Smith, who was starring in a variety show called *Midnight Steppers*. "It was a constant thing," Bessie's niece told biographer Chris Albertson, "to see Lonnie coming in and out of Bessie's stateroom and he kept her company on the whole tour. . . . They really carried on together." Years later, Lonnie admitted, "Bessie was sweet on me—but we never got real serious. Bessie had too many things going for her. . . ." Among other things, an interest in girls as well as boys.

When the depression began playing havoc with the record industry, Johnson turned his talents to double-entendre material like "I Got the Best Jelly Roll in Town" and "Don't Wear It Out." Duets with Spencer Williams and attractive Victoria Spivey, these records prolonged his recording career only slightly. After 1932 he played on a Mississippi riverboat with Charlie Heath's orchestra and in Cleveland with Putney Dandrich's orchestra. Johnson did not return to the recording studios until 1937, when a job at the 3 Deuces in Chicago (with New Orleans drummer Baby Dodds) led to a series of sides on Decca. Thereafter, he made records for many labels, including Aladdin, King, and Rama during the R & B years.

He was approaching sixty when he had the biggest hit of his career, even bigger than "He's a Jelly Roll Baker," cut in 1942 for Bluebird. Anyone who doubts the R & B basis of rock 'n' roll should listen to Lonnie's '48 disk of "Tomorrow Night" on King. It has the repetitive triplets, sounded on a cymbal instead of a high-register piano. To Lonnie's held notes, a female group responds with typical "ba-ba-ba's." As for the sixty-year-old blues pioneer, he sings in a vigorous voice that has a vibrant, metallic quality. Evidence of his jazz background can be heard in the way he comes in before the beat, instead of on it.

"Lonnie Johnson had the misfortune," Samuel B. Charters laments in *Country Blues*, "to be recording when blues were becoming a kind of 'jump' music. 'Jive' was about the latest fad and the blues were going along with it."

Big Bill Broonzy said, "In New Orleans, they played jazz. We in Arkansas, Mississippi, and the delta country sang the blues." As a result of his New Orleans background and not merely because of the times, Lonnie Johnson jazzed the blues.

•

Roosevelt Sykes's launching pad, though he hailed from Arkansas, was Katy Red's, a honky-tonk in St. Louis catering to blues piano players. When the owner of the De Luxe Music Shop heard Sykes in 1929, he was so impressed that he persuaded OKeh to rush Sykes to its studios at 11 Union Square in New York for a recording session. Sykes was immediately hailed as OKeh's answer to Vocalion's Leroy Carr, which he was not. He sang in a thin, high-pitched voice that sometimes sounded as if he were humming through a comb covered with tissue paper. His favorite interjection was "Mercy, Mercy," sometime pronounced "Moisy, Moisy" or "Mersee, Mersee."

Sykes's first record was " '44' Blues." It became his trademark and a blues classic, recorded by him in 1930 as "Kelly's 44 Blues" on

Victor, in 1933 as "New 44 Blues" on Bluebird, and in 1939 under its original title on Decca. Sykes learned " '44' Blues" in his home-town of Helena, Arkansas, from a piano-playing pants presser named Lee "Pork Chops" Green, who had in turn been taught it by Little Brother Montgomery. It was, in fact, Montgomery's composition, developed from already existing blues piano riffs and titled "Vicksburg Blues" by him.

"Just a little old sawmill town" is how Sykes remembered the town where he was born sometime between 1901 and 1906 and to which he returned summers to help on his grandfather's farm. "I just been pickin' a little cotton," he would say in public appearances, "and pickin' a little piano." After his family settled in St. Louis, Sykes decided to become a bluesman when he heard a local piano player after whom he named a blues in 1963. "Red-Eye Jesse Bell" was apparently originally known as "West Helena Blues," and later as "Woman in Helena, Arkansas," before Sykes named it as a tribute to Bell, his early idol.

Not unlike other bluesmen, Sykes changed his name frequently. Recording for Victor in Cincinnati in 1930, the year after his OKeh debut, he called himself Willie Kelly, perhaps because he wanted to continue with OKeh. But he had already made some sides for Para-mount in '29 under the name of Dobby Bragg. He was Dobby Bragg again when he cut for Paramount in their Grafton studios after record-ing for Victor. But when he cut again for Victor in November 1930 and June 1931, he used Willie Kelly again. In 1930 he also used the name Easy Papa Johnson on records he made for Melotone in Chicago. But the pseudonym by which he is best known is "The Honey Drip-per," a name he adopted in 1936 on Decca and kept through five years of Decca releases. He was still "The Honey Dripper" when he moved back to OKeh and its parent label, Columbia, in 1941.

Honeydripper is a blues colloquialism for a virile male. Like all bluesmen who spent time performing in an all-male milieu—Sykes worked the sawmill and turpentine and levee camps along the Mis-sissippi—he developed a repertoire of earthy material. "There's a dance hall on the hill," he sings in "Wild Life." "You can dance all night for a two-dollar bill." And he urges his partner to "twist it."

By 1929, having knocked about extensively with St. Louis Jimmy, a better songwriter than a blues pianist, Sykes settled in Chicago, then the musical mecca of all bluesmen. Although he continued to maintain a home in St. Louis, he became part of the group of Southern exiles who were reshaping country blues for an urban audience. The cover

Roosevelt Sykes at the Ann Arbor Blues and Jazz Festival, 1973 (From *Blues*, photograph copyright © 1975 by Robert Neff. Reprinted by permission of David R. Godine, Publisher.)

of a Decca catalog of 1938 accords him a top spot in a semicircle of seven artists, among them Sleepy John Estes, Rosetta Howard, Georgia White, and Peetie Wheatstraw, a St. Louis buddy who billed himself as "The Devil's Son-in-Law and High Sheriff of Hell."

Sykes displayed his growing urbanity in the lyrics he wrote, more so than in his singing or playing, and melodies like "Last Chance, and My Last Time" reveal pop influences. Some of his later blues follow an 8-bar pop/gospel scheme instead of the 12-bar blues pattern. Images like "Go on, let your hair down," pronouncing Pall Mall "Pell Mell," and references to the telephone ("Baby called me this morning . . .") all reflect his response to a more sophisticated environment. On occasion Sykes eschews the intense subjectivism of country blues for a more philosophical approach, as in "Man in Trouble": "He comes from dust and he's gone with the wind. . . ." He was capable of tart, fresh images like, "You ain't nothin' but a button and can be replaced with a safety pin. . . ."; "I hate to think about another man snoring in my baby's face. . . ."; "I'm way out on a limb and I just can't turn around. . . ."

Despite the urbanization of his outlook, Sykes could not communicate in the world of post–World War II, though he retained enough of a following to continue recording for Bluebird and Victor through the '40s. In 1949 he cut some sides for Regal, one of the new R & B labels, including a version of "Rock It." After that, Roosevelt Sykes & The Honeydrippers tried with United and Imperial, but Sykes had become a bluesman in search of an audience. He sat out the rockin' '50s and when he returned to wax in the '60s, it was to documentary labels like Bluesville, Storyville, and Folkways.

.

During the Decoration Day weekend of 1948, Sunnyland Slim and Tampa Red went to the Plantation Club, a Chicago beer tavern at 328 East 31st Street, to hear Sonny Boy Williamson—John Lee Williamson, the original Sonny Boy, and not William Rice Miller, who adopted the name. It was a trip made in vain for Sonny Boy was the victim of a hold-up shortly after leaving the club in the early morning hours of June 1. Brutally beaten, he managed to walk or crawl to his home at 3226 South Giles where he died of a skull fracture and internal hemorrhaging later that day.

Williamson exercised a sway over the Chicago blues scene of the '30s that was based on two factors: his virtuosity on the "harp" and his generosity. "He worked to help the people with somethin' to eat and drink," Lonnie Johnson told Paul Oliver. Born in Jackson, Tennessee, in 1916, and performing around Memphis as a teen-ager, Sonny Boy was only eighteen when he arrived in Chicago, a gangling six-foot youth with a pencil-line moustache and a ready smile full of big teeth. Though it was the depth of the depression, recognition came quickly to him.

Bluesmen were impressed by his musicianship and showmanship— the way he fluttered his fingers when he used the harp as a responsive voice, rotating and cupping his hand over it to produce muted sounds. "He could blow and sing it at the same time," Big Bill has said. A quick learner, he easily adapted his country style to the popular hokum bands of the day, who used humorous spoken intros to their numbers. Even when the government's wartime rationing of shellac limited blues record releases, he continued recording on Victor, along with Tampa Red and the most popular bluesmen of the day.

During the war, Williamson wrote and recorded a number of topical songs, including "Win the War Blues." His most popular recording was "Elevator Woman," an erotic blues with the curious line: "Elevate me, mama, five or six stories on down." A slight speech impediment caused him to prolong certain vowel sounds and to accentuate some consonants, resulting in a sound that other bluesmen tried to imitate. But it was his harp playing that made him unique and led to his working with Big Joe Williams and other star Chicago bluesmen.

Sonny Boy's murder at the age of thirty-two had tremendous impact on other exiles. We are told that William "Jazz" Gillum, a harp player from Indianola, Mississippi, who worked with Big Bill Broonzy, went into retirement. And Robert Brown, a half-brother of Big Bill, left the record field entirely to become a Chicago policeman.

•

A blues written by Brown and recorded by Gillum, "Go Back to the Country," offered the most evocative expression of the then-current hokum attitude toward Southern migrants. Poking fun at those who kept hollerin' "City lights ain't no good," it ridiculed not only their outcries against high rents and grocery bills, but their desire to keep a hog in the front yard "so you can have plenty of meat."

As a performer, Robert Brown accompanied himself on a washboard equipped with two cowbells and a metal turntable that served as a cymbal. Known as Washboard Sam, he boasted a voice that could cope with the raucous rhythm and percussive jangling of his instrument. Despite the crudeness of this homemade device, Washboard Sam displayed an analytical bent of mind in songs like the topical "C.C.C. Blues" and "Levee Camp Blues," with their detailed indictment of the harsh working conditions of the day. A posed photograph reveals a moon-faced, no-neck man in a double-breasted suit, with wide lapels and a white shirt with a long, pointed collar. His pants are pressed to a knifelike crease and he wears gray spats over black shoes. Spats and a washboard! Could anything better suggest the transitional character of urban blues?

Born in Arkansas—some sources say Memphis—in 1910, Washboard Sam came to Chicago in 1932, the year FDR was elected to his first term. Half-brother Big Bill Broonzy was then working out the ravages of the depressed record business in a steel mill. After a time, Sam recorded a number of sides with Big Bill on Vocalion. But being under contract to Bluebird, under whose aegis he recorded steadily from 1935 into 1942, he used the pseudonyms of "Ham Gravy" and "Shufflin' Sam." He also recorded for Vocalion in '36 as the vocalist of the State Street Swingers, a blues combo that included trumpet, clarinet, and string bass.

Although his first two sides for Bluebird in April 1935 used only guitar accompaniment, he soon added piano, employing through the years such talented eighty-eighters as Black Bob, Joshua Altheimer, Roosevelt Sykes, and others. Discographers Dixon and Godrich assert that he was "perhaps the most popular singer of the late thirties." As evidence, they point out that the Victor catalogue of May 1943 contained only 75 blues-and-gospel records compared to 350 listed 2 years earlier, and of the 75, there were only 2 issued before 1940: "Diggin' My Potatoes" and "Back Door," both by Washboard Sam. "Someone been diggin' my potatoes, tramplin' on my vine. . . ."—rustic imagery and sex.

As late as 1955, when he was on active duty as a Chicago policeman, he took his washboard out of a closet and, along with Memphis Slim, accompanied Big Bill on four sides for Chess. They were not R & B sides, although R & B was then at the peak of its impact.

Whereas Leroy Carr was harbinger of the urbanity of city blues and Washboard Sam might have been the biggest seller in the pre–World War II years, the dominant personality on the Chicago scene was William Lee Conley Broonzy, affectionately known to bluesmen and record buyers as "Big Bill."

Bluebird, Bluebird, please fly down
to me,
If you don't find me on the M.O.,
you'll find me on the Santa Fe.
—TOMMY MCCLENNAN

Big Bill Broonzy

WHEN you write about me," Big Bill wrote in his autobiography, "please don't say that I'm a jazz musician. Don't say I'm a musician or a guitar player—just write Big Bill was a well-known blues singer and player and he recorded 260 blues songs from 1925 up until 1952. . . ."

The dates themselves tell an interesting story. Big Bill began his varied musical career during the Roaring Twenties when Chicago was playing host to King Oliver, Louis Armstrong, and the jazz pioneers who were exiled from New Orleans by the World War I closing of Storyville, the Crescent City's tenderloin of brothels and pleasure palaces. It was also the time when white Chicago musicians—the Austin High School crowd of Benny Goodman, Bud Freeman, Eddie Condon, et al.—were "refining" New Orleans style and evolving two-beat Dixieland. In a real sense, urban blues was the result of New Orleans meeting Mississippi and Arkansas—of jazz meeting the blues —in the unbuttoned atmosphere of Prohibition Chicago.

The end-product of an adjustment that Big Bill made to the world of sound around him may be heard in the five-volume recording he taped during the summer of 1957, just about a year before his death. He plays a bluesy guitar but with a steady down- or uptempo, four rhythmic beats to the bar, and although he uses his instrument as a responsorial voice, his licks have a jazzy quality. His repertoire is broad enough to encompass folk material like "Blue Tail Fly" and "Take This Hammer," popularized by Leadbelly, Josh White, and others during the folk revival of the 1940s.

Although he functioned well into the R & B era, Big Bill's roots reach back from his birth in June 1893 in Scott, Mississippi, to slavery. His mother, who died at 102 in 1957, was born a slave, and an uncle, Jerry Belcher, gave him a vivid sense of life on a plantation. Broonzy learned guitar partly by listening to his uncle play a five-string banjo. "They didn't call what they played blues," he recalls in his autobiographical Verve anthology. "They called it Negro reels." White reels were played at square dances, he explains, and Negro reels at barn dances.

The first blues he ever heard, and one that he recorded many times, was "Joe Turner Blues," as performed by his uncle. He believed that it originated in 1892, a year when people lost everything in a terrible flood. Returning from hunting and scavenging, they would find flour, meat, molasses, and other necessities at their door. Not until their benefactor died did they learn that he was Joe Turner, a white man who used one of the many slaves he owned to deliver provisions secretly to the victims of the flood. "He been here and gone. . . ." as the blues says.

Sixteen children in Broonzy's family survived of a total of twenty-one. Of the seven boys and nine girls, only two were sent to school. The rest, and particularly the older children, had to work. Broonzy received no education, not even in the basics of reading and writing. His brother Frank did the reading and writing for the others. When he was eight, Bill began working as a plowboy on his father's Arkansas farm. Late in life, he still thought of himself as a plowhand.

And he did engage in manual labor during most of his life. He worked on section gangs, yard gangs, and extra gangs laying tracks from Texarkana into St. Louis on the main line of the Cotton Belle. When the drought destroyed his Arkansas farm in 1916—he had married and settled down, playing the fiddle at parties and picnics— he worked in the coal mines until he was drafted. On his arrival in Chicago in 1920, he became a Pullman Company redcap. Later in the 30s, he was employed in the steel mills. In the late 40s, when folk music and R & B came in, he took a job as a janitor at Iowa State College. And in the 50s, he worked in a tavern he owned at Thirty-sixth and Cottage Grove in Chicago. But he always wanted "to get out from behind the plow."

Big Bill had unforgettable memories of the days when blacks had to be wary of individuals known as "man catchers" or "man snatchers." These were agents employed by farmers in need of cottonpickers, or superintendents of sawmill, levee, and railroad gangs in need of laborers. The man catchers would lure men to work by offering attractive pay. At other times they would ply unwary Negroes with liquor and simply cart them off when they were drunk. By the time they came out of their alcoholic stupor, they were miles from home. Not infrequently, there would be no pay after they had finished working. Then they had to trudge the many weary miles back home without anything to show for their toil. That was the origin of the blues, "Going Down the Road, Feelin' Bad. . . ."

Big Bill recalls working with John Estes and Huddie Ledbetter on railroad gangs. Estes became known as "Sleepy" John Estes, according to Broonzy, because he would "fall asleep standin' right on a railroad while we're linin'." As for Huddie Ledbetter, "he was my boss once. He was a caller, the lead man. I asked him—did he think he'll ever work? And he said: 'I hate the guy that invented that word "work". . . .' We always called him *Lead* because lead is something heavy. Lead had some across his lap. He always was sittin' down— Leadbelly. . . ." And singing "Take This Hammer," Broonzy says: "All those guys—same as brothers to me. We lived together, slept together, ate together, worked together—all but Leadbelly. He never worked. He sang and we worked by his singing. . . ."

Religion played an important role in Broonzy's early life and left

an indelible imprint, even though he was not a religious man. Big
Bill's mother drank no alcoholic beverage, except sacramental wine
during church service. When she heard his uncle make reference
to gambling in "Mindin' My Own Business," she drove him out of
the house. As for Broonzy: "At twenty-one I was a preacher—
preached in church. One day I quit and went to music. Be what you
are." He adds, "I'm not a church man. When I wanna hear some real
good singin', that's where I go. As for spirituals, let them alone until
the feelin' comes."

But the feeling never went entirely away. In his five-volume anthology, he includes such spirituals as "Hush! Hush! Sounds like the
Voice of my Lord," and several gospel songs, including, "This Train
(is bound for glory)" and "Anananias (. . . tell me what kind of
man Jesus is)" all done in a swinging four-to-the-bar rhythm with a
boogie feel.

In the course of his conversations with radio interviewer Studs Terkel
and dj Bill Randle, he states that he "would never play a blues in front
of Mahalia Jackson" out of respect for her feelings. When he first
heard soul singer Ray Charles, he said, "He's mixin' the blues with
spirituals. That's wrong. . . . He's got a good voice, but it's a church
voice. He should be singin' in church."

Broonzy also maintained that "the blues won't die because spirituals
won't die. Blues—a steal from spirituals. And rock is a steal from the
blues. . . . Blues singers starts out singing spirituals." He also made an
extremely probing observation regarding New Orleans and Mississippi
blues. "In New Orleans," he said, "they don't raise no cotton. They
raise sugar cane. That's the difference between New Orleans and Mississippi blues. Only time New Orleans cats see cotton is in bales on a
boat or train. The feeling of a man—that's what he sings from. They
didn't play the blues in New Orleans; they played jazz. They didn't
make blue notes. We push the strings; they made them clean."

Once he gave up the church, Broonzy headed for Chicago, admit-
ting that he wanted to get everything white men had, including big
cars and white women. Having learned the fiddle on a homemade
cigar-box violin, and some rudiments of guitar playing from his uncle,
he got Papa Charlie Jackson, also a banjo picker, to teach him guitar.
He was in Chicago for six years before he cut his first sides. It was
a Paramount session some time in 1926.

In 1927 the Mississippi overflowed its banks and wreaked havoc
in many riverside towns. J. Mayo Williams, Paramount's inventive

recording director, got the idea of running a contest for the best blues written about the disaster. He sent a group of the day's most celebrated singer-writers down to Mississippi: Bessie Smith, Blind Lemon, Ida Cox, Ma Rainey, Shorty George, Barbecue Bob, and Lonnie Johnson. Big Bill also made the journey and submitted a song in a competition that carried a $500 prize. Bessie Smith came up with the winner in "Backwater Blues."

A year or two later, Big Bill lost out in a blues contest to another woman. Minnie Douglas was her name and she was born in Algiers, Louisiana, in 1900. Singing on the streets of Memphis as a teen-ager, she was called "Kid" Douglas, but she later became know as Memphis Minnie. A big, handsome woman, with the face of a nurse or school-teacher, Minnie was as tough a drinker and blues singer as any man. In '29 she was signed by a Columbia talent scout who heard her as he sat in a Beale Street barbershop. Her early disks were made with her second husband, Joe McCoy, and were released under the dual credits of Kansas Joe and Memphis Minnie. Her breakout disk came in 1931, an erotic blues titled "Bumble Bee," with the suggestive line, "He ain't stung nobody but me."

Soon Vocalion Records was advertising her as its greatest star and selling her records by mail order. It was about that time, having settled in Chicago, that she entered the contest with Big Bill. The judges who gave her the prize (a bottle of whiskey and a bottle of gin) were Sleepy John Estes and pianist Richard M. Jones, writer of one of the most famous of all blues, "Trouble in Mind." While the judges were carrying Minnie around on their shoulders before an applauding crowd, a disappointed Big Bill made off with the whiskey.

Big Bill had gotten his 1926 recording session only by endlessly bugging J. Mayo Williams, and those first solo records on Paramount were not released. Even after they were recut, they sold so poorly that when ARC (American Recording Corporation) issued a group of solo sides by Broonzy in 1930, they refused to use his name and billed him as "Sammy Sampson." Although he eventually became the most recorded of all the Chicago bluesmen, in the years from 1930 to 1934, he cut for many different labels—Perfect, Gennett, Banner, Champion—under different names: Big Bill Johnson, Hokum Boys, Mellow Boys, Bill and Slim, Big Bill & His Jug Busters, and Big Bill Broomsley. To support himself during that time, he worked as a grocery clerk.

A batch of sides he cut as Big Bill for ARC's dime-store labels— Banner, Melotone, Perfect, Romeo, and Oriole—marked the turning point. And from 1934, as the record business clambered out of the depression, he began recording for Bluebird and had a steady flow of releases until the beginning of World War II.

A historical photograph shows Big Bill as part of a group of bluesmen clustered around Lester Melrose, the Chicago music publisher who arranged recording sessions for Vocalion and Bluebird and who thereby played a major role in developing the Chicago sound of the 1930s and early '40s. Born in Olney, Illinois, in 1891, Melrose worked as a fireman on the B & O Railroad and ran a grocery store. After serving in World War I, he and a brother opened a music store on Cottage Grove in Chicago's burgeoning black ghetto in 1922. This led to his enterprising and bustling association with the record companies, an association that is said to have accounted for 75 percent or more of all urban blues disks produced in Chicago.

In the group photograph mentioned, Melrose is surrounded by Jazz Gillum, Roosevelt Sykes, St. Louis Jimmy, and Washboard Sam, all Bluebird influentials. Big Bill dominates because he is the only one with an instrument. That was appropriate because, through Melrose, he functioned as house guitarist for both Vocalion and Bluebird, also as a "contractor" (to use current lingo) who assembled backup groups for other artists. It was Melrose who arranged for Big Bill's critical ARC sessions.

The transformation of Big Bill's performing style came about largely as a result of two bluesmen, pop-oriented Leroy Carr and jazz-oriented Lonnie Johnson. His efforts at imitating them in his dime-store releases began attracting a public that no longer responded to cryin' country blues. "Young people say you're cryin' when you sing," he later said. "Who wants to cry? Well, back in the early days, what else could black people and bluesmen do but cry? Today they talk to lawyers—and don't sing that way."

Having stopped crying, Broonzy proceeded to develop a pleasant, ingratiating style of delivery, evident in sides he made after 1934 with pianist Black Bob. The change was apparent in the optimistic "The Sun Gonna Shine in My Back Door Some Day," a rewrite of "Trouble in Mind." More popular with record buyers was his rewrite of a suggestive tent-show favorite known as "Take Your Fingers Off It." Even though the *it* referred ostensibly to a diamond ring, no one had any confusion about the intended anatomical reference. Eliminating the double entendre, Broonzy gave the song an almost pop flavor by recasting it as "Take Your Hands Off Her." A favorite of his, he recorded it many times: for Mercury (1949), Melodisc (1951), and Storyville (1956).

The years from 1936 to 1939 were peak recording years for Big Bill, first on ARC and then on Vocalion. These years saw him move from a piano-accompanied bluesman to one for whom rhythmic punch became vital. On a 1938 session ("Sweetheart Land"), he worked with tenor sax and electric guitar. By 1939 he was recording with a combo called Big Bill & His Memphis Five, consisting of trumpet, alto sax, string bass, guitar, and piano. In '42, after he had moved to the OKeh label, Big Bill & His Chicago Five duplicated the instrumentation, except that drums replaced string bass.

Although Sam Charters claims that Big Bill was bitter and cynical about women, he himself suggested for inclusion in his obituary: "Big Bill was a happy man when he was drunk and playing with women. . . ." He recalls three of them in the five-volume Verve anthology. "Louise Blues" was inspired, he says, by a gal "whom I knowed pretty well myself. . . . Johnny Temple was the first to sing about her. Little Brother Montgomery—he knowed her pretty well, too. . . . Roosevelt Sykes made a record. I made a record. My brother made a record. All the blues singers knowed her. She loved music. She loved the blues singers."

Then there was "Willie Mae." "I wrote it with no help," he says. "I started singing it in 1928. Never did record it until 1951. Record company thought it was too personal. If she's a real woman, may be trouble. I'm sure all of the blues singers in Arkansas knew about her. She married a friend of mine—they got along fine—but she still loved to hear us sing and have fun with us. . . . All the blues singers liked her. Her husband didn't say anything about it. He was a good fellow. She was a good Joe."

There was also Georgia White, a gorgeous Georgia peach of a blues singer herself whom Big Bill credits with launching "Trouble in Mind." Richard M. Jones, the composer, was her accompanist, and she sang the popular blues in 1929 with Jimmie Noone's jazz orchestra at Chicago's Apex Club. Georgia had a very sophisticated outlook and performed not only songs like "I'll Keep Sittin' on It if I Can't Sell It," but tough blues about prostitution and lesbianism. "When I say Georgia White," Big Bill murmurs, in introducing his version of "Trouble in Mind," "she was a real, nice-looking gal. All the musicians liked her. But there was no way of getting to her because her husband was always around. He was her valet—dressed her, brought all of her food. Was no chance for anybody getting close to her. . . ."

During the years of his burgeoning popularity, Big Bill had many competitors, among them Jazz Gillum on Bluebird, Peetie Wheatstraw on Decca, and Tampa Red on Vocalion. But his genial personality, his musicianship, and his power as house guitarist gave him a commanding position among Chicago bluesmen and black audiences all through the '30s.

In 1939, John Hammond brought him to New York for the second "Spirituals to Swing" concert. Although he had been commuting from his Arkansas farm to Chicago all through the '30s, he apparently resented being introduced as an ex-sharecropper instead of as the prodigiously productive blues composer and recording artist he was. As a folk revival gained impetus in the postwar years, creating a demand for singers like Leadbelly and Josh White, Broonzy developed a repertoire that helped make him a figure in demand. "Take This Hammer" and "John Henry," which he often recorded, became two of his favorite numbers.

Big Bill lived through the R & B years. When he died of lung cancer in 1958, rock 'n' roll was already gaining momentum—Alan Freed arrived in '54 and Presley in '56. But he made no contact with the style or the audience that went for the electrified, amplified, driving combo blues of Muddy Waters, Bo Diddley, Howlin' Wolf, and B. B. King. Big Bill's response was to move onto the folk concert stage. If there was regression in his turning away from a black audience to reach for a larger, white audience, there was also an attempt by him to dig into the Negro past, into folk origins. Young blacks, emerging into the jagged realities of postwar segregated America, found little to stir their emotions or satisfy their hungers in Big Bill or, for that matter, in Sonny Boy Williamson, Tampa Red, Washboard Sam, or Roosevelt Sykes. Theirs was a new, angry, restless world—and the polish, sophistication, and sly suggestiveness of piano-accompanied urban blues sounded stale.

When Ah leaves from here, gwine out
  on the Ohio (repeat)
If Ah doan fin' no log-camp, Ah'll fin
  a gravel-camp sho.
          —LEWIS BLACK

Uprights in the Turpentine, Lumber, and Levee Camps

Now, she's a running mistreater," Speckled Red sang, "a robber and a cheater. Slip you in the dozens. . . ./ Yonder go your mama going out across the field,/ running and a-shaking like an automobile. . . ."

With its animadversions about "your mother," "The Dirty Dozens" was Red's most popular number in the back-alley jukes of the Midwest, where he became known as Detroit Red, and in the lumber camps of the South, where he developed a walloping, barrelhouse style and where the rough and bawdy humor of blues like "The Dirty Dozens" was boisterously enjoyed. Among the limited number of recordings he made, "The Dirty Dozens" was as big a seller in 1929 as Leroy Carr's "How Long Blues" had been in 1928. Like Carr, who made follow-up versions of his hit and who also recorded "The Dirty Dozens," as did Tampa Red and bottleneck guitarist Kokomo Arnold, Speckled Red followed his initial Brunswick version with "The Dirty Dozens, No. 2" in 1930.

As a song, "The Dirty Dozens" has a most curious, if not startling history. It was originally a mnemonic device designed to instruct the young in biblical lore; first, God created the earth; second, he rested; etc. In a humorous patter, Speckled Red's renditions included vestigial references to the original: "God made him an elephant, He made him stout/He wasn't satisfied until He made him a snout. . . ." In time, the religious-oriented mnemonic developed into a secular—almost sacrilegious—device of verbal abuse. It was not only an erotic vehicle, but an obscene one, involving insults that reached their climax in the most outrageous insult of all: accusing a man of having intercourse with his mother. If "The Dirty Dozens" did not originate the epithet *motherfucker*, it was certainly responsible for giving it widespread currency. Legend has it that in any real trading of accusations, the antagonists usually came to blows before they reached the twelfth exchange of insults.

Speckled Red's recording of "The Dirty Dozens" was much less suggestive than in-person renditions, due to record company bluepenciling. The record session itself was largely an accident, the result

27

of Red's encounter with a Vocalion field unit at the Hotel Peabody in Memphis.

Born in Monroe, Louisiana, in 1891 or '92, Rufus Perryman, as he was baptized, was an albino. He acquired the cognomen Speckled Red because of the freckles in his pink skin. Unquestionably, it was the pallor of his skin as well as his sensitivity to light that caused him to perform in a large, black fedora which sat on his eyebrows and shaded his eyes and the rest of his face.

He was raised in Hampton, Georgia, and, as a boy of ten, moved with his parents to Atlanta and then to Detroit when he was in his teens. Next to Chicago, motor-town had the largest black population of any American city, growing from a mere 5000 blacks in 1910 to over 80,000 in 1926. It had its Hastings Street in the black ghetto where Negroes came for an evening of carousing and where piano-playing bluesmen found an enthusiastic welcome. As a teen-ager, Perryman heard eighty-eighters with colorful names like Tupelo Sam and Fishtail. At Butch's Club, he was so mesmerized by a pianist who called himself Seminole that he began learning by ear some of the blues he heard.

Rejected by a father who could not stand the partially blind, strange-looking lad, Speckled Red became an itinerant early in life and spent much time hoboing on freight trains from the Great Lakes to the Gulf—which accounts, perhaps, for his fondness for Cow Cow Davenport's "Cow Cow Blues" and its railroad symbolism. (Cow Cow, incidentally, was one of the itinerant eighty-eighters whom Speckled Red might have heard in Detroit's many brothels.)

Hardly a levee or sawmill camp was unfamiliar with Red's pug-nosed face, which bore a marked resemblance to a battered Jack Dempsey. For a time, he even traveled with a medicine show that wended its way through Arkansas, Alabama, and Mississippi, accompanying bluesman Jim Jackson, who is remembered for his recording of "Kansas City Blues."

Jim Jackson is sometimes credited with arranging the 1929 recording session that marked Speckled Red's debut on wax. The following year, Red did another session for Brunswick, and then the depression intervened. Eight years elapsed before he recorded again, this time for Bluebird. And once again he disappeared until he was located in St. Louis in 1954. By then he was suffering from arthritis and his voice was hoarse. It was two years before Robert Koester, a record collector and producer, was able to produce sides that he could release on Delmark. In 1960 both Folkways and Storyville released albums from which a new generation of listeners could gather something of the raucous barrelhouse style that was Speckled Red's.

•

What local ballrooms were to the big bands of the '30s and the borscht circuit was to a generation of comics, the lumber, levee, turpentine, and sawmill camps of the South were to the bluesmen who progressed from rural to urban blues styling. A source of "bread," the camps were a proving ground; weary laborers seeking a little entertainment before they tumbled off to an exhausted sleep, were a tough audience.

As men like Roosevelt Sykes and Speckled Red struggled to entertain the noisy, half-bombed laborers on battered uprights, the blues toughened and coarsened. Of course, the frank references to sex were toned down before mixed audiences and on recordings, perhaps leading to the extensive use of double entendre imagery in urban blues. Male-oriented when it came to women, the words and the raucous atmosphere invited the barrelhouse-boogie styling developed by eighty-eighters like Sykes and Red, also by Little Brother Montgomery and Sunnyland Slim, to whom we now turn.

•

Eurreal Wilford Montgomery was born in 1907 on the grounds of the Kent Lumber Company, deep in the piney woods of Tangipahoa Parish, Louisiana, and was raised in the environs of other sawmill lumber camps of Louisiana. The living quarters provided by the lumber companies generally consisted of unpainted wooden shacks without electricity, running water, or sanitary facilities. Each shack had a door and a window—really just two holes in a rectangular wooden box, each shuttered with a wooden flap.

The accommodations for the ten Montgomery children were probably a trifle better than that since Eurreal's father operated a juke joint in Kentwood, Louisiana. There, during his preschool days, Eurreal and the loggers heard migrant bluesmen with colorful names like Son Framion, Friday Ford, and Papa Lord God. Motivated by his musician father, Little Brother Montgomery, as he came to be known, began studying piano at the age of five. He has said that Jelly Roll Morton, who played in his father's juke, gave him his first piano lesson. By the time he was ten, he was proficient enough to take a job as a pianist in a Holton, Louisiana, juke joint.

Having left home in 1917, he went from Holton to Ferriday, where he struck up a friendship with two honky-tonk piano players, Long Tall Friday and Dehlco Robert. Out of the association came a number of blues, including "Vicksburg Blues," which Roosevelt Sykes popularized as "44 Blues." It became so popular that no migrant eighty-eighter could undertake a camp job without knowing it. Little Brother recorded it himself during his first Paramount session in 1930, the year after Sykes cut it. But the classic rendition of this blues is the version he cut for Bluebird in 1935.

Until he was sixteen, Montgomery spent his days wandering about Louisiana and Mississippi, performing in honky-tonks and logging camps. Rootless though it was, the nomadic existence allowed him to hear many piano players and many different blues styles, from East Coast ragtime to fast Western boogie and lumber camp barrelhouse. When he settled down, it was in Northfield, Mississippi, where he quickly achieved recognition.

Until the depression put him in motion again, he lived quietly but spent time in nearby Hattiesburg with two piano-playing friends, Sunnyland Slim and Cooney Vaughn. He apparently had to visit Hattiesburg on the sly because his family did not approve of the two bluesmen. But Cooney Vaughn, who combined New Orleans ragtime with Mississippi Delta blues, deeply influenced Montgomery, so that Vaughn's well-known "Tremblin' Blues" became part of his repertoire.

When he left the world of the sawmill in 1929—by then the South was producing almost half of the nation's lumber—Little Brother joined a big band. The following year, he traveled to Paramount's Grafton, Wisconsin, studio for his first record session. He did not record again until 1931 when he cut for Melotone, one of ARC's dime-store labels, and that was followed by another four years with no releases. Then in 1935 in New Orleans, he cut his "Vicksburg No. 2," prompting Bluebird to do eighteen more sides with him the following year.

Although he settled in Chicago before the outbreak of World War II, he did not record again until 1947. On Century Records, he then cut with trumpet, tenor, clarinet, bass, and drums as the Little Brother Montgomery Quintet, implying an effort to move with the times. But an urban orientation was apparent even in a photo taken of him in the late 1930s, which reveals a suave-looking man in a dark suit, white shirt and a modern bow-tie whose points rest under his shirt collar. Unfortunately, Little Brother made the transition more successfully in his appearance than on wax.

Little Brother recorded as late as the 1960s, cutting new and old items, including "Canadian Sunset" and "Buddy Bolden's Blues," "Ballin' the Jack" and "Pinetop's Boogie Woogie." He was part of the transition, but R & B was beyond his reach.

•

When he came to Chicago in 1940, Little Brother was accompanied by Albert Luandrew, another bluesman who paid his dues working the levee and lumber camps along the Great Muddy. Born in 1907 in Vance, Mississippi, Sunnyland Slim, as Luandrew became known, performed locally before he went on tour with Peter "Doctor" Clayton, an incurable alcoholic who performed in oversized, white eyeglass frames without lenses. When Slim cut his first sides for Victor in 1947, they were released, in fact, under the cognomen Doctor Clayton's Buddy. That year, he also recorded for the newly launched Aristocrat label of Chicago, forerunner of Chess. His vis-à-vis was a man who was to become one of the foremost R & B artists, but the billing then read: "Sunnyland Slim & Muddy Waters." Unfortunately, Sunnyland failed to move with the times as Muddy did.

Nonetheless, he was obviously esteemed by his Chicago confreres. Among those who recorded with him were Big Bill, "harpist" Little Walter, Lonnie Johnson, and bassist Willie Dixon. From '47 to '56, there was no year that he did not have one or two new releases, and they were seldom on the same label. Aristocrat was followed by Hytone, Mercury, Apollo, JOB, Sunny, Regal, Opera, Chance, Constellation, Blue Label, Vee Jay, Club 51, and Cobra.

Sunnyland walked the path of other urban bluesmen. His songs contained occasional topical references, as in "Back to Korea Blues," but his favorite numbers, recorded several times, were traditional blues like "Brown Skin Woman" and "Woman Trouble Blues."

Sunnyland played a jangly, barrelhouse piano, singing with a light-textured growl and talking rather than vocalizing, except when he rose to a *falsetto*. By 1949 his combo generally included tenor sax, and he even experimented with maracas on dates in '54. As the blues adopted electrical amplification, he used an electric piano. Of his style, he said, "I lay it down hard on the piano. The way I do it, I get a person to tap his foot just like a Baptist preacher." The intent was there. But even if his backgrounds were urban, his material and style remained traditional.

•

Arthur "Big Boy" Crudup also worked the lumber and levee camps, and he did it for much of his life. But when he cut his second record, in 1942, he played electric guitar, and the song he wrote and performed possessed a psychological dimension that made it modern—and meaningful to the postwar generation. Lamenting the runout of his woman, he sings, "I was standing, I was list'ning for that Southern whistle to blow," and he speculates, was it "that mean old Frisco train or that low-down Santa Fe?" Crudup was touching traditional blues bases—departing railroad trains, a woman who had left him, feeling unwanted—but his emphasis is on the man's pretense—a concern about which train she took. With "Mean Old Frisco Blues," cut in the second year of World War II, Big Boy was really headed away from urban blues toward R & B.

Arthur Crudup (pronounced Crood-up) was born in Forest, Mississippi, in 1905, the son of a farmhand who played guitar. He acquired the nickname "Big Boy" in his youth. A photo reveals a tall man who looked even taller because he had a small head sitting on a huge, neckless frame. Another distinguishing feature was a mouth that spread across his face, almost from ear to ear, the underlip protruding over the upper in a thick, rubbery, convex curve. He weighed 220 pounds when he arrived in Chicago in 1940 with the Harmonizing Four, a gospel group. After he broke with the gospel quartet, he "lived" in a wooden crate beneath the el station at Thirty-ninth Street and sang on street corners for handouts.

Crudup was thirty-six years old when he made his first recordings for Bluebird in September 1941, playing guitar with accompaniment by Joe McCoy on a brownie bass (a washtub with a rope running through a hole in the center and attached to a broom handle, which served as a fretboard). For a big man, he had a high-pitched, shrill voice and sang in a style imitative of the hollers of field hands. He liked his guitar to ring, and since he was not a bottleneck guitarist, he capoed his instrument far down on the fretboard until he began using electrical amplification.

Reacting quickly to the Chicago scene, he played electric guitar on his second Bluebird date, in April 1942. The six sides included "Mean Old Frisco Blues," with which he became identified. But after each record date, he returned to Mississippi to continue working on his farm and in the lumber camps. His recordings and songs did not give him enough income to support a growing family, eventually thirteen children, four of his own and nine stepchildren.

Except for 1942–3 and 1948, Crudup did one or two sessions a year for Bluebird until 1952. That year, he switched to Trumpet Records (billed as Elmer James), then to Checker (as Perry Lee Crudup), and finally to Ace Records (back to Big Boy Crudup). All these dates were done in Jackson, Mississippi, presumably at the McMurray Studio. In 1953 he returned to Bluebird's parent label, Victor, and recorded in Atlanta for its Groove subsidiary, backed by a tenor sax combo. He followed with another Groove session in Atlanta in 1954, and that marked the end of his recording career. But not of his renown. "The reason I quit playing," he told author-critic Bruce Cook, "is that gradually I realized I was making everybody rich, and here I was poor."

It was an uptempo blues entitled "That's All Right," recorded by Crudup in September 1946, that spread his name far and wide. Elvis Presley, who served as the unexpected herald, told the story to England's *Hit Parade* magazine in January 1957, shortly after his explosive entry on the international record scene.

It happened in 1954, as Elvis told it. He was on the phone with Sam Phillips, the owner of Sun Records of Memphis when Phillips said, "You want to make some blues?" Knowing that Elvis "had always been a sucker for that kind of jive, he mentioned Big Boy Crudup's name and maybe others, too. All I know is I hung up and ran fifteen blocks to Mr. Phillips' office before he'd gotten off the line—or so he tells me. We talked about Crudup records I knew—'Cool Disposition' [cut by Big Boy in '44], 'Rock Me, Mama' [1944], 'Hey Mama, Everything's All Right' [1947] and others, but settled for 'That's All Right,' one of my top favorites."

It was Elvis' first release on Sun—and as close to Big Boy's phrasing, blue notes, and high *tessitura* as he could make it. After RCA Victor bought his Sun contract, "That's All Right" became Presley's second Victor release and the beginning of his fabulous career. When Crudup began hearing his song all over Mississippi, he wrote about royalties to Lester Melrose, who had been his manager and publisher. All that Big Boy apparently received after that was a note from Melrose saying that he would look into the situation.

Later, Presley recorded Crudup's "My Baby Left Me," a 12-bar blues cut also by Creedence Clearwater Revival. Other contemporary rockers who have recorded Crudup songs include Elton John, Rod Stewart, Johnny Winter, Paul Butterfield, Buffy Sainte-Marie, Tina Turner, Canned Heat, and B. B. King (who scored a hit with Crudup's "Rock Me, Mama"). In 1956, Presley sent Crudup a plaque, acknowledging his debt to "That's All Right," and in 1959 he reportedly put up the money to finance an LP by Big Boy, cut by Fireball Records of Nashville and leased to Fire Records.

But Crudup apparently did not receive royalties due him almost from the beginning of his recording career. Not long after Crudup arrived in Chicago, Lester Melrose booked him into a South Side club and arranged for the Bluebird sessions. "The company paid my manager," Big Boy later said, "but he didn't pay me. I was to get 35 percent of every dollar he received. Well, I failed to get it." Finally, in 1947, "after I found out he was gypping me," says Crudup, he broke with Melrose. According to Ben Fong-Torres in *Rolling Stone,* however, "Melrose and later his heirs continued to draw royalties on Crudup's songs until 1971 when a legal action was filed on Crudup's behalf."

It was Dick Waterman, an agent and manager for many bluesmen, who initiated a fight for the royalties after he met Crudup in 1968. Through the American Guild of Authors and Composers, negotiations were conducted with Hill and Range Songs, who are in partnership with Presley and claim ownership of Crudup's songs. A settlement was ostensibly worked out by AGAC attorneys and John Clark, H & R's attorney, whereby Big Boy was to receive $60,000 for royalties due up to June 1971. Big Boy and his four children drove to New York and went to the H & R offices on Seventy-second Street, west of Broadway, in a converted four-story private house.

Waterman described the proceedings to Ben Fong-Torres: "Arthur and the children signed all the papers, which then went upstairs for the signature of Julian Aberbach, President of H & R. We all patted each other on the back and congratulated Arthur that justice had finally been done.

"The next thing, John Clark comes back into the room, looking stunned and pale, and says that Aberbach refused to sign because he felt that the settlement gave away more than he would lose in a legal action. We all waited for the punch line, for him to break out laughing and whip the check out of the folder. But it wasn't a joke. We sat around and looked at each other. How could they do this? How insanely cruel to an old man to bring him to the very brink of going poverty-to-riches and then deny it all?" But Presley's copublishing partners did.

"I was born poor," Crudup once said, "I live poor, and I'm going to die poor." And he did, on March 28, 1974, at the North Hampton-Accomac Memorial Hospital in Nassawadox, Virginia. He was sixty-nine and poor, despite the fact that three years earlier, RCA Victor released an album of his recordings under the title *Father of Rock and Roll.* Although he had recorded continuously for about ten years during the '40s and '50s and wrote some of the frequently-recorded songs of the rock revolution, he never derived enough from music to take him away from his Mississippi farm and the sawmill.

Crudup added something to the rural and sawmill blues he heard in the Mississippi Delta and to the urban blues he heard among Lester Melrose's bluebirds in Chicago that made him father to the "King of of Rock 'n' Roll." As Big Bill Broonzy has said, "You hear Elvis Presley, you hearin' Big Boy Crudup."

As a lifelong sharecropper and piney woodsman, Crudup was un-questionably closer to the soil than to the urban scene; he went to Chicago just to record and did no touring as a performer. His impact on Presley suggests that whereas urban blues, wedded to gospel, produced R & B by introducing a beat and electricity, it was the sound and feeling of country blues, wedded to R & B, that led to rockabilly, the first stage of Rock 'n' Roll.

•

In *Mystery Train: Images of America in Rock 'n' Roll Music,* pub-lished and widely praised in 1976, Greil Marcus writes: "The implica-tion always there when Crudup or Willie Mae Thornton looked out at the white world . . . is that Elvis would have been nothing without them, that he climbed to fame on their backs." And Marcus makes the astonishing assertion: "It is probably time to say that this is non-sense."

Now, we know that Presley did not impress Sam Phillips when he sang big-baritone like Dean Martin or Billy Eckstine, that he had been listening regularly to blues singers against the wishes of his parents, and that he ran fifteen blocks when Phillips asked whether he would like to record some of Crudup. We know also that every one of Elvis' five Sun Records included a song by a bluesman—Crudup's "That's All Right," Roy Brown's "Good Rockin' Tonight," Sleepy John Estes'/Joe Williams' "Milkcow Blues Boogie," Arthur Gunter's "Baby, Let's Play House," and Junior Parker's "Mystery Train." In short, Presley was steeped in the R & B tradition, knew its literature intimately, and had a feeling for it.

After Phillips sold Presley's contract to RCA Victor, Elvis scored a Gold Record with his version of Big Mama Thornton's "Hound Dog," a woman's tough putdown of a no-account man and a song that lacked bite when a man sang, "You ain't nothin' but a hound dog." But Presley was so taken with Mama's sound and feeling that he re-corded it anyway—and I, for one, will argue that he came off second best.

In succeeding releases, Presley cut songs written or originally introduced by Lowell Fulson, Chuck Willis, Lloyd Price, Smiley Lewis and Charles Brown. And it was Presley's adaptation of the sounds of these bluesmen that caught the ears of teen-agers. There is no denying that Elvis *adapted* and brought something uniquely his own to his adaptations. But by the same token, can one deny that he took material from the black culture, learned from renditions by black artists, and found himself as an artist because of that culture? Greil Marcus apparently never asked himself a simple question that would have exposed the absurdity of his position: If Elvis would not have been "nothing without Crudup and Big Mama," is it possible that he was *something* because of them?

Marcus' position is startling because his book is concerned with cultural roots and reflected images. It seems quite evident that had Elvis not become King of Rock 'n' Roll, others who had absorbed the same black musical and cultural influences might have ascended to the throne. Jerry Lee Lewis almost did until his marriage to a teenage cousin brought such a torrent of media abuse that his career was almost destroyed. What makes Marcus' stance so troubling is that it puts him in the camp (where he surely does not belong) of those who have been trying for years to deny and depreciate the undeniable and pervasive impact of black culture on American popular music.

I want you to pull up on your blouse,
let down on your skirt,
Get down so low you think you're in
the dirt,
Now when I say "Boogie!"—I want
you to boogie. . . .
——CHAMPION JACK DUPREE

The Ballin' Towns

BECAUSE OF its intense recording activity, Chicago was the magnet that drew bluesmen between the depression and World War II. But there were several other cities that nourished urban blues and contributed to the frothy mix of boogie, blues, gospel, and jazz out of which R & B bubbled forth.

Situated at important rail junctions or harbors, they were wide open towns, with bustling streets that never slept: St. Louis, Naptown (Indianapolis), Memphis, KC. Their tenderloins housed pleasure palaces, energizing a kaleidoscopic whirl of gamblers, prostitutes, pimps, hustlers, narco peddlers, jazzmen, and bluesmen.

In the 1930s, St. Louis was a base, among others, for men with colorful nicknames like pianist James "Stump" Johnson and singer Charlie "Specks" McFadden; for Walter Davis, who was a dapper dresser and always wore a carnation as he manned the eighty-eight; guitarist-pianist William Bunch, who went by the name of Peetie Wheatstraw and made a striking appearance with his unbelievably high, bullet-shaped head; and pudgy-faced Roosevelt Sykes. All of these and others could be found performing at Charles Turpin's Jazzland Club or the Chauffeurs Club or Katy Red's Honky-Tonk.

St. Louis was a base, too, for the man who became known as St. Louis Jimmy. James Oden, born in Nashville in 1905, traveled periodically to Chicago to record. Oden never became an accomplished pianist, presumably because the town throbbed with so many keyboard giants. His reputation is built on his work as a blues composer, but he did make many vocal records, accompanied either by Roosevelt Sykes or, later, Sunnyland Slim.

Oden was a big-toothed man, with heavy-lidded eyes and pronounced cheekbones. Even early in life he had a receding hairline that made him look as if he wore a skullcap on the back of his head. Two rows of protruding teeth, reminiscent of Satchmo, gave him a constant smile. But it was a shy smile.

Oden cut his first sides in 1932, traveling to the Richmond, Indiana, studios of the Starr Piano Company and recording on Champion, the cheaper Gennett label. The following year, through Sykes and broker Lester Melrose, he cut on Bluebird. When Decca opened its doors, St. Louis Jimmy appeared as Old Man Oden on sides cut in '34 and '37. By '37, after the hiatus occasioned by the depression cutback in releases, a violin background gave way to clarinet and string bass.

It was not until the beginning of World War II that Oden wrote and cut the most important of his blues. Returning to the Bluebird label in 1941 and recording for the first time as St. Louis Jimmy, he waxed "Going Down Slow," a well-constructed blues with expressive imagery and interesting chord changes. The following year brought four more Bluebird sides, including "Poor Boy," another of his famous blues, recorded later by Speckled Red (1956) and Memphis Slim (1961). St. Louis Jimmy recorded "Poor Boy" for Victor in 1946 (unissued), for Bullet in 1947, and with Red Saunders Band for Parrot in 1955. Subsequently, he waxed versions for Bluesville (1960), Delmark (1963), and Spivey (1964). In 1973, versions by Duane Allman and Bobby "Blue" Bland, received such extensive airplay that the classic became one of the year's most-played songs.

After World War II, Oden moved into the R & B scene, recording with Muddy Waters on Aristocrat (1948) and with Sunnyland Slim's Orchestra (1949–51). But he achieved no real acceptance as a record artist and moved from label to label, leaving single disks on Apollo, Savoy, Herald, and other R & B labels.

·

He has been called the "Shelley, Keats, and Rimbaud of the blues." He was a rambler of whom singer-guitarist Johnny Shines reported, "He says, 'I'm gonna take a leak'—and disappears for two weeks." He was a divinely inspired bluesman, but the devil was no figment of the imagination for him. "Me and the Devil Blues" and "Hellhound on My Trail" suggest a man in the grip of evil he could not overcome. He recorded only twenty-nine sides, but the legend that has grown up around him is of epic proportions.

In part, it stems from the fact that, like Shelley, Keats, and Rimbaud, Robert Johnson was dead by the time he was twenty-five or twenty-six. Until very recently, no one knew exactly how it happened, but everyone knew that he was murdered. An oft-repeated story had it that he was stabbed to death or poisoned by a jealous girlfriend. He was an incorrigible cocksman; shy in the presence of other musicians, he knew no boundaries when it came to women.

And now, as a result of the researches of Mack McCormick, a Texas folklorist at the Smithsonian Institution, we know that he was killed, not by a woman, "but by a man who had previously told him to leave his wife alone."

No one knows for sure when or where Johnson was born. It is believed that the year was probably 1914 and the place probably Robinsonville, Mississippi. McCormick's researches have established that he was the "outside" son in a family of ten brothers and sisters. As the result of a racial incident, his father, Charles Dodds, ran off before his birth, and his mother took up with a field hand named Noah Johnson.

Robert Johnson took to the guitar like an eagle takes to flight. Thereafter, he went rambling and performing through all the ballin' towns—St. Louis, Memphis, Houston, and Dallas, as well as the big and small spots in Arkansas and Louisiana.

He did his recording in Texas, the first two sessions in San Antonio or Houston in November 1936, and the last two in Dallas in June 1937. He was dead by December 1937. Don Law of ARC handled the four sessions for Vocalion Records, now owned by Columbia Records. In the two days between his first two sessions in '36, Johnson was arrested as a vagrant. Law found him with a smashed guitar, torn clothes, and a bloody face. Some hours after Law bailed him out, he received a call from Johnson complaining that he was lonesome. When Law probed, he learned that Johnson had a lady in his room who wanted fifty cents and that he was shy a nickel.

In his first session, Johnson cut "Sweet Home Chicago," recorded recently by Taj Mahal; also the famous "Dust My Broom," a hit for Elmore James and a favorite of The Rolling Stones. His "Crossroad Blues," cut on the second session, was revived by Cream. Not long ago, Paul Butterfield adapted his "Walkin' Blues." The *Let It Bleed* album of The Rolling Stones contains "Love in Vain," recorded by Johnson at his last session in '37, which also included the classic "Hellhound on My Trail."

Although unschooled, Johnson created brittle poetic images of great brilliance and intensity, reflecting a sense of personal frenzy. Like Rimbaud, he tried to engulf an eternity of sensual experience in his brief years. There was an ineluctable urge toward self-destruction in the excesses in which he indulged.

As a bluesman, his influence was felt among the R & B generation of Muddy Waters and Howlin' Wolf, whose fierceness was akin to his own. But he also touched the later generation that figured in the white R & B revival of the late 1960s.

•

Clifford Odets could have based his play *Golden Boy* on the career of Champion Jack Dupree, who was both a piano-playing bluesman and a professional fighter for a dozen years. When he decided to give up the ring because of the danger to his fingers, he settled in Indianapolis, locus of Leroy Carr, whom he met briefly and whose moody, bittersweet blues became part of Dupree's repertoire.

There are two stories about how Dupree became a Naptown resident around 1940. One has it that he was thrown off a freight train by a railroad "bull" when the train paused to take on water in Indianapolis. According to the other, he fought his last "major" bout in Naptown, knocking out someone called Battling Bozo. In either event, his decision to remain was the result of meeting an ex-fighter named Kid Edwards, owner of a record shop on Indiana Avenue in the city's black ghetto. Kid Edwards apparently got him some boxing matches, then arranged an audition with Sea Ferguson, a local black impresario, that led to a permanent position for Dupree.

Ferguson was the kingpin of Naptown's black-and-tan night life. In a four-story building he owned near the downtown area, he operated The Cotton Club (named after Harlem's famous night spot), The Trianon Ballroom, and who knows what else? Dupree impressed Ferguson with his personality as well as his bluesmanship. Ferguson liked the friendly-looking man with a pencil moustache, who drank little and was "clean" (no drugs). He hired Dupree first as a performer in his Cotton Club revues and then made him emcee.

The club was known to draw a rather tough, demanding clientele who were not above throwing things at performers they did not like. It was a great experience for the Champion, who really developed as a bluesman and showman from 1940 on. In time he acquired a partner in Ophelia Hoy. Their act was said to have compared favorably with that of the famous comic duo, Butterbeans & Susie.

By the time he settled in Indianapolis, Dupree had been leading a nomadic existence for at least ten years. Born in New Orleans in 1909 or '10, he lost both his parents in a fire in 1911 and was brought up in the Colored Waif's Home, the same orphanage in which Louis Armstrong was raised. By the time he was fourteen, he was out on the streets, sleeping in automobile graveyards. After a while, he encountered a Mrs. Gordon, who had seven children of her own, but who had the compassion to take in the lonely boy.

It is said that he learned to play the piano by watching eighty-eighters perform on New Orleans' Rampart Street, memorialized in his "Rampart Street Special" on Atlantic Records (1959). One of the street's barrelhouse bluesmen, who went by the colorful cognomen of Drive 'em Down, took a liking to the earnest lad and became his only teacher. Dupree paid tribute to him on a June 1962 Storyville disk, "Drive 'em Down Special." While he woodshedded on the piano, Dupree began working out in a Rampart Street gym operated by Kid Green. Before long, he was boxing professionally under Green's aegis and earning thirty to forty dollars a bout. That's how he came to be called *Champion* Jack Dupree.

Upon Drive 'em Down's death in 1930, Dupree left New Orleans, riding the "blinds" (freight cars) and "rods" (under the trains), boxing when he could and performing when he found an accessible juke or barrelhouse. Eventually he landed in Chicago where he made contact with some of the influentials: Big Bill, Memphis Slim, Tampa Red, and Leroy Carr; it was Carr's songs he had first heard Drive 'em Down play. With the recording industry in the grip of the depression, Chicago did not offer anything to make him stay, so he continued his hoboing. It is not unlikely that his wanderings carried him into Mexico, for in a 1942 session on Folkways he recorded "Mexican Reminiscences."

It was Kid Edwards, his Indianapolis mentor, who arranged for Dupree's first recording session. Starting in June 1940, he cut at least sixteen sides for OKeh, including two versions of "Cabbage Greens." Employing vegetable imagery for sex, the blues became an in-demand number that he recorded many times. The 1940–41 sessions also included "Heavy Heart Blues," a song that dealt with the traditional theme of the two-timing woman, but which rose to a rare expression of empathy: "I looked out my window, and I see you on the street./ The load your heart be carrying be too heavy for your feet." It is believed that Leroy Carr's former partner, Scrapper Blackwell, played guitar on the first of Dupree's OKeh sessions on June 13, 1940. Dupree himself played a rolling blues piano with a heavy boogie base.

By 1942 he was "On My Way to Moe Asch," as he explained on one of two dozen sides he cut between '42 and '45 for Folkways Records and its allied Asch, Solo, and Continental labels. Asch paired Dupree with the enduring blues team of "harpist" Sonny Terry and guitarist Brownie McGhee. The latter recorded with Dupree when he made combo sides as Willie Jordan & His Swinging Five (Alert, 1946), Champion Jack Dupree & His Country Blues Band (Apollo, 1949), Brother Blues & The Back Room Boys (Abbey, 1949), and as Meat Head Johnson (Gotham and Apex, 1950). In many of these, Dupree touched subjects of contemporary significance. "FDR Blues" and "God Bless Our New President" were among twenty sides he cut for Joe Davis Records in '46.

It came as no surprise when, in 1953, he began making records for one of the major R & B labels, King Records of Cincinnati. Dupree possessed the flexibility to move with the times, even if he was not a commanding figure. After he left King Records, he recorded on Groove and Vik, newly activated R & B subsidiaries of RCA Victor, but the move resulted in few released sides. An association with the potent R & B label, Atlantic, yielded two albums. The second, cut in London in 1959, contained a memorial blues, "Death of Big Bill Broonzy," who had died the previous year.

From 1959 to 1968, Dupree remained on the Continent, recording at first for Storyville in Copenhagen. He cut almost 200 sides for the label, many of which were never released. The titles give a good indication of the range of his material and the span of his career. There are country blues like "New Vicksburg" and Washboard Sam's "Diggin' My Potatoes"; Leroy Carr pop blues like "Hurry Down Sunshine," "Blues Before Sunrise," and "Midnight Hour Blues"; jazz-inflected blues like Billie Holiday's "Fine and Mellow"; urban classic blues like Pete Chatman's "Everyday I Have the Blues" and St. Louis Jimmy's "Goin' Down Slow"; and quite a number of R & B hits like "Drinkin' Wine, Spo-Dee-O-Dee," B. B. King's "Three O'clock in the Morning," Lonnie Johnson's "Tomorrow Night," and Guitar Slim's "Things That I Used to Do." He even covered a rock 'n' roll hit, The Falcons' "You're So Fine." In a London session in 1966 for Ace of Clubs and Decca records, Champion Jack Dupree revealed how far he had traveled from Rampart Street's barrelhouse blues when he recorded with rock stars John Mayall ("harp") and guitarist Eric Clapton. He was on the road, but not in the vanguard.

•

"Memphis was wide open," bluesman Furry Lewis has said. "The only way the police would bother you is if you was out there fightin' or somethin'." But they did not bother you if you were running a gambling joint or policy game, selling bootleg hootch, or doing a rocking business in segregated pussy. According to Tommy Pinkston, a pit musician in the old Beale Street Palace Theatre, there were several whorehouses staffed by black prostitutes who catered only to whites—white police, white politicos, and white patricians.

Peter Chatman, who became known as Memphis Slim, was born in Memphis in 1915, one year after W. C. Handy orchestrated "St. Louis Blues" in a Beale Street pleasure palace. The palace was the legendary Pee Wee's at 317 Beale, a combination swinging-door saloon, gambling casino, and policy game house. Like The Onyx on NYC's Fifty-second Street in the speakeasy era, it was a headquarters and a hangout for musicians, including members of Handy's marching band. They parked their instruments and picked up phone messages in a back room.

A few years earlier, Handy had written out copies of "Mr. Crump" on Pee Wee's cigar counter for visiting bands; later he published his tune as "Memphis Blues." Handy's marching band had helped elect Mayor Crump, who ran on a reform platform but won on the anti-reform sentiments popularized in "Mr. Crump": "Mr. Crump won't 'low no easy riders here. . . ./ We don't care what Mr. Crump don't 'low/ We goin' to barrelhouse anyhow. . . ."

Where there were easy riders, pimps, and politicos, there was music —and Beale Street was another Bourbon Street (New Orleans), Rush Street (Chicago), and Central Avenue (Los Angeles). Peter Chatman grew up with music in his ears: boogie, blues, barrelhouse, and rag-time. A precocious learner, he was still in his teens when he began playing gigs at roadhouses in Arkansas, where his father owned some clubs. By the time he was sixteen, he was ensconced on Beale Street, following prestigious Roosevelt Sykes into the famous Midway Cafe at Fourth and Beale.

"The Midway sold whiskey," Chatman recalls. "They had gambling and they paid the police off—it was during Prohibition. Beale Street was full of such clubs, though I think the Midway was the most lively. Sometimes I'd be playing there in the middle of the day—it was that busy. We didn't know what time it was, night or day."

Just about the time he was starting at The Midway in 1931, Pete paid a visit to Chicago. He met many of the Southern bluesmen who had settled there, but he decided to return to Memphis and remained long enough to earn the sobriquet Memphis Slim.

It was not until 1939, when Victor had stopped sending recording units into Memphis and juke joints were replacing honky-tonks, that he finally decided to leave Beale Street. When he first settled in Chicago, it was Sykes "who helped me a lot, telling me how to conduct my business, how to get a little money out of the damn cheats. . . . Roosevelt and his brother Johnny (a helluva piano player) used to play for my father, who had clubs in Arkansas and Memphis."

Living within a block of Broonzy on the Windy City's Indiana Avenue, he and Big Bill became fast friends. "After I got my flat at 3216 Indiana, it became a rehearsal place for all the Chicago musicians. When guys like Tony McClennon or Sonny Boy Williamson came up from the South, the representative would bring them to my house and I'd charge them four or five dollars a week. Tampa Red had a place over on State Street, and they'd stay there too. But my house was bigger, so I could accommodate more people. Oh, we had Walter Davis, Blind John Davis, Roosevelt Sykes, Washboard Sam, Curtis Jones, Big Bill, Cookie Malone, Lil Green, Jazz Gillum, Black Bob. . . ."

On his first Chicago club date, Memphis Slim accompanied Big Bill, who had been urging him to stop imitating Roosevelt Sykes. "That was in 1941 on the West Side. His piano player, Joshua Altheimer, had died, and Bill couldn't find anybody to play with. He and I had been jamming at my house, so I knew exactly what he wanted. When Big Bill really got the blues, he didn't give a damn for bars or measures, you just had to follow him. We worked that way for six or seven years—at all different clubs." The clubs included The

Ruby Tavern, 1410 Club, The Beehive—and even Town Hall in NYC.

When Slim cut his first sides in August 1940, he was accompanied by Washboard Sam. It was for Bluebird, and the first side was Sam's "Diggin' My Potatoes, No. 2." On a subsequent Bluebird date, he cut by himself. In December 1941, he waxed for the first time with Big Bill—and that was his last date until the war was over.

When he returned to a Chicago recording studio in 1946, it was on an offbeat label, Hy-Tone, and he cut with an R & B combo: alto sax, tenor, and bass, but no drums. During the next two years, the same combo appeared on the Miracle label, as Memphis Slim & His House Rockers. With Chicago bassist Willie Dixon replacing Ernest Crawford, the titles included "Blue and Lonesome," a blues that Slim recorded a number of times thereafter.

From 1949 to 1954, Slim cut steadily, but kept moving from label to label, from location to location: King in Cincinnati (1949); Peacock in Houston (1949); Premium in Chicago (1951); Mercury in Chicago (1951); Peacock in Houston (1952); Premium and Chess in Cleveland (1952); United in Chicago (1953–4); and Money in Los Angeles (1954). Obviously, he had accommodated himself to the demands of a new listening audience. Obviously, too, he was unable to deliver a best-seller for that audience.

The advent of R 'n' R benched him. Slim did not record again until 1958, when he did a date for Vee Jay, a strong R & B label in Chicago, and an album for United Artists Records, the result of a Carnegie Hall concert. In '59 he went back to the fledgling Vee Jay label, employing a solid R & B combo: two tenor saxes, alto, bass, drums, and his piano. After cutting several retrospective albums for Folkways, he turned in 1960 from R & B in a folk-oriented direction, recording an album for Verve and two *Live at the Village Gate* albums for Folkways with Willie Dixon and folksinger Pete Seeger, the latter of whom received major billing.

Nineteen-sixty also found him on the Continent, waxing an album for Collector in London and another for Storyville in Copenhagen. And then he was back in Chicago, recording a boogie album for Folkways. During the next three years, he cut retrospective albums for American and European blues labels.

By the time he recorded in Paris in 1962, Memphis Slim considered himself an expatriate. Married to a young French woman, he worked steadily at a Paris club when he was not touring Europe. Before long, he lived in one of Paris' luxurious residential districts and drove about in a Rolls or Silver Cloud. His wife preferred their Cadillac. "The Ambassador of the Blues," as he called himself, had no desire to return to the USA. In a *Rolling Stone* interview in 1972, he admitted that he was sometimes "bitter—no, scornful—about the place accorded me and black bluesmen in America," and he cited an incident that had happened in Chicago years earlier.

"Joe McCoy, he was the first husband of Memphis Minnie, wrote a song called 'Why Don't You Do Right—Like Some Other Men Do.' Lil Green made it first, then Peggy Lee did it. . . . Joe McCoy died and we had to bury him at the time his song was play- ing at the Chicago Theatre. We had to beg money from all the musi- cians . . . and he was the writer of this song. When a black person made a record, it was called 'race records.' But when Peggy Lee made it, it was a big hit. She got worldwide promotion while a black person only got it in the backyard of the black belt."

On another occasion, Slim told journalist-author Bruce Cook: "Those companies I recorded for made so much money off of us that we never saw. . . . Unless you were riding on top with a hit record, they wouldn't even talk to you. That's the rat race I'm talking about. I fought the shit a long time and then I got out of it. . . ."

Writer of one of the great blues classics, "Everyday I Have the Blues," Memphis recorded it originally in '48 as "Nobody Loves Me." Lowell Fulson introduced it under its new title on Swing Time in 1950. Two years later, Joe Williams made a best-selling record, accom- panied on Checker by the Count Basie Band. In 1955, B. B. King cut it on RPM Records, adopting it thereafter as his theme and becom- ing so closely identified with it that Memphis Slim's authorship is sometimes forgotten. Slim himself did not record it as "Everyday . . ." until 1961 when he was cutting in Bayonne, New Jersey, for a little- known and short-lived label, Agorilla.

Despite the productivity of Memphis Slim, St. Louis Jimmy, and Naptown's Jack Dupree, it was Kansas City that produced two vocal- ists who were really crucial in the rise of R & B. Native son Joe Turner's proving ground was the Sunset Club, while Oklahoma-born Jimmy Rushing's springboard was the Reno Club and the Count Basie Band.

The Sunset Club, located on Twelfth near the intersection of High- land and Paseo, was part of a roistering complex of speakeasies (dur- ing Prohibition), bars, night clubs, saloons, taverns, and music lounges.

"You could hear music twenty-four hours a day in Kansas City," drummer Jo Jones has said. At the peak of the Pendergast era, nearly 500 palaces of pleasure served a combination of music, liquor, food, girls, and marijuana. "Tricks," as they were termed, were two dollars an orgasm and "sticks of shit," as reefers were called, were three for a quarter. A Prince Albert tobacco can packed full of the stuff cost three to five dollars. Run by gangsters and politicos, the clubs were shielded from police interference by the Pendergast machine until it collapsed in 1938 in the wake of Tom Pendergast's conviction for tax evasion.

Anti-union, the mugs used free food, free liquor, and free "sticks" —not to mention the harder stuff that made Charlie "Bird" Parker a drug addict in his teens—to keep the pay down. "Usual pay was a dollar twenty-five a night," Bird reported later, "although somebody special, like Count Basie, could command a dollar fifty." Jamming was encouraged by the hood owners—it was unpaid entertainment to them—making Kansas City a stellar proving ground for the later greats of jazz: Count Basie, Lester Young, Bird, Ben Webster, and a generation of swing and bop musicians. In the Pendergast era, many of these star performers blew just for a share of the "kitty," a large metal can decorated with cats or "pickaninnies," whose wide open mouths and winking electric eyes were an invitation to give "bread."

Pianist-arranger Mary Lou Williams recalls an evening when "the word went around KC that Coleman Hawkins was in the Cherry Blossom [where Basie was then playing]. Within about half an hour there were Lester Young, Ben Webster, Herschel Evans, Herman Walder, and one or two unknown tenors piling in the club to blow. . . . The Fletcher Henderson band was to play in St. Louis that evening, and Hawkins knew he ought to be on the way. But he kept trying to blow something to beat Ben and Herschel and Lester. When at last he gave up, he got straight in his car and drove to St. Louis. I heard he'd just bought a new Cadillac and that he burnt it out trying to make the job on time. . . ."

It was an unbuttoned, anything-goes time and place, and the revelry was reflected in the swinging KC jazz that emerged. One of the smaller establishments, The Sunset, was owned by Felix Payne, a Pendergast crony, and managed by Piney Brown, probably the only club manager whose name is permanently inscribed in the annals of jazz. On his death in the fall of 1940, a group of jazzmen gathered in a Decca studio in NYC and improvised "Piney Brown Blues." The mourning jazzmen were led by two legendary figures who made the

Sunset jump. Pete Johnson, born in KC in 1904, was a piano player with a pair of mitts that gave his eight-to-the-bar stylings and walking bass the wallop of a big band rhythm section. And Joe Turner, a bartender in the tradition of the big barmen of the West—tall and hefty, six-foot-two and 250 beefy pounds—boasted a pair of pipes that did not require the public address system that blasted his singing into Twelfth Street to attract customers. Together, Turner and Johnson developed a genre of blues-shouting that antedated and became a major phase of World War II R & B.

•

"While Joe was serving drinks," Mary Lou Williams recalls, "he would suddenly pick up a cue for a blues and sing it right where he stood, with Pete playing piano for him. I don't think I'll ever forget the thrill of listening to Big Joe Turner shouting and sending everybody while mixing drinks."

Blue was the color of their music. But it was not the melancholy country blues of Blind Lemon or the caustic blues of Robert Johnson or the prison-death blues of Bukka White or the yearning, moaning blues of all the rural, "harp"-and-guitar performers who wandered through Southern towns in search of a handout. "Roll 'em, Pete," Turner bellowed. "Roll 'em boy, we all jump for joy."

In the midst of the revelry, women would enter Joe's mind. "You're beautiful, but you gotta die some day," he would declare existentially. So why not "boogie my woogie until my face turns cherry red." Cut in 1938 by Joe and Pete, the Vocalion recording of "Roll 'em, Pete" and "Cherry Red" sold so well that it had the same effect Mamie Smith's disk of "Crazy Blues" had had eighteen years earlier. It awakened recording companies to the expanding potential of the Negro record market. The mushroom growth of R & B "indies" developed not long afterwards.

Like an earlier generation of bluesmen, Joe Turner found little fruition in his relationship with women—in song, that is. "Love ain't nothin' but a lot of misery," he would declare, exhibiting no emotion in his characterization of the female as demanding, unpredictable, and untrustworthy. But unlike his predecessors in the blues, he did not cry or get uptight over it. He could love her still, but he "ain't gonna be her low-down dog any more. . . . Turn off the water works," he orders. "That don't move me no mo'." And off he went on the Midnight Cannonball.

Turner's song attitude was calculating as well as cool. "Shake it, Mama," he would urge, "and I'll buy you a diamond ring./ Don't shake it and you know you ain't gonna git a thing." And when he felt real mean: "If you don't mean me any good, I'll cut your head like a block of wood." The blues was moving toward the male boastfulness and arrogance of Muddy Waters, Bo Diddley, and all the "sixty minute" men on the postwar Chicago scene.

Joe Turner did not moan the blues. In a high-pitched, flutelike voice, with little change in dynamics, he shouted his independence. He was the new black man. After years of servitude and demeaning servility, he had self-respect and a sense of his worth. Under the inspiring influence of FDR's New Deal and the sense of togetherness generated by the struggle against the depression, he looked to the future with optimism. Why, in segregationist Kansas City, The Reno Club (the queen of clubs) admitted blacks as well as whites—although a divider was used to discourage mixing.

The sense of freedom apparent in Turner's jump blues was spatial as well as temporal in origin. If it was generated by the freewheeling spirit of Pendergast's Kansas City and the enhanced economic situation of the urban Negro in the late '30s, it also drew vitality from the rolling plains and wide open spaces of the Southwest. It was a new world for Negroes emerging from the viselike restrictions of tenant farming and mill labor.

In 1938, Joe and Pete went to New York—their first trip two years earlier had been a bust—and appeared at Carnegie Hall in the famous "From Spirituals to Swing" concert. Along with Albert Ammons and Meade Lux Lewis, who were also on the program, they were swept up in a renaissance of boogie woogie (1938–41) that yielded a long booking at Cafe Society Uptown and that brought the eight-to-the-bar style into the pop mainstream.

Yet after World War II, when R & B had superseded swing as the music of America's black ghettos, the man who was a harbinger of the style went into a decline. The exuberant barroom voice had not lost any of its vitality or vigor, but by then a new generation of urban bluesmen was riding the speeding train of shout blues and bar blues. Young blacks were buying Eddie "Cleanhead" Vinson and Wynonie Harris, and putting nickels in jukeboxes for Bull Moose Jackson, Big Maybelle, Big Mama Thornton, and others.

It was Ahmet Ertegun of Atlantic Records who rescued Joe Turner from obscurity. By 1954 Turner was a best-selling R & B artist and soon-to-be recognized major figure in the transmission of R & B into R 'n' R.

If Ma Rainey is "Mother of the Blues" and Bessie Smith "Empress of the Blues," Joe Turner surely is "Boss of the Blues." Life has been good to him since the advent of rock 'n' roll. But his thoughts keep returning to the early days in Kansas City, where he was born in 1911, began playing professionally at the age of seventeen—some say at the Kingfish, others the Hole in the Wall, and he says the Backbiters Club—and first teamed with Pete Johnson, who remained his partner into the '50s.

"All the working people came in early to the Sunset," he recalls, "and got high and had a ball. Then things would quiet down and finally there wouldn't be nobody in there except the bartender, waiter and the boss, and we'd start playing about three o'clock in the morning. People used to say they could hear me hollerin' five blocks away. It would be in the still of the morning and the bossman would set up pitchers of corn-likker and we'd rock. Just about the time we'd be starting to have a good time, here would come the high hats and we'd set the joint on fire then and really have a ball till ten or eleven o'clock in the day. Sleep? Who wants to sleep with all that blues jumpin' around?"

.

In the eyes of Basie biographer Raymond Horrick, rotund Jimmy Rushing was "the prime mover" behind the robust singing style, "more so even than the intrepid Joe Turner." As one seldom thinks of Turner without pianist Pete Johnson, so Rushing goes with Count Basie. Joining the Count at Kansas City's Reno Club in 1935, "Mr. Five-by-Five" remained with the Basie band for fifteen years. The Count, with whom he wrote a number of blues, has said, "For my money, Jimmy Rushing has never had an equal when it comes to the blues."

Rushing's association with the Count antedated the formation of the Basie band. It began when the "Kid from Red Bank" played piano with bassist Walter Page and His Blue Devils. In 1927 Rushing became a Blue Devil in Oklahoma City, where he was born in 1903 and to which he had then returned after a two-year sojourn in LA's after-hours clubs. When the Devils broke up in 1929, they were in Kansas City, and Jimmy, along with the Count and others, joined the big, exciting band of Bennie Moten. When it broke up in 1935 after Moten died following a tonsillectomy, Rushing and bassist Walter Page were among the Moten alumni who went with Basie.

Like Joe Turner, Rushing was a big man, but *around* instead of up. A prodigious drinker and eater, he was also a man of prodigious energies. It was his every-night routine to do a full evening's singing and then spend the hours until daylight wandering around Kansas

City, carousing and jamming. His volume, ebullience, and drive unquestionably drew much from the propulsive backing of the Basie band, over whose instrumentalities he soared with ease. Like Turner, he shouted the blues in a big, intense, high-pitched voice, but had a measure of hoarseness and more melody and *vibrato* than Turner had.

Jimmy never attained the renown of Joe, perhaps because he remained a band singer for most of his career. After the Basie bustup of 1950, he did become a soloist and even led his own septet for two years at Harlem's Savoy Ballroom. And when the "indie" labels began to flourish in the '40s, he did a session with Johnny Otis on Excelsior. But unlike Turner, Rushing had no hits of his own. His powerhouse vocals are to be heard on many of Count Basie's most memorable disks, including, of course, "Sent for You Yesterday (Here You Come Today)," with which Mr. Five-by-Five became irrevocably associated.

Until his death in 1972, he continued recording and making appearances at festivals like the annual Newport Jazz event. Though R & B was commercial music, written and produced for a specific market, it had improvisational elements, and it was here that Rushing's influence was felt. He was more of a jazzman than Turner, whose shout style was R & B.

Even as their shout style set a direction for the blues, Turner and Rushing added muscle to pop singing. Frankie Laine was the first of a group of white singers who became known as belters and who contrasted sharply in their drive and decibels with crooners like Como, Sinatra, and Nat Cole. Instead of "mooing" "That's My Desire," a typical Tin Pan Alley ballad of the '30s, Laine spit and stamped it out. By the early '50s, white shouters included young Eddie Fisher, Don Cornell and, on the distaff side, Rosemary Clooney, Georgia Gibbs, and the McGuire Sisters.

*If you don't like my ocean, don't fish
  in my sea* (repeat)
*Stay out of my valley and let my
  mountains be.* —MA RAINEY

The Boogie Woogie Craze. and 1938

C'N REMEMBER," Elizabeth Cotton said, "how we just loved playin' 'round the ol' railroad track in Chapel Hill. . . . Why, I usta steal my mama's straight pins just so's I could lay 'em on the steel rails and watch the trains burn 'em up." Elizabeth was eighty-three in 1975. She wrote her famous song "Freight Train" when she was a little girl growing up in North Carolina, picking it out on her brother's banjo before she was twelve.

Railroad trains are a rich part of our folklore—"Casey Jones," "I Been Workin' on the Railroad," "Wabash Cannonball." Evocative of an era in American life, the Iron Horse fascinated black folks. Trains meant tragedy, a loving man or woman leaving. Trains meant ducking a bad situation—"Gonna leave this Jim Crow town/ I'm sweet Chicago bound." Trains brought men to prison, but they could also "open" prison doors, as in the legend of the "Midnight Special"— "Shine its ever-lovin' light on me!" To a people moored to the soil as slaves or sharecroppers, trains meant freedom.

Many blues memorialize the names of trains, routes, or rail lines: Bessie Smith singing her "Dixie Flyer Blues"; the Illinois Central in Tampa Red's "I. C. Moan"; the Yazoo-Delta as the "yaller dawg" in Big Bill's "Southern Blues"; Leroy Carr in his "Big Four Blues"; Washboard Sam and his "Flying Crow Blues"; Georgia White riding the "Panama Limited." And in the repetitive eight-to-the-bar figures of boogie woogie, many hear the clicketty-clack of train rhythms and the huffing and puffing of steam locomotives.

During and after World War I, Midwest railroads ran excursions for Negro factory workers desirous of visiting relatives in the South. To carry the greatest number of passengers and keep the cost low, baggage cars were used instead of coaches with seats. "Honky-tonk trains," as they became known, carried pianos for entertainment. Albert Ammons, a boogie-woogie giant, played on one of these. And Meade Lux Lewis, closely associated with Ammons during the '20s and '30s, recorded an impressionistic "Honky-Tonk Train Blues" in December 1927, a year before Pine Top Smith aroused public interest in boogie woogie.

Actually, the origin of boogie woogie is shrouded in mystery. There is agreement that it is a rudimentary style, developed by untutored fingers in search of a dance rhythm or rhythmic accompani-

51

ment for a blues melody. Some jazz scholars believe that just as rag-time piano involves imitative guitar-picking in the treble range, so boogie woogie is a guitar derivative in the bass range.

Pete Johnson recalls that, as he grew up in Kansas City, he heard pianists playing something they called Western rolling blues. The style was also known as Fast Western, suggesting possibly its origin. Leadbelly, Jelly Roll Morton, and Bunk Johnson claim they heard boogie woogie in Texas during the first decade of the century. W. C. Handy recalled hearing the sound at about the same time in Memphis. Little Brother Montgomery, who began playing professionally around 1917, in Louisiana, claims that all Southern pianists used rolling basses. Aaron "T-Bone" Walker, born in Texas in 1913, has said, "The first time I ever heard a boogie-woogie piano was the first time I went to church. That was the Holy Ghost Church in Dallas. That boogie woogie was a kind of blues."

What we know with certitude is that boogie was a staple of Chicago house-rent parties (known as "boogies") during the depression years. It is believed that it reached the Windy City shortly after World War I, brought there by itinerant eighty-eighters with strange names like Cat-Eye Henry, The Toothpick, and Jack the Bear, as well as Cow Cow Davenport, who came from Alabama and who had nothing to do with the popular song derivative, "Cow Cow Boogie," though he did write "Cow Cow Blues."

Paul Oliver claims that when Cow Cow was playing at the Star Theatre in Pittsburgh in 1924, he heard Clarence "Pine Top" Smith at a local honky-tonk. "Boy, look here," Cow Cow is supposed to have said, "you sure have got a mean boogie woogie," alliterating the designation of the piano style played at Chicago "boogie" parties. Pine Top Smith is credited with using the term *boogie woogie* on record for the first time. The year was 1928.

Pine Top, so called because he was tall and had red hair, appar-ently took Cow Cow's advice and settled in Chicago. There were two other piano players in the apartment building where he lived: Meade Lux Lewis and Albert Ammons, both of whom drove for the Silver Taxicab Company and became disciples and, later, central figures in the boogie revival of 1938. Pine Top, born Clarence Smith in Troy, Alabama, in 1904, recorded "Pine Top's Boogie Woogie" and other boogie numbers on Vocalion in 1928. By March of the following year he was dead. After finishing a gig, he stopped by at a party given by the Odd Fellows Lodge at Masonic Hall. An argument developed among lodge members, shots rang out, and Pine Top, an innocent bystander, fell dead.

Although some of the St. Louis pianists name Son Long, a little-known piano player, as the originator of boogie woogie, the father figure was a Chicago bluesman named Jimmy Yancey. Born in the Windy City in 1894, he was a familiar figure at Chicago "boogie" parties and occasionally played small clubs like Cripple Clarence Lofton's bar. He did not regard himself as a professional musician. In fact, beginning in 1913 he worked for many years as a grounds keeper for the White Sox ball club at Comiskey Park. But his house, near the ball park at Thirty-Fifth and State streets, was a hangout for Lofton, pianist Doug Suggs, classic blues singer Chippie Hill, as well as Pine Top, Lewis, and Ammons.

In 1938, Meade Lux Lewis composed "Yancey's Special" as a tribute to the man who devised many of the boogie basses he and his confreres used and, in fact, recorded before their mentor did— Yancey himself did no recording until April 1939, a decade after his disciples first appeared on wax. His sessions were not on any of the established labels, but were on Solo Art, a short-lived company established in the wake of the national boogie craze. Curiously, Solo Art was the creation of a New York bartender, Dan Qualey, who was a collector of piano blues disks and who also recorded Ammons, Lewis, Pete Johnson, and lesser-known boogie performers.

After the Solo Art sessions, other companies became interested in Yancey. Before his death in September 1951, he made records for Vocalion, Session, and Atlantic. British critic Max Harrison regards the Session disks as the most "magnificent" examples of Yancey's work. He contends that boogie woogie drew much of its power from its close relation to the life of its audience. Both Yancey and Doug Suggs worked at the White Sox ball park, the latter as a porter, and Lewis and Ammons remained cab drivers until the boogie woogie craze made them professional musicians. Since the musicians worked at jobs like those of their listeners, there were shared feelings between performer and audience.

Although Count Basie recorded "Boogie Woogie (I May Be Wrong)" with a vibrant vocal by the redoubtable Jimmy Rushing in 1936—the year that Meade Lux Lewis cut new versions of "Honky-Tonk Train Blues"—the real upsurge in boogie recording began after the "Spirituals to Swing" concerts at Carnegie Hall in 1938 and '39. (In 1938, Harlem's Cotton Club featured a number entitled "Boogie Woogie," but this was written by two Tin Pan Alley songwriters and was not the Yancey number by the same name.)

Beginning in 1939, The Boogie Woogie Trio (Ammons, Lewis, and Pete Johnson) did much to bring the sound, style, and form to the ears of listeners and audiences around the country. Fresh from their resounding acceptance at Carnegie, they embarked on a cross-country tour. Assisted at first by singer Joe Turner and, after Pete Johnson left the group, by Joe Williams, the trio also made records.

•

Boogie woogie became a basic ingredient of R & B. But before it did, and as it did, the pulsating *ostinato* of eight-to-the-bar rhythms swept into the mainstream of pop. Count Basie, whose band performed at the Carnegie concert, tried for pop hits with "Basie Boogie" and "Red Bank Boogie," and Tommy Dorsey made it big with a simply titled "Boogie Woogie" disk. The swing band that derived the most from the style was the short-lived Will Bradley Orchestra, with Freddie Slack at the piano and Ray McKinley as drummer-vocalist.

Playing the Famous Door on Fifty-second Street in 1940, the Bradley orchestra programmed an experimental boogie-woogie instrumental put together by Slack, McKinley, and the band's arranger. During a drum break, according to legend, McKinley shouted spontaneously: "Beat me, daddy, eight to the bar." Two Tin Pan Alley songwriters who were in the audience, Don Raye and Hughie Prince, instantly went to work on a song built around the exclamation. Recorded by the band, it became the forerunner of a series that included "Scrub Me, Mama, with a Boogie Beat" (a 1940 hit for Will Bradley), "Rhumboogie," "Boogie Woogie Bugle Boy," and "Bounce Me, Brother, with a Solid Four," all 1941 hits for the shrill-voiced Andrews Sisters.

All of these were published by one Tin Pan Alley firm, Leeds Music, now MCA. Leeds grew up on the eight-to-the-bar sound just as Capitol Records, founded in 1942, scored its first best-seller with "Cow Cow Boogie," recorded by none other than Freddie Slack, with a rousing vocal by Ella Mae Morse. In '41 Leeds also published "Boogie Woogie Stomp" by Albert Ammons and "Boogie Woogie Prayer," introduced at Carnegie and written by The Boogie Woogie Trio.

Its interest in black-oriented material made Leeds a maverick among Broadway publishers. The incentive came from its owner,

Lou Levy, who had been a dancer and had performed in blackface in Harlem with the Jimmie Lunceford Band. An early Leeds hit (1939), "T'ain't What You Do (It's the Way that You Do It)," was written by black trumpeter-arranger Si Oliver and James "Trummy" Young of the Jimmie Lunceford Band, which introduced it. In '42 Leeds promoted "Mr. Five by Five," Don Raye-Gene De Paul opus and a best-seller for Freddie Slack on Capitol and Harry James on Columbia; it was later associated with the man who could have inspired it, Jimmy Rushing. The following year, Leeds scored with "Shoo Shoo Baby," written by Phil Moore, and, in '44, with the breezy and amusing "Is You Is, or Is You Ain't (Ma' Baby)?" which brings us to a key figure in the rise of R & B, Louis Jordan, who made a hit recording of it.

Leeds' success prompted other Tin Pan Alley firms to leap on the eight-to-the-bar bandwagon, accounting for "Boog It," co-written and recorded by Cab Calloway, "Boogie Woogie on St. Louis Blues," by Earl Hines, and, unbelievably, "The Booglie Wooglie Piggy," recorded by Glenn Miller.

Like Modern Records of Los Angeles, which released boogie woogie versions of popular classics played by pianist Hadda Brooks, many of the R & B "indies" kicked off their labels with boogie-woogie material.

•

The year that brought the rise of boogie woogie as a national craze, 1938, witnessed significant changes in white-black relationships in entertainment. That year, Fifty-second Street was integrated due to, of all things, an air-conditioning unit. NYC's summer heat was pushing the Famous Door, one of the street's best-known clubs, to the brink of bankruptcy. The Count Basie Band, despite its popularity in many places, had never played a midtown Manhattan club. John Hammond, who had discovered Basie in KC, made a simple offer to the tough owners of the Door: book Basie and let me bring my friends, many of whom are black, and you can have air-conditioning. It cost $2,500 to install a unit, and Basie mounted the tiny stage. His became a name band in '38 largely because of broadcasts from the club. During the "remotes," as radio pickups from locations were then termed, the Door's clientele had to nurse drinks on the street lest they had their eardrums shattered in the small club. And Fifty-second Street, as segregated as the rest of Manhattan's midtown theaters and clubs, opened its doors to Negroes for the first time.

In 1938, too, Billie Holiday joined the Artie Shaw Band, the first black girl to sing regularly with an all-white band. It caused both Lady Day and Shaw no little anguish, even at NY's Lincoln Hotel, where Billie was compelled to use the Service Entrance. Later Billie said, "There aren't many people who fought harder than Artie against the vicious people in music business or the crummy second-class citizenship which eats at the guts of so many musicians. He didn't win. But he didn't lose either. It wasn't long after I left"—Billie quit to ease the pressures that were being exerted on Artie—"that he told them to shove it like I had. And people still talk about him as if he were nuts because there were things more important to him than a million bucks a year."

And 1938 was the year of Slim & Slam's nonsense novelty, "Flat Foot Floogie (with the Floy Floy)," and Ella Fitzgerald's swinging nursery rhyme, "A-Tisket, A-Tasket." In addition to playing the "Spirituals to Swing" concert, which brought Billie Holiday, Hazel Scott, and the boogie woogie piano players to the stage of Carnegie Hall, The Boogie-Woogie Trio appeared before New York cafe society. It was an emergent year for black performers and the future of R & B.

The 1930s were a period of profound sociological and psychological change for Negro exiles from the South, particularly after the country climbed out of the depression. Symptomatic was the FDR-inspired desertion of the Republican Party by Negroes. The President's wife was known to be most ardent in her support of Negro causes, giving black people a feeling that they had a friend in the highest reaches of government. The door to economic advancement also seemed to swing wide open when, in 1935, the CIO unlatched union membership to blacks.

The world of popular music likewise began to reflect a new receptivity. Prior to 1938, record companies generally hired artists, particularly black artists, on a single-session basis, paying a flat fee and no continuing royalty on sales. The artist was then "free" to record for any other label, and the same artist frequently appeared on different labels, though pseudonyms were employed. But by the end of the '30s, Negro artists were becoming so valuable that major record companies began insisting on exclusive contracts.

Anticipating the expanding demand, two of the biggest booker-managers in the "colored" field began discussing merger. Hoarse-voiced Joe Glaser, later head of the still-active Associated Booking Corporation, handled Louis Armstrong, Hot Lips Page, Willie Bryant, Andy Kirk, and Claude Hopkins. He was head of the

Rockwell-O'Keefe Agency's colored band department. Moe Gale had his own agency, managing Chick Webb, Teddy Hill, Erskine Hawkins, and The Savoy Sultans. He also owned the famous Savoy Ballroom in Harlem. With Glaser "controlling" bookings at Sebastian's Cotton Club on the Coast and The Grand Terrace in Chicago, a merger of the two would have created a powerhouse black agency. But Glaser and Gale could not come to terms; the merger talks came to a standstill, and a sigh of relief was heaved, not only by Rockwell-O'Keefe, but by Consolidated Radio Artists and Associated Radio Artists, booker-managers of Fletcher Henderson, Duke Ellington, and others.

Despite the word *radio* in the agency titles, there were no black bands on network radio, even though Fletcher Henderson, Count Basie, Benny Carter, Duke Ellington, Jimmie Lunceford, and Chick Webb had been swinging it before Benny Goodman was crowned "King of Swing." Nor were these stellar aggregations or those of Les Hite, Earl Hines, or Andy Kirk able to secure bookings at the big white hotels or clubs. Motivated by John Hammond, who later became his brother-in-law, Goodman did much to break down segregation by adding pianist Teddy Wilson and then Lionel Hampton to his band. But they performed as a trio or quartet *in front* of the band, not *with* it.

Vibrahharpist, drummer, and pianist—he used only one finger of each hand like mallets on the keyboard—Hampton became a key figure in the transition from big band swing to small combo R & B.

I grabbed ma baby, I danced till the clock struck twelve....
—BLIND LEMON JEFFERSON

Blues Bands
—and Louis Jordan

IN 1943 The Famous Door, one of Fifty-second Street's first jazz clubs, relocated at the northwest corner of Fifty-second and Seventh Avenue, above a Chinese restaurant. I was present at the opening, which starred Lionel Hampton's big band. Even while he was with Goodman, Lionel had recorded with pickup groups and he had made the charts in '39 with "The Jumpin' Jive," a best-seller also for Cab Calloway. His big band, organized in 1940, played with a rhythmic punch and propulsive drive unequalled by any of the white swing bands. (Financed and booked by Joe Glaser, it included Illinois Jacquet on tenor and Jack McVea on baritone sax, both important figures in the R & B era.) At the Famous Door opening, the band, hyped by Hamp's own histrionics on drums and vibes, developed a thundering beat of such proportions that it felt like the whole building was jumping. The proprietor of the Chinese restaurant protested to the owner of the building, who was relieved only when a hastily summoned building inspector assured him that the structure could withstand the strain.

A deeply religious man who attended Holy Rosary Academy in Kenosha, Wisconsin, and St. Monica's school in Chicago, Hampton has said that when he performs, "It's like a spiritual impulse comes over me." This is, of course, characteristic of gospel and blues singers. Singer-writer Alberta Hunter has said, "To me, the blues are—well, almost religious. The blues are like spirituals, almost sacred. When we sing blues, we're singin' out our feelings."

Under Lionel's leadership, the Hampton band *played* its feelings. Recognizing that excitement was its main objective, Leonard Feather contends in his *Encyclopedia of Jazz* that the band "gradually reduced its musicianship and by the early '50s had become as much a rhythm-and-blues as a jazz attraction, with circus overtones." Regardless of this jazz-critic snobbery toward R & B, the Hampton band was not concerned simply with showing off its musicianship. It did not separate itself from its audience as an elite craft group, but sought emotive contact with its listeners. It sought to move its listeners as well as entertain them.

The story is told of a gig that the Hampton band played on a barge on the Potomac River. At the peak of a rousing rendition of "Flyin' Home," a Hampton hit noted for Illinois Jacquet's frenzied tenor solo, Hampton shouted to his bass player, "Hit the water!" The cat was so stirred up that he took the exhortation literally, and leaped overboard. The Hampton band early epitomized the roaring vitality and energy of R & B—and, incidentally, nurtured one of the great R & B ballad singers, Dinah Washington.

•

Early in 1938, Reese Dupree, then the leading booker of colored bands, exulted over the grosses of the Jimmie Lunceford, Willie Bryant, and Lucky Millinder bands at the Strand Ballroom in Philadelphia. Although the year was marked by a recession in music business (and the exodus of Tin Pan Alley songwriters from Hollywood, to which they had sped for the film musical splurge of the '30s),

"COLORED BAND BIZ [was] BECOMING BIG BIZ," as *Billboard* headlined in April 1938. By 1942 the developing R & B explosion forced *Billboard* to institute a separate chart, distinct from pop and hillbilly, to cover "race" recordings. As in the pop area, bands again dominated the new race chart. Apart from Louis Jordan, there was Lucky Millinder, born Lucius Venable Millinder in Anniston, Alabama, in 1900, who became known when he took over as leader of the noted Mills Blue Rhythm Band in 1934. Millinder was a nonperformer who had his start in 1928 organizing shows at the Grand Terrace, a new Chicago club. A frequent visitor to the Grand Terrace was mobster Al Capone, who drove around in a seven-ton armored limousine, ordered all doors closed when he came in with his henchmen, and tipped lavishly.

From the Mills Blue Rhythm Band, Millinder went on to launch his own combo in the early '40s. "Lucky couldn't read a note," says drummer Panama Francis. "But if you gave him a bunch of guys who could read, in one week's time, he'd have them sounding like a band that had been organized for a year. He could remember everything in an arrangement after it was run down once. He was a genius that way."

About the time that he started his own band, Millinder wrote an article for the *Amsterdam News* of Harlem, expressing the resentment of black musicians over the many imitative white swing musicians who were capitalizing on their creativity. But Millinder took the position that much of the responsibility lay with colored arrangers— he cited numerous names—who were working for white bands. R & B was to go through a parallel development, except that the white imitations were without benefit of black collaboration.

Millinder's acknowledged sensitivity to public taste yielded a hit for his band in '42 in "When the Lights Go on Again," a nostalgic pop war ballad, and the following year in "Apollo Jump," an R & B rouser.

Millinder's alumni included some of the giants of R & B: Sister Rosetta Tharpe, blues shouter Wynonie Harris, tenor-sax honker Eddie "Lockjaw" Davis, pianist-arranger Bill Doggett, and saxist-vocalist Bull Moose Jackson, leader of a highly successful R & B combo.

•

Erskine Hawkins came out of Alabama, too—he was born in Birmingham in July 1914—with a band whose members originally worked to pay their tuition at Alabama State. But after they hit New York in 1936 and began playing the Harlem dance spots, the 'Bama

State Collegians incorporated and chose Erskine as their leader. Managed by Moe Gale, owner of the Savoy Ballroom, they became the house band, along with Chick Webb, and were great favorites from 1938 until the ballroom's closing in 1958.

Although he played trombone, tenor sax, and drums, all quite well, Hawkins earned his stripes as first trumpet. "High-note trumpet stuff was very popular at the time," arranger Sammy Lowe told jazz historian Stanley Dance. "Louis Armstrong really started it, but Erskine excited the people in N.Y. On 'Shine,' Louis would usually make 10 high C's and high F's. . . . [At the Harlem Opera House] Erskine would play 100 high high C's and make high F while the band counted them aloud."

Moe Gale got the band a Vocalion recording contract, then a Bluebird tie-up and, finally, a berth on the all-important Victor label. By 1940 the band was traveling at high speed as "Tuxedo Junction," named after a small rail junction in Alabama, became a "race" hit. When the Hawkins record took off, Glenn Miller quickly made a cover version (also on Bluebird) and racked up such sales in pop that he became identified with the tune. It was featured in the bio-pic *The Glenn Miller Story*, but it was Hawkins' theme. As Hawkins always pointed out, the oft-imitated trumpet solo on his disk was not by him, but by William "Dud" Bascomb.

In 1940, Hawkins also scored with "After Hours," a composition written by pianist Avery Parrish, who arranged for the band. After the success of his piece, Parrish remained in California and made good money as a solo pianist in clubs. In a bar one night, he was struck over the head with a bar stool. Attendant paralysis forced his retirement from music, and a fall down a flight of stairs in '59 brought death at the early age of forty-two.

When Erskine Hawkins had "Tuxedo Junction," he "was kind of downed by the critics," Sammy Lowe told Stanley Dance. "They dug Dud and Paul Bascomb, and Julian Dash [a co-writer of the number], but they were always down on him. They didn't realize that the reason the band was in New York in the first place was because of his high notes, which excited the public. You can talk about artistic endeavor all you want, but America is a commercial country where people go for materialistic things, and you don't make any money if they don't recognize you."

Perhaps what troubled the jazz critics was Hawkins' sensitivity to popular taste. The band's arrangements had a simplicity and commercial appeal that won it a large following, and it had crossovers into pop. Nevertheless, when postwar economics wiped out the big bands, ushering in the era of the jazz combos on the one hand and R & B on the other, Hawkins had to slim down to a nine-piece combo. By 1949 he displayed his awareness of the direction of black music in a series of Victor recordings that included "John Henry Blues" and "Memphis Blues."

•

Although Lionel Hampton, Lucky Millinder, Erskine Hawkins, and other blues bandsmen like Budd Johnson, Buddy Johnson, and Erskine Butterfield contributed to the rise of R & B, all dwindle in significance before the jazzman whose ebullience, humor, and ethnic orientation helped usher in the R & B era. Born in Brinkley, Arkansas, in 1908, Louis Jordan did not attract attention until he began playing alto sax and singing novelties in the Chick Webb Band in 1936. By 1938 he had his own combo, The Tympany Five, was playing at the Elks Rendezvous in Harlem and had cut his first sides for Decca Records. Although he recorded steadily for Decca all through the R & B years, leaving at the edge of the rock 'n' roll era in '53, Jordan was not regarded as a rhythm-and-bluesman and certainly not as a jazzman.

Most critics thought of him in the genre of Cab Calloway, whose tremendous acceptance by the white world of the 1930s was then as rare as Lena Horne's. From 1929 for a decade, Calloway was a band-leader whose Alabamians—he, himself, was born in Rochester, New York, and raised in Baltimore, Maryland—alternated with Duke Ellington's orchestra as the house band at Harlem's Cotton Club. When the famous night spot closed in 1940, Cab played extended engagements at The Cocoanut Grove in NYC's Park Central Hotel and at the midtown Cafe Zanzibar. *Metronome* praised the band for its "clean musicianship, jazz licks and brilliant showmanship."

Yet Cab's public image was that of the "King of Hi-De-Ho," the performer (he was also the composer) of "Minnie the Moocher," and the "Dean of Jive," as New York University dubbed him when it gave him an honorary degree. (He claims to have originated the term *jitterbug* with the title of a song he co-authored and recorded in 1934, and he is the author of the *Hepster's Dictionary* [1938], maintained by the New York Public Library as the official reference work on jive language.) Cab Calloway was, in short, a great showman, comic, and personality rather than a singer and bandleader.

Louis Jordan in *Junior Prom*

And this is what Louis Jordan became once he decided that jazz-men "play mostly for themselves," and concluded, "I want to play for the people." Of course, he functioned as a bandleader from the time he organized The Tympany Five, but in an early trade paper ad, he typed himself "The Modern Bert Williams," after one of the most gifted clowning songmen of his race.

According to Milt Gabler, who produced Jordan's records at Decca and then became producer for Bill Haley, an unacknowledged Jordan disciple who signed with Decca in 1954, "Jordan came right out of the Cab Calloway zoot suit era and the costumes were all a put-on. He knew his audience and how to preach to them." Cab Calloway's voice has been described as exuding "a joy and festive spirit which moves one to instant gaiety." This was true, not only of Jordan's singing style, but of his entire personality. The man who performed at one point in an oversized pair of white-frame glasses radiated irresistible good humor.

Of the greatest significance in the parallel trajectories of the two comedy showmen is Jordan's ethnic orientation. Calloway's interest in jive found its counterpart in Jordan recordings like "Knock Me a Kiss," "That Chick's Too Young to Fry," and "Reet, Petite, and Gone." But Jordan's feeling for folk was not merely a matter of hip lingo. His recordings of "I'm Gonna Move to the Outskirts of Town,"

"Early in the Morning," and other blues reveal that, as T-Bone Walker has said, "Jordan plays good blues and he sings them like they were originally sung, too."

The late Ralph Gleason wrote: "The Mills Bros. like the Ink Spots were really black men singing white songs. But Louis Jordan sang black and sang proud." In songs like "Beans and Cornbread," "Ain't Nobody Here but Us Chickens," "Don't Worry 'bout That Mule," "Somebody Done Changed the Lock on My Door," and "Caldonia (What Makes Your Big Head So Hard?)," he manifests a rich appreciation of the modes, manners, and living style of poor black people. R & B was so rooted, too.

The most interesting of Jordan's local-color vignettes was, of course, "Saturday Night Fish Fry," which took a critical turn as he told of the intrusion of police into a simple scene of merrymaking—only black people would be hauled off to jail for becoming boisterous. But since Jordan was primarily an entertainer and not a commentator, a humorist rather than a satirist, he was not bitter or angry, just amused. And that was precisely the stance and social outlook of R & B, too.

For almost a decade after 1942, Jordan's records were seldom off the "Harlem Hit Parade," as black charts were then typed in *Billboard*. Not infrequently he monopolized a majority of the slots with three or four disks, placing no fewer than eleven recordings in the best-selling category in 1946. That he was able to sell over a million copies of "Choo Choo Ch'Boogie" and close to that of "Saturday Night Fish Fry" suggests the breadth of his appeal. You could not sell that many disks in the years from 1946 to 1950 to black buyers alone. Even when he was not selling a million, his '44 disks of "G. I. Jive" and "Is You Is, or Is You Ain't (Ma' Baby)?" were pop jukebox as well as "race" hits. And "Is You Is?" was heard in no fewer than four Hollywood films.

Doubtless there was an element of self-caricature, if not self-depreciation, in Jordan's humor. It might have accounted for his appeal to "ofays." There is also the possibility that middle-class blacks felt that they were laughing at things associated with rural and lower-class blacks. But there was also a measure of strength in the ability to laugh at oneself—and this is what, I think, Jordan may have communicated to black people.

Immediately after Pearl Harbor, Col. Benjamin O. Davis was named a brigadier general, the first black to achieve this rank. Executive Order 8802 forbade "discrimination in employment . . . in defense industry and government." Fraternizing on foreign soil, which had been illegal during World War I, was tolerated, though frowned upon, in World War II. Once the war was over, the political and social strides made by Negroes hardly seemed as formidable as they did during the conflict. But the war years, being "acceptance years," Negroes could, perhaps, look at their past without self-consciousness. Jordan's popularity among blacks was evident not only in the sales of his disks, but in a series of motion picture shorts he made for an "indie" company, aimed exclusively at the Negro market.

Jordan is the pivotal figure in the rise of R & B, not only because he was the musical father of Bill Haley and, strange as it may seem, Chuck Berry, but because his fantastic success on disk, on the radio, in personal appearances, and on the screen fired the imagination of black artists and independent record producers. He demonstrated that, not only was there a market for black-oriented material and black-styled music, but it was a big market, white as well as black.

Jordan's influence on Haley, forerunner of rock 'n' roll, was partly the result of Bill's working as a record librarian at a small Chester, Pennsylvania, radio station. Programming Jordan and R & B disks during the late '40s led Haley to think, as he told me, "Why shouldn't a country-and-western group sing rhythm-and-blues?" The first record he cut for Essex, a small Philadelphia label, was "Rocket 88," a cover of a '51 R & B hit by Jackie Brenston on Chess.

Milt Gabler has indicated that he consciously sought to incorporate the Jordan jump beat into Haley's style. Because none of The Comets, except pianist Johnny Grande, could read music, "head" arrangements were worked out in the studio. "We'd begin with Jordan's shuffle rhythm," Gabler told me. "You know, dotted eighth notes and sixteenths, and we'd build on it. I'd sing Jordan riffs to the group that would be picked up by the electric guitars and tenor sax Rudy Pompanelli. They got a sound that had the drive of The Tympany Five and the color of country and western. Rockabilly was what it was called back then."

As to his impact on Chuck Berry, the writer of "Maybellene" has himself said, "I identify myself with Louis Jordan more than any other artist. I have a lot of flighty things like Louis had, comical things and natural things and not too heavy." And Berry, who is a most guarded man, added, "If I had only one artist to listen to through eternity, it would be Nat Cole. And if I had to work through eternity, it would be Louis Jordan."

•

By the end of World War II, all the ingredients of R & B were available. *Shout-styled blues* had been developed by Joe Turner and Jimmy Rushing, among others. *Boogie woogie* and *shuffle* had demonstrated their metrical appeal. The abbreviation of the big band to the *tenor-sax styled* combo offered *jump* accompaniment to convert blues into rhythm-and-blues. In the wake of Jordan's triumph—and that of Cecil Gant, whom we shall meet again shortly—it was time for the R & B shouters, honkers, and black-oriented record media to make their appearance.

Out of the blues bands already discussed, as well as the bands of Benny Carter, Les Hite, and Earl "Fatha" Hines, came not only some of the top honkers but shouters like Wynonie Harris, Bull Moose Jackson, Savannah Churchill, Ida James, Dinah Washington, and T-Bone Walker. And in six cities with large Negro populations—LA, Chicago, NY, Cincinnati, Houston, and Memphis—a flock of "indie" R & B record labels took flight.

groove 1   **LOUIS JORDAN**

Jordan was sunning himself in his backyard when I arrived at his home in Los Angeles in July 1973 for what may have been his last interview. A good-looking man, he wore a brown straw hat tilted back at a rakish angle. He was bare-chested and wore a stylish pair of walking shorts. He was taking the sun as a cure for arthritis and was wearing copper bracelets on his wrists and ankles as part of the treatment. A trim-looking man, with not a wrinkle or a jowl in a beaming face, he looked neither ill nor his age. He had just passed his sixty-fifth birthday on July 8.

•

"It was a saxophone in a store window. I could see myself in the polished brass—that started me off. I ran errands all over Brinkley [Arkansas] until my feet were sore, and I saved until I could make a down payment on that shiny instrument. My father taught me music. I was still a teen-ager when I played my first gig. It was vacation time, and I blew with Rudy Williams—he was known as 'Tuna Boy' Williams. It was at The Green Gables in Hot Springs. That was about 150 miles west of Brinkley where I was born. Little Rock is in between, and about 100 miles from my hometown. I went to Arkansas Baptist College there and majored in music.

"My first professional job was with The Rabbit Foot Minstrels. Ma Rainey was once the star, and Bessie Smith got her start with them. I played clarinet and danced all through the South. Around 1932, I went North, settled in Philadelphia and got connected with Charlie Gaines' band. I had eyes, you know, on the Big Apple—New York City. But it took several years before I could get a union card in Local 802.

"I worked with several bands. Joe Marshall was one. He was a drummer with Fletcher Henderson. We played the Elks Rendezvous in Harlem for a while. Around 1936 I joined Chick Webb at The Savoy. Played alto, sang, and announced numbers. Chick was a little man, hunchback, but a great drummer. He had big ears for talent—like Ella Fitzgerald, whom he adopted so she could sing with the band. But he was no showman and some people thought I was the leader because I introduced numbers.

"I loved playing jazz with a big band. Loved singing the blues. But I really wanted to be an entertainer—that's me—on my own. I wanted to play for the people, for millions, not just a few hep cats.

"When Chick died in 1938, I cut out and formed my own band.

Louis Jordan
(Courtesy RCA Records)

Nine pieces, and we had a regular gig at the Elks Rendezvous. Four-sixty-four Lenox Avenue was the address. Also played club dates and 'off nights.' Those were nights when a band was off. I played up and down Swing Street, Fifty-second Street. After a while, I cut the nine pieces down to six. Later I added a guitar and made it seven. Once I got known as Louis Jordan and His Tympany Five, I kept the name. But I always had seven or eight men.

"After that Fifty-second Street bit, I started playing proms, like at Yale and Amherst. That's when friends began saying, 'Why don't you get out of New York, Louis? It's taking too long for you to get started.' So they came and asked me if I would play with the Mills Brothers in Chicago. The Capitol Lounge was for white folks. It was across the alley from the Chicago Theater. Not many Negroes came because they felt they weren't welcome. They wanted me to play intermission for the Mills Brothers. I started not to go—that was a big mistake.

"At first I was doing ten minutes; then they raised me to fifteen; then I got to half an hour. The Mills Brothers went over big. 'Cause the people who came to hear them and Maurice Rocco—he was the third act—they had *their* following and he had *his*. And after a while, I had *my* following. The Capitol Lounge couldn't hold two hundred people. But they would have a hundred twenty sittin' down and maybe a hundred eighty standin' at the bar. After that booking, I was gone!

"The Fox Head in Cedar Rapids was a great turning point in my career. It was there I found 'If It's Love You Want, Baby, That's Me' and a gang of blues—'Ration Blues,' 'Inflation Blues,' and others. Now, it was just a beer joint. It ran from a street to an alley. Beer was fifteen cents. The owner was a ham radio operator. He insisted that I stay at his house. He was a wonderful man.

"After my records started to sell, we drew mixed audiences to clubs like The Tick Tock in Boston, Billy Berg's Swing Club in Los Angeles, The Garrick in Chicago and The Top Hat in Toronto. The first time I played the Adams Theatre in Newark, I played with a fellow who sings like Perry Como. He was in Vic Damone's bag. And the second time I played there, I appeared with a society band like Meyer Davis. I was the Negro part, and they played the white part. That's how we did it in the early forties, so that we drew everybody. I was trying to do what they told me: straddle the fence.

"I made just as much money off white people as I did off colored. I could play a white joint this week and a colored next. The Oriental

Chicago was a white theater for the hep crowd. The State
n Hartford was the same. It drew the college crowd. Same
Riverside Theatre in Milwaukee. Any time I played a white
my black following was there. The Paradise Theatre in Detroit
the borderline. The Negroes lived on that side of Woodward,
and the whites on this side. Oh yeah, the Royal in Baltimore was a
colored theater. But white people came to see me. The Beachcomber
in Omaha was basically a Negro place. When I played there, I had
white audiences. Many nights we had more white than colored,
because my records were geared to the white as well as colored, and
they came to hear me do my records.

"For Negroes, there were three basic theaters: Howard in Washington, Regal in Chicago, and Apollo in Harlem. In the big years,
we played the Paramount on Broadway—a four-week engagement
every year—and the Apollo twice a year. We appeared at the Regal
in Chicago every Easter week and the Apollo every Christmas week.

"At the Apollo, I did lose a set of hubcaps. Came out of the stage
entrance on a Hundred-twenty-sixth Street, and they were gone. I
noticed this fellow hanging around and asked if he knew where I
could get a set. Quick as a flash, he showed up with four. I paid him
five dollars a piece. When I turned them over, each one had two little
letters in them: L.J. [Laughing] He charged me five dollars a piece
for my own hubcaps.

"I have read Jack Schiffman's book about the Apollo, and I know
he claims I was temperamental and made a fuss about the place being
too cold or too hot. His father, who ran the theater, didn't care how
you felt as long as you did the show. And I found that out, and it
dragged me. He'd come backstage. And when he did, they'd kinda
clean it up. But as soon as he went up front, it was a mess. He could
have corrected it. But he never did.

"Every time I used to go to the Apollo, I'd get hoarse. Why?
Because it was a filthy theater. And he'd say, 'I'm gonna close it up
for two or three months during the summer and clean it up.' He'd close
it up and set mothballs around, and then open it up next year. The
same dirt was there from year to year. To tell you how I know—I
used to put a mark in it. And I'd come back to play there again, and
my mark would be there. Great theater! Did a whole lot for Negroes,
made a lot of Negro stars. If he'd cared, he would have fixed it up
and made it a first-class theater. If he had cared!

"I think the Schiffmans are rich. I never did get to his son's place
out from Tampa—he's got a ranch, it covers miles and miles. He

sells cattle. Outta sight! He invited me, but I never got a chance to go. Anytime we'd be down there, we'd be playing one-niters, jumping two and three hundred miles, and I had to get some sleep. But they never did fix the theater. It ain't fixed now.

"I played there not long ago. It smells like the Apollo of twenty years ago—and if you care about a thing that you made millions out of, you would have it fixed up. You didn't have to tear the theater out and gut it out. Just fix it up! Fix the heat, fix the drinkin' fountain, just the little things. The same drinkin' fountain is there that's been there for twenty-five to thirty years. They may have changed the spout because it wore out. And I will tell Schiffman that! 'Cause I ain't in the business now. I don't care if I don't play the Apollo no more. And in fact, I don't feel that I should. I've contributed, and at sixty-five years I ought to calm down and enjoy myself. [Chuckling]

"Old man Schiffman was one of the best managers of theaters I have ever worked for. I will give him that. He was a great man. He's eighty years old and he's still great. A good mixer, he could get out of you what you think you can't do. A great manager! But as for the theater—stinks!

"And still it's number one of the Negro theaters. The kids were there that night when I played not long ago. They surprised me, they did. Give me three standing ovations. And I did only one rock 'n' roll number. I did 'Hello Dolly,' 'Let the Good Times Roll' (opened with it), 'Saturday Night Fish Fry,' and 'Caldonia.' That was my program—and they was standin' up when they closed the curtain."

•

Jordan began recording on Decca in 1938 when the label was in its infancy. Although band records by such black artists as Duke Ellington, Count Basie, Jimmie Lunceford, Chick Webb, Andy Kirk, Cab Calloway, Lucky Millinder, Erskine Butterfield, and Erskine Hawkins, among others, became pop jukebox hits, Jordan did not make the lists until 1942, when *Billboard* established a jukebox "Race Chart." By then he had scored his breakout stand at the Capitol Lounge in Chicago. "I'm Gonna Move to the Outskirts of Town" and "What's the Use of Getting Sober?" were the first two numbers to gain such recognition, followed in '43 by "Five Guys Named Moe" and "Ration Blues."

"Caldonia (What Makes Your Big Head So Hard?)," a hit in 1945, was written by Jordan and covered by Woody Herman. "He did his own thing," Jordan said, as we continued talking in his back-yard. "He did it up real fast." Jordan illustrated, imitating Herman's *tempo furioso* and snapping his fingers in rhythm. "Mine was medium tempo—bump-be-dump-ee, bump-be-dump be-doo-be-doo.

•

"Not all of my hits was written by Negroes. 'Knock Me a Kiss' was by a white man, Mike Jackson, though Andy Razaf wrote some special words. Two white guys came up with 'Choo Choo Ch' Boogie.' I believe that Vaughn Horton and Denver Darling were really country-western writers. The song was played to me in the studio. We were recording with Milt Gabler, who handled all my Decca sessions. He brought the words and asked what I could do with them. At that time I had Wild Bill Davis playing piano. All of my things are based on the blues, twelve-bar blues. So I asked Bill to play some blues in B-flat. I was using the shuffle boogie then. He started shuffling off in B-flat, a twelve-bar phrase—and that's how we got the record together.

" 'Blue Light Boogie' was by a colored woman, Jessie Mae Robinson. She was the best-oriented colored songwriter. She didn't write white songs. 'Don't Worry 'bout That Mule' was written by colored. 'Beans and Cornbread' was by a colored boy, Freddie Clark. 'The Chicks I Pick Are Slender, Tender, and Tall,' 'What's the Use of Getting Sober?,' 'Somebody Done Changed the Lock on My Door,' 'That'll just about Knock You Out'—they were all written by Negro, colored, black writers. But that saying, 'That'll just about knock you out,' started from a white man in Grand Forks, North Dakota. The boss of the place had a husky voice. [Imitating] He'd say it all the time. That's where we wrote the song from.

" 'Saturday Night Fish Fry' was the work of a colored girl. 'Let the Good Times Roll' was by Sam Theard, a black comedian. 'Mama, Mama Blues' was by a black writer, and so was 'Small Town Boy.' That was written by Dallas Bartley, my bass man, who comes from a small town. But 'Five Guys Named Moe' was by a white guy. It was done with a Negro feel. [Sings lyrics and some of the instrumental licks] 'Beware, Brother, Beware' and 'Buzz Me' were both written by white guys. 'Early in the Mornin' ' was by a mixed group—Leo Hickman, a white man; Dallas Bartley, my bassman; and me.

"I had five tunes that sold a million records, and "Is You Is, or Is You Ain't (Ma' Baby)?' was by a white man. I was playing at Lakota's Lounge on Wisconsin Avenue in Milwaukee. He was a little humpback fellow about the size of Chick Webb. He'd come in every night and talk to this girl. They'd have dinner and stay for lunch. He just loved me, and he'd hang around so long as I was there. She'd be talkin' to someone else and he'd say to her, 'Is you is or is you ain't ma baby?' And he was strictly Caucasian—no black blood in him at all. Soon I started sayin' it. And he said, 'Let's write a song.' You can't say because of color or race that a person would not say a thing or would not do a thing.

"'Caldonia' was by a black writer, meaning me. Fleecie Moore's name is on it, but she didn't have anything to do with it. That was my wife at the time, and we put it in her name. She didn't know nothin' about no music at all. Her name is on this song and that song, and she's still getting money."

•

Lou Levy, who founded Leeds Music in 1937 and sold it to MCA for $5 million in 1968 (he managed The Andrews Sisters in their heyday) published "Is You Is . . . ," "I'm Gonna Move to the Out-skirts of Town," and other early Jordan songs. Of the substitution of Jordan's wife's name for his on "Caldonia," Levy had this to say: "Louis Jordan was controlled in those early days by Berle Adams and a fellow called Lou Levy. I told Berle that if he would quit his job at GAC [General Amusement Corporation], I would give him my piece of Jordan. I felt that he could always get a job as an agent, but he had a unique opportunity to become the personal manager and partner of a colossal talent like Jordan. I cut out so that Adams could cut in. I later sued Adams on 'Caldonia.' When I got out, I said, 'I'll publish the songs and you manage him.' Then Mr. Adams forgot to remember. They put Louis Jordan's wife's name on the song and gave it to another publisher. But actually Jordan and Adams both got outsmarted. When the Jordans got divorced, Louis tried to get the song back and his ex-wife thumbed her nose at him."

•

"I guess I will live a long time," Jordan said, "without worrying about the money that Fleecie Moore is getting. If I make a deal and it goes down in someone else's favor, I just feel that I never missed what I didn't have. I don't go worryin' about it. I've almost got my present wife doin' the same. It's a hard job to convince a woman not to worry. My wife is nineteen years younger than I am. But I'm tryin' to get her to that.

"I'm glad that you don't think I show my years. For the last twenty-five or thirty years, I have took care of myself. Now you talk to people and they say I was a wild, woolly thing. I was wild onstage, but when

I came offstage, I took care of me. I still do. My wife is goin' to a party; if I don't feel like goin', I say, 'Darlin', call up a girlfriend,' and I stay home and rest. That's the cause of my feelin' good. My voice hasn't left me."

•

How did he feel about the younger generation?

"White kids are today much more open to black culture and the black experience than even the blacks. They're closed up. What proves they're closed up—I saw on TV a group of black people marching and they had a sign, 'Black Will Prevail.' Now, how ridiculous is that! I don't want it like that. I want a man to be accepted for what he is and what he can do, whether he's black, green, or yeller. I don't wanna be tolerated. If you give me a job and I can't do it, fire me and hire a white boy if he does a better job. Not just keep me there because I'm black.

"I was in Tahoe about three weeks ago. Some kids come in, some hippie boys, and they started to sing. All white kids. They felt that way, and they kept it going. First thing you know, they'll have a tune, sit down, and write it. In the forties, there were white guys writing the blues. I know because they hung out with me and asked me to sing their tunes. If you associate with a certain type of person, you begin to think like they think. I was in Philadelphia for years, hung out with wop boys and Jews, and some of them wrote blues.

"My whole theory, my whole life, has been: when you come out to hear me, I want to make you happy. Now I hardly ever do any morbid tunes, or any sad tunes, or any tunes that would suggest that you cry. I wanted to make you smile or laugh.

"Now, I did a tune last Sunday in an album I'm cutting for Johnny Otis, called 'Helping Hand.' It's got some very deep words, written by two white boys. It deals with a rundown woman sitting on her ghetto steps, watching her kids play, wondering if the Lord would take the time to hear her nightly prayer. It went on about the older kids, playing in the street, as she wondered if she'd have money to put shoes on all of their feet. Now, see how deep that thinking is? And this by two young kids, whipper-snappers, as you'd call them. But they're thinkin' and they're writin'. It's not race or creed. It's the way they think.

"I've hung out with some hippies, and they come up with some things that ain't no black boy to think of that. It's not in the white category at all. Maybe it's because their environment is different now. It's mixed. It's not that white hangs on the other side of the track and colored on this side. The white goes on the other side of the track, too. I'd like to go on record by saying this—it's the first time I've ever said this: Do you know? I can go out and get some white musicians that can play *my* music better than I can find colored musicians?

"I finished that album for Blues Spectrum—that's Johnny Otis' label—last Sunday night at eight o'clock. Dig me now. You used to get a white musician to play and it would sound like this. [Sings a square lick] That is gone. Now they feel and interpretate it better than a black. We have called up and gotten colored musicians to come in and do a phrase we wanted to put on a record. We said, 'This is how it goes. How would you play it?' You can't write this phrase down. You have to feel it! They come and say, 'How did you say it go?' No, no, no! They say, 'Well, wait a minute, let me think about it a bit.' And they can't do it. You call up white musicians and they do the job better—better than the colored musician. We have only a few colored musicians that have stuck to the things that we set up a long time ago. We set up a thing that should have been a heritage of us. But we got away from it.

"Now, to tell you what I mean. If I want a drummer, I can find only a couple of drummers in the whole Los Angeles to play my stuff. The Negro drummers are playing rock 'n' roll stuff and they got the feelin' of it. Call in a white boy, and he comes and plays it for you. He adapted himself to it, which we don't do as Negroes. The drummers of today wants to play trumpet, tenor, alto, trombone on the drums. A drum is a rhythm instrument, should be played as a rhythm instrument. When you call somebody to play some shuffle boogie and some real low-down blues, go and get your white boy. In the forties, we were separated. They couldn't play it then, but they can play it now. They learned and adapted themselves.

"But as a black artist, I'd like to say one thing: There is nothing that the white artist has invented or come along with in the form of jazz or entertainment—I'm not talkin' about concert music, the masters. He hasn't invented anything. Rock 'n' roll was not a marriage of rhythm and blues and country and western. That's white publicity. Rock 'n' roll was just a white imitation, a white adaptation of Negro rhythm and blues.

"What the white artist has done—and they started it fifteen or twenty years ago—they started the publicity and eliminating talk of the black artist. They eliminated talking about who did what and how good it was, and they started talking about white artists.

"I went to a concert in Philadelphia, a Dave Brubeck concert.

We had a gang of black kids there from the colleges, and we went to a party after the concert. They said that Dave Brubeck was the greatest piano player they've ever heard. Now how ridiculous can that be! I can name ten pianists that play better than Brubeck. He is a stylist, but not a great pianist. But the publicity has told them—they read the magazines—that so-and-so is the greatest.

"I just got through playing the Newport Jazz Festival in New York City. We did a jam session at Radio City. It started at eleven-thirty P.M., and we were the last to go on at four o'clock in the morning. Now there was a blues singer—I didn't know that he was supposed to be the greatest blues singer from England. I said to him, 'Let's do some choruses together.' And he turned green after I did the second one. I didn't say it—the papers said I just washed him out. Now I am a black artist. He's come along, and the whole world knows that he's the greatest white blues singer in the world. Because they have been told that in magazines, on the radio, on television. And where did he learn it from? I lived in New York for twelve years and I've had white musicians hang around me twenty-four hours if I would let 'em, hang around until they learned something from me. *And then I couldn't go to hear them play!*

"One good thing I had in my life—and I have no regrets—that the people who associated themselves with me let me portray *my* talent. They let me do whatever I felt. Milt Gabler of Decca—he's one of the main fellows in my life. If we were recordin' a tune and I said, 'I would like to do it this way,' he never said, 'No, don't do it that way.' Today, if you get a production manager to produce a record, he wants you to do the record like he wants it done. That is the change that has happened. If I can't play the way I feel, to heck with it. I'll go out like that.

"I worked with Chick Webb and Ella Fitzgerald, and I played jazz. And then I switched over. I didn't think I could handle a big band. But with my little band, I did everything they did with a big band. *I made the blues jump.* After I got into the public, they said I should straddle the fence. I didn't know what they meant at first. But they mean that I shouldn't play just for Negroes, but for the world. Then I decided that when you come to hear Louis Jordan, you'd hear things to make you forget what you'd had to do the day before and just have a good time, a great time.

"I was with Decca Records from 1938 to 1953. When Bill Haley came along in '53, he was doing the same shuffle boogie I was. Only he was goin' faster than I was. He was running around the country.

I got sick on the road. We had thirty-one one-niters, booked three hundred–four hundred miles apart. It meant driving all day and playing all night. Doctors said: 'You cut down or you die.' I stopped playing all those one-niters. Bill Haley was jumping all over the country. My inactivity was the whole thing, not rock 'n' roll. I had two years of ill health, very bad health. I'd go out and play a couple of months, and I'd get sick. Then I'd go back to Phoenix and sit down. I lived in Phoenix for eighteen years. Moved down there before I got sick, but I kept recuperating in the house I built.

"After Decca, I went with Aladdin Records here on the Coast. Two brothers ran it. Both of them died not too far apart. Both were gamblers. One played horses; the other stayed in Vegas. They were the Mesner brothers—had a big house out on Sunset Boulevard, almost at the ocean, near Will Rogers Park. It had everything, even a studio where we could record. They had money before they went into the record business. But they didn't have Decca's juice."

•

In the summer of 1973, just before I interviewed him, Jordan helped Johnny Otis' newly formed Blue Spectrum label by recording an album of oldies that had made him the superstar black artist of the postwar years. With Otis on drums and piano, and talented Shuggie Otis on bass, guitars, and organ, Jordan worked with a Tympany Five front-line: trumpet, tenor sax, and his alto. While the sixty-five-year-old voice inevitably lacked some of the ebullience of his prime years, the appealing blues intonation and infectious good humor were there. And his sax solos, richly improvised, had the sock and raucous shout of pristine R & B.

Otis, who played the Apollo for the first time in 1946 on a Louis Jordan bill—Jordan sent the money to bring the stranded Otis band from Detroit—recalled, "Whenever we played shows with Louis back in the late forties and early fifties, all the members of my group would stand in the wings and watch the master showman at work."

Jordan was performing in Sparks, Nevada, in October 1974 when he suffered a heart attack. After a short stay at St. Mary's Hospital in Reno, he returned to his Los Angeles home to recuperate. On February 4, 1975, he went shopping with his wife. Shortly after he returned home, he suffered a fatal attack. The father of R & B was flown to St. Louis for burial in the Mount Olive Cemetery.

groove 2   **BERLE ADAMS**

"I started with Louis Jordan in 1941. I was an office boy at GAC. They gave me an opportunity to become a salesman if I could sell an attraction to The Capitol Lounge in Chicago. That's where I was located. So after working hours, I would haunt the place and try to persuade the owner to buy a band from me. I did not know whom to offer so I wrote our office in New York, and Dick Gabbe suggested that I submit Louis Jordan and His Orchestra, who were playing at the Elks Rendezvous in Harlem. I persisted and thought for a time that I had made the sale.

"But on the night when one of the owners was supposed to make the commitment, as I was waiting in one of the high-backed booths, I overheard a conversation in a booth in front of me. Mr. Schwartz, one of the owners, was telling a gentleman that he had decided to bring in Louis Jordan. And the gentleman said, 'You're kidding. Louis Jordan doesn't have an organized band. He works with pickup groups on weekends. You don't want him. He's nobody compared to Roy Eldridge.' That was my first encounter with Joe Glaser, who did such a great managerial job for Louis Armstrong and other black artists. I was defeated. The lounge bought Roy Eldridge.

"Months went by and I kept haunting the place, trying to sell Jordan, whom I really knew nothing about. One day, the president of GAC, Thomas Rockwell, came to Chicago. I guess he was told that I knew the people at the Capitol Lounge, and he asked me to go there with him that night. I felt pretty good going with the president of the company, who wanted to sell Mr. Schwartz and Mr. Greenfield on the Mills Brothers. They had been out of the country on a South American tour and during their absence, The Ink Spots had become very popular. Mr. Rockwell saw the lounge as a medium for reestablishing the Mills Brothers. When he told the owners that he could get Station WGN to put a radio line into the place, they bought the Mills Brothers. And Rockwell did convince WGN to do live broadcasts from the lounge.

"The steady attraction there was Maurice Rocco, who did not play standing up, as he later did. He really copied the gimmick from Jordan. But I did some arithmetic and could not see how four shows by the Mills Brothers and four shows by Rocco could keep the lounge audience entertained from nine P.M. to four A.M. in the morning. When

I broached this problem to the owners, they quickly agreed that they needed an orchestra to fill out the extra time. But they would not pay more than scale. And scale then was thirty-five dollars a man per week—a dollar per working hour—plus a dollar extra for the leader. When they agreed to pay Jordan's transportation from New York, I closed the deal. It was a big accomplishment for me personally. After Jordan opened, I received an increase in salary from twenty dollars a week to thirty-five. I was quite pleased.

"In those days, Jordan sang ballads. He billed himself: 'Louis Jordan, his Silver Saxophone and his Golden Voice.' He played intermission music, and the crowds liked him. The stage of the Capitol Lounge was in back of the bar. We couldn't put the drums up there, so all we had was the snare drum, a trumpet, bass, Jordan, and piano. And the pianist had to stand because there wasn't room for the piano stool. Tommy Thomas stood all the time, and that's how Rocco developed his standing style. The Mills Brothers had trouble to keep from falling off the stage.

"It was a very successful engagement, and Jordan and I became very friendly. He had great personality when he sang. I asked him one day why he didn't do any novelty songs. He thought that would be making a fool of himself. But I persisted and suggested that he try a song called 'Cherry, Cherry,' which was then becoming popular on a Harry James record. One day at rehearsal, he and Eddie Rohner, who played trumpet, did try it and they gimmicked up a version.

"Jordan would lean over and ask the bartender for a maraschino cherry. Then he'd hold it up and sing, 'Cherry, cherry, you're so hard to get.' The first time he did it, the place broke up. That's all Jordan needed—a little encouragement. Slowly, guys in the band began coming in with ideas, although they considered themselves musicians rather than entertainers.

"Then we had a problem. Jordan came to me to say that he had to quit; he just couldn't live on sixteen dollars a week. Then I discovered that Jordan couldn't get the musicians to come to Chicago unless they got forty dollars a man. So he was taking the money out of his salary and paying each man five dollars above what the lounge paid. When I learned this, I went to the owners and had them fire the band. Jordan was the attraction after all, and the owners didn't care if we used local musicians so long as they didn't have to pay more than they were paying.

"But when they received their notice, the musicians went to the union, and the union summoned Jordan on the ground that he was playing for below scale. I always had a habit of reading contracts through from beginning to end. I had read the musicians' contract and union bylaws. I found a technicality that prevented Jordan from being fined. But as a result of the interrogation, we learned that the trouble-maker in the band was the bass player. All the others agreed to play for the scale being paid by the lounge. So I gave Jordan the money to send the bass player back to New York—that was required when you brought a musician away from his home base—and we hired Dallas Bartley.

"He was a godsend because he became with Jordan one of the creators of the novelty material that became Jordan's stock in trade. 'Five Guys Named Moe' was one of the songs he brought it. From the lounge, the combo went to a club I handled in Cedar Rapids, Iowa, The Fox Head Tavern. Now, they were not in New York or Chicago. They were not known, and they could make fools of themselves. That was where they developed all the novelty songs that later made Jordan. When they came back to The Capitol Lounge, he had a wealth of material and became a smash overnight.

"That's when I got the idea that Jordan should be on wax. Even though I pointed out that Jordan had once made four sides for Decca, the office didn't feel that they could present a five-piece band to a record company. But I was then in line for a raise. When I asked for permission to pitch Jordan at Decca, they said, 'Okay, if you get a recording contract for Jordan, you won't need a raise.' I could retain the commission from the recording fees.

"I contacted David Kapp in New York, who was aware of Jordan's success at the lounge and who agreed to sign him for four sides at a penny royalty with options. I suggested to Mr. Kapp that we would accept a half penny, instead of the penny they offered, to insure that our option would be picked up after the first four sides were released—in case other new attractions sold as many records as Jordan. (I saw records as a means of exploitation then—to build audiences for personal appearances and to help us increase our fees—rather than as a money-maker.) David Kapp agreed, and that was the way the contract was written.

"After that, J. Mayo Williams, who supervised black talent for Decca, came out to Chicago and brought four songs with him. We rehearsed and recorded them. And the first two sides were 'Knock Me a Kiss' and 'I'm Gonna Move to the Outskirts of Town.' The other record had 'Mama Mama Blues' and 'It's a Low-Down Dirty Shame.' The great Andy Razaf, later Fats Waller's collaborator, wrote special lyrics for the first two sides. Both records were big, but the first one with 'Kiss' and 'Outskirts' was a real smash. It was on the 'Harlem Hit Parade,' as it was called in *Billboard*, among the top three records of forty-two.

"I went into New York for my first visit. When I met David Kapp at Decca Records, he told me that his brother wanted to meet me. This was too much. I had read so much about the great Jack Kapp. Well, after some pleasantries, Jack Kapp asked whether it was true that I had insisted on signing for a half penny a record when I was offered a penny. I said it was true. Then, Jack Kapp asked, 'Don't you feel sorry now? We've sold thousands of Jordan records. You've lost a lot of money for your attraction.'

"I told him, 'If we had taken the penny, you may not have given us those tunes. Now that we're a recording attraction, we're getting more money in clubs. Wherever we go, we've increased our terms. We're very happy. We consider records only for exploitation purposes.' With that, Mr. Kapp rang a buzzer, and when Isabelle Marks came in he said, 'Tear up the Jordan contract. Issue a new one for 5 percent *retroactive*. No young man is going to make a fool of me.' That was the beginning of a very close relationship with the Kapps. And through the years, I guess that I was the spoiled boy at Decca. The Kapps always gave me the right to pick Jordan's tunes by myself, set the release dates, the couplings, and everything else.

"We had a long string of hits. I guess we were on top of *Billboard* listings more than any other attraction over an eight-year period. Not because we knew more than anybody else, but because we had the band so well organized that we were able to do what is known today as market research. After the first couple of hits, we went out on a tour of one-nighters. We had two arrangers with the band, Bill Doggett and Wild Bill Davis. They would alternate. One week, one would play piano and the other do the arrangements; then, we'd switch. All of us looked for material: Jordan, myself, the boys in the band. Much of it came from unknown writers. We favored good lyrics, topical and meaningful, and we got them from both white and black writers. When we found something we liked, an arrangement would be made up and we'd play it on the one-nighters. The songs that the public asked for again and again were the songs that we recorded.

"When we walked into a studio to do a record date, we knew that the four songs would be hits—we had pretested the market. And everything we released was a smash because the public had already determined that they liked the song. They had already judged them and waited for our recording. For eight or nine years, we had the number one record in the R & B charts. It wasn't that we knew more, but that we had researched the market *before* we recorded the song.

"The other thing that was interesting in our story: when the war came along and we were a thirty-five-cent record, Decca would not release any more records because of the ceiling on the price of records. The cost of material was higher actually than the price of the record. They couldn't move us to the seventy-five-cent label. So that's when we made 'Is You Is or Is You Ain't?' with Bing Crosby. Since we needed a record by Jordan on the market, they convinced Bing to cut two sides with him. We found the song out here in Los Angeles. Billy Austin, whose idea it was, was a maintenance man or a superintendent of an apartment building.

"At this time BMI [Broadcast Music Inc.] was subsidizing publishing companies that could deliver performers on the radio. Usually this meant that a company had to hire a professional staff. I went to them with a different kind of proposition. We wouldn't put on a staff, but we would make a motion picture short in which we would introduce new songs. We would then book these shorts into theaters in black communities down South so that, in place of phonograph records, they would be able to see Jordan perform new material on the screen. Bob Burton of BMI approved the idea. The first short we made was 'Caldonia.' That was its title. It was so popular wherever it played that frequently the regular motion picture received second billing on theater marquees to Jordan's short. In this way, we were able to keep Jordan before the public at a time when we couldn't get records released.

"One night when I was dining at Lindy's, Woody Herman came over to my table asking about blues material that he could record. Herman was then playing the Meadowbrook, and Jordan was at the Paramount. I suggested that he catch one of Jordan's shows. 'I can't get Decca to release Jordan's record,' I said, 'so you might as well do it.' Well, he came in the next night, and I had Louis perform 'Caldonia' for him. He practically ran out of the theater and cut it—an entirely different treatment from Jordan's, but a big record for him. Then Erskine Hawkins heard about it, and he cut it for RCA Victor. When these two disks came out, Decca was forced to release Jordan's record.

"Louis never played black clubs. In Los Angeles, for example, he usually appeared at Billy Berg's Swing Club, a white club. Theaters were another story. In LA, we only played the Lincoln, which was black. In New York, we played the Paramount—a four-week engagement every year—and we played the Apollo twice a year.

"Our procedure was to play the black theaters on a percentage basis. Because of the popularity of the attraction, we took a lot of money out of them. We were fortunate in that every year we took a great female singer along with us on personals. Jordan subscribed to my theory that you buy the best talent and give all the acts important billing. We brought Sister Rosetta Tharpe into the theaters for the first time. We introduced Sarah Vaughn and Dinah Washington on their first theater tours. When Paula Watson hit with 'A Little Bird Told Me'—on Supreme Records, I think it was, in '47—we took her with us. We took Ruth Brown on her first theater tour. That was just after she signed with Atlantic. We took Dinah out of Hampton's band and Sarah out of Earl Hines' band. The Will Mastin Trio, featuring Sammy Davis, made their first theater tour with Jordan and remained a featured part of the Jordan theater tour for three years.

"We were the first to bring a white act into black theaters. It was a group called Los Gatos Trio, a spectacular opening act. We always used a white sight act to open the show.

"Louis lasted into the fifties. I was the president and founder of Mercury Records, and I became ill. Had a problem with my spine. Sold my stock in the company because I had to move to California. After I recovered, I became a little wary about being in a personal service business where everything is dependent on your availability. Jordan was very big—one of the big, if not the biggest, black attractions. But I didn't want to travel as much as I had. My doctor didn't think it was advisable. My children were small and I worried about their future. So I decided that it would be smart to affiliate with a large corporation. Fortunately, MCA [Music Corporation of America] came to me at that time with an attractive proposal, and I decided to give up the band.

"It was a very trying situation with Jordan. There was no reason for me to give up the attraction. We had a good relationship. We were making a lot of money. He was at the height of his popularity. When I sat down with Louis to explain my thinking, I never forgot the look on his face. His reaction was: 'You think I'm over the hill.' I responded, 'How can that be? You still have one hit record after another. Your income is tremendous. Your percentages are high, and you can work as many days of the year as you please.' But he kept staring at me and shaking his head. 'You're too smart to walk out on something that's that good. You must see something in the future. You think I've hit the top and that I must start coming down.' I protested that that was not true. He said, 'Then I guess you're tired of this old chick and you've found yourself a new, young bird.' It was really harder to walk away than I made it seem or than he realized. But an aching back is quite convincing.

"When I left the band, Jordan did something he should not have done. All through the years he was not happy with the small combo, but I would not permit him to enlarge. This fight—really just an argument—went on for years. And because of our close relationship, he would accept my decision and thinking. Two months after I left him, he formed a big band. The next thing I heard, he was at the Flatbush Theatre in Brooklyn. I went out to see him. Afterward we had dinner. We had always been direct with each other through the years. When he asked how I liked the band, I said, 'Terrible! You sound like everybody else. You had the most unique sound. You were individual. There was only one. You were that. You were the pace-setter. Everybody imitated you. You had the sound.' His reply was that a guy had to change. I pleaded with him to go back to the small band. But he was adamant.

"The other thing that hurt him was the flow of material. He stayed up there so long as he had great material—and material came to us because he was a big record-seller. As he began to slide, the flow of material stopped. He also lost some of the musicians who had helped bring fresh material into his repertoire.

"Probably time had something to do with it, too. And then Bill Haley came along with a style that he copied from Jordan. Haley picked up where Jordan left off. But years later, I remember being in Chicago. On the radio, I heard Howard Miller, then the big dj, interviewing Kirby Stone. He had just played the Kirby Stone Four's hit record of 'Baubles, Bangles, and Beads' and he was raving about the arrangement, its originality, and asking how Kirby came to it. Stone laughed. 'What do you mean, how we came to it? We just borrowed the sound from a Louis Jordan arrangement. Listen to Jordan, and you'll hear the Kirby Stone Four.' He was one of the first guys to admit it.

"What many people don't realize is that Jordan was not only a showman-singer of novelty songs, but a great blues singer as well. A story comes to mind. We always played the big municipal auditorium in Kansas City on Thanksgiving Day and the Fourth of July. We had those dates locked in. But as we were getting close to one July fourth, I had a call from Johnny Antonelli, who was the promoter there. He confessed that he had made a serious mistake—forgotten that he had a prior commitment to Jordan and booked Lionel Hampton. My reaction was: 'Great! Play them both and we'll have a battle of the bands.' That auditorium could accommodate 12,000 to 14,000, and it was one of the few air-conditioned halls in the South. But Antonelli was upset because he had booked each at a sixty percentage. So I said, 'Talk to Joe Glaser and tell him that together we'll split seventy percent and you'll pay the extra ten percent for your mistake.' Glaser would not go along. So I told Antonelli to buy Glaser out, which he did for three thousand dollars or so, and I took the risk on a seventy-percent basis.

"This was the year when 'Flying Home' was the rage—probably '43 or '44—and Lionel Hampton was flying high. It was the biggest thing that Lionel had. Well, Joe Glaser flew into Kansas City and I flew in. It was a hot, humid day. And the moment I walked in, Glaser said, 'Lionel goes on first.' I said okay. The place was so jammed that people couldn't dance. And Lionel went on first. I watched what happened, but Lionel himself told it to Dave Kapp at Decca about a month later. He happened to go into Kapp's office when Dave was looking at the cover of a new Louis Jordan album. When Hampton saw it, he said to Dave: 'That man Jordan! Let me tell you, Mr. Kapp. We played a battle of the bands about a month ago in Kansas City. Mr. Glaser—smart man—he got me on first. We finished our set with twenty minutes of "Flying Home." We had the crowd going wild, jumping up and down to the beat and screaming. We had them going crazy. And I thought: That finishes Louis Jordan. But do you know what that man did to me, Mr. Kapp? He had only piano, bass, drums. He just sang the blues and he cut my ass!"

"Jordan was a great, great performer. If you challenged him, watch out. I'd always make him go on next to last—and then he really would perform. I recall one time when we were going to play the Palace Theatre in Cleveland. Peggy Lee wanted to do it with us. Now, Cleveland and Detroit are two heavily unionized towns where I never liked to play on percentages. You never knew what might happen by the time you played the date. Carlos Gastel, who was Peggy's manager, said that she was willing to take the risk. I said okay, pay us our price and it can be her show.

"Well, the date arrived, and we sat down to discuss routining the show. I urged her not to let Jordan appear next to closing. I warned her that he would tie the show in knots, especially the first show when the audience would be predominantly black—jitney cab drivers and all the sports who would come to report on whether it was a good show or not. I was trying to be helpful because Peggy and I were old friends. But she reared up and said, 'This is my show and I'm going to close it.' Then I suggested that she let Jordan go on first, with the comic, Georgie Kay, coming between them. But her response was, 'You didn't want to take the risk, so I'll decide how to routine the show.'

"It was just too bad for Peggy. Louis decided to work, and I don't think that anybody could have followed him. Peggy is a great singer and a good performer, but she could never take hold of the audience after Jordan left them in a frenzy. When I came backstage to console her, she said, 'You did this on purpose. You've even taken my husband away from me. You go to football games and you won't let any women accompany you!' That happened to be true. I had eight season tickets to the Rams' games and I insisted that only men come along. Anyway, I finally convinced her to let Jordan go on after her and close the show.

"In one of our first engagements—in Hartford, I believe it was—we were on the same bill with The Three Stooges. They insisted that they were going to close the show. Jordan was just starting in those days. But even The Three Stooges had a real tough time going on after him.

"It's true that a lot of Jordan's material dealt with black situations and customs in a comical way, but I know that Jordan wasn't doing it as an Uncle Tom. He was not trying to attract white followers by poking fun at his own people. He was just dealing with things that came out of his background and that he was familiar with. He was not self-conscious at all. And no black organization ever found anything offensive in his style or material. 'Ain't Nobody Here But Us Chickens' was probably the one record that generated the most discussion. It was brought to us by Milt Gabler, who supervised Jordan's recordings at Decca. And Louis thought it was a very funny bit. I once asked Jordan when he came back from a Southern tour about the reactions of black people. He told me that everybody enjoyed the song and recognized it as a fun song, and kept requesting it over and over.

"Jordan kept an open door when it came to seeing songwriters. And that's why we found so much good material. He never turned anything down. A songwriter would always leave him feeling buoyed up. Afterward, I'd ask him, 'How could you say those nice things when you knew it was a piece of junk?' And he'd say, 'If I said something negative, they'd argue with me and I'd never get them out of my dressing room. So long as I say a good word, they leave.' It seemed to work for Jordan because more and more amateurs came to him with material, and they frequently had fresh ideas even if the song needed to be touched up, which Louis was quite capable of doing. It was unusual for that period. Most artists kept a fence around themselves but not Louis. Of course, a lot of material came to Louis through me. I'd review it and send the goodies to him to review on the road.

"Most Jordan hits were in the R & B field. It was practically impossible to get airplay from white jockeys on the big stations, though occasionally there would be a crossover. 'Choo Choo Ch' Boogie,' 'Beware, Brother, Beware,' 'Saturday Night Fish Fry,' and 'Let the Good Times Roll' were probably crossovers. But there were also a number of important white jockeys that played Jordan: Bill Randle at WERE in Cleveland, Jazzbo Collins in Denver, and others. You see our records were never 'broken' through airplay. By the time they were released, we had a waiting public who had heard Louis do the tunes at his personals.

" 'Saturday Night Fish Fry' was done on one-niters for eight weeks. We knew that we had a hit. That was why we made a two-sided record out of it. Unlike other artists, who frequently learn songs at the date, Jordan knew all the nuances of every song he ever recorded. We could go into a studio and do four songs generally in less than the three hours allotted for the session. All that had to be done was to balance the band. Every man knew exactly what to do. Of course, most artists refrained from publicly performing material they planned to record because they were afraid it would be stolen. But we had material locked up because we owned it and controlled all rights. We were also protected because Jordan had a unique style and The Tympany Five had a unique sound—and neither could easily be copied. Imitated, yes. Copied, no."

2. The Components

With my little band, I did everything they did with a big band. I made the blues jump. —LOUIS JORDAN

*Nothin' comes to a sleeper but
a dream....*
    —LOWELL FULSON AND
    MAXWELL DAVIS

Pvt. Cecil Gant
and the
"Sepia Sinatras"

APART FROM Louis Jordan, it was an army buck private from Tennessee who ignited the postwar blues explosion—just as a heavy-hipped, heavy-voiced, heavy-lidded gal from Cincinnati sparked the predepression spill of "race" records. Pvt. Cecil Gant was to 1945 what Mamie Smith was to 1920. The locus of Mamie's feat was the NY studios of OKeh Records; Cecil's springboard was the LA studio of Gilt Edge Records. Mamie's sales-crackling song was "Crazy Blues"; Gant's was "I Wonder."

Gant was born in 1915 in Nashville, Tennessee, birthplace of Leroy Carr. World War II took him into the service and served to launch his recording career. As he himself reported in the liner notes on an early album, he was attending a street-corner Treasury Bond rally in Los Angeles. During an intermission, he asked if he could play the piano; he was so well received that at the request of the local campaign committee his commanding officer permitted him to perform at all local Treasury Bond rallies.

Late in 1944, Cliff McDonald, a former worker at Allied Record Pressing Co. of L.A., caught Gant at a rally and persuaded him to record "I Wonder," a ballad co-written with Raymond Leveen. McDonald had a studio in his garage and pressed records in a small plant behind it. With the war still in progress, Gilt Edge made the sagacious move of billing singer-pianist Gant as "Pvt. Cecil Gant" and of advertising him as "The G.I. Sing-sation."

There is still confusion about who actually owned the Gilt Edge label on which the Gant disk was released. Some associate it with Bob Geddins of Oakland; others with Bill McCall, an aggressive LA recordman who later developed 4 Star Records into a formidable company. Gant's success in achieving a crossover black ballad was so great that McDonald's enterprise fired the imagination of other would-be "indies" and promoted the rapid rise of small record companies on the west coast.

Billboard, however, was hardly impressed by Gant's four sides. In its issue of January 6, 1945, it dismissed the recording quality as "poor," asserting that the disk sounded "more like something picked up with a machine hidden under a table in a smoky back room."

89

But it thought the sides of interest because Gant was "great guns at piano on the West Coast" and because he was "the composer of the wonder race ballad 'I Wonder.'" It stressed that "the song itself" rather than the "sepia lad's delivery" made the spinning count. As for the other sides: "Put Another Chair at the Table" was "a strictly sentimental cry-in-your-beer waltz, dated in high button shoes"; "Cecil's Boogie" was just barrelhouse piano on a "repetitious blues strain"; while "Boogie No. 2" was "a weak sister to Lionel Hampton's boogie theme," then on the "Harlem Hit Parade."

Yet "I Wonder" had already stirred interest. In fact, it had made the Top Five of the "Harlem Hit Parade" during November and December. The issue with the so-so review also contained a so-so review of a National recording of the ballad by Warren Evans and the Hank d'Amico Sextet. By March 1945, there were two ads for the song in *Billboard*. Gilt Edge Records, of 500 North Western Avenue in LA and 18 East Forty-first Street in NYC, apologized for its inability "to keep up with the unprecedented demand all over the nation." Apollo Record Distributing Company, of 615 Tenth Avenue, NYC, boasted that it was the exclusive distributor of Gilt Edge Records. Listing the titles of six other Gant sides, the distributor noted that "I Wonder" was number one on the Hit Parade—Harlem, that is—three weeks running and twenty weeks in all. By the end of March, a Roosevelt Sykes rendition on Bluebird appeared along with Gant's among the "Most Played Juke Box Race Records." "I Wonder" was a runaway hit—and its impact was felt throughout the record business.

Regardless of Gant's impression on reviewers, Gilt Edge advertised twenty-one different recordings by him in January 1946. By then the company had expanded so that it was pressing 100,000 records a month and boasted distribution outlets in Chicago, St. Louis, and New York, and three in Los Angeles. It was the company that Gant built.

In "I Wonder" Gant had apparently tapped a vein of wartime feeling that found expression in such pop hits as "A Little on the Lonely Side" and "Saturday Night (Is the Loneliest Night in the Week)," a song popularized by a new superstar, Frank Sinatra. By 1945 the war had taken a turn for the better and people were singing "I'm Beginning to See the Light" and "My Dreams Are Getting Better All the Time." But there was still the uneasy feeling expressed by Pvt. Gant: "I wonder . . . my little darlin' . . . where can you be . . . again tonight. . . ."

In personal appearances, Gant dressed in the khaki of a buck private sans jacket. His appeal was broad enough so that he broke attendance records at the Paradise Theatre in Detroit and Club Zanzibar in Nashville, both catering to black audiences, and was able to command a following on white hillbilly stations like WSM's "Barn Dance" and WHK's "Blue Grass Club." Nonetheless, "I Wonder" remained a "sepia" ballad, sung by a "sepia" artist: it did not make the big Saturday night, coast-to-coast "Your Hit Parade," as did the other ballads mentioned above.

Gant was less a bluesman than a crooner. That undoubtedly helped account for sales that reached beyond the black ghettos. Although he played a bluesy, boogie piano, his singing style was modelled on Leroy Carr's—he recorded "In the Evening When the Sun Goes Down"— and was influenced by Bing, then at the peak of his popularity, and by newly arrived Frankie Boy. In short, a sepia crooner with blues inflections and a black sound.

A possibly more immediate influence was Nat "King" Cole, who was then performing in LA clubs. Cole played The Troc in the early part of 1945 and The Swanee Club on Central Avenue toward the end of the year. Although he was doing some singing, Nat thought of himself primarily as a jazz pianist. In '43 he made Number One on the "Harlem Hit Parade" with "That Ain't Right" (Decca) and again in '44 with a Capitol disk of his own song "Straighten Up and Fly Right." But in '45 he cut sides for Excelsior Records in LA, suggesting a transition to the Dentyne style of murmur-singing à la Crosby-Sinatra-Como. Cole did not actually cross the Mason-Dixon line in entertainment until 1947 when he scored with the Deek Watson ballad, "(I Love You) For Sentimental Reasons." Full pop acceptance did not come until after 1948, when he had the good fortune to encounter "Nature Boy" with its winding, exotic melody, and "Mona Lisa," the sophisticated Academy Award-winning song of 1949.

Gant's hours in the limelight were limited. Two years after "I Wonder" made him a star, albeit minor, he was back in Nashville. For a short period before then, he switched from Gilt Edge to 4 Star (and Bronze) Records, cutting over a dozen nondescript sides. In Nashville, during a two-year period between '47 and '49, he recorded twenty-eight sides, including a remake of "I Wonder" for Bullet Records. But in '49 he was back in Los Angeles recording two sides for Down Beat Records and two for Swing Time, and in '50 he was down in New Orleans, cutting four sides for Imperial.

His search for the acceptance and audience that had deserted him continued in '50 and '51. By then he was in New York recording for

Decca. I met him briefly when he came to the office of Leeds Music, publishers of "I Wonder." (I was then the hit-picker of Duchess Music, a Leeds subsidiary.) He was a much-troubled young man, and I could tell that he was bugged by his inability to duplicate (or even approach) the success of "I Wonder." Through the years, I have seen this frustration and puzzlement in the eyes of publishers, writers, and artists, and it is a painful and unforgettable sight. (In the years when I was in music business and had dry periods, I inevitably came down with a bad case of the flu.) But Gant was by then on a major label, and I could detect threads of hope in the overall blanket of depression. Between July 1950 and January 1951, he participated in almost monthly Decca sessions, producing nine disks. These included a cover of Leadbelly's "Goodnight Irene," a 1950 smash for The Weavers. Since Gant was on the same label, his platter was unquestionably aimed at the R & B market. He cut several titles with a then-magic word in them, but "Rock Little Baby" and "We're Gonna Rock" didn't take off. He made a new version of one of his early Gilt Edge sellers, "The Grass Is Getting Greener Every Day," but it really wasn't true for ex-Pvt. Cecil Gant. Some time after his last recording session on January 19, 1951, he died, possibly from the self-destructive habits into which frustration often drives us. Gant's record career, launched when he was thirty years old, lasted a brief six years.

•

The blues-inflected, ballad style of Gant harked back to Leroy Carr, who also enjoyed a brief career that was ended by death at an early age. That style became a basic strain of R & B, finding later exponents in Johnny Ace, Jesse Belvin, and Ray Charles, among others. Musicologist Charles Keil dubs it "the postwar Texas clean-up movement in blues singing," while blues scholar Paul Oliver sees it as part of "the West Coast blues fusion." A fusion it was, mixing elements of country blues, boogie woogie, and jazz in a cauldron fired by the seductive sales of pop balladry. If the Ink Spots were the progenitors, Leroy Carr the father, and Nat Cole an influence, the exponents of the murmuring, gentle *vibrato* ballad style were bluesmen like Charles Brown, Lowell Fulson, Percy Mayfield, and Ivory Joe Hunter. They were the black-ghetto equivalents of the baritone crooners in pop—in short, they were "sepia Sinatras."

Coming from Oklahoma and Texas, along with many Negro laborers attracted by the shipbuilding industry in Oakland and the oil refineries in Long Beach, Bakersfield, and other California cities, these bluesmen worked together at various times. Ivory Joe Hunter

Cecil Gant

used Johnny Moore's Three Blazers as a backup combo on recordings in '45. He, himself, worked as an accompanist to Lowell Fulson. Johnny Moore's brother, guitarist Oscar Moore, was part of the Nat "King" Cole Trio, and Charles Brown was the featured vocalist-pianist of The Three Blazers.

•

Charles Brown seems to have been the most influential, though he was not nearly as successful as Ivory Joe. Brown's first hit, "Drifting Blues," came in the same year as "I Wonder." It was on Aladdin Records, another R & B West Coast label. His gentle voice had a hollowness that made it sound almost like an echo of itself. In a sense, his mellow, after-hours style epitomized the down mood of the group. Not all of them sank to the depths of self-pity, but the West Coast ballad fusion was marked by frustration, a reflection, perhaps, of the postwar mood of many black people for whom the war to rid the world of racial discrimination was promises, promises—and hollow promises at that. And the singers did not shout, declare, or demand; they murmured.

Incidentally, the low-key character of the Charles Brown school of the blues can be acutely sensed by comparing Brown's "Drifting Blues" to a 1952 version by Bobby "Blue" Bland on Modern Records. Bland concretizes the title to "Drifting from Town to Town" and freights his delivery with an intensity that contrasts sharply with Brown's passivity.

Brown's background and upbringing provide an interesting and instructive contrast with those of the bluesmen of the previous generation. Born in Texas City, Texas, in 1922, he was raised by grandparents when both of his parents died. He began studying piano at the age of ten, under the tutelage of his grandmother, Swanee Simpson, who was the first female choir director in Texas. On graduating with honors from Galveston High School, he went to Prairie View College in Hempstead, Texas, and earned a B.S. degree. After teaching for a time at George Washington Carver High School in Bay Town, Texas, he was appointed head of the science department.

On the outbreak of World War II, he became a junior chemist at the Pine Bluff Arsenal at Arkansas. He was doing research in plastics for the war effort when an asthmatic condition forced him to give up his work. It was then that he migrated to LA.

During his high school days, Brown had played cocktail piano at a beachfront club on Galveston Bay owned by a science teacher. Working as an elevator operator by day, he moonlighted at the piano in small clubs and in his uncle's church. Eventually, he entered an amateur contest at the Lincoln Theatre and won first prize by playing a then-popular, Earl Hines boogie woogie version of "St. Louis Blues" and encoring with the "Warsaw Concerto." As a result, Ivy Anderson, then Duke Ellington's vocalist, hired him to play in her Chicken Shack. Cecil Gant was among the regulars who came to hear him play light classics and show tunes.

In May 1944, he joined the pit band at the Lincoln Theatre but left after a brief period to affiliate with Johnny Moore's Three Blazers. Until then, he had done no professional singing. But when the owner of the Talk of the Town Club in Beverly Hills insisted that the trio had to sing, he began singing. The Blazers modelled their vocals on those of the Nat "King" Cole Trio, then working at the 331 Club in Los Angeles and riding high with a Capitol recording of "Straighten Up and Fly Right." But Brown's idol was vocalist Pha Terrell, who sang with the Andy Kirk band and was famous for a high falsetto like that of Bill Kenny of the Ink Spots.

When the group appeared at the Swing Club on Hollywood Boulevard, Frankie Laine was a frequent visitor. According to Brown, in an interview with a *Living Blues* writer, Laine told him: "I wanna sing like a spook." This was not long before Laine made his belting version of "That's My Desire," which launched his career as a singing idol. Before this development, the Blazers made a recording with Laine on Atlas Records; one side was "Tell Me You'll Wait for Me," a ballad written by Brown and Oscar Moore, and recorded later by Ray Charles.

It was while they were performing at the Copa Club in LA that Eddie Mesner, one of two brothers who founded Aladdin Records, came to hear the Blazers and offered them $800 to record "Drifting Blues," the ballad that had become an audience draw on Johnny Moore's playing and Charles Brown's singing. "Drifting Blues," released as a Blazers disk as well as a Charles Brown platter, sold close to a million copies and won the *Cash Box* award as "Best R & B Record of 1946."

Brown broke with the Blazers in 1948, apparently in a disagreement over money. Songs that he recorded on his own underline the emotional dejection that marked his style. "Trouble Blues" made No. 1 on R & B charts in '49, followed by "Homesick Blues," which was a Top Five seller. And 1951 was a good year with such typically low-spirited songs as "Seven Long Days" and "Black Night," both the work of a talented West Coast writer, Jessie Mae Robinson. But after '52 and his record of "Hard Times," black audiences demanded a more aggressive and demonstrative style than Brown's warm romanticism.

It was almost ten years before he was able once again to achieve a chart-climber. "Please Come Home for Christmas" on King Records was a fleeting best-seller. But into the 1970s, Charles Brown continued to play small clubs around the country. There was a demand, albeit limited, for the man who has described his style in these words: "I would not call myself really a blues singer. I think I'm a blue ballad singer because I sing ballads my way and yet they sound bluesy."

•

Lowell Fulson, a part-Indian born in Tulsa, Oklahoma, in 1921, played guitar for the legendary Texas Alexander for three years, and did a stint in the navy, after which he settled in Oakland, California. The death of his brother, Martin, who worked with him in clubs spawned by Oakland's shipbuilding industry, led to associations that modernized his style. One was with Lloyd Glenn, a Texas pianist with a jazz background, and another with Kansas City jazzman Jay Mc-

Shann. But the most important influence, instrumentally, came from T-Bone Walker, whose guitar playing had West Coast musicians agog. Vocally, Fulson's idol was Jimmy Rushing.

By the time Fulson began making records in 1946, the down-home, rural blues style of Texas Alexander had modulated into the more melodic and bland sound of the West Coasters. Mastery of the electric guitar helped make him a pivotal figure in the transformation of the Texas blues of Blind Lemon and Lightnin' Hopkins into West Coast R & B.

After his discharge from the navy, Lowell cut his first sides for Bob Geddins of Oakland, the same city where he worked in the flourishing shipyards. "Come Back Baby" and "Three O'clock Blues," recorded years before it became a hit for B. B. King, booted him to the top echelon of blues performers and made him one of the Bay Area's most important purveyors of postwar blues.

Originally, his disks were released on the Big Town and Trilon labels. But they appeared also on Swing Time, a Los Angeles label owned by record distributor Jack Lauderdale. In '49, Fulson left Geddins and recorded for four years for Lauderdale's label.

Fulson's great years were 1950 to 1954. Working with jump combos and Texas pianist Lloyd Glenn, he scaled the charts with Swing Time Records of "Every Day I Have the Blues," later B. B. King's theme; Lloyd Glenn's "Blue Shadows," a No. 1 disk; and his own classic, "Reconsider Baby." These were the years when the man who later became known as "The Genius," Ray Charles, toured with him as the combo's piano player, later recording such Fulson perennials as "Sinner's Prayer."

"Reconsider Baby" marked the beginning of his association with the Chess brothers of Chicago on their Checker label, though he did most of his recording in Los Angeles, and occasionally in Dallas. He remained with Checker into 1962, and then, between '64 and '66, was associated with the Bihari brothers, appearing on their Modern and Kent labels. Although The Beatles' deluge initially brought difficulties for him, as it did for all bluesmen and American rock 'n' rollers, he staged a comeback in 1965–67. Chartmakers like "Tramp" and "Black Nights" on Kent led to a highly rewarding overseas tour.

Fulson was able to give a good account of himself into the '70s when he made a number of albums for Jewel Records, the documentary label produced by Stan Lewis, a record-store owner in Shreveport, Louisiana. As recently as 1974, he cut an album of new songs, working with Steve Cropper, who attained renown as house guitarist of Stax Records of Memphis.

A man with a pencil-line moustache, wide mouth, and an easy smile, Fulson wrote many blues with Fats Washington, occasionally producing a song like "My Baby" with a near-pop melody. His most appealing number was "Blue Shadows," a No. 1 R & B hit in 1950, the year in which he also made the charts with "Every Day I Have the Blues" and "Lonesome Christmas."

Although he occasionally sang songs on such traditional blues themes as the chain gang, he was mainly concerned with man-woman problems, perhaps because of his own situation. (See Groove 3.) Articulating well, singing smoothly in a voice that sometimes sounded like a low-pitched Billy Daniels, he adjusted early to the R & B era, leaving echoes of himself in Bobby Bland and B. B. King.

.

The bluesman who led the Oklahoma-Texas musical caravan to California and moved further away from it than either Fulson or Charles Brown was Ivory Joe Hunter. In part, the explanation may be that the emphasis in his boyhood home was on spirituals, antecedent of, but antagonistic to, the blues. (Spirituals were the songs of God; blues were the songs of the devil.) One of his early songs, recorded by C & W artist Jimmie Davis, was titled "Lord, Please Don't Let Me Down."

Ivory Joe—that is his baptismal name—was born in 1911 in Kirbyville, Texas, about 135 miles northeast of Houston and sixty miles from Beaumont. Although both his parents died before he was eleven, he remembers his mother as a great singer of spirituals and can recall evenings when the entire family of eleven boys and four girls formed a huge spiritual choir. The family moved to Port Arthur (now renowned as the birthplace of Janis Joplin) where he did not go beyond eighth grade. He began working as a professional musician before he was sixteen, and not long afterward had a program of his own on Station KFDM in Beaumont, the town in which "Rambling Fingers," as he was known, formed his own band.

Two other musical influences were Duke Ellington, whom he admired for "the sharp way he dressed," and Fats Waller, whose stride piano style left a permanent imprint. The impress came from seeing both in films, not in person. By 1936 Ivory Joe was settled in Houston, where his band played the Uptown Tavern for five years.

In 1942 he made the trek to California, working first with Slim

Jenkins in Oakland and then gigging in clubs in San Francisco and Los Angeles: the Oasis, Radio Room, Crystal Bowl, and Cricket Club. In 1945 he launched Ivory Records in Oakland and became one of the first blacks with his own record company. However, it was a short-lived venture largely because of wartime restrictions on shellac. But he produced at least one memorable disk, a Leroy Carr ballad he later recorded on Dot. In *Billboard*'s December 8, 1945, chart of "Most Played Jukebox Race Records," "Blues at Sunrise" was tied for the No. 3 spot with Roosevelt Sykes' "The Honeydripper," Lionel Hampton's "Beulah's Boogie," Joe Liggins' "Left a Good Deal in Mobile," Louis Jordan's "Caldonia Boogie," and Helen Humes' "Be Baba-Leba." On his early recordings, Ivory Joe used Johnny Moore & The Three Blazers, thereby making intimate contact with pianist-vocalist Charles Brown, whose ballad style shaped his own.

At this stage, Ivory Joe was still working largely with blues material, as his disks on Pacific and Excelsior indicate. (He established the Pacific label in Berkeley as a partnership after his Ivory label folded.) Among the numbers he recorded were "Grieving Blues," "Heavy-Hearted Blues," "Tavern Blues," and jump tunes like "Boogie in the Basement" and "Ivory Joe's Boogie." His future direction as a bluesy-pop balladeer, however, was suggested by songs like "I'm So Crazy for You," "Whose Arms Are You Missin'?" and "Why Did You Lie?"

He was known at the time as the "Baron of the Boogie," perhaps because he looked a bit like a foreign nobleman. Sporting a mous-tache, he gazed through rimless glasses that served to accent his heavy eyebrows. A wide, Cheshire-cat smile contributed a hint of exotic menace to his look. But he found a warm welcome, according to the Harold Oxley Agency, which managed him, at such Hollywood clubs as the Sunset, Swing, and Ciro's; at Shep's Playhouse in LA; at Shadowland in New Orleans; at the Zanzibar in Nashville and San Antonio; at The NBC Club in Beaumont; and at the Bronze Peacock in Houston. He fronted a typical R & B combo: piano, bass, drums, and tenor sax.

He was still paying his dues when he was signed by 4 Star Records of Los Angeles. Although he recorded some blues and boogie, the overwhelming number of his releases had a pop-ballad orientation—"Did You Mean It?" and "Don't Leave Me"—and included smart novelties like "Are You Hep?" and "Big Wig." But none of these at-tracted a large listenership, despite his popularity in club appearances; nor did the sixteen sides he recorded for King Records when he used some of Duke Ellington's sidemen. Two titles, "Guess Who" and "Landlord Blues," did make the charts.

His first impact disk came after he signed with MGM Records in 1949. The following year, he achieved best-sellers in four titles, but especially with two original ballads, "I Need You So" and "I Almost Lost My Mind," the last finishing as *Billboard*'s No. 6 R & B Best-seller of the year. Ivory Joe enjoyed his affluence, traveling around the country in a custom-designed bus.

Between '56 and '57, after he had moved to the Atlantic label, Ivory Joe repeated his success with "I Almost Lost My Mind." At that point, Pat Boone came up with a white-buckskin version on Dot, which made the song a top rock 'n' roll hit of the year. Ivory Joe scored again with another original ballad, "Since I Met You Baby." It was not only the No. 5 "Most Played R & B" record of the year, but a Gold Record, presented to him on "The Ed Sullivan Show." Of greater significance was the fact that the song made the Top 20 on *Billboard*'s "*Pop* Honor Roll of Hits," not on a white cover, but on Ivory Joe's own recording.

This was the period when young white artists were covering black records and taking the play and sales away because of the massive exposure they commanded on the country's white stations. In 1956, both Eddie Fisher and Connie Francis recorded "No Other One," a ballad Ivory wrote with Clyde Otis. In '57, Teresa Brewer cut "Empty Arms" when Joe's Atlantic disk began hitting the charts. And in '59, Presley plattered Joe's "My Wish Came True."

By the time he joined Atlantic, Ivory Joe said that he did not wish to be described as a blues singer. He felt that he had acquired wider scope as a songwriter and performer, the result of his feeling, not only for blues, but for country songs, spirituals, and good pop ballads. As for blues, he had never been either a shouter or a down-homer, but had always veered toward a more gentle approach. There was more rhythm than blues in his style.

•

With Amos Milburn, another bluesman out of Texas, we move more completely into the area of commercial R & B. Although he wrote many of the songs he recorded—or rewrote blues that he early learned —his most successful disks were the work of other writers. In this division of labor, the blues sacrificed one of its most fundamental and exciting features: self-expression. The singer might still sing his feelings, but now he had to find material that made him feel.

Born in a Houston family of thirteen children circa 1925, Milburn was precocious in several respects. At five, he was picking out tunes on the piano, and at fifteen, having enlisted in the navy, he saw enough action in the Philippines to earn thirteen battle stars. By the time he was discharged and returned to Houston, his father had died and he became the family breadwinner. Organizing a sixteen-piece band, he performed at Houston's Keyhole and other clubs. To early musical influences were added contact with sophisticated entertainers like the Slam Stewart jazz trio and other visiting artists.

Some time in 1946, an enterprising young Houston woman named Ann Cullum, or McCullum, arranged for Aladdin Records to record Sam Hopkins, who was to Houston blues what Blind Lemon was to Dallas. Texas Alexander, who had just come out of jail—on a trumped-up charge, according to Hopkins—wanted to accompany Hopkins to Los Angeles, but Ms. Cullum was uncomfortable in the presence of gruff-and-tough Alexander and took along suave Amos Milburn instead. She also collaborated on songs with him. Incidentally, this was the Aladdin session at which Sam Hopkins, accompanied by pianist Thunder Smith, acquired the cognomen "Lightnin' " Hopkins.

Milburn's Aladdin session resulted in a relationship that lasted eight years. Although he cut over seventy-five sides from 1946 on, no title gained wide acceptance until 1949, when seven songs hit a sizable R & B audience. "Hold Me Baby," written with Ms. Cullum, and "Chicken Shack Boogie" were the most widely accepted, finishing as the No. 8 and No. 9 titles on *Billboard*'s survey of the year's R & B Best-sellers. Other chartmakers included "Rooming House Boogie," written by gifted Jessie Mae Robinson, who also authored "In the Middle of the Night." That year Milburn finished as the No. 1 artist in *Billboard*'s year-end surveys—in retail sales as well as juke box plays.

There is no indication that Milburn had a drinking problem, as Leroy Carr, Speckled Red, and other bluesmen had, but in 1950 his "Bad, Bad Whiskey," written by tenor saxist Thomas Maxwell Davis, climbed to the top of R & B charts. It launched a cycle of alcoholic songs, none written by Milburn, among which were "Thinking and Drinking" in '52 and "Let Me Go Home, Whiskey" and "One Scotch, One Bourbon, One Beer" in '53. "One Scotch. . . ." and "Thinking and Drinking" were the work of Rudolph Toombs; "Let Me Go Home, Whiskey," a possible forerunner of "Let Me Go, Devil," was by someone who went by the curious name of Shifte Henri. The cycle also included the cry of many an alcoholic, "Just One More Drink," and to cap it all, "Good, Good Whiskey" in '53.

Apparently, Milburn did no recording after '53, by which time the first signs of the rock revolution were looming on the record horizon—Bill Haley's "Crazy, Man, Crazy," among other items. But, perhaps there was anticipation of the development in Milburn's recordings of "Let's Rock Awhile," briefly on the charts in '51, and "Rock, Rock, Rock" in '52. And one should not disregard "Chicken Shack Boogie" and "Let's Have a Party," fast jump records that in the opinion of rock historian Charlie Gillett "achieved more excitement than any of the derivative rock 'n' roll hits by Bill Haley, Boyd Bennett or Larry Williams."

•

During Charles Brown's peak years on wax (1949–51), another Brown became a record best-seller. Roy Brown's career offers illuminating sidelights on the sources and development of R & B.

Born in New Orleans in 1925, Roy organized a spiritual quartet when he was only thirteen. Like many another bluesman, he worked in the fields as a youth, chopping sugar cane, harvesting rice, and picking cotton in Eunice, Louisiana. Attending high school in Houston, where his father's work as a bricklayer took the family, he heard and admired Wynonie Harris, who sang with the Lucky Millinder Band at local dances. Yet his favorite singer was Bing Crosby—and "still is," he said in 1975. To win first prize in an amateur night at the Million Dollar Theatre in Los Angeles, where he migrated at seventeen and boxed for several years, he sang two songs associated with Der Bingle, "San Antonio Rose" and the World War II ditty, "Jingle Jangle Jingle." After being rejected by the armed services because of flat feet, he secured his first major job in a Shreveport, Louisiana, club by singing pop ballads like "Star Dust," "Temptation," and Crosby's record hit "Blue Hawaii." The owner of Bill Riley's Palace Park hired him, as Roy himself told a *Blues Unlimited* interviewer, because of his appeal as "a Negro who sounds white."

It was at the Palace Park that Brown began developing a blues repertoire, learning contemporary R & B tunes like "Jelly Jelly," as recorded by Billy Eckstine, and "When My Man Comes Home," as recorded by Buddy and Ella Johnson. And it was through a series of blues he himself wrote that Roy became a record star. But before he did, he performed for a long period with Joe Coleman's group in Galveston, Texas, singing hit parade tunes, Ink Spots songs and Sinatra ballads—no blues.

By the time he returned to New Orleans in 1949, he had already written "Good Rockin' Tonight," the blues that was to become an R & B classic. Approaching Wynonie Harris, who was then appearing at Foster's Rainbow Room and who later had a best-seller in "Good Rockin' Tonight," Roy was turned away. Through a sympathetic musician, he was able to see instead Cecil Gant, who was then playing at the Crescent City's Dew Drop Inn.

"Gant was terrific," Brown recalls, "he was beautiful, he was responsible for my career." The blues balladeer phoned Jules Braun of De Luxe Records in Linden, New Jersey, waking him in the middle of the night. When Braun next visited New Orleans to record Annie Laurie and Paul Gayten, he also cut Roy Brown at the J & M Studios on Tulane Avenue.

That year (1949) "Boogie at Midnight" made R & B's Top Ten. The following year, Brown had four De Luxe disks on R & B charts, with his own "Hard Luck Blues" hitting No. 1 and "Love Don't Love Nobody" making No. 2. Although his own version of "Good Rockin' Tonight" failed to make national charts, it prompted a cover by Wynonie Harris on King Records, which established the song as a standard. Revived by Pat Boone on Dot Records, "Good Rockin' Tonight" made pop charts in 1959.

With only a brief two-year run on record charts, Roy Brown is little remembered today. Yet in the early '70s, he created a sensation at the Monterey Jazz Festival. Appearing as part of a program billed "Johnny Otis' Rhythm & Blues Hall of Fame," he literally brought the audience to its feet. Few who reacted so spontaneously to his falsetto-shriek delivery of "Rocks are my pillow / The cold, cold ground is my bed," were aware of how potent a bluesman he was in 1949–51. It can be said of him, as he himself said of Cecil Gant: "He did everything from his heart and soul, as if he was pining about something, reminiscing about some sad occasion." His was more of a *cry* style than a *shout* style. A showman who could deliver pop ballads à la Crosby or Sinatra, he sang blues with pop inflections, a strain of R & B that reached peak expression in the work of another New Orleans bluesman, Fats Domino.

•

Most people do not associate R & B with the relaxed, soft, almost crooning style we have been considering in Cecil Gant, Charles Brown, Lowell Fulson, Ivory Joe, and, to a lesser degree, in Amos Milburn. They think of R & B as a loud, high-amp sound—and it obviously was that, too. The shapers of this tougher strain were generally Easterners like Arthur "Big Boy" Crudup and Midwesterners like Big Joe Turner. But California was not without its hard, raucous blues, as some of Milburn's drivers suggest and the local popularity of Roy Milton would indicate.

Holding forth at the Cobra Club in LA—bottled liquor was sold at a streetside, storefront adjunct—Milton delivered a sock kind of jump blues. With a typical front line of trumpet, alto sax and tenor, the group's propulsive force was Roy Milton himself on drums. Although he sang, the group's forte was its rhythmic drive, directed at dancers only.

Recording for several labels—Hamp-Tone, Juke Box, and Specialty—Milton was able to transfer the rhythmic excitement of his "Solid Senders," as he called them, onto wax. In 1946 "R. M. Blues" became one of the "Most Played Juke Box R & B Records" and remained a best-seller all through the summer. Attaining the No. 2 slot, it was unable to dislodge Lionel Hampton's "Hey! Ba-Ba-Re-Bop," Louis Jordan and Ella Fitzgerald's "Stone Cold Dead in the Market," and Louis Jordan's million-copy seller "Choo Choo Ch'Boogie," three disks that made No. 1 in this period.

Nevertheless, "R. M. Blues" reportedly sold over a million records, "the first to do so in the Negro market," according to Charlie Gillett, who also contends that the record gives Milton the right to make "one of the strongest claims as the inventor of the rock 'n' roll beat." Grounds for the claim also can be found in Milton's superimposition of an accented afterbeat on the typical boogie rhythm of dotted eighth and sixteenth notes.

·

About the time that Roy Milton was "sending" them at LA's Cobra Club, two Midwestern blues shouters came together in San Francisco after several years of separation. They became a fixture at the Memo Cocktail Lounge.

During the latter years of the '40s, Joe Turner and his Kansas City buddy, Pete Johnson, roamed up and down the West Coast giving Californians a good taste of the rousing, booming KC blues and boogie. Between '49 and '52, Joe Turner made recordings for several of the newly founded West Coast "indies," including Aladdin, Imperial, RPM, and Dootone. Whether it was the material or the time, none of these samples of robust Kansas City jump-and-shout blues registered with record buyers.

Neither did the disks of Aaron "T-Bone" Walker, who was part of the Texas invasion of California and whose electrifying role in the development of R & B warrants separate consideration.

groove 3   **LOWELL FULSON**

"My name sometimes is spelled with an *m* and sometimes with an *n*. My grandfather used *m*. My mother changed it to *n*. In all of my business and recording, I use *n*.

"I was born in Tulsa in 1921. When I was about five, my father got killed in an accident. My mother moved back into the country where we had some land, in the area of the Choctaw freedman Indian, mixed blacks, between Atoka and Wopanockee. It belonged to my grandfather, and that was where I was brought up, attending a mission school. When I was about eight or nine, I began singing in school programs and doing tap dances. I sang hymns I learned in church— Methodist church—spiritual songs like 'Precious Lord.' My grandfather was a violinist, and I had some uncles on my mother's side who played guitar.

"The first thing I had to do was learn to tune it. They wouldn't let me play their instruments if I got them out of tune. I know guitar players who play for five or six years before they can really tune the instrument. When I first learned to play, I tuned the guitar in what we called 'cross key.' When you didn't clamp any of the four strings, you had an E-natural chord.

"By the time I was twelve, I was singing country-and-western songs. Can't remember any of them now. Learned some of them from Coot Mason, a white boy who played with Jimmie Rodgers. Then I began learning songs like Blind Lemon Jefferson did, Blind Boy Fuller, and others. I never did see none of them, or hear them in person. Learned from their records. Couldn't sing these songs around church or school.

"When I was about thirteen, my cousin got drunk and couldn't play for a small dance party. They heard me fooling around with the guitar and asked me to play. I got to playing, and when he got right they didn't want him to play. Then he come down on me for learning the guitar. It was one of those things.

"I paid three dollars for my first guitar. Got it in a pawn shop. I was a teen-ager, worked all week, made six dollars, and took three to buy a guitar. In those days, I played mostly in churches. But I also played picnics—outdoor dances, we called them. My parents didn't like that.

"By the time I was in ninth or tenth grade, I began moving away from the churches because I was getting paid. But I played no clubs, just country balls, by myself. I was singing Blind Lemon Jefferson songs, Peetie Wheatstraw—'Black Snake Blues,' 'No More Sweet Potatoes,' 'The Frost That Killed the Vine,' 'Blues in the Bottle, Stopper in My Hand,'—things like that. Also did 'Lordy Lord' when Big Maceo came out with it. Like 'Used to have a car painted white and black./ Missed the payments,/ The finance took it back.'

"Around 1938 I went to Ada, Oklahoma. Got a little name playing around there. So I begin playing the white clubs—singing songs like 'Beer Barrel Polka,' 'Silvery Moon,' 'Sunrise Serenade.' But I didn't really like them. I liked the more churchy type of thing—blues, moans, like Baptist hymns—but I played what they liked. About this time, I got with Dan Wright, who had a ten- to twelve-piece band. He had one man who had just one leg and one hand—he made a pack to fit around his waist. He'd just strum, he didn't pick, he comped. That was my first experience with a big band. It was all strings— violins, mandolins, banjo, guitars, drums, and bass—upright bass. They played bluegrass, Dixieland.

"In '39 I got married. My wife didn't want me to play, so I quit and got out of the band. We had a lady pianist in the band, and I guess she was jealous. But the girl was with the band when I joined. I wasn't the best looking, but I was the youngest. And the girl, who was the same age, wound up in later years marrying my uncle, who was a preacher. There was nothing between us, but my wife couldn't understand that. She'd come down on dates and raise so much sand they'd say, 'Lord, Lowell, can't you keep your wife home?' So I quit and goes into the Holiness Church at Ada, and stayed and played there for a while.

"There were men that would come through the town and pick up men to go out to the western part and pick cotton. I thought that this is a good time for me to get away. I'm gonna tell her that I'm gonna go pick cotton, which I never could pick any cotton. I harvested and did farming. But pickin' it off that burr, I just was no good at it. After they'd get done harvestin' it, I'd haul the stuff to town. Anyway, when a truck came through and a bunch of guys got on, well, I got on too. When I said, 'I'm gonna take my guitar,' she said, 'No, you don't need your guitar.' I said, 'Thass right. I don't need it.'

"Nothin' is as hot as those Oklahoma cotton fields. But I knew I had to do somethin' to pay those guys, because they pick you up. I stayed about a week, picking and singing the blues. Guys would try to keep up with me so they could hear me. Finally, I went to town to see a guy they called Shorty Hatchet. Never did know his name. He made homemade beer. I liked it because it wasn't strong. When I told him that I played guitar, he sent me to the back, where I found an old box. As soon as I started singing and playing, they cut the jukebox off. After singing a few numbers, I quit. They wanted more. So I said, 'Put something in the hat.' I took up more money that night than I made all week in the cotton field. So I never went back. I stayed in town and played around.

"And that's how I met Texas Alexander. He had a guitar player named Wolf, who had just left him. He could absolutely sing. When he and I run up to Shorty's place, he sang one and he sounded so good that I didn't want to sing anymore. I was just ready to play behind him. But we would go from place to place. He knew the towns and we made so much money, man, that we traveled all over west Oklahoma and west Texas. I guess that I didn't get back home for over a year. [Laughing] But when I came back, I had to stop playing again. She just couldn't stand it, she really couldn't. So I quit playing and I moved to Texas. That was in 1940 to '41.

"I worked as a fry cook in the city bus terminal. Started as a dishwasher, but I learned things fast. When I was a farmer, I learned to cut meat because we butchered our own hogs. The war just broke out and I got this old cook's job. I was the youngest cook there. I was drawing that meat and cutting that meat up. I didn't play no more music. If I went out to a country ball, maybe somebody would get a guitar and I'd sing a bit. They'd chip in five or six dollars.

"So I got drafted into the service. And they sent me to a baker's and cook's school. I didn't wanna be no cook, so I didn't try to graduate. Then they sent me to Camp Shoemaker right out here in Los Angeles. I arrived on Thanksgiving Day '43. Never forget it. Kept me in the O.G. unit—the Outgoing Unit—stationed at Alameda Naval Air. I was still butchering in the service. If you cut enough meat and get your supplies up, you get a seventy-two-hour pass. I'd be done by Friday and get myself a pass so I didn't have to be back on the base till Monday morning.

"I found me a partner with a guitar, and we went about playing. It wasn't an electric. The streets were crowded, and we sat on top of an automobile playing. Suddenly, the MPs came along and wanted to take me in. I was in uniform. But there were so many people around us, they couldn't. The MPs told me to get off the street. So I began playing at house parties.

"I got me a couple of raises. After third class, you wore an officer's suit—and I wanted to get out of that little blouse then. I made third class and second class, and with first class, you became chief. But I didn't want to be a chief because you couldn't get off for seventy-two hours. So I decided to stay second class. And that's how I met Bob Geddins, who had a good electric guitar—but he wouldn't let me borrow it. They would meet me right at the gate and take me to some house party in San Francisco or Oakland.

"One evening Bob Geddins asked me what I was going to do after I got out of the service. I said that all I was trying to do was keep from going overseas. He said that he thought we could get a recording session. I didn't think I was that good, but I went out and got me an electric guitar with amplifiers. And then they sent me to San Diego. I kept playing, hitting the night clubs when I could. And then I got shipped overseas. That was in about May '45. I wondered what I was gonna do with my guitar and amplifier. The guys said, 'Man, take it with you!' And they helped me get it on board with a footlocker. The U.S.S. *Wayne*, a troopship going overseas. My papers read: Destination Unknown, Somewhere in the South Pacific. When we got to Guam, they transferred me to the U.S.S. *Sparrow*, a submarine tender.

"We were twenty-one days going over. I worked with the chaplain, who put on a little show. I volunteered, and he asked me to audition. Louis Jordan had 'Caldonia' smoking then, and that's what I played going over. Word got around, and that's how I got taken off the U.S.S. *Wayne* and put on the U.S.S. *Sparrow*. Then they take me off there and put me out on the beach—Camp Dille-Guam. I stayed over there until I got forty-four points. Never did get the rating, but I played the music.

"They pulled six pieces out of the regular station band—piano, trombone, alto, tenor, trumpet, and myself. After the war was over, we'd go into different little villages and serenade the natives. I was singing some of those old blues that I made up and later recorded, 'Caldonia' and a boogie woogie tune that was very popular. The only thing about it: when I got ready to come back overseas, I had to leave—they don't make you, but they just about force you to leave your instrument. That's in case somebody else comes over. So I left my guitar with the Red Cross.

"I got discharged in Norman, Oklahoma. That's where my native home is. I gets home and goes right back in the kitchen cooking—thirty-three dollars a week with tax cuts. But this wife still don't want no music. She came over when I settled in a place, but she didn't know I was playing music. She knew I had more money than the base was paying me. Back in that time, second class wasn't getting but seventy-eight dollars—a hundred twenty-five overseas. I was making three times that much. But here I was cooking around Duncan, Oklahoma.

"One day, I said, 'I'm going to California and I'm gonna play music.' I said, 'I forgot. A man told me I could cut a record. And I'm going out there. You can come if you want to. It doesn't make any difference.' So I left.

" 'Man, we didn't think you was ever coming back. You ready to cut?' I said, 'Yeah, what am I gonna git?' 'A hundred dollars.' I said, 'Let's go.' And that's the way it started in '46. 'Crying Blues' was the first side I cut in Oakland by Bob Geddins. Came out on Big Town and Gilt Edge. Both were Geddins' labels. When I met him, he was operating in a little place pressing 78-rpm records for the little itty-bitty record companies. I guess he tried recording a few guys before me, but they didn't do too much. I had to borrow a guitar for that first session. I got it from the chaplain I knew in the service. He lived right down the street from Geddins.

"My first record was me and my brother Martin, just two guitars. I wanted heavier backing so we got Big Dad on bass, a drummer, and Eldridge McCarthy, piano player. He was a good blues man—big fingers and a great big guy. Man, but he could go up and down them keys. He kinda slapped it on the Fats Waller kick. But I went on working in the shipyards—worked until I got 'Every Day I Have the Blues.' In '49 we did it. Fifty was when it jumped off and became pretty big. Recorded in the fall of the year—and this was for Jack Lauderdale on Swing Time. 'Blue Shadows' followed 'Every Day I Have the Blues.'

"Lauderdale came to the house. I was living in a little old project house in Vallejo. I think that even my first records for Geddins also were released by Lauderdale. But after a time, maybe after a year, in '47 or '48, it was just Lauderdale until he stopped recording in '52. Working in the shipyards by day, I got me a job playing at the Club Savoy in North Richmond. Started at ten dollars a night, three nights a week to add onto the shipyard money. Went up to fifteen dollars, up to twenty dollars, twenty-five—wound up getting fifty dollars a night—that's a hundred-fifty dollars for three nights. I kept the place packed, and they didn't want to lose me, which I didn't know that. So I played like North Richmond, Vallejo—and around.

"One morning I went to work. Said, 'I can't do this and play music. May mash my finger.' And I quit. Went back to the house, and my wife wanted to know what I was doing back so early. I told her I quit. She looked at me and said, 'Think you're gonna play music?' Still after all those years—that was about '48 or '49—she didn't want me playing music. Told me, 'You play music and you won't stay here.' I said, 'All right, baby. When you get ready for me, send for me. But don't wait too long because I'll be gone. I'm gonna cut a hit record.' We never did go back together because I know the hassle that I would have to go through. She wasn't the type of person to mix with audiences and see a lot of women shaking hands with me.

"I loved Jimmy Rushing, Mr. Five-by-Five. The first I heard him was in the service, or maybe right after I was discharged. He was with Count Basie. That was in the forties. Never saw him in person, just on records. People used to say that I sounded just like Jimmy on modern type blues, which I never noticed that. On one of my LPs I did go to Chicago. They liked the way it come out—I did it on the Kent label. On 'Every Day I Have the Blues,' I kinda patterned my tone of voice style on Jimmy. I didn't do that 'ahha -ahha- ahha' going down like Jimmy. It wasn't that type of song. I just went on smooth with it. But he was my idol.

"It's true that my style changed when I moved from Tulsa to Oakland. I knew both types of music. I could play by myself and I could play with a band. Well, when you play by yourself, you have to play in just about the worst places—honky-tonks, holes in the walls, and not a lot of money. The smoother the music was, the bigger the houses was, upper class of house you would get into, and the money, and you was recognized. Talking to Bob Geddins, I said, 'We're not making any money without a combo. Let's get a band.' He said he liked it just as it was. But I didn't. That was when little old three pieces come up and I did 'Black Widow Spider Blues.' Then I left him and went on to Trilon because Hugh Martin had a big band; seven or eight pieces is a long way from three pieces.

"I started on the electric guitar when I was in service. The closest to that was a metal guitar with a dialing face—you could change the button. I bought one of those until I went into the service. When I went for the electric, I had to learn to refinger. You couldn't hit the strings hard. Hung me up for about two or three months. After I got discharged, I had to keep on studying. In service I couldn't learn anything from the guys—you couldn't create anything because you didn't have anybody to learn from. In my field, I was just the best—singing the blues and playing the guitar. So if you don't find nobody better, you can't learn anything.

"But after I got out, there were these guys like Pee Wee Crayton, T-Bone Walker, and they made me study a little more and work a little harder until I got to a place where I could sit in with the big fellows—in the big bands. Your timing is different. You gotta be more accurate. I had to learn that. You take a small group; if they're familiar with what you're doing, if you go a little bit ahead of the time, why they fall right in with you. But when you go into band sections, you can't do that.

"Of course, my songs changed as I moved away from my beginnings. Instead of singing 'River Blues,' 'Black Widow Spider Blues,' and that type of thing, you went into a smoother type of blues like 'Trouble, Trouble' and 'Jelly, Jelly.' The first time I heard 'Jelly, Jelly,' Jimmy Rushing was doing it. And then Billy Eckstine came out with that big baritone voice.

"B. B. King wasn't recording when I did 'Three O'clock Blues' in '48 or '49. I gave it to him. Every time that B. B. and I get together, he always says, 'You gave me that big number.' The reason I give it to him—back in Memphis, Tennessee in 1950–51, he had a show on WDIA. He was the only one to play my records. The rest of the jocks wouldn't play them. B. B. came down to the Hippodrome when I was playing in Memphis. The people lined up, and I had to stay there for two nights to get them all into the place. It was B. B.'s playing of my records that did it. When he asked me for 'Three O'Clock Blues,' I gave it to him right there. I didn't have no dreams that he was gonna sell. We shook hands, and the next thing I know the man had a smash. And I said to my brother, 'That's the onliest man that I met that can take my own songs and beat me singing them.' He really did put it over, he put it over beautifully. Of course, he cut it with a band. But his voice part was so much better than mine. It was beautiful.

"Around 1953 I cut four things for Aladdin. Down in New Orleans. I never did hear them played that much to remember. Aladdin was the Mesner brothers. I didn't get acquainted too much with them. Maxwell Davis was doing the arranging. Came into New Orleans and cut me; later the musicians became Guitar Slim's band. They were six beautiful musicians. I wished I would've had more time to get the guys familiar with what I was doing before I went into the studio. We could've had a lots better session with the type of musician they have there. The guys catch on quick and they really have that soul beat—the drumsticks and rock 'n' roll blues—they just have it. The rhythm section is hard to beat in New Orleans.

"Right after that, I went with Checker. Stayed with them longer than with any company, about eight years. I recorded for them in Los Angeles. I could've had a lotta better things with them if I'd'a been a local. You're stayin' in a hotel. You're half gettin' your rest. You're not eatin' properly. You're jumpin' up and goin' down to the studio—and they don't wanna tie the studio up so long 'cause you're pinpointing a hotel bill and expenses. But if you can go home, you don't feel like doin' but three tunes or two tunes and don't wanna do them until next week, well, you just don't do them because you're already at home. Then, if you've got a company that has a recording studio, they always have a rehearsal room. And if you've got a regular band that you work with, you can get your three main guys—that's your rhythm section—to come in and sit down (you give them a little something) and they rehearse with you and get the stuff down. I'd rather get my rhythm section dead-headed first. The horns can read the stuff. I like the horns be dubbed in mostly anyway. I like the rhythm section patterned. And you can't pattern a rhythm section better than for the guys to get familiar with the material you're doing. They have their feelings—and let them put it in instead of playing just dead rhythm.

"It's a funny thing, but most every hit record that I've had I've arranged it myself by ear. 'Blue Shadows'—me and Lloyd Glenn. I told him the way I wanted it played, he told the fellows. Me and Lloyd cut all but one song for Swing Time, for Jack Lauderdale. I met Lloyd in Los Angeles. Jay McShann, the Kansas City piano player, was the first guy that cut me on Swing Time. He had 'Hot Biscuits' at that time—a big instrumental. I was kinda shy—big band with all new faces. And I always felt that I wasn't good enough, I wasn't ready. I was kind of drawn back. So Jay McShann come over, hit me on the shoulder, and say, 'Young man, you got it. Come on, belt it out. Let it go. We with you.' He loosened me up and we went in and did 'Ain't Nobody's Business' and 'Jimmy's Blues.'

"I told Jack that I just had to have a piano player. He got another man, and I didn't like him. So he got Lloyd Glenn, and me and Lloyd rehearsed. He had a very high-pitched voice, but a great feeling for music. He'd say [imitating the falsetto voice]: 'Now, Fulson, put a little more phrasing.' I got used to having him around and loosening up with him. Then we got Big Tiny Wills for rhythm guitar and Billy

Hadnott on bass and Bob Harvey on drums. I got me a regular rhythm section and we rehearsed and now I was ready. I told Jack Lauderdale that I wanted to do 'Every Day I Have the Blues' and he said, 'Well, I got a song I want you to cut for me: "Lonesome Christmas" and "Blue Shadows." ' And they all were big songs.

"Like I told Glenn: this is the way I want to do it. [Sings a slow ascending boogie riff] I didn't want nothin' else. I didn't know music terms so he said, 'Give the bass player two for nothin'.' Earl Brown was the alto sax on the session. Now, he played with me in North Richmond. He was fourteen, in junior high school. He was on all those records. I asked his mother to let him go with me, and I watched out that he took care of his schooling. Later, when I got my big band together, right here in the union hall, the old union hall down on Central Avenue, he was my alto sax. Ray Charles was the piano player because Lloyd Glenn didn't want to travel. Ray was also on Swing Time then, and we stayed together from '50 until '52, when he went on his own. He got too big, and I couldn't pay him the money that he was worth. I told Jack Archer and Billy Shaw, 'You ought to put the cat with a big label. He's great.' And they swung Atlantic Records for him. But I kept that little alto player. That's all I had for a good while—just one horn.

"Then we added three or four horns. I had two trumpets, alto, tenor, and baritone, and three rhythm. We had a good sound. Going back to those times, I made all the theaters: the Apollo, the Howard, the Regal. I took out Billy Ward & The Dominoes when they first had 'Sixty-Minute Man,' the Clovers—and we all worked out of the same office. But they claimed that I had the best band. I had Stanley Tarantine on tenor, Earl Brown on alto, Billy Brooks on trumpet— I had some strong musicians. The Korean War broke up the band, took a lot of my musicians.

" 'Reconsider Baby' was a song I wrote for my first date on Checker —in '54 it was. I was remarried then to a girl from Fort Worth, Texas. That's where I stayed when I wasn't on tour. Hung out at the B & B Cafe. Drink no beer till certain time of the evening. Drink pop through the day. When I called Leonard Chess, he wanted me to come up to Chicago to record. I said, 'No, I don't wanna come to Chicago. I don't like the musicians up there. I got me some good fellows right here.' He agreed to cut in Dallas, and called Sellers Recording Studios. I told the musicians what I wanted as a layman and Jimmy, the piano player, who was blind, told them what to do. Stan Lewis handled the session. I later cut that *In a Heavy Bag* album with

Lewis. He was then working for the Chess brothers in Dallas. But that's how we made 'Reconsider Baby.' It was a big one in '55.

"Stan Lewis is a good man. The only thing I don't like about him is that he works with small labels. If I get heard, let everybody hear me. Not just a few people in the South, a few people in the West. I'm gettin' old. I'm fifty-two, be fifty-three this month [March 1974]. I want a big company or no company. Let the people hear what I'm doing. And if they don't like it, well, I'll try somethin' else. I have a good market overseas. When I went to London in '69—first time I been over there since the war—I had a good ovation. Toured the British Isles—wonderful all over. Same year, I went into Paris. Then I toured France clean up to Nancy. A good tour. Dick Boone was handling it. He passed, and I haven't been back since.

"The Europeans seem like they appreciate you. Man, they'll make you play with encouragement and ovations. And the way they enjoy makes you put all you got into it."

I like low-down music, I like to
  barrelhouse and get drunk too (repeat)
I'm just a low-down man always feelin'
  low-down and blue.
           —"MR. FREDDIE" SPRUELL

T-Bone Walker and the Electric Guitar

A MAJOR FACET of the development of the blues—classic, country and urban—into rhythm and blues is the replacement of the Spanish or acoustic guitar by the electric. Without amplification there would, perhaps, have been no R & B, certainly not as we know it. Starting with the guitar, electrification enveloped bass and organ as well. And the bluesman who was pivotal in the development was Aaron Walker. Known as T-Bone Walker, he pioneered the introduction of electric guitar into combo blues.

Since the Presley and Jimi Hendrix generations never saw T-Bone at work in his heyday, they blithely assume that Presley and Hendrix's acrobatic and provocative manipulation of the instrument is original. But back in the late '30s, T-Bone was playing the guitar as he held it behind his head or back, and thrusting it through his legs in a sexually suggestive way.

Of greater consequence were T-Bone's advanced harmonic chording and his inventive use of jazz-inflected *arpeggios* and runs. So great a master of the instrument as B. B. King has said, "When I first heard T-Bone's single string solo on 'Stormy Monday,' it drove me crazy. I could never believe a sound could be that pretty on an instrument. . . . T-Bone has a way of using ninth chords—nobody's done it ever yet. . . . I like his singing, too, but he always killed me with the guitar. Just completely killed me."

Self-taught, Walker early developed such virtuosity as a guitarist that he experienced no difficulty, as most bluesmen would have, in working with one of the big Negro swing bands. For several years in the early '40s, he toured with Les Hite, whose alumni include trumpeter Dizzy Gillespie, trombonist Lawrence Brown, trumpeter-arranger-bandleader Gerald Wilson, and Lionel Hampton, who was Hite's drummer before he joined the Benny Goodman band.

Regardless of how far he moved musically, T-Bone's roots ran deep in the blues, and, unlike Ivory Joe, he maintained a strong, unshakeable feeling for the bedrock nature of the blues. "I think that the first thing I can remember," he has said, "was my mother singing the blues as she would sit alone in the evenings in our place in Texas. I used to listen to her singing there at night, and I knew the blues was in me, too. When I first started, I used to take an old Prince Albert tobacco can and strum it kind of like a guitar. There wasn't much tone, but the bluesy beat was there and a kind of melancholy note, too, that I like when I sing the blues."

Childhood and boyhood influences were later reinforced by his association with Ma Rainey, the classic blueswoman. He accompanied her as well as Ida Cox, another Bessie Smith contemporary, and Blind Lemon Jefferson. Out of this background came "Stormy Monday," the song for which he is best remembered. "Stormy Monday" can be traced back to work songs and spirituals. If T-Bone drew it out of the folk well, as Ma Rainey did "C. C. Rider," he was certainly responsible for giving it the shape in which it became a classic. Earl Hines recorded it before him in 1943 for Bluebird. T-Bone cut it for the first time for Black & White Records in 1947. Bobby Bland had a chart-maker on Duke in 1962. And among rock groups, The Allman Brothers and Isaac Hayes have recently cut it.

•

Lester Sill, now president of Screen Gems–Columbia, owns the publishing rights to "Stormy Monday." It came about in a strange and interesting way. "In '57–'58 I received a call from Randy Wood of Dot Records," he told me.

"Pat Boone was hot as a pistol then. Randy wanted the original recording of 'Call It Stormy Monday,' the one produced by Ralph Bass for Black and White, for Pat Boone to study. I told Randy to call T-Bone. But Randy said, 'You get in touch with him. And if you can get me a copy of the original, I'll buy you the most expensive suit of clothes at Sy Devore's.' Well, I managed to find T-Bone and went over to see him. He lived right here in Los Angeles. He had only one copy of his Black and White original, and he naturally didn't want to let it out of his hands. I offered him twenty dollars if he would let me borrow it for two hours so that I could make a dub. He agreed, and I rushed over to Bunny Robein's Studio on Fairfax where he quickly made a tape. While I ran the original back to T-Bone, Bunny made several dubs for me.

"The following day I brought it over to Randy, who listened to it and told me to go over to Sy Devore's and pick out any suit I wanted. After a few days, I had another call from Randy. He wanted me to get T-Bone's permission to change one phrase: 'Drinkin' Coca-Cola' instead of 'Drinkin' wine.' Then he told me that he was definitely planning to record it with Pat Boone and suggested that I try to buy the publishing rights.

"After a search, I figured that Paul Reiner, as the owner of Black and White Records, owned the song. When I located him in Cleveland and offered to buy the publishing rights, he said, 'They're yours, I don't want to have anything to do with music business.' Then I discovered that T-Bone had copyrighted the song before he recorded it for Black and White. Since he had never assigned the copyright to Reiner, he was still the owner of the song. So I went to T-Bone, drew up a contract and gave him a fifty-dollar advance.

"When I called Randy to tell him that I was now the publisher, he told me that the Boone version was not coming out. So I called T-Bone and asked him about the royalties he had received as the writer of 'Stormy Monday.' His answer was one word: 'None.' He explained it by saying that whoever had handled his business had passed away. I now arranged for a copyright assignment and immediately notified the Harry Fox Agency. [They automatically collect royalties from all the record companies for publishers, who then are obligated to pay half to their writers.] The first check I received was for forty-six hundred dollars from Capitol on a Woody Herman album. Since then, the song has become a blues standard."

•

The two pioneers of the electric guitar are, of course, Eddie Durham, born in San Marcos, Texas in 1906, and Charlie Christian, born in Dallas, in 1919. Durham was playing trombone in the famous Jimmie Lunceford band when he became interested in the amplified guitar. To give the instrument greater resonance and volume, he experimented with a resonator. Leonard Feather names Lunceford's recording of "Hittin' the Bottle," cut in September 1935, as "probably the first recorded example of any form of guitar amplification."

This was at least three years before electric guitars were generally available on the market. In the interim, Durham had encountered Charlie Christian in Oklahoma City, where the young musician had been raised and led his own combo. "I don't think Christian had ever seen a guitar with an amplifier until he met me [in 1937]," Durham claims. "I influenced Floyd Smith [who later played with Andy Kirk] to get an electric guitar, too."

But by 1938 guitarist Mary Osborne recalls hearing Christian in Bismarck, North Dakota, where a music store carried a window display: "The latest electric guitar model as featured by Charlie Christian." Other musicians recall hearing him play, not the typical four-to-the-bar clunks of band guitarists, but single notes that made the instrument an adjunct of three-part harmony with trumpet and tenor sax. By 1939, John Hammond was flying to Oklahoma City to audition Christian. (Mary Lou Williams of the Andy Kirk band had heard him there.) And in October 1939, Christian, then just twenty, participated in his first recording session with the Benny Goodman Sextet and helped, in Feather's words, "reorient the whole concept of jazz guitar." (By March 1942, he was dead of TB and high living.)

T-Bone Walker knew Christian and, in fact, arranged for him to take his chair in a local band when he left Ft. Worth to go to Los Angeles. (It was 1935 and T-Bone had just been married.) He also roomed with the young guitarist when the Goodman band was in New York playing at the Hotel Pennsylvania, now the Statler-Hilton.

Christian was not the only one who played electric guitar; the guitarists in the Andy Kirk and Les Hite bands used them too. But T-Bone, who began playing one after he left Hite, became the first to use it in blues combos. As Christian is credited with revolutionizing the role of the guitar in jazz and transforming it from a time-keeper to a solo instrument, so T-Bone is recognized as the musician to whom all blues guitarists are indebted. Lowell Fulson, Pee Wee Crayton, Oscar and Johnny Moore, and B. B. King, among others, have all acknowledged that debt.

When the new generation of R & B guitarists came onstage after World War II, their instruments all had a long umbilical cord running to a rectangular black box that grew bigger and bigger with the rise of rock. At first, the bass player continued plucking the strings of the bulbous fiddle for which he had to buy an extra ticket on plane trips. But early in the '50s something called a Fender bass—named after the company that manufactured it—made its appearance. It looked much like another electric guitar and it, too, was amplified, but the notes that came out of it were deep, throbbing, cannonlike bass notes. Now the blues were not only urbanized but electrified.

At least one of T-Bone's recordings with the Hite Band, "T-Bone Blues" of 1940, contains a preview of the future sound of R & B. Here is blues with a beat, the electric guitar of Frank Pasely and, most significantly, horns. But the big band texture had to be thinned down to a combo sound: instead of reed and brass sections of five instruments each, just one tenor sax and, perhaps, a baritone, one trumpet and, maybe, a trombone. And the four-to-the-bar feel had to be replaced by an eight-to-the-bar boogie beat with a strong afterbeat punch.

Two years after he made "T-Bone Blues," recording for Varsity Records in New York, T-Bone cut two sides for the newly formed Capitol label. The accompaniment was by T-Bone's electric guitar plus string bass, drums, and Freddie Slack's boogie piano. "Mean Old World" and "I Got a Break Baby," became, along with "T-Bone Blues," favorites of T-Bone followers; he recorded them over and over, and could seldom make a live appearance without performing them. Although the René brothers and their Exclusive/Excelsior labels were making records in LA before 1942, they were cutting black artists with a view to white sales and did not move into the R & B market until 1945. As black-oriented blues, T-Bone's Capitol sides of 1942 are considered by many to mark the beginning of blues recording on the West Coast.

groove 4   **AARON "T-BONE" WALKER**

"I've just completed two new albums," T-Bone Walker said in August 1973, in a voice that crackled like a supercharged guitar.

.

"I had a big group, fifteen or twenty musicians, different combo every day for ten days. They went through a lot of changes, and I'm anxious to hear just what they did. I'm my biggest critic. Charles Brown was my piano player. He's the leader of the sessions, did all

Aaron (T-Bone) Walker
(Photo by Arnold Shaw)

the directing 'cause he know me, been around me all his life. So he did a good job playin' the piano; he always do a good job. So they got me sittin' around, waitin' to see what's gonna happen. I don't worry about work. I have plenty of work. I have to beg to get off. But I would like to have a real, nice hit record. I'm playin' all the festivals, and in all festivals you don' do mebbe three or four numbers and you're finished—because they got so many of you.

"They won't let me do anything else but my old numbers: 'Stormy Monday,' 'Mean Old World,' 'I Gotta Break, Baby,'—and all the kids are buyin' old blues. And as a matter of fact, that's what keep us goin', old-timers. It's the young kids, likin' the blues. I'm enjoyin' it. Lotta guys say, 'Well, I thought you was over the hill.' I say, 'You never be over the hill in music.' Looka Duke—how old he is. [Ellington died in May 1974.] Must be at least 75 and he's still makin' it. So you never get too old to play music. You might get the way you can't play it.

"Around '47 was when I recorded 'Call It Stormy Monday' for Black and White Records here in Los Angeles. And Black and White sold the masters to Capitol. Capitol put out EPs. I did a session with Freddie Slack right after Capitol had its first hit record, 'Cow Cow Boogie' with Ella Mae Morse and Freddie. I did 'Mean Old World' and 'I Got a Break, Baby' with just a rhythm section; Freddie was playin' piano. Should have been sometime in the summer of '42.

"I was born in Linden, Texas, on May 28, 1910. Waxahatchie is my wife's home. But I was raised in Dallas, and my wife was raised in Waxahatchie and moved to Fort Worth. That's where we got married in 1935. My mother took me away from Linden when I was two. I lived in Dallas practically all my life. When I was a kid, I had a stepfather, and he and his brothers played like a mallet and guitars; and, like, Blind Lemon was a very good friend to my family, a very good friend to my mother, and my mother knows Big Bill Broonzy. I heard them. But my favorite was Leroy Carr. I just loved him. I never met him, but he made a record of 'In the Evening When the Sun Go Down.' When I heard that one, it was dramatic—that's it.

"I was with Les Hite for two years. I started out from here [LA], but they picked me up in Dallas. I went to see my wife—I figured I'm gonna hit the road—so I went in ahead of the band. We played Dallas, Houston, San Antone, and all through the northern states until we got to New York. That's the first time we'd ever been to New York. That was 1939.

"I left Les Hite in Chicago and come on back to California. And then I went on the road with my own band. Started out with eight but one of 'em died—trumpet player died—so it ended up with seven. The kid that run the band for me—the manager—and played baritone, of the name Dick Jim Wynn. Now he's with Johnny Otis.

"But I'm planning on not travelin' no more too much. I'm planning on stayin' around the house—you know like San Francisco and Los Angeles—if I can. I'm gonna try it anyway because I'm under a doctor's care. I go to a clinic every ninety days because I have dizziness and all that.

"When I went from Dallas to Los Angeles, I came with two cars— drivin' one and pullin' one. A feller had a used car lot, and he was moving all his cars to LA. You get a free trip to Los Angeles so I drove one and pulled one. And when I got here, well, I just stayed. Then I went back and got my wife. That was '41. But I come out here in '35.

"I worked for Rhumboogie in Chicago. I did 'I'm Still in Love with You' and 'Sail On, Little Girl,' and they bootlegged the records. It was in '45, and they sold them for five dollars a piece while I was in this club. I didn't get a dime out of it. The man that did it was Charlie Glenn, and I worked for Charlie Glenn in The Rhumboogie

Club. They got the name from out here in LA. Used to be a Rhumboogie long years ago. So Joe Louis opened this Rhumboogie. I stayed
in and out there three years—till the war was over—and then I hit
the road again.

"I worked with Jack McVea—he's on 'Stormy Monday'—he's
playin' tenor sax. That was on Black and White. After that I worked
with Imperial for five years. Talked with Lew Chudd before I went to
Canada two months ago, and he said he would try and get me into Las
Vegas.

"They have a lot of rhythm and blues, like B. B. King, and they're
playin' through these places all the time. I think I'm about the only
one who hasn't. I played Las Vegas way back. Me and Jordan was
down there together, travelin', doin' one-night stands.

"My headquarters is in Boston. My manager is Hemenway. I make
it from there, always go back to Boston, and start to playin' from
Boston and the small towns, and hit the road overseas. I always go
about once a year, European countries. Stayed a little bit in Paris.
I stayed over at a place called Trimaille, Madame de Nis. Memphis
Slim worked there for years, I guess he musta been there five, ten
years. Of course, you know we come to the European countries to-
gether. We worked with the blues package—Helen Humes, Memphis
Slim, Shakey Jake, Sonny Terry and Brownie McGhee, Big Willie
Dixon, Jump Jackson on drums.

•

"I made some records for Atlantic around '55. Saw Ahmet Ertegun
about two months ago in New York; he come to visit me when I
played Carnegie Hall. Golly, it wasn't two months ago. 'Hey, mama,'
[Calls to his mother, who has been sitting in the long living room,
talking to a young man] 'Hey, has it been two months ago when I was
in New York? Haven't been that long? I played Carnegie Hall? Musta
been about a month ago?' [She answers 'Yes' in a low voice.] Musta
been about a month ago. Me and Albert King.

" 'Leroy' [That was the young man talking with his mother.] was
talkin' about me travelin' some time with B. B. King. But I'm trying
to get out of this travelin' business. I ain't in the best of health.

"I like to play the small rooms. Leroy been talkin' to me about the
one that manage B. B. King. But already got a manager. Terrible,
them road managers are. You gotta sign up with them. You gotta
have somebody take care of your business while you're workin', so
you gotta have a road manager when you're on the road.

"I don't think that B. B. King imitated me. I influenced him to play.

I met him in Memphis when he first come up outta Mississippi. I met him at WDIA. I was working there. I opened W. C. Hanley's theater when they had their first show. This is where I met him. I remember he was doin' 'Three O'clock in the Morning' and stuff like that. He's crazy about me. He never goes nowhere unless he brings up my name. Says he gonna write a book. I says, 'Well, go and write it if you wanna write it.' He's a nice cat. Studies a lot. He's catchin' up what he thinks he's lost. He's got plenty of people to help him, and he doesn't have to worry about anything, but just go on and study. Go up on stage and play and come on out. He's got a good connection. He's got a good road manager. Leroy is very good. Leroy worked with me when they was St. Clair and Leroy, a dancing team. So he got this break with managing B. B. King. And he's doin' a good job.

•

"My stepfather played with Coley Jones's String Band. I played with the whole family. Coley used to come over and see my stepfather. His name was Marco Washington, played the upright bass, and they had a string band. Everybody get together on Sundays and play and enjoy themselves.

"I did a record once as Oak-Cliff T-Bone, around 1929 in Dallas. For Columbia, I made 'Wichita Falls Blues' and 'Trinity River Blues,' which top all blues. Just me, piano, and guitar, and they call me 'Oak-Cliff T-Bone, the Cab Calloway of the South.' I also played banjo and ukulele. Picked these up all by myself—no help. I learned the hard way, the real hard way, went through a lotta changes.

•

"I don't know whether I was the first guitar player to use the electric. But I was *one* of the first. The guitar player with Andy Kirk had one. And the guitar player with Les Hite had one—his name was Frank Pasely. He played steel guitar and regular guitar, and I just played guitar and sing. I didn't get to California until 1935. Started playing the electric after I left Les, I think it was 1939.

"I knew Charlie Christian, who played electric with Benny Goodman, all his life. When I moved to California from Fort Worth, I gave him my job in Fort Worth with Lawson Brook. Then I played a little bit with his brother Ed Christian. Three brothers of them played. They never worked together, I mean, not on the road. Charlie never did get a chance; he wasn't but about twenty-three or twenty-four years old when he died. I picked him up at the airport when he came out here to record with Benny Goodman, took him over to CBS, sit there and listen to the session. He was the most amazing guitar player I ever seen in my life. He walked in the studio—he was a little late—and when he got there, they run down a couple of numbers, and he jumped right in like he'd been rehearsing. Great guitar player! Didn't get a chance. And Edward was a piano player and he didn't get too much of a chance. Ed musta been in his late thirties, maybe early forties when he died. But they both died with the same thing. I think it was TB. That's what I heard.

"Charlie had never been nowhere. Maybe he had some bad friends, but he never got any rest. We were in New York together. That's when I was with Les Hite. We all were in New York together—Les Hite, Benny Goodman and Charlie. Me and Charlie lived at the Braddock Hotel, right there by the Apollo Theatre. He just didn't take it easy, was too fast for him. There'll never be another one, though. I know that Barney Kessel tries. He do a good job. He's from Oklahoma, I think. I got one of the guitars that was in his name. I was on the road when Charlie died."

•

To the left, as I entered T-Bone's house from the porch, there was a dark drinking room. The bar had obviously not been used for some time. T-Bone explained that he planned to put it together one day. Hanging on a wall was a plaque from the Pittsburgh *Courier*, dated July 31, 1956: "Battle of the Guitars at The Flame Show Bar. Winner: T-Bone Walker." T-Bone beat Pee Wee Crayton. A Grammy dated 1970, received by T-Bone for "Good Feeling," is labelled *Best Ethnic*. T-Bone has lived in this house, in the Watts area of L.A., for twenty-five years. He has been married to Vida Lee for thirty-eight years; she's fifty-five and he's sixty-three.

"I do anything I wanna do," he said. "But I respect her—I wouldn't take ten thousand dollars for her." His mother still lived with him, as did his nephew, T-Bone Junior or Little T-Bone. He told the story of how once when he was playing Robert's Show Lounge in Chicago, he sent for Little T-Bone, who got off in Kansas City instead of Chicago and went to Marty's Orchid Room where they had played together. He spoke highly of Little T-Bone as a guitarist, also as a gardener and truck driver, all of which functions he fulfills.

T-Bone was proud that all his family is deeply religious and that his daughters, wife and mother never miss church on Sunday. "I'm the only back-slider," he said, with an infectious, wide-mouthed grin.

When I asked him whether he got his nickname because he likes T-Bone steaks, he said that he does like them, but that the name came from a nickname by which his family called him. It was "Tibou," which after a time became T-Bone.

He felt that he had a sound so unique on guitar that if two hundred guitarists lined up and sounded a few chords, listeners could instantly tell which was his.

On New Year's Eve of 1974, T-Bone suffered a stroke. He died of pneumonia at Vernon Convalescent Hospital in Los Angeles on Sunday, March 16, 1975.

Canal Street's of diamonds,
St. Charles Street's made of gold
(repeat)
But when you go "back of town" bound
to see nothin' but old Creoles.
—WILLIE JACKSON

Black Is Green: Preconditions for the Rise of R & B

T HE NEGRO MAKES ADVANCES," was the headline on a January 1943 survey article in *Billboard*. A subhead advised: "Edging into Radio, Films; Bigger Than Ever in Music; And Despite Many Obstacles."

But in his survey, reporter Paul Denis observed: "Negro performers are still segregated in colored locals in most cities where the American Federation of Musicians operates. They are not accepted as members by many AFL theatrical unions. They still are not accepted as patrons in most hotels and restaurants. They still get lower salaries than white entertainers of equal talent. And they still do practically all their business thru white agents because Negro representatives are not 'accepted'."

As for radio: "A Negro cannot be represented in any drama except in the role of a servant or as an ignorant or comical person. Also, the role of the American Negro in the war effort cannot be mentioned on a sponsored program. Negro artists may not be introduced on any commercial network show with the appellation of 'Mr.' 'Mrs.,' or 'Miss' preceding his or her name."

Within a month, the Blue Network labelled these statements erroneous and provided a list of its radio programs that went counter to *Billboard*'s contentions. Considering the small number of shows involved, the best one could say for the Blue—the other three radio networks did not bother to respond—was that it made a case for tokenism.

In June 1943 two members of the Count Basie Band went to the door of the Trianon Ballroom in LA, where the Jimmie Lunceford Band was a walloping success, broadcasting nightly over Station KHJ and the Mutual Network. Although trumpeters Snooky Young and Harry Edison had come on Lunceford's invitation, the doorman refused to admit them. When Lunceford came to the door and explained that they were his guests, the doorman said, "You only work here. They can't come in." Lunceford, who was set for a six-week engagement, immediately notified the ballroom management that he and his men were pulling out at the end of two weeks. His was, in *Billboard*'s words, "an unprecedented move."

Late in 1944, clarinetist Barney Bigard became the center of a controversy about black membership in the Musicians Union. Although the trade regarded him as "colored," Bigard was actually of French and Spanish ancestry. He wanted to be admitted to the white local (Los Angeles had two separate locals). The NAACP entered the situation, addressing itself to James C. Petrillo, national union president, and demanding that the union's Jim Crow policy be abolished. The NAACP noted that of 673 locals, 32 were "colored." Of the remaining 641 "white" locals, 8 had segregated subsidiary branches while many simply excluded Negro members. According to Walter White, national president of NAACP, only 2 locals, those in Detroit and New York, admitted Negroes to full membership. Citing President Roosevelt's wartime Executive Orders 8802 and 9346, White contended that the union's Jim Crow practices were in violation of the Fair Employment Practices Code.

Petrillo gave a typically evasive reply. He stated that where two charters have been granted in a locality, "these separate charters were asked for in that way," and the present situation "is entirely satisfactory to the colored membership." He denied that only two locals admitted Negroes and cited the federation's bylaws requiring that locals not in dual jurisdiction areas admit all eligible musicians. It was pointed out, however, that since each local was autonomous, discrimination against Negroes, particularly in the South, was easily practiced.

In the year of Hiroshima and the end of the war with Japan, Cab Calloway and a friend were in Kansas City and decided to visit with Lionel Hampton, whose band was performing at the city's Pla-Mor Ballroom. Purchasing two tickets, Calloway and his companion went to the door, only to find that the doorman would not honor the tickets. Instead, a representative of the management appeared to explain that "no Negroes were admitted" and to offer the two a refund. What happened after that was a subject for investigation by the NAACP. A security guard claimed that he was pushed to the floor: "I got up and struck Calloway," he said, "and then drew my revolver. I hit him on the head several times." After being treated at General Hospital for cuts on the head, Calloway was booked by the KC police on a charge of intoxication and resisting arrest.

During its out-of-town tryouts, *The Hot Mikado*, with an all-Negro cast, used a Negro pit band. But when the show arrived on Broadway, the black musicians were replaced by an all-white pit band. The explanation was the house-contractor system: all Broadway theater contractors were white and hired only white musicians.

Incidents of discrimination, reported and unreported, could be multiplied without number, but these few serve to indicate that, despite the efforts of administration officials to gain the support of the Negro community for the war effort, local prejudice persisted. For that matter, Negroes were confined to segregated units at the Battle of the Bulge until the Nazis counterattacked. After the battle, in which 2500 Negro soldiers were permitted to volunteer their hides, those who came out of the fierce fighting alive had to return to their segregated units.

And yet, during the war years Negroes made strides in the entertainment field. Denis noted that Lena Horne was currently featured at Manhattan's Savoy Plaza Cafe Lounge, the first Negro ever booked in that swank spot. "The Cotton Club version of slaphappy Negroes," he wrote, "has started to give way to the Cafe Society version of Negroes as serious, formal dress, concert-style creative musicians and singers.

"Negroes have begun to land jobs on radio house bands," Denis reported, "thanks mostly to John Hammond's persuasions. Joe Pines has ten Negroes in his Blue Network band. Irving Miller has two in his NBC band. Raymond Scott uses four in his CBS band."

In Norfolk, Virginia, The Ink Spots, working with the Lucky Millinder band, became the first black attraction ever to play the Palomar Club. In St. Louis, boogie woogie pianist Dorothy Donegan became the first black artist ever to play the Chase Hotel Club. (Donegan was then so hot that the club, paying her $750 a week, agreed to let her interrupt her engagement and fill a one-week stand at Chicago's Oriental Theatre at $1,000 for the week.) In Columbus, Ohio, doors opened, not for artists, but for audiences. For the first time in half a century, Negroes were admitted to suburban as well as downtown theaters. ("This opened up some 60,000 new customers," *Billboard* reported.)

The crux of the situation was wartime economics. Some racial barriers began to come down because the Negro had new purchasing power and represented a sizable new market. Lounges, clubs, and bars mushroomed in defense areas, swelling the demand for Negro cocktail units and combos. But the green stuff entered into the situation, too: black combos were hired for less than equivalent white groups.

Throughout the war years, music trade papers were alive with headlines like "Negro Units Riding High," "Colored Names Biz Up in Detroit, Omaha, Binghamton," "New Spots and More $ $ Open Bonanza for Negro Musickers"; and there was even talk of a radio network for Negroes—it came to naught—with the FCC saying, "Why not?"

In Cleveland: "Race Orks Get New House in Metropolitan," giving the city six theaters catering to Negro audiences and rounding out a chain of flourishing black vaudeville houses that included the Roosevelt in Pittsburgh, Lincoln in LA, Royal in Baltimore, Regal in Chicago, Howard in Washington, Paradise in Detroit, and Apollo in New York.

And in LA: "Growing Sepia Clubs Offer 15 G Weekly Market." A section of the sprawling city formerly known as Little Tokyo had become Little Harlem. Adjacent to Central Avenue, LA's Lenox Avenue, it included Shep's Playhouse, Cobra Club (remodelled from a Japanese street-level store), Rhythm Club, Cafe Society, Club Alabam, The Last Word, and Club Plantation, owned by bandleader Joe Morris, who was soon to open Little Joe's. Significantly, all these places were patronized by Negroes with defense-work money in their pockets.

In Philadelphia, the only large midtown dancery, Town Hall, switched from booking white bands to black. The owners admitted that they discouraged attendance by "ofays" and that "swollen Negro paychecks at local war plants and shipyards" had created prosperous business.

It was a bonanza period for such bands as Lucky Millinder, Jay McShann, Tiny Bradshaw, Jimmie Lunceford, Buddy Johnson, Earl Hines, and Erskine Hawkins, and for such black artists as The Ink Spots, Mills Brothers, King Cole Trio, Lil Green, Fats Waller, Dorothy Donegan, Art Tatum, Maurice Rocco, and the boogie woogie pianists.

The two biggest names were, of course, Cab Calloway and Louis Jordan.

Cab was managed by Irving Mills and booked by GAC, while Jordan was managed by Berle Adams of Chicago. The Windy City was a scene of tense competition for the black market among such bookers and/or managers as GAC, MCA, Consolidated Radio Artists, Frederick Bros., William Morris, Phil Shelly, and Bert Gervis. But there were operators also in LA (Harold Oxley), Philadelphia (Jolly Joyce) and New York (Joe Glaser and Moe Gale, among others).

Apart from reporting the growth of the Negro audience and the expanding demand for Negro performers, *Billboard* itself gave recognition to the new black market. In October 1942 it instituted the "Harlem Hit Parade," a chart that, at first, had as many records by "ofays" as blacks. Until then, records addressed to black listeners were lumped with hillbilly recordings under the catchall classification of Folk. By 1945 the "Harlem Hit Parade" was expanded into several "race" charts: Juke Box Plays, Retail Sales, and others. The change in nomenclature to *rhythm and blues* occurred finally in the closing year of the decade—in the issue of June 25, 1949.

By then the brave, new world anticipated during the war was beginning to fade into the shoddy old cosmos of prejudice and discrimination as usual. "The Negro couldn't get out of the black ghetto," Mike Royko writes in *Boss*. "He merely extended it another fraction of an inch on the city map." Describing developments during the '50s in Chicago, Royko tells how the Mafia murdered its way into control of the lucrative numbers wheels, "taking away the black's own home-grown racket. Most small and large businesses in the black ghetto were owned by outside whites." This was also true to a lesser or greater degree of Harlem and other ghettos in major American cities.

As for more extreme situations: "In 1952 Governor Stevenson had to call out the National Guard when the old Capone suburb of Cicero went berserk and stormed a house bought by a black man." When gospel singer Mahalia Jackson, who was accustomed to adulation from white people in her audiences, tried to buy a home in Chicago, she found that houses prominently displaying "For Sale" signs had *just* been sold. When she finally put a down payment on a home, she began receiving phone calls, warning her that the house would be dynamited if she moved in. Bullets were fired through her windows after she did move in, and police remained posted outside for nearly a year. Eventually, white neighbors began selling their homes and real estate agents discovered that they could not find white buyers.

In 1956, Mayor Richard J. Daley said there was no segregation in Chicago. But, according to Royko, "most restaurants wouldn't seat blacks, most hotels wouldn't accommodate them, and the Loop was considered off limits. As a rule, South Side whites hated blacks more than North Side whites did, because the blacks were closer."

What this meant for Chicago, as for other cities with black ghettos, was that the Negro was being forced back into his own world for entertainment—black bars, taverns, clubs, saloons, and lounges—and when he was too tired or too broke, his home record-player. This phenomenon was the precondition for the rise of rhythm and blues.

.

Enter the jukebox, child of the illegal one-arm bandit. On May 1, 1942, the War Production Board commandeered the facilities of J. P. Seeburg and other jukebox manufacturers for the production of war materiel—this, at a time when the demand for jukes was growing. No army PX was without a box, a link to home for many soldiers. For young people in colleges and high schools, it became a vital recreational facility as youngsters were crowded out of their favorite dance spots by servicemen. "Jukebox Clubs," as they were called, were set up in many areas, with boxes being donated by Kiwanis and various organizations combating juvenile delinquency. Postwar economics, which required many lounges to dispense with live entertainment, prompted tremendous expansion in the jukebox industry.

By the summer of '44, the trade papers were reporting the inability of record companies to keep the country's "hungry Jukes well fed." Jukebox operators were critical of the scarcity while disk manufacturers protested that as much as 75 percent of their output was being apportioned to boxes and as little as 25 percent reserved for retail trade. *This was the gap into which small record companies could and did move*, especially in the area of black records, whose creation and production were curtailed during the wartime rationing of shellac.

The disk jockey was another factor favoring the rise of R & B. His emergence was slow. At first, record companies were wary, afraid that the playing of disks over the air would hurt retail sales. As a young company, Decca not only did not make its disks available to radio stations, but banned plays even when the stations bought them. "For private home use" was its war cry. (The jukebox was then regarded as the medium through which the public could be nudged into purchasing new records.) By the end of World War II, however, the collapse of the big bands and the growth of small stations enhanced the possibility that dee jay turntables might serve as a medium of exposure and promotion. The advent of television cast the die. The decline of network radio shows and the introduction of the transistor gave new importance to the "indie" station and the "Knights of the Turntable," who became the medium through which the small record company could economically reach the public.

As small diskeries rose to meet jukebox demand for records, particularly black records, financing became a problem—so did songs and artists. And here is where a competitor to ASCAP, set up by the country's broadcasters, proved of critical importance. Broadcast Music, Inc. (BMI), chartered as a performing rights society in October 1939, began operations in February 1940 with 256 stations pledging over a million dollars. Its early development was slow until it moved into two areas of American pop neglected by ASCAP: hillbilly and "race," or as they became known in the more enlightened atmosphere of postwar America, country and western (C & W) and rhythm and blues (R & B). Nashville and black songwriters and publishers suddenly found an open door for their work.

And so the stage was set for one of the most interesting developments in American pop music: the mushrooming growth of small, independent record companies.

New York's a pretty city and the lights
*   do shine so bright* (repeat)
But I'd rather be in New Orleans
*   walkin' by candlelight.*
          —GENEVIEVE   DAVIS

Pioneer R & B Labels and Groups

WHEN Cecil Gant's 'I Wonder' broke in 1945," said George Leaner, owner of a record store on Chicago's South Side and later a record producer, "a number of refugees from Europe, who had great ethnic knowledge, saw the possibilities in the blues, and the independent label was born."

The "indie" label was actually born some years before Gant's disk alerted men to the rewards that a small record company might reap. So far as I can determine, at least four labels were operative during the late '30s when the record industry was in the hands of a small group of majors. On the West Coast, there was Exclusive and in New York, Varsity, Beacon, and Keynote.

Exclusive and its sister company, Excelsior, were owned and operated by blacks, the René brothers, originally from Louisiana. Otis, the elder by four years, was born in New Orleans in 1898. Leon was born in Covington, Louisiana, in 1902. Both were university trained: Otis graduated from Wilberforce University in 1921 and earned a B.S. in pharmacology at the University of Illinois in 1924. He immediately moved to Los Angeles where he worked for his uncle for two years before opening his own pharmacy. Leon went to Xavier University in New Orleans, Southern in Baton Rouge, and Wilberforce in Xenia, Ohio. He spent the summer months working for his father, a brick contractor, and, when his parents moved to Los Angeles in 1922, he became a bricklayer by day and studied music at night. After a time, he formed his own orchestra and began writing songs. One of his earliest hits, "When It's Sleepy Time Down South" (1931), became Louis Armstrong's theme. A standard of equal popularity is "When the Swallows Come Back to Capistrano" (1940).

Exclusive Records was founded in the early '30s, apparently as a vehicle for showcasing songs written by the two brothers. During the '40s they began expanding and acquired artists like Herb Jeffries, a Billy Eckstine-type balladeer who scored with "Body and Soul"; Johnny Moore's Three Blazers, who recorded for several West Coast labels; and The Basin Street Boys, a jazzy cocktail combo. They were more interested in the white mainstream market than the regional black market.

During the R & B years, however, they attained a peak with Joe Liggins' "Honeydripper," a record that sold over a million in 1945–6, an unheard-of figure for a blues instrumental. Liggins' instrumental became the first combo blues recording to turn into a runaway R & B hit, antedating Paul Williams' "Huckle Buck" on Savoy (1948) and Bill Doggett's "Honky Tonk" on King (1956). In the late '50s, Leon René came up with two enormous R 'n' R and R & B hits on a new label, Class Records: "Little Bitty Pretty One" and "Rockin' Robin."

On the East Coast, in the late '30s, a reshuffling of RCA Victor executives resulted in the founding of Varsity Records by former A & R chieftain Eli Oberstein. In the R & B field, the label developed its catalogue through making deals with two companies that had been active in the blues area during the '20s but were destroyed by the depression—Paramount, bankrupt in 1932, and Gennett, in 1934.

Oberstein's most important reissues were of the Mississippi Sheiks, a vocal-string group (including fiddles), that originated in Shreveport,

Louisiana, and was extremely popular in the early '30s with more than fifty OKeh releases. They accounted for the ironic blues-ballad hit, "I'm Sitting on Top of the World (Now She's Gone)." For reasons not easy to comprehend—unless he wanted the records to seem like new releases—Eli released the Sheiks' disks under the cognomen "Down South Boys."

When Columbia and Victor lowered the price of their "race" records in 1940, Varsity came upon dark days, and by 1941 it was out of business. Its failure led to the formation of several labels by Joe Davis, an enterprising Broadway songwriter-publisher who bought the Varsity masters. Attracted by Harry Gennett's wartime shellac ration, Davis made a deal: He lent Gennett the money to reopen his defunct pressing plant; in turn, Davis was able to purchase pressings on a cost-plus basis. Using old Electrobeam sleeves and acknowledging the original source of the recordings—Gennett Record Division, Starr Piano Company, Richmond, Indiana—Davis reissued disks by Georgia Tom, Big Bill, Champion Jack Dupree, and other popular blues artists of the 1930s.

Around 1942 Davis launched Beacon Records (renamed Joe Davis Records in '45), a label that developed new black artists, among them, Una Mae Carlisle, The Five Red Caps, and Savannah Churchill. Una Mae Carlisle, born in Xenia, Ohio, in 1926 and dead before her thirty-eighth birthday, was more a jazz singer than an R & B shouter. A discovery of Fats Waller, she imitated his piano style, playing Kelly's Stable and other Fifty-second Street clubs at the height of her career. Although she contributed more sides to the Beacon catalogue than did Savannah Churchill, she never made it on wax. But she was responsible for a number of blues-inflected, pop hits, including "Walkin' by the River" (1940) and "I See a Million People" (1941), both of which she coauthored and recorded on Bluebird.

Beacon rang the cash register with a group called The Five Red Caps, whose disk of "Mama Put Your Britches On," a defense-slanted jump tune by R & B writer Irene Higginbotham, was featured in the company's first full-page ad in *Billboard*. Singing in a pseudo-black style somewhere between The Ink Spots and Mills Brothers—solo voice against sustained harmonies—the group bowed in the fall of '43 with another Irene Higginbotham jump tune, "The Caboose," a black man's "Chattanooga Choo-Choo." By '44 the singing, piano-bass-guitar group was on the "Harlem Hit Parade" and the chart of "Most Played Juke Box Records" with "I Learned a Lesson I'll Never

Forget," by Joe Davis, who wrote some of their other sides. Although they occasionally recorded indigenous numbers like "Boogie Woogie Ball" and "Lenox Avenue Jump," most of their etchings were aimed at a wider (whiter) market, which they, unlike The Ink Spots and Mills Brothers, never reached.

Savannah Churchill, the most accomplished of Beacon's artists, entered show business as the result of an accident. Born in New Orleans in August 1919, she was raised in Brooklyn, attending St. Peter Claver, a Catholic elementary school, and graduating from Girls' High School. Her plan to become a dress designer, pursued after studies at New York University, was early terminated by marriage to her childhood sweetheart. Settling down as a homemaker, she bore two children—and then her husband was killed in an auto accident.

Show business seemed the best way for the widow to raise her youngsters. She managed to wangle a job at Smalls' Paradise in Harlem, not because she sang well, but because she was so attractive. Working as a dancer, she studied singing and eventually impressed Benny Carter, whose band vocalist she became. When the Carter orchestra played Loew's State Theatre on Broadway in March 1944, a *Billboard* reviewer wrote: "The showstopper of the current bill is Savannah Churchill whose swell voice throwing of 'That Ain't Right' and 'Hurry, Hurry' brought the house down. Show ran over because crowd wouldn't let her go. . . . Gal's big voice and delivery of race numbers makes her a natural for night clubs."

Savannah was one of the first artists Joe Davis recorded when he launched Beacon Records. Two years before her impressive showing at Loew's State, he cut four sides with her. Three were new blues (R & B like "Fat Meat Is Good Meat") and the fourth was a pop ballad with a wartime slant, "He's Commander-in-Chief of My Heart." None sold well enough to prompt new sessions. But by 1945 Savannah had interested Irving Berman, of Regis, Arco, and Manor Records, in becoming her manager. "Daddy, Daddy," which she wrote and recorded on Manor after stopping the show at The Bowery in Detroit, made the chart of "Most Played Juke Box Race Records" in October 1945. Two years later, Savannah enjoyed the biggest disk of her career, "I Want to Be Loved (But Only By You)," a blues ballad she wrote, followed by "Time Out for Tears," written by Abe Schiff and Irving Berman, her co-writer on "Daddy, Daddy."

Savannah became a solid nightclub performer, appearing at Ciro's in Hollywood and other chi-chi white spots. After Manor, she recorded on major and minor labels: Decca, RCA Victor, Columbia, Reg, Arco, and Cadence; but she never achieved the renown of Dinah Washington, to whom she was often compared and who crossed into pop. On wax, Savannah remained an engaging R & B balladeer.

On both "Loved" and "Tears," Savannah was backed by a male quartet that became known as the Four Tunes. An early R & B group, The Tunes appeared on wax from 1947 to 1956, the year of the Presley explosion. Although they recorded briefly on Arco and Columbia, most of their work was evenly divided among Manor ('47–'49), RCA Victor ('50–'53), and Jubilee ('53–'56), for whom they cut a total of over 100 sides. Owing a debt to The Ink Spots, some of whose hits they recorded, the Four Tunes scored their biggest success with "Marie," the Tommy Dorsey hit, and "I Understand," both on Jubilee in '53–'54.

•

Between 1942 and 1944, four other East Coast R & B labels set up shop. Savoy, located at 58 Market Street in Newark, New Jersey, was established by Herman G. Lubinsky, a hard-headed, hard-working, highly opinionated recordman who minded the store until a few months before his death in 1974. DeLuxe Records, also a New Jersey company but less important than the others, was the child of the Brauns, a Linden family who even built their own pressing plant. Apollo Records, an outgrowth of a Harlem record shop, involved three partners: Hy Seigal, Sam Schneider, and Ike Berman, whose imperious wife Bess exercised a potent voice in its affairs. Despite its name and proximity to the Apollo Theatre, it had no connection with the temple of black entertainment.

The most important of the four "indies" as a pioneering R & B label was National, a Manhattan company founded by A. B. Green. Its stature is based on the savvy and intuitions of the man who served as its inspired A & R director, Herb Abramson, a fast-talking, cigar-smoking, eye-squinting recordman who later was co-founder of Atlantic Records.

Before it found The Ravens, National contributed disks by Pete Johnson and Joe Turner to the R & B scene, recording them separately and together. These disks were produced by Abramson in 1945, at the time when Cecil Gant was stirring the record world with "I Wonder." Billy Eckstine & His Band was another early National find. Though his orientation was pop and jazz rather than R & B, Eckstine did produce one substantial blues-oriented disk in 1946 in "Jelly, Jelly." At the same time, Herb Abramson was extensively advertising a more ethnic bluesman, "Gatemouth" Moore, who unfortunately did not make it.

Having started as a jazz record collector, Abramson had his ears open for the unusual. In 1947 he recorded a jazz classic with Charlie Barnet, the famous ear-catching disk of "Cherokee." But that year he also accounted for one of the early R & B crossovers into pop, "Open the Door, Richard," which will be discussed at length in a later chapter.

•

When Atlantic Records put together an eight-album *History of Rhythm and Blues,* it turned to the catalogues of two other companies for selections that antedated its first R & B hit, "Drinkin' Wine, Spo-De-O-Dee," in 1949. One was National, from whose vaults it chose "Ol' Man River," by The Ravens as the opening number of volume 1; the other was Jubilee Records, from whom it leased "It's Too Soon to Know," by The Orioles. Although The Ravens are frequently regarded as the grand-daddy of R & B groups, both groups were influential in generating the rise of black/ghetto, street-corner groups as well as in naming such groups after birds. A partial list includes The Cardinals (Atlantic), Swallows (King), Robins (Savoy), Flamingos (Chance), Meadowlarks (RPM), Hawks (Imperial), Wrens (Rama), Falcons (Flick), Larks (Apollo) and Penguins (Dootone). Though neither The Ravens nor The Orioles captured the large white audience commanded by The Ink Spots and Mills Brothers, they both had a following among white listeners—and they produced a blacker sound than their predecessors of the '30s.

The Ravens coalesced in the spring of 1946 and made their debut at the Club Baron on West One-Hundred-Thirty-second Street and Lenox Avenue in Harlem. It could have been the club where bass Jimmy Ricks and baritone Warren Suttles had worked as waiters and sung along to jukebox recordings of the Mills Brothers and The Delta Rhythm Boys. Though Maithe Marshall was the initial lead voice, the group first made it on the recording of "Ol' Man River," which featured Jimmy Ricks' voice—a low, low, vibrant bass just right for *The Showboat* hit associated with the great Paul Robeson. Their rendition of the Kern-Hammerstein standard swung in a jazzy, four-beat rhythm reminiscent of the Delta Rhythm Boys. It immediately established the group, which had made no impression with previous recordings on King and on Ben Bart's Hub label. Ben Bart was co-producer of the side, along with Al Green and Herb Abramson.

From 1947 to '50 The Ravens poured forth a series of attractive sides on National, scoring again in '47 with "Write Me a Letter," a ballad by a new black songwriter named Howard Biggs, who thereafter wrote many of their charts. But much of their catalogue consists of *café au lait* (not quite black) versions of standards like "Wagon Wheels," "Deep Purple," and "September Song," and of cover records of current pop hits like "Someday (I'll Want You to Want Me)" in '49 and "Count Every Star" in '50. Occasionally they even cut a cover of an R & B best-seller like The Orioles' "It's Too Soon to Know." With a sound only a bit blacker than the Mills Brothers, they were bringing white material to the black market—not quite R & B—yet they influenced The Drifters, who adapted their version of "White Christmas" to produce one of their biggest sellers on Atlantic.

The Ravens continued recording into 1957, moving to Columbia Records after National foundered in 1950 and Herb Abramson had left. Then to OKeh, then to Mercury for three years, briefly to Jubilee and Argo, and finally to Savoy.

The other of the two pioneering R & B groups, The Orioles, was the first to go pop. It did not happen in a significant way until the fall of 1953 when "Crying in the Chapel" traveled as fast on pop best-seller charts as it did on R & B lists. In the pre-rock 'n' roll era, it was the precursor of "Gee," by The Crows on Rama, "I Understand," by The Four Tunes on Manor, and "Sh-Boom," by The Chords on Cat, the song of summer 1954 that heralded the rock revolution.

Originally known as The Vibranaires, The Orioles came from Baltimore, where they sang on street corners after Earlington Tilghman (later known as Sonny Til) came out of the service. They were singing on the corner of the Pitcher Street station of the Pennsylvania Railroad when a friendly bar owner invited them into his place to perform. There they were discovered by Deborah Chessler, an enterprising and aggressive songwriter. Changing the name of the group to that of the Baltimore bird, she packed them into her second-hand Ford, drove them to New York City, and parked directly in front of the Apollo Theatre. Not without some difficulty, she managed to persuade Frank Schiffman to audition the group even before they changed their clothes.

Schiffman booked them into the shrine of Negro entertainment, and before long, they were Apollo favorites. According to Jack Schiffman, son of the theater's owners, lead singer Sonny Til affected the girls like an aphrodisiac. When he bent over the mike and leaned to one side, "sensuously gyrating his shoulders and caressing the air with his hands," the girls would shriek, "Ride my alley, Sonny! Ride my alley!"

From the Apollo, Ms. Chessler took the group to two other auditions. One was at CBS for a possible appearance on Arthur Godfrey's famous springboard show, "Talent Scouts." On the basis of audience applause, they came out second to jazz pianist George Shearing. But by the time they had returned to Baltimore, a call came from the Godfrey office based on listener response—and The Orioles flew back to New York to appear on the Godfrey "Morning Show."

The other audition was with Jerry Blaine (who died in March 1973), then in the process of changing the name of his record label from Natural to Jubilee. The Orioles actually had their first release on Natural, but the sides were rereleased on Jubilee, for whom they recorded steadily into 1956.

For their first session, the group cut "It's Too Soon to Know," a ballad written by their manager. Their recording has a very unfinished quality. Both the lead singer and his harmonizer are not sure of their pitch. The tempo is slow, and the rhythm nonexistent. With only guitar accompaniment audible, the disk has an inescapably amateurish quality, which, curiously, may account for the stronger acceptance of The Orioles over The Ravens and The Four Tunes. But the record also had in the vocal of Sonny Til an emotionalism that enraptured white as well as black listeners. Crying "am I the fire or just another flame," Sonny's voice was full of heartbreak and a palpably horny sound.

The personnel of the five-man group remained constant until guitarist Tommy Gaither fell asleep at the wheel of their station wagon one night. The car raced off the highway; Gaither was killed instantly, and baritone George Nelson and bass Johnny Reed were badly injured. Nelson's tart delivery in the bridge of songs was, incidentally, a feature of Orioles disks along with high-tenor Alexander Sharp's voice flying above the group's harmony. "Pal of Mine" was recorded as a tribute to Gaither, who was replaced by Ralph Williams.

Apart from "Crying in the Chapel," a No. 1 R & B hit in '53 and a pop chartmaker, The Orioles had a No. 1 record in "Tell Me So," written by manager Deborah Chessler, and an R & B chartmaker in '49.

•

A third group that was important in the development of R & B but came later was The Five Royales, who cut on Apollo Records. Beginning as a gospel group called The Royal Sons, they contributed gospel excitement, an ingredient as basic to R & B as the passion of The Orioles. In 1953 they placed two sides among the year's "Top Ten R & B Bestsellers": "Baby Don't Do It" and "Help Me Somebody," both of which had greater intensity than most R & B ballads, even in their titles.

The following year, they moved from Apollo to the more formidable King label of Cincinnati, for whom they produced chart numbers in "Think" in '57 and "Dedicated to the One I Love" in '58, a record that has been called "a secular prayer." Although virtually all of their songs were love ballads, some with pseudoreligious overtones, their sound was more raucous than other ballad groups. Lead singer and songwriter Lowman Pauling was a high-spirited shouter. On their King Records, they added tension through the use of a whining electric guitar as a responsorial voice. Three years after their success with "Dedicated," written by Pauling and King's A & R director Ralph Bass, the shrill Shirelles made a best-seller of it on Scepter Records.

Apollo Records was also responsible for The Larks, a Harlem street-corner quintet that produced two moderate R & B hits, "Eyesight to the Blind" and "Little Side Car," both in 1951. Recording without a string bass, the group used their bass singer as a substitute. His deep, four-to-the-bar "doe-doe-doe-doe's" were imitated by other groups of the '50s, notably The Moonglows, who employed the device on their classic recording of "Sincerely."

•

Insofar as solo artists go, Jubilee introduced a young California singer on Josie, a subsidiary, who danced briefly across the R & B stage with several chart-climbers in the late '50s. Bobby Freeman, born in San Francisco in June 1940, sang with the Romancers and Vocaleers before he was discovered by a Jubilee producer who was honeymooning in the Golden Gate city. On hearing Freeman, who was then a high school senior, A & R director Morty Palitz quickly signed him to a contract. In the month (April) that the Army drafted Elvis Presley, Freeman recorded a song that he had written. "Do You Want to Dance" bounded onto R & B charts in May 1958, just about the time that teenage girls were mooning over Presley's disk of "Wear My Ring Around Your Neck." It remained a best-seller for three months, eventually climbing to No. 2 and aggregating sales that made it a Gold Record. By then, *American Bandstand*, with Dick Clark as its host, was making its impact felt as a hit-making program. "I just about lived on that show," Freeman told a *Rolling Stone* reporter in 1974. "Between myself and Frankie Avalon, we were on more than anybody else." Freeman scored again in '58 with two other Josie disks, "Betty Lou Got a New Pair of Shoes" and "Need Your Love." But neither these nor other records approached the mark of his debut disk.

When he appeared briefly on King Records two years later, Bobby attempted unsuccessfully to trade on the popularity of a new teenage dance with "(I Do the) Shimmy-Shimmy." Another rock dance, The Swim, became the subject of a recording Freeman made in 1964. Written by Sly Stewart (later known as Sly Stone) and Tom Donahue, a Bay Area disk jockey, "C'Mon and Swim" made Top Ten on Autumn Records, a local label. The disk failed, however, to extend Freeman's record career, even though his initial hit, "Do You Want to Dance," was successfully revived the following year by the Beach Boys; again in 1968 by the Mamas and Papas; and once again in 1973 by Bette Midler. Freeman remains an artist who has a solid following in the Bay Area and draws well at clubs like the Condor.

•

Apollo Records, guided by domineering Bess Berman, made its contribution to R & B, not so much through blues disks as through its gospel catalogue. Tony Heilbut begins his book *The Gospel Sound* by describing the 1969 funeral of Roberta Martin. Noting that the gospel singer-songwriter drew the largest turnout in Chicago's history of hysterical funerals, he observes that the sound of Martin and other gospel singers accounted for "the beat, the drama and the group vibrations of rock." A discovery of gospel songwriter Thomas A. Dorsey and his associate Sallie Martin, Roberta Martin (no relation) sold over a million records of her Apollo disk "Only A Look."

Apollo's crowning achievement was its eight-year association with the woman who has been called "The World's Greatest Gospel Singer." Mahalia Jackson, born of devout Baptist parents in New Orleans in 1911, idolized blues singer Bessie Smith. Other gospel singers claimed that Mahalia was the first to bring the blues, which she later eschewed, into gospel. Mahalia's childhood influences also included the Baptist hymnology as well as the frenzied shouting of a Sanctified Church congregation next to which her family dwelt.

Although she recorded first for Decca (in 1937), she began her ascension to the throne of Gospel Queen after she signed with Apollo in 1946. While her relation with Bess Berman was marked by stormy sessions—chiefly over royalty statements—it was on the Harlem

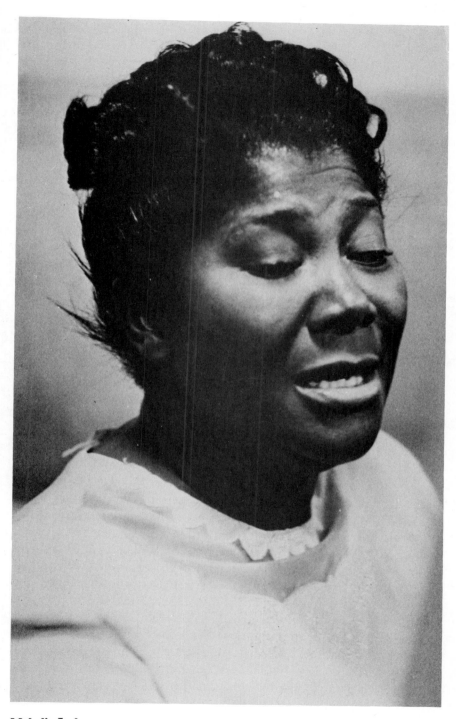

Mahalia Jackson

"indie" label that she became known for "How I Got Over," "Just Over the Hill," and especially "Move On Up a Little Higher," an Apollo record that would have earned a Gold Record had it been a pop disk.

The Bess Berman label helped launch the record careers of two other important artists. Wynonie Harris came out of the Lucky Millinder band to register a "Most Played Juke Box" hit in September 1946 with "Playful Baby," stirring so much excitement that he became the object of a lawsuit levied by Apollo against King Records for stealing him away.

And then there was Dinah Washington, the most expressive blues-ballad singer of the R & B years. Dinah was as great in her metier as Mahalia became in hers. The rich interrelationship of gospel and R & B, of the sacred and secular in black song—is magnificently illustrated in the careers of the two women. Mahalia went into gospel from Bessie Smith blues, which she later characterized as "devil songs of the depression"; and Dinah went from gospel into R & B.

groove 5   **BOBBY SHAD**

Bobby Shad, today the active owner/producer of Mainstream/ Time Records, is a pioneer of blues and jazz recording whose career spans the rise of bop, cool jazz and R & B. In the late '40s he founded the Sittin' In With label (SIW) and recorded many down-home bluesmen in field trips through the Texas-Louisiana triangle of cities— Tyler, Texarkana and Shreveport. In 1950 he launched Peppermint Harris (whose real name is Harrison Nelson) through a series of sessions in Houston. The first took place in a brothel in Houston Heights; it was the only place where he could find a usable piano. Out of this session came "Rainin' in My Heart," a Top Ten R & B disk in the spring of 1950. That year Shad recorded a dozen sides with prolific Lightnin' Hopkins at the ACA Studios in Houston, subsequently cutting another batch in New York City. In 1951 he was back in Houston recording Smokey Hogg. On blues that he wrote, Shad used the pseudonym Robert Ellen. He became widely known as a record producer after he joined Mercury Records as director of blues & jazz records and supervised sessions by Illinois Jacquet, Buddy Johnson and the Platters as well as Dinah Washington. He left Mercury for a brief stint with Decca, but returned to the Chicago-based company in 1957 to launch the Emarcy jazz label and to succeed Hugo and Luigi as eastern A & R director of the company.

•

"I started producing R & B records right after the war—at the end of 1945 when the recording industry opened up again. The majors were neglecting R & B—there was a price-fixing thing—and any independent who had the facilities to get pressings had no problem in selling.

"I was a musician (played guitar), and I knew all the musicians. Someone would say, 'Who knows Coleman Hawkins or Trummy Young?' and I did and ended up doing the record date. That was the beginning of the independent record business.

"I did a lot of recording for different 'indies' before I went with Mercury. The first was Black and White, a company out of Cleveland that was owned by Paul Reiner. I did a bunch of jazz things for him. I also recorded for Manor, Savoy, and Continental Records. I did Charlie Ventura, Rubber Legs Williams, Dizzy Gillespie. I did the first Charlie Parker things.

"Parker wasn't allowed to play because he was delinquent to three locals, which was typical of Charlie. At the time, he was delinquent to the Kansas City local, the Chicago local, and Local 802. I phoned Al Knopf, who was then head of 802, and guaranteed to take X dollars out of his recording dates and pay off all the locals. It was the weirdest deal I ever made. Though Parker was a jazzman, the first artist we did on the date was a bluesman named Rubber Legs Williams. Charlie was on the date, Dizzy Gillespie, Trummy Young—it was a weird blues date. I once read an article by George Wettling, and he said that the best vocal blues he ever heard in his life was a thing called 'That's the Blues,' by Rubber Legs Williams on Continental.

"For Charlie Parker, this was the first date allowed by the unions after the things he did with Jay McShann. Since all the cats were then working on Fifty-second Street where they'd finish at four or five in the morning and this date was at ten A.M., Parker was taking benzedrine all day. He didn't want to disappoint me, and he was trying real hard to stay awake. Rubber Legs didn't know that Charlie was taking the benzedrine in his coffee, and he took a swig. If you take a listen to the record of 'That's the Blues,' you'll hear this guy screaming like he was insane. A day later, he called me and said, 'Mr. Shad,

I don't know what happened to me. But ever since that record date, my heart's been pounding and my head feels like it's coming apart.'

"After that, I did Pigmeat Markham for Manor Records. You know, the 'Here Comes the Judge' stuff. I did spirituals of the time by Ernestine Washington, The Coleman Brothers. This was from 1946 to '49 when jazz and blues were going strong. I did a lot of jazz and blues for Savoy and have lost track of most of it.

"Then I went to work for National Records. This was after Herb Abramson left. I did Dusty Fletcher, the Ravens, and Una Mae Carlisle. I did the Dusty Fletchers after he had 'Open the Door, Richard.'

"Started my own label after I left National; it was called Sittin' In With. And I did all the early Charlie Venturas, Stan Getz, Wardell Gray. It was strictly jazz at the beginning—Gerry Mulligan, Buddy Stewart, Benny Green. But there was no money in jazz. Used to sell seven to eight thousand. That's when the blues thing hit me and I bought a Magnecord, which was probably the first portable tape recorder. Went down South and did a lot of recording with Peppermint Harris, Lightnin' Hopkins, Smokey Hogg. Recorded in Texas, mostly in Houston. But I did some up in Tyler; also in Shreveport, Louisiana.

"The big problem with on-location recording was finding a piano that was in tune. I would go into the black quarter of town and ask the disk jockeys. I would tie up one musician and find a blues singer. One bluesman would tell you about another—it's a whole family— everybody sings blues. I did Curley Weaver, Big Bill Broonzy, Memphis Slim, Mel Walker with the Johnny Otis Band, Little Esther.

"Itinerant blues singers like Lightnin' Hopkins used to hop on buses, perform, and then walk around with a cup. When we picked him up and talked a recording date, he wouldn't sign a contract. He wouldn't accept a royalty deal. He had to be paid cash. Not only that, he had to be paid after each cut. He didn't want to know about doing a tune over. He didn't know the lyrics from one song to another, but made them up as he went along. A typical vagabond. Whatever hit his mind, he sang and recorded. Like 'Coffee Blues'—he's got the blues from coffee because his girl left him. It was out of meter, out of rhyme, and the musicians would go crazy. He had no conception of a twelve-bar blues. It could be eight-and-a-half, thirteen-and-a-quarter or what have you. The musicians would be fumbling all over the place. But he had a wonderful feeling, and if you could stay with him long enough, you ended up with something worthwhile. Smokey Hogg was the same thing.

"Yes, you had to pay Lightnin' after each song. Before he started a new one, I'd pay him a hundred dollars. He did another, I gave him another hundred. He refused to work in any other way. Smokey Hogg was the same type. They were both out of Houston, Texas.

"I did the first things with Eddie Vinson* for Mercury—The Cleanhead. I just can't recall all the companies I made masters for. They were going into business and out. I did the Eddie Vinson things on Capitol. They sold like a million copies, and I think I received like ten dollars as a producer. I did Savannah Churchill for Manor. She became a star. I think I received a big twenty dollars. I was getting great write-ups in the papers and starving to death.

"I had the Sittin' In label for three years, and we did very well. We had a number of big blues records—one with Herb Lance, who became the big disk jockey in Atlanta.

"When I went to Mercury, I took over the whole R & B field. I did Junior Wells in '51–'52 and a load of Sonny Terry and Brownie McGhee. They're still selling records by them that I cut in the fifties. I did Dinah Washington, who used to sing at the De Salle Hotel in Chicago. Then she went with Lionel Hampton. Made a record on Decca of 'Blow Top Blues.' Then she hit on the Apollo label. I'll never forget two great records she made on Keynote with Lionel Hampton, 'Evil Gal Blues' and 'Salty Papa Blues.' Leonard Feather produced. They were great for the time.

"When I started to record Dinah on Mercury, I wanted to take her out of the R & B field. At that time, if you brought a record by a black artist to a pop disk jockey, you were dead. They would refuse to play them. I remember bringing up records, and I would refuse to tell them who it was. I'd say, 'Just listen to the record.' I recorded Dinah with strings and probably cost the company hundreds of thousands of dollars. That was about '53 when I started with the big orchestras backing Dinah. She was a fantastic singer, unbelievable artist. But you had to catch her on the right night. She thought nothing of being up all night to eight A.M. and then recording at ten A.M.

"We did a lot of R & B with her. But we also did Cole Porter in a blues style. Her version of 'Love for Sale' is one of the best records ever made. *Down Beat* said that. That was Dinah at her Harlem best.

* John Hammond advises that he cut sides with Eddie Vinson as early as 1947. He cannot forget the date: it was 104° in the Premier Studio in St. Louis.

"Every singer in the world was influenced by Billie Holiday—whether it's Nancy Wilson or you name them. The ballad influence is there. With the emergence of tape, all you did was take scissors and paste it together. That's how I did The Platters. Cut eight bars, then eight bars, and tack them together. You made a mechanical record. But when you got a singer like Dinah or Billie, there was no such thing as editing. You did a take and WHAM—that was it!"

*Oh, I'm gonna get me a religion, I'm
  gonna join the Baptist Church* (repeat)
*I'm gonna be a Baptist preacher and
  I sure won't have to work.*
              —SON HOUSE

Gospel Song, and Dinah Washington

COY about giving out the exact year of her birth (it was 1924), Dinah Washington was born Ruth Jones in Tuscaloosa, Alabama. Brought up in Chicago, at age eleven she raised her voice and accompanied herself on the piano in a Baptist church on the South Side. For a time, she toured the country, giving recitals in churches with her mother, her music teacher. At fifteen she won an amateur contest at Chicago's Regal Theatre and became involved in night club work. But the following year, 1940, she gave it up to accompany a woman who became one of the foremost figures in gospel music: Sallie Martin, who hired and trained Ruth Jones; later formed the first female gospel group (of which Ruth was part); founded one of the oldest gospel music publishing companies, the celebrated gospel song "Just a Closer Walk with Thee" being its first publication; and, together with Thomas A. Dorsey, launched the Gospel Singers Convention. During the period that Ruth traveled with Sallie as her accompanist, she acquired a reputation for being flighty and volatile.

It was not until 1943 that Ruth Jones made a final break with gospel and moved into black pop. Joe Glaser was the agent of the transformation. When he heard her at Chicago's Garrick Bar, he brought her to the attention of Lionel Hampton, whose booming band she joined that year. It was then that she changed her name.

"Joe Glaser told me about a friend of his," Lionel Hampton said, as he recalled the incident to Stanley Dance, "who had a girl who worked in the washroom of his club. They couldn't keep her in the washroom because she was always trying to sing with the band. They took me down there, and she sang a couple of blues numbers and sounded so good, so I said, 'I'm playing at the Regal Theatre. Come on out and sing with me tomorrow.' Joe Sherman, the club owner, brought her out, and she sang 'Evil Gal Blues,' and, boy, she broke it up! Her real name was Ruth Jones, but I asked her if she would mind if I changed it.

" 'I don't care what you call me,' she said, 'so long as you give me a job!'

"Okay, you're hired. From now on you're Dinah Washington. I don't know why that name came to me, but that's the way it was."

As Dinah Washington, Ruth Jones made her first recordings, not for Apollo as has been frequently stated, but for Keynote, an early "indie" company. Founded by Eric Bernay, Keynote was a jazz label, but it became the first "indie" to break the monopoly hold of the majors on *Billboard*'s "Harlem Hit Parade." In November 1942 a gospel disk, "Praise the Lord," by the Royal Harmony Quartet, inched its way among disks of Capitol, Bluebird, Victor, and the all-powerful Decca, whose releases then dominated the Negro market. It was Leonard Feather, later the encyclopedic jazz critic, who arranged Dinah's debut on Keynote. Working with a sextet from the Hampton band, she cut "Evil Gal Blues" and "Salty Papa Blues," both written by Feather and produced by him.

Dinah had been with Hampton for little more than two years when Apollo Records offered her an opportunity to record on her own. Her first Apollo sides appeared in the fall of 1946. Except for two jive novelties, titled "Me Voot Is Really Voot" and "Me Voot Is Boot," Dinah cut early R & B numbers like "Chewin' Woman Blues," "Rich Man's Blues," and "Wise Woman Blues." The sensuous ballad style that influenced virtually every black female vocalist came later, but even in these blues, her voice had a velvet sheen, and, in its bluer moments, it tore like silk, not satin.

Her Apollo tenure was short lived; an agent named Ben Bart became interested in her work and negotiated a recording contract with Mercury Records, then a fledgling label that had been founded late in 1945 in Chicago. Dinah's first disk on Mercury, "West Side Baby," appeared in 1948. Eleven years elapsed before she reached the large mass market to which her inspired singing entitled her.

During those years, Dinah was the regnant queen of the R & B scene, with three and four Top Ten disks a year. Anything but a shouter, she could swing on rhythm numbers with the best jazz vocalizers. She had a flutelike voice, sinuous, caressing, and penetrating.

Master of all the devices of blues and gospel shading—the bent notes, the broken notes, the slides, the anticipations, and the behind-the-beat notes—she handled them with an intensity that came from her early church training. In time, she developed a style of expressive phrasing that was as unique as Sinatra's.

During the R & B years, she recorded every type of song with great sensitivity. Her best-sellers included R & B numbers like "Baby Get Lost" (No. 1 in '49) and classic blues like "Trouble in Mind" (No. 4 in '52). There were pop standards like "It Isn't Fair," a hit for Don Cornell in '50; and "I Wanna Be Loved," also a '50 revival by the Andrews Sisters—and show tunes like Cole Porter's "I Concentrate on You," a '55 chartmaker for her. She successfully recorded new pop tunes like "Wheel of Fortune," a best-seller for Sunny Gale on Derby and Kay Starr on Capitol, and "Teach Me Tonight," a pop hit for the De Castro Sisters on Abbott and Jo Stafford on Columbia. Dinah could do no wrong even with country ballads like Hank Williams' "Cold, Cold Heart" and "I Don't Hurt Anymore," a Hank Snow hit.

All of her disks were geared for sales in America's black ghettos. In fact, when I suggested to Mercury executives that Dinah could sell pop, they patted me on the head and urged me not to waste my company's promotion budget. This happened in 1959 when I was creative head of E. B. Marks Music and brought "What a Difference a Day Made" to Clyde Otis, then Mercury's A & R director and the only black in such a position in the entire industry.

I was so excited when Otis cut the Marks standard with her that even though field record promotion was the province of other members of my staff, I went on the road. I spent nine weeks visiting disk jockeys—not R & B jockeys but pop platter-spinners. I was having no difficulty getting her record programmed, but a Mercury executive phoned me in New Orleans and suggested, to put it mildly, that I was a misguided young man. Several weeks later, in June 1959, I had the pleasure of being told by the same exec that Dinah's disk had crossed over into pop. "What a Difference a Day Makes"—Dinah used the present tense—not only stayed on R & B charts for seventeen weeks, the longest of all of her chartmakers; it went to No. 9 on *Billboard*'s pop "Honor Roll of Hits" and finished in the "Top 50 Hot Disks of the Year."

The following year, Dinah cut several duets with Brook Benton, who had also just broken big on the pop horizon. "Baby (You've Got What It Takes)" and "A Rockin' Good Way," both long-running

No. 1 R & B hits, reveal a side of Dinah—the tantalizing kitten—not evident on her solo disks. But it was apparent during studio sessions I attended—in the way she fenced suggestions that came from Clyde Otis in the engineer's booth. The tantalizing kitten, the purring kitten—these are sensuous vocal qualities that Dinah brought to black balladry and that left their magic mark on a generation of female singers—Etta James, Ruth Brown, Dionne Warwick, Diana Ross, and Little Esther, who as Esther Phillips made a hit once again of "What a Difference a Day Makes" in 1975.

Dinah could scratch as well as purr. She had paid her dues as a performer, as a woman—many unsatisfying marriages—and as a black artist. And it all came out in one of the most moving records she ever made: "This Bitter Earth" (No. 1 in R & B in 1960). "Mahalia Jackson and Dinah Washington," Tony Heilbut observed in *The Gospel Sound*, "were the only soul forces out there [in the '50s], speaking with the drive and impetus of church and street."

From Mercury, Dinah went to Roulette Records. Arranger Fred Norman, who worked with her at Mercury, also went to Roulette. "Dinah Washington was fantastic," he told Stanley Dance, "the greatest person I've ever worked with. She amazed me at one of our first sessions by making a number in one take. . . . 'That's it!' she said. 'I know.' Another time, when we were making that album *Back to the Blues*, she was singing 'You've Been a Good Old Wagon.' Oh, she was going, singing like crazy, and it was getting so long. 'Jeez,' I said to myself. 'There's got to be an end!' And I cut the band. 'What the ----?' she shouted, exploding. The final version was five minutes long anyway."

At various times, Dinah talked about buying a hotel in Chicago. By the early '60s, she owned a restaurant in Detroit, where Fred Norman came to help her to prepare a record date. As he recalls, "She spent days in the restaurant, supervising and handling the cash register." Norman returned to New York without ever going over songs with her, but she kept the date.

To prepare for a 1963 concert in Chicago, Dinah, who tended to be rather fleshy, began taking pills to bring down her weight. On the evening of December 14, she drank quite a bit. Unable to fall asleep, she also apparently took some sleeping pills. In the combination of alcohol and pills the world lost one of its finest singers, as great among the sultry sirens of song as Sinatra was among the big baritones.

•

In the early '40s before the black-ghetto market opened wide, the catalogs of black-oriented record labels were a mixture of jazz, pop, and gospel. When the owners were not casing Fifty-second Street, as Herman Lubinsky of Savoy did, or Central Avenue in LA, as the Bihari and Messner brothers did, they were haunting the black churches. While Apollo recorded Mahalia Jackson, Manor cut the Silver Echoes, Heavenly Gospel Singers, Sky Light Singers, and the still-active Dixie Hummingbirds. De Luxe recorded The Southern Jubilee Quartet. Golden-voiced James Cleveland, influenced by Dinah's fusion of gospel and blues, became the mainstay of the Savoy label, whose catalogue included Alex Bradford, the Selah Singers, and the Caravans, among others.

Many other independent labels established a foothold in the record field through gospel music before or at the same time that they invaded the black pop market of R & B. Specialty Records of Los Angeles recorded the Pilgrim Travelers, Swans, and Soul Stirrers, the group that nurtured Sam Cooke. Before he conquered the R & B market, Don Robey of Houston, Texas, built his Songbird label on the Mighty Clouds of Joy and the Dixie Hummingbirds, and his Peacock and Duke labels on The Five Blind Boys, still remembered for their classic disk of "Our Father." In the southeast, Ernie Young of Tennessee developed a huge catalogue of gospel on his Nashboro label—Silvertone Singers, Skylarks, Swanee Quintet, Prof. Harold Boggs—before he moved into R & B with Excello Records.

It is impossible to overemphasize the contribution of gospel music to the development of R & B. Like Dinah, most black artists began by singing in church. Sam Cooke, Clyde McPhatter, Lloyd Price, and Jackie Wilson started out as gospel performers. The Five Royales, the Dominoes, the Dells, and Gladys Knight & the Pips all began as gospel groups. Despite the long-standing conflict between blues as "devil songs" and gospel as "God songs," there is a root link between black religion and blues singing.

The link was apparent in the work of Thomas A. Dorsey, who began by accompanying Bessie Smith and Ma Rainey and went on to tour with gospel singer Sallie Martin and the great Mahalia Jackson. Dorsey became the central figure of the Golden Age of Gospel (1945–1960), not only as the co-organizer with Sallie Martin of the annual Gospel Singers Convention but as the writer of "Precious Lord," "Peace in the Valley" and other eloquent gospel songs. "Precious Lord" has been translated into thirty-two languages, and both Elvis

Presley and Red Foley sold a million records each of "Peace in the Valley."

"I'm not ashamed of my blues," Dorsey told Tony Heilbut. "It's all the same talent. A beat is a beat whatever it is." And Heilbut adds: "In the mid-50s, rhythm-and-blues groups began using simple, funky melodies swiped from Dorsey tunes."

The interweaving of gospel and blues comes through when we find that Dorsey developed his gospel song, "I Surely Know There's Been a Change in Me," from the jazz tune "There'll Be Some Changes Made," and later Ben E. King, working with Leiber and Stoller, transformed Dr. C. H. Tindley's sacred song "Stand By Me" into the secular song that was a pop hit in '61.

Big Bill Broonzy was a bluesman one week and a preacher the next, until his father, angered by the mixing of the sacred and the profane, compelled him to stop straddling the fence; then Big Bill chose the blues. Little Richard went through a temporary change of "spirit," registering in a school to become a preacher; his conversion eventually stuck. Likewise, Little Junior Parker at one moment promised God to quit the blues in eight years—"because He made it possible for other people to dig me"—but apparently forgot his resolve to "devote myself to His service."

On the other hand, Arnold Dwight Moore, born in Topeka, Kansas, in 1913 and raised in Memphis, began as Gatemouth Moore and today is Bishop Moore, Pastor of Wesley Chapel Community Church in Chicago. He has himself told of how he acquired his colorful name: "One night during a performance at the 81 Theatre in Atlanta, I was singing 'Star Dust' and while I was doing my song, a drunk woman staggered up to the stage and said, 'Ah, sing it to you Gatemouth, S.O.B.' The drummer fell off his seat, the rest of the band quit playing and the theater went into an uproar. And there I stood in front of a frenzied audience, a new personality named Gatemouth Moore."

And so he remained for more than a dozen years. His later conversion was as spontaneous as his acquisition of his stage name. Performing the blues at the Club De Lisa in Chicago one evening in the 1940s, he suddenly interpolated the gospel hymn "Shine on Me," announced his retirement from the entertainment scene, and walked off the stand. (He has recapitulated the conversion scene in a recent BluesWay album, *After Twenty-One Years*.) Serving an apprenticeship with Rev. Clarence Cobb, he was ordained at the First Church of the Deliverance in Chicago in 1948.

His acquisition of a pastorate was as dramatic as the other major changes in his career. While working as a religious dee jay on Station WBEE, he conducted a service at Wesley Chapel Church on an invitation by Bishop J. W. Stevenson. Some time afterwards, the Bishop dropped dead while conducting a service. The church elders immediately called on Rev. Moore to become officiating pastor, a post he still held in 1974.

•

While the blues was an emotional music, invested with a sense of dedication almost spiritual in character, its outlook was existential. The singing styles, particularly of the rural bluesmen, tended to be cool; they narrated and they were resigned. After they migrated from the rural South, contact with big city mores and modes added hope, polish, sophistication, and "hokum," producing what we have come to know as urban blues.

But it was gospel music that brought an excited vitality into R & B that sharply distinguished it from pop, also from jazz, which became intellectual, cool, and concert-oriented after World War II. The war itself played a significant role, unleashing strong religious feelings even as it provoked uninhibited living.

To those who view R & B simply as a matter of screamers and shouters, there's Dinah Washington. Her unique style was a blend of gospel and blues, but not of gospel as frenzy, exuberance, exhibitionism. Dinah brought intensity, *inner* intensity to R & B.

groove 6   LEON RENÉ

Leon and Otis René of New Orleans, mavericks in the recording business, were enterprising and aggressive at a time when the business was in the grip of a small group of majors who guarded the process of record making as if it were an Oriental mystery.

Otis died in the late '60s; Leon still lives in the West Los Angeles area in a well-appointed home surrounded by spreading carob trees and a well-manicured lawn. He carries his seventy-plus years well and is still active in the music publishing business.

On the upper floor of his home is a spacious office, approached through his private bedroom. The mahogany walls, plush rug, and acoustic-tile ceiling make an excellent setting for a kidney-shaped desk inlaid with leather, and a gilt-trimmed Mason & Hamlin grand piano.

The office is removed from the other rooms so that René can work late without disturbing his wife, Irma.

Above a flagstone fireplace hang a few of his hit songs, mounted on black cork: "Rockin' Robin," "When the Swallows Come Back to Capistrano," "When It's Sleepytime Down South," "I Lost My Sugar in Salt Lake City," and others.

" 'When It's Sleepytime Down South' goes way back to 1931. Otis and I wrote it for a Hollywood stage play titled *Under a Virginia Moon.* Clarence Muse [co-writer] had a small part. The author of the play— the daughter of movie-actor George Fawcett—rejected the song, but it became a standard.

"When Louis Armstrong was playing the Cotton Club in LA, we invited him to a Creole gumbo dinner, Louis's favorite dish. He brought Les Hite, who led the Cotton Club band, and Lionel Hampton, to my parents' home in Pasadena. During the dinner Louis asked Mama, an expert gumbo cook, for a second helping. As she was serving him, he suddenly let out one of those scat riffs, like 'Bop-Bip-Ti-Doo-Dat.' Believe me, it shocked everybody. It was the first time we heard a 'mouth riff.' Mama almost dropped the gumbo in his lap. You see, the radio was on, and Guy Lombardo's band was playing a number. Satchmo couldn't resist filling a spot the band left open. We all flipped when he said, 'Excuse me, Mrs. René, that cat left that break open and I had to make it.' This was the beginning of scat singing. After dinner, we played 'Sleepytime' for him and he promised to record it on Victor Records, which he did. It became a great standard—and his theme song for the rest of his life."

Pointing to the title page of "When the Swallows Come Back to Capistrano," Leon showed me a seven-inch record in a four-colored sleeve depicting the swallows returning to the Old Mission at San Juan Capistrano. As he was putting the record on his player, he handed me a slip of paper; it was an order from the mission for 200 copies. "They sell it down there in the souvenir shop all year round to tourists," he said, and proceeded to describe the song's origin.

"On the morning of March 19, 1939, I was waiting for my breakfast when I heard the radio announcer tell about the swallows, which were, according to legend, expected to return to the mission that morning. Mrs. René was late in serving my breakfast. I had just recovered from a long stay in a TB sanitarium and, on doctor's orders, slept in the garage, converted into a small studio, away from the rest of the family. The waiting made me impatient, and I said to Irma, 'Maybe by the time the swallows come back to Capistrano, I'll get my breakfast.'

"After I said it, I thought, 'Hey! That's a great title for a song,' and took off for the studio. I composed the opening strain in a matter of minutes and rushed back in the house to play it for Irma. When it was completed, I got a friend, Celle Burke, a very fine singer who fronted his own band, to record it. Then I submitted it to Witmark & Son, a NYC music publisher, who accepted it and sent an advance royalty check of $500.00. On the same day I received the check, Irma confessed that it was last day of her Novena to Our Sorrowful Mother. She had been praying for my health and the success of 'When the Swallows Come Back to Capistrano.'

"Many artists recorded it. But The Ink Spots produced the disk that sent the ballad to the top of the 'Lucky Strike Hit Parade' in 1940. I received the ASCAP Award that year for the Outstanding Song of the Year—and 'Swallows' went on to sell over three million records. It's still selling.

"Not often does a writer get a break to be the flip side of a smash hit, but I did with a song titled 'Boogie Woogie Santa Claus.' You've probably never heard of it, but it just happened to be coupled with one of the biggest records of all time. It was released by Mercury around Christmas time of 1950 or '51. Mercury was set to go with 'Boogie Woogie Santa Claus' and ignored the flip side, written and introduced years before by Redd Stewart and Pee Wee King, who had had records also by The Short Brothers (Decca) and Erskine Hawkins (Coral). Neither these records nor their live performances did very much for the song. But when Patti Page recorded it, she had one of the greatest records of her career. I refer, of course, to 'Tennessee Waltz.' This was the song on which 'Boogie Woogie Santa Claus' got a free ride—and what a ride! After Christmas, Mercury recoupled the record, but by then I had earned more royalties [for 'Santa Claus'] than the writers of 'Tennessee Waltz' because I was not only the writer of the words and music, but also the publisher.

•

"Otis and I got into the record business because we found it difficult to get the big record companies to record our material. When the depression came, the majors cut off most of their Negro talent. You just couldn't sell a colored artist to any of the majors—and Decca had all it could handle, although we cut a few sides with Cleo Brown, like 'When,' a mild success.

"I was actually the first to put Nat Cole on wax. It happened when his trio played on Eighth Street at the 331 Club. Nat also worked The Swanee Inn as intermission pianist. Oscar Moore [guitar] and Wesley Prince [bass] began jamming with him and started the trio. They tried New York in the early forties and played Fifty-second Street at Kelly's Stable, but they came back to Los Angeles where they got a much better reception, especially at the 331 Club.

"Jack Gutshall, a jukebox operator, asked me to A & R his new label called Amour Records. He needed new R & B artists for his jukeboxes, so I started scouting for new talent. I recorded Nat at the old Melrose Studio (used by Decca). In those days they were still cutting masters on wax cylinders (unused masters were scrapped and used again). When the session was completed, I played the masters for Jack: 'Black Spider,' 'River Street Marie,' 'I Like To Riff,' and 'Sunny Side of the Street.' He liked the 'hot' numbers, but turned down 'Sweet Lorraine,' which became one of Nat's biggest hits. These were the first sides that Nat 'King' Cole ever recorded. After making these sides, Nat went to Decca, where he recorded 'Slow Down.'

"By this time I had started my own label, Exclusive Records, and signed Joe Liggins & His Honeydrippers and Johnny Moore's Three Blazers. They became top R & B artists in the 1940's.

"In 1944 my brother Otis recorded Nat Cole on a tune he wrote, titled 'I'm Lost,' on his own Excelsior label. Johnny Otis, Jimmy Rushing (using the Basie band as background), and 'Big' Jay McNeely were some of his artists. 'Harlem Nocturne' was one of Johnny Otis's big standards. The following year Capitol signed Nat, and that was the beginning of a great singing career. Until then he was mostly a jazz pianist and lead singer in his trio. Jazz lost a tremendous talent, but he became a 'giant' in popular music.

"One day Glenn Wallichs, who owned Music City, one of the largest music stores in Hollywood, asked me, 'Where do you get your records pressed?' He was thinking then about starting a record company. He was aware of our progress with R & B records and wanted to know how we got started. I told him the key was to get Al Jarvis to play his records on the air. (I had an in with Jarvis because Johnny Mercer and I wrote his theme song, 'Your Make-Believe Ballroom,' for his 'Make-Believe Ballroom' radio show. I recorded his theme with a twenty-piece band, arranged by one of Glenn Miller's arrangers, and featuring The Modernaires with Jo Stafford. Billy May and Buddy

Cole also were on the session.) We told Wallichs how tough it was to get pressings and suggested he build or buy a plant. That's what he did when he founded Capitol Records. He was president for many years.

"Exclusive Records soon became the nation's number one independent R & B record company. Our first session included two smash hits: 'The Honeydripper' and 'I've Got a Right to Cry,' both written and recorded by Joe Liggins, who also backed Herb Jeffries on the same session on 'I Left a Good Deal in Mobile.' When I played the dubs for Jack Gutshall (our distributor), Jack picked 'The Honeydripper' as the hit of the session. Before long 'The Honeydripper' put Exclusive Records solidly in the recording business.

"Jarvis wouldn't play Joe Liggins' record on the 'Make-Believe Ballroom' because it was R & B. He played mostly pop artists, but we knew we had a smash. One day the owner of a restaurant called and demanded that Gutshall take 'The Honeydripper' out of his jukebox. It seemed that the waitresses were reacting too strongly to the infectious beat and were hopping all over the place as the record was played over and over.

"We had great difficulty getting pressings because Allied Records was the only independent pressing plant in Los Angeles, and each customer was limited to only 200 records a week. They had a good thing going, as the only independent pressing company on the West Coast. Nobody was allowed to enter the plant, because they did not want anyone to know the secret of pressing records; the majors were the same.

"Otis and I broke through that wall of secrecy by contacting Jimmy Beard, who worked in the maintenance department of Allied. Jimmy offered to build us a record press for a thousand dollars. We formed a partnership with Gutshall, and hired Jimmy to work at night and weekends to complete the first press for RGR pressing plant.

"The press needed stock, so we went hunting all over town for discarded records, at stores that had old disks that they wanted to get rid of. We paid them one cent each. In those days there were few R & B record stores. R & B records were sold in furniture stores, drug stores, makeshift store fronts, shoe-shine stands—anywhere—to meet the demand for R & B records.

"As sales increased, so did the demand for old records. We went to two cents per record until the supply was exhausted. All the old records were brought to our one-press plant in Culver City where we reheated them on a steam table. The centers were cut out and the stock rolled into a ball and put into the press where the finished record was completed. Since we used old records of different colors, the finished record looked like a rainbow, but it didn't matter if you had a hit like 'The Honeydripper' or 'I'm Lost.' Before long several backyard plants sprung up and we had to furnish them with old records to use for stock. Allied fired Jim Beard when they found out that he was setting up presses for us.

"Because of the demand for 'The Honeydripper' in the midwest, Pullman porters would take records to Chicago from Los Angeles and bootleg them at ten dollars a disk. In Chicago, Harry Rife had a record shop on the South Side next door to the Regal Theatre, and R & B fans would line up for blocks to purchase 'The Honeydripper' by Joe Liggins and 'I'm Lost' by Nat 'King' Cole. Exclusive Records and Excelsior Records had now established a foothold as pioneers in the independent record business.

"The great demand for R & B artists grew, and soon Aladdin got started; then the Biharis launched Modern Records. Before long the majors began worrying about the independent labels. They tried to compete with us, but it was too late—we had a head start and the format for making R & B records. We built our own rolling mills and matrix plants to strengthen our position. We also established an Independent Record Manufacturers Association. I was elected president and Jack Gutshall vice president. It worried the majors for a short while, but our higher retail price and the lack of unity among the independent record labels soon defeated us.

"Victor was selling pop and R & B records for seventy-five cents (our price was a dollar-five). To compete with Victor I set up my own distributing company in New York and Los Angeles, and shipped directly to the distributor. All orders were shipped on a sight-draft bill of lading through the Bank of America, who backed me to the amount of $500,000. Seventy-five percent of each order was credited to my account upon shipment and the remaining 25 percent paid when picked up by the distributor.

"We subleased masters to other companies in England, Europe, and South America. In the '60s, The Beatles, Rolling Stones, Dave Clark Five, etc., learned from our records and imitated them. (The Dave Clark Five recorded Bobby Day's 'Over and Over' and it became the number one best-selling record in America in 1965.)

"When Little Richard went abroad, he was idolized by The Beatles and all the groups. They knew his records better than our kids here, except the black kids who admired him as they do James Brown today.

"Well, after a time, the majors decided, 'If you can't lick 'em, join 'em.' So Columbia and Victor Records finally opened the doors of their pressing plants to all independent record manufacturers. That never would have happened if we hadn't broken through their veil of secrecy.

"We had things going our way until Victor introduced the seven-inch vinyl, 45 rpm record, which revolutionized the record business and made the breakable ten-inch 78 rpm record obsolete overnight. It helped all the record companies because shipping the heavy ten-inch records by air was too costly. Competition with the majors, however, forced the independent labels to use the seven-inch 45 rpm records, and they had to reduce the price of R & B records from a dollar-five to seventy-five cents, retail. This forced many independent labels out of business.

"My two publishing firms, Leon René Publications and Recordo Music Publishers, by this time had built up an extensive catalogue of standards. (My son Rafael "Googie" René is professional manager today.)

"Rock 'n' roll forced us to become inactive for a while. But in 1957 I came back with Class Records and started with an instrumental ('Wham Bam') written and recorded by my son Googie René. I first offered it to several record companies, but they all turned it down, so I decided to put it out on Class Records. In those days R & B disk jockeys still had a free hand in choosing their material; that was before Top 40 listings took over. We were able to get the help of a number of platter spinners like Hunter Hancock, Lonnie Johnson, and Huggy Boy to break a record in Los Angeles. Our distributors worked with disk jockeys in their territories, the same as we did, to break a record nationally.

"Then along came a very talented young man named Robert Byrd. Googie discovered him, and we recorded him on Class Records under the name of Bobby Day. His first hit was the original version of his own composition, 'Little Bitty Pretty One,' published by Recordo.

"Before Bobby came to us he had a group called The Satellites, who made some records for John Dolphin. John owned a record store on Vernon near Central Avenue. 'Little Bitty Pretty One' was on the flip side of my song, 'When the Swallows Come Back to Capistrano,' which we thought was the hit side. But before long the disk jockeys turned it over and 'Little Bitty Pretty One' broke through.

"No sooner was Bobby's disk on the market when Thurston Harris covered us on Aladdin Records. When I say *covered*, I mean copied—note for note. Dick Clark went on the Harris record, and we were in trouble. I wanted Bobby to go on the road and get into theaters like the Apollo and the Regal. But he was making a hundred dollars a week and refused to quit his job. Bobby Day's record was on the *Billboard* and *Cash Box* charts six weeks before the Thurston Harris record was released; but when Dick Clark aired the Harris record on his network show, we were dead. Aladdin sold 700,000 of Thurston Harris and we sold about 180,000 of Bobby Day. But if you say 'Little Bitty Pretty One,' Bobby Day's record on Class was by far the best.

"When I asked Bobby to write another song to follow 'Little Bitty Pretty One,' he came up with 'Over and Over,' which I coupled with 'Rockin' Robin.'

"Here's another story. A mockingbird kept waking my wife every morning, and she asked me to chase him away so that she could get some sleep. I told her I couldn't unless I threw a rock at him. (Imagine the writer of 'When the Swallows Come Back to Capistrano' getting caught throwing rocks at a bird.) But the next night the bird flew into a tree outside my window and woke me up, and about two A.M. every morning thereafter. He was making so many riffs that I called him a rockin' mockin' bird. I finally changed it to 'Rockin' Robin' when I wrote a cute little song about him. I thought so little of the song that I decided not to put my name on it; instead, I gave it to my wife, Irma, and she put my mother-in-law's name down as the writer— Jimme Thomas.

"And, would you believe it? 'Rockin' Robin' has received two BMI Awards—1958 and 1973—and been awarded a plaque by *16* and *Spec Magazine* as the hit song of 1972. 'Rockin' Robin' is a two-time number one best-seller in *Billboard* and *Cash Box,* and one of the biggest songs in our catalogue. When Bobby Day's record came out on Class Records in 1958 backed with 'Over and Over' (a two-sided hit), Thurston Harris covered 'Over and Over.' But he just couldn't duplicate 'Rockin' Robin,' so his record flopped.

"We had a sensational arrangement on Bobby Day's great vocal of 'Rockin' Robin,' but fourteen years later, in January 1972, it became a number one hit all over again with Michael Jackson of The Jackson Five. Motown had a giant billboard sign on Sunset Strip, here in LA, advertising the album *Got to Be There.* It was the 'Rockin' Robin' single that the kids went for. Over fifty recordings have been made of the song, and there is no doubt that it will go down in musical history as one of the all-time great standards.

"K-Tel released the Bobby Day version of 'Rockin' Robin' in a gigantic mail-order package titled *25 Rock Revival Greats.* After that,

Columbia, Roulette, and other record companies began reviving and repackaging songs of the fifties. I believe that 'Rockin' Robin' really started the revival."

groove 7   **JOHNNY OTIS**

Johnny Otis, the Californian who made hit records with Little Esther back in the early '50s, who started Etta James and discovered the Midnighters and Little Willie John, who produced records with Johnny Ace and Big Mama Thornton, and who wrote many R & B hits ("Every Beat of My Heart," "Willie and the Hand Jive," etc.), was talking about his early days in Berkeley. As a teen-ager, he became the drummer in Count Otis Matthews' West Oakland House Rockers. Matthews was a young, fiery, barrelhouse boogie woogie pianist who had come to Berkeley with the mid-30s migration of Mississippi blacks.

"Mixed group?" I asked Otis.

"No," he said quickly. "The House Rockers were all black."

I sat there studying Otis' face. There was nothing about his features or the pallor of his skin to suggest that he was black. I was nonplussed, as I had been from the moment he opened the door of his house in the black district of Gardena, an LA suburb.

He had been so intimately involved for so many years with R & B as a performer, songwriter, talent scout, disk jockey, and record producer that I had expected to be greeted by a black man. Though I could not see too much of his face under a large, black Stetson hat, big black shades, black beard and moustache, he looked white and sounded white. But his wife of thirty years is black, his son Shuggie is black, his grandchildren are black and all the musicians rehearsing in a studio in back of his house were black. More significantly, his use of pronouns, *we* and *they*, left no doubt about his identification: *they* were white and *we* were black.

I could not bring myself to ask a direct question. The enigma was not resolved until he handed me a copy of his book *Listen to the Lambs*, published after the Watts riots of 1965. "My friend, Johnny Otis," black musician Preston Love wrote in a preface, "is genetically white, but in all other respects completely black. His life has been that of a black man joined with other black men to combat the outside —the hostile and unjust white establishment."

Johnny Otis is the son of Alexander and Irene Veliotes, Greek immigrants. His surname Otis is a variant of the last two syllables of Veliotes. Born in Vallejo, California, in 1921, he was raised in Berkeley, where his parents moved a year after his sister Dorothy was born. They lived above his father's grocery store in an integrated neighborhood that early became a black ghetto.

"I did not become black," he writes in his book, "because I was attracted to Negro music. My attitude was formed long before I moved into the music field. Nor did I become a member of the Negro community because I married a Negro girl. I became what I am because as a child, I reacted to the way of life, the special vitality, the atmosphere of the black community." And he adds emphatically: "I cannot think of myself as white.

.

"My first musical experience was with Count Matthews, who did not play like Count Basie. He was a delta bluesman and he played a down-home boogie-blues piano. With Matthews, we played weekend gigs, frequently at the black gym in West Oakland where the guy would pay us off with a jug of wine. The West Oakland Rockers, as we called ourselves, were a rhythm-and-blues band, a boogie combo, and we played house rent parties, too. Head arrangements, of course, which we worked out after listening to Matthews play and sing old blues he brought from Mississippi.

"You know that 'Willie and the Hand Jive' thing I did some time in '58? Well, before that was 'Bo Diddley.' And before 'Bo Diddley' was 'Hambone.' And before 'Hambone,' Count Matthews used to tell me— in the thirties—to play: 'Shave and a Haircut—six bits.' He'd ask me to beat it on the tom-tom. And he had a couple of coffee cans that he'd fill with sand or pebbles. He'd call a chick from the audience to shake the can—shick-shick-shick-shick—and I'd play that 'Shave and a Haircut' rhythm.

"He'd sing, 'Mama bought a chicken,/ Thought it was a duck,/ Stick 'em on a table. . . .' He had a thousand verses. That was always the big number of the evening. And it was the same beat that later 'Hambone' used, and 'Bo Diddley' and 'Hand Jive' and 'Hey, Little Girl.'

"Unfortunately, Count Matthews was never recorded. He should've been. He was a meaningful bluesman. After that, I went through some territory bands. I was the drummer with George Morrison in Denver, Lloyd Hunter in Omaha, and then I came here to LA, with Harlan

Leonard & the Kansas City Rockets. We were the house band at the Club Alabam. Then I was with Bardu Ali's great band at the Lincoln Theatre. Finally, I got my own band, a big band.

"And I got lucky on the first record we cut. Most of the little record companies of the forties were owned by whites. But the René brothers of LA were the exception. Leon René is still active. But I worked with Otis, who died a while back. This was my first session as a bandleader—and I came to the date with three numbers. I thought that union regulations provided for three sides and four hours. But it was four sides in three hours. With twenty minutes remaining, I dug into the book and came up with 'Harlem Nocturne.' That was my first big hit—on Excelsior in 1945. And we went sailing across the country with The Ink Spots and Louis Jordan.

•

"I had a really big band," Otis said, pointing to a faded photograph on his office wall. "You can see—seven brass, five reeds, four rhythm and the Trenier Twins. And sometimes, we also had a female vocalist." Johnny's was the only white face among the eighteen.

His office is in the back of his house, a dozen feet away and several feet above it. To reach it, you have to walk across two heavy wooden planks, stretched over a semicircular pond he constructed at his wife's urging. Fed by a four-foot waterfall he made of rocks and concrete, it is stocked with Japanese rainbow-colored carp. Large lava rocks, gathered on the Mojave desert, serve as a border. The office itself, narrow, cluttered and cold, is under the recording studio Johnny built with the help of his sons-in-law, who are building contractors. Vents left for heat and air-conditioning were then still unconnected. Johnny wore his black Stetson all through our conversation and kept closing the lapels of a well-worn mackinaw jacket around his throat.

•

"Around '47, jobs became extremely scarce for big bands. Just before I returned home to LA, I remember meeting Billy Eckstine during a date in Washington, DC. Standing on a street corner near the Howard Theatre, we bemoaned the fact that we were both 'too late' with big bands. He was having trouble keeping his together, as I was too. And I recall his saying, 'I'm going to disband and go out as a single,' which he did, not long after. It was a happy move, and he soon became the first black singing idol after Nat Cole.

"When I got back to LA, there were no jobs and I had to give up the big band. When I put together a new group, I was still thinking of brass section, reed section. So I used two saxes, trumpet and trombone, and piano/bass/drums/guitar. This became like the standard rhythm-and-blues ensemble. Musically, I went back to my days with Count Matthews. Watching the records that were making it—like my friends T-Bone Walker, Roy Milton, Joe Liggins & the Honeydrippers, Charles Brown with Johnny Moore's Blazers—we began to develop something within something. It was a hybrid form that began to emerge. It surely wasn't big band; it wasn't swing; it wasn't country blues. It was what was to become known as rhythm and blues, a hybrid form that became an art form in itself. It was the foundation of rock 'n' roll.

"In 1948 we opened the Barrel House on One hundred-sixth Street and Wilmington, right across from the Watts Towers. I thought they were ornamental oil wells until I took a close look at them one day. You know they were built by an Italian immigrant who spent years constructing them of scrap metal, small objects, inlaid pieces of glass, and whatnot. The old man died just before the Watts riots, and never saw his work recognized as a state monument. He was a recluse. I tried to talk with him since I do a little art work myself, carve wood and paint. But he just kept to himself."

On Otis' spinet stood two African figures he had carved. And in the living room of his house—through which we had passed—an unfinished painting of a bull fight rested on an easel. In a dining alcove hung a painting of his wife, done some years ago. He had caught the fire in her large, dark eyes, which still gave off sparks when we met.

"Bardu Ali was my partner in the Barrel House. His real name was Bhadru Muhhamid Ali. I played in his band when I first came to LA. He was like a father to me and still is. We wanted to do something that hadn't been done: give the people a pure blues environment. Not that there weren't blues clubs in Chicago, but they weren't R & B clubs—bands with horns and comedy, a certain kind of Skillet & Leroy comedy on stage. We had cartoons all over the walls and sawdust on the floor and barrels for tables. It was a fantastic success.

"I was in it during '48 and '49. I left in '50, and Bardu finally closed the Barrel House in '52 or '53. I left when I got lucky on wax. You know, that string of hits I had with Little Esther and Mel Walker. When I got back to LA several years later and became a disk jockey and got the TV show, Bardu became my manager. We just didn't have time for a club.

"Before I had those hits with Savoy, I did some sides for Modern.

It was in '49. I worked with all three of the Biharis—Saul, Jules and Joe. But we still do things together. In '68 I did an album called *Cold Shot* that got me started all over again. My son Shuggie, really John Otis, Jr., who was then thirteen, made his debut on it. The single, 'Country Girl,' from the album made R & B charts.

"I found Little Esther at a talent show at the Largo Theatre in Watts. First I took her to RCA. And the guy told me, 'She sounds like Dinah Washington, and if we want Dinah Washington, we can get her.' It hurt my feelings and Little Esther's, too. I packed my brief-case and we went back to Watts. That was '49, and we then did at least one session for Modern. And I don't know what's happened to those sides.

"The Barrel House was swinging in those days. One night, Ralph Bass, who was a friend, became so excited over what he heard that he got on the long-distance phone and called Herman Lubinsky, the owner of Savoy. Lubinsky was here a night or two later. During inter-mission, we went across the street and he leaned up against a wall and said, 'You sign this contract and if you give me one hit, I'll triple it.' It was for a one-percent royalty. What did I know in those days.

"Well, I gave him eight hits and he never tripled anything. He and Syd Nathan are probably the world's champions at you-know-what. You look at the R & B charts for 1950, and you'll find 'Double Crossin' Blues' [No. 1], 'Mistrustin' Blues' [No. 1], 'Deceivin' Blues'— all of these were with Little Esther, Mel Walker, and my group. Still in '50, Mel Walker and I had 'Dreamin' Blues.' Then came 'Wedding Boogie'—Little Esther and Mel and me. And before the year was over, Mel and I had 'Rockin' Blues,' which went to number two. In '51, I had 'Mambo Boogie' and 'All Nite Long,' and Mel and I had 'Gee Baby,' which went to number two.

"I don't think that I ever got five thousand dollars all told for all of those records and all that action. I'm not the only one, you know. A lot of us suffered that fate at the hands of those who had us in a helpless position. We just didn't know what the sales were or how to find out.

"When we first recorded 'Double Crossin' Blues' and it began to move, the Robins, who hummed behind Little Esther, got an attorney who summoned me and told me that they were the stars of the record and not Little Esther. On the strength of the record, they were going on tour, and if I wanted to go along as musical director, they'd pay me twenty dollars a night. I had found the Robins through the talent show at the Barrel House. Bobby Nunn, who worked around the club and was one of the Robins, sang the bass voice behind Little Esther. But it was obvious that I couldn't use the Robins any longer. My musicians could do the humming.

"But I did need someone to sing the low Ricky-of-the-Ravens kind of things with Little Esther. And one day, a young man showed up at a rehearsal at my house—that was when I had the chicken farm— and I liked the way he sounded. It was Mel Walker, and from then on he was Little Esther's partner and got some hits on his own. After he began working with us, I discovered that he had been a minor football star around LA in high school, Jefferson High. He was pretty young when he died.

"The chicken farm? I had it right in Watts. Just a few coops so that we would have some fresh eggs. I'd butcher a bird on occasion and give a hen to a member of the band. Then one day, we got to talking about my chickens on the radio show. Well, the next I knew, everybody in Watts came to my house, wanting to buy a chicken. So we started selling them, and I started building additional coops to house them. I used a power saw, and that's how I got these. . . ." [Otis held up his right hand. The two middle fingers were shorter and permanently bent at the knuckles.]

"I'm responsible for what's missing [Chuckling], but a negligent physician is responsible for the paralysis. Friends wanted me to sue him. But what the hell. The money isn't going to restore movement. And I learned to play piano with the three remaining fingers. I picked up the piano after the accident and I do my bit on 'Willie and the Hand Jive' without any trouble, despite those two dead fingers. Hey, let me show you my present chicken colony. It's nothing like the farm we had in the days of the Barrel House."

•

We left Otis' office, crossing the double planks over the pond, trudged up an eight-foot incline and skirted the recording studio. Behind it were two good-sized coops. The one we entered contained a batch of small Cochins, some white and some a veneer black, with fan tails and feathered feet. The locked coop beyond housed thirty or forty chickens, a few strutting roosters, and the rest, russet-colored Rhode Island hens. The Cochins were for show and the Rhode Islands, for eating.

•

"Little Esther had a strut to her voice even when she was just a kid. She made it when she was quite young. A lot of money all of a sudden, you know. She was kinda wild, bent on having a lot of fun.

But she was always a very bright person. Good, sharp intellect and very talented. She's proved it over and over through the years. Dinah Washington was her idol as a young kid. I hear a bit of Dinah's flavor in her. She had a lot of caustic bite, but she was endowed in her own right. I think that Nancy Wilson sounds more like Dinah, certainly in her phrasing.

"Etta James was another great singer I found. It was later, around '55. We were up in San Francisco for a date at the Fillmore. That was when it was black, before Bill Graham took it over and made it a palace of rock 'n' roll. I was asleep in my hotel room when Bardu Ali, my manager, phoned. He was in a restaurant and a little girl was bugging him: she wanted to sing for me. I told him to have her come around to the Fillmore that night. But she grabbed the phone from him and shouted that she wanted to sing for me *now*. I told her that I was in bed—and she said she was coming over anyway. Well, she showed up with two other little girls. And when I heard her, I jumped out of bed and began getting dressed. We went looking for her mother since she was a minor. I brought her to LA, where she lived in my home like my daughter.

"After a while, I wrote a song based on Hank Ballard's 'Work with Me, Annie,' a big R & B number. I called it, 'Roll with Me, Henry.' Took it to Modern and recorded Etta James. That was her name and that's how she started. When Georgia Gibbs covered her, she called it 'Dance with Me, Henry,' and made a big pop hit for us—and Etta, I, and Hank Ballard split the royalties three ways. That's one time when we were not unhappy with a white cover.

"As for me, I went from Savoy Records to Mercury. That was around 1953. Bobby Shad and I got Ben Webster and his tenor sax out of Kansas City. We did some things with an R & B background, which he really loved. He had never worked with a twanging blues guitar before. We did four instrumentals, jazz, and boogies. I played vibes on 'Star Dust'.

"In 1954 I began recording for Peacock Records of Houston, Texas. It was recently sold to ABC Paramount by Don Robey, who was our promoter when we went through the South in the fifties. I never played his club, the Golden Peacock, because we stuck to the big auditoriums. I served as a talent scout for him and a record producer. That was when I cut Johnny Ace, the kid who killed himself playing Russian roulette. I also served as producer for Big Mama Thornton, who made the original recording of 'Hound Dog,' later a smash for Presley. 'Hound Dog' was written by Leiber and Stoller, who brought it to me. I helped rewrite it. We worked together on many songs and artists in those days. The Peacock label lists all three of us as authors. We were co-writers, and there was no problem so long as we were producing R & B artists. But when the Presley record hit with a sale of 6 or 7 million, they disaffirmed the contract as minors and cut me out.

"When rock 'n' roll came flooding in with Presley, the little labels as well as the big began running after young, teen-age kids. I formed Dig, my own label, in '56. Put out many sides, but we couldn't make it. We had a number of local hits, but no national sellers. And in '57 I connected with Capitol where 'Willie and the Hand Jive' caught the following year.

"Rock 'n' roll was a direct outgrowth of R & B. It took over all the things that made R & B different from big band swing: the after-beat on a steady four; the influence of boogie; the triplets on piano; eight-to-the-bar on the top-hat cymbal; and the shuffle pattern of dotted eighth and sixteenth notes. They heard it in Lloyd Glenn's records on Swing Time, 'Old Time Shuffle Blues' and 'Chica Boo.' He used an almost Afro-Cuban thing, like the conga, working against boogie."

•

Otis was illustrating the beat with his hands and nonsense syllables when the phone rang and I heard him tell somebody, "Come on over at three. We're having a pigeon raising class." When I asked about it, he led me out of the office again. We went up the barnyard incline to a wide, tin-roofed structure adjoining the chicken coops and set directly on a hill behind his house. Inside, there were nine coops constructed around a rectangle open to the sky. Different types of birds were in the cages.

"Pigeons are a great study for genetics. They have clutches of babies every thirty days, so it's easy to breed them for different colors, different body formations, and to control the results. I hold this class for the neighborhood kids every Saturday afternoon. I always remember what pleasure I got as a kid out of keeping birds. And I arrange for the poorer kids to have their own birds and teach them how to take care of them. When I get very busy with my music, I can't keep that weekly schedule. But the class seems to mean so much to the kids that I keep it going, no matter how little time I have. They'll be pretty unhappy this summer when we go on our annual tour."

•

Back in his office, I asked Johnny about soul music. He is a rapid well-structured talker, but I was unprepared for the flow of words.

"Soul is a direct outgrowth of R & B. It involves sociology and the unique character of American life, also the normal search of young people of successive generations for their own language. Traditional or folk music, by which I mean music that grows out of the people and the community, is very conservative. Growing out of a way of life, it's slow to change. In C & W you can listen over the past twenty years and find that while it has changed slightly, it still has a recognizable identity. Perhaps, it's moving a little closer to pop, but Buck Owens isn't very much different from Hank Williams.

"But when it comes to black music, there's a radical change from R & B to soul. That's because there are forces at work from without, bringing pressure to bear on the black community. From the turn of the century to now, American pop has become increasingly black. Black men and women have been the innovators, breathing life into new forms. Black artists have always drawn the road maps; white artists have picked up on the music, dug it, copied it, interpreted it, become the kings, and reaped enormous financial benefit. Very often, they have accepted the proffered crowns. Paul Whiteman, 'The King of Jazz'—surely not the king; Benny Goodman, 'The King of Swing'— a fine musician, but surely not the king. Count Basie, Duke Ellington, Jimme Lunceford wore the crowns whether they were invested formally or not. Elvis Presley, 'The King of R 'n' R'—a fine creative artist and a revolutionary figure in American music, but the kings of rock 'n' roll were Fats Domino, Little Richard, Chuck Berry, B. B. King.

"Now, with that pattern in operation, the black artist has to be gun-shy. 'We're gonna come up with something,' he figures, 'that whitey can't rip off.' So soul music became so black and so gospel-tinged that it can't easily be copied. I'm not saying that there's a meeting of black people to decide this any more than there's a gathering of whites to plan rip-offs. It just happens. It's somehow woven into the fabric of our nation.

"Many of our colloquial expressions come from black musicians. Much of our wit and humor comes from black comics and the Jewish way of life, eventually finding their way into the mainstream. But where music is concerned, money is involved and the whites have gotten it. It's a racist situation. It's not a cultural exchange; it's long-distance theft. That's one reason why the music has changed in character at an accelerated pace—a much more rapid pace than folk music would normally change.

"Then there's this other factor that's operative in all societies. Young people want a voice of their own, clothes of their own, and a language of their own. With all the talk of 'Black is beautiful' and 'Let's go back to our roots,' there is still very little homage paid to the black artists of yesteryear by young black people. They've forgotten Big Joe Turner. They've forgotten Louis Jordan, Pee Wee Crayton, Charles Brown, and others. Suddenly, they've remembered B. B. King. But that's because white people began buying his records and he had a big pop hit. He developed status.

"So soul music has gone from the Atlantic-Stax sound of the sixties to something else. It's become more stylized and not as black as it was. A lot of violins and French horns and European influences— pseudodramatic, soprano-voiced males; a lot of primping; affected dance steps and programmed choreography. That's the present-day thing, of course, and to me, all of this tends to dilute the strong, honest black character of American black music.

"At this juncture, I don't see any great Ray Charles or Otis Redding or Nat Cole appearing. I hear an awful lot of stylized jive. Aretha, Stevie Wonder, Marvin Gaye, and Gladys Knight are some of the more recent artists that have been, in my opinion, black and beautiful, to use an overworked phrase. But they are the rare exception rather than the rule. Incidentally, what I've been saying about stylized soul does not apply to the Memphis thing of the sixties—that was great!— the Otis Redding, Sam & Dave era. It had black integrity. I think that black music has to go back—black artists have to go back and try to recapture the pure and honest emotionalism of the past.

"I've just embarked on a project to promote this return to roots. I've established a record label I call Blues Spectrum on which I plan to release traditional black music and pioneer artists. Here, take a look at these."

[Otis handed me six albums: Vol. 1, *Louis Jordan*; Vol. 2, *Charles Brown*; Vol. 3, *Johnny Otis*; Vol. 4, *Joe Turner*; Vol. 5, *Pee Wee Crayton*; and Vol. 6, *Joe Liggins*. Each performed songs associated with their careers.] As I was glancing at the titles, Johnny added:

"But I am still interested in contemporary new talent, as I've always been. Back in 1951 we played the Paradise Theatre in Detroit. It was one of the 'around the world' theaters, as we called the black vaudeville theaters of those days: the Apollo, the Howard, the Regal, the

Royal. I prevailed upon the manager to let me have a talent show, which I tried to do wherever I went, always hoping to find some young, meaningful, aspiring talent. The manager was very cooperative. A one-hour show stretched into an hour-and-a-half, and there was still another hour-and-a-half of kids waiting. In later years, when I thought of what Berry Gordy did in Detroit, I was not surprised. For some reason, Detroit was loaded with talent; it just needed the vision and the creative power of Gordy to help it mature. A tremendous percentage of the young people heard at the Paradise was talented. Three of them made a strong impression. They were Little Willie John, Jackie Wilson, and a group called The Royals.

"I was then serving as a talent scout for King Records. When I phoned Syd Nathan in Cincinnati, he quickly agreed to send somebody to Detroit. That night, as we waited, I wrote a song for Jackie, who seemed to need material. It was called 'Every Beat of My Heart.' Jackie learned it and sang it for the producer Nathan sent, but he preferred the vocal group, probably because King was doing great with Billy Ward & The Dominoes. King was vocal group conscious. He kinda ignored Little Willie John and Jackie Wilson—and poor Jackie, who sang in a very high tenor, really sang his heart out. But he took the song with him and recorded it with The Royals [later known as The Midnighters]. That was '51 and nothing happened. But as you know, ten years later, in '61, Gladys Knight & the Pips found The Royals record and made a smash debut with it on a little label called Fury. And King later signed Little Willie John, who became a giant of an artist."

Now, I started at the bottom and
  I stays right there,
Don't seem like I'm gonna get nowhere.
  —GABRIEL BROWN

The Honkers

"PUSH YOUR PARTNER OUT,/ Then hunch your back,/ Start a little movement in your sacroiliac,/ Wiggle like a snake, waddle like a duck"—and that's the way you did The Hucklebuck.

In 1949 "The Hucklebuck" was an extremely popular song and dance. Catching on in black ghettos as a result of the Paul Williams record on Savoy, the dance became so popular that Tommy Dorsey recorded the tune for Victor and Frank Sinatra, for Columbia. There were also platters by Roy Milton (Specialty) and Lionel Hampton

(Decca). When the year's statistics were compiled, the Savoy disk by Williams stood at the very top of "Best-Selling Rhythm & Blues Records," followed by Charles Brown's "Trouble Blues" (Aladdin) and Louis Jordan's "Saturday Night Fish Fry" (Decca). Savoy tried to capitalize on the seven-month popularity of the platter by issuing a Williams follow-up, "He Knows How to Hucklebuck." It went the way of most follow-ups: one week on the charts, then nothing.

Although Andy Gibson was credited as the composer, the music of "The Hucklebuck" was derived from one of Charlie Parker's bebop originals, "Now's the Time." Bird had recorded his original four years earlier with a group of jazz stars, including trumpeters Miles Davis and Dizzy Gillespie and drummer Max Roach, on Savoy, an important source of Parker and other early bop recordings. Apart from its origin, "The Hucklebuck" was significant as an R & B song and dance because it cut across color lines. It may well be the earliest instance of the crossover that became a pop phenomenon in the 1954–56 period and that spelled the end of R & B as a segregated music.

•

In 1949 Savoy released an instrumental recording entitled "Deacon's Hop," composed by Cecil J. McNeely and recorded by him as "Big Jay" McNeely. It did not make the charts, but it exploited a sound, present also in the Paul Williams disk and in McNeely's earlier Savoy recordings of "35–30" in '47 and "Waxey Maxie" in '48, that had come to identify R & B. As the acoustic guitar and wheezing "harp" epitomized the blues, so were there few R & B disks without a screaming tenor sax solo like that heard on Hal Singer's "Cornbread," another Savoy chartmaking instrumental in '48, or Joe Houston's "All Nite Long" (Modern). Less frequently heard on record was the honking tenor, though one can hear a brief, low three-note repetition and freak high notes on the tenor solo in Hank Ballard's "Finger-Poppin' Time."

I cannot recall the name of the Harlem joint where I first encountered the phenomenon. It might have been Joe Wells's Upstairs Room, Jock's Place (formerly The Yeah Man), or The Shalimar—all on Seventh Avenue in the 1940s. But when we came into the smoke-filled room, we could hear a loud tenor sax on which the performer kept honking one low note. The honking had no particular rhythm; it was just repeated at intervals. Just as we sat down, the saxist switched to a very high note and kept screeching that one note for what seemed an interminable interval. What confused us as we began to see through the curtain of smoke was that there was no sax player visible on the small bandstand. But then we discovered, not without some amazement, that the saxist was lying on his back and kicking his feet in the air as he "played," like a small child having a tantrum. The performer could have been Big Jay, though the incident goes back too far for me to recall. (Disk jockey Norm Nite recalls that in stage appearances, "all the house lights would be extinguished and then Big Jay McNeely's band would begin to play, fluorescent lights reflecting off their shirts, while Jay lay down on the stage and played.")

Jazz historian and critic Leonard Feather characterizes tenor saxists who indulged in this type of playing as "audience getters." Noting that almost all of them were capable of "first-class mainstream jazz work," he continues, "but all of them found that by resorting to such tactics as the use of freak high notes, the relentless honking on a single note for an entire chorus, and the use of low notes with deliberately vulgar tonal effects, they have been able to achieve great popular success, either at the rowdier jazz events or in the circles variously known as rhythm and blues or rock and roll." Aligning them with a group he types "extrovert moderns," Feather enumerates the follow-

Paul Williams

ing as "audience getters": Gene Ammons (Billy Eckstine band, 1944–47); John Coltrane (Miles Davis, 1956–7); Eddie "Lock-jaw" Davis (Count Basie, 1952–3); Paul Gonsalves (Duke Ellington from 1950); and among former jazzmen who achieved greater success in R & B: Sam "The Man" Taylor (Cab Calloway, 1946–52); Al Sears (Duke Ellington, 1943–51); James Moody (Dizzy Gillespie, 1947); and Arnett Cobb (Lionel Hampton, 1942–7).

Adding the names of Willis "Gatortail" Jackson and Lynn Hope, LeRoi Jones observes: "The riff itself was the basis of this kind of playing, the saxophonist repeating the riff much past any useful musical context, continuing it until he and the crowd were thoroughly exhausted physically and emotionally. The point, it seemed, was to spend oneself with as much attention as possible, and also to make the instrument sound as unmusical, or as non-Western, as possible. It was almost as if the blues people were reacting against the softness and 'legitimacy' that had crept into black instrumental music with swing."

Jones does not rule out the audience-getting angle. He sees R & B as a "less personal music" than the older forms of the blues because the pounding rhythm sections subvert the lyric content; R & B is more easily faked; and performances tend to monotony. As for the tenorman who falls down on his back screaming, he concludes: "Even though he might be genuinely moved to do so, [he may be doing it] more from a sense of performance than from any unalterable emotional requirement." But then Jones concedes, ". . . the dramatic or *burlesqued* part of the performance" might be self-expression since it made "the separation from the social implications of the white popular song complete."

An expressiveness as extreme as the honking–falling-down syndrome is unquestionably a social as well as a musical phenomenon. Jones sees it as expression of a threefold separation: from the sound of Western music; from white popular song; and from the Negro middle class to whom R & B was anathema. I buy his thesis and would add that the syndrome was a conscious or unconscious projection of the postwar segregration of black people, an abysmal expression of the separateness of the black ghettos.

The postwar world was one that Negroes viewed with a mixture of disgust and frustration. Not only were they still isolated from the mainstream of society, they not infrequently suffered white violence. In August of '46, Sarah Vaughn was performing at Cafe Society Downtown. One night, as she left the club to walk to the subway, she and her musicians were set upon by about twenty hoodlums. It was just a few weeks afer Josh White had been beaten up on leaving the club. Owner Barney Josephson protested to the police, but, he reported, "The hoods haven't been caught, and the cops just shrug their shoulders."

Down in Atlanta, at about the same time, there was a rash of violence against blacks. Characterizing the attack as Nazi-like, Station WSB launched a campaign in an attempt to stem the development. Tensions between blacks and whites reached a level in Philadelphia that led several radio stations there, too, to embark on campaigns against prejudice. In Washington, D.C., the Washington *Post* supported a drive by Actors Equity to eliminate Jim Crow practices in the theaters; it became a drawn-out battle in the courts and the media as theater owners continued the practice of excluding Negroes. The widespread nature of the problem inside the entertainment field as well as in society generally became clear when *Billboard*, in December 1946, ran a front-page editorial captioned: "Where Does Show Business Stand on Intolerance?"

For black musicians, the postwar world posed distressing situations. Once, it had been claimed that Negro musicians could not read, that they played out of tune, that they were not musically cultured. But these denigrations could no longer be sustained. The postwar generation of musicians was academically trained, at colleges, universities, and institutions like Juilliard. Even when proficiency was the result of "woodshedding," as in the case of genius Charlie Parker, there was a quick leap into the world of Stravinsky, Prokofiev, and other contemporary composers. Yet the doors to the world of prestigious and lucrative music—the broadcasting studios, recording companies, Hollywood studio orchestras, symphony orchestras—still bore big, white-lettered signs: No Admittance.

"Getting the audience" is a good description of many a black musician's motivation. After all the white promises and black sacrifices made during the war, the musician was not playing music. In the monotonous honking and catlike screeching, he was mocking the audience and destroying the music. And what irritation, anger, desperation, frustration, despair, and petulance could be read in the gesture of playing while lying on one's back!

•

Illinois Jacquet is recognized as the father and founder of the honking school. Born in Houston, Texas, in 1921 and associated with several regional swing bands, he came into his own after he moved to

California and joined Lionel Hampton. His tenor sax solo on "Flying Home," a number written in 1943 by Benny Goodman and Lionel Hampton (whose theme it became), drew attention to his capabilities and led to a more lucrative berth with Cab Calloway and, later, Count Basie. The "Flying Home" solo served to launch a school of booming, demonstrative and, erotic tenor sax stylists. But after Jacquet began leading his own band in '47 and making records for Savoy and Aladdin, he became known for freak high notes and other showy gimmicks. These became a staple of R & B tenor saxists, although Jacquet himself remained a jazzman.

•

Earl Bostic, born in Tulsa, Oklahoma, in 1913 and a student of harmony and theory at Xavier University, played alto sax. But he blew with a ferocity that made the usually delicate and sweet alto sound almost like a robust baritone. Of the many sides that became favorites with R & B audiences ("Sleep," "Temptation," "Moonglow," "Blue Skies," "845 Stomp"), his King recording of "Flamingo" proved the most popular. In 1951, it was heard much of the year, as it climbed to No. 1 over a period of twenty weeks. A successful, jazz-inflected songwriter ("Let Me Off Uptown," among others) and arranger for Lionel Hampton and other jump bands, among others, Bostic was an instrumental stylist whose improvisational playing put him on the dividing line between jazz and R & B. Doubtless it was his tone, so full of sand and sex, and the rhythmic backgrounds of his disks that gave him a strong following in pop R & B circles.

•

Since young record buyers, white as well as black, turned to R & B because it was so danceable, instrumental records were very popular through the R & B years. Few registered the success of Bostic's solos. In 1956, nonetheless, pianist/organist William Ballard Doggett, another King artist, accounted for one of the biggest disks of the decade. Born in Philadelphia in 1916, Doggett played with Lucky Millinder's band in 1940, after which he spent two years as an arranger for The Ink Spots. Work with Louis Jordan, who used organist Wild Bill Davis, led Doggett to take up that instrument and to develop a tough, driving style comparable to Davis'.

In 1956 Doggett recorded "Honky-Tonk"; it is likely that the music was improvised since it is credited to four men: Billy Butler, Shape Sheppard, Clifford Scott, and Doggett—all musicians on the session. Released in August '56 as a two-sided disk (rare in those days), it remained on best-seller charts for seven months, much of that time in the No. 1 spot. Between '56 and '59, Doggett succeeded in placing six other instrumentals on R & B charts. "Hold It" (1958) came closest to "Honky-Tonk" in popularity. But none of the others was more than a faint echo of the record that reportedly sold over 4 million copies.

And what was "Honky-Tonk"? A simple, bluesy melody on an appealing riff, performed in a medium four-to-the-bar style. Though Doggett played organ and piano, the record sold on an extended tenor sax solo by Clifford Scott, who, at moments, explored some of the bizarre sounds of the honkers. It was a great dance record for the youngsters who were then mesmerized by "Heartbreak Hotel" and "Hound Dog," Presley's early hits.

•

Among the unsung tenor saxists whose incandescent solos heightened many an R & B and rock 'n' roll record, one should include Maxwell Davis, a Los Angeles resident who worked with B. B. King, Red Prysock, and Sil Austin, among others. In '56 Davis came through with a hit disk of his own in "Slow Walk" on Mercury.

The sound of the red-hot, big-toned tenor was transported into rock 'n' roll by Rudi Pompanelli, a Bill Haley Comet from the early days. Onstage, Pompanelli would bob up and down and swing from side to side in what appeared to be a frantic attempt to scale an unattainable height of frenzy. Many feel that the impact of Haley's records is traceable to Pompanelli's searing solos more than to Haley's bellowed vocals.

A number of saxophonists carried the tradition of the raucous, driving tenor *cum* jazz overtones into the '60s and the soul scene. Sam "The Man" Taylor, born of a musical family in Lexington, Tennessee, in 1916, played with Lucky Millinder 1944–45 and Cab Calloway '46–'52, before becoming a sought-after tenorman in NY recording studios. Sam Butera, who was born in New Orleans in 1927, was a featured soloist with Louis Prima from 1954 until Prima suffered a stroke in 1973; he may also be heard in the instrumental breaks on many R & B recordings.

•

The most impressive of this latter-day group was King Curtis, who became Atlantic Records' studio tenor, soloing on disks by The Coasters, Wilson Pickett, Aretha Franklin, The Rascals, and many others, and who also recorded with groups under his own insignia (King Curtis & His Noble Knights, King Curtis & His King Pins).

Born Curtis Ousley in Fort Worth, Texas, in 1934, he started on alto before switching to tenor sax. Although his scholastic standing was so high that he was offered several scholarships, he went directly from secondary school into Lionel Hampton's band. Settling in New York in 1952, he became the most in-demand tenorman for R & B record sessions.

In 1958 he formed his own jazz combo and played Smalls' Paradise, now Big Wilt's (Chamberlain) on Seventh Avenue. In '62 he moved from the in-circle of outstanding performers into public acceptance with "Soul Twist," an Enjoy recording that became a No. 1

King Curtis

R & B best-seller. Five years elapsed before his name appeared again on hit lists—and that time, it was with a concoction known as "Memphis Soul Stew."

King Curtis was a more sophisticated performer than the early R & B tenormen. To the drive and energy of the honkers and screechers, he added an emotional sweep that made his solos expressive and exciting. In the legacy of disks he left behind, he paid tribute to some of his predecessors, recording Big Jay McNeely's "Something on Your Mind" and Bill Doggett's "Honky-Tonk." In 1971, he was stabbed to death outside a Manhattan brownstone he owned when he told a loiterer to move on. He was thirty-seven years old. It was a tragedy as senseless as the prejudice, discrimination, and violence that generated the phenomenon known as honking.

3. The California Cataclysm

Now, R & B started here in LA. Roy Milton was here, Joe Liggins was here, T-Bone Walker was here, Charles Brown was here, I was here, and others, too. By '48 or '49 it was set—we had an art form, though we didn't know it then.

—JOHNNY OTIS

Well, if a man can make it Los Angeles,
he can make it anywhere,
But you have got to have one of those
Cadillac cars . . .
— CHARLES WATERFORD

Record Company in a Cigar Box

IN the mid-'40s Los Angeles not only had the many black artists mentioned by Johnny Otis, it also had a large black audience in the expanding Watts ghetto.

The urbanization and industrial growth fostered by World War II brought to California over 2 million laboring people, and to Los Angeles alone over 400,000. A large percentage was black, attracted from Texas, Oklahoma, and even Louisiana by the opportunities for employment. War-related industries like shipbuilding and aircraft contributed to the rising employment of blacks. During the '40s, surprising as it may be, the production of cotton in the San Joaquin Valley rose over 1,000 percent. Vegetable truck farming and fruit growing expanded tremendously, and Los Angeles' San Pedro grew as a port.

Although wartime prosperity generated a higher income level for blacks and wartime psychology favored public desegregation, permitting blacks to frequent formerly inaccessible bars, lounges, saloons, theaters, and night clubs, home entertainment was still a staple of Negro life. As black income levels rose, there was a growing demand for records, and not the white records and artists produced by the major companies. Eventually, the majors were to move back into the "race" field, as it was known before World War II, but during and immediately after the war, small independents mushroomed to supply the demand for black music. An unusually large number of these companies sprang up on the West Coast. One of the earliest and most successful was Specialty Records.

The first office of Specialty was, literally, a cigar box. The year was 1944, and Art Rupe (rhymes with *loop*), of Pittsburgh and UCLA, had paid his dues at Atlas Records. Having lost his modest savings at Atlas, his capital was not sufficient to finance both an office and the recording and manufacture of a record. Rupe might have rented desk space to have a mailing address, only he could not afford even that. Instead, for two dollars a month, he rented a box that was kept on a desk. To distinguish his cigar box from those of other box-holders, his had a number and a sticker that read: Owned by Jukebox Records.

"I called it Jukebox Records," he explains, "because the jukebox

179

was the medium then for plugging records. If you got a record into the boxes, it was tantamount to getting it on the top stations today. The jukebox operator was also important because he bought in volume. While a small operator might have twenty or thirty boxes, a big op would have a thousand or twelve hundred locations. It was a sizable sale if you made it."

Rupe's first record was an instrumental called "Boogie No. 1," and it was by the Sepia Tones. He picked the title because of the impact of the word *boogie*. "To a black man," he says, "boogie meant intercourse, sexual intercourse. And my record had both the beat and the sex in the title. We sold 70,000, but never made the "race" chart in *Billboard*. They listed only five records and 'Boogie No. 1' sold primarily in LA, San Francisco, and Texas. It didn't have national distribution."

Neither did Rupe have an easy time getting the record manufactured. "It was pressed by a factory in Los Angeles," he recalls. "But I had to wait in line, go there in the middle of the night. The factory didn't want your business, but they didn't turn it away if they had vacant time on the presses."

The cost of the recording session was $195. Studio rental cost $25. Art hired three musicians, each of whom received $30, except for the leader, who got double. It was a three-hour session and four sides were cut, as permitted by the Musicians Union. Although the musicians received union scale, Art agreed to pay them a royalty, too. Completed master in hand, Rupe rushed over to the pressing plant. He ordered 1000 but, as he recalls, got only 600–700. As soon as he had a boxful, he took it over to Gold Furniture Store and sold a batch for cash. Situated near the black Musicians Union—LA had two locals, one for whites and one for blacks—the store catered to a clientele that was primarily black.

"There was a tremendous demand for this type of record," Rupe says, by way of explaining his quick turnover. "The majors weren't supplying music of this type. With the wartime shortage of shellac and other materials, their pressings went mostly to pop music. 'Boogie No. 1' wasn't really a hit, you follow me? But it sold well because of the sheer vacuum."

Into the vacuum moved a number of family-owned West Coast enterprises. There were the Bihari brothers—Saul, Joe, and Jules—who ran a little restaurant and owned jukeboxes; they started Modern Records. There were the Messner brothers—Leo and Edward—and

Ida Messner, who launched Philo Records, changed within a year to Aladdin Records. There was Paul Reiner and his wife Lillian, who established Black & White Records. And there were the René brothers —Leon and Otis—who had been around for some time with Exclusive and Excelsior Records.

Rupe's entry into the record business, he has said, was an accident, though his feeling for black music was not. Born and raised near Pittsburgh, he lived around black people. "We grew up in what you might call a ghetto area," he said.

•

"We lived in an alley, a street without sidewalks. The name of the alley is fascinating—TubeWorks Alley. And it was called that because it was near a steel mill where they made steel tubes. My father, who came from Austria-Hungary, did not work in the mill, but in a factory owned by Westinghouse. He worked on a stamping machine until he was hurt, and then he got a job as a salesman in a second-hand furniture store.

"My mother, whose folks were from Holland and Hungary, was a first-generation American, born in Pittsburgh. She played the piano, classical and some popular music. She didn't have much time to play, but I thought she was the best pianist in the world.

"In a picture I remember seeing of me with my classmates, I look like a sugar cube in a coal bin. We were all poor and, whether white or black, our culture was the same. The music I heard was black. My black friends had old Bluebird Records and I forget what others— Vocalion and so on. They were real 'race' records. But most of it was what I now realize was country blues. Stuff like Maceo, Bessie Smith, the washboard singers, etc.

"I'm talking about the mid-thirties. Some black people in Tube-Works Alley played the harp or guitar. And I heard a lot of church music. But that didn't impress me as much at that time as did the big bands. I used to get a kick going to band concerts in the park. And, of course, they played mostly marches and light classical music. The bands were all white. The only black musicians I saw performing professionally was when I went to a theater in Pittsburgh and saw Count Basie or Duke Ellington."

•

Having graduated McKeesport High School, Rupe went to Miami U. in Oxford, Ohio, and then to UCLA. He chose California because he wanted to get into the motion picture business. Registering initially for a pre-med course, he switched to business administration. It did not move him closer to his goal. "There was a lot of nepotism in the motion picture business," he recalls. "You had to be related to someone, or know someone and so on. Without some kind of family connection, it was difficult to get into the unions, which were very, very strong. It was a tough challenge, and I wasn't as aggressive as I should have been. I dreamed and fantasized about getting in. But I didn't do, I guess, what was necessary to get into the field."

An advertisement got him into the record business. Atlas Records, a small independent, ran an ad seeking financial partners. Atlas was owned by a songwriter named Robert Sherman (no relation to the Shermans of Walt Disney fame), and the company had three artists: Nat Cole, Frankie Laine, and Al Sack, a fellow who played music in the Lawrence Welk manner.

Unfortunately, Sherman was a better judge of talent than of his own songs. Nat Cole recorded one: "My Lips Remember Your Kisses." "It sold practically nothing," Rupe notes. "The company went down the drain, even though it had good artists. Whenever I suggested something, Sherman would say: 'Get away, kid. You're the silent partner. Stay silent.' But in the three and one half to four months I was with this company, I really came to feel that this was a field I should get into. I was getting out of the university then, and I didn't know where the hell I was going. I was in a hole quite a bit. But I managed to get six hundred dollars together and I decided to go into business for myself. Atlas was a very, very bad deal. I lost my money. But what I gained was an entree into the recording business."

When he started on his own, Rupe concentrated entirely on black artists. The reason was that he felt it was the only area where he could succeed. "I saw the problems of Atlas," he said, "competing with the majors. I looked for an area neglected by the majors and in essence took the crumbs off the table of the record industry. The majors kept recording what we call country blues. The black people, particularly the black people I knew, never lived in the country. They looked down on country music. Among themselves, the blacks called country blues 'field nigger' music. They wanted to be citified. They found a country bluesman like Lee Hooker terribly crude.

"When I got into the business, few white people fooled around with this kind of music. It was called 'nigger' music, and one of my friends called me a 'nigger lover.' I've never forgotten that. Then it graduated into being labeled 'race' music, then R & B music, then rock 'n' roll and now black 'n' soul music. I had no idea that it would ever appeal to many white people."

•

Before he began recording, Rupe made a meticulous survey of the market, trying to find out what records were selling and why. He visited all the stores that sold black disks, spending almost $200 on records and an all-important stopwatch. Then he spent hours playing the records over and over and timing sequences—the length of intros, of choruses, of repeat choruses. He tried to discover correlations in the records that sold and in those that did not sell.

In Los Angeles, the stores that stocked black disks were in the Watts area. "Most of the stores that sold black records," he recalls, "were little, hole-in-the-wall places, owned by black proprietors. Since they couldn't get credit, they could buy only a limited quantity. The white distributors of the time didn't cater too much to them. I doubt that their salesmen even visited them. So it depended on the initiative of the black store owner to find saleable records. And I managed to produce records that they wanted to stock." Speaking of Watts, Rupe said, "It's tragic what has occurred down there. A lot of white people have really been cut off from very, very—*interesting* is too weak a word—I mean it was rich in so many things. It's sad. But now I'm even hesitant to go down there at all. Such are the times!"

At the conclusion of his scientific analysis of best-selling records, Rupe concluded that the secret of sales was in "a big band sound, expressed in a churchy way. I remember being impressed by Lucky Millinder." He also discerned considerable contrast between urban and country music. "The urban music had horns," he says, "and the country music was primarily percussion. The urban was a little more sophisticated, a little more disciplined, a little more organized and closer to the American, popular, Tin Pan Alley structure, except these were twelve-bar versus eight-bar. The structures of urban and country blues were the same, except—and I don't mean this disrespectfully— that one was very elementary and unpolished and the other was the same thing, but polished. The roots were there."

Rupe had no more difficulty finding talent than he had finding out- lets to stock his disks. After-hours clubs were the focus of his search. They were known as "after-hours" because of California's liquor law prohibiting sales after 2:00 A.M. Catering to people who wanted a late drink, the clubs burgeoned. To some, you could bring your own bottle, which had a pseudo-legality. Others continued the speakeasy tradition of flouting the law. It was in these clubs that Rupe went searching for someone who could get the Lucky Millinder sound.

•

"You see, I had a limited budget. I had six hundred dollars to begin with and I spent two hundred buying records and a stopwatch. I was looking for the same sound with a smaller group. I couldn't afford eighteen pieces, so I ended with two small acts. The first was only three pieces—a drummer, bass player, and a girl who doubled on organ and piano, and could play both at the same time. I called them the Sepia Tones. The other act consisted of six instruments— it was Roy Milton's combo. And he succeeded in getting a sound which was as good, and even better than, Lucky Millinder's. It was an uncomplicated sound, and yet it had the full harmonic range.

"Roy had two sounds, like other black bands. During regular hours when he gigged in a white club, he played white music, Tin Pan Alley songs. Then, after hours, he went down to Watts and played for black people. That's the Roy Milton that I recorded. But before I went in with Roy to a studio, I did things differently—at least one of my contemporaries told me at the time that it was different. Most black musicians were good at improvising and very seldom would play the same thing twice. If they felt good, you got a superb performance; but if they felt bad, it would turn out bad.

"I couldn't afford to gamble. So we rehearsed and rehearsed and rehearsed. I did the same thing with the Sepia Tones before Roy Milton. It's something that I insisted on. Many of Roy Milton's men did not read music, so they had to memorize every note and every nuance—and timing. When I walked into the studio, believe me, the first take would have been it, except that the engineer had to learn what we were doing. You follow me? Everything came out to the second. All I had to do was make sure that they did precisely what we had planned. And then I had to make sure that it sounded extemporaneous.

"If you give me points for anything, I would give myself points for being a record producer and, way down the bottom, as being a very bad businessman. And that's as candid and as honest as I can say— although some people considered it just the opposite. Many of my competitors thought I was a better businessman—well, no, Ahmet Ertegun and Jerry Wexler [of Atlantic Records] and people like that, knew I was a good producer. Ahmet told me how lucky I had it because I went to New Orleans or produced out here [in LA], and I got musicians who did this thing naturally. But he had to take New York jazz people and make them try to copy our type of urban blues.

"Well, New York was the altar. You know they were really sophisticated. You have to dig real deep into the bowels of Harlem to find gutsy blues. I mean New York was the epitome of the change that I was telling you about—the black urban wanting white music form expressed in his black way.

"Roy Milton was recorded in July or August of 1944. I didn't know that much about it, but I heard later that the René boys were recording from 1942 on. You see, the big problem was that the four major companies had a monopoly on the manufacture of records. The making of a disk, that is, the actual physical pressing—though it's relatively simple—was sort of a closely guarded secret. They had the highest security at the plants, so that no one knew how to press a record—*really*.

"The reason the independents started out here was a fellow named Jimmy Beard, who worked in one of the record pressing factories. You can do all the recording you want, but if you can't get records pressed, you're nowhere. Well, Jimmy decided to establish a factory of his own and he built a press. It's like an oversized waffle iron. You heat the press, pour in some dough, and squeeze the lid down on it. You get a waffle if you use dough and you get a record if you use a black shellac mixture. After Beard put one of these things together, he went around soliciting business. The majors weren't going to give him pressing orders since they had presses of their own. So he went to Atlas Records, Excelsior, and people like me. He made the independent record industry possible because he pressed records for anybody who could pay for them.

"There was also Greg Lee, who worked in the same plant originally as Jimmy Beard. In the manufacture of records, you start with a master. That's what comes out of the recording session. Then, there's a mother, like a photographic negative, from which a metal stamper, or die, is made. Greg Lee made the stampers that were put into press or waffle iron and gave the batter its grooves and sound.

"Another man who contributed to the growth of the independent record business was Jack Gutshall. He was a Los Angeles jukebox operator who became the first independent distributor. When he heard a record he liked, he would contact jukebox friends in other cities. Many of the original 'indie' distributors were jukebox operators like Gutshall. I got going before he became active in distribution.

My seventy-thousand sale of 'Boogie No. 1' was spread out over a period of a year and a half or so. It gave me enough capital so that I could record Roy Milton about five months after the first release. When I recorded Milton, I still had my office in a cigar box, but I was doing a lot better because I could get records pressed and sold soon after I had a master.

"With the increased distribution that I could get through Gutshall in other cities, Roy Milton's first record became what was probably, up until that time, the biggest record of urban black music that had ever been made. I'm talking about 'R. M. Blues.' "

Rupe's large-scale success with his first release brought an influx of capital to the small Jukebox label. Several people with money came knocking at his cigar box, and soon he had a number of partners. By the time "R. M. Blues" was climbing the "race" charts, Rupe found that his partners were asserting themselves in a way he had not anticipated, and control of the company was slipping away from him. Fortunately for him, he acted quickly and, in 1946, established a new label without partners. Since he was still determined to concentrate on black artists exclusively, he called the label Specialty.

Roy Milton & His Solid Senders became one of Specialty's most accepted artists. Milton was really the West Coast counterpart of Louis Jordan, but lacked Jordan's showmanship. In 1949 he gave competition to Paul Williams' smash disk of "The Hucklebuck," partly because his version contained a vocal describing what became the biggest R & B dance of the 1940s. (The piano triplets make one think it's an early rock 'n' roll record.) All through '50, '51 and '52, Milton and his city blues were consistent sellers, scoring with "Information Blues," "Best Wishes," and "So Tired."

The popularity of "The Hucklebuck" led Jimmy Liggins & His Drops of Joy, another Specialty instrumental group, to try a takeoff in "Shuffleshuck." It was a much more furious disk than Milton's, distinguished by the type of screaming sax solo associated with Big Jay McNeely and the honkers.

"Big sellers sometimes are not planned. They just happen. That was the case with Camille Howard's 'X-temporaneous Boogie.' I don't know that it ever made the charts, but it was a big, big seller for us. And not just in '48, but for years. It was selling even in the fifties. We called it 'X-temporaneous Boogie' because that's what it was. You see the Musicians Union called a recording strike at the end of

1947. Like all record companies, we tried to stockpile enough masters to tide us over the period when we couldn't get musicians.

"On December 31, 1947, I was in the studio all day, recording all of our artists. At about eleven P.M. I began cutting Camille Howard's Trio. She was Roy Milton's pianist—and we formed a trio that consisted of Camille, bassist Dallas Bartley of Louis Jordan's Tympany Five, and Roy Milton on drums. Camille sang and we recorded a number of blues ballads. When she had completed the numbers we planned, the clock stood at eleven-fifty-five P.M.

"We weren't going to give up even those five minutes, so we let Camille and the trio extemporize a boogie. As she finished, we could hear the church bells and horns of New Year's Day 1948 sounding outside the studio.

" 'X-temporaneous Boogie' made it possible for Camille to step forward as a solo act. Funny thing is that nothing Camille recorded after that compared with that boogie. And we did quite a lot of recording with her—vocal as well as instrumental. Oh, yeah, in '51 she did make the charts with a number called 'Money Blues,' but that never approached 'X-temporaneous Boogie' in sales."

•

Rupe made his first trip to New Orleans in 1952. "The only reason I went South," he says, "was because I was very impressed with Fats Domino. I really dug him, liked his sound." Rupe confesses that he did not make the trip without some uneasiness. All his friends—his black friends—told him, "Man, it's out. A 'fay [white boy] messin' with spades [blacks] will end up in the pokey, in the jug."

But he had come to feel that his LA musicians were getting somewhat glib. "I didn't feel the spontaneity that I felt originally," he says. "Either I needed a change or they needed one." In Fats Domino, he heard something different.

"I think I heard a church sound," he says, noting that his main interest as a record producer was in gospel music.

"Not rock 'n' roll but gospel—the forerunner and the roots of the blues, country and urban, and of rock 'n' roll. I started recording Gospel in 1947—eventually cutting The Pilgrim Travelers, Swan Silvertones, Chosen Gospel Singers, and Soul Stirrers [whose lead singer was Sam Cooke]. I feel that one of the most electrifying sounds on wax was that of Alex Bradford, a great gospel shouter who sold an enormous number of records of 'So Close to Heaven.' He had a way of suddenly giving out with an unexpected *falsetto* note that electrified his listeners. You can hear it in 'Somebody Touched Me.'

Incidentally, before every record session, Roy Milton loved to listen to gospel records. He'd bring some of his favorites or just have the engineer pick some out of our catalogue. Does anyone need anything more to indicate the close relationship between gospel and R & B?"

•

It was during his trip to New Orleans that Rupe found Lloyd Price, who was born in the Crescent City in 1933—one of ten children—and who accounted for one of Specialty's biggest sellers, "Lawdy, Miss Clawdy." As a boy, Lloyd sang the gospel in church. His parents taught him guitar and piano, and in high school he mastered the trumpet. When he was still in his teens, he had a five-piece R & B band and began displaying the resourcefulness that allowed him to weather the turbulence of the times.

He arranged for his band to appear on local radio, and he himself began writing jingles for the station. One of the jingles evolved into "Lawdy, Miss Clawdy." Rupe released Price's recording in May 1952. It went to No. 1 on R & B charts, remaining for six months. The number of disks he sold led Rupe to believe that whites were buying it as well as blacks, and the story has been often repeated about white women who went into New Orleans record shops to buy the record ostensibly "for their black maids or housekeepers." What was, perhaps, more interesting was that the piano player on the record was Fats Domino, who had a number of releases on Imperial and a hit paralleling Price's. His "Goin' Home," also released in May, went to No. 1.

Price's second release on Specialty was a two-sided chartmaker, though neither "Oooh-Oooh-Oooh" nor "Restless Heart" did nearly as well as "Miss Clawdy." It made clear, however, that as a singer, Price combined Joe Turner's exuberance with the type of sensuous balladry that became Sam Cooke's trademark. And Price was a precursor of Otis Redding, the great Georgia songbird.

Rupe's relationship with Price ran for little more than a year. The Army sent greetings, and Lloyd was soon making music in Korea and Japan—literally, for he organized a band with which he toured American bases. On his discharge he settled in Washington, D.C., and established a record company, KRC Records. By 1957 he had a hit on Am-Par Records (an ABC division), having sold them "Just Because," a song he wrote and recorded on his own label. It was the succeeding ABC release that sent his career into orbit; "Stagger Lee," a rewrite by him and his longtime partner-manager Harold Logan of the old folk blues "Stack-O-Lee," went to No. 1 in '59.

(There were really two versions of "Stagger Lee." For an appearance on the Dick Clark show, Price modified his original recording and softened the bluesy tale of a stolen girlfriend, lost money, and murder into an argument that was amicably settled when the girl returned to Stagger Lee. The beat and sound of the refined record remained earthy R & B but the substance became romantic pop. The record, as first released by ABC, is audible in an anthology of Price's *Greatest Hits*, while the genteel "American Bandstand" hit version is to be found on ABC's *Rock 'N' Soul, 1958*.)

In 1959 Price also had No. 1 disks on R & B charts in "Personality" and "I'm Gonna Get Married," both written by him and Logan. When *Billboard* compiled its year-end statistics, "Personality" was listed No. 3 among "Hot 100 Records of the Year" and No. 5 among "Top Tunes of the Year." "Stagger Lee" also placed among the top thirteen on both charts, indicating that Lloyd Price had made the crossing into rock 'n' roll. In truth, were it not for his first disk, "Lawdy, Miss Clawdy," it would be difficult to think of him as an R & B artist.

·

Rupe's ongoing contact with the musical life of New Orleans was partly through Dave Bartholomew, a former Duke Ellington trumpeter in whose band Fats Domino played piano, and it led to his recording a number of other important rhythm-and-bluesmen.

Larry Williams, born in the Crescent City in May 1935, initially became a Specialty artist because he had served as Lloyd Price's valet. With Price out of his reach, Rupe persuaded Williams to cover Lloyd's first ABC hit, "Just Because." His second release, "Short, Fat Fannie," became a national R & B hit, entering the charts in June 1957 and climbing to the No. 2 spot. "Bony Moronie," another song he wrote, made the lists in November 1957, but failed to approach the popularity of "Fat Fannie." The following year, "Dizzy Miss Lizzy" an obvious imitation of his big hit, and of Price's, made no impression on the record-buying public.

·

Rupe's most significant discovery in the southeast came "knocking" at his door. Richard Penniman, born in Macon, Georgia, in December 1932, was washing dishes in the Greyhound bus station in Macon when, at the suggestion of Lloyd Price, he sent Art a demo tape of a song he had written. When, almost a year later, Rupe expressed a desire to record Little Richard, as Penniman became known, he discovered that he was under contract to Peacock Records of Houston. In fact, Penniman had had four releases on RCA Victor in '51–'52 (as the result of his winning a talent contest at Atlanta's 81 Theatre) and four releases on Peacock in '52–'55. After Rupe bought Richard's contract from Don Robey of Peacock, he sent Bumps Blackwell to record him at the Cosmo Studios in New Orleans.

The hit that came out of that session happened to be the ninth number, although only eight had been scheduled. Little Richard described the development as follows: "We met in New Orleans and I cut some blues songs. During a break in the session, someone heard me playing 'Tutti-Frutti' on the piano and asked about it. We ended up recording it, and it sold two hundred thousand copies in a week and a half." Little Richard had, perhaps, forgotten that they also ended up changing his original version. Blackwell apparently thought that the original was too risqué and enlisted the services of a writer, Dorothy LaBostrie, who was hanging around the studio, to tone down Little Richard's words.

"Tutti-Frutti" struck R & B charts in November 1955, five months before Elvis had his first national chart disk, and bounced up to No. 2 in a twenty-week period. From then through 1958, Little Richard gave Specialty eleven best-sellers, most of which made the Top Ten in R & B. These included "Long Tall Sally" b/w "Slippin' and Slidin'," and "Rip It Up" b/w "Ready Teddy"—both No. 1 disks in '56. The following year, "Lucille" b/w "Send Me Some Lovin'," and "Jenny Jenny" b/w "Miss Ann" made No. 2. Toward the end of '57, "Keep A Knockin' " made No. 5 while in '58, "Good Golly, Miss Molly" made No. 6. All of these were cut at Cosmo, the studio in New Orleans where Fats Domino did virtually all of his recording. Although the two men used the same band—musicians led by Dave Bartholomew, Fats' collaborator on his original songs—the sounds they achieved could not have been more different.

It was partly a matter of the two voices: Fats had a friendly baritone and Little Richard's sound was strident and slam-bam. Fats' Cajun-inflected speech had an appealing musicality; Little Richard was a shouter. For Fats, the band played New Orleans jazz with an after-beat while he boogied and barrelhoused at the piano. With Little Richard's crashing piano triplets, the band picked up drive and went "a-womp-bomp-a-loo-bomp a-lomp bomp boom" and "bama lama, bama loo."

The contrast had a lot to do with the personalities of the two Southerners. Little Richard represents a triumph of style over substance. His songs were lightweight fare, but great vehicles for his manner of performing. In person he was a cauldron of sweat, a dynamo that gave off electric sparks, banging the keys with his heels

Little Richard

and rump and resorting to all the exhibitionistic gambits that Jerry Lee Lewis later imitated. Wearing his black hair in an exaggeratedly high pompadour, he appeared in eye-dazzling costumes that suggested effeminacy. On wax he came across with such a display of fire that young people responded violently. He exemplified the excitement, exhibitionism, and energy of R & B.

But he took the curious position in a *Rolling Stone* interview that he was not a rhythm-and-bluesman: "One of the big problems with record companies," he said, "is they all try and make me a rhythm and blues artist, and I'm not. I came from a family where my people didn't like rhythm and blues. Bing Crosby—'Pennies from Heaven'—and Ella Fitzgerald was all I heard. And I knew there was something louder than that, but I didn't know where to find it. And I found it was me."

That his frenetic style was the man and not a put-on is suggested by his spectacular turn to religion. It happened after he recorded "Good Golly, Miss Molly" early in 1958. He was sailing on a ship near Australia when he rushed to the rail, tore one ring after another from his fingers—he loved gaudy jewelry—and hurled them into the sea. He was through with the entertainment scene! On his return to the USA, he enrolled at an Alabama college, paying his entire tuition in advance for a four-year course that would make him a minister.

It is known that Joe Lutcher, another Specialty artist, worked at converting Little Richard, but it has also been suggested that the launching of the Soviet satellite *Sputnik* in 1957 shocked Little Richard into accepting the call to the ministry. According to another story, an airplane engine caught fire on one of his flights and Little Richard promised God that he would quit the evil world of blues if he were saved. There is even a rumor that Little Richard joined the church because he had learned that ministers do not pay income tax.

Whatever the truth, Little Richard's stage appearances are frequently filled with religious references. "We all belong to God," he says between songs. "God is a God of beauty, of love, of peace, so I think that we are all together in this bouquet—God's bouquet. He's not a God of one race. He's a God of all races, and I don't think that God intended us to have hatred against any race. I mean a black man can be prejudiced, a white man can be prejudiced, and if I'm a militant against a man, I'm prejudiced."

Little Richard also talks of his music in religious terms. "I believe my music is the healin' music," he says. "Just like Oral Roberts says he's a divine healer. My music uplifts the soul. You see everybody's movin', they're happy, it regenerates the heart and makes the liver quiver, the bladder splatter, and the knees freeze."

By the time he returned to the recording scene in the '60s (after his religious conversion), there was little market for excited scatting like "Bama Lama Bama Loo," released in the year that The Beatles took the American entertainment scene by storm. It was, in fact, his last release on Specialty. Of course, the R & B revival of the late '60s opened new doors for him, like those of the Ambassador Hotel in Hollywood and the International in Las Vegas. Nonetheless, reissues of his recordings and new versions of his old hits (on Vee Jay, OKeh, and Reprise) found a limited market, and in person, the "Bronze Liberace," as he sometimes called himself, was too mannered and too freaky—with his vest of tiny mirrors and his rainbow-colored fingernails—to command the solid following of a B. B. King or Fats Domino.

Yet he was more of an influence than either of those men. His gospel dynamism, showy exhibitionism, and sheer animal vitality "spoke" to artists as different as Elvis Presley, Otis Redding, Jerry Lee Lewis (who told me that he had to wipe pounds of nail polish off the keyboard when he followed Richard onstage), Bill Haley, Marty Balin of The Jefferson Airplane, The Rolling Stones, and The Beatles.

"I gave The Beatles their first tour before they made a record," he told rock historian David Dalton. "I carried them to Hamburg, Germany, to the Star Club. . . . I gave Mick Jagger his first tour with The Rolling Stones. . . . You know, I put James Brown in show business and he never mentioned my name [on the Mike Douglas Show]. I put Jimi Hendrix in the business—he played in my band for two years before he made a record. I put Don Covay in the business, Otis Redding was in the business because of me, Billy Preston met The Beatles through me."

Some of these rhythm-and-bluesmen and some of these rock 'n' rollers copied his frantic mannerisms, and all recorded his songs, frequently scoring pop hits when he registered mainly with black buyers. In the Specialty records he made between 1955 and 1958, R & B reached a peak.

•

Several other artists helped establish Specialty as an outstanding R & B label between 1949 and '51. In the spring of '50, Joe Liggins & His Honeydrippers filled the glasses with "Pink Champagne," a "torch ballad" (he lost her) with a boogie beat that went to No. 1. In the fall of the year, Percy Mayfield, a murmuring, Nat Cole-type singer and the father of Curtis (*Superfly*) Mayfield, duplicated Liggins's success with "Please Send Me Someone to Love." It was a provocative combination of a love ballad and antidiscrimination song that climbed the charts for twenty-seven weeks and made No. 1. It was also a rare kind of song with its warning that hate would destroy the world, for R & B had little social orientation. "Lost Love" ran a close second for Mayfield in the winter of '51.

The references to ballads, in the romantic not narrative vein, require mention of Sam Cooke, whose recording career began in the mid-'50s on Specialty when he sang with The Soul Stirrers, a gospel group. Cooke had one chartmaker as a Specialty soloist, but that came after he had left the label and made his mark on another small independent, Keen Records. That story, later.

•

Through the years, Rupe was assisted by several record producers— Bumps Blackwell, Johnny Vincent, and Harold Battiste among them —making it possible for the label to find and record talent "on location" in Dallas, Houston, Shreveport, and Jackson. In addition to its stable of artists who made the charts, Specialty built a rich storehouse of early blues pioneers like Smokey Hogg and urban bluesmen like Roosevelt Sykes, Big Maceo, Joe Turner, and Clifton Chenier.

Specialty continued to flourish into the rock 'n' roll era, scoring with the now-classic recordings of Little Richard. By the end of the '50s, after he lost Sam Cooke (who left The Soul Stirrers to sing pop) and Little Richard, Rupe deactivated the label and adventured instead in the worlds of motion pictures and real estate. The fifties revival brought him back into the record field, but only as a reissuer of recordings that were landmarks of the R & B era and that helped lay the groundwork for the rock revolution.

I flagged a train, didn't have a dime,
Tryin' to run away from that home
of mine.   —MEMPHIS MINNIE

Record Company on a Railroad Track

SITUATED in Los Angeles' Watts district, the two-story red-brick building squats alongside a railroad spur that crosses South Normandie Avenue. A wide stairway takes you from street level up to a long hallway with offices on both sides. The reception room is at the head of the stairs, across the hallway. The pressing plant is underneath, occupying the entire street-level footage of the block-square building. It is here that the Bihari brothers operate Modern Records and its subsidiaries.

Several freight trains stand on the railroad tie. You can imagine some of the down-home bluesmen riding in from Texas or Oklahoma on the "rods" or "blinds"—men like Smokey Hogg, Lightnin' Hopkins, Jimmy McCracklin, Lowell Fulson, and others whose records the Biharis have released. The Biharis themselves came from Oklahoma in 1941; their father was a feed grain farmer and salesman. Still active in the company are three brothers, Jules, Joe, and Lester, and three sisters, Florette, Roz, and Maxene. Saul Bihari, one of the founder brothers, died in February 1975 at the age of fifty-four, three years after a stroke had forced his retirement.

Modern's extensive catalogue, including subsidiary labels like RPM, Kent, Crown, and Flair, runs the gamut from boogie and blues to R & B and R 'n' R. Among its key artists are transitional bluesmen like John Lee Hooker, Pee Wee Crayton, Elmore James, Jimmy

Witherspoon, and Etta James. As Little Richard was Specialty's towering R & B figure, so B. B. King is Modern's.

Joe Bihari, a slim, handsome man who looks much younger than his years, traces the beginnings of the company back to March 1945. *Billboard* announced the event in its issue of April 21, 1945. As Joe told me,

.

"My brother Jules operated jukeboxes in all-black locations, and it was difficult to get R & B records at that time. His feeling of frustration was crystallized by the shortage of one particular record, Cecil Gant's 'I Wonder.' It was a monster. No matter how many copies he got, he still needed more. Finally, one day he said, 'Let's make records ourselves.'

"I was still in high school, Saul was at business college; but we all pitched in. We took the name Modern Music from a Galveston jukebox company where brother Lester was working. I undertook the selling, Saul took charge of manufacturing, and Jules handled the recording. He had been wanting to make records, and I guess the success of that ex-pressing plant worker who recorded 'I Wonder' in his garage gave him the confidence to try it.

"As a matter of fact, he searched out the fellow who produced the Cecil Gant recording. He was a former employee of Allied Record pressing who built a studio in his garage and set up a small pressing plant behind it. Jules was enterprising, and he quickly learned the process of making matrices from a master and the stampers from the matrix. He was soon able to press records himself, and he did so for a time in the early days. It was not too long before our volume required better productivity, and around 1947 we bought a pressing plant from Mercury Records at Robertson and Santa Monica boulevards.

"The first record that Jules cut was just a girl playing the piano and 'Swingin' the Boogie,' as we called it. The girl was Hadda Brooks. Jules got to know her because she ate in a restaurant we owned in the Little Tokyo neighborhood on San Pedro Street. She worked as a rehearsal pianist at a nearby dance studio. Jules had her swing the boogie to the accompaniment of bass and drums. The disk was a hit—and we were in the record business. In those days, a record would last five to six months, and you could sell a hundred thousand without making any kind of splash at all. While there was some airplay, it was the jukeboxes that made a hit—and we got quite a play on them."

.

Lester Sill, now president of Screen-Gems Columbia Music, was a salesman for Modern Records in those days. He recalls,

•

"I covered the territory from Fresno in the north of California way down to San Diego at the Mexican border. When I ran into salesmen of the major companies, they were mystified about where I went and baffled that I sold records. Obviously, you could not sell R & B disks the way that Capitol, RCA, Decca, and Columbia—Mercury was just beginning—merchandised their disks.

"When I went to San Diego, I would arrive on a Sunday, early enough to see the very few disk jockeys who played black records. There were few and they were all white. I remember only Henry Louis, who is today an engineer at A & M Records. San Diego did not have too many platter spinners like Hunter Hancock of KPOP or KDAY of Los Angeles, who loved to spin R & B records. (There were a few dee jays like Gene Norman of KFWB and Frank Bow who played jazz records, but also occasionally programmed an R & B disk. Although Bow was basically a Dixieland buff, he loved Hadda Brooks records. And in LA, in addition to Hunter Hancock, we had Joe Adams, who recently was Ray Charles's manager. On Saturday mornings, Joe would broadcast from Santa Monica with a live, all-black show.)

"The disk jockeys were a pipeline to the jukebox operators; the boxes made the hits. In San Diego, after I saw the dee jays on Sunday, I visited the jukebox ops on Monday and all through the rest of the week. Selling them was easier if I could say, 'Listen to Henry Louis, and you'll hear the new Hadda Brooks, Charles Brown, or Johnny Moore & The Three Blazers.' In addition to the jukebox ops, I made a hundred stops: shoeshine stands, candy stores, Woolworth's, Newberry's. Everybody sold records in those days—there were few record stores as such. And black people, particularly, bought records in the same stores where they bought groceries, furniture or fruit.

"I covered Central Avenue in Los Angeles, which was the main artery of black business and entertainment. It took me five days to visit all the outlets from Washington and Central to 103rd and Central. Except for John Dolphin's, there weren't too many stores that sold just records. Dolphin bought radio time and had a disk jockey working in his store window on Central Avenue.

"Dolphin was, unfortunately, murdered one Saturday morning. He was a music publisher or song broker on the side. A songwriter came in to collect royalties allegedly due him. Dolphin was apparently drunk. There was an argument. And the guy shot him with a 22. It was unpremeditated, and he went up for manslaughter. John Dolphin did a lot for black music. And his gimmick of having a jockey right in his store window was a pattern followed later by other R & B record dealers.

"The radio stations of the day were not too receptive either to the music or the employment of blacks. I remember when Hunter Hancock started his show. He had to buy time himself on the station. Then he walked up and down Central Avenue selling slots to advertisers. There was also Earl McDaniel, who moved to the Hawaiian islands. He didn't concentrate on R & B as Hunter did, but he would play a black record that had a chance of going pop. He was the one who broke 'Loop-the-Loop Mambo' by The Coasters so that white-oriented KFWB began programming it. It went to number one here in LA.

"In '48 to '49 I began to produce records. The Biharis let me cut Hadda, B. B. King, and other artists. Hadda had 'That's My Desire' before Frankie Laine launched his career with a belting R & B version. Hadda could sing pop songs, but she gave them a sultry R & B sound. We sold a lot of her albums—they consisted of three 78s and the worst artwork you ever saw.

"Hadda had a classical background and her first big sellers were classics in boogie. Hazel Scott did the same thing in a more sophisticated style. One of Hadda's biggest sellers was 'Humoresque Boogie.' Then Jules Bihari asked her to sing. She balked at first but then she tried—and she did develop a sound of her own. She had a throaty, gritty voice that had a seductive, after-hours quality. She was an attractive chick. In person, she made guys feel they had a bedroom invitation. She took the Biharis out of the restaurant and jukebox business and put them into the record field."

•

In Joe Bihari's recollection of the postwar years, there were just three record distributors around the country then.

•

"One was Paul Reiner, who went into record-production himself with the Black & White label. There was Jack Gutshall here in LA, who was a jukebox distributor and started a record company. And there was Julius Bard in Chicago. We sold to all of these, and they sold to operators around the country. After a time, my brother Saul made a trip across country and set up independent distributors for us. Naturally, he went to jukebox operators and showed them how they could make money at the distribution end. By then, there were some small companies starting up, like M. S. Distributing in Chicago (Milt Salstone), who became a giant distributor. Joe Kaplan launched Pan American in Detroit. Bill Davis founded Davis Sales in Denver. In San Francisco, there was Melody Sales.

"Around 1948 Saul set up a sales and promo office in New York. Once we had national distribution, we needed more product and we began buying masters. From Herb Rixey and his Blue Bonnet label in Dallas, we got Smokey Hogg's first masters in '48. From Bob Geddins in Oakland, we leased disks by Roy Hawkins and Jimmy McCracklin & His Blues Blasters, who began recording for us in '49. And from Bill Quinn of Gold Star Studio in Houston, we purchased thirty-two Lightnin' Hopkins sides in '51. Except for Hawkins, these were down-home bluesmen who recorded with guitar/piano/drums accompaniment.

"Smokey Hogg, who came from Cushing, Texas, became known as 'Smokey' because of his blurred delivery. We cut many sides with him in '48 and even put him on R & B charts with 'Little School Girl' in '49–'50. He was not an easy man to record because, like most country bluesmen, he sang without a beat. There were constant variations in rhythm even though he recorded with drums—it bothered Hadda Brooks no end when she played piano on one of his sessions. But he had a following among those who loved buzz-tone Texas blues, and he continued making records into the mid-fifties, sometimes for us, sometimes for other LA labels, like Specialty and Imperial.

"Pee Wee Crayton was another Texas bluesman with whom we had at least one best-seller. He came from Austin or Rockdale, and his real name was Connie Curtis Crayton—'Pee Wee' because of his size. He was part of the northwest migration that ended in the Bay Area of San Francisco. He was working in the New Orleans Swing Club when my brother Jules heard him and took him to LA to record for Modern. His brand of blues was quite different from Smokey Hogg's down-home variety. Before he came to us, he cut some records for 4 Star with a typical R & B combo (tenor sax plus rhythm). His blues was mixed with jazz. Although he had learned guitar from Elmore James, the Mississippi bottleneck guitarist (who later became one of our artists), he was influenced by T-Bone Walker. He used some of T-Bone's modern riffs, performing on a custom-made Fender Telecaster. Friends also remember him playing around the Waco and Dallas-Fort Worth area with R & B bands, one of which included avant-garde saxist Ornette Coleman.

"We recorded Pee Wee with saxes right from the start in '49. Before the year was over, he was on the charts with 'I Love You So,' a song written by Paul Gayten, who later worked with Annie Laurie, a Dinah Washington-type singer. Although he continued cutting for us into '51 (when he switched for a single release to Aladdin) and he recorded after that for Imperial, Vee Jay, and John Dolphin's Hollywood Records, 'I Love You So' remained his biggest seller and really his only hit.

"Roy Hawkins also came with us in '49 after we had leased several of his records from Bob Geddins, who lost many of his artists for lack of national distribution. Hawkins was recording with saxes when he cut in Oakland, and he continued in an R & B groove with us. In '50 we had a Top Ten disk with 'Why Do Things Happen to Me?' which he wrote. The following year, he had 'The Thrill Is Gone,' an important song—not that it did too well for him—but because it became a big hit almost twenty years later for B. B. King.

"I guess that the most important bluesman we acquired through leasing or buying masters was John Lee Hooker, who came from the Mississippi Delta but recorded in Detroit. My brother Saul bought several dozen Hooker masters from John Caplan and Bernard Besman, who continued recording him in Detroit and peddling his masters to different companies—King, Regent, Savoy, Sensation, Regal, Chess—frequently under other names."

•

Hooker was a Clarksdale, Mississippi, bluesman (born in 1917), who settled in Detroit in the period when the lure of high wages on the auto makers' assembly lines doubled its population. Hastings Street was the Central or Lenox Avenue of the Motortown, crowded with one bar on top of another and the hangout of bluesmen who drifted in or settled here. Big Maceo camped at Brown's Bar, and there was even an off-beat recording studio in the back of Joe's Record Shop.

Hooker did a few sides in '52–'53 in Philadelphia for the Gotham label (under the pseudonyms of Johnny Williams or John Lee) and in Cincinnati for DeLuxe and Chart; and from '55 to '58 he cut for Vee Jay in Chicago. His major recording, however, took place in Detroit. "Boogie Chillen," cut on his first session in November 1948, was a substantial seller and became a perennial for him. But he made R & B charts for the first time with "Hobo Blues" in May '49, and toward the end of the year scored with "Crawling Kingsnake." His biggest record for Modern came in '51 with "I'm in the Mood," which he wrote and which climbed to No. 2. (His co-writer was the ubiquitous "Jules Taub," one of several company names—the others were Sam Ling and Josea Taub—used by Modern to reduce royalties paid to songwriters and publishers.)

Whether he had a contract or not, Hooker was a freewheeler. "I did some records as Johnny Williams," he told Charlie Gillett. "I did some as Texas Slim. At that time I was hot as a firecracker and they would give me big money to do some material. Use a different name. Money's pretty exciting y'know, so I was Texas Slim for King, John Lee Hooker for Chance and Chess and DeLuxe, and Johnny Williams for Gotham and Staff." Leadbitter and Slaven's discography reveal that he was also Birmingham Sam for Regent and Savoy, The Boogie Man for Acorn, John Lee Booker for Chance, Johnny Lee for DeLuxe, and John Lee for Gotham.

Hooker is unquestionably one of the most-recorded bluesmen of the World War I generation, outnumbered only possibly by Lightnin' John Hopkins. Unlike most of the delta and many of the Texas bluesmen, he developed a style that involved a steady dance beat—boogie, of course—and showmanship. None of his songs ends abruptly or dribbles off. They fade gently or terminate with some clanging guitar chord. Hooker works at setting and maintaining a mood, and this is another respect in which he differs from other down-home bluesmen.

A superlative guitarist, he uses his instrument not only to maintain the beat, but also to respond, comment, and enhance the mood he seeks to establish. His songs have a fragmentary quality. They frequently begin with a statement like "Don't leave me baby/ Because I need you." Then working against a steady boogie beat of sixteenths and dotted eighth notes, he unfolds the story through repetition, not of the entire statement, but of fragments of it. He has a good singing voice, but he talks his lines, occasionally recalling Josh White.

"Fancy chords don't mean nothin'," he says, in a song entitled "Teaching the blues." "Throw the fancy chords away. . . . Get this beat . . . this slow beat . . . this big beat. . . ." An after-hours, moody bluesman par excellence, Hooker has more than 400 released sides.

•

"In 1948 we also started making field trips," Joe Bihari continued. "If I'm not mistaken, I went down to Atlanta early in 1948 and did about eight sides with Pinetop Slim. The following year, I took a swing from Chicago down to Kansas City and later, in '51 and '52, made some trips through the Mississippi Delta. I generally lugged my own equipment, a Magnecord, and I would rent an empty store or garage to record. But I recorded Elmore James, who came from

Mississippi, in Chicago at Bill Putnam's Universal Studio. His first sides came out on Meteor, a label started by brother Lester on his own in Memphis. (Lester also operated as our scout in the area.) After that first session, we released James on Flair, a new label we launched around '54. Modern and RPM, which we started around '50, had such a flow of releases that we had to diversify not to gum up our distribution. James then began calling himself Elmore James & His Broomdusters—after 'Dust My Broom,' the famous Robert Johnson blues, the first number he ever recorded while he was still in Mississippi. He played bottleneck guitar and was really a wailer with a very intense delivery. That first session I did with him in Chicago yielded 'I Believe (My Time Ain't Long),' which was, perhaps, his biggest number."

•

Elmore James was born in the Mississippi Delta—in Canton in 1918—and settled in Chicago in 1953, not long after he had cut his first sides on Trumpet Records, a Jackson, Mississippi, label owned by Mrs. Lillian McMurray. In the Windy City, he became part of the electric blues crowd that included Muddy Waters and Howlin' Wolf, and that cultivated a tough shout style necessary to command audience attention in a rowdy bar like the Tay May Club.

Before he moved to Chicago, James gigged frequently with Willie Rice Miller (the second Sonny Boy Williamson), who played on his Trumpet disk of "Dust My Broom" and on whose radio program out of West Helena, Arkansas, James appeared frequently. James himself served as a disk jockey on Station WOKJ in Jackson, Mississippi, and operated a radio shop for a time. Deeply influenced by pioneer blues-man Robert Johnson, he used Johnson's walking boogie bass in much of his work. Even though he remained a jangling, bottleneck guitarist, he quickly adapted to the musical demands of the Chicago scene, working with an electric bass and horns, and adhering to a danceable beat.

Although he did most of his Chicago recording for the Biharis (1953–57), he also cut sides for Chief, Vee Jay, Checker, and Fire. In the latter '50s, he used guitarist Homesick James on most of his sessions. By then his emphasis on traditional blues subjects—deceiving women, economic worries, emotional wounds, and a blues world— was considered old hat by a younger and more militant crowd of record buyers. He was able to secure releases only on lesser "indie" labels like Bobbie Robinson's Fire, Enjoy, and Fury Records, cutting in NYC as well as Jackson, Mississippi. He died in Chicago in 1963.

James left his mark on a generation of young Chicago guitarists, including Buddy Guy and J.B. Hutto & His Hawks. "I was just a kid," Hutto told journalist-author Bruce Cook. "But I'd sneak into places like Sylvio's [in Chicago]. I remember one night I had a long talk with old Memphis Slim and that got me decided that playing the blues was what I wanted to do. So I took up the drums, and I fooled around with that until one night I heard Elmore James. He was just getting started and he was real heavy. He played it different from anybody. Old bottleneck guitar had died out by then. And Elmore was the first I ever heard go at an electric guitar with a bar. Well, I never heard anything like that before. So I got me a guitar and a piece of pipe, and I went to work with the two of them."

Ike and Tina Turner

When B. B. King is asked about the guitarists who impressed him most during his formative years, he names three: T-Bone Walker, Frenchman Django Reinhardt, and Elmore James.

•

"Operating out of Memphis, brother Lester hired young Ike Turner as our talent scout," said Joe Bihari.

•

"Ike wasn't more than sixteen then. He would send dubs of things he cut to us, and if we liked them we'd make a deal or sign the artist. That's how we acquired B. B. King. We had Bobby 'Blue' Bland before he went to Duke Records, also Johnny Ace, who played piano in

B. B. King's band. Through Lester, we made a deal with Sam Phillips, who built the Sun studio around 1950 but was using it to produce masters for other companies. We released Howlin' Wolf before litigation about his contract gave him to Chess.

"B. B. King had his first chartmaker, 'Three O'Clock Blues,' late in 1951, helping us to establish our RPM subsidiary on a firm foundation. But before that we had chartmakers with Jimmy Witherspoon, who sang with Jay McShann; with Little Willie Littlefield, a Texas bluesman, on 'It's Midnight'; with Helen Humes, who sang with Count Basie and sold big on 'One-Million-Dollar Secret'; and with Jimmy Nelson, who had a moment in the limelight with '99 Blues.'

"Most of the artists came into the studio with their own material, usually things they wrote or picked up. The only thing we might have done—they might not have constructed the tune properly—we'd change certain lyrics. On some songs, they had them in their head, but couldn't quite get it together, and there was help. We worked with artists in recording sessions. We rehearsed with them and changed things. You might notice the name of Jules Taub on some songs. That was a pseudonym for Jules Bihari, who worked with the artists. To copyright the songs, we generally had to have them taken off the disks by an arranger."

⋅

Jules Bihari described his recording technique in *Blues Unlimited* as follows: "I don't think you have to be a genius to record blues. All you have to do is stick a microphone out there and let them play. The thing about it is, in recording a blues singer, if you try to be a producer like quite a few people are, as soon as they sing four bars and make a mistake, or if you don't like the way the engineer is changing the dial, or something like that, you stop. This way you may lose the whole effect. I believe in recording a blues singer: you sit him down, let him sing, and regardless of the mistakes he makes, let him finish out his song. Then do it over until you capture one little thing in that record."

⋅

"Spoon," as Jimmy Witherspoon is known, came from Gurdon, Arkansas (where he was born in 1923 or 1924), and the choir of Gurdon's Baptist church. After spending the war years in the Merchant Marine, during which time he became enamored of the sounds and styles of Jimmy Rushing and Joe Turner, he joined Jay McShann's Kansas City band. Over a period of several years, while he occupied the chair that was long Walter Brown's, he practiced adding jazz rhythms to gospel inflections. When he stepped out to record on his own for Supreme Records, he possessed a warm, swinging style that instantly won him a wide following.

"Ain't Nobody's Business," one of the most-recorded blues and later Billie Holiday's signature, was a winner for him. In 1949 his disk was No. 1 on R & B charts, racking up a record for remaining a best-seller over a period of almost nine months. It holds the record as the longest-lived of all R & B chartmakers between 1949 and 1971. The follow-up on Supreme, a version of Leroy Carr's "In the Evening When the Sun Goes Down," did not do nearly as well, but it, too, was a chartmaker. That same year, 1949, "Spoon" produced two other chart records, but they were on Modern. "No Rollin' Blues" and "Big Fine Girl" were back-to-back, with one side making the charts a week before the other. The sides were apparently recorded at a Gene Norman "Just Jazz" concert, with backing by Gene Gilbeaux's bop-inflected quartet. Jimmy came up with another chart record for Modern in '52 with "The Wind Is Blowin'."

"Spoon" has a big, heady voice in the swinging tradition of Jimmy Rushing and Joe Turner (to whom he has paid tribute in recordings of "Piney Brown" and "Wee Baby Blues"). But he uses his pipes with taste and the soulful feeling of a Ray Charles, probably as a result of his early church experience. Unlike Joe Turner, Witherspoon could not make the transition to rock 'n' roll, and he lingered instead for years in the shadows of the chitlin' circuit. In 1959, however, an appearance at the Monterey Jazz Festival reawakened record people to his capacious talents, and he proceeded to make jazz-oriented albums for Atlantic (with Wilbur De Paris) and Verve.

·

In Joe Bihari's recollection, B. B. King's first hit, "Three O'Clock Blues," was recorded at the Memphis YMCA on a portable recorder. "They had a large room," he told me, "with an out-of-tune upright piano. At that session, we cut Johnny Ace, Roscoe Gordon, and Bobby Bland—possibly also Ike Turner. By then we were recording on tape, not disk. Apart from B. B.'s debut hit, we got 'No More Doggin'' by Roscoe Gordon, which came onto best-seller lists just as 'Three O'Clock Blues' was beginning to fade.

" 'You Know I Love You,' B. B.'s next smash, was recorded at a music teacher's house in Memphis. His name was Tuff Green, he played bass, and he was on the very first record B. B. ever made, for Bullet. Ike Turner played piano.

"When B. B. was playing in Houston the following year, we went down and recorded 'Please Love Me.' We used the A.C.A. Studio and a band led by tenorman Bill Harvey. The drummer was a Conga man. 'Woke up This Morning,' also on the R & B charts in '53, was done on this date."

•

B. B. King went on to become one of the most consistent sellers of any R & B artist. An examination of *Billboard*'s R & B chart yields the following statistics: two on the charts in '54; three in '55; three in '56; one in '57; two in '58; four in '60; two in '61; two in '62; one in '65; two in '66; two in '67; and one in '68. B. B.'s string of hits continued into the late '60s after he switched to Bluesway Records and in the '70s after he moved to the ABC label.

The advent of Elvis Presley and the rise of rock 'n' roll in '56 motivated the Biharis to turn away from singles to LPs; Crown Records became the main album outlet. About that time Kent Records became the company's singles label and B. B., who had been on RPM, appeared on Kent after 1957. In 1961 B. B. secured a release from his contract, but only after he had cut so many masters that Kent was able to release B.B. King sides as late as 1970–71. In '70 Kent had a modest chart record in "Worried Life" by King and, in '71, "That Evil Child." A $2-million lawsuit, brought by King against the Biharis for unpaid royalties, will, perhaps, have been settled by the time this book is in print.

B. B. was born Riley B. King in Indianola, Mississippi, in 1925. (He became B. B. King after he billed himself as the "Beale Street Blues Boy" when he was disk jockeying on Memphis Station WDIA.) He started toying with the guitar when a sanctified preacher brought the instrument to his aunt's home. He had to sneak practice sessions while the adults were occupied. In this period, he was digging country bluesmen like Blind Lemon, the original Sonny Boy Williamson, and his cousin Bukka White. But the people who influenced him were more modern bluesmen like T-Bone Walker, Lowell Fulson, and Johnny Moore & The Three Blazers.

He adds: "Then, I was somewhat jazz-minded, too. . . . I was crazy about Charlie Christian and one of my favorites, real favorites, was Django Reinhardt." He heard Christian with Benny Goodman at ten cent movies. Basie was a favorite because he liked Jimmy Rushing; and he listened to Duke Ellington, digging him "because a lot of times he had people like Al Hibbler."

B. B. is that rarity in the arts, a self-taught primitive who possesses a discriminating ear for new sounds and who has grown. In truth, he has never stopped growing or seeking new musical worlds to conquer, but he integrates what he learns into the framework of his basic orientation as a bluesman.

In a visit I paid to his suite at the Las Vegas Hilton—it was then still known as The International—I found him immersed in a rather demanding book on composition. It was a volume of *The Schillinger System of Musical Composition*, a mathematical approach to the art

B. B. King

and as remote as one could imagine from the horizons of a Mississippi bluesman. For a moment, I thought that B. B. was trying to be friendly since I was co-editor of the two hefty volumes, but I quickly discovered that he was unaware of my connection with the work. Somewhere in his peregrinations, he had met a musician who told him of the *System* and of disciples that included a generation of swing arrangers, Hollywood film composers, and, most notably, George Gershwin. B. B. bought the books and spends spare hours studying them.

In his early days and for many years after he developed a following in America's black ghettos, he was (to use his words) "well, a little bit, well not actually ashamed. But I was almost afraid to say that I was a blues singer." That changed with the rise of rock 'n' roll and, most dramatically, after The Rolling Stones, The Beatles, and other British rock groups came to this country. "I'm not speaking racially," King told Ralph Gleason. "I'm just talking about when people as a whole just wouldn't accept us, in some of the places the door's now open for me to go into. People like Mike Bloomfield, Elvis Presley, The Beatles, Fats Domino—and people like that helped us quite a bit."

And since the R & B revival of the late '60s, he feels that he is in a position to realize his yearning "for the *whole world* to be able to hear B. B. King sing and play the blues." His audience has continued to grow as a result of a coast-to-coast tour with The Rolling Stones, appearances on network television, and regular bookings in Las Vegas. In the 1970s he has had record hits in "The Thrill Is Gone" and "To Know You Is to Love You."

The significant fact is that B. B. has not accommodated his work to audience tastes, but has compelled audiences to come to him. He is still "twinging" Lucille, as he calls his guitar. ("Twinging" is B. B.'s onomatopoeic word for the cry-and-whine sound of his guitar. Lucille acquired her name years ago when she was almost destroyed in a club during a fight between two boozers over a girl called Lucille.) As a masterful blues guitarist, B. B. still uses her as a seething, responsorial voice. He still begins every show with Memphis Slim's song "Every Day I Have the Blues," and his programs include songs like Joe Turner's "Sweet Sixteen" and Richard Nighthawk's "Sweet Little Angel." As he performs, he closes his eyes frequently and screws up his face in an expression of intense pain. It is an expressive face of the blues, but it is electric blues with a beat—R & B.

From a technical standpoint, B. B. is today at the other end of the blues spectrum from the Chicago blues of Muddy Waters and Howlin'

Wolf. Although he came with them from the Mississippi Delta, the influence of jazz-oriented bluesmen like T-Bone Walker and Lonnie Johnson moved him in a fresh, advanced harmonic and melodic direction. Ninth chords are a staple of B. B.'s style instead of minor (blue) notes played against major chords (I,IV,V), as in delta or country blues. King uses single-string runs and jazz-blues riffs, making the instrument less percussive and more melodic. Instead of pushing the strings and producing a raw, distorted, sharp-flat tone, he employs *vibrato* to sound precise, clear, ringing notes. His vocal style also contrasts with that of the Chicagoans. Like most jazz singers, he sings behind and over the beat. He seldom talks the lyrics; singing more, he "worries" the words more. And he uses *vibrato* extensively to achieve a mellow tone. In short, B. B.'s style is more musical and more polished, whereas Muddy and the Wolf project power, energy and excitement. It is the difference, perhaps, between performing with a band in a concert hall or a Vegas showroom rather than with a combo in a noisy South or West Side Chicago bar.

•

During the transition years, 1954–56, when white artists were ripping off R & B records, the Biharis fared better, perhaps, than some of their competitors. Shirley Gunter & The Queens had been on the charts for only one week in October '54 with "Oop Shoop" when The Crew Cuts, who had done the same thing to black groups on Savoy and Atlantic, covered their record and took the song away from them. Whatever the Biharis lost in revenue on the Shirley Gunter disk was recouped from publisher royalties they collected on The Crew Cuts disk.

On the other hand, The Teen Queens (Betty and Rosie Collins) more than held their own on the Bihari's RPM label against Dot's Fontane Sisters' version of "Eddie, My Love." The Teen Queens disk not only remained on R & B charts for three months of 1956; it crossed over into pop.

The Biharis also attempted to reverse the cover syndrome with two black groups, The Cadets and The Jacks. The two were identical in personnel, except that the addition of a fifth voice to The Jacks helped produce a different sound. Recording on Modern, The Cadets covered R & B disks like Nappy Brown's "Don't Be Angry" on Savoy, The Marigolds' "Rollin' Stone" on Excello, and The Willows' "Church Bells May Ring" on Melba. And in '56, they produced a chartmaker in "Stranded in the Jungle," taking it away from The Jayhawks on Flash. The Jacks (on RPM) had fewer releases. They did "Smack

Dab in the Middle," a number that Joe Williams popularized with Count Basie's band. It was on the other side of "Why Don't You Write Me?" which The Jacks took away from a group called The Feathers in '55.

•

In 1955, too, the Biharis recorded young Etta James on Modern. "The Wallflower" was conceived by Johnny Otis, who arranged the session, as an answer to "Work with Me, Annie," a giant hit for The Midnighters on King. Soon after Etta's disk made R & B charts in February 1955, A & R directors Hugo and Luigi rushed Georgia Gibbs into a Mercury studio and came out with "Dance with Me, Henry," "The Wallflower" under another name. It finished as one of the smash pop hits of the year. Although Etta and the Biharis lost record sales, they shared in the writer-publisher royalties on the song. Royalties on the million-copy Gibbs disk were split as follows: Etta, Johnny Otis, and Hank Ballard (as the original writer of the song) divided the writer royalty while King Records' Lois Publishing Company, as publishers of "Work with Me, Annie," and Modern Music Publishing, as publishers of "The Wallflower," divided the publisher royalty.

There are two versions of how Johnny Otis found Etta James, who became one of the towering females of R & B, along with Dinah Washington, Esther Phillips, and Ruth Brown. One oft-repeated story has it that he heard her in an LA club where she was working with a group called The Peaches. Johnny claims that when he was appearing at the Fillmore in San Francisco—it was then still a black ghetto auditorium—she came to his hotel and insisted on auditioning for him. In either case, Johnny decided to do a date with her and recorded "The Wallflower," which they wrote together, in Modern's Culver City studios. Incidentally, "The Wallflower" was originally titled "Roll with Me, Henry," since it was an answer to "Work with Me, Annie," but the Biharis thought the title too suggestive.

Shortly after the success of "The Wallflower"—it reached No. 2 on the charts—Etta went on tour with Little Richard. "I was so naive in those days," she recalled recently. "Richard and the band were always having those parties. I'd knock on the door and try to get in, and they'd say, 'Don't open it! She's a minor!' Then one day I climbed up on a transom and looked in, and the things that I saaaw. . . ."

It was not only the things that she saw, but some of the things she experienced that soon had young Etta involved in a very expensive habit. After two best-sellers in '55—"Good Rockin' Daddy" and "The Wallflower"—there were no records for five years. In 1960

Etta pulled herself together and began recording again, this time on the Argo label, a subsidiary of Chess.

And there was a waiting audience. During '60, '61, and '62, Etta was seldom without chartmakers. Among the many best-sellers she produced—ballads like "All I Could Do Was Cry" and "At Last"— the biggest was "Something's Got a Hold on Me." And something had. Again, there were four years of record silence. In '67 Etta returned again, that time on the Bihari's Cadet label. Again she had chart-makers—"Tell Mama" among others—and again there was a hiatus.

When Etta reappeared on wax in 1973, it was on Chess. Setting aside the stridency and little-girl pouting of her early hits, she chanted and cried and pleaded as the unabashed gospel shouter she had been as a youngster in the choir of LA's St. Paul Baptist Church. She was closer to Aretha Franklin than Dinah Washington, though there were echoes of both in her delivery. A portion of the proceeds from her '73 album went to the maintenance of methadone programs in Los Angeles and New York.

•

Jesse Belvin's days on Modern were as short as his life, but he struck pay dirt with his first recording, "Goodnight, My Love." It was not only an R & B best-seller in 1956, but was adopted by super-dee jay Alan Freed as the closing theme of his program. Before he had a hit on his own, Belvin co-authored one of the great rock 'n' roll hits, "Earth Angel," the song that established The Penguins.

Born in Texarkana, Arkansas, in December 1933, he settled in LA at the age of five and sang in his mother's church choir at seven. At sixteen, he joined Big Jay McNeely's band and participated in his first record session. In '53 he went into the army. The following year, he wrote "Earth Angel" with two army buddies. His Modern record hit so impressed Alan Freed that the WINS disk jockey arranged for him to come east. By '58 he was signed by RCA Victor, where there were visions of transforming him into a great black balladeer à la Billy Eckstine or Nat "King" Cole. Belvin was in a line of black ballad singers that went back to Leroy Carr and Charles Brown, and stretched through Ivory Joe Hunter, Cecil Gant, and Percy Mayfield to Sam Cooke—warm, tender, tasteful singers who delivered with great inner intensity. He was on the way in 1959 with hits like "Funny" and the longer-lived "Guess Who," the latter written by his wife JoAnn, when he was killed in a car crash on February 6, 1960. He was just twenty-six years old.

•

Modern Records drew its releases from so many disparate sources that its large catalogue runs the gamut from ethnic rural blues to rock 'n' roll. Today, in 1978, it remains one of the very few companies of the R & B era that not only continues in business but, like Specialty, is still owned and operated by the original founders. This is not true of Chess, Atlantic, Peacock, King and Savoy, other R & B giants. Although Saul Bihari, who spearheaded the establishment of Modern, is gone, other members of the Bihari family remain active.

groove 8   **JIMMY WITHERSPOON**

Jimmy Witherspoon is a big bear of a man, friendly and outgoing, with a bushy, walrus moustache, thick eyebrows, and brown eyes that can narrow to probing slits. He was appearing in Las Vegas on a bill with The Average White Band when I talked with him.

"I joined Jay McShann's band in Vallejo, California, around 1944. I just got out of the merchant marine, and Walter Brown had just left the band. I was wearing a Lieutenant junior-grade uniform. I was a chief cook and steward in the merchant marine, but I looked like a Japanese admiral with my braids and all. That time, they wouldn't let too many blacks do anything in the navy. I was just a cook and steward.

"No, I wasn't singing in the navy. But when I was in Calcutta, India, I ran into Teddy Weatherford, the great pianist from Chicago. He had this big band with Burmese and English musicians. They were playing Benny Goodman's 'Why Don't You Do Right?' So I walked up and sang with them.

"On my return I settled in San Francisco. My mother lived there. Weekends I worked in a club in Vallejo called The Waterfront. I had a day-job as a boiler in a shipyard. This stuff has never come out in my bios. I was burning steel to make the plates that go into bulkheads. I did this until I joined McShann, who had the greatest blues band. I received the best schooling in the world.

"Did I know Johnny Otis? Did you read his bio *Listen to the Lambs*? I'm the one who discovered him. I know he was born in Vallejo, but I didn't find him there. It was in Omaha, Nebraska. I used to sing in a place called The Blue Room. Johnny Otis was the drummer. I was always going around with musicians in Los Angeles. Harlan Leonard, who had a great band out of Kansas City, was playing at the Club Alabam, and Jessie Price was his drummer. When Jessie was leaving to go into the service, I told Leonard about Johnny Otis: 'He's a white cat who's passing for black—and a great drummer.' Harlan said that Jesse had told him about Otis too, and asked me to tell Johnny to come on out. That's how he got to Los Angeles.

"I stayed with Jay McShann about four years, singing all of Walter Brown's blues. Jay McShann told me, 'Spoon, they know me by "Confessin' the Blues," so you sing it with Brown's sound, but the rest, you go your own way.' He recorded 'Ain't Nobody's Business' with me. And that's something bandleaders wouldn't do for their vocalists at that time. That was my big one. Jay McShann is playing piano; his brother, Pete McShann, was the drummer on the date.

"I ran into Jimmy Rushing and Joe Turner in LA. At that time, I was working in the Owl drugstore washing dishes. I used to hang out at Lovejoy's Breakfast Club. Art Tatum used to come in, Joe Turner, Slam Stewart. It was an after-hours joint. I sat there all night. Then I'd have to go and wash dishes all day at the Owl drugstore— on Eighth and Broadway. I was making seventeen dollars a week, sixteen sixty-two after tax. And they all thought I was a musician.

"T-Bone was working in Little Harlem. He was the first artist, asked me to come up and sing. I always wanted to be a singer. At that theater where they did the broadcasts, they'd ask you to sing—pretend that they'd pick you out of the audience. But they didn't. You had to audition and rehearse.

"I have no musical training, but I did sing in the church choir in Gurdon, Arkansas, when I was a kid. I still sing in church when I visit with friends and go to services with them.

"I liked Jimmy Rushing, but Joe Turner was my idol. I knew him from 'Wee Baby Blues.' Then I saw him at the Mayan Theatre in LA with Duke Ellington in *Jump for Joy*. That just did it for me. He's a blues singer! Before that, I didn't dig the blues because I'd been told that it was a dirty word. You couldn't sing in church and sing the blues. That's the way it was at that time, but no more. The ministers look at it different. It's an American art now. [Chuckling]

"Walter Brown made the first records with Jay McShann. But I'm on all the Aladdin Records he cut—'Ernestine Blues' and others. We did some on Premier Records, too. That was the beginning of Mercury Records. Berle Adams was running it. We cut those in St. Louis. We cut 'Hard Working Man Blues' on Philo, which later became Aladdin.

"The first records I made on my own were on Supreme, including my biggest, 'Ain't Nobody's Business.' The label was owned by a dentist named Al Patrick. God Bless him—he just died about six months ago. I don't know why I should be blessing him; he never did pay me no royalties. But I'm that much human, I hope.

"You know a lot of artists, especially young artists, are always complaining about who's gonna rip them off. And I tell them this: I got ripped off. But first you got to be known. They're taking a chance when they record you, too. So what you gonna do is give me a name, which I would have never had without them recording me. Like 'Ain't Nobody's Business' did it for me. The Los Angeles *Times* ran a survey, showed it still holds the record in rhythm and blues: on the charts for thirty-four consecutive weeks. The only record that comes close is Paul Williams's 'Hucklebuck.'

"But I didn't get one penny royalty. Patrick paid me a flat fee for the session. I was supposed to get so much on each record sold, which he never paid me. So he had arrangements all made up for me to record. He had an interesting writer by the name of Percy Mayfield to write the tunes. They had the session all set and everything. So I pull rank on him—'Not until you pay me some money,' I says. What happened was that when I didn't show up that night, he let Percy Mayfield sing in order to save the session. And that's what started Percy singing 'Please Send Me Someone to Love.' That was supposed to have been my tune. The date was at Radio Recorders on Santa Monica Boulevard.

"After Supreme and Philo Records, I met Jules Bihari. Joe Bihari was just a kid. Jules was a jukebox repairman. He made that company, gave his whole family jobs—I love him. He did give me more money than anybody else. The time I had 'Big Fine Girl' and 'No Rollin' Blues,' back-to-back, he had a standing thing; that was a thousand dollars a month, that I received, like a royalty. I take that back—he did give me money for about a year. But you must remember, at that time they wasn't getting much for records either . . . seventy-nine cents and sixty-nine cents and fifty-nine cents. And what Bihari gave me wasn't bad at all.

•

"Tell you something that people forget to write about. They all talk about the blues singers—Kansas City, New Orleans, Texas— but most of your blues singers were recorded in Los Angeles because this is where all the independent companies were. And the big majors wouldn't record no blues singers. So the independent companies really came through—Roy Brown, Amos Milburn, Charles Brown, Roy Milton, Lightnin' Hopkins, John Lee Hooker, Johnny Otis. Modern Records discovered all of these. Mercy Dee. Jules Bihari discovered more blues singers, Modern Records discovered more blues singers than any other record company in history, including Lomax.

"Lomax's a phony—and quote me—for going to the prisons, recording these men, and not giving them one penny. On these things, you see Lomax as the writer. The prisoners wrote these tunes. Although they say, he preserved the history. Hell, I'm the one who preserved the history. I'm a living legend, so I don't need Lomax to rip nobody up. He did it for himself. Look at the royalties. [Chuckling]

"I just played the Smithsonian Institute [sic] in Washington, D.C. I sang all the old blues: 'Trouble in Mind,' 'See See Rider,' others. A great feeling!

"Before I went with Jay McShann, I was singing for black people. That's how I found a lot of the songs. A lot of them was putting down the blues. Blacks was trying to lose their identity, and rightfully so. Now I can see what they were trying to do, including my mother. They wanted us to be just like the white kids, and they had been taught that blues was a dirty word. I learned the blues from singers like Joe Turner. Didn't hear them on the radio or on a record player. The jukebox brought it to us.

"I was singing a tune the other night, along with the band. The cats thought I was making it up. But this is old blues, years ago, in the twenties or the thirties. Tell you who wrote it: Dr. Clayton. People thought I was making up something to feel good, except some of the older ones who had heard it. But we heard all these old tunes on the jukebox. Bumble Bee Slim, Tampa Red—they were all on the jukeboxes in the black area, not on the radio. Hell, no.

"I saw this transition. I was in Houston, Texas, when Little Richard came along with 'Long, Tall Sally.' The blacks was starting a thing in America for equality. The radio stations and the people in the South was fighting us. And they were hiring program directors to program the tunes, to let the white kids hear what they wanted them to hear. They banned Little Richard's tune in Houston. Who comes off television with Tommy Dorsey but Elvis Presley—shakin' and twistin'. And how are you gonna stop RCA Victor and NBC? Elvis Presley— I give him credit for opening up more doors for black artists.

"Can you believe that Mike Douglas was using stars from Leonard Chess's label when he first started? Then he got very middle class. Of course, that's what you do when you get rich. That's what I'm gonna do—I'm gonna get middle class and wear polyester suits.

"You don't have no place in America where you can hear the blues today. It's a shame. But back in the forties and fifties, in Nashville, Tennessee, there was Randy's Record Shop on the radio. He used to play all R & B. Somebody should protest. I'm gonna protest because I happen to know the head of the FCC right now. I did the Black Caucus thing, you know. I think all American music should be heard daily on all the radio stations.

"And now I'm doing a Saturday night show from twelve to three A.M. I'm playing everybody in blues. Also Ben Webster, Art Tatum, but mostly blues. And I've learned more about blues since I have this show than I ever knew before. I never knew Mercy Dee, one of the greatest blues singers of all time. [Born in Waco, Texas, he recorded sides on Spire, Imperial, Bayou, Colony, Specialty and Rhythm from '49 to '55.] I didn't really get hip to Lightnin' Hopkins till I got my show. That man was a giant.

"Bo Diddley—I think he can't sing the blues. I'll tell you what he did do. He created a rhythmic thing. I remember I was in Chicago the first week his record came out. 'Man,' I said, 'there's this cat on Chess Records that's doing a rhythmic thing, and he created something.' But vocalwise—you know. . . .

"Chuck Berry is a country singer. People put everybody in categories, black, white, this. Now, if Chuck Berry was white, with the lyrics he writes, he would be the top country star in the world! And the way he sing it!

"Let's get back to this stereotype thing. Like rhythm and blues. That only started because blacks were doing it. Then there was Rock 'n' Roll—that was when Elvis Presley started. That changed the whole thing to denote white and black. They call me an R & B singer. I'm a singer! I can sing ballads; I can sing church; I can sing Dixieland. It's true I'm not doing many ballads—like the things I did in Sweden with Benny Golson. They were all right, but it wasn't me. I'm a blues singer—and a prophet—philosopher, rather.

"The manager I got right now—somebody told him about me. He subsidized me for three years. He wouldn't even let me record, wouldn't let me do nothing but play the right places. I had the talent; but you have to have some money, and sincerity behind you, too, which I never had in my career. Steve Gold is forty-six years old. He's been a CPA, an executive with Warner Brothers. And he dug me. He flew in the other night to see me here in Vegas. That's the first man who really cared about my career—I mean *cared*. I'm not jiving. We fight. I fight with my old lady, but I love her. [Laughing] That doesn't alter the fact that we disagree. But I've had nobody in my o dig me like Steve Gold has. And it can't be for monetary 'cause a cat my age . . . I hope he makes it back. [Chuckling] e also said, like you, that he was investing in a gilt-edged bond. making me blush. You can't see the blood running through my veins, but I am blushing.

"I love T-Bone. He's on my album. He did his theme and I sung it. 'Evening . . . every night you come and you find me. . . .' I was at his funeral, biggest funeral I ever seen in my life. The man was loved by everybody. He'd give you the shirt off his back—he would do it physically, I don't mean just figuratively speaking. He was a sick man—he's been a sick man for the last twenty-four years. And he was a decent man. He didn't want nobody to know it; he didn't bug his wife, his kids.

"I want you to hear this pathetic thing. He did this album with Leiber and Stoller. (They wrote for me when they were in high school, for Modern Records.) When he passed, I talked with his wife. 'I want to ask you something personal,' I said. 'It's a damn shame a man had to sing when he was sick.' I could tell. She said, 'You right. He could hardly make it when he went in and did the album.' I'll probably do the same thing. I mean, I could tell on the album that this man was so ill. Great album! It's a double album, called something like *T-Bone Steak*. Get it!"

groove 9   **B. B. KING**

His valet opened the door when I rang the bell of Suite 2149–50 at the Las Vegas Hilton. There were two bells, in fact, one on each side of the corridor, and you went through double doors into an entry hall with a large bedroom on each side. The curtains and venetian blinds of the valet's room were closed, shutting out the bright, two-o'clock, desert sunlight. I sat down at a round dine-and-work table on which lay a pile of small objects—keys, coins, etc.—that had been removed from pants pockets before retiring. After a while, I heard a door open, footsteps through the entry hall, and B. B. King entered the room. He had put on some weight since my last visit with him, about a year earlier. His voice had the chestiness of a man who had just arisen, but he looked wide awake, and except for an occasional get-up yawn and eye-rub, he was quite alert.

•

"This list of recordings," he said, as he glanced at a listing of his disks in *Those Oldies But Goodies*, "is not complete. I did four sides, not two, on my first date. It was for Bullet, a Tennessee company. But in addition to 'Miss Martha King' and 'Got the Blues,' I did 'Take a Swing with Me' and 'How Do You Feel When Your Baby Packs up to Go?' Bullet was in Nashville, and I was a disk jockey in Memphis at that time. Wantin' to record, I talked with my bosses at radio Station WDIA and they made the contact for me. We recorded the four sides in the studio of WDIA. On my first session, I had tenor sax, trombone, trumpet—Ben Branch on tenor, his brother Thomas on trumpet, and a girl on trombone. It was Tuff Green's band, and he was on bass. Phineas Newborn played the piano. It was his first date, and we had to get union permission because he was too young to have a union card. We called him 'Finas,' which is his name—and they changed it in later years to Phineas. We had his father, Phineas, Sr., playing drums and his brother, Calvin Newborn, playing guitar. We didn't have charts, but I had an idea of what I wanted. Then Ben Branch, who was like a conductor, got with Tuff Green, and we had a head thing going.

"Ike Turner did not have anything to do with my first date for RPM, but later we did some things together. Ike had been playing with Robert Nighthawk and people like that around Clarksdale, Mississippi. He was a great pianist. (I still like his piano playing.) Later he played with Howlin' Wolf—did his first sides, I believe, around Memphis. And he did some things with us some, and cut with Kent Records, another Bihari label. But I was with them before Ike became their Memphis talent scout. I used Tuff Green's band again when I made my first sides for RPM around 1950. Finas Newborn was on 'B. B. Boogie' and 'Mistreated Woman'—those were my first cuts for RPM.

"When I was growing up around Itta Bena, Mississippi, and Indianola, I sang in the church choir. My folks split up before I started school, and my ma died when I was nine. I went to church with her a lot, but after she died I became a tenant farmer. Yes, at nine, and with all the chores, planting and hoeing and picking cotton, I did not have much time for school or church. But I was listening to records. I was crazy about Blind Lemon Jefferson. Also, I liked Lonnie Johnson. I still have records of both that I listen to quite often. I also liked jazz—Charlie Christian and Django Reinhardt.

"I got to hearing Django through a friend who was in the service and was stationed in France. I got started playing guitar when I was

B. B. King

about fourteen after an uncle in Indianola taught me the basic chords. When that friend came back from France on furlough in '44, he brought back some records by Django. And it was about the same time that I started listening to Charlie Christian. Later, when my friend was mustered out of the army, he brought me some recordings put out by the Hot Club of France.

"It is true that I did not begin playing the blues until I myself went into the army. I played mostly spirituals and sang songs I heard in church. I was not trying to make a living with the guitar, and I was performing the things that my family, aunts, and uncles, and their friends were familiar with. People of the Sanctified Church thought of the blues as devil songs. But I was listening to the blues from the time I guess I was seven or eight years old. But I didn't really start trying to play the blues until I was old enough to go into the service. My buddies were not interested in spirituals. When I came back home, I still would not play blues around the house. I used to go off weekends to neighboring towns and play blues on street corners. Made more money that way than I could collect in a week of picking cotton.

"Of course, all of us who lived in the delta and played guitar would, as we would say it, fiddle around with a bluesy tune, just for amusement. Even now, if you went around the delta, you would find many homes with an old piece of guitar. That was about the only instrument that most of them could afford. That and a harmonica. But the 'harp' was so small, it would not be around very long. But you could find an old guitar, usually with strings broken, tied back together and with a clamp that would be between the knot and the body of the guitar. Sometimes there would even be pieces of wire that you tied onto the string to hold it together. The sound of one of those old guitars is fantastic. You just can't reproduce it—the sound that you'd get with one of those instruments with the round hole in them.

"No, I did not hear any of the great bluesmen of those days live. When men like Sonny Boy Williamson and others performed, they would come into Jones' night spot in Indianola. I would know about them from the placards. But at that time I unfortunately did not have the money to go to hear them. Another thing, it seemed to me that I did not really belong. I was a little shy about going into some of the places. I remember Count Basie came into town, Duke Ellington. Johnny Jones, which was our man around town, brought all kinds of entertainment. But I didn't go, except for Sonny Boy Williamson, and then I went and peeked through the window. Also saw Robert Nighthawk that way, and Muddy Waters, I think. But I did not go to hear the big bands that came into Jones' club. You see, even though I'm from Indianola, I lived eight miles outside of town. The dances started about nine o'clock and went to one A.M. But you had to catch a ride, if you could on Saturday, about noon. Otherwise, you had to walk. And how much dancing could you do after an eight-mile walk and then an eight-mile back after one A.M.?

"I was in the army only a short while, really just for basic training. After two months, we would be reclassified and go back to the plantation. If you left, you had to go back into the army. There was an arrangement between the army and the plantation owners, because they was raising cotton for the army. I was considered a very skillful tractor driver, one of the top ten of all the tractor drivers. You had to have the basic training just in case they had to call you. But we were not eligible for any of the service benefits. I trained at Camp Shelby in Hattiesburg, Mississippi.

"And it was at that time I made up my mind that I wanted to become a blues singer. When I returned to Indianola as a tractor driver, I was making about twenty-two fifty a week. We had been picking cotton for thirty-five cents a hundred. That had gone up somewhat. Like in the hills of Killmichael, which was about a hundred miles east of the delta where I was living, we'd pick cotton for thirty-five cents a hundred. It was kind of hard to make even a dollar a day. But now the war is going on, and instead of seventy-five cents, it's about double. Sometimes, you could make even two fifty a day. Well, on the tractor we were making four dollars or so a day. It finally wound up where we were making close to thirty dollars a week. That was good money at that time. The delta blacks were picking cotton for a dollar fifty to two dollars a hundred. A good cotton picker could make himself seven or eight dollars a day, especially if he could pick three to four hundred pounds. That's a lot of cotton picking.

"I left Indianola in 1946, hitchhiking to Memphis. I had been singing with a gospel quartet called the St. John Gospel Singers. There were a lot of groups around, and material would pass from group to group so that we did some new gospel songs. We picked most of our material from what we heard on records, radio, jukeboxes. Poor people were beginning to afford a radio and they got to know the name groups and their songs. CBS and a few of the networks were presenting groups like The Trumpeteers and the Golden Gate Quartet. Then, out of Nashville, we could hear the Fairfield Four. The Soul Stirrers came into our area, and that was when I first met Sam Cooke—around 1948, I guess.

"When I first settled in Memphis, around 1946, I did stay with Bukka White for about a year. He influenced me from the time I was a little boy—as a person, not really as a musician. He played with a slide most of the time, and I just loved the sound of that. I still do. I could never use a bottleneck on my fingers as he did, so I learned to trill my finger. That's how I get the *vibrato*. My ears would tell me that I was doing what he was. Robert Nighthawk was a master bottleneck performer. There were others, like Robert Johnson. But I did not take any repertoire from Bukka. Not only was he my cousin, but he had the kind of personality that made me want to laugh. I could never do anything wrong or anything that he wasn't pleased with. For some reason, I had great respect for him and still do—just love him as a person. When we were kids, he'd always come by with candy, and if there was an argument he could always straighten it out without anybody being angry. I idolize him as a man and like to hear him play. But his playing did not influence me, with the exception of my trying to imitate his bottleneck sound. We were in two different worlds. [Bukka White died February 26, 1977, in the City of Memphis Hospital at the age of sixty-seven.]

•

"The distinctions that I hear writers make between blues and rhythm and blues I regard as artificial. Most of the people that we hear playing the blues came from the same area, even though they may be living in other areas. We hear of the Chicago blues because many of the Mississippi crowd lives in Chicago. When I was on the radio in Memphis, we used to get *Billboard, Cash Box*, and they classed things that Louis Jordan was doing as rhythm and blues. Or they would call it 'race.' And that's how you could distinguish what he and others like him did, from so-called pop. But today, for instance, James Brown is considered rhythm and blues. Aretha Franklin is considered soul or rhythm and blues—and I am considered blues. [Chuckling] In Memphis, I was considered rhythm and blues. I personally think that it's all rhythm and blues because it's blues and it has rhythm. I guess that you could break it down if you wanted to. I remember that Dinah Washington was considered R & B or 'race.' But Dinah sang anything that anybody else sang. She just sang it her way. She was doing all of the popular tunes of the late forties and early fifties. So were Ella Fitzgerald, Nat Cole, and Louis Armstrong— these were the top black recording artists. Louis Jordan, too, and The Ink Spots. But they were classed differently. Ella was more pop than most of the black female singers, but she still covered most of the bluesy tunes. But Dinah stayed with them, and Louis Jordan stayed with them, and they came up with some very big records. I remember Dinah covering 'Three Coins in a Fountain.' Mercury Records was using her to sell records to black record buyers. But when she did these pop tunes in her way, they were classed as rhythm and blues.

"It's true that after the big band era, blues singers started being accompanied by horns and rhythm groups instead of just guitar and harp. But the reason that this happened was because, before that, the blues singers just could not afford to be backed by bands. They wanted it. In the delta, there was a band called the Red Caps that had all kinds of instruments. They were playing like Jimmie Lunceford. They were stationed right there in Greenville, Mississippi. They were among the lucky few that could afford band instrumentation. Incidentally, the Red Caps I'm talking about were not the Red Caps of Steve Gibson that had 'Wedding Bells Are Breaking Up That Old Gang of Mine.' But they played the socials around Greenville, and they had a very varied repertoire. They played bluesy things and jazz. What I'm trying to say is that if we had the money or even a music store where we could borrow instruments—why we had to go twenty-five miles to the nearest music store. We did not have one in Indianola. Greenwood or Greenville was the nearest place. And when you went to one of these stores, you had to pay cash. They didn't know you, and you didn't have any credit. At that time, a horn was costing like $100. Gosh, in those days, it would take me five months to make $100. Out of the twenty-two fifty a week I was making, after you bought groceries and other necessities, you could save only seven to eight dollars. So you bought whatever instrument you could afford—and that was the guitar. As for a piano, you could forget about that. Or an organ. But my aunt had one that you had to paddle with your feet. It's so funny to see people now playing notes on an organ with their feet. Well, then you had to use your feet to get air flowing through the organ pipes. I don't know how she got that organ. My aunt was one of those people who said that a person had to have something for themselves. And she did. She had a phonograph, or as we called them, a Victrola. When I was a good boy—and I stayed a good boy around her—she would let me play the Victrola. And that's how I got into those old blues records like Lemon Jefferson. I had a chance to fool with the organ, and that's how I learned to play a few chords.

•

"Yes, I heard Ivory Joe in the late forties. In fact, when I first started, I played one of his tunes, 'The Moon Is Rising.' That was not the actual title. But the first words were, 'The moon is rising,/ The sun is sinking low,/ I can't find my baby,/ I wonder where did she go.' He had another part where the lady is bow-legged and sticks way out behind. [Laughing]

"Bull Moose Jackson was a favorite somewhat. He had a few tunes that I liked. One of them was, 'I love you, yes, I do . . .' I liked everything he did, but I liked him as a saxophone player. But nobody likes everything. Whole lot of things I made myself that I don't like. I thought it was good when I was making them. Later on, you listen to them and you wonder why you made them.

"I like the things that Wynonie Harris did. In fact, I recorded one of his tunes. Can't remember the title. But he did have 'Playful Baby,' which I did not record.

"John Lee Hooker was like Lightnin' Hopkins—a freelancer. Their tunes came out on many labels. I remember during the years in which I was a disk jockey in Memphis, I'd get these Hooker and Hopkins records, and every one seemed to be on a different label. And they were also recording under different names.

"When you mention Amos Milburn, I immediately think of 'Chicken Shack.' Most of the artists seem to be associated with just one tune. For instance, if you say 'B. B. King,' they say, 'The Thrill Is Gone.' Of course, that was the one that made people get to know me.

"To me, Joe Turner is 'Sweet Sixteen,' which is one of my favorite songs. But for most other people, Joe Turner is 'Shake, Rattle, and Roll.' I like the old Joe Turner with Pete Johnson. Things like 'Cherry Red' started me listening to him.

"My first hit record was Lowell Fulson's tune, 'Three O'Clock Blues.' I always did like his work. In fact, I idolized Lowell. But I probably like his singing better than his playing. It's nice of him to say that I do 'Every Day I Have the Blues' better than he does, but he had a hit on it. Several of us had hits on that Memphis Slim tune. But Lowell was the one who influenced me to do the tune. He and Joe Williams. You know, a lot of people don't know that Williams cut 'Every Day I Have the Blues' before he made it with Basie. He first made it with King Kolak's band. That was the one, along with Lowell's record, that made me think that I could get a hit on it. And luckily I did. But then, when Joe Williams got with Basie, he did it again, and that was the master one. But Lowell is a great artist. He is one of the sleeping giants in the blues.

"There were three or four Little Walters, but I loved the one that played harmonica. I was crazy about him. I can hear him in many of the 'harp' players of today. He could do things that a lot of people still can't do today with the instrument. I had two favorites on harmonica: Little Walter was one and the other was the original Sonny Boy Williamson. If you want the real down-home blues, you can hear it in Sonny Boy, and if you want a mod thing for today people, Little Walter is the one.

"The Biharis—Saul, Joe and Jules—were my friends. The company was never bigger than the artist. I could always talk to them, I could always see them. I never thought that I would have left the company [RPM]. What caused me to make up my mind was when they went into a cheap line of albums selling for like ninety-nine cents. Then I found that I was not getting recognition as an artist—you couldn't play the albums on jukeboxes; radio stations wouldn't play them. I worked with all of the Biharis, but Jules was, to me, a gem. I loved him and still do. Joe was also my man. I was crazy about them.

"Before the recent turnaround in the places that black artists can play, I played the 'chitlin' circuit' for many, many years. There were the black theaters, like the George Washington Carver, in the black ghettos. In these same towns or cities, there would be one little night club like Jones' night spot in Indianola (later called the Club Ebony and still there), the Elks in Greenville, Bond's in Hattiesburg, Club Harlem in Mobile, Alabama, the Dew Drop and the Brown Eagle in New Orleans, Sunbeam's in Memphis (later called Club Domino). These places attracted the bluesy crowd, the folks who came to hear the blues and maybe some jazz. I would play a Club Harlem in Miami and the Palms outside of Miami. In Chicago we would play the Burning Spear. We would stay in these places just one or two nights, and that meant a lot of traveling.

"When I first started traveling, I had a band. Johnny Ace, who later became a teen-age star as a singer, played piano. I had Billy Duncan, Earl Forest on drums, Richard Sanders, and others. After I scored with 'Three O'Clock Blues' in '52, I signed with Universal Attractions in New York. They wanted me as a solo act because they had a lot of other black bands. So I gave up my band; gave it to Johnny Ace, which was how he got started. He called the group Beale Street Boys.

"When I went on the road myself, with Universal handling the bookings, I was making about a thousand dollars a week. The best I ever made in that period was two thousand dollars a week. But when you got through paying your agency, your manager and others, you'd come out with about half of the top figure. The artist paid for everything and still does. Yet it was money like I'd never seen before. So I worked with bands like Lucky Millinder's, Tiny Bradshaw, and others. At the Apollo in Harlem, I worked with Charlié Barnet. But I was always featured. I was like a guest artist. And I never did get the experience as a rhythm guitarist. That's the one thing I regret and hate even today.

"Then finally I started working with Bill Harvey and his band out of Memphis. When we got together, we were booked for like a hundred seventy-five dollars a day. Then it went to about two hundred seventy-five, finally about three hundred dollars a day. There were six men and me. Of course, we also had a driver and a valet. In '55 I started my own road band, and I've had a road band ever since.

"When I first started performing, it was me alone. Then I got a trio on the radio: Johnny Ace on piano, Earl Forest on drums. It was hard to keep a bass player. Later on is when I got Billy Duncan on tenor sax. That's when I made 'Three O'Clock Blues.' We recorded our first hit in the YMCA in Memphis. One of my biggest hits, 'Darling, I Love You,' was recorded at Tuff Green's home, the same fellow that made the first record with me.

"By 1955 I was pretty well known, and we were booked for like five to seven hundred dollars a day. That was our guarantee. Then it went up to a thousand and, if we were lucky, twelve hundred. But then I had my own bus and a very big group. We ran it up to about thirteen pieces, and we kept that until I went broke. [Chuckling] Then I dropped down to five: organ, drums, tenor, trumpet, and alto. Kept that for a while, and when things started to pick up, we added more men. I like the big band sound. I guess one of the reasons is my being brought up in the church. I can always hear the choir singing behind me, and that's what I hear when the horns are playing behind me. The little tricky things they do, like rhythms within rhythms—this is what puts spice on. Blues is usually slow, melancholy, and if you have some little figures going on with the horns, it makes it more interesting.

"The blues is the blues. They don't change. But sounds do change. And I've just had to make some changes in my band after working with some men for many years. For some time, I've been asking them to listen to the sounds behind James Brown, behind Aretha, behind Wilson Pickett. Audiences feel the difference. But it was like I wasn't saying anything. Each year, I give my men four weeks off, two with pay and two without. This was to give them a chance to make a change if they wanted to. And this year, I felt that I had to. It wasn't easy, especially since some of the men are Memphis friends from way back. I understand their feelings. But you either change with the times or you find yourself looking at empty seats. . . ."

There's one thing in this world I cannot
understand,
That's a bow-legged woman crazy 'bout
a cross-eyed man. —BLIND BLAKE

Two Other Family-Owned Record "Indies"

ON MARCH 1, 1947, the No. 1 song on *Billboard*'s "Honor Roll of Hits" was "Open the Door, Richard." It was not so much a song as a bit of comic nonsense with erotic overtones, or a riff based on the routine. For years, the routine had been the mainstay of a black comedian named Dusty Fletcher, though it apparently was devised by another comic named James Mason. In black vaudeville theaters, Fletcher used a stepladder, climbing it to knock at an imaginary door and to urge Richard to open it. But Richard was occupied in a way that was easy to surmise, and all that Dusty could do was keep shouting, half-singing, "Open the Door, Richard . . . Open the Door, Richard." The musical riff for these words became so familiar to radio listeners in 1947 that NY Station WOR banned all airings of the tune and requested comedians to lay off "Richard" gags.

By then there were as many as fourteen different versions. Among the majors, Capitol offered a disk by the Pied Pipers; Decca, by Louis Jordan; Victor, by Count Basie; Mercury, by Bill Samuels & the Cats 'n' Jammer Three; and Columbia, a disk by the Three Flames and another by the Charioteers. Eight "indies" sought to mine a bit of silver out of what seemed an endless vein. Apollo was on the market with a Hot Lips Page recording; King, with Hank Penny; Manor, with Big Sid Catlett's Ork; Majestic, with The Merry Macs; Empey with Tosh "One-String" Weller & His Jivesters; and National, with Dusty Fletcher himself.

It was none of these, not even the best-selling Fletcher disk, that started the commotion. The first record was by former Lionel Hampton saxist Jack McVea on Black & White of Los Angeles. Tenor-saxist McVea, who functioned as leader of Black & White's studio band, was responsible for the musical riff that became so popular. And the idea of recording the comedy bit was either his and/or Ralph Bass's, B & W's A & R man and one of the truly inspired producers of R & B disks.

It took a bit of doing and a lawsuit to unravel the writer credits on "Open the Door, Richard," but eventually songsheets and records carried four names: words by Dusty Fletcher and John Mason, music by Jack McVea and Dan Howell. Some said Dan Howell stood for

226

Lou Levy, owner of Leeds-Duchess; others said it was Dave Kapp of Decca; and still others that it stood for nobody, but was just a way of retaining a portion of royalties in the firm's treasury.

At the moment "Open the Door, Richard" touched the top of the "Honor Roll of Hits," it was in the company of such white pop pleasantries as "Zip-A-Dee Doo-Dah," from the Walt Disney film *Song of the South*; "A Gal in Calico," from the film *The Time, The Place and The Girl*; and "Anniversary Song," as sung by Al Jolson and mimed by Larry Parks in the film *The Jolson Story*. But there was also a black ballad, "(I Love You) For Sentimental Reasons," with an inchoate lyric, launched by Deek Watson & His Brown Dots on the Manor label, and quickly covered (and taken away from him) by the King Cole Trio on Capitol, Ella Fitzgerald and the Delta Rhythm Boys on Decca, and white artists like Dinah Shore, Fran Warren, Eddy Howard, and Charlie Spivak & His Orchestra.

At the moment, too, when "Richard" was the runaway sensation of pop music, five black artists each shared a slice of the "race" market: Count Basie (Victor), Tiger Haynes' Three Flames (Columbia), Dusty Fletcher (National), Louis Jordan (Decca), and Jack McVea (Black & White). *Billboard*'s March 8 chart of "Most Played Juke Box Race Records" carried disks of "Richard" by the artists listed in that order. The only other titles that were being "most played" for black listeners were "Ain't Nobody Here But Us Chickens," "Let the Good Times Roll," and "Texas and Pacific"—all three by Louis Jordan.

Together with "(I Love You) For Sentimental Reasons," "Open the Door, Richard" became the first rhythm-and-blues song since "I Wonder" to gain smashing acceptance in the mainstream white market. Not surprisingly, perhaps, the publisher of all three was the Leeds-Duchess combine, in which I then functioned as publicity and advertising director. And "Richard," about which I wrote a byline article in *The New York Times Magazine*, marked the beginning of my interest in chronicling the history of contemporary American music. The across-the-board sales of two black-oriented songs as well as the popularity of Louis Jordan among whites as well as blacks, suggested that the pop mainstream was receptive to the R & B current, a situation that contributed to the rapid rise of R & B record labels.

•

Black & White Records, responsible for initiating "Richard's" phenomenal invasion of the day's comedy and consciousness, tried to capitalize on its acceptance by rushing out a sequel. "The Key's in the Mail Box" by Jack McVea & His Door Openers (a billing obviously designed to establish McVea's connection with the forerunner) fared like most follow-ups: it was a bomb.

"Paul Reiner, who owned Black & White," commented Johnny Sippel of *Billboard*, "was a novice in the record business, and he thought that every record sold like 'Richard,' which easily went over 500,000. Reiner began rushing out record after record, and he literally released himself out of the business. He put out so many new records that he quickly ate up every cent he made."

A family-owned enterprise, with Paul Reiner as president and his wife Lillian as vice-president, Black & White was founded in the year that saw the end of World War II and the beginning of the atomic era. Despite its name, Black & White was really not an R & B label. Although its releases in 1945 included disks by Roosevelt Sykes and St. Louis Jimmy (who recorded a new version of his hit, "Goin' Down Slow," under the name of Poor Boy), B & W's roster was weighted on the pop side. Al Sack, musical director of the label, was also musical director of several CBS programs, including "The Tony Martin Show." Nevertheless, the label made a significant contribution to R & B, largely through the talents of Ralph Bass, the man who, after leaving Black & White, helped build two of the biggest R & B "indies," Savoy Records of New Jersey and King Records of Cincinnati.

While "Richard" unquestionably stirred excitement, Bass's work with T-Bone Walker was more significant. During 1945 T-Bone cut some sides for Rhumboogie Records of Chicago, which suggest that the Texas bluesman who had been a jumpin' jazzman and big band guitarist-vocalist was returning to root material. It was Bass who assisted T-Bone in finding himself in 1946–47.

On his first date for B & W, Walker worked with a solid five-piece R & B combo led by tenorman Jack McVea. By mid-'47 Walker produced one of the great standards of the R &B era, "Call It Stormy Monday." There had been other versions of this old blues—notably an Earl Hines disk with a Billy Eckstine vocal on Bluebird in '42—but it was Walker who gave the classic rendition and made the blues his own. Nevertheless, most bluesmen were influenced by his virtuosity as an electric guitarist rather than as a songwriter or singer.

•

Just a few doors away from Black & White, at 4918 Santa Monica Boulevard, Philo Records opened shop at about the same time. It, too, was a family undertaking, with Leo Mesner as president, Edward

Mesner as vice-president, and Ida Mesner as secretary-treasurer. Unlike Black & White, Aladdin Records (as Philo became known early in 1946) existed well into the rock 'n' roll era and produced hits into the late '50s until it was bought by Lew Chudd of Imperial Records. In 1975, Bill Hancock, an area musician and avid R & B record collector, acquired the old logo and official rights to its name—though not its catalog—and began issuing new disks under the label that became defunct in 1958.

One of Aladdin's earliest noisemakers (while the company was still known as Philo Records) was a disk of "Be-Baba-Luba" by ex-Basie vocalist Helen Humes. Known also as "Be-Baba-Leba" and written by Humes, it employed some of the devices and offbeat intervals of the then-new jazz development known as bebop, later as rebop, and finally simply as bop. At about the same time, Lionel Hampton co-wrote and recorded "Hey! Ba-Ba-Re-Bop," which also employed nonsense syllables associated with the new jazz. The Hampton number became a bigger seller than the Humes tune, but the hit version was cut by the Glenn Miller Orchestra under Tex Beneke. By the time "Hey! Ba-Ba-Re-Bop" was a best-seller, Tina Dixon had written and recorded "E-Bop-O-Lee-Bop" with The Fleming Trio on the René's Excelsior label. It was the least successful of the three.

All of these tunes served to emphasize something Johnny Otis has noted: "The R & B thing didn't really develop till the mid-forties, when interest in swing and the big bands began to slacken. The bop thing came along then, and played a part in R & B, too."

"Be-Baba-Luba," a substantial seller for Philo Records, turned Helen Humes from jazz balladry to R & B, at least temporarily. Helen later recorded R & B songs like "I Just Refuse to Sing the Blues" for Mercury, but her natural province was that of Mildred Bailey, the "Rockin' Chair Lady," with whom she has generally been bracketed. In jazz critic Stanley Dance's view, "Helen Humes' voice is richer and more vital though it has a similar soaring quality."

Aladdin's early orientation was jazz rather than blues, with an artist roster that included, besides Humes, The King Cole Trio, cool tenorman Lester Young, and KC pianist-bandleader Jay McShann. But shortly after the name change to Aladdin, they began recording influential bluesman Amos Milburn, who came from Houston where he was born in 1924. Working initially in a down-home boogie style, Milburn cut extensively during '46 and '47, making over fifty sides in '47 alone. It was not until '48, however, that the burgeoning R & B market opened for the Texan who had begun moving in a Charles

Brown ballad direction. By 1949, a year-end survey gave him Top Ten R & B best-sellers in "Hold Me Babe," cut in cocktail lounge style, and "Chicken Shack Boogie," a record that greatly influenced Fats Domino.

In 1950 Milburn achieved a No. 1 best-seller with "Bad, Bad Whiskey," written by tenorman Maxwell Davis, who functioned as Aladdin's house bandleader and whose productivity as a songwriter/instrumentalist/bandleader/contractor makes one think of Willie Dixon of Chicago's Chess Records. Although Milburn recorded songs with other typical blues themes, listeners seemed thereafter to prefer him on an alcoholic kick. His best-sellers in '52 and '53 were "Thinkin' and Drinkin'," "Let Me Go Home, Whiskey," and Rudolph Toombs' "One Scotch, One Bourbon, One Beer." After the success of the last, Milburn used three glasses as props in his personal appearances.

Two other important bluesmen, both from Texas, contributed to the growth of Aladdin. Charles Brown, pianist of Johnny Moore's Three Blazers, produced best-sellers, starting with his famous "Drifting Blues," tear-stained with self-pity and named "The Best R & B Disk of 1946" by *Cash Box*. Brown, who walked the line between urban blues and white torch songs, pursued the genre in romantic ballads·like "Get Yourself Another Fool," "Seven Long Days," and "Black Night," a No. 1 R & B song in '51.

By contrast with Brown, Lightnin' Hopkins, who came from Centerville, Texas, was a down-home bluesman. He began his long recording career, developing one of the largest catalogues of any bluesman, by recording for Aladdin in '46. By '47 he was back in Houston, recording for Gold Star at the Quinn Studios; the thirty sides he did there were later bought by Modern Records. Although he recorded half a dozen sides for Aladdin in '48, working still in Houston, he branched out after that. To list all of the labels he recorded on would be to enumerate virtually every R & B "indie" in the country. If anyone helped Houston become a bluestown that could compete with Dallas, it was Hopkins.

Another Texas bluesman, Mance Lipscomb of Navasoto, has said of Hopkins, "I can't get along with Lightnin'. You have to handle him like a soft-boiled egg. And there's Howlin' Wolf. He's another one. He's got that mean look. He talks mean, too."

"Homesick Blues," a '49 chartmaker for Charles Brown, was the work of Floyd Dixon, who began recording on Aladdin two years later. Inevitably, Dixon was influenced by Brown's pop-flavored style and even imitated his manner of mooing words—an echo of Leroy

Carr's ballad mode by way of Ivory Joe Hunter. (The parallel progression in pop was from Crosby's crooning to Como's cool balladry.) Dixon's brief recording career was focused on a single subject: early in '51 he made R & B charts with "Telephone Blues," and the following year rang the bell with "Call Operator 210," his best-known hit.

In '51, too, Aladdin registered a notable success with Milburn's favorite theme (drinking), only the singer was "Peppermint" Harris and the record "I Got Loaded." Harrison Nelson, to use his baptismal name, who had previously attracted notice with "Rainin' in My Heart" on the Sittin' In With label was also part of the postwar Texas invasion of California. "I Got Loaded"—the very lingo suggested his urbanity —was a No. 1 R & B hit, but "Peppermint" never again approached that mark, although he tried to with other boozy ballads: "Have Another Drink and Talk with Me" and "Three Sheets to the Wind."

Aladdin had another Harris, but he came along late in the company's history. His record was what is known in the business as a "fluke." In the year that Paul Anka lamented "Diana's" being too old for him, the Everly Brothers urged Little Susie to wake up, and Jerry Lee Lewis was shouting, "Whole Lotta Shakin' Goin' On," there was a record in which a group murmured or mooed in the background and Thurston Harris simply kept repeating, "Little Bitty Pretty One" —that was the title—"Won't you come with me?" The record's success was an enigma, though unquestionably young people sensed something erotic in the invitation and the words gave the more timid a handle with which to approach a potential playmate. (If you got turned down, you were only joking and you didn't have to feel insecure.) Not only was "Little Bitty Pretty One" one of the year's Top 30 R & B disks (taking the play away from writer Bobby Day's disk version), it also received extensive play by Top 40 dee jays. Thurston Harris was unable, of course, to repeat his voodoo, so he became one of the day's many one-shot record stars.

Unlike many R & B labels that could not cope with the rhythms of rock 'n' roll, Aladdin experienced no difficulty in making the transition, and it even became a pacemaker. Two Aladdin groups may be regarded as harbingers of the change—The Five Keys and Shirley & Lee.

The Five Keys, who hailed from Newport News, Virginia, began as the Sentimental Four. They were two sets of brothers: Rudy and Bernie West, and Ripley and Raphael Ingram. Imitating the Orioles, they sang in churches and on the corner of Twenty-fifth and Jefferson

Avenue in Newport News. They eventually entered amateur night contests at the Jefferson Theatre, beating over thirty contestants on three consecutive Wednesdays. As a result, they secured a week's booking at the Royal, the Howard, and finally at the Apollo, where Eddie Mesner of Aladdin signed them to a recording contract.

With their second release, they achieved a million-copy seller in a remake of "Glory of Love," an old Billy Hill ballad, vintage 1936. It finished in the Top Ten of 1951's R & B hits. Naturally, in subsequent releases, they pursued the pattern of gently coloring white love-ballads black. At times they turned to standards like "Red Sails in the Sunset" and "These Foolish Things"; at other times, they covered current ballad hits like "Be Anything, But Be Mine." They also sought to revive R & B weepers like Ruth Brown's "Teardrops from My Eyes." But they could not duplicate the success of "Glory of Love."

Nor did The Five Keys do so when they moved to Capitol in 1954, becoming the first R & B group to record with a major label. Under the aegis of Dave Cavanaugh, a Capitol A & R director who billed himself as Big Dave, and with an assist from Howard Biggs, former arranger of The Ravens, they developed a blacker sound. It led to their biggest hit after "Glory of Love." "Ling Ting Tong," their first Capitol release, climbed to No. 5 whereas "Glory" had gone to No. 1. The Keys could probably have done better had their sales and plays not been undercut by the cover cut by Otis Williams & the Charms on DeLuxe.

The Five Keys produced still another chart song in their second Capitol release, a moving Chuck Willis ballad called "Close Your Eyes." Featuring a highly emotional performance by lead singer Maryland Pierce, the song made Top Ten in 1955's R & B hits. The cover by the Admirals on King did not compete in the way the Charms' disk of "Ling Ting Tong" had. In 1967, incidentally, Peaches & Herb were able to score a best-seller with a revival of "Close Your Eyes."

In 1955, the year of "Close Your Eyes," the Five Keys and other groups began using a type of rhythmic accompaniment that later led to their being called "Doo-wop" groups. It was done vocally—"A-doo-doo-wop, A-doo-doo-dang, A-doo-doo-wang"—sometimes chanted by the bass alone and sometimes by three voices behind the lead. It added drive and danceability, particularly to ballads and especially when the instrumental accompaniment was just piano/bass/drums/tenor sax or nonexistent.

By 1956, however, the Keys were recording with a bigger complement of instruments. They accommodated gracefully to the big band sound of "Out of Sight, Out of Mind" and "Wisdom of a Fool," neither of which made R & B charts. They continued recording for Capitol into 1958, after which they moved to King. According to Steve Propes' authoritative book on collecting, *Those Oldies But Goodies*, the Five Keys are the most sought-after group—the Five Keys on Aladdin, not Capitol—with an original Aladdin record of "Red Sails in the Sunset," blue label with silver print, commanding a price of $100.

•

The other Aladdin group that both anticipated and became a part of the rock revolution was a New Orleans duo named Shirley & Lee, who produced one of the great standards of teen-age music, "Let the Good Times Roll." Aladdin typed them "Sweethearts of the Blues," exploiting a nonexistent romance between Shirley Pixley Goodman and Leonard Lee. They gained acceptance in R & B circles with their first boogie-styled disk, "I'm Gone." It was the work of Leonard, who thereafter wrote most of their songs, and Dave Bartholomew, the New Orleans arranger-conductor known for his longtime collaboration with Fats Domino.

The duo transformed the call-and-response patterns of gospel and blues into a girl-and-boy dialogue, with Shirley's shrill, little-girl voice making an appealing contrast to Lee's low-keyed, sad-sack delivery. More significantly, they created an image for themselves, a rare procedure in R & B, and thereby developed a following. They accomplished this through a series of songs in '53 that told the story of a courtship. Young record-buyers assumed it was theirs, and they did nothing to discourage the idea. But the courtship was only on wax. "Shirley Come Back to Me" was followed by "Shirley's Back," "The Proposal," and, finally, "Two Happy People." They personalized and particularized other songs with titles like "Lee Goofed" and "Lee's Dream," and made their records a form of self-expression, as pioneer blues singers had originally done and rock singers were later to do.

They also early caught the party mood of teen-agers with "Feel So Good," a Leonard Lee rock 'n' roller that remained on R & B charts for one week short of six months in '55–'56. Their follow-up hit, "Let the Good Times Roll," the title of a 1970 film, was banned by most white stations. The reason given was "suggestive lyrics." There weren't any, but Shirley & Lee did communicate an erotic feeling. Nevertheless, "Let the Good Times Roll" made *Billboard*'s pop "Honor Roll of Hits" in the year of Presley's emergence with "Heartbreak Hotel," "Don't Be Cruel," and "Hound Dog." Having touched a root strain in teen-age feeling, the song outlasted many of the year's big hits, among them the Platters' "Great Pretender," Gene Vincent's "Be-Bop-a-Lula," and Frankie Lymon's "Why Do Fools Fall in Love?"

Before the year of "Blue Suede Shoes" was over, Shirley & Lee gave Aladdin another chart song in "I Feel Good." But it was not as potent as its forerunners. They continued recording into '57 and '58, but "The Sweethearts of the Blues" merely seemed to be repeating themselves without freshness or impact.

•

Nineteen fifty-five was the year that panic raced through the ranks of the country's established pop singers, not to mention songwriters and publishers. During the preceding summer, The Chords' (and The Crew Cuts') "Sh-Boom" and Joe Turner's (and Bill Haley's) "Shake, Rattle, and Roll" had signaled a possible shift in taste. The music trade papers were announcing that teen-agers demanded music with a beat; next, that R & B was no longer a stepchild; and finally, that R & B was beginning to invade the pop market. By '55 it was difficult to shrug off the omens of change, what with the fantastic acceptance of "Rock Around the Clock" and *Billboard*'s slogan under the "Honor Roll of Hits": "Keep Pop Alive in '55."

One of the indications of white panic was the rush of pop artists to cover potential black hits. Aladdin figured in the syndrome with a song called "Ko Ko Mo," recorded by a duo named Gene & Eunice. The original recording on a label named Combo was apparently taken over by Aladdin. On January 26, 1955, "Ko Ko Mo" made R & B charts for the first time; then it climbed slowly during a seven-week period to the No. 7 slot.

But the advance rumblings of a hit began to resound in record distributor circles. And on January 15 *Billboard* carried two huge, full-page advertisements: Mercury announced its cover of "Ko Ko Mo" by The Crew Cuts, backed with a cover of the Penguins' "Earth Angel"; in the second full-page ad, RCA Victor thundered that "Ko Ko Mo" was Perry Como's new release! The following week, Combo Records ran a small ad in a feeble attempt to retain some portion of the market for itself. Fighting the massive power of white radio and TV, Gene & Eunice were no match for Como, whose record finished in the year's Top 30—a bizarre casting if there ever was one.

Gene & Eunice were able to capitalize only briefly on the excitement created by "Ko Ko Mo." Their succeeding disk, "This Is My Story," not a rocker like their debut hit, made R & B charts, but never rose above No. 13. Like Shirley & Lee, they continued recording on Aladdin into 1958. After they moved to Case Records for a number of inconsequential sides, they disappeared from the record scene.

Aladdin, too, was gone by 1959. A product of the R & B years, it was unable, despite its hits, to grow big enough to survive, or unwilling to continue the struggle. It was swallowed by Imperial Records, the company built by Fats Domino's hits.

groove 10   **RALPH BASS**

His middle name should be "Laugh." He has one of the heartiest, and when he is not laughing at something you have said, he is cackling about something he has said or, for that matter, is just thinking. One of the great pioneers of the R & B scene as a record producer and a man whose hit disks would easily run to a page of titles, Bass began his recording career in California at Black & White Records. In 1974 he administered the Chicago office of Chess Records. A rapid, nervous talker with a sensitive memory, he leaves you with the sound of his laughter echoing in your ears.

•

"Syd Nathan [of King Records], Herman Lubinsky [of Savoy Records], they're all the same except for a few personal traits. Like Lubinsky was the cheapest motherfucker in the world. Both Nathan and Lubinsky thought the same way. You couldn't make a Goddamn phone call with Lubinsky. 'Write a letter!'—unless it was life or death—'Write a letter!' If you went out with Lubinsky for dinner in a strange town, he would go down the streets and look at all the menus pasted on the window. Then we'd finally go to the place that looked like the cheapest. He would invariably open the same way. He would always order first. He'd say, 'I'll have *hamburg*.' He used to call meat loaf hamburg. Well, that's the cheapest thing on the menu. So I'd say, 'Nooo . . . I'll have a T-Bone Steak, medium rare.' And he would look at me and say, 'Make mine a steak, too.' [Cackling]

"But despite it all, I have no ill feeling toward any of them. I'd say to myself—I have a pet theory: They work so hard making money, and they were financial geniuses for their times. Syd Nathan . . . I could tell you some real weird things about Syd. . . . He'd tell his attorneys where the holes were [loopholes in a contract]. He would find them and tell them. And Lubinsky was a tyrant. Everybody was afraid to cross him.

"One time there was a lawsuit over a very famous group called

The Robins. It was my group, not Leiber or Stoller. Lester Sill became involved later on. They were handled by a man named Ed Fishman. He was a West-Coaster. Looked like Paul Whiteman. I remember one of the big R & B guys of the day—the early fifties—came off the road. He had found that Fishman took 50 percent of the deposits, instead of the usual 15 or 20 percent. For weeks, he couldn't find Fishman. He was in the hospital where nobody could get to him. But one day, this cat went to the office—he was trying to get his share of the money—and he charged right past the receptionist and secretaries with a gun in his hand. When Fishman saw the gun, he suddenly had a heart attack. [Laughing] Fishman was afraid the guy was gonna kill him. He gambled all the money away at the racetrack.

"Well, to get back to the lawsuit over The Robins. I had made an audition record with a little girl who was only thirteen years old—Little Esther Phillips. And I was recording the Robins with Johnny Otis' band at Radio Recorders. The sides were for Savoy. The girl had won contests at a little movie theater in Watts on 103rd Street. I thought as a fifth side, we'd do this thing by a pretty good blues writer. We changed the lyric of 'Double Crossing Blues,' and the thing we changed sold the record—about the lady bear in the forest. The Robins backed Little Esther. And Bobby Nunn, the bass singer, did the bear part. It was a boy-and-girl thing. Anyway, I sent the record to Lubinsky and asked for five dollars to pay for the kid's expenses—lunch and all that, coming to Hollywood from Watts. He shouted, 'Whadiya mean five bucks? For what?' He wouldn't give me the five bucks.

"Meanwhile, there was a disk jockey in Newark, New Jersey—one of the first black dee jays, B. Cooke. He came to Lubinsky's office and said, 'Hey, Herman, there isn't a single smash record out there. Do you have anything?' Lubinsky let him listen to the things I had sent from the Coast. Cooke came running out of the room, asking, 'Who is this girl?'

"'What girl?' Lubinsky asked. The records had no titles and no artist name. The guy grabbed the record and ran out shouting, 'I guarantee that it's an instant hit.' He played it once and, boom! the station switchboard lit up. He ran a contest to name it—that's when it became known as 'Double Crossing Blues.' In fact, everybody who was involved with the record got double-crossed, [Laughing]—the songwriter, Johnny and I, The Robins, everybody connected with it.

"Anyway, Lubinsky calls me up in the middle of the night. Eight o'clock his time was five o'clock our time. 'Get that girl!' he shouts. I asked, 'What girl? The one you wouldn't give me the five bucks for?' He didn't answer. All he said was, 'She's gonna be the biggest thing in the country.' I was half asleep. 'What are you talkin' about?' He starts whispering, 'Go, get her signed. I'll send you some money. Or get some money from Jack Rosen.' (He pressed records for us—had a plant on Orange and Santa Monica Boulevard.) 'But sign her!'

"I drove out to Watts where Johnny Otis lived and woke him up. It was tough getting him up because he worked most of the night at his club, The Barrel House. 'Little Esther?' he said. 'You mean to tell me that record is a hit?' I said, 'Look, man, get your Goddamned clothes on. Let's go find her mama and get these contracts signed.'

"Mama was a domestic who worked in Pasadena. So we drove out there. She signed, and we got Little Esther to sign. We didn't go through the guardianship bit. That's how I happened to take her away from Savoy years later when I went with Syd Nathan at King Records. But the fact was that Herman, who wouldn't give me five bucks to make an audition disk with the kid, now had one of the biggest R & B stars in the business. At one point, we had three of her records riding the R & B charts at the same time. When I went on the road with her and Johnny, we broke records all over the country. It was a record that needed only one air shot—one of the few records that was an *instant* hit.

"Herman and I went to Atlanta, Georgia. Jake Friedman had Southland, one of the biggest distributing outfits in the South. Herman wouldn't call and tell him that we were in town. We sat in the hotel room and listened to the one station that played R & B—WAOK, one of the first black-owned stations in the country. Within two hours after they played Little Esther, Friedman was on the phone. He had tracked us down.

"It was the lady-bear line that cracked everybody up. Little Esther asked: 'How come you're out in the forest looking for bear?/ Ain't got no lady-bears out there.' Well, *bear* was a jive term for an ugly broad. Whites wouldn't know what it meant, but it cracked all blacks up. It came from a comedy team that worked at Otis' Barrel House; the ugly bear that would pounce on the first man she saw and drag him to bed with her.

"You want to know why I left Lubinsky? He had something on all the help he kept. But he could never get anything on me—all my life, I always kept my private life to myself. I never socialized with any of the people I worked with—musicians, writers, owners. It didn't make any difference. My own life is my own life. He could never get anything on me.

"Savoy had a record shop at 54 Market Street in Newark, New Jersey. The offices of the record company were upstairs. An Italian boy ran the record shop for Herman. He was a good-looking kid. There was a burlesque house around the corner, and he used to make it with the broads. Anyway, Herman found out about it and threatened to call his wife. The kid stayed and worked all hours—until midnight, I think, the store remained open—and he got very little salary.

"Herman had a bookkeeper who liked to drink. One day, Lubinsky sent him out to collect rents at some apartment houses he owned. Charlie took ten bucks out and bought some whiskey. Maybe he spent twenty bucks at a bar. Anyway, he came in short. Lubinsky had him arrested, he was sentenced, and then he was paroled to Lubinsky. [Chuckling] Charlie worked his days out, again for little money.

"I was out on the West Coast and Lubinsky wanted me to come into New York. I took my wife into New York, and we talked it over. He promised to pay for my moving, to draw up a written contract, and to my getting a piece of the action as well as salary. I wanted a production deal and he said okay. Believe you me, it was no easy thing finding an apartment in New York at that time. It was the middle fifties, and we spent two weeks looking. It was a great expense to us, and finally we went back to the Coast and moved our sons. When the bill for moving came, Herman said, 'I never said I'd pay for it. I'll pay half.' Then when my first salary check arrived, it was about thirty percent less than it was supposed to be. Herman said, 'That's what we agreed upon.' Well, now I'm in New York and what was I supposed to do? I'd already made my move, and he backed away from what he promised. I said to myself, 'Okay, if that's the way, then I know what to do. I can't trust this man as far as making a deal unless it's in writing.'

"But there was a catalyst that made me quit him. There were a handful of companies then. I was a top producer and had all these hits behind me. Today, I could name my price with any company I wanted. In those days, most of the companies were family-run. And even Syd Nathan had his brother, and his sister, and his brother-in-law—they were all stockholders. The Bihari boys at Modern and the Mesner brothers at Aladdin.

"I had a label called Portrait. After I left Paul Reiner [Black & White Records], I was doing a lot of jazz and I had recorded Errol Garner. He came in from Paris and was playing at a spot called The

Tattle House, a little striptease joint in Culver City. I wasn't working for Lubinsky at the time, but I joined him soon after I cut Garner. In those days, pressing plants wouldn't press anything unless you paid cash. When you had a hit on your hands, you were in trouble without money. Garner's 'Penthouse Serenade' and 'Stairway to the Stars' were tremendous for the time.

"I had two brothers-in-law who were partners in the label, and one of them came into New York. We were settling our affairs because we were going to break up the company and sell the masters. Meanwhile, there was a birthday party at the Baby Grand, which was next to the Apollo in Harlem. Willie Bryant and Ray Carroll were disk jockeys in the window—they broadcast from there. And the party was to celebrate their being on the air for so-many-and-so-many years.

"Herman said, 'Look, I can't be there. I want you to represent me. Our New York distributor will be there, and you pick up the tab. I'll let you have it.' The party didn't start until twelve o'clock at night. Meanwhile, I was rehearsing a couple of blues acts on 125th Street. So I told my wife—we lived in Brooklyn—'Don't expect me. I'll be home late, three or four o'clock in the morning.' I let her have the car, and I took the subway.

"I came home about five or six o'clock in the morning. My wife wanted to know where I was. I reminded her that I was at the Baby Grand. She said, 'No, you weren't. My brothers came to the house, and I called Herman and he said, "I don't know where he is." ' He sends me out to represent him and then tells my wife that he doesn't know where I am! I was furious.

"It was Friday night—Saturday morning, that is. I didn't go to bed. I got showered, shaved, and dressed. I was going to whip the shit out of him. I knew that he came into the office on Saturday, but not until about ten o'clock. It was too early, so I stopped off at Universal Attractions. I sat talking to Ben Bart, who said, 'You look like you're crazy.' I said, 'Yeah, I'm gonna whip the shit outta Herman Lubinsky. I'm gonna kill him. He's trying to break up my home. He's doing the same damn thing he did to Charlie and the others. Now, he's gonna try to blackmail me.'

"Lubinsky had some kind of political job in Newark. He was a commissioner or something. Bart said, 'You hit him, and he'll arrest you! A man like Herman—there's only one way you can hurt him, and that's through his pocket. Quit! And don't worry about another job. I'll get you one. There are two companies interested in you now.' So I just didn't come in after that.

"After a day or two, Lubinsky called up and talked to my wife, asked why I wasn't coming in. She said, 'I don't know why.' And Herman shouted, 'Tell him, he's fired!' About two weeks later, when I went into the office to get my last check, Herman grabbed me: 'Aren't you coming in tomorrow?' I said, [Laughing] 'No, you fired me!' I got my check, walked out of the door, and never came back. Later on, whenever Lubinsky and I met by accident at conventions or something, he'd always grab me and ask, 'What did I ever do to you?' He knew what he did. [Laughing] I would never tell him, never give him the satisfaction. He knew he did wrong, and I knew he did wrong. I messed his mind up. I'll tell you one thing: I could always go back—to him and anybody I ever worked for. I always had that thing about myself. Leave the door wide open. You never know when you want to come back. It was that way with Leonard Chess—and here I am back [1974].

"Anyway, Irving Green, who had Mercury at that time—knew his father Al Green at National very well—Irving met with me and with his attorney, Irwin Steinberg, who is now head of Mercury. I didn't dig Steinberg; he was too square for me. There's a difference between an attorney, in those days anyhow, and a record producer. We're not a champagne and caviar set; we live with reality. I told Irving what I wanted: a contract before I start, a production deal, and the whole bit. He said, 'I'm going to Europe for about three weeks. Don't do a thing until I come back. We'll have contracts made.'

"Well, after a few weeks, Jack Pearl got hold of me, told me Syd Nathan was in town, and asked me to talk with him. Money was running short. I got a written contract and became one of the first record producers to have a production deal. It wasn't much—a half a cent a record—but it was unheard-of in those days. And a publishing firm, Armo, of my own. They established a new label for me, which I called Federal. I produced The Dominoes, the Midnighters, the Five Royales, James Brown, Ike Turner, Etta James, Johnny Otis, Little Esther. Those were some of the acts I brought to the label.

"I know that other stories have appeared in print. Like Syd Nathan found The Dominoes. I never cared about claims that others made. But finally in my old age, I guess, I'm saying, let's get the history of our business straight. Now it's an important thing; it wasn't then. Who the hell gave a damn?

"There was an article in *Cash Box* about Buck Ram finding and forming The Platters. Bullshit! I found Tony Williams in an amateur show at the Club Alabam. Me and Hunter Hancock started that amateur show specifically to find talent. Johnny Otis's band played. When I heard Tony sing, he didn't even win a prize. But I took him to my office—I was working for Syd Nathan at the time—handed him a contract and signed him. Then I said to him, 'Look, man, singles are not making it. Groups are the thing.' At that time, I had the Dominoes and I had Hank Ballard & the Midnighters—Hank was not in the first group. There was a jive-assed group called The Platters, and I put Tony with them. The lead singer was arrested and busted on some charge. What happened was: The Platters had interested Buck Ram in managing them, really coaching them. He came to my office on Pico Boulevard in LA and asked for some of the records made by The Platters. I had done two sessions with them. Sold a little bit on the West Coast, but couldn't kick them off anywheres else. I told Ram, 'Coach them. Give them material. Tony Williams is sensational. And I don't have the time to spend with them.'

"To me, Williams was a modern Bill Kenny. I knew that he wouldn't appeal to blacks as much as to whites. He had that kind of a peg. Then Ram took it from there. I did 'Only You,' in fact, the original version. What happened was that I used to use the group to back some of my other singers. Ram wanted a hundred dollars for the group when they sang backgrounds, but Syd said, 'Look, I can get any group to *ooh* and *aah* for fifty bucks.' So he gave them a release. I was damn mad—but when I got mad, he wouldn't call me. That's how I lost Clyde McPhatter & The Dominoes. But every act that was on Federal I found.

"I found James Brown in Macon, Georgia. I heard a dub in Atlanta—something Brown had made. I drove down to Macon with a disk jockey named Joe Howard. We went looking for him, didn't know where to find him. Went to a radio station, and somebody told us that a man named Fred Brantley, who owned a club in Macon, could help us. Brown wasn't really working in the club. But that's how I found Soul Brother No. 1.

"When Syd Nathan heard 'Please, Please, Please,' he thought it was a piece of shit. He said that I was out of my mind to bring Brown from Macon to Cincinnati—and pay his fare. And we put out that first record on Federal, not King. But then after 'Please' began to sell and made the charts—that was in 1956—Syd sang a different tune. Not to me, mind you. [Laughing] One day, when I returned from lunch, I entered the building through the loading dock. I could hear

Brown's record of 'Please,' and there was Syd playing it for some distributor. He wasn't in his own office where I might have heard it. It just so happened that I accidentally did.

"Brown was way ahead of his time. He wasn't really singing R & B. He was singing gospel to an R & B combo with a real heavy feeling. It was too much, and he didn't have another best-seller for over two years. Then 'Try Me' came along and went straight up like an arrow to number one and sold and sold. But that was in '58–'59 and soul music was coming in. We called his albums *Cold Sweat*, *Raw Soul*, and *Pure Dynamite*—and he sure was. He wasn't singing or playing music—he was transmitting feeling, pure feeling.

"Earl Bostic on King was a monster as far as instrumentals were concerned: 'Flamingo,' 'Sleep,' and others. He never sold blacks as much as whites. He was one of the first black instrumentalists to sell to whites. I was responsible for his style. I heard something. That's what made him—the sound he got. He played alto, but with a raspy buzz that made him sound almost like a tenor sax. He was a great musician, but we found the formula for him.

•

"I'm saving the story of how I got into rhythm and blues for my own book, but I'll tell you this. I was born and raised in New York, then went out to California. I played fiddle in my teens in New York. When I was fifteen or sixteen, we used to go to Harlem. That's where I heard Chick Webb, The Duke, and all the other greats. On the way to gigs, my friend and I would stop off in Harlem for some bathtub gin. I was still going to high school—Stuyvesant in Manhattan. Harlem was the end of the world when you didn't drive a car. And who had a car in those days? You went by trolley or subway or El. I was fascinated by what we heard—the sound of blues. We played what was known as Society Band style. Once when we played the roof garden on the old Astor Hotel, we were told *not* to mess with the broads, *not* to try to socialize with any of them. [Laughing] Musicians, in those days, were considered bums. If you went out with a girl and the father found out that you were a musician, that was it. No way!

"Then you must remember, I'm half Jewish. When you hear a cantor chanting in a minor key, it's not that different from blues in a minor vein as sung by black singers. You can sense the sorrow. That's why songs written in a minor key are hard to sell. They have that soulful, sad sound. Well, it wasn't that far from my kind of sound.

"You know the old saying?—every black can dance, every black can sing. That's nonsense. It's a matter of culture, of what transpired in your house. Blacks live with music all their lives. Their children hear music almost from the moment they're born. If other ethnic groups were brought up the same way, they, too, would be like that. The Italians were. It doesn't belong to any one race or people, but that is how it happened for blacks. There was something about black music that fascinated me, but I couldn't dig pop music. It was too artificial.

"When they danced to a blues, it wasn't dancing really. It was a result of what they were hearing, and their bodies reacted to it. Like their feet were not responding to commands of the brain. It was the sounds and the feeling that made them move. And that's the thing that became soul, if you want to call it that. I hate to use the word *soul*, really. I think that Perry Como has his kind of soul, Italian soul. After James Brown, the word *soul* became attached to it for the same reason that rock 'n' roll became the tag after Freed. If Freed knew what the hell he was saying, it would never have been called *rock 'n' roll*. I did 'Work with Me, Annie,' and my buddy Henry Glover did 'We're Gonna Rock All Night Long' with Wynonie Harris. We weren't talkin' about rock 'n' rollin'; we were talkin' about sex. But we were selling to a dull audience in those days. And Freed picked up on *rock 'n' roll* at the time that I was being lambasted for dirty lyrics on 'Work with Me, Annie' and 'Sixty-Minute Man.' The problem was that white kids were listening to these things for the first time. It was all right so long as blacks were listening, but as soon as the whites started listening, it was no good. Then it became a big, political thing. When Freed named it, he just took the idea from a Wynonie Harris lyric. If whites had known at that time, they would not have permitted the name 'rock 'n' roll to be used.

" 'Work with Me, Annie' stirred a big fuss in LA. Some phony politician who was running for office in the valley started the thing. One of the parents evidently heard their kid, who was nine or ten, play the record. If they can't understand something, it has to be dirty. That was the first time that a kid of that age was listening to music. Then, they had a PTA, some churchman—and I said, 'Hey, I've got to be on the panel. Let me defend myself.' I know that the producer of the show got letters upholding my position.

"On the panel, I said, 'Anytime you don't understand a lyric, then you want to attach something filthy to it. Look, a lot of pop songs are really dirty—"Makin' Whoopee." Listen to the lyric. What do you get for makin' whoopee? A baby. But, no, that's cute. Well, why shouldn't "Work with Me, Annie" be cute?' Actually, the word *work*—I gave that line to Hank Ballard. He came in with a song called, 'Sock It to Me, Mary.' I told him that that was too strong. [Laughing] Now, of course, it doesn't mean anything. The wife of Eddie Smith, who was our engineer and now is an engineer at Bell Sound, happened to come into the control room while we were trying to soften Ballard's lyric. Her name was Annie and she was pregnant. I said, 'I got it. *Work with Me, Annie.*'

"But there was nothing wrong with the word *work*. Like when somebody was blowing a solo, we'd say, 'Work with it, Baby.' Or when someone was dancing, we'd say, 'Work with it.' It was a common expression. If they wanted to make something of things, what about that billboard on Wilshire Boulevard? It was selling some kind of beer—and there's a broad with her breasts hangin' out. What the hell does a girl with her breasts hangin' out have to do with selling beer? [Cackling] The fact is when you hide something, that's when you make it dirty. If it's out in the open, done with good fun, we crack up. There's nothing wrong with sex if it's done with a sense of humor."

.

"I had my first record with Paul Reiner at Black & White. He came out of Cleveland. He was the first national distributor for independent labels. And the reason he got involved was that you couldn't get records during the war years. You had to order five hundred records to get fifty. How I got involved was another story. It involves much of my personal life. I remained with Reiner for about three years.

"My biggest thing during that time was 'Open the Door, Richard.' You say that you worked with the firm that published it, Duchess Music. Out here in LA, there was a cat named Goldie Goldmark whose office was on Hollywood and Vine. Now, who the hell knew anything about publishing in those days? This was 1946 or 1947. I did 'Open the Door, Richard' with a cat named Jack McVea. I was doing some blues with him. I got bored to death because everything sounded alike, and suggested that he do 'Richard,' which I had seen him do live. Then, I sent the tune to Goldmark since I knew it had to be cleared either through BMI or ASCAP for performances. I really picked Goldmark's name at random from the book and sent Jack McVea over to his office.

"There was litigation on the song, as you know. Dusty Fletcher, who recorded 'Richard' on National, had to admit that he took the routine from a cat named James Mason. That's why they had to settle. The publisher also put one of their own writers on the thing. For what

reason I didn't know then. We know now why it was done. I didn't
get a dime out of the tune. The publisher didn't even send me a bottle
of Coca Cola to say thanks. [Laughing] We couldn't find enough
presses on that record. I spent nights checking available plants, trying
to get enough product to meet the demand.

"Cecil Gant's trail-blazing 'I Wonder' came before 'Richard'—
while the war was still on. It was owned by Bill McCall with Cliff
McDonald, a great studio man. Later, McCall founded Starday Records and Don Pierce came into the picture. He had some bread. Gilt
Edge, on which 'I Wonder' appeared, was an LA label, like most
independents of the time. The big, first surge of R & B was on the
West Coast in LA, not in New York. The only one in New York was
Al Green, and he was out of it by the mid-forties. He was an alcoholic;
it killed him.

"Between Black & White and Savoy, I had my own labels, Portrait
and Bop. Three years with Paul Reiner and four with Lubinsky, then
eight with Syd Nathan, and after that, Chess.

"Henry Glover worked for Syd Nathan before I did and after. He
was originally a trumpet player and arranger with Lucky Millinder.
Glover was responsible for bringing Millinder and Tiny Bradshaw to
King. Syd also got some of the bands through Al Green, the Detroit
man who owned the Flame bar. Al also had Jackie Wilson, and Nat
Tarnopol owes his success to Green. He was his office boy in Detroit,
and when Green died Tarnopol got Jackie Wilson. Todd Rhodes was
managed by Al Green. All of these worked with Glover, except for
Wilson, who became the mainstay of Brunswick Records.

"The first act I recorded for King was Clyde McPhatter & the
Dominoes. Little Willie John and other prior things were Glover's.
My acts were the quartets. Earl Bostic was already with the label
when I arrived. He was going to quit, and Syd sent me to New York
to see what I could do with him, and the first thing I did was 'Flamingo.' I did one session at one time with Bostic and Bill Dogget
together. But 'Honky-Tonk' was produced by Glover. I got lost in
the shuffle at that time with an Ike Turner record called 'I'm Tore
Up.' I lived with Ike in East St. Louis for about three months. In
fact, I taught him how to write songs other than blues. [Chuckling]

"They were good days. But I didn't make the money I should have.
We did all the suffering, all the pioneering, and the owners collected
the money. I lived on the road for three and a half years (in a suit-
case). It was while I was with Nathan. I was separated from my wife,
and it didn't matter where I went. I'd flip a coin. And when I found

talent, I'd take them to Cincinnati. I found all types of talent, including at least one hot hillbilly songwriter-singer.

•

"To do it, you had to have a God-given thing. Don't ask me what the hell it is. I can't tell you. It was a kind of thing where you felt something. I remember once when Syd Nathan said to me—I was feeling pretty bad because I was cold—and he said to me, 'Ralph, a baseball player bats three hundred—and he's a bitch. I don't expect you to come up with hits every week.' But I was getting hit after hit and then, suddenly, I was cold. And Nathan said, 'When your Goddamn dick gets hard and your skin crawls, that's when you know you've got something.'

"None of my people ever sounded alike. I recorded Moms Mabley before anybody knew who the hell she was. She had a sound! Moms ain't funny. It's her delivery, it's the sound that she has. And it was something that I heard—and that I would hear—that would say, 'Hey, this is different!' Now, it may not sell, but the mere fact that it was different—that was one of the criteria that I had. And I was very successful.

"But getting back to the money: I don't feel bad about it. I have a saying: 'I'd rather have twenty bucks in my pocket and walk on top of the ground than to have left 10 million under the ground.' You know all these guys I worked for didn't believe in finding tax shelters for their money. They would hide it in safety-deposit boxes under all kinds of names. And when they died, nobody could find them. [Laughing heartily] So what good is it? They loved to carry money on them. Like Herman Lubinsky, if he didn't have a thousand dollars on him or a big, fat wad, he didn't feel good. He was a little cat. Ever notice that about little men? They either become dictators or record men. [Chuckling]

"When he was at the Barrel House one night, in Watts, he flashed all his money. I ran to Johnny Otis and asked him for a couple of cats to walk us out of here. He had diamonds on his fingers. [Laughing hysterically] You know it's a strange thing. I've been in the worst joints in the world. In fact, Henry Glover would say to me, 'Ralph, I'm black and I wouldn't go to none of them places you go to.' I've been in some bad places where they couldn't understand what I was doing there: 'What's this white boy here for?' They either thought that I was the man looking for *the shit*, or I was the man looking for the cat who had *the shit*. But despite it all, whether I lived under a tent of grace or whatever it was, I never got mugged or had a real bad experience. I had some narrow escapes, but nothing ever happened to me. I guess the Lord takes care of fools, sinners, and children, and I'm a little of each.

"I was blessed. I feel that I have left something behind me. I don't give a damn whether everybody knows about me. I used to go into a theater and see an act that I created, I found, I produced. When I say 'created', I don't mean it that way: they had it. I found the act, I produced their records, and they were big. I didn't care about the publicity. My thing was getting my cookies—listening to the audience scream for them. And I knew I had accomplished something. You have to remember that if you went to these places in the fifties where a black couldn't go and didn't have access—theaters, clubs, except their own joints—when an attraction came to town, they would come from 150 miles. I've seen them come with a handkerchief full of pennies—to get in, they saved for that one night, they were in their own world, they found peace, happiness and relaxation—that was when I felt that I was really doing something in my kind of way. And we did as much to break down the barriers as the lawmakers, the enforcers. . . . We did it in a natural kind of way. And I feel deep down that I played a small, but important part in the evolution. And so I feel that it's been a constructive kind of life for me . . . where I've given something. . . ."

Here comes that Greyhound with his
tongue hanging out on the side, (repeat)
You have to buy a ticket if you want
to ride. —TOMMY MCCLENNAN

Bay Area Blues

SOME TIME in 1945, Bob Geddins, a Texan who ran a record store in Oakland, California, rented a studio at Station KSFO in San Francisco and recorded a local gospel group, The Rising Stars. Taking a dub back to his store, he played "If Jesus Has to Pray, What about You?" through a loudspeaker into the street. Passersby who flocked into the store to buy the disk were required to put down a fifty-cent deposit for future delivery. Geddins had started himself in the record business.

By the following year, he had built a small pressing plant, assembled from parts acquired from the Los Angeles firm that had been doing his pressing. After a time, he could produce 500 78-rpm disks a day. Today, bony-faced and gaunt, the father of thirteen children, and still a resident of West Oakland, he prides himself on having been one of the first blacks to own his own pressing plant. He has many other things to feel proud about, too.

The story of Oakland blues is the story of Bob Geddins. During the '40s and '50s, he accounted for the bulk of recording in the area, launching a series of labels (Big Town, Art-Tone, Cavatone, Down Town, Irma, Plaid, Rhythm) and producing and leasing masters to such LA-based record companies as Swing Time, Aladdin, Modern, Special, Imperial, and Fantasy—and even to Checker in Chicago. Through the years, he discovered and/or developed a score of down-home bluesmen: K. C. Douglas, Jimmy McCracklin, Juke Box Bonner, Johnny Fuller, and Lowell Fulson, among others.

Working with these and other artists, sometimes writing for them, he created such hits as "Tin Pan Alley," by Jimmy Wilson; "I Want to Know," by Sugar Pie De Santo; "The Gamble," by crippled Ray Agee; and "The Thrill Is Gone," by Roy Hawkins. It is no wonder then that Joel Selvin of the San Francisco *Chronicle* and a devotee of Bay Area blues has called Geddins "as great a blues genius as there ever was." And Lee Hildebrand, a Bay Area musicologist, has written, "It can be said of Geddins that as a composer and producer of blues records in the '50s, his contributions are exceeded only by Willie Dixon of Chicago."

"I was born in Marlin, Texas, in 1913," Geddins told me. "And I began digging the blues when I was very young—Peetie Wheatstraw, Bumble Bee Slim, Walter Davis, and others. Later, Muddy Waters was my favorite." Geddins is a light-skinned black, a slender, energetic man, and an animated talker who gestures expressively with both hands. His face is a triangle, rising from a small chin to a large dome of a head. He squints constantly through large, shell-rimmed glasses.

•

"I moved to California around 1933 and was a city worker for six years, attending Frank Wiggins School to study electronics. My mother lived in Oakland, and I visited her on vacations. In 1942, along with thousands of Negroes who left Texas, Oklahoma, and Louisiana to find work in the wartime shipyards, I settled in Oakland. Working in the shipyards during the day, I took training in TV at the Central Trades, attending Laney College for two semesters. After the war, I went into business with a man named Wolf in the Seventh Street Record Shop. Repaired TV's before that. When I wanted to go into the record business, Wolf refused and I went out on my own.

"That's when I cut The Rising Stars. 'Brother Noah' was on the

Bob Geddins (Photo by Tony-Ray Jones, courtesy Joel Selvin)

back of 'If Jesus Has to Pray, What about You?' Those were the days of the big Jubilee quartets like the Deep River Boys, Charioteers, and the Golden Gate—they were all on the radio, coast to coast. RCA Victor had the Golden Gate. When the Rising Stars went traveling around the country, Victor wanted to buy my first record. I made six masters with the Rising Stars, and I cut other gospel groups like the Starlight Gospel Singers and the Pilgrim Travelers.

"Lowell Fulson was the first great bluesman I put on wax. Around 1946, it was. T-Bone Walker was then the big artist among black people and blues guitarists. He had a lot of new chords, and I taught them to Lowell. Bought him an electric guitar and amplifier—cost a hundred eighty dollars. And he did a lot of rehearsing in the Seventh Street Record Shop. I wrote his first two sides, 'Crying Blues' and 'Miss Katie Lee Blues,' and they hit off. That was about the time I put up my record-pressing plant. Stepfather and two or three guys lent me some money—maybe six to eight thousand dollars—and I bought presses from an outfit in LA. They sold me a lot of junk. I drew diagrams, and the Oakland Iron and Metal Company built new presses from the junk, from scratch. While I was traveling, Lowell's contract ran out with my Big Town label. He'd already had 'Trouble Blues,' a big one for him. My partners signed him to Trilon. That's when Lowell got mad and went to Jack Lauderdale, who was releasing my records in Los Angeles on Swing Time. Trilon sued Lauderdale. But I cut five or six sides with Lowell after that, including 'Three O'Clock Blues.' Oakland and San Francisco didn't know nothin' about blues until I started recording them."

Johnny Fuller, who grew up in Vallejo and who recorded for Geddins in the mid-'50s, does not recall hearing blues in the Bay Area until after the war. Johnny Otis, who was born in Vallejo and raised in Berkeley, claims that this is not so. If Geddins did not bring the blues to the area, he was surely responsible for establishing a medium of exposure that attracted bluesmen and that sensitized young black musicians to the sound. The basic factor was, of course, the wartime influx of blacks who knew the blues. Their desire for entertainment and their elevated economic circumstances promoted the rise of local clubs like Rhumboogie, Three Sisters, Esther's Orbit Room, Slim Jenkins's, and Manhattan in Oakland; Jimmy's 250 Club and Club Savoy in nearby Richmond; and Shelton's Blue Mirror, Club Long Island, and Tin Angel opposite Pier 23 in San Francisco. These provided employment for blues performers whom Geddins recorded, first, in the back of his radio repair shop at 711 Seventh Street, a few doors from Slim Jenkins' club; later, at his Down Town Recording Co. on San Pablo Avenue, just off Thirty-fourth Sreet; and finally, at his studio at 539 Eleventh Street.

The first major bluesman he committed to disk apparently just wandered into his record store after being mustered out of the service in Oakland and taking a job in the shipyards. Geddins was quick to detect the talent in Lowell Fulson, influenced early by the legendary Texas Alexander, with whom he worked before entering the service. But Fulson played with big bands when he was stationed on Guam. Swing inflections and jazz accents imparted sophistication to his original down-home, moaning blues style. As a guitarist, Fulson quickly became involved with T-Bone Walker's single-string style and modern chording, though his tendency to push the strings gave him a vestigial rural sound.

Geddins cut a dozen impressive sides with Fulson in 1946, recording him with just piano (played by King Solomon), just a second guitar (his brother Martin Fulson), or with a Texas blues combo (piano, bass, drums). Seeking wider distribution and capital, Geddins leased alternate takes of these sides to Jack Lauderdale of Los Angeles, who released them on Swing Time. Between '47 and '49, Fulson remained in Oakland, but his recordings appeared mostly on Swing

Time rather than Geddins' Big Town, and two sides were even released by Aladdin. That Geddins produced these seems likely, and he did issue some Fulson sides on some of his other labels: Trilon, Down Town, and Cavatone. In fact, Fulson's most important side of these early years, "Three O'Clock Blues," appeared on Down Town. By 1950, however, Fulson was in Los Angeles, recording exclusively for Jack Lauderdale until Swing Time folded and Lauderdale went into the motel business.

The Trilon label on which Fulson & the Ful-Tones appeared in 1947 was one of Geddins' many joint ventures and, apparently, a disastrous one for him. In addition to producing masters, Geddins undertook to set up distributorships.

.

"I traveled all through Texas, and my partners were supposed to make payments on my car and pay my expenses on the road. Lowell was known in Texas because of his work with Texas Alexander, and I must have sold fifty thousand Trilon records—his and others.

"When I returned to Oakland, feeling pretty good, I walked into a mess. My partners did not make payments on my car or even my road bills. I was traveling so long that my salary was attached—and I was flat broke. Without telling me, my partners arranged an auction and managed to be the only bidders. They ripped off a hundred and nine masters for nine hundred dollars. That was what I owed. Jack Lauderdale flew up from Los Angeles but did not arrive in time to make a bid. He tried to buy some of Lowell's masters, even offered as much as two thousand dollars; but he was turned down. Then, after my partners gypped me out of all that money, they tried to gyp the US government out of taxes and got closed down a few years later."

.

This was not the last time that Geddins was ripped off. His besetting problem was simply a lack of capital and, perhaps, a lack of business acumen. To feed a large, growing family and accumulate enough "bread" to make records, he generally ran a shop in which he sold records and repaired radios and TV sets. But he could never get far enough ahead to avoid taking in partners. Lacking capital for adequate advertising and national distribution, he constantly leased or sold his masters, which eventually resulted in his losing his artists. It was also his misfortune that he became involved with partners who took advantage of him. "Born for Bad Luck," he told me, was to be the title of a story he was planning to write. Nevertheless, Geddins has a remarkable resilience and he never stayed down too long. New labels, new artists, and new songs have given his career a longevity spanning more than thirty years. In July 1974, just after he had had twenty-six teeth pulled in a single dental session and while he was still putting ice packs on his jaw, he mumbled about new talent he was planning to record. And in 1976, he told me that he had a batch of new songs to record and could write a new song "every fifteen minutes."

It was his well-attuned ear for talent that led him to find Jimmy McCracklin soon after he lost Fulson. Along with Lowell Fulson, McCracklin dominated the Bay Area blues scene through the '50s. In Geddins' recollection, his meeting with McCracklin, who is still an active musician-songwriter-arranger, was again an accident. It happened in 1945 in Los Angeles, where McCracklin "was selling an ole record under his coat." The recording was a Globe disk of his "Miss Mattie Left Me." It prompted Geddins to invite the St. Louis bluesman to Oakland.

McCracklin, who recorded for Excelsior and Courtney that year, did not record for Geddins until 1947. "Railroad Blues," followed by "Jimmy's Blues," came out on Geddins' Cavatone label and also were released in LA by Aladdin. During the next two years, McCracklin & His Blues Blasters cut for Geddins' Down Town and Trilon labels. The eight Trilon sides appeared also on Modern in LA, and by '49–'50 McCracklin had five releases on Modern and the adjunct RPM. All of these were made with simple down-home accompaniment of guitar, piano, and drums. It was, perhaps, his desire to record with horns that led McCracklin to switch to Lauderdale's Swing Time label in 1951.

McCracklin made the national charts for the first time in 1958 with an out-of-Chicago Checker release of "The Walk," a song he wrote that became a favorite of teen-age dancers on Dick Clark's "American Bandstand." His reputation blossomed in the 1960s with four chart-makers released by Imperial of LA. The biggest record of his career, however, was made by Geddins at the beginning of the decade. "Just Got to Know," on Geddins' Art-Tone label, climbed to the No. 2 position on *Billboard* R & B charts in 1961. Although none of his other disks approached its popularity, "Just Got to Know" gave his work the impetus that has kept him an active performer into the present. In recent years, several of Geddins's kids—all seven of his sons are musicians—have been touring with McCracklin.

"When I was a kid in St. Louis," McCracklin has said, "Walter

Davis made me fall apart. But when I came out of the armed forces, I started boxing. I was going good as a light heavyweight—called myself Jimmy Mackey—until I had an automobile accident. I had twenty-three consecutive victories before I left the ring." A mashed eyebrow over his right eye is a reminder of those years.

"A blues is a message," McCracklin says, "a story you tell. That's what counts, not how well you play. . . . No artist takes off without walkin' behind somebody. I followed Walter Davis, who became a preacher, and learned some piano from J. D. Nicholson. . . . The way he sings, B. B. King should be a deacon or a preacher. He's one big man who is never too busy to talk to his old friends. . . ."

•

Although McCracklin was an old friend of "The Boss of the Blues," he was not an influence. Three other Geddins artists, however, either helped shape B. B.'s style or supplied him with material. Lowell Fulson was a precursor in the vibrant sound he achieved by pushing the guitar strings. And B. B. derived three of his most important songs from Fulson recordings—"Three O'clock Blues," "Blue Shadows," and his theme "Every Day I Have the Blues." Another Geddins discovery who provided B. B. with a hit was Roy Hawkins, about whom little is known. Hawkins was first heard on disk when Geddins released a series of sides on Down Town in 1948. Following his usual destructive procedure, Geddins leased these to Modern Records to which Hawkins moved after 1949. And it was on Modern that Hawkins made the national charts, first with "Why Do Things Happen to Me?" which climbed to No. 3 on *Billboard*'s R & B chart in 1950, and then with "The Thrill Is Gone" in 1951. The latter, also written by Hawkins, did not do as well for him as "Why Do Things Happen to Me?" which he wrote in a hospital as he lay recuperating from a car crash. But it was "The Thrill Is Gone" that became, in 1970, one of B. B.'s biggest hits. At that time Hawkins visited Oakland in the hope of finding a copy of his original record. After contacting old friends and scouting record shops in Oakland's black ghetto, he returned empty-handed to LA where he also had no success in locating a copy of his twenty-year-old disk.

The third B. B. King influence who came out of Geddins' stable was Lafayette Thomas, a guitarist born in Shreveport, Louisiana, in 1932. Thomas served as Geddins' studio guitarist, playing on innumerable sessions. But he also played with Jimmy McCracklin's band for about fifteen years. McCracklin claims that when his band worked in Houston in 1948, B. B., then an unknown, hung around "Thing" (Lafayette's nickname), mesmerized by the high, whining sound that Thomas produced on his instrument.

"I know that Thing showed B. B. a lot," McCracklin told Joel Selvin. "B. B. kept him up nights, trading licks, and working to get that sound." And Thomas himself recalls that B. B. whistled the sound he was struggling to learn. "He said, 'Oooooh, I never get that!' But when I heard him later, I said that sucker got it."

Today, Lafayette Thomas works on a conveyor belt in an Oakland water-hose factory. He plays an occasional gig, though he feels that he "can play anything!" and that includes "all that Wes Montgomery stuff."

•

When blues balladeer Johnny Ace, a teen-age favorite, accidentally shot himself to death on Christmas eve in 1954, Bob Geddins seized the occasion to write a song, "Johnny Ace's Last Letter." He had just recorded a new bluesman, Johnny Fuller, born in Mississippi and raised in nearby Vallejo, California. Summoning Fuller, he quickly recorded his new ballad-eulogy with him. Recoupling "Fool's Paradise," Fuller's first side, with the Johnny Ace ballad, he rushed the disk out on his Rhythm label. Aladdin Records of LA eagerly leased the master. Although it did not make national best-seller lists, Fuller claims that it sold a million. What seems more credible is his oft-repeated statement that club owners asked him not to perform the song because of the tears and hysterical reactions it brought from female customers. There was a Johnny Ace cult as there was a James Dean cult.

Fuller's style may have contributed to feminine emotionalism. For a seven-year period, Fuller broadcast gospel music over two Bay Area radio stations. The balladeers after whom he modelled himself were soulful bluesmen like Johnny Ace himself and Charles Brown. (Brown, incidentally, also recorded "Fool's Paradise," Fuller's first side.) In short, Fuller sang ballads with an intensity that suggested, though it fell short of, the impact of Ray Charles.

Yet he achieved his biggest seller with a novelty song written by Geddins. In an audacious move for the time, Geddins put "Haunted House" on both sides of a record, devoting one side entirely to the eerie sounds one might hear in a haunted house. Whether or not the disk sold 3 million, as Fuller claims—again it did not make national charts—it led to his embarking on an international tour with Frankie Avalon, the nasal-voiced teen idol of "Dede Dinah" and, later, "Venus" fame. Fuller stopped touring in 1959 and now works full time as a mechanic in a Sears automotive shop.

For Geddins, "Haunted House" proved something of a bonanza. It was revived in 1964 by Gene Simmons, who sold so many Hi Records that he was awarded a Gold Record. In 1970, it reappeared as a recording by the Compton Brothers, who made Top Ten in the country field with the novelty.

•

Of the numerous songs he wrote, "Tin Pan Alley" stands out in Bob Geddins' memory, perhaps because it was so long in the making. "I wrote it back in 1948 or thereabouts," he told me, "and recorded it with Turner Willis, who started with me in '45 on Trilon and Big Town. Nothing happened with any of his sides. And nothing happened with Bob Geddins' Cavaliers on Cavatone. Yeah, I made some records under my own name and leased them to Modern. Around 1949, it was. I played, I sang, I wrote, I produced, I manufactured—you name it; I did it all.

"Well, in 1953 I recorded 'Tin Pan Alley' with Jimmy Wilson. Put it out on Big Town. It started moving fast around the Bay Area. Soon I was getting calls from Los Angeles. Central Sales was the big distributor down there, and they were phoning orders in. Bill McCall of 4 Star Records in LA called me. He was a sharp operator. Wanted to buy the song and the Jimmy Wilson recording. He tried to tell me it was getting too big for me. I listened, but I didn't sell. Leased it to him. As I sat in his office, he got an order for twenty-seven hundred copies. I received a thousand dollars on a rate of a nickel a record. Later, he sent me a recording machine and amplifier. It was a big one, and there were cover records by Ray Agee, James Reed, Johnny Fuller, Junior Parker, and Pee Wee Crayton. I always knew it would be a big song, but I had to wait five years to prove it."

•

In 1976 Bob Geddins was still hoping to prove some things. In a sense, he was ahead of his time. He was a producer rather than a manufacturer, though he tried, with limited capital, to be both. Lack of national promotion and distribution prevented him from achieving the status of the Biharis of LA, the Chess brothers of Chicago, and Syd Nathan of Cincinnati. His contribution to rhythm and blues was largely ancillary, partly because of his economic situation—horns upped the cost of a session—partly because artists gravitated to the Hollywood labels when they had developed the appeal to reach a

Chris Strachwitz
(Photo by Arnold Shaw)

larger audience; and partly because the Bay Area seemed to have a feeling for down-home blues. Even though he was interested in more modern sounds, no one has made a greater contribution toward the perpetuation of that feeling than Bob Geddins. "Piano and guitar blues," he says, "those were the good ones."

•

As a purveyor of down-home blues, Chris Strachwitz runs a close second, and, in a view of the '60s and '70s, equals and, perhaps, surpasses Geddins's role. Strachwitz is a connoisseur and a musicologist of the blues, a folklorist and a field collector, and a record manufacturer interested in documenting the art and preserving the work of its pioneers. In 1957, a young Texas bluesman named Juke Boy Bonner cut some sides for Geddins in a then-popular Jimmy Reed style. Nothing happened, and Bonner returned to his home in Houston where he has since burgeoned as a poet. But in 1964, long after anyone had heard or thought of Bonner, Strachwitz rediscovered him and

recorded two albums. Call it avant garde in reverse. Strachwitz rec-
ognizes the blues as a minority art, perhaps revels in that fact, and
has not in a decade of scrambling ever attempted to reach for majority
acceptance. Today, with over 150 albums in his catalogue, he is able
to function without checking his daily bank balance.

But curiously, it was the more commercial form of the blues,
rhythm and blues, that aroused and developed his abiding interest in
indigenous and ethnic black music. Born a count in Poland, he fled
shortly after Hitler invaded his country in 1939. For a time, he lived
with an aunt in Reno, Nevada. Then settling in California, he attended
high school in Santa Barbara from 1947 to 1951.

.

"All teen-agers feel isolated and alone," he told me, in the Oakland storefront warehouse that houses the files and album stock of
Arhoolie Records. "But I felt I was an outsider as well. Not only my
background, but my accent, which is still with me but was surely
more noticeable then. It set me apart and made me a loner. I spent
much time listening to the radio and, at first, developed a love for
hillbilly music. But after a time, Hunter Hancock on Station KFVD
out of Los Angeles gave me contact with music and artists with whom
I developed a deep feeling of kinship. I can never get the sound of
his theme on 'Harlem Matinee' out of my ears—it was Johnny Otis's
'From Blues to Ballads, from Bebop to Boogie.' The alienation and
deprivation of blues artists was very real to me then, and it is even
now.

"The first record that I really dug was Hal Singer's 'Corn Bread,'
a honking instrumental disk on Savoy with the likes of Big Jay Mc-
Neely and Joe Houston's big tenor sax. That was around 1949–50—
up until then I was a hillbilly freak. This new interest grew during
the years I was attending Pomona College from 1951 on. I used to
go to the Olympic Auditorium to hear Big Jay." [Posters on the upper
floor of his warehouse include a colored placard of a concert at the
South Gate Arena, Oct. 17, 1952 by the "Deacon of Tenor Sax &
Band, Big Jay McNeely, Exclusive Imperial Records."] "Oh, the pure
excitement of that crazy music—I can hear McNeely at the big
Rendezvous Ballroom in Balboa. And Lionel Hampton, with the
clarinetist squealing and his cheeks puffed out like a balloon. Lowell
Fulson alternating with Chuck Higgins at a concert—the cops all
around—and an audience mostly of Pachucos and Chicanos, about
25 percent black, and, like, I was the only Anglo.

"Gene Norman was another disk jockey I listened to. He ran a blues show with Hunter Hancock emceeing. When KFVD went off the air at night, I'd pick up KFOX out of Long Beach. On Station KWBR in Berkeley, there was Jumpin' George [Oxford]. And then weekends I'd go down to LA to snoop around [Johnny] Dolphin's Record Store on Vernon and Central Avenue.

"At the Palomar Gardens in San Jose, I heard Smiley Lewis, who had a big one on Imperial in 'I Hear You Knockin' '; Joe Turner; Jimmy Wilson; and Joe Houston and his fat, open-toned tenor. I can't forget a concert at the big Oakland Arena, filled to the rafters by Fats Domino and Bill Doggett. Heard The Staple Singers there— great!—at an all-gospel concert. Around 1955–6, at Sweet's Ball-room, there were Jimmy Reed and Guitar Slim with his 'The Things I Used to Do.'

"After college I began teaching German in a school in Los Gatos. Would go up to Berkeley weekends. In 1958 I met Sam Charters, the blues scholar and writer, who lived there, and he told me, 'I found Lightnin' Hopkins in Houston.' It gave me an idea. I had been corresponding with Paul Oliver, the British blues scholar. In the summer of 1960, Paul and I went on a field trip through the South, looking for blues artists whom the world had forgotten and should have known. I met Paul in the lounge of the Peabody Hotel in Mem-phis, and later we met up with Mack McCormick, the Texas blues collector. In Navasota, Texas, we found songster Mance Lipscomb, who was working in the fields as a sharecropper and sometimes sing-ing at night for local dances. I rented a tape recorder and taped him. It became my first album release and the beginning of Arhoolie Records. Mack McCormick was responsible for the name, which is slave jargon for cornfield holler, and he wrote the liner notes for *Mance Lipscomb, Texas Sharecropper and Songster*. I printed those notes on a card that slipped inside the front cover. But I had to dis-continue the procedure because it was so expensive. [Lipscomb died in Navasota on January 30, 1976.]

"My second album was *Big Joe Williams: Tough Times*. I met Big Joe through Bob Geddins. After I bailed him out of an Oakland jail, I taped some powerful blues with him. I did this before I went on the field trip with Paul Oliver. Bob Geddins was active in Oakland long before my time—the only black man to make records and, in the postwar years, the only man to do any recording in the Bay Area. His hangup was that he lacked cash and partnered with different people, some of whom took advantage of him. He usually set up studios as an adjunct of his record stores.

"Lowell Fulson was and is an important bluesman whom he first recorded, and in '48 in Houston he cut Wilson Smith—Thunder Smith —for his Down Town label. If there is such a thing as Oakland blues or Bay Area blues, Geddins helped discover and shape it. Certainly, Bay Area blues is different from LA blues, and I like it better because it's closer to the raw, rural beginning of the blues. As it says on the album of *Oakland Blues* I issued: the horns here 'play mean and rough, not smooth and pretty as in LA.'

"Through the years I've taped or reissued such pioneers as Bukka White, Fred McDowell, Blind Boy Fuller, Li'l Son Jackson, and Lightnin' Hopkins. I've released at least three LPs of country blues and half a dozen albums of Cajun music. Oakland and Richmond have a large population of Louisiana black emigres—and their god is Clifton Chenier, King of Zydeco. That's a bastard music derived from a mixed marriage: blues and Cajun swamp music. Chenier sings in patois and plays a powerhouse accordion. I have ten albums of his, some of them taped live at a church in Richmond where his concerts are fantastic sellouts.

"I've recorded and reissued albums by many of the transitional bluesmen, the so-called urban bluesmen like Sonny Boy Williamson, Washboard Sam, Memphis Minnie, Tampa Red, and Piano Red. The closest I have to rhythm and blues is Big Mama Thornton (two albums by her), Joe Turner, Big Joe Williams, and, of course, Lowell Fulson.

"In its early period, R & B had guts. It had the drive and thrust and excitement of Sanctified Church rhythms. It lost all this in the rock 'n' roll era. But it actually started losing the blues, real blues feeling, when the schmaltzy vocal groups came in around 1956—I hated them and still do.

"I think back to the days when the guys would jam a microphone into the horns and blow wild. I can see Big Jay McNeely playing on his knees, hear the bashing drums and three blasting tenors, and feel the floor bouncing up and down. He'd play 'Dirty Boogie,' and the kids would be unzipping their flies. Big Jay became a Seventh Day Adventist, which was just right. Joe Houston was more primitive and powerhouse. Louis Jordan may have started it, but he didn't have the toughness of Muddy Waters. I don't mind R & B so long as it's blues as well as rhythm. Otherwise, I'd rather take my blues straight."

•

Considering the exciting and crucial role that the Bay Area played in the development of rock of the '60s and '70s, it is, perhaps, surprising that neither Geddins nor Strachwitz developed a record company of the stature of Modern or Specialty of Los Angeles.

As regional entrepreneurs with limited capital, both inevitably looked to Bay Area dwellers for immediate sales, Geddins more so than Strachwitz, who built up a mail-order business. Strachwitz was basically concerned with documenting the history of ethnic blues, and he developed a catalogue rich in delta blues, old timey LP's (as he terms them) and blues classics. Geddins catered more to the war-time migrants, an older generation of blues lovers who brought a taste for downhome blues from Texas, Oklahoma, Arkansas and Louisiana.

Another explanation is to be found in the Bay Area's position as an outpost of Los Angeles. The film capital was the center of West Coast blues recording, with its many studios, pressing plants, distributors and enterprising labels. Oakland and San Francisco served as a proving ground where contemporary bluesmen like Lowell Fulson remained only until they could make it in the "big town."

Even though Strachwitz developed a large mail-order business that brought him orders from blues aficionados around the world, he, too, sought local sales to augment his gross. Nothing is so revelatory of the downhome musical taste of Bay Area residents as the popularity of the hybrid blues form known as Zydeco. A phonetic corruption of the Creole French word for snap beans, les haricots (a traditional dish at New Orleans barbecues), Zydeco took hold in Oakland at the same time that the Haight-Ashbury district of San Francisco became the haven of the hippies and Acid Rock.

So popular is the sound that its most celebrated exponent, singer-accordionist Clifton Chenier, has for more than two decades packed to overflowing the churches and halls where he regularly performs. Known as the King of Zydeco and the King of the Bayous, Chenier was born, like his Bay Area followers, in Louisiana (near Opelousas) in 1925. He came to Oakland by way of Cleveland and Los Angeles where he paused to cut a single for Specialty. Strachwitz's Arhoolie catalogue includes ten collections of Zydeco music by Chenier. Singing in French, English and Creole patois, he shouts, moans and cries like any bluesman. Perhaps Zydeco is the Bay Area's version of R & B. But R & B as such never really had a chance in the Bay Area.

From
Fats Domino to
Sam Cooke

IN 1949 Lewis Chudd, a former radio executive who had founded Imperial Records in LA four years earlier, went down to New Orleans in search of talent. At Station WNOE in the Jung Hotel, he met a disk jockey named Duke Field, who was known as Poppa Stoppa. "He told me about a fat kid," Chudd said, as we talked in the Brown Derby in Beverly Hills,

•

"whom he heard in Good Town, an unpaved, black section of New Orleans. We took a taxi. Because of the prejudice against white and black mixing, we lay on the floor until the cab dropped us at a club, a bar, or just a joint owned by an Italian named Duke Pania. I think it was called the Hideaway Bar or Dewdrop Inn.

"There I heard a kid who worked Friday and Saturday nights for five dollars. Lloyd Price was on the same bill, and he was accompanied by the stout youngster we came to hear. I was offered Price, but I wanted the fat man who played the piano. He was so shy that he wouldn't come over to our table. I had Dave Bartholomew with me. He was a former Duke Ellington trumpet player who had his own band and was very popular in New Orleans. Fats played the piano in his band. With Bartholomew's and Pania's help, I finally got to talk with Fats Domino—that was his name—and signed him to a contract."

•

Lewis Chudd came to the record business via radio. In the mid-'30s he produced a popular radio program entitled "Let's Dance"—it was the launching pad of the Benny Goodman Band—and served as a key executive, opening the NBC facility at Sunset and Vine in Los Angeles. After a stint in the Office of War Information, he founded a jazz label, Crown Records, which he then sold to Irving Felt, who later ran Madison Square Garden in NYC. Chudd launched Imperial Records in 1945 with an eye on the Mexican market; Fats Domino helped establish the label as a giant in R & B.

His first disk, made in 1950, hit Top Ten in R & B. The semi-autobiographical "Fat Man" bore the credits of Antoine Domino and Dave Bartholomew, the latter functioning in a multiple capacity: as collaborator on this and virtually all of Fats's original songs, as leader

261

of his backup band, and as producer of his recordings. With the possible exception of "I'm Walkin'," all of Fats's disks were recorded in New Orleans under Bartholomew's supervision and all of them were cut at the same studio. Cosimo Recording, owned by Cosimo Matassa (who went broke in 1966), was the Nashville of R & B artists in the '50s. Not only Fats, but Bobby "Blue" Bland, Big Joe Turner, Ray Charles, and Lloyd Price used the studio.

Fats's style changed little from his earliest disk. Playing a driving, boogie-oriented piano that modulated into shuffle (another eight-to-the-bar pattern), he sang in a slightly nasal, high-pitched voice with a catchy jump beat. Although his style has been called New Orleans dance-band and Cajun boogie, it was the sound and character of his voice, youthful in its plaintive and pleasureable moments, that made him one of the biggest record sellers of the R & B years, and the R 'n' R years, too. In truth, he is one of the few black artists of the '50s who bridged both classifications.

Fats had a kind of ebullience, humor, and vitality that was beyond racial classification—and his intonations were appealingly childlike.

Fats Domino

His accent was Cajun, that exotic mixture of French and down-South English, and his singing style was not marked by any characteristically black or bluesy qualities. But his instrumental backing was typical R & B, including hot tenor sax solos by either Lee Allen or Herb Hardesty. He was one of the first black singers (along with Lloyd Price) to cross over without losing his original black following.

Born in New Orleans in February 1928, Antoine "Fats" Domino was one of ten children—seven boys and three girls. Although his father played violin and he had an uncle who played with Kid Ory's jazz band and "Papa" Oscar Celestin, Fats mastered the piano on his own. Before he was in his teens, he was boogin' the ivories in local honky-tonks for handouts. Apparently, he never completed primary school—something that may account for his inordinate shyness—but took a job in a bedspring factory to help support the large family. When a heavy spring fell on a hand, causing an injury that almost terminated his piano playing, he gave up factory work.

The bluesman who most influenced his style—piano style, that is— was Amos Milburn, the Aladdin artist whose record of "Chicken Shack Boogie" was one of Fats's favorites. But his meeting with Dave Bartholomew was pivotal in his career. As Fats tells it: "One night I dropped by a club to hear a new band that was playing there, and I asked the cat if I could try sitting in. He said, 'Sure, man,' and that's how I met Dave Bartholomew." Bartholomew, in turn, has said that he was so impressed by Fats that he immediately got in touch with Lew Chudd, who flew to New Orleans to hear Fats. Fats's dependency on Bartholomew stems in part from his inability to read music. "When I get an idea for a song," he has said, "I sit down at the piano and sing it into a tape. Then I've got it so that I can talk with Dave about it. Dave works on all my recordings and on my band arrangements, and we're together a lot of the time."

In his climb to popularity, Fats was a comparatively slow starter. After "The Fat Man" made R & B lists in 1950, he had five record releases before "Every Night about This Time" made the charts. Again, there were five releases before "Rockin' Chair" made Top Ten. But when "Goin' Home" made No. 1 in 1952, he was on his way. That was the year when Lloyd Price had a crossover disk in "Lawdy, Miss Clawdy" on Specialty Records. (Art Rupe found Price because he so much admired Fats Domino and went to New Orleans looking for someone like him.)

Fats did not cross over into pop until 1956 when he had No. 1 R & B hits in "I'm in Love Again" backed with "My Blue Heaven," a ballad of the '20s, and "Blueberry Hill," a C & W song introduced by Gene Autry in 1941. The impetus to record the last came from a Louis "Satchmo" Armstrong disk that Fats loved. In actuality, the transition in Fats's popularity came in 1955, the year of Bill Haley's "Rock Around the Clock," when Fats' "Ain't It a Shame?" was covered by Pat Boone. Although Fats's year-end ratings were entirely in R & B and Boone rated No. 10 in the "Year's Top Pop Tunes" of *Billboard*, Fats was not completely frozen out of the pop market and began to make a strong appeal to the young buyers who were gaining control of the record market.

The year of Presley's breakout, 1956, confirmed that appeal. While the Fontane Sisters covered "I'm in Love Again" on Dot, it was Fats's disk that dominated the pop market and made the tune (written by Bartholomew and himself) one of "1956 Top Pop Tunes." As for "Blueberry Hill," Fats had it all to himself, placing the oldie in the Top 50 of the year's "Top Pops." By then it was clear that Fats was really no longer a rhythm-and-bluesman. He was a rock 'n' roller, by virtue not of a change in his style, but the acquisition of a mainstream audience and his choice of repertoire. Except for his first few disks, he had never been a blues shouter or moaner. His approach to problems, furthermore, had a juvenile simplicity that, coupled with his flat-top hairdo and young sound, gave him easy access to the teenage market.

From 1955 until he left Imperial in 1962, Fats kept its cash register ringing steadily with one best-seller after another, aggregating no fewer than forty-three chart records, eighteen Gold Records, and a sale of over 30 million disks. In the '60s, like most American rock 'n' rollers and rhythm-and-bluesmen, he was buried by the British avalanche. Although it destroyed his power on wax, it did not eliminate his effectiveness in personal appearances. In fact, during the '70s he became a mainstay of the Las Vegas lounges. Despite his success and popularity, he remains a shy man who is ill at ease with strangers.

•

In 1957, at the moment when Fats was at the height of his record popularity, Imperial Records latched onto a teen-age singer who became the other mainstay of the label. Lew Chudd became interested in Ricky Nelson, then on Verve, when Nelson covered Fats's disk of "I'm Walkin'." If trade rumor is accurate, Verve had failed to sign Nelson to a contract when they released "I'm Walkin'," so that he was open to an offer from Chudd. Ricky was the real-life son of Ozzie and

Harriet as well as on their popular TV series. Sharing "I'm Walkin' " with Fats, but making an appeal to the younger record buyers, Ricky became a vital figure in the onrushing wave of teen-age singers (the soft-rock backlash) that included Paul Anka, Frankie Avalon, Connie Francis, Fabian, Ritchie Valens, and the college kid in white buckskins, Pat Boone. Nevertheless, in the interchange of artists and audiences that occurred in the late '50s, Ricky made R & B charts, beginning with "Be-Bop Baby" in 1957 and continuing into 1963, when he switched to Decca, with "Fools Rush In."

While Imperial releases included disks by R & B artists like T-Bone Walker, Smokey Hogg, and Jimmy McCracklin, only two other artists made an impact on the R & B market. Smiley Lewis, a Texan born Overton Lemon, was a Fats Domino disciple, but with a more gutsy delivery. In 1955, he recorded a song written by Dave Bartholomew and Pearl King. "I Hear You Knockin' (But You Can't Come In)," with its double entendre, finished as one of the year's "Top Pop Tunes." But Lewis, whose record climbed to No. 2 on R & B charts, was forced to share the honors with virginal Gale Storm on Dot. Her then-popular TV series, "My Little Margie," on which she competed with Doris Day as a pure-in-heart maiden, gave her the edge in the pop market.

"Smiley Lewis was a versatile singer," Lew Chudd observes. "Starting in 1950, he remained with me for about seven years. By 1957 he was recording country songs like 'Someday You'll Want Me' and 'You Are My Sunshine,' and he sang them well. Although Fats had no difficulty in appealing to the new taste of record buyers, most black singers had to make some kind of an adjustment."

Imperial's other R & B act was The Spiders, who came out of The Pelican Club in New Orleans. A bluesy group, their first record hit so hard that they looked like the find of the decade. It was a back-to-back best-seller, with both sides making R & B charts, though "I Didn't Want to Do It" appropriated a much larger audience than "You're the One." During the next three years, The Spiders had thirteen releases, but of the twenty-six sides only one other demonstrated any real buyer impact. Although it was entitled "Witchcraft" (not the Sinatra hit of 1957), the group seemed to lack it and they went down in the annals of R & B as a one-record group.

In the early '60s, Lew Chudd sold Imperial Records to United Artists Records and returned to the field from which he had come. He now owns several radio stations.

•

Dootone Records was established in Los Angeles in 1954 by Doot-sie Williams, who found much of his talent among street-corner singing groups in Watts. Williams invaded the R & B market with five groups, at least three of which originated at LA's Fremont High School—the Penguins, Dootones, and the Medallions. The most successful, the Penguins, was not unlike Chudd's Spiders. It created a classic R & B disk in "Earth Angel," its one resounding hit.

The Penguins did not reap the full reward of its presentation of the Jesse Belvin ballad, for its record was quickly covered by as many as twenty other artists—mostly white, of course. The disk that clobbered them in the pop market was by a white group out of Canada, the Crew Cuts, who had already ripped off "Sh-Boom." Their Mercury recording of "Earth Angel" finished in the "Top 30 Pop Records of the Year," while the Penguins merely fattened their sales from the spillover into the pop market of a No. 1 record in R & B. "Earth Angel" was outsold in the black market of 1955 only by Johnny Ace's "Pledging My Love," Fats Domino's "Ain't It a Shame?" and Chuck Berry's debut disk, "Maybellene."

The Penguins (who took their name from the penguin on the pack of Kool cigarettes) never again came within waddling distance of a best-seller, even though they had releases, not only on Dootone, but on Wing, Mercury, and Atlantic Records late into 1958.

The other four Dootone groups largely ate up the money that the Penguins put into the company till. There were the Medallions, a Fremont High School quartet led by Vernon Green. After being well received locally for their disk of "The Letter," they tried desperately but unsuccessfully to capitalize on the teen-age passion for cars exploited by Chuck Berry in "Maybellene." Their records in this genre included "Buick '59," "Coupe de Ville Baby," and "'59 Volvo." They postdated their cars with the hope that the disks could be revived five years after their initial release. But the disks were duds. Led by Don Julian, the Meadowlarks were no more successful than the Medallions, though they were more concerned with romance than transportation. And the Cuff Links and the Dootones accounted for so limited a following that their disks never made the charts. As the Penguins were a one-shot group, so Dootone seemed to be a one-hit company. But a catalogue of party records and albums by black comics kept the company in business.

•

Dot Records was not originally a West Coast company, and its relation to R & B is peripheral. Beginning as an offshoot of a mail-

Sam Cooke

order business in Gallatin, Tennessee, about thirty miles northeast of Nashville, it became a Hollywood label when owner Randy Wood moved to the Coast. Wood built Dot into a $5-million enterprise—that's what Paramount Pictures reportedly paid for it—by covering R & B records with white singers, notably TV star Gale Storm ("I Hear You Knockin'") and Pat Boone, who scored hits with Fats Domino's "Ain't That a Shame?" Little Richard's "Tutti-Frutti," and Ivory Joe Hunter's "I Almost Lost My Mind." All the same, Dot had one group that is remembered from the R & B years.

The Del-Vikings are noteworthy as a pioneer black-and-white group. There were only a handful of such mixed groups in the '50s. The Mariners, a pop group featured on "The Arthur Godfrey Show," the Crests and the Roomates of New York, and The Marcels of Pittsburgh are among the few that come to mind. The five members of The Del-Vikings, three blacks and two whites, originated in four different states, mostly on the Eastern seaboard. The group coalesced while the five were in the air force and stationed in Pittsburgh, Pennsylvania. When they won first prize on "Top in Blues," an air force show, they decided to record "Come Go with Me," written by Brooklyn-born bass singer Clarence E. Quick. The "studio" they were able to commandeer was the basement of a Pittsburgh disk jockey named Barry Kaye. His friendship led to a release of their disk on Fee-Bee Records, a local label. The record made enough noise in Pittsburgh to come to the attention of Dot Records, who signed the group and released the disk nationally.

"Come Go with Me" climbed to No. 10 on R & B charts. The follow-up disk, "Whispering Bells," also written by Clarence Quick, did not approach the popularity of their initial release, but Mercury Records was sufficiently impressed that they made an attractive offer. Since four members of the group were underage when they signed with Dot, they were legally free to accept the Mercury offer. During 1957 there were Del-Vikings releases on both Dot and Mercury, but the legal entanglements were eventually resolved in favor of Mercury. Nevertheless, the group never duplicated the success of their basement-cut recording.

•

The Keen label of Los Angeles came into existence in a strange way, and its importance in the R & B area is based on one artist: the late Sam Cooke, whose ambition led to its formation. Cooke, who influenced Otis Redding, David Ruffin, and Jerry Butler among recent singers, was himself the culmination of a blues-ballad tradition that had its inception with Leroy Carr and numbered Cecil Gant, Charles Brown, and Dinah Washington among its celebrated exponents. But more so than any of the others, Cooke added a gospel eloquence and melodic majesty that raised his balladry from entertaining R & B to expressive soul music. And he had a charismatic attractiveness that not only "sent" girls at the Apollo Theatre, but stirred men when he sang in church.

The Cooke story begins with the signing by Specialty Records of a great gospel group known as the Soul Stirrers. It was an old, well-established group, founded originally in 1934 in Trinity, Texas, and operating out of Chicago in the 1940s. Regarded as "the real creators of the modern quartet sound," according to gospel historian Tony Heilbut, and boasting one of the great leadsingers in Rebert H. Harris, the Soul Stirrers vied with The Pilgrim Travelers for the gospel championship in the late '40s. For five years beginning in 1944, they recorded for Aladdin Records. When Art Rupe signed them on Specialty in January 1949, Sam Cooke replaced Rebert Harris as leadsinger (and when Cooke left, he was replaced by Johnny Taylor, one of Stax's major soul artists).

For Cooke, his association with the Soul Stirrers was the culmination of many years of work as a gospel singer, work that left its imprint not only on his pop style but on his psyche. The son of a Chicago Baptist minister, he sang in his father's church choir and, before he was ten, in a family quartet known as the Singing Children. Attending Wendell Phillips High School in Chicago, he sang with a gospel group attached to the Highway Baptist Church. Known as The Highway QC's, they were sponsored and trained by R. B. Robinson, baritone of The Soul Stirrers. During the years when he sang with the Soul Stirrers, Cooke became "the greatest sex symbol in gospel history," according to Heilbut. "He was a bobby-sox idol, even in gospel, the first singer to bring in the younger crowd as well as the older shouting saints."

After singing with the Soul Stirrers for over seven years, Cooke approached Specialty Records about making some R & B disks. Well aware of the opposition of black people to mixing sacred and secular music (gospel and the blues), and fearful of the effect of Cooke's "defection" on the Soul Stirrers, Art Rupe rejected Cooke's request at first. Then he relented, but after he cut some R & B sides, he refused to release them. In his book on The Drifters, Bill Millar claims that the disks were released under the name of Dale Cook and that Sam was compelled to leave the Soul Stirrers when members of the gospel group discovered that he had recorded "worldly material." It was at this juncture that Cooke caught the ear of Specialty Records producer Bumps Blackwell (later Little Richard's manager), who left the company to form Keen Records.

The fledgling label's first release in September 1957 was "You Send Me," a ballad written by L. C. Cooke, Sam's brother. The same year, 1957, was a breakout year for many young artists: Paul Anka with "Diana," Johnny Mathis with "Chances Are," Jerry Lee Lewis with "Whole Lotta Shakin' Goin' On," the Crickets with "That'll Be the Day," Buddy Knox with "Party Doll," and the Everly Brothers with "Bye Bye, Love." It was also the beginning of an exciting career for Cooke, whose record zoomed to No. 1 on R & B charts and finished among R & B best-sellers just behind Presley's "Jailhouse Rock" and the Coasters' "Searchin' "/"Young Blood." But somehow the record did not cross into pop, at least not on the charts, though its enormous sale, reportedly in the millions, suggests that it attracted a large white audience, large enough to outsell Teresa Brewer's cover platter on Coral.

Certainly, Cooke's style, voice, and language had little black or blues coloring. He did not have Clyde McPhatter's stridency, Bobby Bland's paternal bluesiness, Little Richard's frenzy, or Jimmy Reed's down-home funk. He was really closest to Nat "King" Cole, but embodied a sensual intimacy foreign to Cole's cool lyricism. He enunciated in clear, Midwestern accents without sand, grit, or gravel. Though he employed *melisma*, giving the opening words, "You—oo—oo send me," an unforgettable sound, he did not *worry* words extensively, as bluesmen did, or indulge in *curlicues, flowers, and frills*, as gospel singers did. He sang in a soft, sensuous style, so gentle and sex-steeped that he reminded one of Sinatra of the war years. Displaying a feeling for rhythmic phrasing, he also managed to combine vulnerability with ego. Perhaps his most engaging quality was a kind of emotionalism that manifested itself, not in shouting or dynamic crying, but in a deep-down, gospel intensity—the intensity of a man so possessed by his feeling that his listeners could not help sharing them.

That this was, indeed, Cooke's design as a singer becomes clear from a statement that he made concerning the problem of "making your audience feel what you feel." He said, "If you have ever attended Baptist services, you well know what I mean. You have to stir up the emotion of the congregation and literally lift them from their chairs. To do this, you have to muster all the sincerity in your body and project it to every solitary person in the room." And you didn't have to be raucous, frantic, or exhibitionistic to accomplish this. Like Sinatra, Cooke seduced, did not rape, his audience.

From "You Send Me," Cooke's career took a steady upturn. Specialty Records suffered a quick change of attitude as "You Send Me" zoomed in sales; they rushed out "I'll Come Running back to You," a side that Cooke had cut during the period when he was begging to make secular records. "Running" made Top Ten in R & B. Keen scored again with "Win Your Love for Me" in '58 and "Everybody Likes to Cha-Cha-Cha" in '59. The latter was written by Barbara Campbell, co-writer of "Wonderful World," Cooke's last release on Keen. Curiously, Campbell's collaborators on "Wonderful World" were two men who later became record tycoons: Lou Adler of Ode Records and Herb Alpert of A & M Records and the Tijuana Brass.

By 1960 Cooke was of interest to the country's major labels. RCA Victor signed him that year, hoping to make him their answer to Columbia's Johnny Mathis, which he did, indeed, become. During the early '60s and into 1966, two years after his untimely death, he had one smash after the other, most of them moving into the Top Three of R & B. Cooke himself wrote many of his hits, including "Twistin' the Night Away," "Having a Party," and the seductive "Bring It on Home to Me."

What with his popularity, influence on other singers, and creativity, Cooke had the makings of a superstar. And like some superstars, he developed an arrogance that may have contributed to his undoing. The end came suddenly in 1964 when he was shot to death in a Los Angeles motel room by a white woman. The woman claimed that he had tried to attack her, and a coroner's jury returned a verdict of justifiable homicide.

The truth will probably never be known. But in commenting on the suspicious turn of events, Rebert Harris, the man whom Cooke succeeded in The Soul Stirrers, has said, "That don't make no kind of sense. Here's a man who has to run from women, and they say he's raping some woman in a fleabag hotel, shoot!" And Tony Heilbut observes in *The Gospel Sound*: "It's rumored that Sam, like the late Otis Redding, was really the victim of a mob killing. Sam Cooke's enterprises were big business." By the time he was killed, Cooke had branched out from singing into recording (Sar was one of his labels), producing, publishing, and managing talent.

Shortly before his death, Cooke spent a period of weeks attending gospel concerts given by his old group, The Soul Stirrers. He was frequently called on stage to join in singing some of the gospel songs with which he was associated: "Touch the Hem of His Garment," "Nearer to Thee," and "Jesus Wash Away My Troubles." Occasionally audiences manifested their displeasure that a pop singer was singing gospel, but according to Rebert Harris, who acted as emcee, Cooke received his worst setback at an anniversary concert in Chicago. "When Sam hit the stage," he reported, "the crowd went dead and stayed dead. . . . Folks were hollering, 'Get that blues singer down! Get that no good so-and-so down! This is a Christian program!' It pierced me to my heart. It shamed me how he was rejected by the home people. He walked off stage, tearin'. He was hurt badly."

•

Cooke was a formidable figure in the latter days of the R & B era. But it is difficult to view him as a rhythm-and-bluesman, even though he cut songs like Willie Dixon's "Little Red Rooster" in 1963, at the height of his popularity. While gospel excitement, rhythms, and intensities, were facets of R & B even in its inception, they became the dominant characteristics in the soul era. And Cooke, along with Clyde McPhatter, Jackie Wilson, Roy Hamilton, and others, was a transitional figure in the development that culminated with Ray Charles and James Brown.

4. The Midwest Mavericks

More than King Records and Vee Jay, the Chess brothers tapped the richest vein of delta blues and, through Howlin' Wolf, Muddy Waters, and Bo Diddley, behemoth bluesmen, promoted the transformation of urban blues into the abrasive, electrified, ensemble rhythm & blues of Chicago.

—A.S.

*I'm goin' to Detroit, get myself a
good job* (repeat)
*Tired to stay 'round here with the
starvation mob.*
—BLIND BLAKE

Record Company
in an Icehouse

WHEN the late Syd Nathan left the department store business in 1945 and set up a record company in a defunct icehouse on the outskirts of Cincinnati, the city rang with the sounds of country music. WCKY, a 50,000 watt, clear-channel station, programmed C & W records for four to five hours a day (even into the 1960s). WLW featured a program that was to Midwest listeners what "Grand Ole Opry" was to Nashville.

In 1937 John Lair, who had for years produced WLS's "National Barn Dance" in Chicago, came to WLW and launched "Renfro Valley Barn Dance." Lair brought from the Windy City such sterling country stars as Red Foley, Slim Miller, and Girls of the Golden West—and soon developed in Aunt Idy and Bill Clifford country comics in the style of Minnie Pearl. By the time Lair moved his "Renfro Valley Barn Dance" from the Cincinnati Music Hall to the actual Renfro Valley in Kentucky, WLW had a country show of its own. "Boone County Jamboree," as it was originally called, became the *"Midwestern Hayride"* in 1945, the same year that Syd Nathan founded King Records.

It was natural for Nathan to draw talent from the artists who broadcast from the Emery Auditorium in downtown Cincinnati— and the Delmore Brothers, Grandpa Jones, and Hank Penny, among others, soon became King artists. In time, Nathan developed a formidable array of C & W talent, including Moon Mullican, Cowboy Copas, Hawkshaw Hawkins, and Wayne Raney, the last an influential disk jockey as well as a songwriter and recording artist.

Cincinnati was not only on the rail route that brought white country performers and folk into town from Nashville and points south, it was also part of a large industrial complex that included Covington and Newport, Kentucky, just across the Ohio River, and was a way-station on the road to cities whose iron and steel mills produced one-fifth of the nation's metals. In 1945, Cincinnati also had a postwar black population that attracted the country's black territorial and name bands to the city's Cotton Club.

It was there or at a dance at a local arena that Syd Nathan approached Lucky Millinder about recording for his new label. "Lucky told him," said Henry Glover, long a King producer, "that he was

275

under contract to Decca, which Syd must have known. But he suggested that Nathan talk to his vocalist, Bull Moose Jackson, which he did, and then to his arranger—meaning me—which he did. I scratched out some songs and arrangements, like overnight. We did a session a day or two later, and out of it came 'I Love You, Yes I Do.' That was the beginning of Bull Moose Jackson & His Bearcats. It was also the beginning of my association with King Records, which ran for about ten years, into 1956. After a five-year hiatus with Roulette Records—I found Joey Dee at the Peppermint Lounge in NYC and wrote and recorded 'The Peppermint Twist' with him at the height of the Twist craze—I went back to King. When Syd Nathan died and King Records was bought by Starday, then by Lin Broadcasting, I went with Starday."

"I Love You, Yes I Do" became one of 1947's "Top Race Records," as they were still being called then. During the next two years, Bull Moose Jackson had a flow of releases on the Queen label, established by Syd Nathan to separate his R & B releases from C & W releases on King. In 1948 Bull Moose registered with black record buyers on "All My Love Belongs to You" and "I Can't Go on without You," both written by Henry Glover and Sally Nix, co-author also of "I Love You, Yes I Do." "Sally Nix" was one of Syd Nathan's pseudonyms, though he generally wrote or cut in as Lois Mann, his wife's maiden name. His major publishing company was called Lois Music.

In 1949 Bull Moose scored with two ballads. "Little Girl, Don't Cry" was co-authored by Lucky Millinder. "Why Don't You Haul Off and Love Me," Bull Moose's final chartmaker until the 1960s, was a country tune co-authored by Wayne Raney. Curiously, Bull Moose, who came from Buffalo by way of Cleveland and worked with The Harlem Hotshots, did not have a black sound. A hefty man with a heavy, low-slung jaw, Benjamin Jackson was a Crosby-style crooner, though his heady baritone was closer to Vaughn Monroe and the styling of his records was imitative of Tommy Dorsey's sentimental balladry. A mooing sax section sounded behind Bull Moose while the band played in typically slow, swing style.

The contrast with West Coast R & B was striking. Bull Moose appealed to the couples who smooched on the dance floor and came to romance rather than dance. Some of his records took a more earthy turn—"I Want a Bow-Legged Woman" and "Big Ten-Inch Record," for example. But Bull Moose was more lover-boy Benjamin than horny Bull Moose. As black and white listeners became interested

**Syd Nathan, Carl Haverlin,
and Herman Lubinsky**
(Collection,
Fred Mendelsohn)

in a more gutsy sound, the market for Bull Moose's romantic, swing-era balladry evaporated. Still, in 1961, when Seven Arts revived his debut disk, "I Love You, Yes I Do," it made R & B charts again.

•

Henry Glover's background was in the Swing era, the mid-'30s to mid-'40s. Born in Hot Springs, Arkansas, he finished his schooling at Alabama A & M, a state-supported college for Negroes. He went on to Wayne University in Detroit where he was eight credits from a master's degree when he became ill—"sick of education," in his words, "and attracted by the excitement of playing and traveling with a big band." He had studied trumpet with the man who taught W. C. Handy, and was taking a major in education to teach music. He had written some arrangements for Jimmie Lunceford while attending Wayne, and over a period of years after leaving school, he worked with the big blues bands of Buddy Johnson, Tiny Bradshaw, Lucky Millinder, and Willie Bryant.

These black bands were not as well known as those of Count Basie, Duke Ellington, and Jimmie Lunceford, or of such war babies as Lionel Hampton and Billy Eckstine. They played the country's black ghetto theaters and dance halls. Although all of them performed romantic songs in slow, let's-get-acquainted tempos, they featured hot saxists and were evaluated by their success "in blowing dancers off their feet," as LeRoi Jones puts it. The duration of a set was a factor, so was tempo; but most decisive were the screeching, honking, un-buttoned solos by hot tenormen like Illinois Jacquet, Eddie "Lockjaw" Davis, and Eddie "Cleanhead" Vinson.

That King Records became a major purveyor of big band rhythm and blues was, perhaps, inevitable once Henry Glover joined the company. But its location in Cincinnati was also unquestionably a factor. The Todd Rhodes Band out of Detroit, one of whose records became dee jay Alan Freed's theme—was on R & B charts in 1948 with "Blues for the Red Boy," and in '49 with "Pot Likker," written by Glover. Todd's female vocalist was robust La Vern Baker, who cut her first sides on King ("Trying," "Lost Child," and others) before she made her mark on the Atlantic label.

Tiny Bradshaw had King best-sellers in 1950 with "Well, Oh Well" and "I'm Going to Have Myself a Ball," and in '53 with "Soft," a typical, riff-styled swinger, which served thereafter as his theme. Out of the Bradshaw band emerged tenor saxist Sylvester ("Sil") Austin, whose roaring solo on Bradshaw's "Ping-Pong" was a high point. Lucky Millinder, who moved from Decca to RCA Victor in '49, landed on King in '51 with a giant record, "I'm Waiting Just for You," written by Glover, Millinder, and Carolyn Leigh. Later, she was responsible for the words of "Young at Heart" and other sophisticated lyrics.

Shortly after he joined King Records, Glover moved to Cincinnati "because Syd Nathan had built one of the finest recording studios in the country and staffed it with Eddie Smith, a former musician who was a brilliant engineer. "You know," Glover says with a smile,

.

"Sam Phillips has received great recognition because he did the novel thing of recording R & B with white country boys. He deserves credit, considering that Elvis Presley, Jerry Lee Lewis, Roy Orbison, Carl Perkins, and Johnny Cash all emerged from the Sun label. But the fact is that King Records was covering R & B with country singers almost from the beginning of my work with Syd Nathan. We had a duo called The York Brothers who recorded many of the day's R & B hits back in '47–'48. They sounded something like the Everly Brothers, whom they probably influenced. We were more successful in doing the reverse—covering C & W hits with R & B singers. In '49, as you already know, Bull Moose Jackson's hit "Why Don't You Haul Off and Love Me" was a cover of a Wayne Raney country hit. And Wynonie Harris' "Bloodshot Eyes"—on R & B charts in '51—was originally a Hank Penny country record. I'll confess that we didn't think we were doing anything remarkable. It's just that we had both types of artists, and when a song happened in one field, Syd Nathan wanted it moved into the other.

"You see it was a matter of Cincinnati's population. You couldn't sell Wynonie Harris to country folk, and black folk weren't buying Hank Penny. But black folk might buy Wynonie Harris doing a country tune. And since Syd published most of the tunes we recorded, he was also augmenting his publishing income and building important copyrights. He was a smart businessman and didn't miss a trick."

•

Nathan was also asthmatic during all the years I knew him. Overweight and a careless dresser, he hardly looked like the man who could transform a defunct icehouse into one of the country's giant record independents. Nathan developed a plant in which he could record, master, press, and produce finished disks, including the printing of album covers. He was one of the Henry Fords of the record industry.

"Multiple talents," he said to me during one visit I paid to his plant. (It could have been when I sold him an R & B disk I had produced.) "I'm interested in singers who can write songs, record producers who can arrange and write. I'm a multiple talent." There was a gleam of pleasure in the nearsighted eyes behind the thick glasses. And he added after a pause, "You're a multiple talent."

Henry Glover was a multiple talent—arranger, songwriter, record producer. As a songwriter, he ranks with the leading creators of R & B material, though he little likes the R & B handle. He feels that it was a "tongue-in-cheek, trade name given to Negro music to keep from saying 'race'," and that "soul was an expression of black resentment toward that designation." Glover's biggest, if not his best, song is "I'll Drown in My Tears," a 1952 best-seller for Sonny Thompson, with a vocal by Lulu Reed. Thompson's was another of the swinging blues bands nurtured by Glover. Glover's lachrymose ballad became a standard in 1956 when Ray Charles made the definitive version. "Rock Love" was another important Glover copyright, converted into a pop hit by the Fontane Sisters on Dot during the period when white artists were ripping off incipient R & B hits.

•

The culmination of King Records' activity as purveyor of jump blues came in 1956 with a Bill Doggett disk, "Honky-Tonk." Doggett was a musician who had played piano and arranged for the original Ink Spots and had worked with Louis Jordan, Lionel Hampton, and Lucky Millinder, whom he assisted on technical problems. "Honky-Tonk" consisted of a long, rasping, big-voiced tenor sax solo by Clifford Scott, supported by hand-clapping, electric organ, and a gutty guitar playing a boogie counter-figure. Stretching over both sides of the single, it was doubtless a studio-created instrumental since writer credits include Henry Glover, guitarist Billy Butler, Shape Sheppard,

Clifford Scott, and Bill Doggett. I have not been able to verify that one side of the disk was recorded live at a dance played by the combo. Syd Nathan claimed that the record sold over 4 million disks, which would make it the biggest seller issued by King Records, if not the biggest seller of the R & B era. In any event, it climbed to No. 1 on 1956's R & B charts and stayed on the charts for twenty-eight long weeks.

"Slow Walk," the follow-up, exploited the same elements as "Honky-Tonk": Clifford Scott's robust tenor sax, Billy Butler's boogie guitar, and Bill Doggett's high-flying organ. Though there was some similarity in the bluesy melody, "Slow Walk" was the work of Irving Siders, Connie Moore, and tenor saxist Sil Austin, whose Mercury recording of the instrumental paralleled Doggett's disk in its advancement on R & B charts. Doggett continued pouring out instrumental records during 1957, 1958, and 1959 with evocative titles like "Ram-Bunk-Shush," "Monster Party," and "Rainbow Riot." Only "Hold It," a '58 release, was a best-seller, but it never approached "Honky-Tonk" in sales or on the charts.

King was less successful with solo singers than with jump blues. But early in its existence, it made the charts with several male vocalists: Lonnie Johnson, Ivory Joe Hunter, and Wynonie "Mr. Blues" Harris.

Lonnie Johnson was well on in years when he began recording for King in 1947. Born in New Orleans in 1889, he was a country bluesman who had been an OKeh competitor of Blind Lemon Jefferson in the late '20s. A versatile guitarist, Johnson had gone electric by the mid-'40s. But, for his first two years with King, he cut with a typical down-home backing of piano/guitar/bass. In 1949 he added drums and scored his first R & B chartmaker in "Confused." In '51 he cut for the first time with a tenor sax. His biggest disk came in '52 when he recorded with a Todd Rhodes combo that included four horns, two brass, and two saxes. "Tomorrow Night" was a revival of a Tin Pan Alley ballad of 1939, but the sixty-three-year-old Johnson sang with a full voice that was reminiscent of the big blues of Big Joe Williams.

For Ivory Joe Hunter, King Records was prelude to his really big disks, as were earlier recordings on Ivory and Pacific, his own labels. Recording for King from 1947 to 1949, he achieved chartmakers in "Guess Who?" replete with a crying violin and triplet figures, "Landlord Blues," and a cover of Jennie Lou Carson's country ballad,

"Jealous Heart." After recording "I Quit My Pretty Mama," he quit King and went on to score giant R & B best-sellers with "I Almost Lost My Mind" and "I Need You So" on MGM Records, and "Since I Met You Baby" and "Empty Arms" on Atlantic. Ivory Joe was not only an appealing performer, but a gifted songwriter—all of these were his own compositions. The breadth of his appeal is suggested by an event that occurred just before his death in 1975. The "Grand Ole Opry" presented a testimonial program of his songs, and Ivory Joe, confined to a wheelchair by the ravages of cancer, appeared on stage to receive an ovation from the Nashville audience.

Unlike Lonnie Johnson and Ivory Joe, Wynonie Harris was a consistent seller for King and achieved his musical maturity on the label. Wynonie used "Mr. Blues" as a middle name, wore loud clothes, and, according to Jack Schiffman of the Apollo Theatre, had a set of vocal chords "made of steel." A tall man, he had a face-high forehead, a devilish grin, and tremendous energy. Manager Harold F. Oxley thought so highly of him that in *Billboard*'s "Encyclopedia of Music, 1946–7" he divided a full-page advertisement between Wynonie and Pvt. Cecil Gant, then the "I Wonder" sensation. By that time, Harris, who first attracted attention as a vocalist with Lucky Millinder and other blues bands, had made records for Bullet, Apollo, Hamp-Tone, and Aladdin. In 1947 he mounted the charts briefly with "Playful Baby" and "Wynonie's Blues," benefitting on the latter from the backing of Illinois Jacquet's wailing tenor sax.

The switch from Aladdin to King in 1949 brought him rapid recognition as an R & B vocalist. Although his first disk was a cover of Stick McGhee's hit recording of "Drinkin' Wine, Spo-Dee-O-Dee," he was able to climb to No. 4. With a remake of Roy Brown's classic "Good Rockin' Tonight," Wynonie tapped an erotic, double-entendre vein that yielded a series of best-sellers. On "Good Rockin' Tonight" you can hear the string bass walking the boogie, the cymbal splashing, the beat emphasized by hand-clapping, and the tenor sax honking and heating up the proceedings. It was an early "good time" record, later a staple of rock 'n' roll, and *rockin'* meant the same as *swingin'* had to an earlier generation, affording the male an opportunity to prove that he was "a mighty man."

Before 1949 was over, Wynonie had a No. 1 hit in "All She Wants to Do Is Rock." This was followed in '50 by two double-entendre songs, "Sittin' on It All the Time" and "I Like My Baby's Pudding." Neither achieved the success of his '49 best-sellers. In 1951 he tried to hold onto a slipping audience with "Bloodshot Eyes," a shouting version of the Hank Penny country hit. But "Lovin' Machine," a title that anticipated a Jacqueline Susann novel, proved his last chartmaker.

•

In 1951 Ralph Bass, one of R & B's most accomplished producers, joined the Nathan ménage, and a new subsidiary in which he had an interest, Federal Records, was established. Bass was responsible for developing a number of hit groups on both labels. One of the first that he brought onto Federal was the Dominoes, known after mid-'52 as Billy Ward & His Dominoes. The group hit the charts with their first release, "Do Something for Me," but the second, "Sixty-Minute Man," not only made No. 1 in 1951, but remained a best-seller for over thirty weeks. In a provocative bass voice, Bill Brown offers "Fifteen minutes of kissin', fifteen minutes of teasin', fifteen minutes of squeezin', and fifteen minutes of blowin' my top." And the sixty-minute man uses a phrase that came to identify the new teen-age music: "I rock 'em and roll 'em all night long."

The Dominoes serve to emphasize the very close relationship between gospel music and R & B. Clyde McPhatter, the group's lead singer, sang gospel hymns with the Mount Lebanon Singers, a group that rehearsed on the steps of Harlem tenements on 127th and 131st Streets. Along with other members, he participated in gospel fests at the Golden Gate Ballroom, competing with well-known spiritual groups like the Selah Jubilee Singers and the Brooklyn Crusaders. Eventually, much against the will of his religious parents, he entered the weekly amateur night contest at the Apollo Theatre, and he won. His association with the Dominoes came through Billy Ward, a gospel-singing Juilliard graduate who was seeking a high tenor voice like that of Bill Kenny of the Ink Spots for the Ques, a group he coached and accompanied on the piano. When Ward auditioned McPhatter, he decided to build a new group around him. The Dominoes were initially a spiritual aggregation, and they won first prize singing gospel on Arthur Godfrey's "Talent Scouts." When they made their first appearance at the Apollo, they sang opposite the popular Orioles, their program embodying raucous gospel/jubilee-styled material.

If the spiritual orientation of The Dominoes is not evident in "Sixty-Minute Man," it can be heard in "Have Mercy, Baby," also a No. 1 R & B hit that was almost as long-lived a best-seller as the erotic number. Although Rose Marks, manager of the group, appears as co-author of "Sixty-Minute Man," it is believed that Billy Ward was the sole writer, as he was of "Have Mercy, Baby." Recorded in an up-tempo shuffle, "Have Mercy, Baby" is a highly-charged disk, with a torn-up tenor sax solo, handclapping, and raucous shouting. It ends with McPhatter wailing and crying in a manner suggestive of the uncontrolled emotionalism of the Sanctified churches.

By July 1952 The Dominoes were recognized as one of the leading groups in R & B. When they nosed out the Five Keys and the Clovers in a Pittsburgh *Courier* poll, many regarded them as the top group. Beginning in 1953, they turned from recording new R & B songs to pop standards like "These Foolish Things (Remind Me of You)" and pop hits like "Rags to Riches," a best-seller for Tony Bennett. As their style changed, they switched from Federal to King, the company's parent label. Then, in '55, they left, moving to Jubilee for a few sides, to Decca in '56, and in '57 to Liberty. Unquestionably, the turn to a more pop orientation was the result of the increasing receptivity of the white market to black groups. The black shading gave a new attractiveness to such pop standards as "Star Dust" and "Deep Purple," both of which they recorded.

The Dominoes turn-away from gospel-inflected R & B was connected also with the departure from the group of Clyde McPhatter, who had been feeling that his remuneration was inadequate. Dictatorial Billy Ward allegedly paid him and other Dominoes $100 a week, with deductions for taxes, food, and hotel bills. McPhatter chafed, as did the others, under a disciplinary system where fines were levied for infractions. It led to a blow-off, which resulted in Ward's firing the entire group. But apparently Clyde had already indicated his desire to leave, for he was teaching his dance routines and vocals to Jackie Wilson, who succeeded him as leader of the group in 1953; Clyde went on to form the Drifters that year.

•

The story of the Charms, another potent King group (on their DeLuxe label), sounds as if it were concocted by a press agent. But it was told to me by Syd Nathan when I visited him in Cincinnati and dined with him at a private Jewish club to which he belonged. Peering at me through thick glasses that enlarged the pupils of his eyes to a fishlike size and gulping air as he wheezed asthmatically, he told me of how he had received a phone call one morning from his Hollywood distributor. The long-distance call brought a tip on a song that looked like it might break big.

•

"He played the record over the phone for me. It was nothin'. I liked the song—it was called 'Hearts of Stone'—but I knew I could make a better record. But with whom? The Dominoes were gone; the

Midnighters were on a winning streak, but in another groove. As I was sweating the situation out, I happened to glance out of the window. There, across the street from the factory, a bunch of *schwartzes* were playing stickball. I figured, what have I got to lose? So I opened the window and shouted and waved to them. They didn't want to leave the game.

"Finally, I went down and tried to explain that I wanted to hear them sing, that we were trying to form a new group. They didn't believe me and went back to the game. When they got tired of playing, I got them into the studio. I was looking for just one good voice. As luck would have it, there was one—Otis Williams. They were skeptical, but they came back the next day to rehearse. I had some sandwiches sent in, and that's when they began to believe that I meant business. They learned 'Hearts of Stone' by ear from the Coast record. Then they began working on an arrangement. They were one of the first groups to use 'Doo-DOO-Wah's' as a background rhythm riff. The lead voice had a black sound, but it was light and sad and young. He was not easy to understand and their record had an amateurish quality. Maybe it was closer to rock 'n' roll than R & B. But it went to number one and stayed on R & B charts for nearly six months."

Now that I have told the story of the Charms as I heard it from Syd Nathan, I will confess that I discovered recently that the Charms had actually recorded at least two sides before Syd "found" them. These were cut in 1953 for Rockin' Records and taken over by Nathan to build DeLuxe, the label he bought from a company in New Jersey. "Heaven Only Knows" backed with "Loving Baby" became DeLuxe 6000, and Nathan himself cut and had released no fewer than eight sides with them before "Hearts of Stone" came along. *Sic transit* the legends of record business!

The Charms maintained a following on wax for about four years. "Hearts of Stone" had a quick follow-up chartmaker in '55 with "Two Hearts" and "Ling Ting Tong," a nonsense novelty that was a bigger hit for the Five Keys on Capitol. By the time that they covered "Ivory Tower," a pop hit for Cathy Carr on Fraternity Records and for Gale Storm on Dot, the group was known as Otis Williams & the Charms. Otis' voice had a coffee-and-cream richness on "Ivory Tower," while the record had the high register piano triplets that were becoming a mark of the day's rock 'n' roll records. "United," in '57, was their terminal best-seller.

In 1954 Ralph Bass signed the Five Royales, a one-time gospel group that had produced a series of hit records on Apollo, including two No. 1 hits: "Baby, Don't Do It" and "Help Me Somebody." Into 1956 King released records regularly, but the group seemed to have lost its touch, and Bass worried that he had lost his. Then, in '57 they produced a best-seller in "Think," followed in '58 by "Dedicated to the One I Love." Lead singer Lowman Pauling, who wrote both songs, delivers attractively in a vibrant, heady tenor with a chesty vibrato. On "Think," a whining electric guitar responds to Pauling, the group, and tenor sax, and it takes the instrumental break usually reserved for the tenor in "Dedicated to the One I Love." The group sings "footballs"—sustained whole-note "oohs"—behind Pauling in "Think"; a female trio echoes him on "Dedicated to the One I Love." Revived successfully in the early '60s by the Shirelles, "Dedicated" has a chromatic melody rare in the simplistic field of R & B, and the arrangement on the Five Royales' disk also involves a rather unusual key modulation. Both disks are among the most musical and best structured of the R & B years.

•

With the acquisition of the Five Royales, Syd Nathan felt obligated to change the name of one of his groups, and so the Royals became the Midnighters. Although the Royals had had a moderate hit in their first release—a Johnny Otis song, "Every Beat of My Heart," revived in the '60s by Gladys Knight & the Pips—and in "Get It" in '53, they were not nearly as popular or as well known as the Five Royales. The first disk they cut as the Midnighters, however, brought a surprising change. (It was actually issued under both names.)

Drawing upon the quite erotic "Get It," they produced "Work with Me, Annie." Despite severe criticism of the song's sexual connotation—Ralph Bass rejected meanings that bluenoses read into it—and an apparent move by Federal Records to recall the disk, it quickly climbed to No. 1 and remained on best-seller charts for six months. On the heels of its success, the Midnighters cut "Sexy Ways," also a chartmaker, and dealt with the results of Annie's activities in "Annie Had a Baby." This, too, climbed to No. 1. There was still another follow-up in "Annie's Aunt Fannie," but apparently listeners were not interested in the lady's relatives, regardless of how earthy they might be.

"Annie" stirred so much controversy and interest that a number of other groups—in the tradition of country records—produced answer disks. The El Dorados on Vee Jay cut "Annie's Answer," while the

Platters, then on the Federal label, replied, "Maggie Doesn't Work Here Anymore." Neither found much acceptance. Enormously popular, however, was "The Wallflower," which was so closely identified with the original "Annie" song that Hank Ballard was credited as a co-writer by Johnny Otis and Etta James, who cut and co-authored. "Wallflower" faced the same censorship as the "Annie" songs, but that did not hurt its popularity with R & B record buyers. It climbed to No. 2. And it naturally attracted a white cover in the peak year (1955) of white rip-offs of black hits. In the Georgia Gibbs version, sexual overtones were eliminated by calling the song "Dance with Me, Henry." It became one of the Top Ten pop hits of the year. The Midnighters produced their own answer, "Henry's Got Flat Feet," which might also be a description of their disk.

Hank Ballard, born in Detroit in 1936, was the creative force behind the Midnighters, writing some of their hits and singing lead. He had a high-pitched tenor reminiscent of Lowman Pauling and Clyde McPhatter. Despite the group's enormous sales and popularity in '54, five years passed before it again registered on wax. It came back on the charts in 1959—by then on King and billed as Hank Ballard & the Midnighters—with a Henry Glover ballad, "Teardrops on Your Letter." Hardly a number one would associate with the rocking rhythms and earthiness of the "Annie" songs, "Teardrops" was backed by a Hank Ballard rocker entitled "The Twist." Yes, it was *the* twist song that became such a smash in 1960 for Chubby Checker, a former chicken plucker, and that accounted for one of the biggest dance crazes of the '60s. Ballard's version was definitely the "B" side to "Teardrops," which went to No. 4 on R & B charts. Reissued at the height of the craze, "The Twist" did better, but not nearly as well as Chubby's version. (Checker devised his name as a variant of Fats Domino, but he is really not plump, and was and is a fantastic dancer.)

"Teardrops" was the prelude to two years of chart-busting disks for Ballard & the Midnighters. "Finger Poppin' Time" was a raucous, rocking, party platter from its initial group shouts of "HEY now! HEY now!" "I feel so goo—ood," Hank sang, supported by the group's "oohing" and stretching of words—and a knocked-out sax screeched and hung on the rhythm of "HEY now! HEY now!" It was "fing-er, finger poppin' time"—whatever that meant. To teen-agers, it meant the excitement and merriment of a wonderful party. The names of kids coming to the shindig were mentioned, just as rock 'n' roll dee jays did in playing a request record.

"Let's Go, Let's Go, Let's Go," an even bigger 1960 hit, traded also on the evocation of a rocking party atmosphere. "There's a thrill up on the hill!" Ballard sang and, to a rocking boogie beat, shouted, "All right, we're gonna ball!" None of the group's '61 hits approached the popularity of either of the so-called party records, but they made the transition from R & B to R 'n' R.

•

The range of King's considerable contribution to the rise and flowering of R & B is well documented in two Columbia albums that comprise what is, perhaps, the best small R & B collection. Syd Nathan was extremely fond of a young man named Seymour Stein, who went to work for him after a stint in *Billboard*'s charts department. (There were rumors at the time of a tie-up between charters at *Cash Box* and *Billboard* that resulted in manipulated statistics.) It was through Stein, who wrote the informative liner notes, that Columbia was able to issue *18 King Size Rhythm & Blues Hits* and *Anthology of Rhythm & Blues*, Vol. I, all drawn from the catalogues of King and its subsidiaries. No other collection quite approaches these in communicating the rowdy, robust, down-to-earth, party spirit of R & B. Included are artists for whom King provided a springboard into other record pools: Joe Tex with "Another Woman's Man"; the Platters with an early version of "Only You"; and Otis Redding with "Shout Bamalama," which reveals an early indebtedness to Little Richard's frantic styling and rhythmic exclamations. Included also are three selections by a powerhouse balladeer who came to the Nathan ménage in 1955 and who had one of the most consistent best-seller records of any King artist except James Brown.

His name was John Davenport, but he became known as Little Willie John. He was discovered in Detroit by Johnny Otis, peregrinating talent scout extraordinaire, who brought him to the attention of Syd Nathan. Willie John made the charts at the age of seventeen with his first record, "All Around the World." Before it stopped selling, he had another popular record in "Need Your Love So Bad." Later that year, he produced his best-known ballad, "Fever," a No. 1 song he co-wrote. It stayed on the R & B charts for six months of 1956. Apart from an intriguing background, stark in its sound and rhythmic simplicity, "Fever" was fresh in concept and potent in its gospel-like expression of sensual love. Although the time was early for soul, Willie John crossed the dividing line between R & B and Soul—in his intensity, if not in the background and beat of the record. (Two years later, Peggy Lee had perhaps the biggest pop hit of her distinguished career in a version of "Fever" that was patently modelled on the arrangement on Little Willie John's disk.)

He followed "Fever" with "Talk to Me, Talk to Me," a song possessed of a plaintive quality and a ballad sound that anticipated Sam Cooke. Little Willie John had a more gritty and penetrating voice than Cooke's, but he communicated as much fervor, if less tenderness. Through 1958 and '59 he produced chartmakers in "Let Them Talk," "Heartbreaker (It's Hurtin' Me)," and other blues ballads. Then, in '60 he demonstrated his versatility and the power of his pipes with a version of an old Tin Pan Alley standard used by Fred Waring as the theme of his Pennsylvanians; "Sleep" became a best-seller with R & B listeners.

James Brown

Little Willie John's name disappeared from record charts after 1961, though in that year he had a winner in "Take My Love." But it was not that record buyers tired of him; that year, he lost his temper in a street brawl and killed a man. He died of pneumonia in prison in 1968.

•

The King stable nurtured quite a number of other artists. There was saxist Earl Bostic, who made it with a version of "Flamingo." Hefty Annie Laurie had a ballad hit in "It Hurts to be in Love." Donnie Elbert was striking in his high-pitched, almost *falsetto* rendition of "What Can I Do?" And then there was the preeminent vocalist of all. James Brown came to the label in 1956 through Ralph Bass, and his first record, "Please, Please, Please," was marked by an unbuttoned emotionalism that soon brought him recognition as "Soul Brother No. 1."

If you want to have plenty women,
*   why not work at the Chicago mill?*
You don't have to give them nothin',
*   ooh well, jest tell them that you will.*
—PEETIE WHEATSTRAW

Storefront Record Company

CHESS RECORDS and its subsidiaries, Checker and Cadet, were born in a street-level store at Seventy-first and Phillips in Chicago. Their studio was in the back. To add echo, inventive Leonard Chess hung an open microphone in their tiny toilet. (Columbia Records later used a five-story stairwell at 799 Seventh Avenue in NYC as an echo chamber.) For tape echo effects and distortion, they suspended a ten-foot section of sewer pipe from the ceiling of their so-called studio. They drove around the South Side of Chicago peddling and delivering their finished records from the trunk of their car. They had 180 accounts in that area alone because, according to the late Leonard Chess, "every porter, Pullman conductor, beauty and barber shop was selling records in those days."

Their original label was not called Chess but Aristocrat. They launched it in 1946–7. It was really an offshoot of The Macomba, a South Side night club the Chess brothers operated at Thirty-ninth Street and Cottage Grove. The Macomba presented performers like Louis Armstrong, Lionel Hampton, Billy Eckstine, and Ella Fitzgerald. The apparent interest of several record company talent scouts in a newcomer named Andrew Tibbs provoked the Chess brothers to record him themselves. The catalog number of "Union Man Blues" backed with "Bilbo's Dead" was 1425, the number of the house on South Karlov Avenue in Chicago's Jewish section where Phil and Leonard Chess first settled in 1928 when they emigrated from their native Poland.

Aristocrat Records was not too successful. Nonetheless, in the three years of its existence, it "discovered" one of the most important of all postwar delta bluesmen. Leonard Chess has said that McKinley Morganfield, better known as Muddy Waters, just walked into their storefront office off the street. Doubtless, some Chess artists did, among them Willie Mabon of Memphis, Tennessee, Bo Diddley of McComb, Mississippi, Sonny Boy Williamson of Glendora, Mississippi, and Chuck Berry of East St. Louis, Missouri. The street-level storefront, with its similarity to Negro storefront churches, seemed to invite black artists in a way that offices in a tall building would not. All the same, there is reason to believe that another blues emigré from the Mississippi Delta, Sunnyland Slim, at least sponsored Muddy if he did not introduce him to the Chess brothers. A talent scout for Chess apparently went to hear Muddy at one of the small Chicago clubs where he was then playing. And the following day, a friend came looking for him—Muddy drove his uncle's coal truck during the day—to tell him that he was wanted at the Chess studios.

In addition to Muddy, the Chess brothers nurtured and showcased the ample talents of Howlin' Wolf, Little Walter, and Bo Diddley, three other funky bluesmen, as well as the less popular talents of down-home performers like Willie Mabon, Sonny Boy Williamson, and Lowell Fulson. As King Records of Cincinnati became the disk forum for the big-band, blues-band strain of R & B, so Chess was the focus of the electric, Chicago, ensemble style of R & B.

"We're doing the stuff," Muddy Waters said, "like we did 'way years ago down in Mississippi." But the stuff was electrified and the rasping, rural voices were accompanied by a roaring combo—piano, bass, drums, harp, amplified guitar, and horns.

Leonard Chess did not just sit in the label's storefront office waiting for bluesmen to come stomping up from the South. Twice a year, he lugged a heavy Magnecord recorder, a primitive two-piece model, into his car and drove deep into Mississippi, Arkansas, and Louisiana seeking talent. On occasion, he would set up his tape recorder in a cotton field, run a long extension cord into the plantation manse, and record a bluesman in the field.

It was on one of these field trips that Leonard discovered Howlin' Wolf in West Memphis, Arkansas, and recorded "Saddle My Pony" backed with "Worried All the Time," the Wolf's first two sides. Ike Turner was on piano and James Cotton on harp. On another trip, he was able to tape sides with Arthur "Big Boy" Crudup in Jackson, Mississippi. (The sides appeared under the name of Percy Lee Crudup, perhaps because Big Boy recorded for Victor.) Probably Leonard's most rewarding trip was a 1951 visit to Memphis, Tennessee, when he acquired Jackie Brenston's "Rocket 88," a bouncing boogie instrumental,.through Sam Phillips of Sun Records. In the year of Johnnie Ray's "Cry," the Clovers' "Fool, Fool, Fool," and Earl Bostic's "Flamingo"—other No. 1 R & B chart disks—"Rocket 88" finished among the Top Ten best-sellers.

Several years later, in Shreveport, Louisiana, Leonard was introduced to Fats Washington by Stan Lewis, a top dee jay known as Stan the Record Man. When Chess exhibited a favorable reaction to a song that Washington auditioned for him, the writer offered to sell it for $25. "I refused," Leonard said later. "I'd learned some hard lessons on buying songs. If the song is good, a writer will sometimes later say you approached him first. So I suggested Stan buy a piece. He did." It was a valuable piece. Chess cut "I'll Be Home" with the Flamingos, and Pat Boone covered it, yielding a big best-seller.

•

Chess Records succeeded Aristocrat in 1949–50, its blue and white label with the chessboard motif appearing for the first time in June 1950. The Chess brothers were off to an auspicious start with their first release. They had arranged a session for jazz tenorman Gene Ammons, booking time at Chicago's Universal Studio. It was, of course, to be a "head" session—no charts—with Ammons improvising on ballad standards like "Pennies from Heaven," title tune of a '36 Bing Crosby film. At one point, Ammons and pianist Junior Mance began toying with "My Foolish Heart" by Victor Young, title tune of a then-current Susan Hayward film and audible on the air on a Billy Eckstine disk. It resulted in the one side that made the charts. Through it, the new label secured national distribution, something never achieved by Aristocrat Records.

In the three succeeding years, Chess and Checker (formed in 1952) established themselves as new labels of consequence with Top Ten best-sellers. Jackie Brenston's "Rocket 88" was followed in 1952 by Little Walter's "Juke" and in '53 by Willie Mabon's "I Don't Know." Mabon was a Memphis-born lad who came to Chicago with his

292 THE MIDWEST MAVERICKS

family in 1941 when he was only sixteen. Already a harmonica wizard, he mastered the piano while attending Du Sable High School in Chicago. Before he cut his first record for Apollo in '44, he was a newsboy, baker, mechanic, plumber, and a U.S. Marine. It was his own song "I Don't Know" that landed him a Chess recording contract in '52. The following year, he again had a No. 1 R & B best-seller in another original ballad, "I'm Mad." Devoid of down-home blues influences, he was a modern rhythm-and-bluesman who worked in the blues band tradition and recorded with horns almost from the start.

•

In a *Billboard* interview, Leonard Chess called Willie Dixon "his right arm." Born in Vicksburg, Mississippi, in 1915, Willie is remembered by Little Brother Montgomery as a fat boy of seven or eight who chased after the flat-bed truck on which his band rode and played to advertise the evening's concert. At fourteen Willie spent a year in the county farm, known as The Ballground, for stealing bathroom fixtures from an empty house. When he came to Chicago in 1935, he was interested in boxing and won the Golden Gloves the following year. Guitarist Leonard Castor, known as "Baby Doo," used to bring his instrument to the gym where Dixon worked out. They began harmonizing and that was the end of boxing.

When Memphis Slim & His House Rockers recorded for Miracle Records of Chicago in 1947, Willie played bass. That year, he also recorded on his own with the Big Three Trio, cutting his own song "Wee Wee Baby" for Columbia. Dixon came to Aristocrat Records early in its existence to produce and play on a Robert Nighthawk session in which "Little Black Angel," became, in the atmosphere of the time, "Little Angel."

"Everything was head arrangements," Dixon later recalled. "You have to get a feeling and a mood. You can't work a session like that from something on paper. A man feels different when he's on the street from when he comes into a studio to cut."

Dixon went on to become Chess's leading talent scout, an accomplished record producer—the Lester Melrose of Chicago's postwar years—and a bassist who played on hundreds of sessions with artists from Muddy Waters to Otis Rush. In addition, he wrote over 200 copyrights, accounting for some of the best-known songs of Muddy Waters, Little Walter, and many other Chess artists. Dixon is still active today as a performer, recording artist and record manufacturer with his own label.

After a time the Chess brothers moved their ménage to East Forty-ninth Street, where they effectively made the transition from R & B to R 'n' R. Two men were pivotal in this development: Chuck Berry, who became the singer laureate of the teen-age generation; and Alan Freed, the disk jockey who first called teen-age music rock 'n' roll and revolutionized the craft of platter chatter. In 1954, the Moonglows, who had recorded for Champagne and Chance Records, scored their first hit in "Sincerely," co-written by lead singer Harvey Fuqua and Alan Freed. The following year, Freed was present at the recording of Chuck Berry's first hit, and he contributed greatly to the success of "Maybellene," which, along with "Rock Around the Clock," sounded the tocsin of the rock revolution.

In the 1960s, the Chess brothers also expanded into the jazz field, releasing hits by Ramsey Lewis, Ahmad Jamal, Wes Montgomery, and Ray Bryant. Leonard Chess died of a heart attack in October 1969 at the age of fifty-two. By then the brothers owned L & P Broadcasting, with stations in Chicago and Milwaukee, and had sold their recording labels for a figure in the millions to the GRT conglomerate, which moved the enterprise to NYC. Phil Chess continued with the new administration for a time, but soon left to run Station WVON, regarded as the leading black station in the Midwest. Marshall Chess, Leonard's son, gave familial continuity to the firm as a producer and vice-president. Ralph Bass returned to Chess as a producer and head of the Chicago office.

Although the firm continued to be receptive to the work of rhythm-and-bluesmen like Muddy Waters and Howlin' Wolf, and released recordings by these pioneers during the post-Beatles R & B revival, it was sharply criticized for a lack of sensitivity. In the year of Leonard's death, Phil Chess had to browbeat Howlin' Wolf to get him to record with a psychedelic combo; afterward, the Wolf characterized the results as "dogshit." Blues critic Pete Welding denounced *Electric Mud* and *After the Rain*, LP's by Muddy Waters, as exercises in "bad taste."

The most bitter criticism of the Chess brothers came from Etta James, who recorded for them and produced a series of chartmakers between 1960 and 1963— "All I Could Do Was Cry," "Something's Got a Hold on Me," and "Pushover," appeared on their Argo label. Previously, Etta had rocked the R & B world with "Wallflower" on Modern Records. In 1973, when the new Chess organization brought her back in the studio and mounted a huge campaign to reestablish her, she said of the old Chess management: "The Chess brothers didn't know A from Z in a beat. Leonard Chess would get in the booth with me while I was recording, and when I would get to a part where he thought I should squawl or scream "wheeawow!" he'd punch me in the side. I mean literally *punch* me. Or he'd pinch me real hard, so I'd go "yeeeeow." And whatever tune had the most "ooooch" or "eeech" or whatever, that's the tune he thought was going to be the hit.

"Then he'd sit there and listen to the playback, and he wouldn't pat his foot until I'd seen him sneaking a look at *my* foot. He'd have to look around and see if my foot was patting. And if he couldn't see it patting, he'd say, 'Etta, I don't think that tune's any good.' And then I'd wait until some old jive tune that wasn't anything came on, and I'd pat my foot and say, 'How do you like that one?' And he'd say, 'That's it! That's going to be the hit record! Believe what Leonard tells you!' He knew nothing about it."

Nevertheless, in 1960 Etta James had two songs on R & B charts. In 1961 she had four, including "At Last," a No. 2 hit. In 1962 she had three, including "Something's Got a Hold on Me," which went to No. 4. And in 1963 she had one—a total of ten chartmakers in three years. When she began recording again in 1973, she praised Gabriel Mekler, her new producer, saying, "This is the first time I've been able to pick my own tunes and do what I wanted to do. . . ." Without discounting Etta's impact and appeal—she anticipated Diana Ross in her style of little-girl purring—Leonard Chess must have either been a very lucky recordman or had his finger on the public's pulse.

Ralph Bass, who worked as a producer at Chess, told rock writer Michael Lydon: "Leonard was one of the greatest men I ever knew. The cat had a feeling for little people that was so beautiful. He had an understanding about human nature; no education, but he could quote parables to make a point. He had a grasp of how people worked, and he had a way of having people loyal to him."

•

"I wanted to get out of Mississippi in the worst way," said Muddy Waters. "They had such as my mother and the older people brainwashed that people can't make it too good in the city. But I figured if anyone else was living in the city, I could make it there, too."

Born in Rolling Fork in the delta country of Mississippi in April 1915, McKinley Morganfield was raised in Clarksdale, 100 miles to the north. He went to live there with his grandmother after his mother died during his preschool days. McKinley acquired the name by which he is known at an early age because he loved nothing so much as playing in the muddy waters of a nearby creek. Learning harmonica

Muddy Waters

first, he took up guitar after forming a band in 1932. Its members were Henry Sims, pioneer Charley Patton's old fiddle player, and guitarist Scott Bowhandle, who taught him the instrument.

Muddy considers his style a mixture of three influences. "I had part of my own," he has said, "part of Son House, and a little part of Robert Johnson. . . . I never actually seen Robert to play. . . . I thought he was real great from his records. Beautiful. Really though, it was Son House who influenced me to play."

Muddy did meet up with House somewhere in his early playing days. "For about four weeks in a row," he told former *Down Beat* editor Don de Michael, "I was there every night. You couldn't get me out of that corner, listening to what he was doing." In short, all of Muddy's influences were deep-South, red-clay, and he likes to say he remains, as he sang on a Chess record in 1951, "just a country boy."

Not really. Muddy responded to the toughness of Chicago, the rawness of its winters, and the rowdy character of its black ghetto clubs with a blues that is raw, rowdy, and tough. He seldom strays from the form and structure of traditional 12-bar blues, though he sometimes stretches it to 13 or 14 bars, grounded on a boogie beat and boogie progressions. He gives it an urgency in the way words spill out without spacing and through the electricity of his whining, bluesy guitar. The country blues shouter, declaiming in a pit-of-the-stomach, guttural baritone, acquires drive and intensity as he dominates an amplified combo. It is a harsh style and it gave him a commanding presence in rough, noisy bars like the Tay May Club or Smitty's Corner at Thirty-fifth Street and Indiana.

Although Muddy's impact is unquestionably a matter of music and sound, he did touch a theme of consequence to the "new" black male. During slavery and long after emancipation, Negro society was a matriarchic world. Always able to support her children either as a domestic or prostitute, mama was dominant, and the male was a floater with little respect or self-respect. World War II, with its increased employment opportunities in urban industry, put money in the man's pocket. A segment of the population took on middle-class values, *white* middle class, that is. The Negro male prided himself that he held a steady job and was the head of the house.

The outlook of lower-class Negroes, as anthropologist Charles Keil has pointed out, emphasized a different concept of manhood. It was close to what is currently known as *machismo*. What counted was that man was a sharp dresser, spent his money freely if not ostentatiously, and was a knockout in bed. Virility counted, not respectability. It was to this concept of manhood that Muddy addressed himself, and built a black following with erotic songs like "I'm Ready," "I've Got My Mojo Working," and "I'm Your Hoochie-Coochie Man."

In 1940 Muddy journeyed north from Mississippi to St. Louis to see what things were like in a large city. The following year, still edgy about making the big move, he traveled about with a tent show. Finally, in 1943, when he was twenty-eight, he summoned up courage and made for the Windy City to which an earlier generation of blues singers had migrated.

In the Chicago of 1943, urbanized bluesmen like Big Maceo, Tampa Red, Sonny Boy Williamson, and Big Bill Broonzy were still the dominant figures. "But not too many help you," Muddy told author Peter Guralnick. "It was pretty ruggish, man." For a period of two years, he drove a truck by day and tried to find his musical way playing house rent parties and the small lounges. In 1943 the uncle for whom he worked as a truck driver gave him an electric guitar. ("You can't hear an acoustic in a bar," he later said.) And Big Bill Broonzy, who served as a link between generations, helped him, as he later helped Little Walter.

In 1947, Big Bill presented Muddy at Sylvio's, the club at West Lake (later a Howlin' Wolf base), and persuaded Mayo Williams to produce some records with him on Columbia. The sides were never released. Later that year, however, Muddy cut his first sides with Sunnyland Slim at the piano and Big Crawford on bass. The label was Aristocrat, and between '47 and '50 Muddy made as many as eighteen sides for it. They sold lightly even though the songs included "I Can't Be Satisfied (Looking for My Baby)," later one of Muddy's most popular titles. It is, perhaps, no wonder that "I Feel Like Going Home" was the backing for this number—though Muddy had no intention of returning to the South and, in fact, generally avoided Mississippi later when he was on tour.

Nevertheless, blues historian Pete Welding contends that these two sides "launched Waters' career as an important recording artist and were responsible for initiating the modern electric blues style since labelled 'Chicago Blues' . . ." And Muddy confirms: "After the record hit, I was building the group with Little Walter, Jimmy Rogers, Baby Face Leroy, and myself. But I still had to go down there and record with just Big Crawford and myself. Leonard Chess wouldn't upset things. He wouldn't mess with 'harp' or the extra guitar. He wanted to keep the combination that had made the hit record—just Big Crawford's bass and my guitar."

The record may have gained widespread sales beyond Chicago, particularly in the South, as Welding states, but Muddy's first chart song was "Louisiana Blues." He recorded it early in 1951 on Chess. Ironically, the chartmaker is quite unknown compared to "Rollin' Stone," his very first Chess side. Despite its renown (as the source of the name of one of England's most important rock groups), "Rollin' Stone" did not make the charts at all since its sales were regional and covered a triangle roughly outlined by Chicago, St. Louis, and Memphis. In this period, the group Muddy was working with (Little Walter from Louisiana on "harp," Jimmy Rogers from Georgia on guitar, and "Baby Face" Leroy Foster from Alabama on drums) called itself the Headhunters. Out to make a name for themselves, they went from bar to bar and club to club on the South and West sides of Chicago, trying to engage other combos in "cutting contests," as they were once known in New Orleans.

Though Muddy recorded for Chess steadily through the '50s and '60s, and though his backup groups included distinguished older and younger bluesmen—pianist Otis Spann, "harpists" Walter Horton and James Cotton, bassist Willie Dixon, guitarist Buddy Guy, among

others—he enjoyed only limited success as a recording artist. Of the noted rhythm-and-bluesmen, he probably had the fewest best-sellers— only twelve chart songs over a span of two decades. Not one of the twelve made the top three positions on R & B charts. The biggest was "Just Make Love to Me," which climbed to No. 4 in '54. Of the songs most associated with Muddy, only "I'm Your Hoochie-Coochie Man" was on the charts, but even that was for a period of only four weeks and never above the No. 8 spot. Hardly an adequate reflection of the controversial excitement created by the record, or of its popularity. One looks in vain at the charts for well-remembered titles like "I'm Ready," "Got My Mojo Working," "Mean Mistreater," and "Tiger in Your Tank."

Yet through the '50s, when he played Smitty's Corner, the big street-level club on Thirty-fifth and Indiana, few bluesmen were as popular or exerted as much influence as the man with the hooded eyes and protruding lips who looks like an Indian in profile and an

Oriental in full face. Paul Butterfield, who later organized a white blues band, made the scene with Nick Gravenites, later of the bluesy Electric Flag, while he was a student at the University of Chicago. So did guitarist Mike Bloomfield, who cut a *Fathers & Sons* album with Muddy during the blues revival in the late '60s. And through Muddy's band passed the current generation of modern Chicago bluesmen, including Junior Wells, Buddy Guy, Earl Hooker, James Cotton, and others—all of whom drew something from music that English blues historian Paul Oliver described in the following words:

"As the music warmed up, Muddy began to comment, give encouragement, working himself up to a pitch of excitement that made a tremendous impact. . . . There was no doubting who was king—the effect was stunning. And frightening, too. The sheer physical drive of band and blues singer chilled the spine. Muddy roared, leaped, jerked in fierce and violent spasms. When he came off the stage, he was in a state of near trance and the sweat poured off him. It was close on half an hour before he unwound. . . . For most of the following day, he lay in a shaded room with an icepack on his head. . . ."

Oliver heard Waters at the F & J Lounge in Gary, Indiana, a club then frequented by Negro steelworkers and servicemen. It was off limits to "ofays," and there was not a white face in the audience, except those of Oliver and his wife. This was Muddy's own audience, and it remained his audience until the folk revival of the '60s and the British blues revival. Muddy did not cross over on wax because his hard rhythm and blues—forerunner of hard rock—basically appealed to a black audience and because he was fundamentally an in-person performer.

"I like to think I could really master a stage," Muddy has said. "I think I was a pretty good stage personality and I knew how to present myself right. I never developed an act of any kind. I just had a natural feel for it." And he had something else. "It was sex," according to Marshall Chess. "If you had ever seen Muddy then, the effect he had on the women! Because blues has always been a women's market. On Saturday night they'd line up ten deep."

But Muddy's records did reach out in a strange way. Across the Atlantic, young British musicians listened and were enthralled by the raw vitality, the shattering intensity, the unbuttoned sexuality. The early recordings of both The Beatles and The Rolling Stones reveal their indebtedness. Nevertheless, Muddy's first tour of England in 1958 was a flop. The story has often been repeated of the traditional English critic who was driven to a downstairs men's room by the

Howlin' Wolf

sheer volume of Waters' electrified combo blues. In England, as in the USA, Waters' impact was an in-group phenomenon: black people here and white musicians in Great Britain.

That changed, of course, after the mid-'60s' British invasion of American pop when Mick Jagger, John Lennon, and other mop-haired Englishmen revealed the source of their inspiration and voiced their unremitting reverence for Muddy and other black bluesmen. Then, white youngsters leaped parental barriers of segregation, opened their ears, and made Muddy, B. B. King, James Brown, and others welcome on their turntables and in concert halls and arenas.

In 1969, Don de Michael characterized a Muddy Waters appearance in Chicago as one in which "he nearly brought about the physical collapse of the Auditorium Theatre." It was a rendition of "Got My Mojo Working" that peaked audience excitement. "For nearly ten minutes after he left the stage," de Michael wrote in *Rolling Stone*, "the audience roared its delight. They stomped, shouted, clapped, whistled, screamed, jumped up and down in aisles and seats. Pleadings from the stage to calm down were to little avail."

And this was not a segregated club on Chicago's South Side, but a huge theater frequented by a mixed audience, preponderantly white.

.

"There are certain people," Howlin' Wolf once said—and there is no mistaking that he meant Muddy Waters—"who think they are better than you."

"Wolf?" Muddy sniffed. "I was here before him. I had this town served up in my hand."

It was a long-standing rivalry. As late as 1969 at the Ann Arbor Blues Festival, The Wolf stayed on stage long beyond his allotted time in an effort to prevent Muddy from participating in the program. And Muddy told interviewer Peter Guralnick, "I never did quit trying to be friends. I never did let on that I knowed."

Muddy was a friend when The Wolf came to Chicago from Memphis. Being the dominant figure on the Chicago blues scene in the early '50s, he helped The Wolf get his first club job. But I regard The Wolf as the more original of the two and, perhaps, the most underrated of the R & B generation of bluesmen.

The backgrounds and early influences of the two men were similar. Both were born in Mississippi, The Wolf (curiously) being named Chester Arthur Burnett after the twenty-first President of the United States. Five years older than Muddy, Burnett was born in Ruleville, in the eastern part of the state near West Point. Rolling Fork, where Muddy was born in 1915, is in the western sector, almost on the Mississippi River. Both grew up in the delta area where the blues originated. But whereas Muddy was raised in the town of Clarksdale, The Wolf grew up on a Ruleville cotton plantation. In fact, the howler was a farmer, entertaining on the side, until he was almost forty years old.

Both men shared an admiration for Robert ("Hell Hound on My Trail") Johnson. The Wolf actually worked with the inspired, demon-driven bluesman, who was killed by a jealous husband in 1938 when he was just twenty-four. "Me and him played together," The Wolf told blues historian Pete Welding. "And me and him and Sonny Boy Williamson [Rice Miller] played together awhile. I met Robert in Robinsville, Mississippi—his mother and father stayed out there. I worked a little while with him around through the country. We was playing around Greenwood, Ita Bena, and Moorehead. We didn't stay too long because I would go back and forth to my father to help in the farming."

But the bluesman who turned The Wolf on, as pioneer Son House had done with Muddy, was another Clarksdale-bred bluesman, Charles Patton, known for the growling intensity and involvement of his style. Patton lived on Dockery's Plantation in Ruleville, Mississippi, near Young and Mara's plantation where The Wolf's family moved in 1923 shortly after his thirteenth birthday.

"It was Patton who started me off playing," The Wolf told Welding. "He showed me things on the guitar, because after we got through picking cotton at night, we'd go hang around him. . . . He used to play out on the plantations, at different homes. . . . There were no clubs like nowadays. He mostly worked by himself. It took a good musician to play behind him because it was kind of offbeat or off-time."

But after a time, The Wolf's preference shifted to a duo called the Mississippi Sheiks, consisting of Memphis Slim and his brother. The Wolf came to feel that Patton's music was "what you would nowadays call old-fashioned folk singing," whereas The Sheiks had a beat and sounded modern. Yet he has said that he "got the most from Charlie Patton and Lemon Jefferson—from his records. . . . What I liked most about Lemon's playing was that he made a clear chord. . . . As a kid I also heard records by Lonnie Johnson, Tampa Red, and Blind Blake. . . . I also ran with Tommy McClennan later." And still later, at the time when his sister was being courted by the second Sonny Boy Williamson, he got Rice Miller (his real name) to teach him harmonica.

The Wolf's strangest influence, and in a sense the most decisive, was white blues yodeler Jimmie Rodgers, the country singer from Meridian, Mississippi. The Wolf tried desperately to emulate the tubercular trainman who called himself The Singing Brakeman and who is recognized as the "Father of Country Music," but he did not have the pipes. "I couldn't do no yodelin'," he often said, "so I turned to growlin', then howlin', and it's done me fine."

There are times, as in "Smokestack Lightning" and "Moanin' at Midnight," when The Wolf almost sounds as if he is yodelling. But it's a deep, dark sound that comes out of a more than six-foot, 250-pound body, and nothing describes the heavy moaning better than the word *howlin'*. It's a sound that's unique with the man, a wolflike growl compounded of agony and aggression, but not without moments of pain and hurt.

Chester Arthur Burnett was known for a time as Bull Cow. It suggests something of his size. But he began calling himself Wolf because of the lasting impression made on him by stories he heard from his grandfather about Mississippi's marauding wolf packs. And the addition of *Howlin'* projects just the right image of the man and his style. Bluesman Johnny Shines of Memphis, who revered The Wolf and tagged after him, has said that when he first met him, "I was afraid of him just like you would be of some kind of beast or something. . . . A guy that played like Wolf, he'd sold his soul to the devil."

The Wolf got his first guitar when he was eighteen years old, purchased for him by his father. "We were living out there on the Quiver River on Boosey's Plantation," he recalled. "At that time I was working on the farm with my father, baling hay and driving tractors, fixing fences, picking cotton, and pulling corn. There was a lot of music around there, work songs. . . . They'd get me out there and sing as they worked—plowing songs, songs to call mules by. . . . They'd make up the songs as they go along."

Having learned the rudiments of the guitar from Charlie Patton— he didn't get his *time* right, he confessed, until the 1940s—The Wolf decided to try Patton's way of life. Between farm chores, he played the plantations in Mississippi and Arkansas. His repertoire consisted of Patton blues he picked up: "Spoonful," "Banty Rooster," "High Water Everywhere," and "Saddle My Pony"; also "Sittin' on Top of the World" from the Mississippi Sheiks; and traditional blues. But they came out sounding different. His problem with *time* resulted in out-of-meter versions that developed later into the offbeat, contrapuntal style that one hears in his records.

In 1933, when his father moved to the Arkansas side of Big Muddy, he went to Memphis. He recalled watching jug bands perform in the Square on Beale Street. But he remained a country farmer and played the plantations. It was tough work, he said: "The people played me so hard. They'd look for you to play from seven o'clock in the evening until seven o'clock in the morning. That's too rough! I was getting a dollar and a half."

"Blues is problems," he said at one time. And with a fierce realism that marked his work and personality, he added, "Singing about them doesn't make things easier. It just takes your mind off it. You singing ain't gonna help you none. The problem is still there."

He had just about decided to form a band and lighten his work as a performer when World War II intervened. He was in the service for the duration. On his discharge in 1945, he returned to farm work. Then, in 1947, he moved to West Memphis, Arkansas, bought himself an electric guitar, and decided to pursue a career as a musician. He was thirty-seven years old.

In 1948, he formed his first band, with Little Junior Parker and

James Cotton on "harps," and began broadcasting daily over Station KWEM in West Memphis. He made his first recordings in sessions arranged by Ike Turner, Tennessee talent scout for the Bihari brothers who also played piano on some of the numbers. In 1951 Crown or RPM Records released a dozen sides by The Wolf. But Turner was also producing sessions at the Memphis Recording Service of Sam Phillips, who was leasing masters to the Chess brothers in Chicago. The apparent success of Chess's first release, "Moanin' at Midnight" backed with "How Many More Tears," led Leonard Chess to make a trip to West Memphis and to bring The Wolf to Chicago.

By the time he was settled in Chicago in 1952, the country farmer had developed into a modern bluesman. He not only produced his own radio show, but solicited advertising and signed up sponsors. And his band was completely electrified and amplified. Connoisseur Pete Welding feels that The Wolf's move to Chicago resulted in "strong, well-focussed recordings," and he credits Leonard Chess with this advance: "As a result of recording Muddy Waters and others, Chess had developed a real understanding of rural-based urban blues . . . and he lavished considerable attention on the recording of Wolf's music, providing supporting musicians sensitive to its demands." But even if The Wolf's Memphis recordings were "undistinguished," as Welding believes, his sound and style made their impact.

Almost immediately after he arrived in Chicago, he began playing at a club on Thirteenth and Ashland, following appearances by Muddy Waters. Before long, his local popularity grew so that he could be heard either at Sylvio's on the West Side or the Big Squeeze Club on the South Side.

For his first record session in Chicago, he brought guitarist Hubert Sumlin North. Sumlin and his biting blues guitar became, in fact, a mainstay of The Wolf's band, along with Willie Johnson, who had been part of his Memphis combo. On many of his recordings, one hears also the substantial bass of Willie Dixon, who contributed to The Wolf's repertoire "Down in the Bottom," "Red Rooster," "Back Door Man," "Tail Dragger," "Built for Comfort," and "Wang Dang Doodle," among other songs.

Howlin' Wolf made R & B charts late in 1951 with "How Many More Tears," even before he came to Chicago. Five years of steady recording and popular appearances in Chicago clubs passed before he again scored a chartmaker with "Smoke Stack Lightning." Except for a short-lived "Evil" in '69, that about summarizes his track record on record charts, but not his importance or influence. Like Muddy's, The Wolf's music reached across the seas to inspire the generation of British rock 'n' rollers who upset the traditional balance of trade, musically speaking.

The Wolf has been called "the raunchiest and funkiest" of the delta-Chicago group of rhythm-and-bluesmen. In many ways, his tough, aggressive style is less accessible to white listeners than even that of Muddy Waters. His big voice, more than a match for the amplified instruments behind him, is startling in its metallic raspiness. It goes through you like a dentist's drill. When he demands—"Babe, where did you spend last night?"—or accuses—"You've got yourself a youngster and can't stand me no more"—his voice has a wolflike ferocity. But the growl can also modulate to a moan, making him sound like an animal in pain, or to a plea in "Louise" that is agonizing in its primitive plaintiveness.

Although he worked with traditional blues, boogie shuffles, and hammering triplets, The Wolf also frequently resorted to a form that is mesmerizing in its monotony. A favorite device—audible in "Smoke Stack Lightning" and "No Place to Go"—was to set up a short, rhythmic phrase as an *ostinato*. You can't call it a riff because he did not vary, manipulate, or resolve it. He just repeated it from one end of the record to the other, its offbeat rhythm inviting counter guitar slashes and shrill "harp" responses. In some passages, there are two or three rhythms at work, giving his rendition a contrapuntal quality rare in the blues. And his records have a sound, distinctive and ear arresting. In his best-known songs like "Killing Floor," "Evil Is Goin' On," and "Sittin' on Top of the World," Delta blues peaked in raw, electrified blues with a beat.

•

Part of the saga of the black entertainer's struggle against economic exploitation is a lawsuit brought by Howlin' Wolf. In the $1-million suit, The Wolf accused Arc Music Corp., Chess Records' publishing arm, of working with the Chess brothers to defraud him of his rights and interest in songs recorded by him for Chess between 1952 and 1970. Through the initiative of the American Guild of Authors & Composers, which began demanding an accounting in 1966, Arc Music paid The Wolf $3,302.45 in accrued royalties in 1969, shortly before Chess Records was bought by GRT Corporation. But in 1971, The Wolf was moved to enter into an agreement with Arc Music as a result of representations he later claimed were false. Among other allegations was The Wolf's contention that Arc Music had requested that companies outside the USA not remit royalties on his songs so that Arc could in turn evade payment to him. In addition to asking damages in excess of $1 million, The Wolf sought to recapture all of his original copyrights.

About the time that he launched the lawsuit, The Wolf had several heart attacks. Then in 1973 he was in an automobile accident. Hurled through the windshield of his car, he suffered severe kidney injury, which required regular dialysis treatments. Although the condition slowed him down, it did not stop him from pursuing an active program of public appearances. But he could no longer make his trade-marked entrance: crawling on all fours with a wolflike gleam in his eyes. On January 10, 1976, he died in Hines Veterans' Administration Hospital near Chicago after undergoing an operation to relieve pressure on the brain. He was buried in Oakridge Cemetery in Hillside, Illinois, a week later.

•

When Elvis Presley came to New York in 1956 for his first appearance on TV—it was the Tommy Dorsey Show, and I attended rehearsals in the Nola Studios on Broadway—he spent many hours at the Apollo Theatre. Of all the cats he saw and heard at the Harlem shrine of black entertainment, he most dug Bo Diddley. The third of Chess's major R & B men was a striking figure on stage, appearing generally in a black, long-sleeved shirt and a wide-brimmed, black Stetson hat. A tall, heavyset man, he was a dynamic performer who struck angular poses as he played and sang. In 1956 he set the Apollo's all-time attendance record to date.

What intrigued Presley, as it captivated a generation of rock 'n' rollers, was the sawing, twisting rhythms of Bo Diddley's playing. The beat has been variously described as jungle rhythm, voodoo chant, Latin-American, African drum rhythm, and an adaptation of the old jingle, "Shave and a haircut—SHAM . . . POO." When I asked him what it was after a performance at the Flamingo in Las Vegas (where he wore that big, black Stetson as we snacked in the coffee shop), he grinned a broken- and uneven-toothed smile and said, "It's a mixture of several different beats." He would not identify the components. Identifiable and unique it is in its drive and strutting ferocity—so much so that among black musicians it is known as "the tradesmen's knock." The pattern that Bo originated in his first Chess releases was copied by, among others, Duane Eddy on his "Cannon-ball" instrumental, Dee Clark on "Hey Little Girl," and Johnny Otis

Bo Diddley and Chuck Berry

on his smash, "Willie and the Hand Jive." But Otis told me that he knew the rhythmic pattern from his teen-age days in the Bay Area when he played with Count Otis Matthews.

Born Ellas Bates in McComb, Mississippi, in December 1928, Bo was given out for adoption by an indigent mother. His legal name became Ellas McDaniel after the family that raised him. ("They never deprived me of knowing who my mother was," he has said.) There are many stories as to how he got the nickname Bo Diddley. Some have said that it started in his childhood. Leonard Chess claimed that he called him that because he was an inveterate storyteller—what's Polish or Yiddish for *storyteller*? McDaniel himself has made several explanations, none of them complete.

"I got the name Bo Diddley from fightin'," he has said, referring to the years between fifteen and eighteen when he was an amateur boxer and a Golden Gloves contender. Alluding to his penchant for designing weird-looking guitars, including a rectangular instrument, he told rock critic Lenny Kaye, "I guess that's why they call me Bo Diddley 'cause I always jump out the bag with some new crap. . . ." He told Paul Oliver that his nickname came from a scat phrase for his unique rhythm, "Bo didley, bo didley-um-dum." If you get the impression, as I did during an interview, that he derives pleasure from acting the sly comic, you are right.

When he was playing The Flamingo, he was made an honorary member of the Las Vegas sheriff's department and given a metal star, which he pinned on his Stetson. Chuck Berry was on the same bill with him. Bo waited until Chuck had his back turned, then snuck up behind him, tapped him on the shoulder, and said, "I've been lookin' for you." He positioned himself so that the first thing Chuck saw when he turned was the sheriff's star.

At about the time he entered grade school, the McDaniels moved to Chicago where Bo grew up in one of the toughest neighborhoods. Almost each block was a different gang's territory, and a kid crossed from one to the other at the risk of having his clothing torn and being severely beaten. Diddley grew up without scars only because of his music. When he was facing attack from an unfriendly quarter, he offered to entertain.

His first instrument, studied in grade school and throughout secondary school, was not the guitar, not the fiddle, but the violin. His lessons, given by a Prof. O.W. Fredrick, who "kicked my ass," were in the classics. Eventually, he played in the Sunday school orchestra of the church that paid for his lessons. Learning guitar was his own idea when he was in his teens, and it was not well received by his family. But it was a more formidable weapon than a violin for dealing with street gangs.

"I've always been a string fanatic," he says, "loved string instruments. When it's something you gotta blow, I don't want no part of it. And I'm a lover of basic bottom. I don't like a lot of keenin', screamin' guitars. If the bottom is right, crazy."

As he mastered the instrument, he began playing the streets for handouts, an activity that continued through the years in which he made a living at various jobs. After his second marriage in 1949, he formed a street trio that included Jerome Green, a former jazz fanatic whose maracas became an integral part of the Bo Diddley sound and rhythm.

"Oh, I played the street corners," he told Lenny Kaye, "until I was about nineteen or twenty, from about fifteen on. Then I walked the streets around Chicago for about twelve years, before I got somebody to listen to me." Finally, he got a job performing at The 708 Club—and that's where his recognition started. Then one day he walked into Chess's storefront office and told him he wanted "to do my thing."

He chose Chess, he has said, because "everybody else slammed the door in my face."

The day he cut his first sides, he went home "and told my mother they done stole my songs, that they tricked me. [Laughs] Boy, I was mad till I heard it on the air. I said they done ripped me off . . . 'cause, see, I was one of those dudes that don't trust nobody." He still doesn't, especially record companies.

The two sides he cut in the spring of 1955 made the charts. Backed by Jerome Green on maracas and Frank Kirkland on drums, "Bo Diddley" was a Top 10 R & B best-seller of the year. With the addition of Lester Davenport on harmonica and Otis Spann on piano "I'm a Man" also made R & B charts, climbing to No. 2. Later, it became the swaggering theme of Muddy Waters. It was four years before Bo produced a comparable seller in "Say Man," a song in which he and Jerome Green traded put-downs.

Bo achieved only limited air exposure, but the energy and excitement of his personal appearances and the sheer danceability of his style gave him an appreciative audience not only among blacks, but among white rock 'n' rollers as well. There was also an element of youthful fantasy in lyrics like "Cops and Robbers," "Bo Meets the Monster," and "Bo Diddley's a Gunslinger."

Bo was not strictly a blues singer. Neither was he a rock 'n' roller like his Chess confrere Chuck Berry, with whom he cut an album and made frequent appearances. His was not a youthful style nor could he become, as Berry did, a teen-age idol. He was a raucous Chicago bluesman—great in bars and lounges—a vigorous rhythm-and-bluesman whose personal rhythmic concept proved an enduring influence in R 'n' R. He still makes occasional in-person appearances.

·

Little Walter walked in the shadow of both Muddy and The Wolf, one of many talented sidemen with whom these giants surrounded themselves. Born in Alexandria, Virginia, in May 1930, Marion Walter Jacobs played harmonica on the streets and passed his cap for coins from the time he was eight years old. At sixteen he was one of the many indigent musicians who hung out at the Maxwell Street Market in Chicago, an area of vacant lots around Halstead, Peoria, and Sangamon streets where black ghetto dwellers came to buy things from pushcart peddlers and where young, unknown musicians played for handouts.

At seventeen he made his first recordings, cutting two sides for an in-and-out Maxwell Street label, Ora Nelle. The following year he recorded with Sunnyland Slim & Muddy Waters, as they billed themselves, on Tempo Tone Records. In 1950 Muddy performed as part of the Little Walter Trio on Regal Records with Leroy Foster on drums. That year Little Walter made his first recordings as part of Muddy Waters's band, thereafter alternating with Walter Horton on Muddy's sessions until his premature demise around '59. He was one of many bluesmen—others were Pine Top Smith, Scrapper Blackwell, and Sonny Boy Williamson (the first)—who suffered violent deaths on the streets of Chicago.

Although Little Walter played sideman to Muddy, he also had his own band and made a number of hit records on Checker, the Chess subsidiary. In 1952 he enjoyed no fewer than three chart disks under his own name, with "Juke," an original blues instrumental, occupying R & B best-seller lists for a sixteen-week period. To capitalize on its popularity, Checker used the designation Little Walter & His Jukes on succeeding disks. In '53 and '54 he was on R & B charts with songs like "Blues with a Feeling" and "You're So Fine," both of which climbed into the Top Ten. In '55 he bettered his success with "Juke" when Willie Dixon's song "My Babe" became a No. 1 best-seller for him. Even after the rise of rock 'n' roll, he was able to produce chart records, with "Key to the Highway" of '58 approaching "My Babe" and "Juke" in popularity.

Little Walter would probably have achieved greater recognition if he had been more of a vocalist. But his voice was the "harp." He played with great conviction, sensitive dynamic shadings, and a feeling for varied textures. In the era of electrified instruments, he amplified his sound by cupping both the "harp" and microphone between his hands. Echoes of his sound may be heard in later "harpists" like James Cotton and Junior Wells, who was also a precocious performer and played with Tampa Red and Big Maceo when he was only fourteen years old.

•

On a number of his '55 Checker disks—"Diddley Daddy" and "Diddy Wah Diddy," among others—Bo Diddley was backed by a vocal group called the Moonglows. Hailing from Louisville, Kentucky, they started as the Crazy Sounds after organizers Harvey Fuqua, lead, and Bobby Lester, first tenor, migrated to Cleveland and joined with Prentiss Barnes, bass, from Gary and guitarist Billy Johnson. They made their first recording for Champagne Records, an abortive label launched by disk jockey Alan Freed, who changed their name to the Moonglows to tie in with his Moondog Show on Station WJW. The two sides, "I Just Can't Tell A Lie" and "I've Been Your Dog (Since I've Been Your Man)," were credited to Al Lance, apparently a pseudonym for Freed.

The Moonglows next recorded for Chance Records, to whose owners they were introduced by Freed. Accompanied by Red Holloway's Orchestra, they cut five disks—songs mostly by Harvey Fuqua and Freed—none of which produced enough income to free Fuqua and Lester from full-time jobs in a Cleveland coalyard. (Bobby shovelled and Fuqua drove a truck.) When disk jockey Art Sheridan and his associate Steve Chandler shuttered Chance in December 1954, Freed brought the group to the Chess brothers.

On "Sincerely," their first Chess side, the Moonglows employed a style of vocalizing later known as "blow harmony" and imitated by The Dells, The Spinners, and other R & B groups. Akin to crooning, it involved a sensuous, closed-mouth, mooing sound. "Sincerely," highlighted also by Fuqua's pleading tenor, established them as an important R & B group and initiated their acceptance by rock 'n' roll fans. Breaking into R & B charts in November 1954, the ballad remained a best-seller well into the spring of '55. Written by lead singer Harvey Fuqua, whose uncle was one of the original Ink Spots, "Sincerely" benefitted tremendously from the powerhouse exposure it received on the turntable of Alan Freed—listed as a co-writer—who was by then on Station WINS in New York. The ballad's popularity was also hyped by a cover disk on Coral Records by the McGuire Sisters.

Here are some interesting comparative statistics, taken from *Billboard*'s year-end survey of 1955's top records (numbers = rank):

	GROUP	RETAIL SALES	DISK JOCKEY PLAYS	JUKE BOX PLAYS
POP	McGuire Sisters	8	2	3
R & B	Moonglows	9	5	7

The McGuire Sisters' record was somewhat bigger in pop than the Moonglows in R & B, but the contrast in sales was staggering. The McGuires sold over a million disks while the Moonglows did not go beyond 250,000.

Recording as the Moonglows on Chess, the group also appeared as the Moonlighters on Checker. Two lead singers, Bobby Lester with the latter and Harvey Fuqua with the former, helped secure some differentiation. After "Sincerely," the Moonglows managed to maintain a succession of hits until 1958. The follow-up to the hit ballad was "Most of All" in '55. In 1956 the group scored with "See Saw," followed in '57 by Percy Mayfield's sociological ballad, "Please Send Me Someone to Love." By the time the group had "Ten Command-ments of Love" it was known as Harvey & the Moonglows and it had crossed the line into rock 'n' roll. But that year, 1958, it broke up. Harvey Fuqua, who married one of Berry Gordy's sisters, became a producer, first with several labels in which he was partnered with Gordy (Tri Phi and Harvey Records) and then with Gordy's spec-tacularly successful Motown conglomerate.

•

Like the Moonglows, the Flamingos emphasized romantic ballads, contributing a sense of emotional involvement and warmth rare in pop quartets. But unlike the Moonglows, the Flamingos came from different areas: lead Nathaniel Nelson from Chicago; tenor Terry Johnson from Baltimore; bass Jacob Carey from Pulaski, Virginia. Starting on Chance in 1953, they produced six disks, one of which, "Golden Teardrops," was a local noisemaker. When the Art Sheridan label folded, they recorded briefly on Parrot Records, joining the array of artists that covered Gene & Eunice's "Ko Ko Mo."

The move to Checker Records brought them, in 1956, their first national hit, "I'll Be Home," also a pop hit for Pat Boone. It was their only Checker chartmaker of six releases. Decca tried with them during 1958, but they were back again on Checker the following year. They scored their biggest success in '59, by which time they were recording on George Goldner's End label. Adapting an old film ballad (vintage 1934) to an R & B beat and a "sh-bop, sh-bop" vocal background, they converted "I Only Have Eyes for You" into one of the year's big R & B hits. By then, their lead singer was Tommy Hunt, who had replaced Nate Nelson, who had succeeded Sollie McElroy. And they, too, like the Moonglows, had moved into the rock 'n' roll scene.

•

Otis Rush, who recorded eight sides for Chess in January 1960 but had only one release ("So Many Roads, So Many Trains"), has not received the recognition warranted by his talent. Blues historian Paul Oliver attributes this to his lack of showmanship. Rush himself blames long-term contracts with record companies that would not release his recordings or him; also, his lack of adequate equipment. Guitarist Mighty Joe Young, who played with Rush at such Chicago clubs as the Castle Rock and Pepper's, told *Living Blues*: "Otis was the hottest thing in Chicago [after "I Can't Quit You Baby" hit the charts], Otis and Magic Sam. But he was with Cobra Records and Cobra wasn't no Chess. With the right company at that particular time, he coulda been a real big artist. Then Chess got him [in 1960] and just drug their feet. But the man had the talent."

Born in Philadelphia, Mississippi, in April 1934, Rush came to Chicago in 1949 and went part-time to Dunbar High School on the South Side. In the four years before he played his first gig at the Club Alibi at 2711 Wentworth, he labored in the steel mills and stockyards. Then he also worked at Campbell Soup and the Wilson Packing Company. Finally, in 1955 he began playing music full-time at the 708 Club at 708 East Forty-seventh Street, to which Mighty Joe Young came all the way from Milwaukee to hear him. "He had a heck of a voice," Young recalls. "He became a wonderful guitarist later."

As a blues guitarist, Otis became interested in the use of minor chords, an innovation, since blues are traditionally built on the three basic chords of the major scale. Apparently, other Chicago guitarists, for example, Jody Williams, were likewise experimenting with the sound of minor keys. Willie Dixon claims that he introduced minor tones when he produced "Hoochie Coochie Man" and "I'm Ready" with Muddy Waters. "At that particular time [1954]," he informed *Living Blues*, "I was trying to get the Chess company to go with minor tones for blues."

While he was playing at the 708 Club, Otis approached Chess about a recording contract. He was turned down, according to Willie Dixon, then associated with Chess, because he was "too close" to Muddy. Not long after, Dixon left Chess and began working with Eli Toscano, who operated three labels in a partnership with Joe Brown: Abco Records, superseded by Artistic and Cobra. Dixon early recorded Otis, along with Buddy Guy, Magic Sam and Betty Everett. Rush's first Cobra session, held during the summer of '56 at the Kimball Hall Studio, yielded "I Can't Quit You Baby." Dixon recalls that before they had pressed records, he and Toscano brought a dub to disk jockey Big Bill Hill, who spun records over Station WOPA in the window of a cleaning establishment. The station switchboard "lit up like a Christmas tree," Big Bill reported, employing one of music business's cliches describing a record that elicited a quick response from the public. By October, the blues ballad was on R & B charts where it moved up to No. 9 and brought Rush's name onto the national record scene. Unfortunately, it was his only chart-maker, although Cobra released sixteen sides over a two-year period.

Willie Dixon received credit as the writer of most of the Cobra songs and co-produced and played bass on the sessions, most of which were held in Cobra's hole-in-the-wall studio on Roosevelt Road. It was Dixon, too, who arranged, on his return to Chess, for Rush to record on the giant label in 1960. "That was a bad day," Rush has said. But out of the frustrating association came "So Many Roads, So Many Trains"—not a chart-maker but regarded as one of his best sides.

"After Chess wasn't releasing anything on me," Rush told *Living Blues*, "from there to Duke, and that was another sad day." Under contract to the Don Robey label for five years, from 1962 to '67, he had just one record release. In desperation, he did a session for Vanguard Records in 1965, even though he was still tied to Duke. He was not satisfied with the session and nothing happened with the records. In 1968 he recorded an album for Cotillion Records, a subsidiary of Atlantic. Working at what was then one of the hottest studios in the country, Fame Recording in Muscle Shoals, Alabama, and guided by guitarist-producer Mike Bloomfield and his Chicago friend, gravel-voiced singer Nick Gravenites, Otis failed to produce a hot LP.

The Atlantic deal was set by one of the best-known and most powerful agents in the entertainment field, Albert Grossman, who also made an arrangement with Capitol Records whereby Otis Rush Productions would deliver finished masters. After Nick Gravenites produced the album in San Francisco at a cost of $36,000, Capitol declined to release it. Otis Rush continues to be in demand for in-person appearances in many areas of the country, but lingers still in the limbo of talented artists who somehow cannot find the large audience which should be theirs.

His observation on his career: "I got burnt messin' with a lot of assholes. I mean the record companies."

•

In an overall view, the Chess brothers built one of the magnificent labels of R & B, an achievement comparable to that of Syd Nathan at King, Art Rupe at Specialty, the Bihari brothers at Modern, Don Robey at Peacock/Duke, Herman Lubinsky at Savoy, and Ahmet Ertegun and Jerry Wexler at Atlantic. But more than any of the other "indies," they tapped the richest vein of delta blues and, through behemoth bluesmen like Howlin' Wolf, Bo Diddley and Muddy Waters, promoted the transformation of urban blues into the abrasive, electrified, ensemble Rhythm & Blues of Chicago.

*I left my babe in Mississippi, picking
cotton down in New Orleans, (repeat)
She say, "If you get to Chicago, please
write me a letter if you please."*
—TOMMY MC CLENNAN

Chicago's Black-Owned Record Company

VEE JAY RECORDS was launched in Chicago late in 1952 or early '53 and went bankrupt in 1965, but it looked for a time as if it might become what Motown later did, the first major black-owned record company. Within two years of its first releases, it owned a building on Michigan Avenue, directly across the street from Chess Records. The company was founded by Vivian Carter Bracken, husband James Bracken, and Calvin Carter. The Brackens owned a record store in nearby Gary, Indiana, and Vivian was a local disk jockey. Periodically, they made trips into Chicago to stock their store with records. After a time, they began cutting masters in their own home. When they decided to launch a label, they moved to Chicago. Calvin Carter, Vivian's brother, selected the name Vee Jay, based on the first initials of his sister and brother-in-law's names.

The company began operations in the period when the great promises of World War II were seen by many blacks for what they were—opportunistic white come-ons. The black community, which had acquired some mobility—geographically, economically, and to a lesser degree socially—was by then sequestered in urban ghettos. Wartime prosperity was a matter of the past. And so black music took the angry form of bop, the frustrated form of cool jazz, or the indigenous, self-contained form of rhythm & blues. But blacks with capital were moving to invade the white world of Big Business.

Vee Jay's initial release was by the Spaniels, a group that started singing together in Roosevelt High School in the Brackens' home town. Because so many black groups were named after birds—the Orioles, Flamingos, Penguins, and others—they chose, instead, to name themselves for a dog breed. The Spaniels had a languid manner, and their vocal style has been described as the coolest of the cool. Vivian Bracken, who managed the group, placed their first disk with Chance, the short-lived Chicago label. "Baby, It's You" also appeared on Vee Jay, but it sold better on Chance, which then had better distribution.

"Goodnight, Well It's Time to Go," an early 1954 release, became the Spaniels' most popular disk and a giant of a record in the white rip-off years. The McGuire Sisters did not do as well with their cover

315

as they did with "Sincerely" and other copies. Written by James Hudson, lead singer with the Spaniels, and Calvin Carter, who produced their sessions, "Goodnight, Well It's Time to Go" was also covered in the C & W field by Johnnie & Jack on RCA Victor.

Originally titled "Goodnight, Sweetheart, Goodnight"—the title was changed, perhaps, to avoid confusion with a ballad of the 1930s, but it was an evocative change—"Goodnight, Well It's Time to Go" beautifully caught the ambivalence of the lover, reluctant to go home but too cool to admit his reluctance. It mirrored a mood of the time, at least among a sector of American blacks: the feeling that they had been betrayed once again, but were reluctant to show that they cared. Those who cared enough to seek a change were moving toward black nationalism, joining the Black Panthers, following Martin Luther King, participating in the Freedom Marches, or involving themselves in the action that led in '55 to the Supreme Court decision desegregating schools. The others were cool; and "Play It Cool," with comic overtones, was the Spaniels' follow-up release.

Although they never scored another best-seller approaching the popularity of "Goodnight, Well It's Time to Go,"—it was Vee Jay's first Top Ten hit—The Spaniels remained active to the end of the decade. But in 1955, the makeup of the group changed, with only lead singer James "Pookie" Hudson remaining. This, perhaps, accounted for the group's decline. By 1958 depressed sales led to their recording pop ballads like "Stormy Weather" and "People Will Say We're in Love." By the time Vee Jay went under, partly as a result of mismanagement (rumored to involve rip-offs by key personnel), the Spaniels had vanished from the recording scene. They surfaced again briefly on record charts in 1970 with a song titled "Fairy Tales" on Calla, an offbeat label.

•

Second to the Spaniels in the rise of Vee Jay were the El Dorados, a group that coalesced at Englewood High School in Chicago and originally called itself the Five Stars. Vivian Bracken, who signed them after they won a talent show at a local club, changed their name. The El Dorados were as ebullient and outgoing as the Spaniels were cool and detached. Although they remained on the label from '54 into '58 and had almost as many releases as the Spaniels, their claim to fame is based almost entirely on one smash record: "At My Front Door." Coauthored by John C. Moore and Vee Jay prexy Ewart G. Abner, Jr., it was a bright, up-tempo, well-harmonized number that is still remembered for a Bo Diddley-type lick on the words "crazy little mama-doll." The song's concept was designed to inflate male egos: crazy little mama-doll was back at his front door *begging* to come in. The disk went to No. 2 on 1955's R & B charts, a feat never duplicated by the group.

.

There was still a third group with but one Vee Jay smash to its credit, but the Dells were a long-lived quintet who had record releases into the '70s, on other labels. In their early years, each of the boys sang in a church choir in their hometown of Harvey, Illinois, and they began singing together at Thornton Township High School. Studying the records of the Moonglows, Flamingos, Five Keys, and Clovers, they sang on the streets of Chicago. Hanging around the Chess offices on South Michigan Avenue, they met Harvey Fuqua, and he made a drastic change in their style. "Before the Moonglows came to town," baritone Michael McGill has said, "we sang only two-part harmony. But they had us sing with each of them, tenor with tenor, baritone with baritone, and they showed us how to sing five parts." By 1954 they were calling themselves El Rays and managed to interest the Chess brothers (mentors of the Moonglows) in recording them. Their Checker disk of "Darling, I Know" demonstrated that they needed more experience.

When Vivian Bracken signed them to Vee Jay the following year, El Rays became the Dells. Their second release was an R & B chart-maker. "Oh, What a Night" was written by two members of the group, lead singer Johnny Funches and first tenor Marvin Junior. It involved an interesting use of call-and-response in that the lead singer kept repeating, "Oh, what a night" while the group responded, "To hold you . . . to squeeze you."

There was more creative direction in Vee Jay records than in disks produced by other R & B "indies." Records cut by Vee Jay groups— and this was a group era in R & B—were true vocal records with lean instrumental backgrounds. Voices were used inventively to establish rhythm and to fill spaces generally assigned to instruments. Credit for this creativity should go primarily to Calvin Carter.

Although the Dells made the charts again on Vee Jay only briefly with a disk of "Stay in My Corner" in 1965, they established an enviable record when they reappeared in 1967 on the Cadet label. From 1968 into 1971, they managed fifteen chart climbers, including No. 1 disks with a new version of "Stay in My Corner" in '68 and a new treatment of "Oh, What a Night" in '69. And they were still work-ing as a group into the mid-'70s when the Four Seasons scored with a song of the same title.

•

Mismanagement accounted for the brief association with the label of the all-important group out of Atlanta, Georgia, Gladys Knight & the Pips. "We all started in church," Ms. Knight has said. "Most of what I believe they call R & B singers today started in church. And really, I believe this is where the soul sound came from. It's the delivery, the way it's done." Gladys was only four when she sang before the congregation of Mount Moriah Baptist Church in Atlanta. Her precociousness seemed natural since both her father and mother had been members of the famous Wings Over Jordan Choir. By five Gladys had made a tour with the Morris Brown Choir through Ala-bama and Florida.

A family party at which Gladys sang with her brother Merald and several cousins led to the formation of the group. They called them-selves Gladys Knight & the Pips as a gesture to cousin James Woods, who volunteered to manage them and whose nickname was Pip. Early in 1961 they recorded a Johnny Otis song, "Every Beat of My Heart,"

The Dells

for a local label, Huntom Records. Play in Atlanta prompted a scout for Fury Records of New York to bring the group to the attention of owner Bobby Robinson, who flew the group up to the Big Apple and rerecorded the song. On its rerelease by Fury, "Every Beat of My Heart" made national R & B charts.

But in the meantime Huntom Records, which had not signed a contract with the group, was pressing records and selling them to Vee Jay. "Letter Full of Tears," the group's second release, was even bigger than "Every Beat," climbing to No. 3 on national R & B charts. By then Fury Records sued Vee Jay, forcing the Chicago company to give up all rights to the group. Fury was a short-lived label, and Gladys Knight & the Pips did not appear again on best-selling charts until 1967, by which time they were recording for Soul Records, a Motown subsidiary.

In "Letter Full of Tears" Gladys sang with an emotionalism that anticipated Aretha Franklin's soulfulness while a female backup group added heat with shouts and echoes of a gospel intensity. It came as no surprise that in 1974 Gladys won the accolade of "Best Selling Female Soul Artist."

Vee Jay's roster included outstanding solo artists as well as substantial groups. Jimmy Reed, of Leland, Mississippi, was the first of three to add stature to the fledgling label with a chart-climber in 1955. Reed was working in a Gary, Indiana, steel foundry when he came to the attention of the Brackens. During lunch hours he would sing the blues, accompanying himself, down-home style, on guitar and harmonica. "You Don't Have to Go," his initial hit, made Top Ten, but is not as well remembered because his follow-up, "Ain't That Lovin' You, Baby," was later recorded by many rock 'n' roll singers.

Reed sounds like a typical, old-style country blues singer—there is a harmonica interlude instead of the tenor sax solo of R & B disks—and he worked with horns only once, in 1962. A steady boogie beat and bass guitar accompaniment by Eddie Taylor made his disks danceable and attractive to young R & B fans. A more interesting feature, seldom commented upon, is that Reed's voice is frequently "shadowed" by another voice. It is not clearly distinguishable from his since the sound is a unison echo, but it adds thrust and clarity to his delivery.

Recording steadily for Vee Jay into the year of its demise, Reed was a regular occupant of R & B charts, usually in the Top Ten, from 1955 to 1961. His greatest acceptance came in '60 and '61 with "Baby, What You Want Me to Do?" "Big Boss Man," and "Bright

Lights, Big City"—songs later recorded by rockabilly vocalists like Jerry Lee Lewis, Charlie Rich, and Elvis. Apart from his own popularity, Reed is important because of the influence he exerted on modern Southern bluesmen like Lightnin' Slim and Lazy Lester. Young Chuck Berry is said to have heard a kindred voice in Reed's easy, humorously infectious style. Reed was a potent figure in the mid-'60s' R & B Revival and he had a part in shaping the style of Slim Harpo, an Excello Records chartmaker between '66 and '68. In the humor of Harpo's "Baby, Scratch My Back," No. 1 in 1966, one can hear echoes of Jimmy Reed, who died in his sleep in August 1976 after a performance at the Savoy Club in San Francisco. He was fifty years old. (L. C. "Good Rockin' " Robinson, a Texan who became a Bay Area bluesman in 1940 and who visited with Reed that night, sitting in on several numbers, himself died of a heart attack the following month at the age of sixty-one.)

John Lee Hooker, who was born in Clarksdale, Mississippi, in August 1917 and who became a Detroit dweller during the city's auto-industry boom in World War II, had been recording for at least eight years when he came to Vee Jay. But Hooker, who was as prolific as he was illiterate, seldom maintained allegiance to any one label. "I was after the big bread," he told rock writer Michael Lydon, as he had told Pete Welding. "I didn't care what they called me, or who they were. If they'd pay me, I'd play. I never changed my style, but I'd change my name."

And that he did during the years in which Bernard Besman was making records with him. Hooker was recording ostensibly for Modern Records, whose Detroit distributor was Besman, but he also appeared as Birmingham Sam on Regent and Savoy Records, Johnny Williams on Staff, Texas Slim on King, John Lee Booker on Gone, The Boogie Man on Acorn, and more. But between '49 and '51, he had three chart records for Modern, all recorded by Besman in Detroit, of which "I'm in the Mood" (1951) was the biggest.

When Hooker came to Vee Jay late in 1955, the company insisted on recording him in its Chicago studios. Partly as a result of this and Hooker's own development, his Vee Jay disks display a polish that contrasts sharply with his earlier recordings—though some connoisseurs prefer the earlier work. Hooker's repertoire was rooted in such traditional country blues as "Hobo Blues" and "Crawling Kingsnake," both of which were Modern hits in 1949. His style was ethnic and delta oriented, involving foot-tapping (audible on his disk of "Boogie Chillen" of '48), unison guitar accompaniment, choking or hammering on the strings, and sometimes songs developed on a single chord.

Gone were much of the rural abrasiveness and slurred unintelligibility of his earlier disks. He also pursued a much more rhythmic style that gave his records dance appeal. In 1958 he was on the charts with "I Love You, Honey," two years later with "No Shoes," and in '62 with "Boom Boom," the most popular of the three. He recorded for Vee Jay from '55 into '59, and again from '60 into '64. Some of the Hooker disks released by Vee Jay in the '60s were recorded live at programs of the Newport Folk Festival. An extremely versatile performer, Hooker was able to function both as a commercial R & B singer and an ethnic bluesman.

.

Vee Jay had still another bluesman who hailed originally from Mississippi. Though born in Sunflower, near Ita Bena in the northwestern part of the state, Jerry Butler thinks of himself as a Chicagoan —and properly so, since he was only three when his parents settled on the Windy City's North Side. The early death of his father, which left his mother with four young children to raise, forced Jerry, the oldest, to look for a paying occupation. After attending Washburn Vocational School, he studied to become a master chef and ice sculptor.

He was not yet a teen-ager when he joined The Northern Jubilee Gospel Singers, who chanted in Chicago's Traveling Soul Spiritualistic Church. Curtis Mayfield's grandmother was the pastor, and this was the beginning of a long-standing relationship between Butler and Mayfield. Eventually, the two became part of the Impressions, a group formed after Butler left the Quails, an R & B group, and Mayfield left the Alphatones. The nucleus of the Impressions was a group called the Roosters, whose members included Sam Gooden and the Brooks brothers, Arthur and Richard, all from Chattanooga, Tenn.

The Impressions' audition at Vee Jay Records in 1958 was making no headway until they performed "For Your Precious Love," a ballad written by Butler and the Brooks brothers. Then Calvin Carter could not record them fast enough. Within one week, Vee Jay had records on the market, so certain was Carter that the ballad would be a hit. "For Your Precious Love" broke like a souped-up hotrod and raced to the Top Ten within five weeks. Unfortunately, in the haste that attended the release, Carter sowed the seeds of the group's destruction. Without consulting its members he had the credits read: Jerry Butler & the Impressions. (The disk appeared on the Abner label, a subsidiary named after Ewart Abner, president of Vee Jay.) Seven months later, Jerry, who was as upset by the billing as the other members were, was out of the group. "I just split," he said, "because I saw this was getting to be a thing where we were busy worrying about who was getting top billing or equal billing," instead of concentrating on the singing. Even then, at the age of eighteen, Butler was already known as The Iceman, partly because of his cool demeanor. His singing, however, was anything but cool.

Once Butler left the Impressions, the group tried unsuccessfully to land another recording contract and then just folded. At that point, Butler and Mayfield began working together, the latter as guitarist and writer-collaborator. It took a bit of time before they connected with "He Will Break Your Heart" on Vee Jay, a No. 1 R & B hit in 1960–61.

Vee Jay production played a part in making the record a bestseller. Use was made of a shadow voice to heighten the impact of Butler's voice and a Latin-styled beat gave rhythmic lift to the disk. Compared to a vast number of R & B songs, "He Will Break Your Heart," by Butler, Mayfield, and Calvin Carter, was rather sophisticated, making expressive use of an extended theatrical metaphor: the new lover just playing a part he had long rehearsed.

Yet Butler emphasizes that the lyric came from experience. "The whole thought of 'He Will Break Your Heart' was something that I'd lived. You go into a town. You're only gonna be there for one night. You want some company. You find a girl, you blow her mind. Now you know this girl just hasn't been sittin', waitin' for you to come in. She probably has another fellow. They're probably planning to go through a whole thing, right? But you never take that into consideration. . . . But looking at it from the standpoint of the guy that's been lovin' this girl for years—that was basically the reason for the lyric. The melody came to me while shooting down the highway from Philadelphia to Atlantic City with Curtis Mayfield. I just sang it, and Curtis put the chords to it. Basically, what comes from the soul is melody. I think that lyrics come from experience and thoughts."

Butler finds the same down-to-earth statements in country-and-western music. "And that's one of the reasons," he commented in *Rolling Stone*, "why I believe those are the only two real forms that are gonna be around, C & W and black popular music, blues or rhythm-and-blues. They stay around because they talk about everyday

The Impressions

situations; they talk about true-to-life things. They don't get hung up in fantasyville and they don't get hung up on Broadway. They talk to people about things that happen to people."

Butler contends that it was as a result of his goading that Curtis Mayfield began writing about life. " 'Cause when Curtis first started writing," he says, "he used to write very abstract, like 'Gypsy Woman.' He was writing shit that was very fairytale-ish. I kept saying, 'You're writing about shit that you read about or that you dreamed about, but you're not writing about what you *live*. And then he wrote 'It's All Right' and 'Woman's Got a Soul.' He started to come toward himself in 'People Get Ready.' He started to come from stuff that he was *seeing* to stuff that he was feeling."

In 1961, the year that Butler had a Top Ten seller in "Find Another Girl," Curtis Mayfield regrouped the Impressions, adding Fred Cash, one of the original Roosters, to Gooden and the Brooks brothers. ABC signed them, scored with Mayfield's "Gypsy Woman," and two years later achieved a No. 1 R & B hit in "It's All Right," another Mayfield copyright. Powered by Mayfield's writing, singing, and producing talents, the Impressions were able to maintain a huge following into the '70s. After 1968, their releases appeared on Curtom Records, a Curtis Mayfield enterprise that had its beginnings with Curtom Publishing Company, a music house he founded with Butler in 1961.

Virtually all of Mayfield's early songs were love ballads, but he soon turned to socially-oriented material in numbers like "Choice of Color," No. 1 in 1969, and a series of songs on poverty, black pride, and discrimination. As a writer, Mayfield has continued to add to his laurels during the '70s, reaching a high point in '72 with his score for the hit film *Super Fly*, the tale of a black cocaine huckster. In dealing with the drug scene, Mayfield tackled the white enslavement of blacks through narcotics and did not flinch at attacking the *laissez-faire* attitude of the New Left as a contributing factor to the continued victimization of blacks.

On his own, Jerry Butler went through a trying period in which he and/or Vee Jay worked at developing disks that would cross over into pop. In 1962 he competed with Andy Williams on "Moon River," the year's Academy Award song. The following year, he also had a chart song, pop as well as R & B, in "Make It Easy on Yourself," an early ballad by Burt Bacharach and Hal David. In a backward look at this period, he has said: "At the time I started . . . your ultimate goal was to be a Nat Cole or a Sammy Davis. . . ." "Moon River" was to him a gambit "in hope of getting into the mainstream of things. We thought it would open up the doors to the pop stations for us." Acknowledging that it was "prostitution in a sense," he adds, "But I feel that, with me music is more than just what I like—it's a business. . . . I'm too honest to bullshit myself that everything I do is simply for the sake of art. That's crap 'cause I gotta live and I have a family to support."

After Vee Jay went bankrupt, Butler moved to Mercury Records, where he began working with the producing-writing team of Kenny Gamble and Leon Huff. The three were able to keep Butler a best-seller into the '70s both in pop and R & B with original songs like "Hey, Western Union Man" and "Only the Strong Survive," No. 1 hits in '68 and '69 respectively.

•

Dee Clark, born Delectus Clark in Blythesville, Arkansas, in November 1938, came to Vee Jay late in the '50s when the dividing line between R & B and R 'n' R had begun to blur. As the source of R 'n' R, R & B itself underwent a transformation as crossovers increased. It became more sophisticated, with string sections adding their swirl to the horns that gave R & B its bite.

Clark's background was ghetto Chicago—his family moved from Arkansas when he was a child. When he was still a teen-ager, he not only sang on the streets but recorded on OKeh with a group called the Hambone Kids. After he won a talent contest in '55, a local disk jockey named Herb Kent brought him to the attention of Vee Jay. His first releases appeared on Falcon Records, a subsidiary whose name was later changed to Abner Records.

"Nobody But You," his initial chartmaker and a song that he wrote, made R & B's Top Ten in 1958. Neither of his follow-ups, "Just Keep

It Up" and "Hey, Little Girl," both from the inspired pen of prolific Otis Blackwell, were as popular, though both also made Top Ten in R & B. "Hey, Little Girl (In the High School Sweater)" ran into censorship problems when parents called radio stations to object to the hardly objectionable lyrics.

Clark's best-remembered song is a weeper ballad that he wrote. "Raindrops" had an unusually strong melody, excellent record production—rain effects and swirling strings—and it demonstrated Clark's vocal versatility. Possessed of a high, clear, imperious baritone in the Clyde McPhatter groove—he almost sounded feminine in his top notes—he could also emit catlike wails in the style of Little Richard or James Brown. In fact, in 1957, when Little Richard quit singing to enter the ministry, Clark took over his band, the Upsetters.

Dee Clark helped Vee Jay make the transition from R & B to R 'n' R. Betty Everett also contributed with "The Shoop Shoop Song" ("It's in His Kiss,") as did Gene Chandler with "Duke of Earl." Both of these artists later scored on other labels: Everett on Uni and Fantasy; Chandler on Constellation, Checker, Brunswick, and Mercury. The group that really projected Vee Jay into the rock 'n' roll era was the Four Seasons, a white group that came up with two smash sellers in 1962: "Sherry" and "Big Girls Don't Cry." Startling though it may appear, Vee Jay was also the first company to release records by the Beatles in this country. Through a deal negotiated by Randy Wood, who moved from sales manager to the company's presidency in 1963, four Beatles singles were released in 1963–4. That was before the Beatles exploded with "I Want to Hold Your Hand" and before Capitol Records, which had turned down the earlier releases, exercised its overall option with EMI Records of Great Britain.

Despite its outward appearance as a thriving and enterprising company with all signals *Go*, Vee Jay suddenly folded in 1965 amidst rumors and charges of maladministration and manipulation of funds. After a time, Randy Wood and a former comptroller bought the defunct company's masters. Wood, with whom I taped the interview that follows, is no longer associated with the company, except in a consultant capacity. Recently, ABC Records released an informative collection: *14 Golden Recordings from the Historical Vaults of Vee Jay Records.*

•

Although it was the most successful, Vee Jay was hardly the only black-owned company in Chicago. J.O.B. Records, founded in 1949 by Joseph Brown, was a partnership involving major participation by bluesman St. Louis Jimmy Oden and minor participation by bluesman Sunnyland Slim. The name J.O.B. is said to have been derived from the initials of St. Louis Jimmy's real name, James Burke Oden. Brown, who came of Cherokee Indian stock, was born in Wagoner, Oklahoma, in 1904 and died in 1976. The company recorded so many little-known artists that Brown branded as a lie the accusation that he would cut anybody who paid for a session. J.O.B. Records did, however, produce one No. 1 R & B hit. Titled "Five Long Years," the Eddie Boyd recording was on national charts from September 1952 into early '53. Boyd was a delta bluesman, born in Clarksdale, Mississippi, in 1914, who cut his first session in Chicago in 1947 with J. T. Brown's Boogie Band, ubiquitous Willie Dixon on bass. His debut disk was released by Victor for whom Boyd thereafter cut a dozen released sides into 1949. His J.O.B. hit led to a contract with Chess Records with whom he remained for five years and enjoyed two R & B chartmakers, "24 Hours" and "Third Degree," both Top Ten in 1953. Boyd continued recording into the '60s with many different "indies," most in Chicago, and at least one (Palos) in Texas and one (Bob Geddins' Art-Tone) in Oakland, California. J.O.B.'s Brown continued producing disks on many different "indies": Abco, Fury and Ruler among others. But as he was a manufacturer in search of sales, Eddie Boyd was an accomplished bluesman in search of listeners.

•

What makes Vee Jay's demise regrettable is that its growth, in just over a decade, was little short of phenomenal. By the time it entered the recording scene in '53, R & B was developing a following among white teen-agers. Vee Jay found a way of reaching this expanding audience not only through artists like the El Dorados, Dells, Dee Clark and Gladys Knight & the Pips, but through delta bluesmen like John Lee Hooker and Jimmy Reed. Its versatility was all the more impressive because its product was firmly grounded in and did not depart from its black roots. Unfortunately, the tensions and dialectics of white-black relationships figured in the demise of the company as well as its growth. Perhaps Vee Jay's experience as a black-owned company that failed helped Berry Gordy build the black-owned enterprise that today is the fabulously successful Motown entertainment complex.

groove *11*   **RANDY WOOD**

"I didn't join Vee Jay until June of 1960," said Randy Wood, as we talked in his home in the Hollywood hills.

"I became president of the company about two and one-half years later. But I did go into the archives to reconstruct its history. Their first artists were the Spaniels. 'Baby, It's You' was the first release, Vee Jay 101. Recordmen remember catalogue numbers better than titles. Calvin Carter not only produced the Spaniels but sang with the group.

"Jimmy Reed was one of the company's early discoveries. What's interesting is that they were auditioning a fellow named Eddie Taylor and Jimmy came in as a backup guitarist. Calvin liked Eddie Taylor, but he was more impressed by Jimmy Reed, so much so that he asked Jimmy whether he had any other songs 'that he had composed.' And Reed replied, 'No, but I have some songs that I writ.' And they ended up signing Jimmy.

"The company had a phenomenal track record, usually producing a hit with an artist's first or second release. Like 'Goodnight, Sweetheart, Goodnight,' the Spaniels' second or third release, was a smash that went into the Top Ten in R & B. I went into the statistics at one point. But apart from charts—and they were not as sophisticaed as they are today—it was conceivable that you could sell several hundred thousand records of a disk that no one in pop radio ever heard of.

"The company started as a gospel label. The Brackens had small retail record shops in the suburbs of Chicago, as far out as Gary. They had customers for gospel records, but just didn't have sufficient product. Companies like Apollo and Savoy then had limited catalogues. And people interested in gospel music collect records the way kids collect their favorite rock artists. James Bracken told me that that was one of the principal reasons for their forming Vee Jay. They knew of gospel groups around Chicago that they could record for very reasonable costs.

"For example, they had an artist named Maceo Woods who was with them for the better part of ten to twelve years. He has never had a single big record, but his albums were consistent sellers in the gospel field. It was either Maceo Woods or the Staple Singers that made the original record of 'Amazing Grace,' which has since been a best-seller five or six times. Twice for Judy Collins and twice for the Royal Scots Guards Band. It's a P.D. [Public Domain] thing, which I heard in Baptist churches in Harlem when I was a kid. The first Vee Jay gospel album, catalogue-wise, was called *Amazing Grace* by the Staple Singers.

"You are, doubtless, right about the Staple Singers being on Warner Brothers Records with Cal Lampley. But after they left Vee Jay, they went to Columbia, the Epic subsidiary, I think. It's interesting to note the influence that group had on the pop records made by Vee Jay. When I joined the company, we were in the middle of a big record by Jimmy Reed. It could have been 'Baby, What You Want Me to Do?' The next big record was 'He Will Break Your Heart,' by Jerry Butler, which went about eight hundred fifty thousand copies. [It went to No. 1 on R & B charts] Over the past fourteen years, it's been covered by God knows how many artists. And as an oldie, Jerry's record has probably passed the 2 million mark. The intro on the original Jerry Butler record is a four-bar phrase that Calvin heard and took from a Staple Singers gospel record.

"The overlapping of those two creative concepts is quite revealing. Somebody suggested to me that the only real heritage that our country has, the only art form that is basically ours, is the Negro spiritual. And thinking about it, one has to recognize its truth. Every other facet of our culture, be it painting or music, is an offshoot from some other nationality that's migrated to this country. But this is an art form that was created right here on the plantations and in the fields. Gospel was not simply praise-the-Lord kind of crap and it's-a-terrible-thing-that-we're-being-beaten-by-straw-bosses. It was also a form of entertainment and relaxation. The entertainment, for blacks in any event, had to be created in the home. That's why even today the record is so vitally important in minority communities.

"Living in England for a time, I saw evidence of this. Take people in this country and England who work for comparable salaries, whether it's pushing a truck in the garment center or being a box-boy in a supermarket. There is no money available to go into a night club or a sophisticated saloon to hear a live artist. The ghetto communities—black, Mexican, and Puerto Rican (and Mexicans and Puerto Ricans are heavy into black music as well)—spend proportionately more money on records than do whites. One cat will call up a friend, 'I've got the new Aretha album,' and the other will say, 'I've got Isaac Hayes,' and suddenly they get a party together that way. Black music is really an integral part of the way blacks live.

"When I started at Vee Jay, it was not in a creative capacity. I headed up their marketing for the West Coast. They had Red Schwartz for Philadelphia, Steve Clark in Atlanta, and they moved me from New York to California to cover the eleven Western states. The company never had a sales manager. Ewart Abner doubled in brass. That was in June 1960. By October 1960, after I had been waiting years to move out of New York, I was commuting every three weeks to New York. I lived there for practically a week on each trip. I was involved in distributor changes, packaging concepts, resurrecting neglected masters, and extracting what we felt were good sales items to perpetuate the catalogue.

"I brought the Four Seasons to Vee Jay. They were originally on RCA Victor as a group called the Four Lovers. That painting on the wall is Bob Crewe's present to me for 'Sherry,' their first hit. They had two in '62; 'Big Girls Don't Cry' also made number one. The writing and creative genius were reflected in all four members, but principally in Bob Gaudio. Dee Clark was with the label from '58 on and had some substantial sellers, the first being 'Nobody But You.' His biggest record was 'Raindrops' in '61. We also had Gene Chandler, who had a biggie in '62 with 'Duke of Earl.' There was J. B. Lenoir, a good singer who was unfortunately bitten by the Ray Charles bug and never really made it.

"On the distaff side, we had Christine Cottrell, who had the original record of 'I Am a Woman,' later covered by Peggy Lee. Priscilla Bowman had the original record of 'Hands Off'—I think that Jay McShann received top billing—which later became a big hit for Dinah Washington. The Jay McShann-Priscilla Bowman record went to number one in '55.

"The longevity of this catalogue is absolutely amazing. The blues cult reappears every five years. In '63 Abner made a deal with Dave Hubert to distribute masters that Hubert had acquired and produced for over a period of seven or eight years. One of the artists in that pact, Hoyt Axton, was later signed by us. We recorded two or three albums with him and now he's getting to be a monster. He was a giant as a writer, and now Hoyt has emerged as an artist. We tried. Capitol tried. And now A & M has come up with the right combination.

"The single most important influence in my life, as far as music is concerned, was a man named Eric Bernay, one of the legends in our industry. He was probably the first independent record company. If I remember correctly, the masters of Keynote Records were sold to Mercury and became the basis of the Mercury LP package catalogue.

Eric had a store on West Forty-fourth Street called The Music Room. It was 129 West Forty-fourth. It was next door to an avant-garde bookstore called Book Fair, which stocked leftwing literature. For folk music, The Music Room was the place to go.

"I was born in Harlem. My parents were poor. I had to work after school. One of the places where I worked was Lehman Music at 68 West 125th Street. It's there today. After that, I went to The Music Room. But let me go back to 1935–36. I couldn't have been more than six or seven years old. We had one luxury in our apartment, and that was a radio. When the weather was bad or there were riots in Harlem—and we had hunger and race riots—my mother simply wouldn't let us go out.

"I learned two things that have stayed with me. One was how to cook—because when things really got boring, I watched her. The other was music. I used to listen to Martin Block—he was *the* original disk jockey. Martin's taste was very good. He played Paul Whiteman, Jimmie Lunceford, Don Redman, Count Basie, Ellington, Red Nichols & the Five Pennies, Ella Fitzgerald and Chick Webb, John Kirby— that was my introduction to music. I did take piano lessons for about six months.

"At first my interest in music was as an escape. But eventually it became an integral part of the way I lived. Eric [Bernay] was the first person to have a profound influence. I wandered into his store one day soaking wet. I was five-foot-five and weighed about 118 pounds. I was thirteen years old and probably looked like I was ten. I told him I wanted a job. And his wife, now his widow, Isabelle, put me to work packing classical sheet music in the back of the store. But I also had an opportunity to hear 'Songs of the Lincoln Brigade,' 'Ballad for Americans,' and music that somewhat shaped my future.

"After that I spent several years in the navy and merchant marine. On my release, I went to work for People's Songs. I became very friendly with Josh White, who taught me how to phrase, the difference between folk music and blues, and how there was a logical and co- hesive marriage between the two. I also had the pleasure and privilege of spending a lot of time with Pete Seeger. All of this led me to try promoting those concerts they used to run at Town Hall at midnight thirty years ago. I did one with Josh White and ended up managing Oscar Brand for about two years and producing his radio show.

"At the same time, I wound up managing and living with Leadbelly for about a year and a half. And that was a trip and a half! That led to my being involved with Brownie McGhee and on the fringes of

Sonny Terry. By then Sonny had gone into a show called *Finian's Rainbow*, and he was somewhat on his way to becoming a folk star. I was only eighteen or nineteen. One of my first introductions to black music came as a spin-off of being involved with Brownie. His brother was Stick McGhee, who hit on Atlantic Records with 'Drinkin' Wine, Spo-Dee-O-Dee.' That was the first time I heard of Atlantic Records. Just about that time I became involved with a song called 'The Roving Kind,' which was adapted by Oscar Brand from a folk tune and was a hit for Doris Day on Columbia. While Oscar was working at Plum Point in New York, I met Milt Okun's father and then eventually Milt. This led to my first record venture. Crest Records, I think it was called, and our first release was 'The Roving Kind,' as sung by Oscar Brand. The Ray Charles Singers were the background group—this is the white Ray Charles who was connected with 'Your Hit Parade.' Milt and I produced the record.

"I was then working for Columbia Records. This was around 1948 or '49. I had gotten married, and I needed a steady income. Columbia paid thirty-nine dollars a week for doing clerical work in the order department. But they soon found out that I could promote and, after Christmas, they moved me to the promotion dept. The first record I worked on was 'Buttons and Bows,' by Dinah Shore. It was #38234. The second record was #38301, and that was Kay Kyser doing 'Slow Boat to China.' The next one was #38324, which started very slowly and I regarded as a smash hit. It was 'I've Got My Love to Keep Me Warm,' by Les Brown, a revival of a rhythm ballad of the '30s. It also created a solid friendship between me and Les Brown. With all the internal crap that went on at Columbia—and I was too young to understand it—there was a cutback and I had to look for another job.

"And so I ended up as a salesman and then a buyer for a shop called Coin's, on Cortlandt Street in lower Manhattan—58 Cortlandt Street. That happened in May 1950, and I was a bit depressed about going back to the retail end, except that a very positive thing happened. At 68 Courtlandt, I met and became very close friends with Dave Rothfeld, who is now head of the entire music division of Korvette's. He is without a question the most astute and important record buyer in the United States. Korvette's does about $35 to $40 million just in records alone, and it's all as a result of Dave Rothfeld's second sense.

"From there, I went to Folkways, remaining for a period of two years. Folkways was the creature of Moe Asch—'The Asch we want mo' of.' It was a very interesting experience, because meeting Moe

Asch's father was a trip and a half. I mean Sholem Asch, one of the most prolific writers of the twentieth century. He was a fascinating man. Among other things, he was seventy-seven and he had a wife of thirty-five who was the happiest woman in the world. Obviously, he was doing something right. Serving as Folkways' sales manager broadened my perspective on the record business greatly. I traveled, not only around the country, but worked conventions—not just rack-jobber conventions but library, school, and educational conventions. I went up into Montreal where we exported finished product. Folkways was three people—Moe Asch; Marion Distler, that wonderfully dedicated woman now gone; and Randy Wood.

"At Moe Asch's I developed some rich insights into the business. Asch was one of the first to record Nat 'King' Cole. But he also recorded some of the most obscure African music, Haitian music, Indian music—ragas and things like that. He didn't actually record them. The American composer Henry Cowell did. In an effort to know what I was selling, I carefully read the liner notes and booklets that came with these albums. I learned so much that at one point I was lecturing in the dance classes at the New York High School of the Performing Arts on rhythms and music to be used in interpretative dancing and the development of primitive to jazz concepts in dancing.

"Something else comes back to me at this moment. In the merchant marine I met Woody Guthrie and Cisco Houston, separate and apart from any other connection. Cisco is a faint memory for me because he died around '44, I think, of tuberculosis. We all know what Woody died of—mostly a broken heart, like Alan Freed later did.

"So folk music and jazz and blues—and there are white blues as well as black blues—have all played an integral part in my life in music. Given a preference, I think I lean more to Vivaldi and Scarlatti. I like Janis Joplin, but I can't really handle Bessie Smith. I understand the art form and where it comes from. But that sound is alien to my ears. I could handle Bobby Short singing 'Give Me a Pigfoot and a Bottle of Beer,' but not Bessie Smith.

"Today there's that girl from Scotland, Maggie Bell. Absolute dynamite. It's not a question of recording techniques. It's a matter of blending the guttural sounds that we associate with the blues with a kind of musical sophistication. The blending of the two results in a very pleasant form, I think, anyway.

"I can handle gospel, not intellectually, but musically. Intellectually, it's a bunch of bullshit, as far as I am concerned. But the nuances and the approach to music of The Staple Singers is fantastic. They have managed to bridge the gap. They have taken what is fundamentally a gospel sound and given it pop appeal—those rhythm patterns, the reading of the lyrics (grass-roots mentality)—when it comes out of your speaker, it's something that anybody can relate to, anybody from ten to seventy years old. It's something that doesn't identify itself as to color; it bridges all the gaps. And that's what music is all about.

"I left Folkways in '52 to go to work for Liberty Music Shops on Fiftieth Street and Madison Avenue. After nearly two years, a friend told me that his brother-in-law was opening a shop on Thirty-fourth and Fifth Avenue. Maybe I could moonlight. Well, this guy opened a store, ran a few ads in *The New York Times*, and suddenly he became one of the biggest accounts in New York: The I. Stock Music Shop. His father's name was really Isidore Stock. I was working at Liberty during the day and showing him at night how to set up inventory controls.

"After a while, he asked what I was making at Liberty, which was about a hundred fifty a week, and he offered two hundred. I asked for a piece of the action, but he said, 'It's just my father and me,' and offered funny money. It sounded interesting. That plus the fact that the store was at 131 East Thirty-fourth and I lived at 129 East. So I took it.

"After I left Stock, I opened a mail-order thing of my own. This lasted for about a year. I wasn't properly capitalized for it. Then I went to work for a man named Aaron Wall on Fifty-seventh Street. He had taken a lease on a place called Rabson's. It was on Fifty-second and then moved to Fifty-seventh—one of the first discount stores in the radio-music area. He also owned Strand Music. After a while, he offered me the option of coming over to Strand or leasing Rabson's record department.

"I frankly did not want to work for anybody. So I put the money together, and a friend of mine and I ran it. It was not the best record location in the world, but I was diagonally across the street from Carnegie Hall, and I had interesting experiences. I met Errol Garner, Leonard Bernstein, Don Shirley, Andy Williams, and I started to develop acquaintances all over the music area. Also, the building housed Steve Allen and record producer Bob Thiele on the second floor. On the third floor, Archie Bleyer had Cadence Records. Dave Kapp was on the sixth floor with a new company of his own. Frank Loesser had his own publishing company on the seventh floor.

"In this period, I was studying with Andy Williams' vocal coach and thinking of singing with the Sauter-Finegan Band. I had become friendly with Archie Bleyer, Bob Thiele, and particularly Dave Kapp. I had known Kapp before as a result of arranger Bill Finnegan because Dave had been at RCA Victor, to whom Bill was contracted. Dave used to come down from his office when he had free time and wander around my record department, trying to figure out new products. He had Roger Williams, Jane Morgan, and others.

"I used to make suggestions to Dave about things he could record. And for one Roger Williams date, I recommended an instrumental, 'Almost Paradise,' originally recorded, I think, by the Norman Petty Trio. Dave's single knocked the Petty disk on its ass and became one of the biggies of the year—probably 1957. Mickey Kapp, Dave's son, and I became friends, too. About two months later, Dave came into the store with Jay Lasker to tell me he was doing a date with Roger and wanted to know what was moving. I told him about a new Percy Faith disk that was just beginning to sell—'Till.' I didn't know that Randy Wood, my namesake at Dot, was covering it with Billy Vaughn. Dave's 'Till' album went to about a hundred fifty thousand initially. Dave got hung up on the song and recorded it with other artists on his label: Jane Morgan and the Troubadours.

"All of this was a prelude to Kapp's approaching me about a job. One day, he did ask what I was taking out of the store a week and offered to match it. I laughed and said, 'Add about fifteen dollars a week and I'm your man.' And so I went to Kapp Records. Dave had made so much money at that point that it was a matter of investing it or paying it out as taxes. The first thing I did was buy a label for him called Unicorn. Believe it or not, I was the Kapp A & R classical producer. Unicorn had one big record in its catalogue: Haydn's *Trumpet Concerto*. Unicorn was actually an offshoot of the string section of the Boston Symphony Orchestra. It was called the Cambridge Music Society. Now that the Kapp label had a foot in the classical door, Dave asked me one day, 'What do you know about opera?' I told him, 'Instrumentally, I love it. Vocally, I can't stand it.' And so I produced twelve operas without words, among them, *Traviata, Aida, Carmen, Il Trovatore, La Forza del Destino*. Domenico Savino helped at the music end and I even wrote the liner notes.

"When I was working at Columbia, in my lean days, I used to moonlight at the Metropolitan. For three bucks a night, I'd run across the stage with a spear—you know the bit. The three bucks on top of thirty-nine dollars helped; it could last me for two days. I don't like the art form, except for Mozart, who had a great sense of humor. I love Wagner orchestrally, but vocally, it's a chore for me. Italian opera is so saccharine—those stories should be on daytime TV and the chick should burn her fingers while she's ironing a *shmatta*.

"So I'm at Kapp Records making a hundred ninety a week, and I learn that Imperial Records is looking for a sales manager. I found out that the first thing you don't do is tell the truth when you're negotiating for salary. When Lew Chudd asked me how much I made at Kapp, I quoted two hundred fifty bucks. And that's what I got as sales manager and East Coast A & R man. But I took the Imperial job mostly because I wanted to settle in California. I was still living in New York, but I started commuting. I'd spend a week in California with Chudd, then go out on the road for two, and be home about one.

"The A & R man on the coast was Henri René, who had come over after a long, long career at RCA Victor. I wound up with Georgia Gibbs, and he got Annette Kleinberg, who was one of Phil Spector's Teddy Bears. It became clear after a short time that things were not going to work out. A music publishing friend, Jackie Gayle, suggested that I work with him and Nat 'King' Cole, which I did for about six months, while I was still with Imperial.

"It was not long before the thing with Chudd blew up. And then I learned that Vee Jay needed a sales manager and wanted him to locate in California, which was just what I wanted. I went to see Ewart Abner in Chicago. When I told him what I was making, he said that they couldn't afford it and offered two hundred dollars a week. I told him I couldn't afford to work for that—by then, I had two kids. So he got hold of Jimmy Bracken and we went down to Batts, a nearby Chicago restaurant. Later, I used to hold my sales meetings at the place. Bracken was a lovely man, but he was out to lunch all the time. And while Abner and I talked salary, he sat watching a baseball game on TV. Once in a while, he'd look over and say, 'Yeah, yeah,' and that's how Abner okayed my salary figure. I was supposed to meet Abner for a final conversation at the ARMADA [Association of Record Merchants & Distributors of America] meeting in Atlantic City. When I arrived, Abner was in the hospital, suffering from nervous exhaustion. After a week or so, he called me and I moved out to California. And so, in June 1960 I became the West Coast regional rep for Vee Jay.

•

"I see a distinction between 'race' records and rhythm and blues records not merely in terms of time but audience, if you will. The 'race' records of the thirties and forties were made for a black audience; R & B records are disks that are conceived for a black audience, but have a potential for crossing into the white market. Jimmy Reed and John Lee Hooker do what they have always done. The music and the changes are essentially the same, though Jimmy Reed displays some creativity at the lyric end. The man who bridges the gap for me is B. B. King. In the early fifties you began to feel the transition, the general population move toward black-oriented music: i.e., Fats Domino, Little Richard. Periodically a Larry Williams record would cross over from what was essentially a black-programmed record to a pop record.

"My early sales contact was with folk-blues artists like Josh White and Brownie McGhee and Sonny Terry. I did not get into hardcore blues until I went to work for Imperial just about a year before I became sales manager of Vee Jay. When I got to Imperial, Fats Domino had made the transition. He retained his black customers, but went on to sell records consistently to white listeners. Even today you have a certain amount of black-oriented product that never makes it into pop. But the number of radio stations playing records that you can hear only on those stations are rapidly diminishing.

"There are several reasons. Take the Motown artists who were originally black-oriented marketwise. That's no longer the case. The Four Tops, who are now on the ABC label, are played immediately, not only on the black stations, but on the white ones as well. So with The Temptations, The Miracles, The Supremes, and Marvin Gaye. I am sure that when a Marvin Gaye or Stevie Wonder disk comes into a white station, there's a fight among the jockeys as to who plays it first. So the potential and the horizon for black artists have broadened greatly.

"These days the only stations that expose black material not heard on white stations are the so-called underground stations. In California, there are stations like KMET and KPPC. Not long ago I assembled a series of ten albums to be reissued from the Vee Jay catalogue. Among these are two sets of double-record albums based on masters going back as far as 1955–6 through about '63. One of the albums is just called *The Blues*. It utilizes disks of Priscilla Bowman, Harold Burrage, J. B. Lenoir, Jimmy Reed, John Lee Hooker—there are sixteen different artists among the twenty tracks. To me, this is grass-roots blues. You will not hear that kind of music on key stations in Chicago, who must perforce program a more sophisticated type of music.

"In 1961 we came out with a Jimmy Reed release on Vee Jay. Although I was still nominally sales manager, I doubled in brass and even did a movie sound-track recording for the company out here in LA. The Reed release was a two-record set called *Jimmy Reed at Carnegie Hall*. At the same time, we issued an album that had only one record—it was one of the two—and we called it *The Best of Jimmy Reed*. When Reed played college dates, the audience was preponderantly white, but his selling pattern was white and black. He sold well in Miami, New Orleans, Atlanta. But in Texas his sales were unbelievable. Now blues are indigenous to black people. Perhaps, they were indigenous to *all* the people in that area. If our initial order on an album was twenty-five thousand units, you could figure that Houston and Dallas would account for about twelve hundred as a 5-percent market. But Reed sold four thousand units.

•

"I became president of Vee Jay in August of 1963. Abner, who hired me, was removed as president, and I was installed. And that was a bit of trauma. At that point, my leanings were toward leaving, but Abner almost insisted that I stay: to look after what he referred to as his baby. I was scared to death. I knew how to sell, I knew how to market, but to assume fiduciary responsibility was something more than I felt I could cope with. All of us sat around a table and the conversation went: 'You do it,' 'No, you do it. . . .' I suggested Jay Lasker for the presidency. They felt, and wrongly so, that it would not be the proper image for them. [Lasker was white.] I suggested Calvin Carter, and he said, 'No, not me, no way.' And I wound up with it.

"In some ways, it was good and, in many, bad. I'm not even referring to the eventual demise of the company so much as to the internal bickering that went on, the constant black-and-white confrontations, which I had never been exposed to in my life, even though I was born in Harlem and raised in a ghetto. I never saw that incredible amount of hostility. And it stemmed from the black facet of the company, not the white. And the white finally reacted in kind.

"As the president, I had to walk a very peculiar line because I was neither white enough nor black enough. You know Broonzy's lines: 'If you're white, you're right./ If you're brown, stick aroun'./ If you're black, get back . . .'? Well, it was that philosophy in reverse. Jimmy Bracken was Chairman of the Board, and Vivian held some titular title—who the hell knows what? But Vivian had her own things going, and Jimmy had a variety of interests and really couldn't be active. And when he was active, he managed to create unrest. I found out later why it happened. It didn't come from him. He was parrotting things that came from the outside influences, outside elements. Jay Lasker was executive vice-president; Steve Clark was vice-president; Calvin was vice-president; Mark Sands was comptroller, but not really an officer. That was the chain of command, and it was a mixed group.

"We were trying to reconstruct the company from every standpoint —the location of masters to what our real obligations were to creditors, suppliers, artists, etc. When I took over as president, they came in swarms out of the woodwork. We found one pressing plant to whom we owed a quarter of a million dollars. We had hassles with Bob Crewe and the Four Seasons and their lawyers. Out of bad, some good comes, and I developed friendships with several accountants and lawyers. At one point, we had no fewer than sixty-four legal actions going. It's frightening to think of it even now.

"All of this had accumulated over a period of four years. The pressing plants went along with the program for many reasons, some that I'm aware of and some that I can only surmise. Ewart Abner had the whole thing in his head. And how you can run a company that's doing $2 to $3 million a year—keeping the facts and figures in your head—is an enigma. I guess he had that sixth sense of knowing what to put where, which is, perhaps, the qualities that make a president. But they also serve to fuck up that company pretty badly. And to add to everything else, we had Internal Revenue threatening to close us up on an almost daily basis. We had four or five creditors threatening to throw us into bankruptcy. And our comptroller said, 'Go ahead, we'll beat you to the courtyard and do it ourselves.' Chapter Eleven as opposed to involuntary bankruptcy—things that I then didn't understand.

"Then we had hassles with the artists, particularly Jerry Butler and Betty Everett, Dee Clark, Wade Flemons, and others. I got along rather well with Jimmy Reed, but fortunately he was on the road. I say 'fortunately' because it would have been just another problem.

"One of the fellows who tried to be helpful was Al Smith, a musician who brought Jimmy Reed and Al Taylor to Vee Jay. He died not long ago. He managed John Lee Hooker and Betty Everett as well as Reed. He and I became pretty good friends, and he ran interference for me as much as he could. Jerry Butler had become a very astute businessman. Although we were very friendly, he was concerned with protecting his interests, and rightly so. Except for the Four Seasons, he was the biggest artist that Vee Jay had, and he had a bit of a clout. Also, we had nothing but heartaches from Eddie Harris.

"The pressures that were brought to bear made it increasingly difficult to operate the company. On top of that, there was a family situation. Every time I wanted to fire someone—not to replace him, but just to save money that was being needlessly expended—I would get arguments from Jimmy Bracken, occasionally from Vivian, and from Calvin Carter. They had no concept of profit and loss and didn't seem to understand that if we cut off four or five pieces of dead weight, it would save the company in overhead and salaries forty or fifty thousand dollars. We could use that money to produce or acquire product that would yield income and help make the company healthy again.

"There was a tremendous strain on Jay Lasker and myself because we were commuting almost every week between Chicago and California. We lived here in LA and ran the company in Chicago. It created a gap between Jay and myself that led to several nasty confrontations and one in particular that almost completely destroyed our friendship. That bickering and that hassling carried on through the success of Vee Jay with the Beatles and what-have-you.

"The end result was that in February 1965, Vee Jay bought out Jay Lasker, Steve Clark, and Mark Sands for a total of a hundred thousand dollars and some fringe benefits. They were going to buy me out; I had reached a point where I felt things were impossible. I was being shoved around by both sides. But what happened was regretful. We could have wound up with Johnny Rivers when he really exploded. He was managed by Lou Adler and Bobby Roberts, who is Jay Lasker's brother-in-law. Well, considering the state of things, Jay couldn't allow Lou to bring Rivers into Vee Jay.

"We literally could have been millionaires. We were in the midst of a deal where a film company was going to acquire Vee Jay. It would have been a stock deal and given us something like seven hundred fifty thousand in cash to be divided among seven of us. Also three- to five-year firm contracts with the balance of the sales price to be paid out in stock, which would have given us about one and a quarter million each over a period of five years. The one who fucked it up was Jimmy Bracken. In the middle of a corporate stockholders and board meeting, he announced that he didn't want 'any more cooperations.' It took me a few minutes to realize that he was talking about 'corporations.'

"I can almost understand why he said it. We had set up a separate sales company as a tax shelter. Vee Jay acted as the producer, another company served as the manufacturer, and a third as the sales agency.

It was strictly a paper transaction. The manufacturing company could not be a stockholder in either of the other two; otherwise, the government would have outlawed it as a tax device. The tragedy of the thing is that this setup was formulated in December of 1963 or January 1964, and in June of '64 the government did away with the excise tax, which negated the reason for it anyway.

"It was this kind of bickering and hassling that was principally responsible for the demise of Vee Jay. The product was there. In June 1965, the Brackens decided to bring Abner back and to remove me. They brought him back in, and in October 1965 Abner picked up and moved the company back to Chicago. Four months later—I had been gone for the better part of a year—they filed Chapter Eleven in Chicago; and in August 1966 it was adjudicated bankrupt. The courts would not even let them stay in Chapter Eleven. They were put into bankruptcy and the assets of the company were then placed in the hands of the court. Warner Brothers sent someone in, so did ABC, to evaluate the catalogue; but they couldn't because they didn't know what was there. Almost thirteen years of the company could not be pieced together, except by two people, Abner or myself. The courts tried for a solid year to sell, but they couldn't dispose of the company free and clear; they could sell only on the basis of right, title, and interest. The court could not warrant that Vee Jay owned many things—they weren't sure.

"The end result was that a representative of the court bought it as a nominee—in Chicago, you can do anything. After trying to sell all over Hell's half-acre, the only buyers he could find were Betty Chappetta and myself. She had been comptroller for about a year and a half before the company went under. So we bought it. A year and a half later, I sold my interest out to her under some very strange circumstances, too. The company is still functioning. I've been involved with it off and on. I sold my interest in 1968 and got involved again in 1969 in what might be described as a consultant or advisory capacity.

"Betty Chappetta owns it now. But a company called Modern Distributors has spun off the masters into several companies. So there are three or four companies that in one way or another hold some degree of title to the masters. Betty and I set up Modern Distributors when we purchased Vee Jay's assets.

"It's sad to think what it could have been."

5. East Coast R & B

World War I started bluesmen moving up North, and No. II made it a mass migration. There were three paths. Up from Mississippi and Alabama, they headed into Chicago— and we had the strong Delta influence on Chess Records. From Oklahoma, Texas, and the Southwest, they went to California—that was T-Bone Walker and the honky-tonk, jazz combo influence. And from the Carolinas, Florida, and Georgia, they came up to giving us a mix of Gospel and Pop.

—JERRY WEXLER

Savoy Records of Newark, New Jersey

"**R**ALPH BASS was one of a group of men," said Johnny Sippel, now of *Billboard* and formerly of Mercury Records,

"who were white and intelligent, even learned, and who became so involved in R & B they went black—and I mean *Black*. They talked black, affected black mannerisms, and some of them married black women. The younger of the Mesner brothers, owners of Aladdin, did. So did Monte Kay, who wed Diahann Carroll when she was a complete unknown and mixed marriages were a no-no. Ralph Bass divorced a white wife to marry a black gal.

"Just think of it! Paul Reiner of Black & White Records, Herman Lubinsky of Savoy, Freddie Mendelsohn of Regent and Herald, Leonard Chess of Chess and Checkers, Jerry Wexler of Atlantic, Art Rupe of Specialty—all of them were bright, well read if not erudite, and all of them became so profoundly enmeshed in R & B, they literally changed color. And all of them happened also to be Jewish."

Strange it may be. But I would postscript Johnny's observation with two thoughts. The '40s were still a time when even bright Jews could not easily find a place in the WASP world of communications—advertising, book publishing, journalism, broadcasting, and even higher education. In motion pictures, they could make it as administrative and creative people, but not too readily as actors. (John Garfield was the exception.) The music business, however, was wide open for Jews as it was for blacks.

A second thought. There were quite a number of non-Jews who were as immersed in black music as any of those mentioned. Ahmet Ertegun, now President of Warner Communications, comes quickly to mind. John Hammond of Columbia is another. There's Dave Dexter, a thirty-year man at Capitol until he was given six-weeks' notice in 1974. And Johnny Otis, whose beautiful marriage to a black girl was not accepted by his mother for eighteen years.

In 1942 Herman Lubinsky, who ran a small record store in Newark, New Jersey, established Savoy Records at 58 Market Street. It was the first R & B label of consequence, in terms of both the artists it developed and its longevity. It is still flourishing today, though Herman died of cancer in March 1974 and the label is now owned by Clive Davis.

"Sepia" seemed to be the accepted trade term for Negro artists in 1942. In *Billboard's Band Year Book* for that year, I found Maurice Rocco advertised as "America's No. 1 Sepia Personality," Louis Jordan promoted as "No. 1 Band in Decca Sepia Series," and Count Basie voted "1942 Sepia King of Swing" in a WNEW poll by Martin Block.

The market for "sepia" records was obviously in a period of tremendous expansion. In *Billboard's Music Year Book* of 1943, I noted record releases on Brunswick by Pine Top Smith, boogie woogie pioneer, and Sonny Boy Williams, a new "King of Boogie Woogie." Bluebird was rereleasing Washboard Sam, Tampa Red, Jazz Gillum, and Lonnie Johnson, and presenting a new rhythm-and-bluesman, Arthur "Big Boy" Crudup. Decca disks included Sister Rosetta Tharpe, on secular as well as gospel material, the Harlem Hamfats, Lucky Millinder, and the King Cole Trio. (Nat was then appearing at the 331 Club in LA.) There were sundry platters on Beacon by the Jubileers, etc.

In January 1943, Savoy was the only "indie" to make the "Harlem Hit Parade." The Bunny Banks Trio's disk of "Don't Stop Now," with a vocal by Bonnie Davis (Savoy 101), invaded the major-dominated chart on January 30, 1943, and climbed to No. 1 on April 10. Beacon covered it with Beverly White at a time when Decca Records monopolized eight out of ten listings on the parade with the Ink Spots, Lionel Hampton, Lucky Millinder, Bea Booze, Ella Fitzgerald, and Charlie Barnet.

By 1944 the "indies" were beginning to give the majors some competition. Beacon was on the "Harlem Hit Parade" with the Five Red Caps, Exclusive with Ivy Anderson, Hit with Cootie Williams, De Luxe with Billy Eckstine, and Keynote with Lester Young, Lionel Hampton, and Cozy Cole.

·

I always meant to ask Herman Lubinsky, whom I knew rather well, how he came to choose the name Savoy Records. He kept putting off answering letter queries, and by the time I went back to New York in June 1974 to interview recordmen, he was gone. The obvious answer did not occur to me until I was working on this chapter.

One of Harlem's entertainment landmarks was, of course, the Savoy Ballroom, located at 596 Lenox Avenue from 1926 until it was torn down in 1958 to make way for a public housing project. Billed as the "World's Most Beautiful Ballroom" when Moe Gale opened it on March 12, 1926, it featured battles of the bands during the '20s. In the '30s and the era of the big swing bands its slogan became "The Home of Happy Feet"; swingsters referred to it as "the track." Among the famous dances that were developed or associated with The Savoy were the Lindy Hop, Peckin', Truckin', and the Suzy Q. In 1934, Chick Webb recorded a dance tune with music by saxophonist/swing composer Edgar Sampson, and words by talented lyricist Andy Razaf. Benny Goodman cut it for Victor two years later and soon everybody was singing, "SAA—VOY . . . tah-dah-dah-TA-TA-TUM—SAA—VOY . . . tah-dah-dah-TA-TA-TUM." It was "Stompin' at the Savoy," a swing standard of the '30s.

As the founder and owner of Savoy Records, Lubinsky was more of a wheeler-dealer than a creative recordman. Either by accident or intuition, he employed a series of extremely good record producers. Late in 1945, he hired Teddy Reig, a bear of a man, who continued Lubinsky's initial work of recording all the talented jazzmen he could bring into a studio from Fifty-second Street. "Sorry, It's Nix," a Savoy ad read in '44. "Nix" meant "No" on Swing Street—and Savoy was not accepting any new accounts until production could be stepped up. The ad listed records by tenor-saxist Ben Webster, the Cozy Cole Orchestra, pianist Johnny Guarnieri, tenorman Coleman Hawkins, trumpeter Hot Lips Page, guitarist Tiny Grimes, altoist Pete Brown, singer Billy Daniels with the Stuff Smith Trio, all of whom were Fifty-second Street regulars.

Reig was succeeded by Lee Magid, who moved the company in an R & B direction. Magid brought artists like Varetta Dillard to the label. Fred Mendelsohn, a husky but gentle man who had worked at times for Lubinsky, was the next to join Savoy, and he has remained with the company, succeeding Lubinsky as president when he died. Mendelsohn's experience with other "indie" labels like Regent, Regal, De Luxe, and Herald gave him the background to produce some of Savoy's biggest R & B hits like "The Hucklebuck," one of its hottest noisemakers.

On the West Coast, Lubinsky availed himself of the substantial talents of Ralph Bass, who produced a series of Savoy best-sellers in 1950–51. These involved a trio of performers who were responsible for three of the ten "Best-Selling R & B Records of 1950": "Double Crossing Blues" (No. 2), "Cupid's Boogie" (No. 5), and "Mistrustin' Blues" (No. 10). The trio was Little Esther (who sounded like Dinah Washington), baritone Mel Walker, and Johnny Otis, who was the sole writer of all three hits and the impresario of the Rhythm & Blues Caravan, a successful touring show. The following year, without Little Esther, Otis and Walker had a Top Ten R & B best-seller in "Rockin' Blues," also written by Otis.

On several of his Savoy disks, Otis's billed trio was backed by an unbilled background group known as the Robins. They cut their first disk for Savoy in the year before Johnny had three smashes, making the charts, albeit briefly, with "If It's So Baby." Six other Savoy disks added nothing to their renown. But in 1954, they attained their majority on Spark, a West Coast label, splitting up thereafter into two groups: the Robins and the famous Coasters. Success came to them through two young songwriters, Jerry Leiber and Mike Stoller, who not only wrote their songs but produced the Spark sides. And Leiber

Little Esther

and Stoller made their debut as songwriters in '49 through Johnny Otis.

•

Little Esther was a young teen-ager when her collaboration with Otis and Mel produced a Savoy best-seller. The sudden sunlight of success was blinding and, as with Frankie Lymon later, a bit too much for an adolescent. Before long, she, too, became a heroin addict, saddling a career of great promise with a destructive burden.

When she reemerged as Esther Phillips in the '60s, a personal appearance in Houston led to her recording for an offbeat label, Lenox. In the year that surfing songs became a craze, Esther selected, among other numbers, one that seemed to have autobiographical overtones. "Release Me" had been a country hit, recorded by such Nashville artists as Ray Price and Kitty Wells. Singing with poignancy and intensity, Esther Phillips produced one of '62's No. 1 R & B hits and transformed the song into a standard. Those who heard something of Dinah Washington's bittersweetness in her voice also detested an acid stridency that was part of Dinah, too.

But Little Esther was not released, despite accolades showered on her by the Beatles, who featured her on a BBC-TV show in 1965. Around 1966 she turned to Synanon for help. She remained at the drug rehabilitation institution for three and a half years, during which she also made some records on Atlantic and Roulette. One of her sides for Atlantic in '66 was "When a Woman Loves a Man," the ballad that served to rejuvenate Aretha Franklin and launch her superstar soul career. Another in '70 was "Set Me Free," recorded shortly after she left Synanon. They did not command the large audiences of her earliest releases.

"All that I will say about the Synanon trip," she said recently, indicating a distaste for the subject, "is that I learned some hobbies there. When I get tense and need to settle down, I do crossword puzzles and jigsaw puzzles. I hook rugs too. . . . I'm sick of talking about it."

In 1972 and '73 Esther made albums for Kudu, a subsidiary of CTI Records owned by Creed Taylor. *From a Whisper to a Scream* contained "Home Is Where the Hatred Is," a powerful song that she could well have written about her travail, but that was, in fact, authored by Gil Scott-Heron, a young poet-novelist. "A junkie walking through the twilight," it went, "I'm on my way home./ I left three days ago, but no one seems to know I'm gone./ Home is where the hatred is, . . ."

Big Maybelle

Esther Phillips has a host of admirers who hope that Little Esther is home and on the way to the wide recognition that her vocal talents merit. In truth, at the LA NARAS Awards in 1973, when Aretha Franklin rose to accept the Grammy for "Best Rhythm & Blues Performance by a Female Vocalist," she announced that the award should have gone to Esther Phillips, who had been a nominee.

Big Maybelle, who started her recording career in 1953, came to Savoy Records in '56. The R & B charts of her debut year reveal three titles: "Grabbin' Blues," "Way Back Home," and "My Country Man," all on OKeh Records, the Columbia blues subsidiary. Born Maybelle Smith in Jackson, Tennessee, Big Maybelle was then a twenty-nine-year-old woman. Problems, both personal and professional, pyramided, and Big Maybelle became a junkie. As with Little Esther's, her struggle to withdraw from the habit wreaked havoc with her musical activities. Soon after she joined Savoy in '56, "Candy" proved her most viable product. There followed almost five years of Savoy recordings, during which she displayed a remarkable sensitivity in handling ballads, many of them standards like "Mean to Me," "All of Me," and "It's a Sin to Tell a Lie."

Big Maybelle sang in the choir of Jackson's Sanctified Church as a small child. When she was just nine, she won a singing contest sponsored by the Memphis Statewide Cotton Carnival. She was still a teen-ager when she began singing with Dave Clark's Memphis Band. Then, in the swing era, she became featured vocalist of the Tiny Bradshaw Band, touring extensively and singing in the country's large ballrooms, theaters, and clubs.

Big Maybelle affirms once again that R & B was something more than loud, raucous music, as its detractors want us to believe. It was driving music. It was rousing, carousing dance music. But just as there is soft rock and hard rock, so R & B has two strains: tender, internalized balladry and tough, exhibitionistic bounce.

Anyone who wants to experience a study in contrast should listen first to a screamer like "Maybelle Sings the Blues" and then to her handling of an old 1928 hearts-and-flowers ballad, "My Mother's Eyes." Here we have this hefty, two hundred fifty pound, middle-aged woman who can caterwaul and screech like Little Richard and the most strident blues shouters. Suddenly, she turns into a little girl, tenderly recalling her mother. Thus, a trite, corny ballad that was right for the whining, nasal *vibrato* of George Jessel, who introduced it in a film *Lucky Boy*, becomes one of the most moving and delicate expressions of daughterly love one has ever heard. This is R & B balladry at its best. (Monotonous and repetitive as R & B tends to be as up-tempo jump music, so it becomes subtly and richly chorded in the ballads, with moody inner voicing and blues-rooted harmonies. At this level, R & B harks back to the spirituals and reaches for the expressiveness of gospel and jazz.)

Disrupted as her work was by bouts with "horse," Big Maybelle was in and out of the music scene—mostly out—for almost ten years. After "Candy," she did not make R & B charts again until 1966 with "Don't Pass Me By." By then she was recording for an offbeat label, Rojac, which gave her a modest '67 R & B chart climber in "Ninety-six Tears." And then, in 1972, at the age of forty-eight, she died.

•

On March 29, 1952, Lee Magid, then handling A & R chores at Savoy, visited the Apollo Theatre to catch the amateur hour contest. (Few Manhattan managers, bookers, recordmen, or out-of-towners missed the weekly Wednesday night contests.) Varetta Dillard did not win that evening, but she did impress Magid enough for him to go backstage and invite her to make a test recording. Varetta was then twenty-four years old, having been raised in the Bronx and graduated from Morris High School with a commercial diploma. Although she had distinguished herself in typing, shorthand, and bookkeeping and quickly found remunerative employment, she had her eyes set on a musical career.

Singing in a style that invited comparison with Dinah Washington, she produced R & B best-sellers from 1952 to '54. In her first year, it was "Easy, Easy, Baby," by gifted Rudolph Toombs; in '53, "Mercy, Mr. Percy," which carried an echo of "Lawdy, Miss Clawdy"; and in '54, she had "Johnny Has Gone." She developed a large enough following in black ghetto markets to continue recording for Savoy into the late '50s. But she was never able to hit the top, as Dinah Washington did, possibly because she was an echo of Dinah.

•

Still another Savoy singer who enjoyed a brief moment of glory on R & B wax was Nappy Brown, who came from Charlotte, North Carolina with a gospel group and who almost made the transition to rock 'n' roll. Part of his impact came from his ability to attract white cover records. Although these generally took the play away from the original black disks, white covers created a whirl of excitement that added momentum to the original. Nappy sang in a robust, melodic style, reminiscent of Joe Turner, that almost caught the ear of young record buyers.

In 1955 Nappy made the charts with "Don't Be Angry," a song co-written by him. It remained on R & B charts for almost four months, climbing to No. 2. By then, the Crew Cuts had scored with "Sh-Boom" and were casting about for another R & B number to cover. They chose "Don't Be Angry," but it never made it in the pop market. It did make enough noise, however, to permit Herman Lubinsky, an alert and hard-working entrepreneur, to hype New York publishers on Brown's next release. It was "(My Heart Goes) Pitter Patter."

I had then just joined Edward B. Marks Music Corporation as vice-president and General Professional Manager, the music business title for those charged with finding and developing hit songs. Within days after I settled in a long, narrow office on the sixth floor of the RCA Building, Herman's crackling voice was on the phone. The Brown disk was still being pressed, but from the way Herman talked it was the next "Shake, Rattle, and Roll," a recent smash for both

Varetta Dillard

Joe Turner and Bill Haley, or "Sincerely," which had scored for the Moonglows and the McGuire Sisters.

Middle-aged, a loud talker, and a man who felt that he had proved himself, Lubinsky was then acting the man-about-town. Although he was married and lived in Newark, he kept a bachelor apartment in Manhattan. During his campaign to sell "Pitter Patter," I was invited for cocktails, as was Herbert E. Marks, the president of the firm. Having fought his way to eminence in a very tough field, Lubinsky was never an easy spender. But record producer John Hammond remembers him as a man who was helpful to many jazz musicians; apparently, Herman guarded his generosity. He was a hearty, energetic and dedicated man, and I liked him.

Like most "indie" record companies, Lubinsky's outfit had its own publishing setup and generally owned the copyrights its artists recorded. By selling the song to us, he acquired a potent promotional arm to move it into the more remunerative pop area. (He also received an advance or bonus, and a slice of our income as a continuing royalty while his own record remained royalty free.) As for us, I would have a finished record, instead of a demo to audition for A & R men—and a disk by a black artist was then the most viable instrument for promoting a song. Also, the more noise the Nappy Brown disk made in R & B markets, the easier it would be to negotiate a white cover disk.

Lubinsky's campaign was helped by the writers of "Pitter Patter," Rose Marie McCoy and Charlie Singleton, both of whom frequented my office. (Singleton later co-wrote "Strangers in the Night.") And so I bought the song for Marks Music. Unfortunately, Nappy Brown's disk remained on R & B charts for only three weeks, never climbing higher than No. 10. Nevertheless, I was able to persuade Hugo and Luigi, then A & R chieftains of Mercury Records, to cover the song with Patti Page. (It was my initial recording for Marks Music, and a quite impressive beginning, considering Patti Page's stature. Damita Jo's disk of "If You Go Away" was my last record contribution to the company when I left in '66 to become a full-time writer and composer.) The title of the song was changed to "Piddily Patter Patter" because it was regarded as more contemporary than "Pitter Patter." The Page cover made noise without becoming a hit. But it was an important acquisition for Marks, which had been dormant for a number of years, and it served notice to the industry that one of the oldest Broadway music publishing firms was aggressively back in the pop business.

Nappy Brown had to wait three years before he came up with a new best-selling disk. That time he reversed the cover process. He took "I Don't Hurt Anymore," a country ballad that had been a 1955 hit for Hank Snow, and recorded it as "It Don't Hurt No More," giving it a slightly erotic slant by the change in the pronoun and an R & B sound through the use of the double negative. Like many R & B artists, Nappy went with the decade. His last chartmaker—and a slight one it was—"I Cried Like a Baby," came in 1959, the year that many recordmen and disk jockeys were really crying like babies over the payola investigation.

That investigation really marked the end of the R & B era, though in a sense the end was in sight after Elvis Presley broke in 1956. It was hardly the end for Savoy. Lubinsky turned back to gospel music, an emphasis he maintained even through the resurgence of R & B in the late '60s, developing one of the largest catalogues of gospel records.

groove 12   **FRED MENDELSOHN**

For some years, Savoy has been located at 56 Ferry Street, not far from the Newark station of the Pennsylvania Railroad. It's in a dull, gray-painted four-story building whose dust-encrusted windows give it the look of a deserted factory. Just beyond is the trestle of a spur of the railroad. As you pass the gray structure and almost walk under the trestle, you come upon a short, brick-red stairway. Up the seven steps is a weatherbeaten door with a small, hardly visible sign identifying the gray ghost as Savoy Records.

There is no anteroom. You burst right into a medium-sized room, cluttered with desks and tables, jammed with boxes and piles of circulars. The passageway into the bulging stockroom beyond is narrowed by four- and five-foot stacks of maroon record cartons. Fred Mendelsohn, who succeeded Lubinsky, never had an office of his own; he sat across from the large desk that was Herman's in a room just to the right of the stockroom. Curiously, the walls of Lubinsky's office—every visible inch—were covered with paintings that Herman kept buying from some unknown Manhattan modern artist.

•

"In 1949 three of us—the Braun brothers and myself started a rhythm and blues label [Regal] in Linden, New Jersey. We developed artists like Larry Darnel, Paul Gayten, Annie Laurie, Chubby Newsom, a great blues singer. We had a big record with Doc Sausage called 'Rag Mop,' which later started the Ames Brothers.

"I always liked blues, heard it on the radio even though I was brought up on the Lower East Side in Manhattan. When I was a kid, I worked in a drugstore in a black neighborhood in Brooklyn. I heard one record constantly, 'Careless Love.' It was on an old 78 Decca blue label. I know because I went out and bought it. Though I can't recall the name of the artist, it was a typical down-home blues.

"With the Brauns, I went down to Atlanta. We brought along our own Magnecord recorder and rented a store. We cut artists like Pig 'n' Whistle Red, Blind Willie. Later we recorded bluesmen in Chicago, again renting an empty store. Once we recorded in our distributor's office, working after hours. There was nothing to set up but our Magnecord. The artist generally accompanied himself.

"Shortly after we started Regal, we made a trip to New Orleans. In The Dew Drop Inn, a club owned by Frank Pania, we heard Larry Darnel. This was *the* club for black artists. Darnel was doing a song called 'I'll Get Along Somehow,' originally popularized by Andy Kirk. He added a recitation that sent the dames screaming and hollering. We brought him up to New York and recorded the song as a Part 1-Part 2 record, something unheard-of in those days. We also cut a ballad, 'For You, My Love.' And we put both records out at the same time, also something that was unheard-of. *Billboard* had an R & B chart of ten records. Darnel had two at the same time—in the number one and number three slots. He was very successful and a fine showman. Had he recorded at another time, perhaps he would have achieved much greater recognition—I mean, in the white market.

"In New Orleans, Paul Gayten had a band. Played all the black clubs. His vocalist was Annie Laurie, a big woman. They had made a number of powerful records. 'True' was one of them. I brought them up to Jersey with me, and we recorded a song, 'I'll Never Be Free,' which hit all the charts. Gayten, incidentally, wrote 'For You, My Love,' a hit for Darnel and later for Nat 'King' Cole.

"The first time I met Gayten was in 1947. He had a small combo and was working at Foster's Hotel, a block away from The Dew Drop Inn—in the black quarter, of course. Annie Laurie, his vocalist, was the one singer that Dinah Washington always went to hear. I recorded Annie in later years when I was with De Luxe and she came up with a smash called 'It Hurts to Be in Love.' This was about 1957.

"De Luxe was originally owned by the Braun brothers. They sold the label to King—Syd Nathan in Cincinnati—and that was when we went into the Regal operation. Regal actually started in the same offices as De Luxe in Linden, New Jersey. When we recorded Larry Darnel, we went into a more sophisticated style of recording than the storefront bit. We worked in a studio we had in Linden.

"There was no way of promoting a record in those days, and we did no promoting. We simply sent the finished record to our distributors. In those days, there were very few R & B shows around the country, and most of them were run by white disk jockeys. Our distributors brought a new record to these shows.

"Now in Atlanta, if Zenas Sears played your record, it was a hit—automatically a hit. He was on every night, and he had a tremendous following. Nobody else in Atlanta played the records he put on. The same thing was true in New Orleans where a cat who called himself Poppa Stoppa made your record a hit if he played it. In those days, that's the way it was—one disk jockey and one program on one station in the whole area. But it probably had more impact than today when you might have five stations in the same city playing the same thing. There's no individuality to programs these days. But these fellows had personality.

"After a time, the Brauns wanted to expand and went into a kiddie line. Irene Wicker was a very popular kiddie artist in those days, and we put out a four-record album—seven-inch records but at 78 speed. We sold them by the hundreds of thousands, but somehow we were losing money. Then the government came in and wanted to tax us on the jackets plus the records. Jules Braun, one of the partners, was a lawyer, and he decided that we were going to fight—and that led to the dissolution of Regal Records.

"In 1952 I started Herald Records on my own, operating it from Elizabeth, New Jersey. To get pressings, I went to New York to a

Fred Mendelsohn, James Cleveland, Bill "Hoss" Allen
(Collection, Fred Mendelsohn)

small plant run by Al Silver and his brother-in-law. When they heard some of my records, they offered to come in with me. I started with Little Walter. But I didn't stay too long. When I returned to work for Herman Lubinsky at Savoy, Silver and his brother-in-law continued Herald.

"Before I went into business with the Brauns, I had a pop label called Regent. Started it in 1947 and had a big hit, 'You Call Everybody Darling,' by Al Trace. My partner then was my accountant. He didn't know anything about the record business, and he was happy to sell out to Lubinsky. And I moved to Newark and became Lubinsky's partner in Regent. But I also worked for him in Savoy.

"Teddy Reig was working for Lubinsky then, making the jazz things and recording Charlie Parker, Lester Young, Dizzy Gillespie, and those things. I cut Paul Williams doing 'The Hucklebuck,' a monster of a record. Lubinsky had already had Hal Singer on 'Corn Bread,' an earlier instrumental hit. He got very hot in the R & B area at this time, especially when Ralph Bass on the Coast came through with those Johnny Otis and Little Esther hits, one after the other.

"Lee Magid was with Lubinsky shortly before I returned. He contributed the hits by Varetta Dillard. 'Mercy, Mr. Percy' was probably her biggest. Then I brought artists like Big Maybelle, Little Jimmy Scott, and Nappy Brown to the label. Although Lubinsky started simply as a small-label man, recording some jazz, some pop, and some gospel [on the King Solomon subsidiary], he became a big force in R & B during the 1950s. In '59, after rock 'n' roll was in, we had 'Bad Boy' with The Jive Bombers.

"But then in 1960 we went almost exclusively into gospel, dropped all the R & B artists. Payola was rampant. In order to get plays, you had to go out and promote with money. Many companies were cited for it. Lubinsky didn't appreciate that type of operation, and we didn't have it in the gospel field—and still don't. There are not that many companies and not that many releases. Jockeys are happy to get new gospel releases.

"Although Lubinsky had recorded The Davis Sisters and made some great gospel standards with The Ward Singers, we now came up with James Cleveland. He has become the giant, the 'King of Gospel.' There's nobody bigger. And we now have about forty albums with him. He also presents new artists. On the album he sings one of the songs, and the artist takes it from there. The fact that he is on the album sells it and introduces a new artist. The follow-up is an album by the new artist alone. There's no promotion. You send the new releases to the jockeys and wait. At times, a record will not take off until six months after it's released, but then it will go on selling for sixty years.

"To go back to 'The Hucklebuck.' There was a musician and arranger named Andy Gibson who adapted a Charlie Parker tune called 'Now Is the Time' and called it 'The Hucklebuck.' He brought it to Lubinsky after lyrics were added to it, but Lubinsky was so incensed that it was a takeoff on 'Now Is the Time,' which he had published, that he refused to have anything to do with it. But I had already recorded it on Fifty-seventh Street, so Lubinsky refused to release the record.

"Juggy Gales, who was the publisher of 'The Hucklebuck,' began romancing Lubinsky—got him to a point where he would buy Lubinsky a deluxe dinner if it was a flop and Lubinsky would buy the dinner if it was a hit. It ended with Lubinsky paying for the dinner. 'The Hucklebuck' was one of the biggest sellers that Savoy ever had. We used an eight-piece group. Paul Williams played tenor and baritone sax, mostly baritone. There were four rhythms plus tenor, baritone, trumpet, and trombone. That was the makeup of the group.

"I remember being in Cincinnati once where a disk jockey named Ernie Waits invited me to go across the river to hear a girl. Her name was Maybelle Smith, and I was so flipped by her that I gave her money and brought her into New York. I had Leroy Kirkland rehearse her. I was doing some independent things then, and we recorded her for OKeh Records. Called her Big Maybelle. Although her records sold, OKeh let her go when her contract was up and I brought her to Lubinsky.

"One of the first things I did with her was 'Candy.' Even though it was a pop song, her treatment made it number one in the R & B field. She became a tremendous act in person as well as on records—great crowd-pleaser. She had a great blues sound, but with a jazz feeling. Unfortunately, she was unheralded and really remained undiscovered despite her tremendous talent.

"I found Nappy Brown in a gospel group I recorded for Lubinsky. He had a sound that led me to ask him whether he had ever sung blues. We made several records with him, rhythm and blues, and they were just so-so sellers. Then we did a novelty, 'Don't Be Angry,' which took off and attracted a pop cover. You were associated with his next noisemaker, 'Pitter Patter.' After that he recorded 'Night Time Is the Right Time,' which has become a solid standard. It was recorded by Ray Charles and almost thirty other artists.

"I first heard Little Jimmy Scott when he sang with Lionel Hampton. Had a big seller called 'The Masquerade Is Over.' No, before that, he was responsible for 'Everybody Is Somebody's Fool.' The label didn't even give him credit—it just read: Vocal Refrain. I convinced Jimmy to leave Hampton, and we recorded him solo. His records were not earthshaking, but he developed a very solid following. He had style and a sound and a way of phrasing that has been copied by many, many singers. He was really an innovator who did not reap the fruit of his genius.

"Little Esther was still in her teens when she had the big hits with us. The big criticism of her was that she sounded too much like Dinah Washington, and she probably still does. But sounding like Dinah was, after all, not bad, considering her singing talent.

"When Johnny Ace died, I wrote a song made up of all the titles of Ace's songs. We called it 'Johnny Has Gone.' That became a hit for Varetta Dillard, helped a bit by a little lie. We spread the story that Varetta was Johnny's girlfriend, which she wasn't."

groove 13   LEE MAGID

"I joined National Records in 1943–44 when I was eighteen or nineteen. Herb Abramson had just left—he studied dentistry—to open an office in Washington, D.C. I actually joined through Jerry Blaine, who was national sales manager. I was his promotion man, cracking records in New York and Jersey, cracking R & B on pop.

"Before that I was a song plugger. This is how it happened. I was interested in a singer Ralph Young, who sang with Les Brown. Yeah, the same guy who's now part of Sandler and Young. Met him at 1674 Broadway where I had a little office with three other guys. There was Dick Linke, who later managed Andy Griffith and Jim Nabors; some guy who was involved in distribution; and a songwriter. Les Brown opened an office near us with Solly Loft, the song plugger, and Eddie Marmor. Their errand boy was Buddy Stark, who later became a big man at Gimbel's Department Store. Stark introduced me to Ralph, who hung around the office, and Young introduced me to Jerry Blaine.

"Blaine recorded Ralph under the name of Rudy York—I don't know why. Jerry liked the way I was running around—I was cracking Ralph's records at all the stations. I was doing what I could just to help Ralph along. He got on 'Gloom Dodgers,' a hot little show, while

I was *toomeling* with his records. Jack Carter and Morey Amsterdam were emceeing it, and Vera Holly was on the show.

"Nobody in those days cared about disk jockeys. Maybe Martin Block and Fred Robbins. William B. Williams, I think, was just beginning. Alan Courtney was the other guy on Station WOV. I kept in touch with all of them. I was doing record promotion, which was another area, when I was a song plugger. Jerry said one day, 'Why don't you take a job here at National?' I said, 'Fine.' I needed the money anyway. Jerry got two other accounts for me, so I was making thirty plus thirty plus thirty-five dollars. That was a hundred five bucks clear, which was a lot of money in those days. In addition to National, I handled Rondo Records. They had organist Ken Griffin, who later had a hit with 'You Can't Be True, Dear.'

"One day, Al Green, who owned National, said, 'Hey, kid, you're doing a helluva job for my label.' I took The Ravens, I took Billy Eckstine and cracked them on white stations. The only black artists who ever got played in those days were The Ink Spots, Mills Brothers, Ella Fitzgerald when she hit with 'A-Tisket, A-Tasket.' Nat Cole a little bit, and Louis Jordan wasn't as strong until two years later when he had 'Saturday Night Fish Fry' and 'Brother, Beware.' Anyway, Al Green asked me to run their publishing company. So I took care of copyrighting and all the paperwork.

"One thing led to another, and suddenly I found myself in an A & R position. I used to hang around the studio, and Al Green showed me all the detail stuff—with the union, the contracts, the W-2 forms, deductions. Sylvia Langler was secretary with the company and later married Al Green, the father of Irving Green, who ran Mercury Records for years. But this Al Green was not the Al Green who ran The Flame Bar in Detroit. This Al Green was originally from Chicago where he was a union organizer of the painters. He came from a rough, rough school. He had a plant that was pressing pots and pans, or something. Some guy talked him into converting it into a record pressing plant, and he wound up with a big plant in Phillipsburg, New Jersey. He became the biggest independent record manufacturer. National could deliver a record in a day and a half to two days, which was something in those days.

"If Billy Eckstine recorded, like, 'A Cottage for Sale' or any of those big Ellington numbers, I'd make a trip out to the pressing plant, carry the masters with the matrix, and get it into the baths overnight. Could deliver strike-offs in which you didn't have to wait for the whole processing. They still do it today, but in those days it was, like, a novelty.

"The first session that I produced for National was Dusty Fletcher when Brother Bones hit with 'Sweet Georgia Brown.' Since we had the pressing plant, we could hold back everybody else's records—pass their action, I mean without telling them, and get ours out. That was the secret of success. You take everybody's orders, you don't deliver them while you're pressing your own. Suddenly, you hear that distributors are calling from everywhere saying, 'I don't understand it. This guy's got a hit—and he can't send the merchandise.' So Al Green would pick up on that, and say, 'Shit, we'll go in the studio and do our own.' He'd black out the other cat who's got the money to pay for pressings. But he'd say, 'The hell with it. It's worth more money to me to go ahead and send our product out.' And that's what he used to do.

"And so we did 'Sweet Georgia Brown' and sold and sold. And it wasn't even a good version. Dusty was a simple, nice man who did a comedy *shtick* on a stepladder for years. The bit with 'Open the Door, Richard' was his whole thing. And here's the follow-up—he just couldn't read. The other side, whose title I can't remember, was pretty good. I remember specifically calling in Babs Gonzalez, who had a vocal group called Three Bips and a Bop. He was always hangin' around Broadway, *noodging* everybody to do a session. He claimed he could whistle, so I brought him in. And he couldn't whistle nothin'. Green kept looking at me in the booth and said, 'We'll just mark it off as an education. We'll come off with the record without this bum whistling.' So I called in Buddy Tate, who played tenor with Basie, and he blew the fills. That was my first lesson in learning that you can't believe a guy, no matter who the hell he is, until he proves himself to you first.

"The next session I did was with The Ravens. I got a call one day, and I had to go to St. Louis. I'd never been on an airplane. But I had to go to record The Ravens on 'Race Track Blues.' It might have been a radio station, but I remember a little studio. Howard Biggs, who was their arranger, played piano. Jimmy Ricks, the lead singer, was great. Mate Marshall was the lead tenor; Warren Evans was second. There was a replacement for Ollie Jones, who had left them. Warren I remember because he had a cute personality. The songs were 'Race Track Blues,' 'Send for Me if You Need Me,' 'Write Me a Letter' (I think), and either 'The House I Live In' or 'Deep Purple.' I remember bringing the masters back with me on the plane. We had a meeting to listen, and I remember Warren Troob, who was the National attorney, sitting in with us.

"I did so many sessions after that I can't remember them. Joe Turner was one of our artists. Buddy Stewart was alive with songs like 'Laughin' Boy.' We had Charlie Ventura when he had an all-star lineup: Eileen Barton with "If I Knew You Were Coming, I'd've Baked a Cake,' and we could have had so many others if Al Green didn't listen just for numbers. He was a heavy drinker and a rough guy, and you couldn't be too creative under him. I left after two years.

.

"Sid Siegel, who owned Seeco and Tico Records, kept urging me to produce masters for him. I started Dawn Records with a group I called The Starlighters, some guys from the Bronx. I recorded a chick, Helen Thompson, who came from Georgia. She had a Ruth Brown quality and sold pretty well. But everybody was giving me funny counts, and I didn't see a fast enough return for me. Then, Herman Lubinsky offered me a job at Savoy Records, and I stayed there for about five years.

"I did everything there: The Ward Singers, who originally cut for a Philadelphia label—Clara was tops in those days; The Gay Sisters out of Chicago—we had hits with them: 'God Will Take Care of You.' We had a thing that we picked up from heavyweight boxer Joe Walcott, who used to say, 'God Is on Our Side.' We had a song written around the idea. I did The Four Buddies: 'I Will Wait.' I cut Billy Wright: 'Stacked Deck,' 'Hey, Little Girl,' 'Blues for My Baby.' Billy was from Atlanta, Georgia and I used to go to Atlanta and record a lot of guys. Recorded at WGST, the radio station. Zenas Sears was the guy. Him and Ed Luykens, who was called Jack the Bell Boy.

"Let me go back to National for a moment and tell you who my engineer was. At Apex Sound on Fifty-seventh Street, 119 West, the owner was a guy named Bob Schewing, who passed away years ago. But my engineer was a young cat, Tommy Dowd, who really knew what was happening. He's Atlantic's rock. We had great rapport. And probably, if I hadn't got into a lotta areas and lived with an ego trip, I could have stayed with a guy like him and built a big company. Because a lotta artists have passed through me that have gone to other companies. I think that one day before me and Tommy split from this world, we should get in a studio and do one for nothin'— and show them. I always felt that. Now, it's Tommy with Ahmet Ertegun, Tommy with Jerry Wexler. For me, I believe in Tommy.

All the other guys have learned, too, they've come along, and everybody has become individually great. But Tommy has been unique. He's special.

"And I gotta say this for Herb Abramson, who built National and started Atlantic with Ahmet. In his early days, Herb had a feel for talent. If not for Herb, there'd be no Ravens. He discovered them for National. They were originally cut on a Hub label. And Herb had those vibes out and picked them up. Same with Billy Eckstine. Herb grabbed him out of the Earl Hines band and interested Al Green. He was right there on the ground floor of R & B.

"I gotta say this for even guys like Teddy Reig, who produced for Savoy before me. He had a great ear. Teddy was just Teddy, a bandboy or something hanging around the business. Got into whatever games he got into. But Teddy produced the Paul Williams 'Hucklebuck' out of Detroit. And him and Herman never hit it off—too many angles being shot by too many people. But Teddy for years later produced all the Basie records. Whether they liked working with him or not is a different story. If you take it from where he came from—just that without all the personality shit that people get involved in—he was a good man in the studio. Just that everyone got hungry and wanted to grab pieces of everything—and that's what tends to ruin the business.

"Some of the other things I produced for Savoy were Tommy Brown, who years later hit at the same time that Chuck Willis came around out of Atlanta, and Titus Turner, who was then called Mr. T. Billy Wright was God in Atlanta, Georgia. He was the greatest blues singer there was.

"At Savoy, I did all the record promotion. I did everything. My number one man was Willie Bryant, and Ray Carroll. They were then WHOM. They started in the studio on Fifty-second Street, 136 West, on the second floor, right above the old Hickory House. Before that it was Symphony Sid and Ray Carroll—when I was with National. Sid was always the *macher*. He was the hippest guy in the business; whatever was supposed to be the thing today, he was there and gone and back. But it was Sid and Ray, and then it became Willie and Ray. And then they moved up to The Baby Grand in Harlem, right in the front window for Jack Krulick. They had a radio show, and anytime I needed a record busted: Willie and Ray and boom! Later, they moved to WLIB or WWRL in Long Island City.

"I used to cover the Apollo Theatre all the time and The Palm Cafe down the street, too, where years later Sugar Ray's sister had a disk jockey show on WOV. Believe it or not, Joe Petralia, the promotion guy, was the program director on WOV. He used to program a lot of my stuff. Jack Walker was one of the guys working for Willie and Ray. He had an untimely death; he was killed. Fat Jack Walker with the pear-shaped tones—he was the kid hanging around, pulling out the records, and he later became the big boy on the Harlem scene.

"Never missed Wednesday night at the Apollo. Looking for talent, I'd cover every joint in Harlem, Brooklyn, the Bronx, Long Island. Wherever there was something, I'd be out there—and I'm still out there. Just surprising to me how many people are not there. You know, they just sit back with their accountants and their lawyers, and they wanna know where the music business has gone.

"In the Apollo, I discovered a girl—she was sixteen years old— by the name of Varetta Dillard. She limped slightly on one leg, but she sang her tail off, that kid. She didn't win the prize, but I heard her and I said, 'That's the one.' And I brought her to New Jersey and I cut a demo with her, and I recorded a thing with her. ['Please Come Back to Me.'] It was an original song she'd written, and suddenly Lubinsky's name got on it. What'd I know? I rewrote half the song with her, but who knew and who cared in those days? You were out there trying to make it. She sold a lotta records, and she had a quality somewhat between—she had a young soul—somewhat between Ruth Brown and Dinah Washington.

"I wrote quite a lot of songs. They're all somewhere with Savoy Records or Savoy Music. God knows when I'll ever get a statement. I should call Herman and tell him to send me some money. I talked to him a few months ago, and he was going into the hospital for a prostate massage. I guess it's all the assholes he's been dealing with that came back. Anyway, he's one of those old, hardcore guys like Syd Nathan of another era. But he keeps a tight rein. And that's the way it's supposed to be. I don't care. Maybe he ain't right with this and maybe he ain't right with that, but then who is? Unless you're dealing with your top companies.

"Incidentally, prior to going with Savoy, I had a company—was it before or after Savoy?—me and Larry Newton—Central Records. He was in trouble with Derby, and he called me. I guess it was after I left Savoy. I recorded a group called The Charmers. Sold a helluva lot of records. Still get calls—I don't know where those damn masters are. I better call Larry one day and find out whatever happened to them.

"But getting back to Varetta Dillard, we were really cooking with her, and I became her manager. And that was the time when I decided I wasn't making enough money at Savoy. Honestly, I was only making seventy dollars a week and I could steal three dollars a week over what my transportation cost. . . . I was commuting from New York to Jersey because I had an office at 1650 Broadway and I had started my own music company. So I grabbed whatever copyrights I could because I felt I wasn't getting enough out of Jersey, except running there on certain days of the week, close to payday—all I remember, I was in the studio day and night with groups. We were forever cutting gospel, which was all right with me.

"I started a group called the Wanderers, which later went to MGM, and then, years later, I put them on Decca and we recorded a song, 'Say, Hey, Willie Mays.' I also had a group called the Blenders, which was some of the former Raven members. Ollie Jones, for one, who wrote 'What'd I Say?' for Ray Charles. Good writer and a wonderful guy. I heard he's living in Philadelphia now as a chef. He always came up with ideas. He always handled it well. A lot of the other guys, they'd get overambitious and they're a pain in the ass. You wanna chase them no matter how creative they are.

"At Savoy we cut a lot of jazz. We had the Shearings, Marian McPartland, Errol Garner even singing. We had Johnny Guarnieri, but he was cut before I got there.

"In R & B we had Johnny Otis, of course, with whom we cut 'Double-Crossin' Blues.' I cut Little Esther. It was the last session before she and Herman got into a big hassle about contracts and stuff, with her mother. . . . Also cut the Walker Brothers. Mel Walker was a great singer, another guy that was influential and started with the Johnny Otis situation.

"Huey Smith was one of the musicians I used on trips to New Orleans. He later came up with a novelty smash. In New Orleans we used to rent a little studio called Cosimo's. And after a time, the owner Cosimo Matassa suddenly became a guy who wanted to get into the record production business. Everybody got on the bandwagon. Used to go down to collect money from a distributor, while you're down there, record a session with part of it, and bring the rest of the money home, or deliver product or take samples around of things that you've cut.

"Detroit was my main thing. I recorded a big smash hit—it must have sold close to a million—'My Kind of Woman,' with The Emmett Slay Trio. Emmett was a guitar player, and he had a Louis Jordan kind of blues vocal quality. There was an organist there called Bob White, not Wyatt, who had that Ray Charles screamin', like Little Richard or Bobby 'Blue' Bland. He was something else, this cat, and I put them together, him and Emmett, and I wrote part of the thing with them. I took the idea—I gotta be honest with you. Big Maybelle had a big smash called 'Gabbin' Blues.' So I took the idea where the guy was talkin' and the other guy is answerin'—with her it was her subconscious talkin' to her—so I had an idea; I said, 'Jesus, whatta thing!' and we had a smash.

"Also cut guys like T. J. Fowler, a helluva band out of Detroit, played great boogie piano. La Vern Baker, who was Little Miss Sharecropper. She was with The Todd Rhodes Band, with us. So that goes back. Little Miss Cornshucks was a different thing entirely, one of the greatest blues singers before Ruth Brown, and everything that Ruth Brown became is everything Little Miss Cornshucks had. Atlantic signed Ruth Brown, and they did 'In the Rain' and 'So Long.' It was Ahmet Ertegun who knew all about Cornshucks. She was a little black chick with two buckets and pigtails—come out in the Apollo Theatre—and in rags and sing her ass off.

•

"Going back before Alan Freed, in Detroit, the big jockey was Ed McKenzie, called himself Jack the Bell Boy. He had a chick named Penny Pryor, used to program the stuff. There were a lotta black cats like Eddie Durham. Alan was big in Akron first and then went to Cleveland.

"Atlanta was the big breakout town. We'd break every thing with Zenas Sears and Ed Luyken. And, man, that was it! The same happened with Alan Freed. In New York, Willie Bryant and Ray Carroll, no question about that. In New Jersey, there was a guy called Mr. Blues. He was a white cat, Jewish boy, can't remember his name. Nobody knew he was white until years later; he walked out, and somebody said, 'That's him.' But we bought his radio time on WNJR, I think it was. Then there was—what's his name?—started Dot Records down in Gallatin, Tennessee . . . Randy Wood. He had a big R & B outlet. He started from scratch, and his one-stop—Randy's Record Shop. We'd send him some stuff.

"In the Baltimore area, there was a station in Annapolis, Maryland—WWAM, I think. And in Washington I'd make a deal with Waxie Maxie—Max Silverman. He had a guy in his window, Tex something or other. And Hal Jackson in the early forties, who is now at WLIB. I recorded groups of his for National and Savoy. They had an Ink Spot-ish kind of quality. I remember a guy by the name of James Griffith; he sang so good.

"Then after that I left Herman because I had Al Hibbler. Well, I had written a song, 'I Played the Fool,' and I offered it to Herman to give it to Varetta Dillard. I started a group called the Marshall Brothers. When The Ravens broke up, I took Mate Marshall, his family, his brothers, and we had a great group, and they recorded some songs of mine. But Herman wouldn't go for it, said, 'No, Lee, you can take it anywhere else. It's a little too white.' That's how he used to talk, like I wasn't thinking R & B, he says, which is a lotta bunk. He just couldn't hear nothin' else except one bag. So I wrote under my daughter's name.

" 'I Played the Fool' made the number one song in 1953. It really helped Atlantic Records, that song, because they were in a lotta trouble at that time. The Clovers cut it, and it made all the charts, pop and R & B. I think it was one of the few crossovers in those days. I had Art Mooney, Sunny Gale, a lotta people jumped on it. And I made myself; I gotta say this: I put Hal Fein in the R & B business.

"Hal Fein was working for Sammy Kaye's music company, and he came to me for a song. I wrote that song in ten minutes. I was feeding my daughter a bottle—I was living in the Bronx, I had gotten married—and I wrote it for him. I had written a thing called something about a fool that the Marshall Brothers recorded on Savoy. It was never promoted—I had a couple of breakouts, but Herman wouldn't do anything. He felt that I was learning to fly and maybe I wanted to do something else. So he didn't go out too well, and I got upset because he wouldn't ship the record to all the distributors. So I rewrote the song a different way, called it 'I Played the Fool' and put my daughter's name, Diane Alexis, on it. And I gave it to Hal Fein, who wanted to get in the R & B business. Ollie Jones did the demo for me, and Kenny Watts played the piano. Hal Fein got me a two-hundred-fifty-dollar advance. I had never seen an advance in my life. I used to *give* them, but I never saw them. And it got me started in my married life, and the song became a smash. And I got myself a check for twelve thousand five hundred dollars one day.

"That was in 1953. And it got me to California for the first time. I took my wife and my kids—they were, like, little babies—and I saw California and I locked it in my brain. I says, 'One day, that's where I'm gonna be.' I had enough of an incentive to leave Savoy, and that's what I did. I was never exclusively with Herman. But the minute he found out I was doing a session for somebody else, he'd go crazy, especially if it made a little noise.

•

"I signed Al Hibbler, and it took me six months to convince Decca. This guy was singin' at The Baby Grand and knockin' me out. And the rest is history—'Unchained Melody,' 'After the Lights Go Down Low,' 'He,' 'They Say You're Laughing at Me,' 'Stella by Starlight,' 'Pennies from Heaven,' on and on. Al was to me the greatest male singer that ever lived!

"After that, Al Green called me from Detroit. He managed The Flame Show Bar. Morris Wasserman was the owner. Terrific, great blues talent was all sittin' in Detroit. The guy that had the photography concession in the place was Berry Gordy. I didn't know until years later. And his sister was the one I used to flirt with—sold cigarettes— I never knew. And Maurice King—all the guys I used to use on my sessions—turned out to be key Motown people. That's years later.

"Me and Al Green were very close. He had paper on Johnnie Ray. That situation was another thing. I helped him get some money. Bernie Lang, who managed Johnnie, and Danny Kessler, who signed him to Epic, got into some kind of swindle with Al. Bernie was given Johnnie through Danny Kessler, but Danny had no right to take him because Al Green had him. It was that kind of situation. Al was the one who brought Danny to Detroit. I like Danny and I always liked Bernie—he used to hang around my office when he had nothing to do. Al Green and me became pretty close because Al knew I was close to these guys. And I made them settle the thing. When Johnnie hit with 'Cry' and 'The Little White Cloud That Cried,' they deposited thirty-five thousand dollars in Al's account. So me and Al became buddies.

"That was when I was managing the Emmett Slay group and other things. Al was bankrolling me and lending me money because I didn't have it. I had signed a white chick in Detroit . . . now I remember— that's when I joined Larry Newton. When I left Savoy, Larry and me got together and started a company called Central Records. And I says, 'There's a chick I saw in Detroit when I was with Savoy. She's white with a black sound.' Anyway her name was Patti Jerome, and she wrote a song and I recorded it in the back of a place called Sam's Record Shop on Woodward Avenue. Not even on Woodward—in the black part of town. Can't remember the name of the street, but I'm sure that today there are a lot of bodies lying around there. It was a song called, 'No Mama, No Papa,' and I gave it to Hal Fein. He had made me some money with the other, and he was already now starting to feel his oats. He left the Sammy Kaye music company, and he came up with a Dakota Staton record when she had just signed with RCA. She also came out of The Flame Show Bar.

"Anyway Al Green called me. Said, 'There's a chick out here can go white. Nobody knows what to do with her.' I'll never forget what he said: 'A tonk broad.' Relation to honky-tonk—I'd never heard the expression before. And he sent the girl in. She borrowed twenty-five bucks to come in and meet me in New York. I had Varetta Dillard working The Baby Grand. And Varetta and me were having hassles already. She'd gotten married. She was sort of goofing. I wasn't too happy with her.

"So in comes this girl. Nipsey Russell was the emcee. So I says, 'Nipsey, put her on the stage for me.' Willie Bryant was there in the front. And this chick got up there, and I'll never forget it. She sang 'There'll Never Be Another You' as a ballad and up-tempo the second chorus. And then 'Birth of the Blues'—and forget it! The house came down! She was the prettiest thing I'd seen—her hands, her diction. I says, 'Female Hibbler! No question! She could be the greatest!' And she also took me a long time to get started. The chick was Della Reese.

"I learned what a tonk broad was. When I started talking about managing her, she looked me straight in the eye: 'Do you want to manage me or just fuck me?'

"Erskine Hawkins was a friend of mine because Al Hibbler was booked out of the Gale Agency. Erskine was always around. He was their favorite band. Moe Gale himself was handling Erskine—you remember, he had 'Tuxedo Junction.' So I says to Erskine, 'Hey, man, you need somebody with your band because nothing too much is happening with the horn.' I says, 'There's a girl in town. Put her with your band. I don't care what the price is. I'll record her, and you won't be unhappy.' He auditions Della—flips! And she wound up doing 'Teach Me Tonight' for six months. But at least she kept out of my pocket. She was now making, believe it or not, eighty-five bucks a week. But she had a big band behind her.

"Then I cut a demo with her. First cat on the eighty-eight was Mal Waldron. He couldn't make it, though he later joined Billie Holiday and became a big jazz player on his own. The styles didn't match. Howard Biggs, the pianist for The Ravens, just didn't show up. So I got ahold of Sid Bass, who had an original song he had written with Roy Jordan—Kiss something.

"The first record was 'In the Still of the Night,' which Della used to do. It was a smash for Jubilee. I sold her to Jerry Blaine. I got turned down by Herb Dexter, and I went right past him to Jerry. And she was a smash. Then Morty Palitz, formerly with Decca, came in, and we did a lot of records with her. And from Jubilee after 'And That Reminds Me,' she went to RCA Victor. That's history!

"Now I had Al Hibbler and I had Della Reese. Everybody is coming to me. It was that kind of situation. And I got so involved in management that I wasn't really producing any more records, except that I was there supervising all the dates with all my people. And that's what happened with Earl Grant, Sam Fletcher, Lou Rawls, Ossie Smith. . . . Along with Hibbler and Della, they were the tops of a lotta artists.

.

"Disk jockeys in R & B? There was one man in Atlanta who left and went to Louisville, Kentucky. He was very big in R & B—Johnny Martin. He covered the Kentucky-Cincinnati area. He was in Atlanta before Zenas. In Nashville, there was a cat by the name of Hoss Allen. Another jockey who came later, but was around the Fort Worth area in R & B—James Clemons on KNOK. Also in Beaumont, Texas, there was Boyd Brown on Station KGET.

"There was a time when you could send a guy two thousand free records to crack your record. You'd make the chart in one day. That was their hustle. Instead of cash, they get X-amount of free records. If they didn't have record shops, they'd have a guy behind the counter that they could *schmear*. For singles, they might pick up fifty cents a piece. For albums, there'd be another number. So they were sent free merchandise. They would transship it all kinds of ways. They'd send it to St. Louis and have the guy from St. Louis send it to Omaha, or whatever, so that nobody knew where it was coming from. Today, it's no different. Especially if you had your own pressing plant, there was no problem at all. I don't know why it shocks everybody. But then some days you wonder some people discover their kid smokes marijuana—like nobody ever smoked it before! These things do exist.

"You know they talk about airline tickets now. The guy would spend two weeks with his wife in Florida. The bills were sent to the company. Or they would hold a mortgage on the guy's house. I remember this—since both guys are gone—Jerry Blaine held the mortgage on Alan Freed's house. And that was his wedge. *You better play my fuckin' records.* Without saying it that way, but you'd better!

"I remember even to get an artist to record—they'd sit back, make believe they got sick, and all that horseshit. Then you'd have to *schmear* them, drop a few thou in their lap to make them sing. Bring the cash right there to the studio—and they don't get paid till they open their mouth and it's first take. Then, give them the money.

"Today, it still exists. The reason for success with a lot of performers —I don't give a shit what type of song they're singing—the success of a company is to be able to do something at long distance in the dark, when there's no union man sitting around hocking you, and where all the guys locally get frustrated and say, 'Hey, man, how come he's not using me? I can play as good as the other cat.' And that's how you make your hit records. The name of the game is below the line and above the line.

"And that's how independent production has become successful. Most of the things are not recorded, and who gives a shit? The union has drove everything out of proportion where guys say—and they won't say it because they're in New York or Hollywood—'Fuck the union!' It's really what they're sayin' because they ain't really doin' nothin' to help. The whole thing is a big farce. I think it's all right when you set a figure and establish a two-week vacation and hospitalization. Beyond that, it's all bullshit.

"That goes for any field. One day a guy will be smart and open a little hacienda in Mexico where the union is five bucks a man or whatever it is, and keep a rhythm section and let them build a farm. And you're better off. Or take a rhythm section to Japan. There's no union at all. You can get anything you want. As long as your rhythm is together, if that's the kind of rhythm. . . . Maybe you want Japanese rhythm. You don't have to bring anybody. But that's where it is."

I got a jazz-playin' piano and a great
* big rockin' chair,*
You can rock in rhythm by the music
* you hear.*   —BUMBLE BEE SLIM

Lenox Avenue and Broadway R & B

"THE KIND of records we have to make," Ahmet Ertegun of Atlantic Records told his associate, Jerry Wexler, "must work like this. There's a black cotton picker who lives in a cabin twenty-seven miles outside of Opooloosa. It's Friday night, and the cat is all tapped out. It's ten o'clock, and he's lying back in his chair, dozing and listening to the radio. Then our record comes on. He listens. Then he gets up, gets dressed, borrows a car, borrows a dollar, drives the twenty-seven miles to the town, and buys the record."

And Jerry Wexler said, "Ahmet was onto something. To black people, music is like holy communion. It's bread, I mean in the transcendental sense. It's the biscuit, the wafer. . . ."

•

When Ahmet Ertegun and Herb Abramson incorporated Atlantic Records in October 1947, they were financed by a Turkish dentist, Dr. Vahdi Sabit, of Washington, D.C. Ahmet's deep interest* was in jazz. He and his brother Nesuhi had come to the USA when their father was Turkey's ambassador to this country. They had spent their early years searching for the New Orleans pioneers of jazz and working to put men like Bunk Johnson and Kid Ory back into action. They also wanted to record them. But in Washington, D.C., where he was studying for his Ph.D. at Georgetown University, Ahmet spent much time at the Howard Theatre and at Max Silverman's Quality Music Shop, not far from the Negro vaudeville house.

By the time that Atlantic was founded, Ahmet had begun to realize that most people were not interested in early or even contemporary jazz. The records that sold at Max Silverman's store were by Helen Humes ("Be-Baba-Leba"), Dusty Fletcher ("Open the Door, Richard"), Big Maceo, Washboard Sam, Leroy Carr, and other contemporary bluesmen. Charles Brown's disk of "Drifting Blues" flipped Ahmet. These were the type of record that his partner, Herb Abramson, had been making since 1944 as A & R director of National Records. Not jazz, but blues with a contemporary feeling or pop tunes with a black sound and blues feeling like the Ravens' "Ol' Man River."

Despite Abramson's recording background—he was a record collector, too, just like the Erteguns—the first recordings that came out of Atlantic's tiny offices at the old Jefferson Hotel on Broadway and Fifty-sixth Street, now the site of the MONY building, were by jazz artists. Abramson and Ahmet recorded the band of Joe Morris, an ex-Lionel Hampton trumpet player who had assembled a group of jazz all-stars like Philly Joe Jones (drums), Percy Heath (bass), and Ray Charles (piano)—yes, *the* Ray Charles. Fledgling Atlantic sides included a swinging quartet led by Tiny Grimes, one of Fifty-second Street's regulars; progressive jazz by Boyd Raeburn; symphonic jazz

---

* In 1946 Ahmet recorded Little Miss Cornshucks. "I'd never made a record before in my life," he told me. "I did it just for fun—a piano player, a KC saxist, no rhythm section, and Cornshucks just singing the blues."

Ruth Brown

piano by Erroll Garner; and experimental jazz by alumni of Stan Kenton's big band.

A yearful of records were well made and sold—but in quantities that hardly paid their modest overhead at the Jefferson Hotel. Then Abramson and Ahmet made a recording of "Drinking Wine, Spo-Dee-O-Dee," an old blues refurbished by Stick McGhee, who cut it, and J. Mayo Williams, who had nurtured a generation of down-home bluesmen at Paramount and Vocalion during the '20s and of urban bluesmen as Decca's blues producer during the '30s. The Stick McGhee disk hit R & B charts in April 1949 and remained on best-seller lists for over six months, aggregating a sale of over 300,000. It was an eye-opener to Ahmet. As Atlantic's first R & B hit, it set the future direction of the company.

During the R & B years, Atlantic became the preeminent R & B label, surviving into the present under the Ertegun management. Grossing $1 million in '53, it earned over $20 million ten years later. Between 1950 and 1966, it scored over 100 Top Ten R & B hits. Its closest competitor was Mercury, a major company. Among R & B groups, two Atlantic aggregations, the Drifters and the Clovers, achieved more Top Ten disks than all the rest, including the Midnighters, Platters, and Dominoes.

Unlike Chicago and Los Angeles competitors, who had a pool of migrant country bluesmen to draw upon, Atlantic had to search out and create new talent. And the talent was recorded with black musicians who played on Fifty-second Street, jazz musicians who early gave Atlantic recordings a more hip and polished sound than those that came out of other sectors of the country.

·

Atlantic made its first major acquisition in 1949. Ruth Brown, a petite singer born in 1928, had sung in a church choir in Portsmouth, Virginia, where her father was the choir director. After a time, to escape her father's censure, she sang blues "behind the fence where the boys smoked cornsilk." Her first professional job was as female vocalist with the Lucky Millinder Band. When Ahmet and Herb Abramson went to hear the slim, trim, sloe-eyed miss at the Crystal Caverns in Washington, D.C., she was singing pop ballads of the day, albeit with the inflections that came from the church and a blues band. However, when Ahmet asked her to sing a blues, she replied, "I don't like blues."

Ahmet later said, "The blues we made with Ruth Brown came out like urbanized, watered-down versions of real blues. But we discovered white kids buying them because the real blues were too hard for them to swallow."

Even if Atlantic distributors found that they could sell Ruth's pop disks, and jukebox ops found that they could place them in white locations, the white radio world would have none of them. This was a problem that Atlantic faced not only in 1949, when Ruth Brown had her first chartmaker in "So Long," but throughout the '50s and into the rock 'n' roll years. Ruth herself did not make the Pop Forty until 1957 with "Lucky Lips," a song written by Leiber and Stoller.

"So Long," incidentally, was not the "So Long" used by Russ Morgan as his theme, nor the "So Long, It's Been Good to Know You" of Woody Guthrie, nor the "So Long, Oo Long (How Long You Gonna Be Gone?)," written by Kalmar and Ruby in 1920 and sung by Fred Astaire and Red Skelton in the Kalmar-Ruby 1950 biopic. It was an old blues ballad on which Ruth was curiously backed by an Eddie Condon Dixieland combo.

Ruth's follow-up hit, "Teardrops from My Eyes," was the biggest of a recording career in which she cut almost 100 solid sellers. Written by the late Rudolph Toombs, "Teardrops" was sung by Ruth against a "pop but blues-directed dance band arrangement," as Ahmet described it, and was scored by Budd Johnson. It was a departure that was to become a mark of Atlantic recordings.

Ruth also had No. 1 R & B disks in the suggestive "5-10-15 Hours" (1952), "Mama, He Treats Your Daughter Mean" (1953), "Oh, What a Dream," and "Mambo Baby" (1954); and she commanded a fervent following until the end of the '50s, when "I Don't Know" was on the R & B Top Ten. Delivering in a sandy voice with squeaky little curls, she sang with a beat that invited the designation "Miss Rhythm." A precursor of Little Esther, she recalled Hadda Brooks. Her diction was clear, and her pronunciation only delicately black. But her backgrounds were R & B, including the triplet figures, boogie basses, and horny tenor sax solos.

•

As the market for R & B expanded, Atlantic's other great rhythm-and-blueswoman, La Vern Baker, came to the label from King Records and The Todd Rhodes band. Born in Chicago in 1929, La Vern began singing in the Baptist church she attended, and she displayed such vocal ability that she made her professional debut while still a teen-ager. She was only seventeen when she drew such crowds at Chicago's Club De Lisa that she was retained for six months. During the years in which she paid her dues as a club singer, she was known as "Little Miss Sharecropper," a pseudonym she chose probably because of the popularity of a singer known as Little Miss Cornshucks. Eventually, La Vern found her way to the Flame Show Bar in Detroit, where owner Al Green became her manager. He was able to secure a Columbia Record contract for her, but it proved a dead end. Her association with King Records in 1953 was even briefer and equally unrewarding. From 1954 to the end of the decade on Atlantic, however, La Vern produced a steady stream of best-sellers, scoring her mightiest hit, as Ruth Brown had, with a ballad. "I Cried a Tear"

La Vern Baker

('58–9) was in waltztime, no less, and it was her closest approach to a pop style. Her loudest noisemaker was her third release, "Tweedle Dee," written by Winfield Scott and delivered with all the guts and drive of her chesty contralto to a Latin-inflected riff. How memorable and horny, her "hompy-om-bom-bom" fill! The record became something of a *cause célèbre* because the white cover by Georgia Gibbs, as imitative a treatment as could be derived from the original, became a Gold Record and destroyed any chance of La Vern's disk going pop. Indeed, Baker went to her congressman and tried to get him to introduce a bill making it illegal to copy arrangements, a practice not forbidden by law even today.

La Vern's other notable disks include Winfield Scott's sing-along novelty "Bop-Ting-a-Ling," in 1955; Lincoln Chase's "Jim Dandy," a real screamer in '56–7; and a version of the famous blues, "See See Rider," in 1962. Mercury Records released a Georgia Gibbs copy of "Jim Dandy," but by then young buyers were more interested in the black original than the white copy, and the airwaves in New York were also beginning to change color. Gibbs fell far short of the million-plus sales she had racked up on "Tweedle Dee."

"See See Rider" was quite a departure to anyone who knew the authentic Ma Rainey blues. While La Vern sang with the raucous commitment of a pioneer blues shouter and a tenor sax heated the proceedings, the background was a carefully worked out arrangement, scored for band and a female chorus by Ray Ellis, a well-known pop arranger. Ellis developed an *ostinato* composed of a swinging-eight figure against a solid-four beat and used the chorus to echo La Vern on a "See See Rider" riff. There was more beat than blues, and a sophistication of styling that brought the original blues decades away from its rural beginnings.

The style anticipated the Motown development of the 1960s when black song and sound were "popularized" and "manicured" with the help of musicians from the Detroit Symphony Orchestra. Ahmet Ertegun frankly felt that the use of schooled studio musicians and written scores prepared by pop arrangers was "one of Atlantic's first and really major departures." Later, when Atlantic began releasing Memphis-made Stax Records and Aretha Franklin came to the label, the process was reversed and Atlantic producers went South (to studios at Muscle Shoals, Alabama, and elsewhere) to get improvised, studio-developed "head" backgrounds. But from early in the decade to the end, Ertegun and his associates worked to evolve a blues-orchestrated style with the help of such black arrangers as Jesse

Stone, Howard Biggs, and Budd Johnson, and, later, white Ray Ellis and Stan Applebaum.

Atlantic also sought to develop a new breed of sideman who could read as well as play real blues. Other Eastern companies like Herald, Rama, who also recorded blues singers in Manhattan, produced a more primitive black sound, but Atlantic's choice was obviously commercially sound, for it outstripped all of its competitors and developed into a major label that was sold in 1969 to Warner Communications for the sum of $15 to $20 million.

.

"In an era when groups were in," Jerry Wexler has said, "we were the specialists in the single artist." During the R & B years, Atlantic developed at least five major male singers: Joe Turner was signed in 1951, Ray Charles in '52, Clyde McPhatter in '53, Chuck Willis in '56, and Ben E. King in '58. The '60s brought such formidable figures as "Preacher" Solomon Burke, "wicked" Wilson Pickett, and high-voltage Otis Redding, among others.

When Ahmet approached Joe Turner backstage at the Apollo about making some records, the Kansas City bluesman was rather depressed. His hour in the limelight seemed to have passed, despite the renown he had attained during the years of his collaboration with pianist Pete Johnson in the boogie craze of the late '30s. He had been jumping from label to label—Aladdin in 1949, Imperial and Bayou in '50, Colonial and RPM, also in 1950. Though he had produced well-sung sides, they found no real acceptance. In '50, on still another label, Freedom Records, he made the charts briefly with "Still in the Dark." But the disk was a dud. Although Big Joe still had the big pipes of a man who stood six-foot-two and weighed over 250 pounds, he was then forty years of age and had been singing for over twenty. Record buyers seemed to be searching for new heroes. But Ahmet refused to take "No" for an answer.

Writing under the pen name of Nugetre (Ertegun spelled backwards), Ahmet himself produced "Chains of Love," with music by Henry Van "Piano Man" Walls. It opened the door to Turner's full-scale acceptance by a new generation. Breaking R & B charts in June 1951, the blues ballad remained on best-seller lists to the end of the year. (Five years later, Pat Boone revived "Chains of Love.") Ertegun provided Big Joe with a follow-up in "Sweet Sixteen," topped the following year by "Honey Hush," written by Lou Willie Turner. The forty-year-old bluesman made no concession to his new environment or his new audience, but sang in the big, hearty, heady baritone that

Ray Charles

had once overwhelmed listeners in his days as a singing bartender in
KC. In truth, "Honey Hush" backed with "Crawdad Hole" was recorded in New Orleans without the supervision of any Atlantic executives. Turner was making an appearance in the Crescent City and cut
with a local band that included Lee Allen on tenor sax and Fats
Domino on piano.

The year 1954 brought the biggest record of Turner's refurbished
career: "Shake, Rattle, and Roll." Written by Charles Calhoun, it
was as earthy and as vital as any of the old-time blues—so much so
that when Bill Haley & His Comets covered Turner, they moved the
song's setting from the bedroom into the kitchen. Contrasting Turner's
original and Haley's imitation, one can hear R & B modulating into
R 'n' R. Black youngsters did not buy Haley, but white teen-agers did
purchase Joe Turner.

The acceptance achieved by the "Boss of the Blues," as Turner has
been called, on "Shake, Rattle, and Roll" led to a series of Top Ten
R & B best-sellers in the succeeding two years. In 1955, he had "Flip,
Flop, and Fly," an attempt to capitalize on the '54 hit, as well as
"Hide and Seek." Of five '56 titles that included even a rock 'n' roll
song, "Lipstick, Powder, and Pain," the biggest was "Corrine, Corrine," a reworking of the old blues. But as teen-agers took possession
of the music market and developed a partisanship for young and frequently amateurish singers, Big Joe's years began to tell. He had the
vitality and drive, but not the sound of youth—and R 'n' R was music
by, for, and of teen-agers.

·

Ray Charles came to Atlantic from several small West Coast labels
and from a direction that combined the shaping influences of Joe
Turner, whose background was that of an urban bluesman, and of
Ruth Brown and La Vern Baker, both of whom were blues band
vocalists. Ray knew the songs of Charles Brown and other urban
blues balladeers in the tradition of Leroy Carr—he once got a job in
Seattle by singing "Drifting Blues"—and he was on the road with
Lowell Fulson. But he also worked with hillbilly and R & B bands,
traveling through Florida, Tennessee, and other Southern states.

His major influence, after the beginnings, was Nat "King" Cole.
Understandably so, since from 1948 on Cole was the sole black singer
making it big. Hits like "Nature Boy," "Mona Lisa," and "Too
Young" were not only R & B best-sellers, but Top Ten in the white
pop market as well. It comes as no surprise that Charles's own first
combo was modelled on the piano-guitar-bass setup of The King Cole

Trio and that he affected a singing style similar to Cole's astringent, jazz-inflected baritone.

In the Seattle area, where he pursued his solo career, Ray's combo became the first black group to perform on a sponsored TV show. Charles' first recordings, made about the same time (1949) for Downbeat Records, reflect his Nat Cole jazz and blues orientation. Although he cut from '49 to '52 for Rockin' and Sittin' In With, his major output was on Swing Time, the Los Angeles label from which Atlantic purchased his contract for a mere $2,000. Two of the sides that Charles made for the Jack Lauderdale label, "Baby Let Me Hold Your Hand" and "Kiss Me, Baby," bounced briefly on R & B bestseller lists.

Although Atlantic released sides in 1952 and '53, it was not until '54 that Charles began selling disks (with "It Should've Been Me") and not until '55 that he managed his first hits. It was then that he formed his own permanent band—a big, horned blues band. In "I've Got a Woman" and "This Little Girl of Mine," he also returned to roots, taking gospel songs and developing them in a blues setting with a beat. It was an audacious move since to black people blues were still profane songs, while gospel was sacred, church singing— and the two genres were not to be mixed.

Ray had actually created a new genre, later designated "soul." In his gritty baritone, he sang with conviction and passion, with a dedication to the spirit and a feeling for the flesh. The excitement of gospel wedded to the sensuality of the blues produced a mind-shattering combination, which he successfully pursued in "Hallelujah, I Love Her So," and on which he peaked in "What'd I Say?" his first R & B bestseller to make No. 1. By then, he had been on Atlantic for seven years and, as he said in a final side, "I'm Movin' On." The R & B years were over for him, as they were for black music, and, when he moved to ABC Paramount Records in the '60s, he turned his capacious talents to C & W material, and achieved the first gold records of his career.

In 1959 Atlantic titled a Ray Charles album *The Genius*. Considering the handicaps he had to overcome, it hardly seems hyperbole. Born in Albany, Georgia, in September 1930, Ray Charles Robinson (as he was christened) became totally blind at the age of six and an orphan at fifteen. Yet he was able to master piano and saxophone, as well as the art of orchestration, and by seventeen he had organized and led the trio that became his springboard to an amazing career. Not even a bout with drugs (for which the greed of others was totally

Clyde McPhatter and The Drifters

responsible since he was unable to inject himself) could dim the remarkable creative talent with which he was endowed.

·

Steeped in gospel music and endowed with the voice to employ all the musical devices of the preacher's art, Clyde McPhatter was the inspired lead voice, first of The Dominoes, then of The Drifters. From 1956 to 1959, as a solo Atlantic artist, he produced disks whose sound was echoed in the records of Dee Clark on Vee Jay and Bobby Day on Chess. Jackie Wilson, who replaced Clyde in The Dominoes, later said, "I fell in love with the man's voice. I toured with the group and watched Clyde and listened . . ." and learned.

Born in the tobacco town of Durham, North Carolina, in November 1933, Clyde Lensey McPhatter was the son of George McPhatter, who preached in the Mt. Calvary Baptist Church, and of Eva McPhatter, who played the church organ. At five he was singing in the church choir, along with his three brothers and three sisters, and at ten he was the soprano-voiced soloist. Four years later, when the family was living in New Jersey and he was attending Chelsior High School, he formed his first professional gospel quartet, The Mt. Lebanon Singers. Although he began working as a clerk on graduation, he continued singing with gospel groups both in Jersey and in Harlem.

In 1950 he became associated with The Dominoes. Despite its name, it was composed of students of a gospel singing instructor named Billy Ward. McPhatter's soaring vocals contributed mightily to the success of such No. 1 King Records hits as "Sixty-Minute Man" (he could "rock 'em, roll 'em all night long") and "Have Mercy Baby." But he was frequently at odds with Ward, who was reportedly a petty tyrant who ruled the group with a system of fines for breaking regulations. One day when he was especially upset by the supposed disregard of regulations, Ward fired McPhatter. Ahmet Ertegun, who loved McPhatter's singing, noticed his absence from the group when he went to hear them at Birdland, the jazz club—"an odd booking" in Ahmet's words, "for the Dominoes."

As Jerry Wexler recalls, "Ahmet exited Birdland like a shot and headed directly uptown. He raced from bar to bar looking for Clyde and finally found him in a furnished room. That very night Ahmet reached an agreement with McPhatter under which Clyde would assemble a group of his own. They became known as The Drifters.

"In short order, in May 1953, Clyde had a group. After weeks of rehearsal, we did our first session. In those days, our office was at 234 West Fifty-sixth Street, over Patsy's Italian restaurant. At session time Ahmet and I placed one desk on top of the other in a corner of the room. [During office hours, they occupied the center of the medium-sized room, angled toward each other.] Tom Dowd, our gifted engineer, set out camp chairs and microphones. The control booth was approximately four feet wide by fifteen feet long. A small RCA portable, four-position, mono-mix, served as our console. Tom sat at it with room for one person next to him. Ahmet or I would sit and the other would hover over the other two."

After the same numbers were done in a professional studio, Audio Video, on June 29, 1953, it was decided that the group was not good enough, so Clyde went hunting for new personnel. That was when he found Willie Pinckney—the bass heard on the hit recording of "White Christmas"—baritone Bubba Thrasher, and tenors Gerhart Thrasher and David Baughan. From their very first release, "Money, Honey," the group was in the money and maintained a Top Ten position in R & B for the two years of McPhatter's vocal leadership.

Featuring a bagpipe effect ("ah-OOM, ah-OOM") that innocently established the fiscal nature of the song, "Money, Honey" made an acidulous comment on the connection between love and loot. McPhatter's approach was slyly humorous as he played the tomcat who had come to a most serious decision: no love for a pussycat without loot. It was a triumph of songwriting (by Jesse Stone, originally a KC pianist) as well as a triumphant performance.

After a stint in the armed forces, McPhatter stepped out on his own with "Seven Days," a Top Three R & B hit in 1955. Having added gospel fervor to the Ink Spots sound of The Dominoes, McPhatter adopted a more mainstream approach. "It was his dream," Wexler has said, "to transcend the R & B category and take a place in show biz alongside of Perry Como and Nat Cole." It was a dream he was never to realize, partly because of changes in the musical climate of the late '50s and partly because of his premature death.

"Seven Days," with a chart by pop arranger Ray Ellis, was the first of series of R & B best-selling romantic ballads for Clyde. There was "Treasure of Love," a rather mediocre song by two Tin Pan Alley writers. Jerry Wexler is proud of the disk because, as he explained, "if you listen carefully, you will hear triplets against the shuffle; it's not supposed to work, but it does." "Treasure of Love" was followed by "Just to Hold My Hand," by Don Robey, the versatile owner of Duke-Peacock Records of Houston; "Long Lonely Nights," a cover of a Chess Record by Lee Andrews & the Hearts, with McPhatter singing in a surprisingly low register; and in '58–'59, the biggest record of his solo career, "A Lover's Question."

"A Lover's Question" was the work of two men who soon became known in areas other than songwriting: Brook Benton was about to break out on Mercury Records with a No. 1 R & B/pop hit in "It's Just A Matter of Time"; and Clyde Otis, who signed Benton to Mercury, was just about to become known as the first successful black A & R chieftain of a major label. Writer credits on the song list Brook Benton and Jimmy Williams, apparently a Clyde Otis pseudonym. "A Lover's Question" grabbed the listener's ears with an innovative opening that involved two unaccompanied voices—the bass setting up a rhythmic *ostinato* and McPhatter slipping smoothly into the song. Artful arranging by Ray Ellis—a Columbia Records arranger-conductor who was permitted to freelance at Atlantic—provided an appealing setting for McPhatter's silvery baritone. Its sales garnered a Gold Record.

Although Atlantic recorded McPhatter all through 1959 and his records continued to command an audience, he had passed peak acceptance, and never rose to it again. Teen-agers, black as well as white, were buying youthful sounding rock 'n' rollers. By 1960 McPhatter had left Atlantic for MGM Records. Before the year was over, he moved to Mercury, remaining on the Chicago-based label through the years when the Beatles and a succession of British groups monopolized American airwaves. Somehow, Clyde's Mercury records were not as strong on songs or even as mirrors of his great vocal talent. He was hardly ready for death—he was just forty-one—when it came suddenly in June 1972.

In his book *The Drifters*, Bill Millar names Ben E. King, Smokey Robinson of the Miracles, Sammy Turner, and Marv Johnson among the vocalists who patterned themselves after McPhatter. "Most important," he concludes, "McPhatter took hold of the Ink Spots' simple major chord harmonies, drenched them in call-and-response patterns and sang as if he were back in church. In doing so, he created a revolutionary musical style from which—thankfully—popular music will never recover."

•

Ben E. King took over McPhatter's lead slot with The Drifters, after it had been occupied by three others—David Baughn, Johnny Moore, and Bobby Hendricks. Born Benjamin Earl Nelson in Henderson, North Carolina in 1938, King sang in a church choir as a schoolboy, came to New York at age nine, and dropped out of Seward Park High to help in his father's restaurant. He joined the Five Crowns around 1958 when Lover Patterson, who handled the group, heard him in the luncheonette. By then the Crowns, who started on Rainbow Records, had recorded on Old Town, Riviera, and Gee. King can be heard on the single disks they made for R & B Records and Trans-World, and he went with them when the Five Crowns became The Drifters in March 1959. During '59–'60, when Leiber and Stoller produced and The Drifters regularly made the charts, Ben E. King sang lead baritone on "Dance with Me," "True Love, True Love," "This Magic Moment," "Lonely Winds," "I Count the Tears," and "There Goes My Baby" (No. 1 in '59), and "Save the Last Dance for Me" (No. 1 in '60).

By January 1961, Ben E. King was on the charts by himself with "Spanish Harlem." A story was circulated that the song, by Phil Spector and Jerry Leiber, was intended for The Drifters, but became a solo cutting for King when the other members failed to reach the Atlantic studios in a New York snowstorm. Interesting though it may be, the tale has no foundation. King had actually made solo recordings for Atco, the Atlantic subsidiary, before he cut his lyrical song about "the rose that grew in Spanish Harlem."

King's follow-up hit in 1961 emanated from his gospel background. A rewrite of a hymn of the same title, "Stand By Me" was a dramatic, emotion-wracked record that suffused a secular plea with sacred feelings. It was King's biggest chartmaker, approached only by "Don't Play That Song" in 1962. After that, though he enjoyed Atco releases into 1970 and all of them reached the charts, King became another casualty of the Beatles invasion.

•

Chuck Willis died even younger than Clyde McPhatter. He was just thirty in April 1958 when he succumbed on an operating table after a car crash near his hometown of Atlanta, Georgia. An OKeh artist from 1951 to '55, he attained his maturity as a recordmaker between '56 and '58 on Atlantic. An accomplished songwriter, he won national recognition with an old blues—Ma Rainey's "C. C. Rider." This was an achievement of skillful arranging by Jesse Stone, who handled many Atlantic sessions, and sensitive studio work by Jerry Wexler.

Latin instruments and meters were among the exotic sounds that Atlantic introduced into R & B. "C. C. Rider" opens with the velvet vibrations of a marimba, its south-of-the-border rhythm enhanced by a female group softly sighing, "C. C. Ri-i-i-i der, C. C. Ri-i-i-i der." In 1957–58, a dance called The Stroll was beginning to captivate teenagers, and the walking rhythm and easy tempo of "C. C. Rider" accidentally proved perfectly suited to it. Suddenly, Chuck Willis was the "King of Stroll," and adorned in exotic turbans that also earned him the cognomen "Sheik of the Shake," he became a performer in demand.

A follow-up folk-blues, "Betty and Dupree," sought to capitalize on the impact of "C. C. Rider," but it did not win nearly as many followers. Just before his death, Willis recorded two songs that inevitably acquired ironic overtones after his demise: "What Am I Living For?" and "Hang up My Rock-and-Roll Shoes." A back-to-back record—the former title was not written by Willis—the disk vied with "C. C. Rider" as an R & B chartmaker. Although Atlantic issued a number of disks posthumously and two sides made the charts, no cult developed around Willis as it did around Johnny Ace and Otis Redding following their deaths.

All of these sides are missing from Atlantic's valuable eight-volume anthology, *History of Rhythm & Blues*. Possibly, the company felt that Chuck was not an R & B singer. He was basically a balladeer of the Johnny Ace genre, singing in a soft, cool, flat, almost melancholy voice—perhaps too tender and gentle to be called soulful—though it communicated a shyness that had great romantic appeal.

•

Of three important groups—not counting the brief tenure at Atlantic of the Cardinals, Diamonds, and Five Keys—Atlantic's first successful quartet was The Clovers. John "Buddy" Bailey, cool lead, and Harold Jerome Winley, dumb-sounding bass, started singing together in a Washington, D.C., high school in 1950–1. Before the group came to Atlantic, they had cut at least two sides for another Manhattan "indie," Rainbow Records, delivering "Yes, Sir, That's My Baby" in a style imitative of The Orioles, then the hot R & B group.

A Baltimore-Washington record distributor, Lou Krefetz, who found the Clovers in Washington's Rose Club and became their manager, brought them to Ahmet Ertegun. As he recalls, they wanted to sing like the Ink Spots, hoping to cross over into pop as the Spots and the Mills Brothers had done. Ahmet gave them a song he had written, "Don't You Know I Love You?" and tried to move them in a black-ghetto direction. The result was that they became one of the first groups to serve as a bridge between R & B and pop.

Although "Don't You Know I Love You?" sounded not nearly as black as Ertegun had wanted, it went to No. 1 on R & B charts in 1951, as did "Fool, Fool, Fool," their follow-up, also written by Ertegun. Both of these mark a departure in group recording, thanks to the creativity of Herb Abramson and Ahmet Ertegun as producers. Though they were sweet, romantic records, they were also solid dance disks. The new emphasis was apparent from the opening vocal lick ("Ooh-diddley-do-DAH-do-day, Ooh-diddley-do-DAH-do-day") delivered by bass Harold Winley on "Don't You Know I Love You?" By comparison with today's soul disks and even with the records by blues bands of the '50s, The Clovers songs have a rather empty, almost amateurish sound. But the beat was there, despite the stark simplicity of the tubby drum and tinny piano background. Young black dancers reacted, as did other groups, among them Billy Ward's Dominoes and the Midnighters, and they helped make the Clovers one of the most imitated groups of the day.

Along with Ruth Brown, The Clovers put Atlantic Records into business. From 1951 to 1956, the group had the most consistent record of delivering best-sellers of any R & B attraction of the time. The first four titles—"One Mint Julep" and "Ting-a-Ling" followed by "Fool, Fool, Fool" and "Don't You Know I Love You?"—occupied best-seller charts for extended periods of fourteen to twenty-two weeks.

"One Mint Julep," by the late Rudolph Toombs, was quickly covered by Louis Prima on Columbia Records, one of the earliest instances of a white cover of a black record. There was also a pop version by Buddy Morrow & His Orchestra on RCA Victor. The

Clovers themselves did not make pop charts until after the advent of rock 'n' roll with "Love, Love, Love," a song by Teddy McRae and Sid Wyche, two black Tin Pan Alley writers.

In 1956, their remarkable run of chartmakers came to a halt. The two succeeding years were dismal, despite driving records like the erotic "Down in the Alley." But by '56, doubtless because the pop market was opening to records by black artists, the Clovers were moving in a white direction. This is suggested by their slow-shuffle record of "Blue Velvet," popularized earlier by Tony Bennett, and their harmonically sophisticated disk of "Devil or Angel," a hit for Bobby Vee in 1960.

Though "Down in the Alley" was released in 1957, it was actually written and recorded four years earlier. The work of Jesse Stone and the Clovers (shangity-shangity-shang), it had frankly erotic lines like, "We'll go rockin' and reelin' . . . down in the alley. . . ." In this song—and in "Ting-a-Ling," by A. Nugetre (1952) and "Good Lovin'," by Leroy Kirkland, Danny Taylor, and A. Nugetre (1953)—the Clovers anticipated the sexual candor of the "Annie" songs of Hank Ballard on King Records.

Their last chart song, "Love Potion Number Nine," (1959) is in the same funky groove, though marked by comic overtones with which songwriters-producers Leiber and Stoller imbued many of their songs. By '59 the Clovers were no longer on Atlantic, and the record was, in fact, produced for United Artists Records. "Love Potion Number Nine" made pop charts late in '59, a tribute to the song and its producers, rather than to the group, apparently past its prime.

•

By 1953 Atlantic had acquired its second important vocal group, the Drifters, formed as already noted when Billy Ward dropped Clyde McPhatter from the Dominoes. Starting with "Money, Honey," the Drifters achieved an even more formidable array of best-selling disks than the Clovers had, placing songs on R & B charts from 1953 to '67, all of them Atlantic releases. This longevity on one label would seem to contradict the name selected by the group. But although the name remained, its magic commanding a devoted following into the rock 'n' roll era, the personnel changed through the years.

After Clyde McPhatter was drafted in 1955, Johnny Moore became lead singer, accounting for such platters as the two-sided hit, "Adorable" backed with "Steamboat," and Leiber and Stoller's "Ruby, Baby." But the original personnel changed even during the production of "Money, Honey," the group's first smash, because producers Ertegun and Wexler did not like the backup sound behind McPhatter. Later there was Bobby Hendricks, who became a one-hit chartmaker on his own with "Itchy Twitchy Feeling" on the short-lived Sue label.

Clyde McPhatter, who wrote "Three Thirty-three," a record suppressed in 1954, was co-author with Gerald Wexler of "Honey Love." Apparently, the Atlantic executives felt that the words of the latter were less "suggestive"—to employ the epithet used to damn R & B records in those days—than those of "Three Thirty-three." If this is the case, there can be no question about the erotic overtones of McPhatter's delivery. Squeals, gasps, and growls, all almost orgiastic in sound, leave no doubt that "Honey Love" means sex.

As for "Three Thirty-three," the words may now be heard in the Drifters' collection of *Their Greatest Recordings*. All they said was that one could find "good times, cheap wines, young chicks . . . and a whole lot of ecstasy" in Room 333. In light of the nudity and four-letter words now visible and audible on stage and screen, characterizing such lyrics as suggestive is not inaccurate. They *were* suggestive, not explicit. But in the wake of the attacks, bans, and censorship levelled against the "Annie" songs and some of Muddy Waters's early records, Atlantic execs were uptight over possible adverse reactions to the group. And so they held back "Three Thirty-three." But then The Drifters' "Such a Night" ran into censorship, not because of their disk, but as a result of Johnnie Ray's cover.

Among the most curious records in the Drifters' repertoire, recorded when McPhatter was still lead singer, was a back-to-back version of two Tin Pan Alley standards, Irving Berlin's "White Christmas" backed with "Bells of St. Mary's." The disk made No. 2 on R & B charts in 1954 and became, thereafter, a best-seller every Yuletide until black nationalists began objecting to the association of Christmas with *white*. McPhatter "worries" (in blues terminology) so many words of the song that his gospel intensity borders on mockery. But it is obvious that record buyers accepted this exaggerated intensity as emotional sincerity.

The movement of black groups away from the Tin Pan Alley orientation of both the Ink Spots and the bird groups and toward gospel involvement proceeded apace with the Drifters. Bird groups like the Ravens and the Orioles had a blacker sound than either the Ink Spots or the Mills Brothers—so much so that pop program directors who disliked the sound or feared alienation of white listeners dismissed their disks as "jungle music." However, by the time the Drifters began hitting the charts (1953), white teen-agers were beginning to favor the emotional intensity and gospel excitement with which the original Drifters imbued their records.

Clyde McPhatter was not the only member who served an apprenticeship as a church singer; the other three members were also deeply involved in gospel song. As children, tenor Gerhart Thrasher and baritone Andrew, his younger brother, sang with The Silvertone Singers and The Thrasher Wanderers in their native town, Wetumpka, Alabama. (Pioneer Moses Asch of Folkways recorded the latter group during a field trip.) Bass Bill Pinckney, who came from Sumter, South Carolina, toured the South with several gospel groups, including the Singing Cousins, Wandering Four, and the Jerusalem Stars, writing and arranging original material for the last mentioned. Thus, Bill Millar is on solid ground when he writes: "The Drifters virtually destroyed the distinction between the sacred and the profane, and created the means by which Aretha Franklin and Ray Charles could become the most popular singers in the world."

After the Presley-rockabilly riptide of 1956, the Drifters disappeared from best-seller charts and broke up. But manager George Treadwell, who controlled the name and had advance theatrical bookings, lassoed another group called the Five Crowns and renamed them the Drifters. In '59, Ben E. King became lead singer, and Leiber and Stoller entered as producers, enhancing the soulful vitality of the new group with the innovative addition of a string section. It was, perhaps, the first time that strings were heard on an R & B disk, and record-buyers eagerly bought the fresh sound. "There Goes My Baby" mounted R & B charts in June '59 and soared to No. 1. The following year, "Save the Last Dance for Me," with an arrangement (cum strings) by Stan Applebaum, also made No. 1.

In 1961 after baritone King left the Drifters to make it on his own with "Spanish Harlem," Rudy Lewis became the lead voice. In "Up on the Roof," No. 4 in '62, he was backed by a female group that included Dionne and Dee Dee Warwick. The same personnel, with Leiber and Stoller still producing, accounted for "On Broadway," a Top Ten disk in 1963. By then, the records of the Drifters had acquired a Broadway sophistication and teen-age orientation that was a far cry from their early R & B disks. Rudy Lewis died in 1964, apparently on the very morning that the group was scheduled for a recording session. Despite the unhappy turn of events, they went ahead with the session and produced an intensely emotional version of "Under the Boardwalk."

The session's producer was a creative young songwriter, Bert Berns, who himself died of a heart attack not long after. Berns, who produced many Drifters sessions between 1963 and '66, introduced a social orientation with songs like "My Islands in the Sun" and "Up in the Streets of Harlem." But he also waged a planned attack on the pop market with versions of "Vaya con Dios," "Desafinado," "I Wish You Love," "Who Can I Turn To?" and other pop songs that were not released, including "More" and "What Kind of Fool Am I?"

•

Shorter lived than both the Drifters and the Clovers, the Coasters, Atlantic's third vocal group, brought into the latter days of R & B a quality rare in the blues and in R & B—humor, comedy, laughter. More significantly, their comedy, like the best humor, was socially oriented and frequently took a satiric turn or became timely commentary. It was basically a question of material, and the Coasters were fortunate in having the inventive minds of Jerry Leiber and Mike Stoller working for them. But the material also had to be handled cleverly, and here, again, the group was blessed with the creative direction of Leiber and Stoller, who produced their records.

In 1953, after they had created such R & B hits as "Hard Times" for Charles Brown, "Hound Dog" for Big Mama Thornton and "K. C. Lovin' " (later known as "Kansas City") for Little Willie Littlefield, Leiber and Stoller started their own label in partnership with Lester Sill. Situated in Los Angeles, Spark Records fared well as a regional R & B label, particularly with a group called the Robins. (Ralph Bass claims that the Robins were originally his group.)

"Smokey Joe's Cafe," a 1955 hit for the Robins, led to the association of Leiber and Stoller with Atlantic Records and to the formation of the Coasters. Instead of becoming A & R executives with the company, as was normal in those days, L & S worked out an independent production deal. A typical arrangement in the record business today, it was one of the first instances of such a setup, anticipated only by Ralph Bass's arrangement with King Records, though Ralph was actually on staff in addition to having a production deal.

As for the Coasters (a name chosen because of their geographical origin), they came into being as a result of binary fission. Two of the Robins chose to remain with the original group, recording with a new personnel for the Whippet label of LA. Carl Gardner, lead singer, and Bobby Nunn, bass, left to form the Coasters, recording for Atco, a subsidiary formed by Atlantic to reduce possible intralabel competition with the Clovers and Drifters.

"Smokey Joe's Cafe" set the mold for the comic style that The

Coasters developed to a high degree of perfection. Here was this cat eating at Smokey Joe's when a cute chick sat down next to him with her knees touching his. It looked like the beginning of something. But suddenly there was Smokey Joe himself, a knife in hand, saying in a cool, bass voice: "You better eat your beans and clear out!" The chick was his wife. The situation was played, not for drama, but for comedy. L & S used a descending guitar run to suggest the cat's initial erotic excitement, then the collapse of his hopes. Over and above its story interest, "Smokey Joe's Cafe" was a solid, hard-driving dance record, replete with afterbeat handclapping from its opening rhythmic vocal lick, "ooh-WAH-AAH- at Smoke-y Joe's Cafe . . ."

The Coasters

"Down in Mexico," really the Coasters' first Atco release since "Smokey Joe" was a takeover from Spark Records, poked satirical fun at Mexican tourism. The scene was a honky-tonk in Mexicali, and the supersalesman (really a pimp) was a colorful figure "who wore a red bandana, played a blues piano, donned a purple sash, and had a black moustache." When the luscious chick appeared, bongos set up a palpitating rhythm that humorously underscored the tourist's excitement. The record made Top Ten in R & B.

It was their succeeding record, a two-sided hit, "Searchin' " backed with "Young Blood" that catapulted the group into a two-year run (1957–9) of smash records. "Young Blood," first to attract record buyers, presented four guys going gaga over a chick until papa appears; the tale ends in unrequited lust. L & S adopted a catchy device of individualizing each guy's reactions through variations in vocal timbre and expression. When they first spot the chick on a street corner, each shouts "Looka there," but the lead singer's voice is excited, the tenor silly, the baritone cackles, and the bass sounds determined. When disk jockeys turned the No. 1 disk over, "Searchin' " extended its life on the charts.

The two records that followed marked the high point of the Coasters–L & S collaboration. "Yakety-Yak," No. 1 in 1958, and "Charlie Brown," No. 2 in '59, were masterful probings of teen-age problems and adolescent psychology. L & S were, naturally, on the side of the kids. "Yakety-Yak" opened tough—"Take out the papers and the trash!"—with the quartet barking orders that parents give to youngsters. There was the usual threat when chores were not done— "No cash and ain' gonna rock 'n' roll no more." The young reaction came in two sneering words, "Yakety-yak," followed by the bass mimicking "Don't talk back!" Apart from its unconventional structure—the title of the song simply appearing as commentary—"Yakety-Yak" was a trenchant, if humorous, presentation of the tension between generations.

"Fee-fee, Fi-fi, Fo-fo, Fum,/ I smell smoke in the auditorium," set the stage in "Charlie Brown" for an intriguing, ingratiating, and sly portrait of a youthful cutup—he smokes in school, plays dice in the gym, writes on walls, calls the teacher "Daddy-o," and then asks innocently, "Why's everybody always picking on me?" His friends call him a clown and expect him to get conked, but their emotions are mixed. "Charlie Brown" was not merely an R & B chartmaker; it made an appearance on *Billboard*'s pop year-end surveys: No. 13 on "The Hot 100 Pop Records" and No. 19 on "Top Tunes of the Year."

Playlets was the word Mike Stoller used to describe the Coasters' songs. And that's what most of them were—three-minute comic skits in which every resource of intonation and instrumentation was used to poke fun at palpable targets: TV Western heroes in "Along Came Jones"; phony exotic dancers in "Little Egypt"; middle-aged hipsters in "Shoppin' for Clothes"; etc.

Lead singer Carl Gardner and comedy singer Billy Guy remained with the group, but tenor Leon Hughes was succeeded by Young Jessie and later by Cornell Gunter, and bass Bobby Nunn was replaced by Will "Dub" Jones. But the spirit of high comedy with which Leiber and Stoller imbued Coasters recordings remained. R & B was seldom more artful.

•

My first contact with Atlantic came in 1954, shortly after Jerry Wexler joined the company. I recall climbing several long, steep flights of wooden stairs in a four-story building on West Fifty-sixth Street squeezed between other narrow structures occupied by printing companies and the like. The building had an elevator, but either it was out of order or it moved so slowly that it was less harrowing to walk. Atlantic occupied the top floor, with the rear section serving as a stockroom. The front was a tall, good-sized room with several large desks and a rickety grand piano. At night, as Wexler indicated, the desks were pushed into a corner to turn the office into a recording studio.

There were only two people in the office when I arrived to negotiate a deal on "Sh-Boom," a song owned by Atlantic's publishing company, Progressive Music and recorded by a group called The Chords on Atlantic's Cat label. (I did buy 50 percent of the copyright for Hill & Range Songs, of which I was then General Professional Manager. Atlantic, later a million dollar corporation, then welcomed the $6,000 advance they received for giving up 50 percent of what became the No. 1 song of summer '54 and is generally regarded as the first rock 'n' roll hit.)

My negotiations were with Jerry Wexler and Miriam Abramson, soon to be the ex-wife of Herb Abramson, co-founder of Atlantic. Mrs. Abramson served as business manager, bookkeeper, and office secretary. Wexler, formerly a *Billboard* reporter and more recently publicity and ad director of the MGM publishing companies, was a man with a raucous voice and a roaring laugh. He wore glasses that kept slipping down on his nose so that, when he talked to me, he often did it looking over the top of the black plastic frames. White, well-read, and Jewish though he was, his speech was ghetto-Harlem.

When Herb Abramson was mustered out of the armed services in 1956 he returned to A & R work at the company he helped found. Soon after, Atlantic moved to a building at the northwest corner of Sixtieth Street and Broadway, across from the Colisseum on Columbus Circle. Although his acumen in picking material and in directing sessions helped build the new Atco subisidiary, Abramson experienced considerable tension with his partners. Unquestionably, the source of the tension was the torn relationship between Herb and his ex-wife, whose divorce settlement included stock in the company. After a comparatively short time, Abramson sold his stock and left to form a short-lived label, Triumph Records, which he operated in the old President Hotel on West Forty-eighth Street.

Herb was a nervous man with a high-pitched laugh. He could not stand still, and when he sat and talked with you his glance kept wandering as if to follow his racing thoughts. For that matter, nervousness, hyperactivity, and restlessness were marks of all the male Atlantic executives—Jerry Wexler, Nesuhi Ertegun, and Ahmet Ertegun.

Ahmet practically stutters as his speech seeks to keep up with his thoughts. He is a curious contradiction, a member of the New York jet set and a dedicated lover and student of black music, going back to its red-clay beginnings. His wife is constantly in the society columns. In addition to being Madison Avenue dwellers, they spent their summers on Fire Island—not with the hoi polloi in Ocean Beach, but in an elegant home they owned in the expensive and secluded reaches of Talisman.

Once when I was at Ocean Beach, I took a long walk along the ocean's edge. It was several miles to Talisman. Ahmet's house was about a quarter of a mile from the ocean. As I approached, I could see him wandering about in a glass-enclosed room. I discovered that he had been working on a new song. It was quite incongruous, this millionaire jet-setter spending a Sunday afternoon as A. Nugetre, writing an R & B song in an idiom and with a feeling that grew out of ghetto Harlem.

•

If there was a more enigmatic character than Ahmet, it was Phil Spector. For a brief period in 1961, he was ostensibly an A & R exec at Atlantic. Fearlessly, I called for an appointment and duly arrived to audition a demo. I intercepted him in the crowded Atlantic anteroom where he looked at me as if I were holding a knife instead of a demo record. It made no impression that I was the first publisher of Jeff Barry ("Tell Laura I Love Her"), with whom he was then beginning to collaborate. (They later wrote the moving "River Deep, Mountain High," an Ike & Tina Turner disk whose failure to make it so disenchanted Spector that he quit the record business, for a time.) That morning in Atlantic's frantic anteroom, Spector did not seem to remember that we had an appointment, and I never got to play anything for him.

Born in the Bronx in December 1940, Spector attended Hollywood High School, as Leiber and Stoller had. He was discovered by Lester

Sill, mentor of L & S, with whom he later founded an important R & B label, Philles—Phil + Les. It was Sill who put him under the steward-ship of L & S. Singing initially with and producing a group called The Teddy Bears, who had a modest R & B hit in "To Know Him Is To Love Him" (his first song), he later developed such artists as The Crystals, The Ronettes, and The Righteous Brothers. He is as inno-vative as he was precocious and as weird as he is creative. He experi-mented with extensive overdubbing, the unconventional use of instru-ments (like half a dozen drums on a date), and evolved the "wall of sound" concept—surrounding a singer and overwhelming the listener with an unabating continuum of sound.

Jerry Wexler has said of him, "Phil Spector was a Pygmalion. He took raw clay, and fabricated it and molded it and breathed on it and it came to life. He is a person who presides over studio happenings. He confects it, he gets it together in the studio."

.

The quiet man on the Atlantic scene was Tommy Dowd, an engi-neer who worked with the company from its earliest days. Tall, thin, and soft-spoken, Dowd was the unchallenged man-at-the-control-board at Atlantic sessions. Tommy never talked about his contribution, but it was known both inside the company and outside that there are few men who knew as much about recording black music as he. Begin-ning in 1963, when he co-produced a Drifters session with Bert Berns, he has developed into one of Atlantic's outstanding producers, an activity at which he still excells as a vice-president of the company.

The Atlantic catalogue is an enormous library of black music, as rich in jazz as it is in R & B, and since the advent of British rock, as rich in this area with the Rolling Stones and Led Zeppelin as in the others. With Atlantic, R & B attained a variety and sophistication that took its sounds away from the original. The Motown Sound, drawing on the string section of the Detroit Symphony Orchestra, was a natu-ral consequence.

groove 14   **AHMET ERTEGUN**

Chairman of the board today, Ahmet Ertegun was co-founder with Herb Abramson of Atlantic Records. Knowing of his deep interest in jazz, a dedication that antedated his migration from his native Turkey to the USA, I asked how he became interested in rhythm and blues.

.

"I am sure that you are aware that Atlantic's first releases were jazz instrumentals. That happened, not only because Herb and I were avid jazz collectors, but because of the situation in the recording field in 1947. As we were incorporating that fall, a recording ban was impending. Rushing to stockpile as many masters as we could, we turned to instrumental groups to which we had easy access—Tiny Grimes, Joe Morris, and Frank Culley. And our releases during 1948 were instrumental jazz and blues records.

"By the following year, we were in R & B. We moved into R & B because we dug the blues, the soul of jazz. All kinds of blues! Not just the big city, vaudeville blues of Bessie Smith. Country, delta blues where it all started. The more down home you get, the funkier you get. The more big foot—all expressions for getting down to soul; big foot, mud, red clay. Where does it all come from? It comes from being black. And from being black is where this music emanates. Being black, you go to the very blackness of being black. It's the trouble blacks have had since they were brought here. And those black people who grew up in red clay and up to their knees, working all day on some plantation. That's why it's referred to as big-foot music, funky music, down-home music, gutty music—real black music in a black environment under the worst possible conditions.

"It's sad music and it's happy music. Also secret language music. It has two things. By the fact that it's a lament, it has the dignified beauty of black people expressed in it. And because of its obvious innocence and sincerity, it captivated the world. It isn't because it's got a drum that came from Africa, but because it has a soul that came from suffering.

"That is the reason this music has become the music of the world. It's the music that The Beatles imitated, and The Rolling Stones to an even greater degree. Of course, they've added. Everybody does. But there's a basic core. Jazz is certainly a development from the blues.

"In the thirties and forties, not a jazz player would play blues changes. And if they did, they'd try to hide it. They must have felt that blues were retrogression. It was only with the advent of people like Ray Charles, who was not only a great blues singer and player, but a great jazz musician, that black performers came to realize that blues was their heritage. There was nothing wrong in loving that heritage, which is beautiful. The blues is undeniable. If you like American music, you must love the blues because the blues is the most important thing in American music. And jazz phrasing comes from blues phrasing and from gospel phrasing. The looseness of rhythm is a result of subconscious imitation of Negro gospel and Negro blues singing.

"When I was studying for my doctorate at Georgetown University in Washington, D.C., I hung around a record store not far from the Howard Theatre. That's where I got my doctorate in black music, at the Howard Theatre. What I learned at Max Silverman's Quality Music Shop was that black people didn't buy jazz. They bought country blues singers like Washboard Sam; they bought city bluesmen like Charles Brown; and they bought rhythm-and-bluesmen like The Ravens. My Atlantic partner, Herb Abramson, had been making these records on National. When we cut Brownie McGhee's brother, Stick McGhee, doing an old blues, our direction was set. 'Drinkin' Wine, Spo-Dee-O-Dee' was our first R & B hit in 1949.

"Black people were clamoring for blues records, blues with a sock dance beat. Around 1949, that was their main means of entertainment. Harlem folks couldn't go downtown to the Broadway theaters and movie houses. Downtown clubs had their ropes up when they came to the door. They weren't even welcome on Fifty-second Street where all the big performers were black. Black people had to find entertainment in their homes—and the record was it.

"Even radio was white oriented. You couldn't find a black performer on network radio. And when it came to disk jockeys on the big wattage stations, they wouldn't play a black record. We had a real tough time getting our records played—even Ruth Brown, who didn't sound particularly black. All the jocks had to see was the Atlantic label and the name of the artist—and we were dead. We'd say, 'Just listen and give your listeners a chance to listen.' But they had a set of stock excuses: 'Too loud'; 'Too rough'; 'Doesn't fit our format.' They'd never say, 'We don't play black artists.' But then they'd turn around and play a record of the very same song that was a copy of our record, only it was by a white artist.

"The breakthrough didn't come, as you might expect, in the North. No, it was 'prejudiced' white Southerners who began programming R & B. They began playing Fats Domino, Ivory Joe Hunter, Roy Milton, Ruth Brown, Amos Milburn because young white teen-agers heard them on those top-of-the-dial stations and began requesting them. What the hell was Elvis listening to when he was growing up?

"From the beginning, our records were really accessible to white listeners. Our artists weren't down-home bluesmen. They didn't come from red-clay country. And our backup groups were either studio musicians or jazzmen. Working with these sophisticated cats, we did try to get an authentic blues feeling. And how could you beat a polished performance of down-to-earth blues material? It has mass appeal, white as well as black.

"We worked at getting a strong and clean rhythm sound. This was partly a matter of engineering. We were among the first independents to mike instruments in the rhythm section separately—a separate mike for drums, bass, and guitar. But to get that clean rhythmic punch, we found it necessary to use written arrangements. This was a major departure in R & B recording. Experienced black arrangers like Jesse Stone, Howard Biggs, Budd Johnson, Bert Keyes, and Teacho Wilshire, later white arrangers like Ray Ellis and Stan Applebaum, helped develop a blues arranging style. Some writers have described the Atlantic Sound as R & B with strings or arranged R & B, and there's some merit in that.

"In later years, the Atlantic Sound acquired what Jelly Roll Morton spoke of as 'the Spanish tinge.' Leiber and Stoller introduced a shuffling Latin beat in some of The Drifters' records. Bert Berns also had a big feeling for Spanish music. W. C. Handy used the habanera rhythm in his 'St. Louis Blues.' In the late fifties the samba beat, guaracha, baion, and other Afro-Cuban rhythms added color and excitement to the basic drive of R & B.

"Atlantic grew and survived when most other independents disappeared because it had great flexibility and responded to change. A record company needs engineers, creative producers, and smart promoters. But more than anything else, it needs artists. We established a reputation early for paying established artists top royalty—and we did pay. This trade secret attracted many performers to our doors. And after we signed them, we worked to make them feel at home and to search out the best material we could find for recording. We're probably too big now to cultivate the family feeling that was ours for years, but we still like to think of ourselves as a big, happy, soulful family."

groove 15   **RUTH BROWN**

"When I made my first recording in 1949," Ruth Brown said, as we sat in the back of the Aladdin Theatre in Las Vegas during a rehearsal of the black *Guys and Dolls,* "I was on crutches. And that date was delayed for a year while I recovered from an automobile accident."

"You see I was singing at the Crystal Caverns, located at Eleventh and U Streets, Northwest, in Washington, D.C. At that time, it was being run by Blanche Calloway, a sister of Cab Calloway. One night, a disk jockey who is now associated with the Voice of America, Willis Conover, came in. He was with the great Duke Ellington, who had just finished a late show at the Howard Theatre. They came in to hear the pianist at the club, Calvin Jackson. After I sang, Willis Conover took me over to the side with Blanche Calloway, and asked whether I had any aspirations to record. Of course, I was delighted. He said that he knew Herb Abramson and Ahmet Ertegun at Atlantic Records, and he placed a call to Herb at his home right from the club. The following day, Abramson phoned Waxey Maxey, who had the big record shop, and asked about me. Waxey told him that I was well-liked. Herb and Ahmet made a trip from New York to the Crystal Caverns soon after. And that's how I got my recording contract with Atlantic.

"But it took a while before I actually got into a studio for my first session. Enroute to New York with Blanche Calloway, we were in a car crash that hospitalized me for a year. During that time, I was

Ruth Brown (Collection, Jan A. Shields)

in a hospital in Chester, Pennsylvania, just outside of Philadelphia—
Room 222. I can never forget my nurse, God bless her, a Mrs. Gross
who was just beautiful to me. So very pleasant! I spent Christmas,
New Year's, Easter, Thanksgiving and my twenty-first birthday there.

"Finally, I did get to New York—and on crutches. Atlantic had
not planned a session for me. They brought me in merely to sit and
see what goes on at a recording session—I had never been in a studio
before. That day, they were doing a special session with Eddie Condon's jazz combo—Bobby Hackett, Ernie Caceres, Big Sid Catlett,
maybe Barney Bigard. They were doing something, as I remember,
for the *Cavalcade of Music*. After a while, Ahmet Ertegun indicated
that they would like to try something with me, just to see what I
sounded like, what my voice texture was like on disk.

"Herb Abramson actually picked the song. When he asked me
about songs I was familiar with, he mentioned 'So Long.' It was one
of my favorites. Abramson and Ertegun knew it from a record by
Miss Cornshucks, a very popular black singer of the day. But I knew
it from a record by The Charioteers, which I had listened to every
morning on our local radio station in Portsmouth, Virginia, during
my years in junior high school.

"There was no arrangement. They just gave the piano part to Joe
Bushkin. He ran a few bars and they said, 'O.K., let's try it.' The musicians had been recording for quite a while, and I don't know that
they were so pleased to have to put up with me. But after I sang
the first eight bars, Big Sid said: 'Oh, hold it. Wait a minute. Let's go
back and do this right. The kid can sing.' And so my test record became my first release. It actually was supposed to remain in that group
of tunes for the *Cavalcade of America*. But when they listened to it,
they decided to pull it out and release it as a single. And that was the
first time the record public heard Ruth Brown.

"Herb Abramson not only picked 'So Long'; he was responsible for
the selection of all my hits. He had a vast knowledge of music and
musicians, their life-style and whole history. I loved him. He had a
knack of knowing just what was right for me. Like Jerry Wexler has
been with Aretha Franklin. Herb was that way for me. I missed him
a great deal when he went away. But he was a dentist and he was
called into the service during that Korean thing. While he was away,
some changes were made over which I had no control. I was very
close to Herb and Miriam at that time, visited his home, and he had
such a collection of records that he made me knowledgeable of many
of the artists of the earlier blues days—like Bessie Smith, Ma Rainey,

and others. My knowledge of them was richly enlarged because of what he had in books and periodicals. He really was my buddy at Atlantic.

.

"All of my childhood was spent singing spirituals—not gospel so much. I was born in Portsmouth, Virginia. My mother was a farm girl from North Carolina and I worked the farm every summer. My father, Leonard Weston, was a dockhand but also a choir director of the Emanuel African Methodist Episcopal Church, which is where most of my musical training took place. While my father was a Methodist, my mother's people were Baptists. Consequently, I was christened in the Methodist Church but my grandmother on my mother's side insisted that I be baptized their way. So I was also baptized in the creek at revival time.

"At my grandmother's insistence, I also spent seventeen days on the Mourner's Bench. I remember it well. It was in a lovely, rural, hillside Baptist church in Macon, North Carolina. That's where I got my first chance to testify, to work in the service of the Church. The Mourner's Bench is a bench where sinners sit in the rural churches in the South; they listen to preaching for days and nights until they feel the Holy Spirit enter their body. We would go to the church early in the day and take our lunches and dinners with us on the wagon. When there was a break, everybody would come out, the tables would be set under the trees and the food set out. After eating, you would go back into the church and remain there. You sat while the deacon and the elders did their singing and praying for you. You sat until you felt the Holy Spirit enter into you and you were ready to give your life to Christ; then you stood up.

"The first time we did, my brother and I just got tired of sitting. We had planned the night before exactly when we were going to get up. We had watched the elders and the deacon, how they danced, and we knew just what they were going to do. We had a dance routine and everything. We had practised. But, of course, my grandmother was too wise to let us get away with that. If I remember correctly, that was the best licking I ever got in my life. 'For hopping up and playing with God,' my grandmother said. 'You don't do that!' And so we had to go back to the Mourner's Bench again and start from scratch. This time I stayed there until I did feel something.

"My father was a fantastic singer, never professional, but he had a great baritone voice. Everything that I learned musically came from him. Not the correct way, because we never learned to read music and all that. But singing around the house and singing with his group in the church. When I was ten or eleven, he started taking me around to neighboring churches to hear an all-male glee club he sang with called the Hiram Simmons Glee Club.

"I don't believe that Mr. Simmons ever made a name in the music world. But his name was law in churches wherever gospel music was done in the tidewater area. He wrote hymns and spirituals—beautiful choral music—that were just unreal. As a child, I remember that my father taught me, 'There Is a Hill Far, Far Away.' When I sang it, I was so small that my father used to put me on the piano. I am sure that somewhere there is a book crowded with fantastic music written by Mr. Hiram Simmons—that no one has seen or heard. It was music that I grew up on. If anyone is ever in the small town of Portsmouth, Virginia, or Norfolk, Virginia, and you go back to the people who came along in the late thirties and early forties, Hiram Simmons's name would come up in bright lights. He wrote anthems for male groups— one hundred untrained voices, one of which was my father's. I regret that at that time, there was no such thing as a tape recorder. I would love to have something in my father's voice, some music of Hiram Simmons. My father was tremendous and Mr. Simmons was great.

"I was with the Youth Choir at a time when the minister was the Rev. Charles E. Stewart. I was always positioned directly behind his chair. Each time he would turn and say, 'Well, I know little Weston is there.' That's what they called me since my father was big Weston— and he did have a great, big baritone. I had a pretty high soprano voice. Later, I became a contralto. [Chuckling] I am almost basso now with this Las Vegas throat.

•

"I sang with the Lucky Millinder Band before I worked at the Crystal Caverns. Without my father's knowledge, I began working local clubs at night, USO shows and the like. Like on Thursday nights, I was supposedly going to choir practice. But I was really singing in a little club called the TWA [Tidewater Athletic] in Newport News, Virginia. Many servicemen frequented the club and they used to have talent shows out at Langley Field Air Force Base. That's how I became involved in USO shows under the direction of a gentleman named Lavoisier La Mar, who had come from the New York 'Y' to work with the youth in Portsmouth. From USO shows, I started picking up little jobs at local clubs. My first job in Norfolk, Virginia, was at Percy Simon's Big Track, located on Church Street.

"Jimmy what's-his-name, who owned the TWA, knew a club

owner in Petersburg, Virginia, whose name was Moe Barney. Proprietor of Barney's Theatre, he had a small club upstairs that held about a hundred fifty people. It was in the black neighborhood and catered mostly to black clientele. But most of the good jazz musicians came by. That's how I met Piccolo Nelson, Richard Morgan, and Little John, who played bass. They had a small group called The Silhouettes and I started to work with them. Moe Barney took a liking to me and recommended me to a friend who had a club in Detroit, Michigan. The Frolic Show Bar was owned by Bennie and Hymie Gassman, who booked me when Moe Barney phoned them.

"While I was singing at the Frolic Show Bar, Lucky Millinder came into Detroit to play the Paradise Theatre. Stan Kenton was on the same bill. One night, a guitarist who was working with the Kenton Band came into the club and went back and told Lucky Millinder about me. When he brought Millinder into the Frolic Show Bar, Lucky hired me. That guitarist, incidentally, was Chico Alvarez, who is now an officer of the Musicians Union here in Las Vegas. It's just unreal!

"A few nights ago, he came into Circus Circus where I'm appearing regularly while I'm rehearsing as one of the leads in the black *Guys & Dolls*, [which opened in Vegas on February 14, 1977]. Chico came in to collect dues from some of the musicians. He said: 'I'm Chico Alvarez' and I said: 'I'm Ruth Brown.' I thought for a moment. 'Chico Alvarez! Now, wait a minute! You can't be the same Chico Alvarez that was with Stan Kenton years ago!' He said: 'Yes, I am!' I said: "Well, the name may be a little different now: Brown instead of Weston. But I'm the same vocalist you brought Lucky Millinder to hear in Detroit.'

•

"I left Detroit with Lucky's band. Traveled with him for about a month without ever getting to sing. Just running up hotel bills and such. At that time, he had two singers: Bull Moose Jackson and Ernestine Allen. We finally got to Washington, D.C. Never forget it. It was the Fourth of July, 1948. They played a place called Turner's Arena, which was *the* spot for dancing then. That was the first night I had an opportunity to sing, and I sang the Lonnie Johnson hit, 'Tomorrow Night,' and Dinah Washington's song, 'Evil Gal Blues.' When I finished my two songs, Billy Mitchell, who played tenor and Al Gray, who has been with Count Basie for years, asked me whether I would go to the refreshment stand and bring some Cokes back for the fellows in the band—which I did. I didn't see anything wrong in that. But as I was coming back, Lucky Millinder looked down from the bandstand and saw me coming through with this tray of sodas—and he just went off on me. He came to the side and said: 'I hired you as a vocalist, not as a waitress. And on second thought, I don't think that you can sing anyway. You're fired!'

"I thought he was joking—I really thought he was joking. And so I got on the bus with the band and they went around to the Howard Theatre in the black section of Washington, D.C. There was a bar near the theater called Cecilia Stage Door where all the musicians gathered. After the bus parked, we were told that it would be leaving in an hour-and-a-half. I went in as usual with the rest of the band to eat. When it was time to leave and I headed for the bus, Lucky Millinder was standing in the doorway. He said: 'I said you're fired!' And he told the band valet to take my bags off the bus. I said to him: 'What about my pay?' He said: 'You owe me for room rent and food. What pay?'

"I think I must have had about four dollars if I had a penny. I stood there in disbelief. I could not believe that he was just going to leave me there like that. I was pretty close to home—about two hundred miles. But my Dad had said, and how could I forget those words: 'Once you leave, don't call back here for anything.'

"The bus eventually did pull off and leave me standing there. I'd never been in Washington before. But after the bus left, a young man named Tommy Mosely came out of Cecilia Stage Door. He had won the Horace Heidt Amateur Contest and was traveling around with him. I had met Mosely while I was in high school in Newport News, Virginia. He walked up to me and asked: 'Aren't you Ruth Brown and didn't I meet you in the TWA Club in Newport News?' I shook my head and when he asked what had happened, I broke down in tears.

"After he heard my story, he said: 'There's a lady here who's a very beautiful person. Maybe she'll help you.' He took me to Blanche Calloway at the Crystal Caverns and asked her to hear me sing. That night I sang, 'It Could Happen to You,' which I had learned from a Bing Crosby record. Miss Calloway said: 'You're good. But my show is loaded. I'll let you work long enough to earn your fare back home.' I got thirty-five dollars a week, and she took me to a house where she was rooming and introduced me to the landlady who gave me a room for seven or eight dollars a week. That's where I was working when Willis Conover came in with Duke Ellington. And that's where it all really started.

"Miss Calloway offered to represent me. She was the one who phoned Mr. Schiffman at the Apollo Theatre in New York. His first question when she asked him to book me was whether I had made any records. He took Miss Calloway's word that I was going to record for Atlantic—and booked me into the Apollo. I was supposed to go on with a fantastic singer, a singer that I was in awe of, Billie Holiday. Two days before I was supposed to open, a telegram came saying that because of Miss Holiday's wishes, he had to change my booking and would put me on the following week with Dizzy Gillespie.

"We waited the extra week and started for New York—and then the accident occurred. We didn't do the Apollo that time. But I went from the hospital into the Atlantic session that gave me 'So Long.' After that, hit records for five or six years. In that period, I was never out of the Top Ten in R & B.

"I guess my first number one song—on the charts, that is—was 'Teardrops from My Eyes,' about a year after 'So Long.' It was written by my good friend Rudy Toombs, a man who was full of life, effervescent and happy. He showed that in his songs—all bouncy and jolly. The things he was doing were different rhythmically from what I was into. I was more of a pop torch singer. I preferred the ballads. But since Ahmet Ertegun and Herb Abramson seemed a step ahead of what was going to be the accepted sound, I went along with them and picked up on tunes that Rudy wrote for me.

"We worked together on 'Teardrops' for at least a week. At that time, working on one tune for a week was quite a long time. Usually, they would bring a song in and we would work, maybe a couple of hours, and they'd say, 'Let's go into the studio tomorrow.' That's the way it was done. And it was different then because when you went into the recording studio, all the musicians were there and you did the whole and total recording. You made a mistake—stop the tape, go back and do the whole thing over. Which is much different from the way they do it now. Like the last recording I did, I didn't recognize it when I heard it. When I sang, there was only a rhythm section behind me. The other instruments were put on at another time, and then they worked the whole thing over with an engineer.

"I don't know whether 'Teardrops' was one of my best ventures, because actually I wasn't a rhythm singer. A lot of musicians used to say that I had an ear even if I didn't read music. I also had a sense of timing that was very natural because of my church singing. When 'Teardrops' was played back after I recorded it, it just scared everybody. It was just phenomenal. It seemed to start a whole trend of things because a number of singers covered it afterwards. Ella Fitzgerald did it and Louis Jordan cut it with his Tympany Five, and there were others I can't recall. It had a long run on the charts.

"From that tune on, Rudy Toombs was sort of assigned to me. And we had a series of hits together. That was the beginning of the change in my style. And it was with 'Teardrops' that I started to get some big theater engagements. When I played the Earle Theatre in Philadelphia, Frankie Laine, who was then the biggest of the baritones, was at the top of the bill. He was known as *Mr. Rhythm.* 'Teardrops' got such a response from the audience, with the handclapping and the dancing in the aisles, that one day when he introduced me, he said: 'I think I'll call her Miss Rhythm.' And that's how I got the title.

"In that period, I started doing one-nighters, like from New York through the Litchman Theatre chain to Washington, Baltimore, Richmond, and a small theater called the Booker T. in Norfolk, Virginia, which was like home to me. Then we expanded and did one-night dance dates into the Carolinas, north and south, down to Georgia, Alabama, Tennessee. Sometimes we did as many as sixty-five to seventy one-nighters without a day off. It was exhausting, since you spent the day riding in a bus or behind the wheel of a car. But at night, it made up for that because we went into towns where we had to get in early enough to find places to live in the homes of people. There were no hotels or motels for us. And then we would end up having some very personal friends at the dance that night, friends who would prepare food and bring it to us at the dance. You really got to know people on a one-to-one basis. I have a lot of people who have remained my friends through the years from those one-nighter tours. You don't see much of that anymore. Everything is done on such a big scale. Coliseums and auditoriums that hold ten thousand people and more. A lot of small towns just don't get a chance to see artists in person. If I had the chance, I would love to repeat that experience. I don't know that I could put up with that amount of action. I'm not as young as I was then. But for what it did for me inward, I would love to go back and play some of the small county halls and the Elks homes, the school auditoriums where most of the dances were held, and the tobacco warehouses. Mostly the tobacco warehouses, with the cotton in one corner and the tobacco pushed back. Our stage was usually the back of a tobacco truck, with bricks under the wheels to keep it from rolling. Big difference now!

•

" '5-10-15 Hours' was another big one for me—No. 1, I think, in 1952—and it was another of Rudy Toombs's tunes. Unfortunately, he died a very early and a very hard death. I've never seen it reported the way it happened. He was hit in the head by someone who was trying to rob him. I don't think he was dead when they found him but he was too far gone to live. Very sad. Very talented man. He could sit down at the piano and produce a new song within a matter of hours. He was a forerunner of many of the R & B writers—the Singletons, McCoys, and I remember seeing him sit down at the piano with Bobby Darin before Bobby started to really produce songs like 'Splish, Splash.' Bobby wrote a song for me many years later, probably in 1958, called 'This Little Girl's Gone Rockin'.'

" 'Daddy Daddy' was another Rudy Toombs number (singing 'Daddy, Daddy, Daddy, love me long . . .') I haven't thought about that song in a long time, but it comes back like yes, yes, yes. It should have been bigger than it was. But the record that followed, 'Mama, He Treats Your Daughter Mean' was a monster—the biggest record I ever had—I mean for air-play and the exposure I got. That really made the name of Ruth Brown light up. It gave me the chance really to tour this entire country. Even now, more than twenty-four years later, whenever my name is mentioned, people say without fail, 'Mama, He Treats Your Daughter Mean.' I don't know what it was about that record. The rhythm pattern was similar to what everybody was doing, except that maybe it was a visual thing. Whenever I did the song in a club, I worked with a lighted tambourine—it had fluorescent paintings on it. They always knew I was going to sing 'Mama' when I lifted the tambourine over my head—it was a signal. Once when I went south with Billy Eckstine, George Shearing and Basie—I think it was Charleston, South Carolina, I had to repeat 'Mama' eight times in a row before I was able to leave the stage. There were times I sang it to keep down riots—Kansas City, I did it when Jackie Wilson didn't show and sang it time after time to hold the audience down. In Nashville, Tennessee, the microphone system went out, and I sang it without mikes. But people knew what I was doing and they joined in and sang it. That quelled a riot—they were going to fight had it not been for 'Mama.' When kids I'm working with in *Guys & Dolls* at the Aladdin Theatre here in Vegas bring their parents to meet me—and their parents are my generation—they always ask in amazement, 'Are you the Ruth Brown that sang "Mama, He Treats Your Daughter Mean"?' Then they tell their kids: 'Ruth was the Aretha Franklin of our time.' No matter where I perform, how classy or not, I can't get offstage without doing 'Mama.' It was written by Herb Lance and Johnny Wallace. Johnny's brother Dakota Wallace was a prize-fighter, and Herb is a disk jockey in Atlanta. Yeah, Major Herb Lance, that's him!

"You know when I opened here at Circus Circus, people kept calling the management and saying: 'She can't be *the* Ruth Brown who sang "Mama." Who is this that's pretending to be Ruth Brown?' And so they took down the sign that just read RUTH BROWN and put up another sign: 'THE REAL RUTH BROWN SINGS BLUES.' I guess I've been left out of a lot of those books on the fifties. I sure have felt left out, like I don't exist. But at Circus Circus, I keep getting calls for all those songs I recorded in the fifties.

"Like 'Oh, What A Dream,' which is my favorite, my very favorite. It was written by Chuck Willis who passed. He was very soft-spoken, unassuming, a humble man, but emotionally bubbling over with talent. He expressed that in his songs: he sang his life. We were very good friends. He was running over some material at Atlantic one day, and I asked him when he was going to write a song for me. He thought I was kidding. But when I convinced him I was serious, he said: 'I just happen to have something that might be for you. I haven't finished it.' He had it on one of those long, yellow ledger pads—just the words— and it was in an unfinished form. He just hummed and sang it. When he put it together, he made a demo. I recorded it and it was an instant hit. It was covered by Patti Page and others. That was the period when we began getting covered and clobbered, around '54. La Vern Baker and myself. Yes, they did what you might call a job on us. There was nothing we could do because an arrangement can be identical. Our problem was that they got played by the big stations who wouldn't play us. We wouldn't get exposure on the top TV shows. Up to today, I've never done one. But along with 'Mama,' 'Oh What A Dream' remains one of my most requested numbers.

"Before 'Dream' I had 'Wild, Wild Young Men.' [Chuckling] The next line was, 'Got to have a good time. . . .' The tempo of my record was up so high, it was so fast, that bandleaders used to say it's impossible for anybody to sing a lyric and be understandable at that tempo. But I was able to do it. I believe that was written by Ahmet Ertegun himself, who was the epitome of determination, And very knowledgeable—I had no idea of how knowledgeable he was. Good song.

"The 'Young Men' didn't do so well. But 'Mambo Baby' after 'Oh

What A Dream' went right to the top. That was by Charlie Singleton and Rosemarie McCoy, who produced a lot of big numbers.

•

"After 1955, things began to slide. For a long while I was the only female on the Atlantic label. I started with Ivory Joe Hunter, Joe Morris and Laurie Tate. But after '55 or so, Atlantic started to stretch out. Their roster began to expand. And there was like a toss-up for material. After that, my material didn't seem to be as good as it had been. But who can say what happened. I was never a gut-blues singer. After '55, I was not making the charts the way I had, even though I continued recording for Atlantic until 1960.

"Oh, I had 'Jack O' Diamonds,' which was written by Lloyd Price about the time that he started sliding—I guess, around 1959. It got a good bit of air-play. And I had 'I Don't Know,' which was written by Brook Benton. Something happened there. A whole batch of records came out with a defect. They had to be called in and that sort of slowed sales. But it was because of that record that Brook and I went out together, touring the country.

"Of course, I had a son born in '57 and I guess I started doing less and less of the road thing and one-nighters. I had two sons and a marriage that dissolved. Until then, my sons had been like backstage babies, living in a drawer, somebody holding them in the wings while I performed, in and out of train stations, no roots. I decided that I had to slow down and try to bring up a family. I stayed around New York City where there wasn't that much work for the type of singer that I was. I eventually remarried and moved to Suffolk County with my police-officer husband. Made an attempt to become a suburban housewife [chortling and laughing at length]. I thought I would stay as close as possible until my children were out of high school and into college. I worked in day-care, pre-school programs, with jazz workshops in the colleges around upstate New York.

"In September of '75 when my friend Redd Foxx came through and did a show at Westbury Fair, he invited me out to California. I came out for two weeks and went into a show he was doing called *Selma*. I was doing the part of Mahalia Jackson. I haven't been East since. And now I'm doing General Cartwright in *Guys & Dolls*. I haven't even had a chance to get back to LA since we opened here—six-night schedule. I've got an apartment to close up and a son that's going into U.S.C. in September [1977]. My older boy is in Washington, D.C., at Howard University, finishing this year. But Washington was where it all started for me—at the Crystal Caverns."

groove 16   **JERRY WEXLER**

Jerry Wexler, who refers to himself as a "reformed stickball player," joined Atlantic Records in June 1953. He claims he was brought in "on blind faith" by Ahmet Ertegun and that he "faked it for a while." He spent his youth in the Washington Heights section of Manhattan, playing stickball on Bennett Avenue, frequenting the area's pool-rooms, and swimming in the nearby Hudson River with its soggy bottom—I know because I swam in it, too, just at the point where the Manhattan tower of the George Washington Bridge rises today. Jerry managed to escape the more seamy phases of street life because he was an avid reader and, in 1935, became an equally avid jazz fan. There-after, he spent his nights and early mornings at Nick's Dixieland em-porium in Greenwich Village. After his discharge from the army in '46, he secured a degree in journalism from Kansas State University. It got him a short-lived thirty-five-dollar-a-week job at BMI. From 1948 to 1951, he worked as a *Billboard* reporter. He took a walk when, at the height of the McCarthy Red Scare, he was asked to com-pile a dossier on Pete Seeger and The Weavers. A year and a half of work as publicist and assistant to the general manager of the MGM publishing companies—a position I held a few years before him—led to his association with Atlantic Records.

Jerry Wexler
(Photo by Arnold Shaw)

"Yeah, it's true that I once changed the bass line of a record by dancing in the studio. What differentiates R & B from jazz and pop is a strong bass line—that's what we always looked for in recording R & B. Well, we were doing a date down in Memphis at the Stax Studios and the MGs [Memphis Group] were delivering a light after-beat. I went into the studio from the control room and did the Jerk for them. That's the dance that was the big favorite of the kids at the time. It turned the rhythm around, forcing them to play a heavy after-beat and one that was slightly advanced. You can hear that pushed afterbeat on a lot of records that Booker T. [piano], Duck Dunn [bass], Al Jackson [drums], and Steve Cropper [guitar] made after that. It was a great session, and we got several big hits for Wilson Pickett out of it. In addition to his imperishable record of 'Midnight Hour,' there were 'Don't Fight It,' 'I'm Not Tired,' and 'It's a Man's Way.'

"I've sung, too, on some Atlantic Records—*shouted* would be a more accurate description. When we were recording Joe Turner's great come-back hit, 'Shake, Rattle, and Roll,' we decided in the middle of the session that we needed a group to act as a responsorial voice. So Ahmet, I, and Jesse Stone, who wrote the song, became Joe Turner's backup group. I can never forget the look on Big Joe's face when the three of us came loping out of the control room and began shouting responses to him. The record was a smash despite us.

"What I am trying to say is that we did what we dug. We were fans of the music we recorded, fans who had the rare privilege of making records that we liked and enjoyed. And the weird thing is that we made money—lots of money—out of doing our thing. We built a pretty big company, an eighty million dollar giant, without the help of banks or any outsiders. And we did it because each of us, Ahmet, Nesuhi Ertegun, and I—later Tom Dowd and Arif Mardin—oversaw every phase of what we were producing. Each of us picked the material, the musicians, the arrangers, the artists—and the studio when we couldn't or didn't want to use our own at 1841 Broadway. We weren't segmented, as at the big companies, where different departments with different philosophies and tastes make a mishmash product. We picked the pictures used on albums, selected the liner note writers, and approved the album covers. What came out was a very personal thing, a part of us.

"Of course, we consulted. And each of us respected the other guy's ideas, right or wrong, if he felt strongly enough about something. Like one day, a song plugger named Bert Berns came into my office to play some demos. I felt that there was something unusual about him. A paunchy, nervous cat with a shock of unruly black hair, he hardly looked like the creative and musically educated man that he was. He had a formal background at the Juilliard School of Music. Well, he became my protégé. But the first record we made with him in the studio, Phil Spector and I produced with two cats long since forgotten. It was 'Twist and Shout'—he was a co-writer, under the pseudonym of Bert Russell, with Phil Medley. Spector and I ruined the fuckin' record. Bert was sitting there, and we wouldn't let him open his mouth. He was, like, a beginner, and Spector and I were the big shots. Then Bert went out and cut the number with the Isley Brothers on Wand, and it was a smash.

"That was before I signed Bert to us in 1963. He began by working with The Drifters when Leiber and Stoller decided to start their own Red Bird label. On one of his important sessions, Bert produced 'Under the Boardwalk,' a hit for the group in '64. The following year when Bert wanted to go out on his own, we formed Bang Records, named after *B*ert, *A*hmet, *N*esuhi, and *G*erald, meaning me. We also backed his publishing company WEB 4, named after *W*exler, *E*rtegun, and *B*erns. The business suffered a great loss when a heart attack knocked him over on December 27, 1967.

"Of course, The Drifters were the greatest group ever, not only of our groups, but of all R & B groups. You see, The Clovers wanted to be a pop group. Buddy Bailey, the lead singer, had no funk in him at all. Ahmet forced them to sing gospel and blues changes by writing all their early numbers. But when you hear them sing 'Skylark' or 'Blue Velvet,' that's where their hearts were really at. When Buddy Bailey went into the army and Charley White took over, they began sounding funky because White had funk.

"The Coasters were the California raunch of Leiber and Stoller. Billy Guy, the main lead singer of their comedy songs, really was an expression of Jerry Leiber, who grew up in a black neighborhood in Baltimore and had a feeling for funk talk and funk thinking. If you ever listened to a demo by Jerry, that's Billy Guy—the sound and the comedy. But L & S were very creative in the studio, really masterful producers.

"As for the Drifters, they were Clyde McPhatter. They sang exquisite, pure gospel harmony. Clyde would give them their parts in the studio. His voice was naturally high and not a *falsetto*, and he could stir the others with the intensity of his feeling. The group was the all-time great R & B group.

"In the early Drifters days, the route to the acceptance of R & B was quite circuitous. You'd get a record on WWRL in New York and hope that the program director of WMCA or one of the other power-house stations might hear it (and like it) as he drove home late at night. And if it went onto his playlist, maybe some adults would hear it. But you never expected the kids to pick up on a Solomon Burke or Wilson Pickett. Maybe in the South, for, despite the Ku Klux Klan and bloodshed, the Southern white is a helluva lot closer to the Negro psyche and black soul than your liberal white Northerner.

"Solomon Burke was a preacher, pagan preacher, but a preacher. As a teen-ager, he was known as 'The Wonder Boy Preacher' and had his own church in Philadelphia—Solomon's Temple, it was called. Onstage, he wore a crown and robes. When he entered, the black audience stood up just as a congregation would in a church. And he had that church sound on his records, even when he was singing of secular matters. To a white, middle-class teen-ager who had never experienced the jubilation of a Sanctified Church service, Burke was too far out. But he could connect with a white Baptist Southerner. Black or white, they talked in tongues.

"You find talent in unexpected ways sometimes. Like, I got to know of Burke through a very knowledgeable reporter on *Billboard*, who became a Burke fan when he was recording for Apollo. Paul Ackerman kept bugging me about signing him and actually was re-sponsible for my recording 'Just Out of Reach,' Solomon's first side. Paul heard the song—it was a C & W tune—on a 4 Star record.

"Once I even found a song in the mails. You know it's standard procedure in the business not to accept manuscripts that come through the mail from unknown sources. That's to avoid irresponsible law-suits by amateurs. But in my early days at Atlantic, back in '53 and '54, I looked at everything. This song came in 'over the transom' from a little, old lady named Blanche Carter, who lived somewhere in Georgia. It was called 'Devil or Angel,' and I cut it with The Clovers. In over twenty years, it was the only song that I received unsolicited that I not only cut, but that became a hit. The Clovers were covered by one of the pop rock kids. I must admit to a little bit of pique that people don't remember that we had the original record, just as we did on 'Blue Velvet,' by the Clovers, which was copied by Bobby Vinton.

"Talking about strange happenings—one of the strangest sessions Ahmet and I ever produced was a Ray Charles date in Atlanta, Georgia. Ray was on the road and phoned Ahmet, and we flew down to cut 'I Got A Woman.' The only studio we could find then was at radio Station WGST. Unfortunately, the control room was also the station's newsroom. We had to stop every hour so that they could broadcast the news. With any artist except Ray Charles, it might have been a disaster. With Ray, there was no problem because by the time he went into a studio, he had been performing the number for days or weeks in live appearances. All we had to do was balance the instruments and get a good take from an engineering point of view. He and the band had done their homework.

"Sometimes you can be creative as a producer and enhance the artist's performance; like when Ivory Joe Hunter cut 'Since I Met You, Baby' for us. He had a blues called 'Sant Fe Blues'—he used to pronounce it 'Sant Fee Blues.' In the right hand, he had a little lick, a bell-sounding kind of walk-down. Now, 'Since I Met You, Baby' was a regular twelve-bar blues, but we made him put in that effect, that little lick, as a response. [Wexler sings "Since I Met You, Baby" and then motions with his right hand, as if he were playing a lick on the piano.] And that's what made the record and the song.

"La Vern Baker was probably the first artist I cut when I went to work for Atlantic. Can't remember the tune, but I can tell a story on myself. Lincoln Chase, who is a tremendous writer, wrote 'Jim Dandy,' and La Vern recorded it. I thought it was a piece of crap—pop vaudeville without any soul. I talked Ahmet into holding that record in the can for a year before he put it out. I was all wrong. It was a fantastic record. Not as big as 'I Cried A Tear,' La Vern's biggest hit, but it was one of her solid sellers.

"Many fans think of R & B in terms of the 1950s, but it was really hot in the forties. World War I started bluesmen moving up North, and number II made it a mass migration. There were three paths. Up from Mississippi and Alabama, the center of America, they headed into Chicago—and we had the strong delta influence on Chess Records. From Oklahoma, Texas, and the Southwest, they went to California—that was T-Bone Walker and the honky-tonk, jazz combo influence. And from the Carolinas, Florida, and Georgia, they came up to New York, giving us a mix of gospel and pop.

"Shuffle was the crucial rhythm—Texas Shuffle, Kansas City Shuffle. Back in 1934–5, you had the Harlem Hamfats on Decca. They were essentially a New Orleans transplant and the antecedents of Louis Jordan with their shuffle style. If you want to go back that far, into the thirties, you'd have to say that R & B started with the major record companies. Milt Gabler of Decca has not received the credit he should, not only for Louis Jordan, but for the growth of black music and

R & B. The majors had a lock on black music until World War II. Then they walked away from it, and gave the small independents like Atlantic the opening to move in. But the majors established the parameters of R & B—good-time bands playing shuffle on nonblues changes. Incidentally, I don't go for this soul classification, which *Billboard* has been using since the sixties. I think that's an elegant variant for which there is no need. Rhythm and blues is good enough—it's earned its stripes.

•

"Yeah, I've been called 'honky' and I've had blacks ask what gives me the right to produce music by black artists. But that's only a recent happening. It's only since the growth of black pride, 'Black Is Beautiful,' and black nationalism. But we were producing black music long before blacks had the good feelings about themselves that they now rightly have and long before whites accepted that music. Today, R & B is one of the strongest trends in popular music, and maybe Atlantic played its part in building an audience for it.

"I've been recording black music now for over twenty-three years. I don't go to the office any longer—I'm now a consultant to Atlantic, operating on a freelance basis. And they pay me well for the freedom they've given me to devote my time to producing. I have wanted to get out of administration and the executive bit for a while. Until I did, I was involved in staffing the company, hiring executives, running the office, and all the day-to-day administrative bullshit. Now I'm free to do what I love most: find artists and record them.

"It's interesting and troubling to look back. When Atlantic started in the forties, we were one of numerous independents spread out clear across the map of the country. And now they've all disappeared—some died, some dropped out, some were bought out, some just went broke —all except us and the Bihari brothers [Modern/RPM/Kent] on the West Coast—and now Saul Bihari is gone. Those were great years for black music—the forties and the fifties."

groove 17   **LESTER SILL**

Lester Sill, today president of Screen Gems-Columbia, the music division of Columbia Pictures Industries, started in the record business in 1945. From that year until 1951, he worked for the Bihari brothers of Los Angeles, first as a salesman of Modern Records, RPM, and their other labels, and then as a producer of artists like Hadda Brooks,

B. B. King, and others. We spoke in his present office on Sunset Boulevard.

•

"In 1952, I went into the record distributing business myself, and my shipping clerks were Jerry Leiber and Mike Stoller. I met them in a curious way. When I was still selling for Modern, I was on Fairfax Avenue one day and went into Norty's Record Shop. The moment I was inside the door, one of the stock clerks came running over to me. He had a song he had written that he wanted me to hear. You couldn't be in the record business without having songs pitched at you constantly. I probably would have brushed the kid, but he fascinated me. You see, his eyes didn't match—one was brown and one was blue. He grabbed me by the lapels. I couldn't take my eyes off his eyes and he managed to *shlep* me into a back room where I auditioned his song. *A cappella*, of course.

"But it had something. And I invited him to come down that night to a Modern recording session where the Biharis were cutting a group called the Robins. The song I had auditioned was called 'Back in the Good Old Days.' It was recorded that night. Head arrangement, of course. The stock boy who grabbed me was Jerry Leiber. He was going to Fairfax High School at the time, or to LA City College. That night, at the session, I met his collaborator, Mike Stoller. When I left Modern and went into the distributing business, Jerry and Mike came to work for me as shipping clerks, Jerry more regularly than Mike.

"During this period, Jerry got a call one day from Johnny Otis. He was doing a session with Willie Mae Thornton, and he needed a song. Jerry had just finished his lunch, and the brown paper bag was still lying on the counter. Jerry phoned Mike, and they discussed ideas for a song. Then, he wrote the lyric on the lunch bag. I gave him some time off so that he could run over to Radio Recorders and see Otis. The song was 'Hound Dog.' They were about seventeen then, and they had already had 'Kansas City,' which they wrote when they were fifteen or sixteen.

"At that time, we were living on Sycamore Street, near Melrose in Los Angeles. Jerry would come over to the house quite often. He loved my wife's cooking, and one day he asked if he could move in with us. We had three kids at the time, but somehow we made room for Jerry. He became part of the family and wore my clothes—that is, whatever happened to fit him. One morning he came running into the living room looking for a pair of shorts. He had just taken a

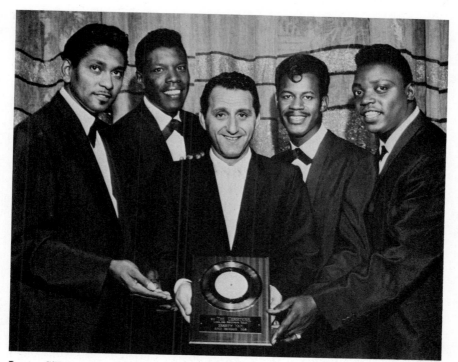

Lester Sill and The Coasters (Collection, Lester Sill)

shower and had a sheet wrapped around his body. After my wife told him where to find his shorts, he turned around and walked toward the bedroom unaware that the sheet did not cover him completely and that his entire backside was showing as he walked away. When we started laughing and he realized what was going on, it was one of the few times I have ever seen Jerry Leiber embarrassed. When we moved from Los Angeles to the Valley, he got his own apartment.

"During the time Jerry was living with us, I gave up the distributing business. Jerry, Mike, Mike's father Abe, Jack Levy, and myself started a publishing company called Quintet Music, Inc. We cut simple demos with Mike playing piano and Jerry singing; or we would go and bring in some small groups to cut a demo. We had the same problem then that most publishers have today: getting the A & R man to listen and record your song. Jerry, Mike, and I then decided we would produce our own masters and attempt to lease them to some record company. The first master we produced was 'Black Denim Trousers and Motorcycle Boots,' sung by a group we found called The Cheers. On the same date we also produced The Cheers doing 'Bazoom.' Both of these were giant hits. I imagine this made us the first independent producers. If not the first, certainly the first successful independent producers.

"Arnold, I believe that you were general professional manager at Hill & Range when the Aberbachs got in touch with us about 'Black Denim Trousers.' They wanted to buy all or a piece of the copyright. Mike and Jerry went to see them in New York and made a deal. We sold only the foreign rights. The Aberbachs paid a hefty sum: fifteen thousand dollars. And this was just for foreign—nothing from American records, performances, or sheet music. We used the money to buy out Mike's father. The Aberbachs more than made their advance back. The song was a smash all over Europe and even in France, where, of all people, Edith Piaf recorded it.

•

"Not long after that, Mike and Jerry decided they wanted to move to New York. They asked me to move with them. They had no family; I did. My family and I decided to remain in Los Angeles. Jack Levy and I then sold our interest, allowing the boys to pay us out over a period of a few years. When they moved, we had offices on Melrose and La Brea, which I took over. Shortly after that, I met Lee Hazelwood through a mutual friend. Lee and I founded a publishing and production company called Gregmark Music. Our first act was Duane Eddy. We produced fifteen straight chart records with Duane. About two years later, Phil Spector stopped up to see me at 1610 Argyle, where we had just moved.

"Yes, he left mother Bertha Spector, after whom he later named his publishing company. [Mother Bertha Music] Actually, he had left her some time before he began living with us. I used to take him down to Phoenix with us, where we recorded Duane Eddy. He absorbed everything we did like a sponge. I met Phil right after he made 'To Know Him Is to Love Him' with the trio he called The Teddy Bears. I saw him at work in the studio then, and he amazed me with what he was doing with vocal harmonies. He looked like he was twelve years old. It was Bunny Robein's studio on Fairfax.

"He was interested in the sound that we were getting on the Duane Eddy records. That was the work of Lee Hazelwood, who was an ex-disc jockey. He was incredible when it came to sound. He taught me about echo and reverb and every aspect of sound. He was one of the greatest in this area. After we recorded Duane Eddy in Phoenix, we brought the records back here and overdubbed them at Gold Star. The records were released through Jamie, a Philadelphia outfit owned by Harry Finfer and Harry Lipsius, who used George Goldner as their distributor. It was a mixed bag of pickles. If I knew what I know now, I could have made a fortune. But all we got was a small percentage. Lee and I then split up. But we still jointly own Gregmark Music.

"Phil and I then started Philles Records, a title derived from the first syllables of our names. It was an instant success. Harry Finfer and Harold Lipsius also distributed the Philles label for us. Things began to get a little hectic, and the pressure became too much for me. So I sold out my share of Philles to Spector. Phil, as you know, is now practically a household word in the music business. Lee is now living in Sweden, producing TV shows, while Duane is working for MCA Music.

"About 1954 or 1955, Leiber, Stoller, and I started a label called Spark Records. We went on to have several hits. Then we went to a convention in Chicago where I played some new releases for our distributors. Ahmet Ertegun of Atlantic heard them. He came running down the hall, sort of out of the woodwork, and flew Jerry Leiber and me into New York. Atlantic bought Spark Records, which included The Coasters. I was glad to sell it since we weren't being paid by many distributors. We were a small company, and we were getting killed. We thought there would be a problem about having The Coasters on Atlantic, that they would get lost in the huge roster of R & B artists. So Atlantic set up a subsidiary label. This was the beginning of Atco— The Coasters and Bobby Darin.

"After Lee and I parted company, I took a semihiatus for about a year and a half, after which I was approached by Don Kirshner, then president of Screen Gems-Columbia Music, Inc., and now the Rock Concert impresario, to come into the organization as a consultant. It was to be a temporary situation because I didn't want to get locked into a big company at that time. The end result is that after twelve years, I am still with Screen Gems-Columbia Music, the music division of Columbia Pictures Industries."

groove 18   **OSCAR COHEN**

A rotund man with a pleasant mien that melts into an easy smile, Oscar Cohen is today president of Associated Booking Corporation, the country's biggest black talent booking agency. He started as an office boy when Joe Glaser founded the company in Chicago. For decades, wherever Glaser went Cohen was sure to follow, and when Joe died of a massive stroke, Cohen became head of ABC. His office is high up in an aluminum-and-glass building on Fifty-seventh Street and Park Avenue in Manhattan. A large room, it is sparingly but elegantly furnished. Cohen's massive desk is completely clean, not even a memo pad on its highly polished surface.

•

"In '46 or '47, we got into the rhythm and blues thing. I went to Washington, D.C., and signed up a group called the Dominoes. They had a smash hit recording, 'Sixty-Minute Man.' In the group was Jackie Wilson, Clyde McPhatter, and Billy Ward, who led and coached them. When I heard the record, it was not yet a hit. But I told Glaser I'd like to go down to Washington—I was a kid then and didn't even know that the Howard was a black theater—and try to sign them up. Backstage, I met Billy Ward and Rose Marks, who were running and handling them. Ward was a tough taskmaster, and, in fact, the boys lined up for an inspection before they went out onstage. Discipline was a very important factor to him. Glaser had to get into the act before we finally signed them. But we had them from almost the beginning to the end, including the period when Billy fired the whole group for some infraction of his rules.

"Rose Marks was the manager of the group then. Although her name appeared on 'Sixty-Minute Man' and other songs, I think Ward really wrote them and just put her name on.

"When I was Joe Glaser's office boy, Associated Booking had jazz artists mainly. We switched over to R & B when the record business changed. Jazz became dull. But it was also a matter of our expanding. Let's see: In the mid-forties there was the Gale Agency and Universal Attractions (which was Ben Bart). Harold Oxley was a West Coast office with a few attractions. Pete Cameron worked for him, and he had Joe Liggins, who scored with 'The Honey Dripper.' In those days, Billie Holiday was going strong. We handled people like jazz xylophonist Red Norvo—singer Mildred Bailey, his wife, was dying in those days; she died around 1950. Glaser had about twelve of the *Esquire* Jazz Award winners.

"We got involved with La Vern Baker at the end of her hit-record run. We handled Lonnie Johnson, Memphis Slim, Big Joe Turner here and there, and Big Bill Broonzy throughout his entire career. Big Bill was one of Joe's [Glaser] big favorites.

"Coming up a bit in time, I found The Chords singing in the street. I didn't talk to Jerry Wexler and Ahmet Ertegun for fifteen years over that. Joe Sully and I were walking on Broadway, and there were five kids singing on a street corner. It was on Fifty-fifth Street when the MONY building hadn't yet been erected. I took the kids across the street to Fifty-sixth Street between Broadway and Eighth Avenue, where Ahmet Ertegun and Miriam Abramson (who later divorced Herb) were in an office. We walked up the four flights. In fact, that night Jerry Wexler came in. He had just quit The Big Three publishing company to join Atlantic Records. It was his very first night.

"I was going to Australia with Louis Armstrong for Joe Glaser. So I said to Ahmet and Miriam—Herb Abramson wasn't there, he was in the army—'Look, I want this song ("Sh-Boom") and you can have the other side, "Little Maiden." ' And we shook hands, and I went to Australia. By the time I got back, The Crew Cuts had covered 'Sh-Boom' on Mercury and it was the biggest thing in the country. And I collected exactly nothing."

At that point in the conversation, Oscar Cohen picked up his phone and asked Joe Sully, who was still working at ABC, to come into his office. Sully quickly verified that the two of them had found The Chords on Broadway and added, "I couldn't understand frankly what he was so excited about, but he persisted."

"I persisted," Cohen said, "because I heard a hit record. Not that I knew. But I had a feeling. And the Atlantic guys didn't know either. Otherwise, why would they have put it out on their unknown Cat label when they could have had it on Atlantic?

•

"In the beginning of R & B, the jazz musician was more sophisticated. R & B was viewed in the same way as rock 'n' roll when it came in. The older agents and musicians and acts looked and said, 'It'll just last a year or two. It's a fad.' But it was part of Americana. Years ago, to make a record happen, you had to have a white disk jockey. Today, you're better off with a black one, because then it goes pop. Today, Gladys Knight & The Pips are pop. In those days, Gladys would have been rhythm and blues, and the white guys would shy away until it hit a chart.

"Thinking back—when I was fifteen years old, Joe Glaser used to pick me up at my house in the Bronx. My friends never saw a Cadillac. We were poor kids. He picked me up every Sunday morning to go see the first show at the Apollo Theatre in Harlem. We did this every Sunday for twenty years. Saturdays, I used to go into the office until five o'clock. We didn't work too late on Saturday. And on Fridays, we used to catch the first show at the Apollo. We did that for twenty years. We caught the Apollo bill twice a week: the first show on Friday and the first show on Sunday. Regardless of who was playing there, we went. And we saw every show for twenty years.

"I remember meeting Bobby Schiffman—he's Frank Schiffman's son—when he was in knickers. I was in knickers, too. Joe Glaser brought me to the theater. Bobby, being the son of the theater's owner, came with his dad. And Bobby has been more successful than his dad, who retired a few years ago, settled in Miami, and died recently. For some years, there have been rumors that the State of New York planned to buy The Apollo, apparently to erect a state building in its place. But there would be a new Apollo in it. It is a New York landmark after all. I hear periodically from Bobby about new talent, also because I still keep the baseball boxes that Joe Glaser held all his life.

"Each year I make at least one special trip to Chicago. It's special because I make it on the anniversary of Joe's death. I try to visit with him at least once a year. I go to the mausoleum and sit and talk with him, bring him up to date on what's happened in the past year to the business he built. . . ."

*I don't want no Northern yellow, no
Northern black or brown* (repeat)
*Southern men will stick by you when
the Northern men can't be found.*
—IDA COX

The Street-Corner Groups and the NY "Indies"

ON a sunny afternoon in the 1950s, if you walked west on Manhattan's 115th Street, you might encounter a dozen vocal groups raising their voices on the corners between Fifth and Eighth avenues. The Willows, the Channels, and the Wanderers are some of the groups that actually emerged from this one street.

"The Five Crowns were supposedly the first 115th Street group," writes Philip Groia in *They All Sang on the Corner*, a fact-crammed account of NY's R & B groups of the 1950s. "The Harptones were the best and later the Drifters (Crowns) were the most successful." Many of the groups, like the Channels on Whirlin' Disc, never attained more than local fame. But The Willows, who started on Lenox Avenue between 114th and 115th streets, hit the charts with "Church Bells May Ring," on Melba, and are treasured by collectors for their first disk, "My Dear Dearest Darling," a street song, on Allen Records.

One hundred and forty-second Street was also the birthplace of many groups: the Vocaleers between Lenox and Seventh avenues, and the Crystals on Amsterdam and St. Nicholas. Then there was the St. Nicholas Housing Project at 131st Street where the Dovers were born between St. Nicholas and Seventh avenues; and the Cadillacs, on the corners of Seventh and Eighth avenues.

In the Washington Heights area, between 145th and 170th, from Edgecombe Avenue overlooking High Bridge Park west to Broadway—an area known as Sugar Hill among blacks—the Velvets, Savoys, and the all-important Teen-agers came into existence.

On Park Avenue and 119th Street, under the elevated tracks of the New York Central Railroad, the Schoolboys, the Jesters, and the Desires found a "man-made echo chamber." Under the Manhattan Bridge at Monroe Street, on NY's Lower East Side, the Harps practiced daily.

Across the East River, in the Bedford-Stuyvesant section of Brooklyn, the Chips rehearsed at Clifton Place and Grand Avenue while the Mellowlarks began singing together after playing basketball in a school yard.

During the 1950s, New York streets in underprivileged and segregated areas like Harlem, Spanish Harlem, and Bedford-Stuyvesant echoed with the songs of young vocal groups. Public housing projects and high schools were the spawning grounds of hundreds of such groups, while street corners, subways, park benches, school yards, and community centers served as free rehearsal halls.

When a singer left a group, he could look for a new association just by wandering the streets and "sitting in," to use a jazz expression, with other groups. Visiting was also a common occurrence. The Willows, a 115th Street group, told Groia, "Sugar Hill was like one small neighborhood. Groups were, in a way, parts of families. Everybody would go and see the other guy perform. Even though it was six or eight miles, we would walk up there and walk back, just singing all the way. . . . If we did take the subway, it would be for the echo chamber."

In short, group singing was a way of life among young blacks and browns in the '50s. And it was a way of life because it was a way out of the ghetto, poverty, and segregation; a way to secure recognition from one's peers; a way of moving into and being accepted by the white world; a way of making money other than slaving at some servile job, playing ball, putting on boxing gloves, or stealing.

"Man, we were stone hooligans," bass Chuck Barksdale of the Dells noted in a *Hit Parader* article. "We broke out car windows and threw pumpkins at buses. We were bad, man. But we were always singing." And singing provided an exciting, escapist camaraderie for under-privileged black youngsters, whether or not it led to a record contract.

Money was not that easily come by, even for those who got to make records. These were young men and women with little under-standing of business, and they dealt with older and shrewder entre-preneurs. They needed a personal manager, who might take 10 percent or as much as 50 percent. A booking agency like Moe Gale's or The Shaw Management would take 10 to 15 percent. A choreographer, who became necessary for club dates, would refuse a flat fee and demand a percentage—leading choreographers like Cole & Atkins would not accept less than 5 percent. Then there was an arranger who was required, not only for record sessions, but for the songs used in a forty-five-minute stage or club appearance. When they deducted all the percentages, groups frequently ended up with little more than 50 percent of their earnings—and that had to be divided four or five ways.

Roland Martinez, originally a singer with The Vocaleers (a group that did not make it), and later a bass guitarist and manager, has told how Apollo Records paid each of the Vocaleers $5.00 for two re-corded sides and $11.00 for another. When the quintet seemed dis-satisfied, Apollo owner Bess Berman explained that the company had picked up the bill for recording (studio, engineer, musicians, arrange-ment) and that they were getting "something for nothing—exposure."

•

Partly as a result of the street-corner groups, the R & B develop-ment peaked in New York (where they originated), and in nearby Newark and Philadelphia between 1950 and 1955. Atlantic Records set the pace, Savoy ran a distant second, and then, in terms of best-sellers, came OKeh, Jubilee, Deluxe, Regal, and Herald Records. But the years saw a mushrooming of numerous independents, men in tiny, one-room offices in the West Forties and in the Tin Pan Alley buildings at 1619, 1650, and 1674 Broadway—all hustling and wheeling and dealing to grab the brass ring of a hit on the record merry-go-round.

During the war years, the major record companies (clustered in NYC) prepared the ground for the emergence of the "indies" in two ways: they released records by urban bluesmen, thus nurturing an audience for R & B; and they did not sign any new black talent, except for dance bands, from which some of the solo singers arose. A glance at the 1943 *Billboard* yearbook reveals OKeh releases by such old-timers as Big Bill Broonzy, Memphis Minnie, and Roosevelt Sykes, the Honey Dripper. Brunswick dug into its vaults for disks by Sonny Boy Williamson, Speckled Red, and boogie pioneer Pine Top Smith. Still riding high with The Ink Spots, Mills Brothers, and Delta Rhythm Boys, Decca Records went back to Blind Boy Fuller and Peetie Wheatstraw, but was enterprising enough to move ahead with the Harlem Hamfats and Louis Jordan. Bluebird offered the longest list of holdovers—Jazz Gillum, St. Louis Jimmy, Lonnie Johnson, Tampa Red, Tommy McClennan, Big Maceo Merriweather, Washboard Sam, and Big Boy Crudup whose all-important disk of "Mean Old Frisco" was released that year. With Savoy Records operating mostly in the gospel field, Beacon Records (owned by Joe Davis and boasting the Five Red Caps and Savannah Churchill) was the only "indie" that showed in the *Billboard* list of "Records Released" that year.

It was not until the market for R & B began growing swiftly that the major companies came crowding back into a field that they had ceded to the independents. Columbia activated OKeh in 1951, placing a Philadelphia promotion man, Danny Kessler, at the helm. His recollection of those days constitutes Groove 20. RCA established Groove Records in 1954, a tale told by Bob Rolontz in Groove 22. Early in 1958, Decca revived Brunswick to house superstar Jackie Wilson, who built a flourishing label on his own.

From the early '40s, there were, of course, "indies" operating in the Big Apple—Keynote, Varsity, Beacon, Apollo, DeLuxe, Manor, Savoy, and National, among others. The postwar years saw the establishment of Atlantic in 1948, and in the following year Jubilee came into existence, an offshoot of Cosnat Distributing Corporation. Founded by former bandleader Jerry Blaine, Jubilee and its sister label, Josie, accounted for the Orioles, regarded as the first *pure* R & B group, and later, in the '50s, for the Four Tunes and the Cadillacs. The latter were managed by an enterprising woman songwriter, Esther Navarro, who cut demos with them which she peddled to Blaine.

The Cadillacs heralded the era of car-named groups like the Belvederes, El Dorados, Fiestas, Fleetwoods, Impalas, and Imperials, and of car-oriented songs, which reached their peak in Chuck Berry's "Maybellene." Coached by Cholly Atkins, whose former dance partner Charles "Honi" Coles had become manager of the Apollo Theatre, the Cadillacs became exemplars of precision choreography. They were noted also for the elegance of their "threads"—in square lingo, clothes. As for recordings, the Cadillacs are remembered for "Gloria," a romantic ballad in which they employed melodious, close-mouthed, blow harmony à la the Moonglows, and for the jump tune about a Speedy Gonzalez-type lover, "Speedoo," which became known as "Speedo" because of lead singer Earl Carroll's pronunciation. Eventually, there were two groups known as the Cadillacs, the result of a controversy between Esther Navarro and Jerry Blaine about ownership of the name.

•

In 1949, the year that Chess was started in Chicago and Peacock in Houston, portly Larry Newton launched Derby Records in the West Forties and made the charts briefly with two minor artists, Freddie Mitchell and Jimmy Preston. Among the Derby groups who did not make it on wax, but who attained some recognition, was the Majors, not to be confused with the Majors of Philadelphia, who had "A Wonderful Dream" on Imperial Records. The Brooklyn Majors, led by Bernard "Jimmy" Beckum, began as spiritual singers, serving St. Marks Holiness Church as the resident gospel group. Then known as the Brooklyn Crusaders, they sang regularly on Joe Bostic's "Gospel Show" on Station WLIB. They also toured with such gospel groups as the Mighty Clouds of Joy, Zion Kings of Harmony, Staple Singers, and the Caravans. Between times, they sang barbershop and R & B, occasionally functioning under other names. An appearance on the Arthur Godfrey "Talent Scouts" led to their recording for Derby Records as the Majors. Although they had releases on the label into '52 and '53, cutting songs by lead singer Beckum and sounding like the Ravens, they were unable to crack the charts or make it for Larry Newton, who went on to become head of ABC Records and now runs Ray Charles' own recording company.

•

Derby Records led indirectly to the formation of Glory Records. Phil Rose, founder of the latter and now a Broadway theatrical producer—*Raisin in the Sun, Purlie*, etc.—paid his dues as a record producer with Newton. After a stint as A & R head of Coral Records' R & B division, he established the Glory label and accounted for the development of two important groups and several well-remembered songs.

Shortly after I took over the creative reins of Edward B. Marks Music in 1955, I became interested in "Soldier Boy," a song recorded by the gospel-inflected Four Fellows on Glory. This was in the period when major artists and record companies were ripping off disks on R & B labels. I liked the song and thought it had great potential as the Four Fellows disk climbed R & B charts. It eventually reached

No. 4 over a fifteen-week run, but the song did not make it, even though the war in Korea gave it timeliness. Some time during those weeks, I approached Phil Rose and arranged for E. B. Marks to take over promotion. Although I was able to persuade half a dozen artists, black as well as white, to record the song—Ella Fitzgerald, Mel Williams, Sunny Gale, and Eydie Gorme, among others—no one came up with the blockbuster version that spelled *hit*. But the many recordings did help to establish the song as a standard that was cut several years later by Presley.

My activity on "Soldier Boy" led Phil Rose to offer "The Banana Boat Song" to me when he cut it with the Tarriers, a group that included Alan Arkin, later the film actor. We worked out an arrangement whereby the copyright was owned and jointly promoted by Bryden Music, Phil's publishing firm, and E. B. Marks. The Tarriers disk was on R & B charts for only one week when Harry Belafonte rushed into the RCA Victor studios and cut "Day-O," his own version of the Caribbean folk song. Harry hit the charts only two weeks after the Tarriers, but came up with one of the big pop hits of 1957. It led to a lawsuit by Phil Rose against RCA Victor, which was pressing Phil's record by the Tarriers. Rose's claim that the major was stalling on Tarriers pressings to gain headway for their Belafonte disk was not sustained by the courts.

In 1950 Rainbow Records released the first recording of a group called the Clovers, the Washington, D.C., quartet that quickly moved to Atlantic Records, where they blossomed as one of the leading groups of the '50s. Eddie Heller, founder of Rainbow, introduced a number of other groups that became chartmakers on other labels. Atlantic became the beneficiary also of the talent of the Five Crowns, who recorded on Rainbow for a number of years from 1952, but came into their own when they changed their name to the Drifters. Still a third group that started on Rainbow, but came up with hits three years later on another label was Lee Andrews & The Hearts. In the early days, Eddie Heller always had a sly smile playing around his eyes and mouth, but by the time he was working for RCA Victor in the '60s, he had a receding hairline and looked like a man suffering from ulcers. He died at a rather early age.

In 1952, Al Silver started Herald Records in a Greenwich Village basement and, without any recording background, developed an almost uncanny ability to find hit talent and make hit records. (See Groove

21.) About the same time, the Weiss brothers, Sam and Hy, began operating Old Town Records out of the cloak room in the defunct Triboro Theatre on 125th Street and Third Avenue. They took the name Old Town from a stationery company for which lean, balding, and bespectacled Sam Weiss worked full-time while pudgy Hy Weiss— he of the perpetually worried look—ran the label and found talent like the Solitaires, the Fiestas, and Robert & Johnny. (See Groove 23.)

Lanky, wall-eyed Sol Rabinowitz, now a vice-president of CBS International, established Baton Records in 1953 and succeeded in producing enough best-sellers to remain in business until 1960. (See Groove 24.)

All of these Grooves, apart from the first-hand information they provide about given record labels, afford the reader an in-depth view of the problems, perplexities, and tensions of the small R & B entre- preneur in the 1950s.

•

In 1956, on one of his WINS programs, Alan Freed announced the death of Billy Brown, a young Harlem singer. Brown, just twenty, was the baritone of a street-corner group called the Harptones, who had played their very first gig at a show presented by Freed at the Jersey City Armory in the winter of 1954. Residents of Harlem will tell you that Brown's funeral procession, as it wended its way through 118th Street, drew a crowd worthy of a city notable.

The Harptones were Harlem favorites—a local underground group, in a sense, since none of their many recordings ever made the charts. Organized in 1953 by Raoul Cita, who acted as arranger, songwriter, and manager, they spent their time listening to records by the Five Keys of Newport News on Aladdin, the Larks on Apollo, and the Swallows of Baltimore on King. Naturally, they tried to imitate sounds they heard and liked on these records. When they were not rehearsing in the school yard of Wadley Junior High on 115th Street and Seventh Avenue, or participating in "battles of the groups" at community centers, they worked at polishing Cita's arrangements in a basement on 119th Street.

After a time, they began gigging around New Jersey, Brooklyn, and Manhattan, occasionally earning as much as $100 (distributed among six) for two nights of singing. They were then known as The Harps. Finally, they entered a Wednesday amateur night at the Apollo and won with a rendition of "A Sunday Kind of Love," a blues ballad introduced in 1946 by Claude Thornhill with a vocal by Fran Warren. An MGM Records man who happened to be in the audience invited them to audition for the company. A few days later, as they were doing some last-minute rehearsing in the hallway of the building that housed MGM Records, they were heard by Leo Rogers, an amiable fringe promoter. Rogers was able to talk them out of doing the audition. Instead, he persuaded them to sign with Bruce Records, a small company whose partners included Rogers; Morty Craft, an eagle-eyed arranger; and moneyman Monte Bruce.

At that time, the Harps became the Harptones in order to avoid being confused with a similarly-named group from Newport News, Virginia. "A Sunday Kind of Love," their first Bruce release, never made best-seller lists largely because of the company's limited distribution. But the disk was a hit in Harlem and established the song so firmly among R & B groups that it has been periodically recorded and revived. The Harptones' follow-up song, "My Memories of You," written by Cita, enjoyed the same limited acceptance, but it also became an underground R & B classic. Bruce Records released five other records by the group without being able to develop an audience beyond the Eastern Seaboard.

The Harptones continued to make records to the end of the decade, moving from label to small label—Dave Miller's Essex in Philadelphia, Paradise of the Weiss brothers, George Goldner's Rama and Gee labels, Andrea, Raven, and Tip Top. They always seemed on the edge of breaking into the national arena, as when Morty Craft, then head of Warwick Records, cut "No Greater Miracle" in 1959 and Bruce Morrow of Station WINS made it a "Pick of the Week." But constant changes in personnel and weak management ultimately militated against the quintet's breakthrough.

As for Bruce Records, it suffered the dismal fate of most "indies." Local popularity of the Harptones led to its acquiring and recording a number of other groups and soloists. But none approached even the limited sales of the Raoul Cita quintet. Cita, who served as arranger and organist for the label, likewise continued to operate on the fringe of a big breakout without ever being able to make it. Willie Winfield, lead tenor of the Harptones through the years, is today a funeral director, but he puts together a Harptones group to sing on special occasions.

•

Of all the New York independent record makers, the most interesting and, perhaps, most successful (apart from the Atlantic, Savoy, and Jubilee recordmen) was the late George Goldner, who built several flourishing labels with street-corner groups. Goldner spent time prowling the streets of Harlem and the black ghettos and Spanish sections of Brooklyn, in a search of amateur Puerto Rican and Negro groups. But several of his most successful groups were brought to him. Rama Records, established in 1953, began as a Latin label. And it was a Latin talent agent, Cliff Martinez, who interested him in a street-corner group he heard at an Apollo Theatre amateur night. They called themselves the Crows in an obvious attempt to capitalize on the success of the Ravens, the Flamingos, and the high-flying Orioles.

The first record of the Crows, "Seven Lonely Days," hardly fore-shadowed the fate of their second release, "Gee." Written by Viola Watkins and two members of the group, lead Daniel "Sonny" Norton and baritone William Davis, "Gee" leaped onto the charts in the spring of 1954 and eventually zoomed to the No. 5 spot. It never attained the national acceptance of "Sh-Boom," a summer '54 hit, largely because it was not covered by a strong white group like the Crew Cuts, whose version of "Sh-Boom" stirred interest in the black original by the Chords. Yet "Gee" was one of the first young songs to cross over from R & B into pop. It made it possible for the short-lived group to ride around Harlem in a big '55 Chrysler with the words "The Crows" blazoned on the sides.

To commemorate the Crows' one big hit, Goldner named the label he established in '56 Gee Records. It was on this label that Goldner achieved a crossover that went to No. 1 on R & B charts and No. 5 on pop. "Why Do Fools Fall in Love?" by Frankie Lymon & the Teenagers finished not only as one of the year's top R & B disks, but Top Pop as well. This was in the year that Elvis exploded on the record scene with "Heartbreak Hotel," "Don't Be Cruel," and "Hound Dog," and pop music went through the greatest upheaval since the advent of Swing.

In 1955 George Goldner signed a group called the Valentines to his Rama label. They were important, not only because they produced a minor hit in "Lily Maebelle," their first Rama release, but because their lead singer, Richard Barrett, became a Goldner producer and a valuable source of new talent. Founded in 1952 as the Dreamers, the Valentines sang on Harlem street corners until they were joined by Barrett, who came from Philadelphia and worked as a landscape gardener on Sugar Hill. Their first association was with Old Town Records, for whom they recorded a local best-seller in "Tonight, Kathleen." When they moved to Rama, the baritone spot was taken over by David Clowney, who had just left a Detroit group called the

Pearls and who became a star in 1959 as Dave "Baby" Cortez with "The Happy Organ." In person, the Valentines were less effective as singers than as dancers, especially in a number titled "The Woo-Woo Train." Although they were successful enough to appear in shows presented by Alan Freed and Tommy Smalls, they were out of business by 1958.

To launch his Gee label in 1956, Goldner selected a group called The Cleftones, who came together while attending Jamaica High School in Queens, New York, where they were known as The Silvertones. Gee 1000 was a song titled "You, Baby, You," written by the group's second tenor. Their second release, "Little Girl of Mine," written by lead singer Herbert Cox and Goldner, made the national charts and gave them a Top Ten platter in R & B. Five years elapsed before they scored again with "Heart and Soul." But the group continued to perform weekends into the '70s while its members spent the rest of the week working at such substantial jobs as computer analyst and IBM technician.

•

It was another group, however, that gave stature to the Gee label and became one of the most talked-about young groups of 1956 and the era. Richard Barrett of the Valentines, who either coached and/or produced Little Anthony & the Imperials, the Isley Brothers, the Flamingos, Arlene Smith of the Chantels, and such minor groups as the Dubs and the Millionaires, brought the Teenagers to Goldner.

Teenagers was an apt title for the superstar group since the five singers, a mixed bag of blacks and Puerto Ricans, were all in their early teens—all except Frankie Lymon, who was only twelve when baritone Joe Negroni formed the quintet from youngsters attending schools on Sugar Hill. Singing on the streets of Harlem, they attracted the interest of Richard Barrett one day when they happened to break out in song under his window on West 161st Street.

Barrett auditioned them at Edward W. Stitt Junior High on West 164th Street, where they sang a song written by young Frankie Lymon in his fifth-grade class. It was based on a poem Frankie had read entitled "Why Do Fools Fall in Love?" Barrett was so impressed that, after coaching the group so that Frankie copied his phrasing, he arranged an audition with Goldner. Legend has it that lead singer Herman Santiago had a cold that day so that Frankie Lymon, the youngest of the young, sang lead. Legend has it, too, that Barrett had to threaten not to rehearse the Millionaires, a group for which Goldner had high hopes, in order to force the Gee owner to record the Teen-agers. And the story goes that the Teenagers cut their smash recording of "Why Do Fools Fall in Love?" during the Millionaires' dinner break.

The rest is history, tragic history in its way. From life in Washington Heights' "railroad flats"—tenement apartments that had no windows except for the living room in the front and the kitchen in the rear—members of the group were suddenly catapulted into a world of affluence, earning $1000 a week. Suddenly, they were on the Ed Sullivan Show, playing the Brooklyn Paramount, touring with Bill Haley as part of Alan Freed's "Biggest Rock 'n' Roll Show of 1956," appearing in Freed's film *Rock, Rock, Rock*, and making a record-breaking stand at the London Palladium. Young Lymon, then only fifteen years old, was smoking long Cuban cigars, and the group behaved so riotously that they were ejected from hotels in Manchester and London.

By then, they had had several chart songs. "I Want You to Be My Girl" and "The ABC's of Love," both written by Richard Barrett and George Goldner, commanded a sizable audience but not the 2 million buyers of "Why Do Fools Fall in Love," on which Goldner also appeared as a co-writer. (Although Goldner did write a number of songs by himself—"Maybe" for the Chantels among them—the "cut-in" was quite common on small independent labels, affording the owner a reduced royalty and, if he sold his label or it went bankrupt, a continuing royalty on the song for the life of the copyright. Alan Freed's name appeared on songs to which his contribution may have been promotional rather than creative, and B. B. King, among other bluesmen, constantly found himself with company co-writers during his tenure on Modern Records. To which, company co-writers always respond: the songs needed fixing.)

After they returned from their triumphal tour of Great Britain, The Teenagers split up and Lymon made abortive attempts to make it on his own. The teen-age tenor voice with the built-in cry somehow lacked the appeal it had when it soared over the voices of Herman Santiago, first tenor; Joe Negroni, baritone; Jimmy Merchant, second tenor; and Sherman Garnes, bass. Moreover, it was not easy to create or find another song that posed the incongruity of a teen-ager asking, with the wisdom of the ages, "Why do fools fall in love?" The song had a kind of natural innocence, despite its apparent cynicism, that made it a young hit—a youngster could identify when he suffered unrequited love.

Lymon's failure may have had something to do with his becoming a heroin addict and fading into the degrading existence of a Harlem junkie. "I'm Not a Juvenile Delinquent," sang the Teen-agers in the film *Rock, Rock, Rock*. But Frankie Lymon lacked the experience and the character not to become one. When he was found dead of an overdose in the bathroom of his grandmother's apartment in February 1968, he was just twenty-six years old. The world was too much with him, and much too soon. And there were some adults who would have to assume responsibility for the poverty in which Frankie lived for several years prior to his death, as well as the cause of that death itself.

"They were always careful to keep the kid happy," Lymon told music journalist Gene Lees some years after his fall from fame. "They bought him what he wanted. What did I want? What would any kid of thirteen want? Certainly I didn't want to think about bank accounts and taxes and getting the proper receipts and that sort of thing. They would pat me on the head and tell me how great I was. I was merely a pawn in a big chess game."

•

Of the many groups that appeared on Goldner's several labels (End and Gone as well as Rama and Gee), three others were standouts. The Chantels, a Bronx quintet, are less memorable for their achievement than for their influence. Composed of five fine black women, they were forerunners of such vibrant female groups as the Crystals, the Ronettes, and even the Supremes. Formed while they were singing in the choir of St. Anthony of Padua in the Bronx, they adapted the name of a rival basketball team, St. Francis de Chantelle, for themselves. Their accompaniment was simple—piano, bass, drums, and organ, seldom horns like many R & B groups mustered. But they achieved a sound that still impresses today. The source of their power was lead singer Arlene Smith, whom a *Rolling Stone* reviewer characterized in these hyperbolic terms: "Arlene sounds like 20 Arethas (and I dig Aretha), 80 Dionne Warwicks and 300 of anybody else you can name."

Signed by Richard Barrett, who heard them in a rehearsal studio at Fifty-third Street and Broadway—a studio that overlooked the marquee of the Broadway Theatre, where Sammy Davis, Jr., was starring in *Mr. Wonderful*—the Chantels ignited in 1958 on the End label with a tender, impassioned "Maybe," written by George Goldner. They hit again, though less impressively, with "Every Night." But devotees still prize no-chart records like "The Plea," "Whoever You Are," "If

You Try," and "I Love You So." Before the group broke up, they moved to Carlton Records, where they produced a substantial best-seller in "Look in My Eyes" in 1961.

The Flamingos, who started around Chicago, were longer lived, operating into the '70s, and had greater national impact than the Chantels. With their members coming from different areas—lead Nat Nelson and baritone Paul Wilson from Chicago, tenor Terry Johnson from Baltimore, bass Jacob Carey from Virginia—the group registered their first seller in "Golden Teardrops" on Chance Records in 1953. By the following year, they were recording for Parrot Records, where they covered Gene & Eunice's "Ko Ko Mo" and Eddy Arnold's "I Really Don't Want to Know," and sold records on "Dream of a Life-time." Their first national seller came in 1956 on Checker Records with "I'll Be Home," a disk on which they answered their preceding disk, "Please Come Back Home." "I'll Be Home" might have done better for them had not Pat Boone covered the title and made a Top 30 tune of it. Unfortunately, the Flamingos were unable to repeat in a two-year period, and by 1957 they were on Decca with a series of no-impact releases.

Their most fruitful period was 1959–60, during which they recorded for End Records and placed four disks on national R & B charts. The biggest was a remake of a Harry Warren ballad, introduced in 1934 by Dick Powell and Ruby Keeler in the film *Dames*. "I Only Have Eyes for You" made the rarified atmosphere of the Top Three in R & B. But they also had national best-sellers in "Nobody Loves Me Like You," an up-tempo tune by Sam Cooke, and "Mio Amore." The style of the group changed as Sollie McElroy's lead on "Golden Teardrops," gave way to Nate Nelson's lead on the End hits, modulating from theatrical thrust to a soulful tenderness.

As with most of the young groups and their young audiences, romance was the staple of the Flamingos. Parents were greatly concerned in those years because kids seemed to be rushing things and, instead of dating casually, became involved in "going steady." Regardless of whether the older generation felt that they were "Too Young," adolescent love seemed to be taking an early serious (read *sexual*) turn. Presley exploited the mood by asking his female followers, when he went into the armed services, to "wear my ring around your neck." The Flamingos captured the romantic yearnings of their followers in renditions that were warm and dreamy eyed. The feelings they evoked were a far cry from the man-woman emotions and problems that figured in earlier blues and rhythm-and-blues.

Unrequited love was as vexing to the day's teen-agers as was loneliness, a less frequent theme of young R & B. "You don't remember me," sang the Imperials, "but I remember you"—and "Tears on My Pillow" became an unforgettable memory of the 1950s. The nasal *falsetto* that brought female teen-agers to the verge of tears belonged to Anthony Gourdine. He was a Brooklyn lad who had gone to Boys' High School and had early found a berth with the Duponts, a group that played one of Alan Freed's bashes at the Brooklyn Paramount and was then quickly forgotten.

After the Duponts and graduation from Boys' High, Gourdine joined the Chesters, whose members included second tenor Ernie Wright and bass Clarence Collins. The trio was the nucleus of the Imperials, who became known as Little Anthony & the Imperials because that was what Alan Freed called them—and Gourdine really was the littlest of the group. Goldner heard another Frankie Lymon in Little Anthony, and Richard Barrett, who signed the group to End Records, coached Gourdine in the gimmicks that became the earmarks of his style: a staccato delivery emphasized by pregnant pauses.

"We cut 'Tears on My Pillow,'" Clarence Collins recalls, "at the old Bell Sound Studios on a four-track machine. It was sort of like an audition, with lots of groups waiting to use the studio. The engineer would come out and say, 'All right, you guys next.' One of the groups that was there that day was The Dubs, and they came out with 'Could This Be Magic.'

"We used five pieces. Buddy Lucas was the leader. He was on sax. He would say, 'Okay, it's in G,' and then the band would learn the tune. Fast. And we worked out our harmony in the studio."

Goldner was not wasting any time. Union regulations that permitted the recording of only four sides in three hours were meaningless. Something of the pressure under which the sides were cut and the spontaneity with which they were put together entered into the final product. The R & B disks of the late '50s had the tension and impetuosity of the young people for whom they were made. Also an amateurish sound that set them apart from the polished, well-arranged, well-rehearsed, and, to them, "manufactured" records to which their parents listened.

Little Anthony & the Imperials did not have many national chart songs. But "Tears on My Pillow" in 1958 (what lovely self-pity!) and "Shimmy, Shimmy, Ko-Ko-Bop" in 1961 (no content, but what a beat!) were potent enough to establish them as one of the standout groups of the day. And they lasted, scoring a No. 3 R & B best-seller on DCP Records in '65 and making regular appearances at the Sahara in Las Vegas into 1977. Their personnel has changed, but Little Anthony is still singing "Tears on My Pillow" and the memory of the Alan Freed years remains fresh in the minds of young parents, now with teen-agers of their own. Who of these parents can forget that fateful day in November 1959 when Alan Freed, dismissed by Station WABC for refusing to sign an affidavit that he had never received payola, announced during the playing of "Shimmy, Shimmy, Ko-Ko-Bop" that he was going off the air.

It was a fateful day, not only for Freed, but for R & B. By then the airwaves were full of young sounds, black as well as white. But the payola scandal temporarily had greater impact on black "indie" stations as well as black artists.

Some time between the end of the fifties and 1964, George Goldner apparently lost a huge sum of money. In '64, he entered into a partnership with Leiber and Stoller, who set up a recording company named Red Bird. Why it went out of business around '68 is something of a mystery since Red Bird took off with a flock of hits by the Shangri-Las, Dixie Cups, and other new groups. The following year, Goldner launched Firebird Records on his own, but he died on April 15, 1970, aged fifty-two, before he was able to get his new enterprise off the ground. "He was not entirely punctilious about royalty payments," Bill Millar, author of *The Drifters* has said. "But he cut some nice records, and he did more for integration than the Supreme Court."

•

Bobby Robinson was one of the first of a rare breed of black owners of record labels. And he very likely had more labels than George Goldner. Founded in 1953, Red Robin was, perhaps, the first. But there were also Enjoy and Everlast. The most successful were Fire and Fury, many of whose recordings were cut in New Orleans.

A Sugar Hill street-corner group may have launched Robinson as a record entrepreneur. The Vocaleers, who harmonized on 142nd Street between Amsterdam and Broadway, came to Bobby's attention at an Apollo amateur night. And he signed them to Red Robin even though they took second place. Philip Groia types their first release, "Be True," a "milestone in R & B group singing—Joe Duncan could be heard warbling the blues, almost pleading; Herman Duncan answered virtually every phrase in a *falsetto* voice; the timing was slow, the keys blues, and the mood forlorn and sad; a *true hallway sound!*" But it was a subsequent release, "Is It a Dream," that made R & B charts in 1953. Groia also claims that the Vocaleers rivalled Jackie Robinson and Willie Mays as Harlem folk heroes between 1952 and '54. But by 1954 the group was out of business, torn asunder by the dissension that plagued many groups—conflict about who was to sing lead, etc.

Nineteen fifty-nine was a good year for Bobby Robinson. Wilbert Harrison of Charlotte, North Carolina, came to him apparently through the good offices of Herman Lubinsky of Savoy Records, who would not have sent Harrison had he properly evaluated the North Carolina singer and a Leiber-Stoller song titled "K. C. Lovin'," originally recorded in 1952. Harrison had been working in Miami where he had won an amateur contest singing "Mule Train" and cut records for the Rockin' label. Gigs in Newark, New Jersey, led him to Savoy. Bobby changed the title of the Leiber-Stoller tune from "K. C. Lovin' " to "Kansas City" and cut it in March 1959. It went to No. 1 on national charts.

That year, Bobby Robinson found Buster Brown, who came from Criss, Georgia, and who had been working in clubs in Georgia and Florida before he settled in New York in the late '50s. When Bobby heard him sing the blues and play the harmonica at a Harlem club, he invited Brown to cut a demo. It led to his recording "Fannie Mae," a song that was on national charts for twenty-five long weeks and became a No. 1 R & B hit for Fire Records. (Brown died in 1976.)

The following year, Robinson came up with another No. 1 hit in "There's Something on Your Mind," a song written by tenor-sax honker Big Jay McNeely and a hit for the sax man on Swingin' Records. Bobby Marchan's '60 disk on Fire Records was even bigger. Marchan, who came from Youngstown, Ohio, began as a gospel singer and worked with several groups before he cut as a solo performer for Robinson. During 1958 he was part of The Clowns, a New Orleans singing group that worked with Huey "Piano" Smith, known for his Ace recording of "Rocking Pneumonia and the Boogie-Woogie Flu." Marchan sang with the group when they recorded Smith's follow-up hit, "Don't You Just Know It?" As a solo recording artist, he made the charts only once again, with "Shake Your Tambourine," in 1966, but by then he was recording for Cameo Records of Philadelphia.

In 1961 Bobby Robinson scored with the most interesting singer of his career, though not the most successful. Lee Dorsey, who came from Portland, Oregon, started life as a boxer. Fighting under the name of Kid Chocolate, he won so many bouts that he became a contender for the light heavyweight crown of the world. Returning

Gladys Knight and the Pips

from a four-year stint in the navy, he left Portland and began boxing around the country. A chance meeting at a New Orleans party with Allen Toussaint, a successful songwriter, led to his making contact with Robinson, who happened to be recording in the Crescent City at the time. Dorsey had written a song titled "Ya Ya," which Robinson cut with him on his Fury label. It went to No. 1 on best-selling R & B charts. Robinson tried a follow-up in "Do-Re-Mi." It sold, but not nearly as well as "Ya Ya." Dorsey did not return to the charts until three years later when he scored with "Ride Your Pony" on Amy Records.

It was in 1961 that Robinson introduced the most important group with which he was associated. Gladys Knight & the Pips are superstars of pop today. Gladys was still in primary school in Atlanta, Georgia, when she won first prize on "The Ted Mack Amateur Hour." Raised in a family that prized education, she had to continue her schooling, but was permitted to become soloist of the choir at Mount Moriah Baptist Church. She was also singing with a family group that included her older brother, Merald, and two cousins, William Guest and Edward Patten; they became known as the Pips when still another cousin, James Woods, whose nickname was Pip, took over the group's management.

In 1961 the group recorded Johnny Otis's ballad "Every Beat of My Heart" for an Atlanta label, Huntom Records. The disk stirred so much interest locally that a scout for Fury Records arranged for an Atlanta disk jockey to forward a copy to Bobby Robinson in New York. Robinson flew the group up to Manhattan and rerecorded the side exactly as they had cut it for Huntom Records. It resulted in a hit for Fury Records, but also required a lawsuit by Robinson to force Vee Jay, as distributor of the Huntom label, to recognize his ownership of the group. Gladys Knight & the Pips' follow-up disk on Fury was a much better seller than the controversial platter. "Letter Full of Tears," released in December '61, reached No. 3 in R & B. Five years elapsed before they had "I Heard It Through the Grapevine" on the Soul label, a Motown subsidiary; the disk sent the group into superstar orbit.

Bobby Robinson introduced at least one other artist who became a major figure in R & B. Saxist Curtis Ousley, better known as King Curtis, cut "Soul Twist" for Robinson's Enjoy label in February 1962. Although he cut many other chart-songs and became Atlantic Records' studio hot tenorman, "Soul Twist" was the King's signature. He was stabbed to death in 1971 when he asked a man loitering around a Harlem apartment house he owned to move on.

•

Of the artists on the reactivated OKeh label, the most colorful by far was Jalacy Hawkins of Cleveland, Ohio, better known as Screamin' Jay Hawkins—and he was a portent of things to come in black music. Born in 1929 and placed in an orphanage at an early age, he began playing the piano just about the time he started school. But like Lee Dorsey, Hawkins went into professional boxing, winning the Golden Gloves in 1947. In 1949 he whipped middleweight champ Billy McCan of Alaska. Again, it was a chance meeting that changed him from a prizefighter into a musician and showman. After a stint in the army and while he was performing in a small Atlantic City club, he met jazz guitarist Tiny Grimes. As a result, he joined the Grimes jazz combo, which played Fifty-second Street in its declining days. Legend has it that Hawkins acquired his cognomen while performing in Atlantic City. Either in jest or because she was drunk, a woman in the audience kept urging him to "scream the song." To humor her, Hawkins began screaming, an act that prompted him to start calling himself Screamin' Jay Hawkins.

If this sounds incongruous, it is not in terms of Hawkins's concept of showmanship. "To be effective," he has said, "you have to do the unexpected." As an example, he indicated that he might have "a huge kettle on stage, with colored lights and dry ice underneath to make it look like it was cooking." Long black hair of a woman—his wife—would hang over the side. "I'd drag her slowly out by the hair," he explained. "Nobody would know what was happening."

For many years, Hawkins was carried onstage in a coffin. The mirrored lid would open slowly and a gloved hand would crawl over the edge before he emerged. The National Casket Company was so concerned about the effect of his ghoulish entrance that morticians were requested not to lend, rent, or sell a coffin to Hawkins. During his performance, Hawkins would wear a swirling black cape like Dracula and wave a wand around which carved snakes swivelled up to a hollow-eyed skull mounted at the top. Beneath the grinning skull hung a bell that rang as he shook the staff.

The macabre style of his performance may have developed as a result of the recording that brought notoriety to Screamin' Jay in 1956. It was a song entitled "I Put a Spell on You." Hawkins was to have sung it as a ballad, but he and the boys "had a taste," a not-uncommon procedure at jazz and R & B dates. What hit the grooves was not a ballad, but something compounded of voodoo and sex that ended in an inchoate gurgle of passion. There was an ominous threat in Hawkins' cry of "I put a spell on you," and the most extreme expression of possessiveness ever heard on a record. At moments, Hawkins' laughter sounded maniacal and his catlike screeches, much like those of James Brown, suggested a man going out of his mind with unfulfilled yearning.

There were stations that banned the record. "They said it had cannibalistic sounds on it," Hawkins later said. OKeh Records attracted attention to the offbeat disk by running a trade-paper advertisement in which it promised to find a job for any disk jockey who got fired for spinning the record. Well, in the tense and embroiled atmosphere of Presley's shattering emergence on the record scene in 1956, a disk jockey did get fired. When the shocked platter-spinner wrote to OKeh, company executives thought it was a put-on. The plaintive letter was passed from OKeh exec to exec and finally turned over to the trade papers, where it may not have helped the dee jay get a job, but where it did add to the upheaval occasioned by the record.

The controversy made a career for Screamin' Jay. The record of "I Put a Spell on You" set the style. A combination of spiritualism and sex, his screamin' delivery, bizarre costuming, ghoulish expressions, and voodoo religious overtones anticipated Jimi Hendrix and James Brown. He was on the surrealistic borderline between R & B and soul.

•

The reactivated Brunswick label, owned by Decca, was built by Jackie Wilson of Detroit. In fact, Brunswick *was* Jackie Wilson. Like Lee Dorsey and Screamin' Jay Hawkins, Wilson began as a prizefighter—and he won the Golden Gloves at the age of sixteen. But he also grew up singing in the church. His feeling for gospel singing took him out of the ring and into the Falcons, a group that modulated into the Midnighters on King Records. He also worked with the Dominoes, from whom he learned what gospel-rooted Clyde McPhatter and director Billy Ward had to teach. Like Clyde and Solomon Burke and Sam Cooke, all R & B preachers, he was a master of *melisma*, the flowers and curlicues of gospel singing. In the space of one syllable, he could jump octaves and sing through a dozen notes. A towering figure in the history of American Pop who has influenced Tom Jones, among others, he was a transition figure in the history of R & B. He brought not only a big operatic voice to R & B, but a degree of involvement, of gospel intensity, and of unbuttoned emotionalism that eventually spelled the difference between R & B and soul. Let him tell his own story.

groove 19   **JACKIE WILSON**

He is slender, moves young, and looks younger. But he is in his forties and has a flock of kids from several marriages. He is an attractive man with a slightly Oriental cast of features that is given emphasis when he smiles. It is a quick, wide-mouthed, eyes-narrowed smile. He is affable, but not very verbal. Onstage, he dances as much as he sings—both tremendous expenditures of energy—and he comes offstage apour with sweat. He cannot wear an outfit more than once even though he works in leathers and buckskins that are less absorbent than cotton.

His dressing-room door remains open, and there is a constant flow of fans and artists. Minutes after we started talking on the first of several nights, someone poked his head in and said: "Tom Jones is coming to the next performance!" That announcement was repeated periodically by different people during the next hour, along with the information that the Temptations would also be there. Tom Jones was then appearing at Caesar's Palace across the Las Vegas Strip from the Flamingo. A large illuminated sign carried not only his name but a ten-foot figure of Jones in a typical, discus-throwing position. The Temptations were featured at the Las Vegas Hilton along with Bill Cosby.

On the Flamingo marquee, Jackie Wilson's name appeared in the bottom fourth. He was singing in the lounge, not the main showroom, along with Fats Domino, who performed in the early part of the evening while Wilson appeared at 2:00 A.M. and 4:00 A.M. Some evenings, he did three late shows.

After a while, Wilson turned to Johnny Roberts, who watches over him like a mother hen, and asked, "Temptations or Jones? Which do I introduce first?" Roberts, who looks like a middle-aged bookie, but who has the wisdom of years as a manager and booking agent, said quietly, "The Temptations."

•

"I was born and raised in Detroit. Ma did some singing. I never studied music. Didn't like instruments. But I sang in church—Mother Bradley's Church—spirituals and gospel. I liked that. Gave me good feelings. But I grew up listening to the Mills Brothers, Ink Spots, Louis Jordan, and Al Jolson. As soon as I could, I entered amateur contests at the Paradise Theatre. Won many, many times.

"Once Johnny Otis was there and heard me, around 1951. He got in touch with Syd Nathan, King Records. Syd sent Ralph Bass. He heard me. He heard Little Willie John. He heard The Dominoes. He passed me and Willie John, signed The Dominoes. But Billy Ward, who ran The Dominoes, took my name and number. I went to work at Lee's Sensation Club. Must have been seventeen.

"I organized a group we called the Falcons. Not the Falcons with Wilson Pickett; they came after I left Detroit. We had a spiritual group. Some of the cats later became the Midnighters with Hank Ballard. After a year, Billy Ward phoned me. Was sure he never remembered me, but there he was on the phone. So I became part of The Dominoes in 1953. Clyde McPhatter was lead singer. I also sang lead.

"I learned a lot from Clyde—that high-pitched choke he used and other things. I know they say Little Richard when they say Jackie Wilson. But he did not give me anything. I liked the Dixie Humming-birds and Ira Tucker, who could really scream. 'I Just Can't Help It' was one of his songs. I recorded it. Used Jimmy Jones, you know, the deep, deep bass voice of The Hummingbirds. I liked James Cleveland, a fine gospel singer, and recorded one of his songs, 'I Don't Need You Around.'

"But Clyde McPhatter was my man. Clyde and Billy Ward. Billy was not an easy man to work for. He played piano and organ, could arrange, and he was a fine director and coach. He knew what he wanted, and you had to give it to him. And he was a strict disciplinarian. You better believe it! You paid a fine if you stepped out of line. But he was a nice man. And I stayed with the Dominoes until 1956.

"Then I went solo into The Flame Bar. Al Green ran it—not the Al Green of National Records—and he had La Vern Baker and Johnnie Ray. Della Reese came later. He knew talent. Detroit was the Paradise Theatre, The Flame Bar, and Al Green. Berry Gordy came later. But he hung around the Flame and his sister worked in the club. I made some demos for Al and, he took them into New York. 'Reet Petite' was one, a song by Berry Gordy. That's how I got with Brunswick Records. I think I was the only new artist on the label for a long time.

"After Green died, Nat Tarnopol took over. He was about my age, maybe two or three years older. He worked as Green's assistant and ran Pearl Music and Merrimac Music, Green's music publishing companies.

" 'Reet Petite' was my first record. It never showed on R & B charts. It went pop and sold a quarter of a million. "To Be Loved" was my first R & B chart-song. I still do it in my act after sixteen years. It was by Berry Gordy, his sister Gwen, and Tyran Carlo. They wrote 'That's Why,' 'I'll Be Satisfied,' [both made the charts] and my first big, big number one hit, 'Lonely Teardrops.' That was 1958, the year I took an apartment in New York—in the same building as Sidney Poitier. My ma still lives in a house in Detroit.

"Berry Gordy was a hustler and very aggressive. I hear he was making masters in those days for several labels with Marv Johnson and with the Miracles, and I think his sister started a Detroit label called Anna Records. By 1960 he was in business for himself.

"My next number one R & B hit was 'You Better Know It' [1959], something I wrote with Norm Henry. And the other big ones were 'Doggin' Around' and 'A Woman, A Lover, A Friend,' both number ones in 1960. 'Doggin' Around' was also a Gold Record in the pop market.

"Nineteen sixty was the year we had a problem in New Orleans. At this theater, the girls were getting excited and jumping up on the stage. I didn't mind, but the police did. They started pushing the girls around—to get them off the stage. They were rough. And so I shoved a cop. The next you know, they arrested me for assaulting an officer. Nat Tarnopol called Johnny Roberts in New York. I guess he was with the Milt Shaw Agency then—that was Billy Shaw's son. Johnny came flying down and took care of things. We've been together ever since. When he tells me something, I know that's it. I don't have to start figuring what it is.

"We also had some trouble in 1961. That was when some crazy chick took a shot at me and nearly put me away for good. It took some time, some good doctors, and a lot of help from the Man Upstairs before I got out of the hospital and back to where I could perform.

"But do you know? In both those years, 1960–61, my records were hitting the charts as if nothing happened. I had five best-sellers in '60 and six in '61. And in '63 I had 'Baby Workout,' number one, and in '67 '(Your Love Keeps Lifting Me) Higher and Higher,' another number one. My fans have been good to me.

"Yeah, it's true I've recorded some things you don't expect from an R & B singer. But I don't know that I am an R & B singer. Sure, black people buy my records—just look at the R & B charts—but so do white people. I've had Gold Records, and I played the Copa in the early sixties before they were saying, 'Black Is Beautiful.' Some people say I'm a soul singer—and there is a lotta gospel in me.

"But in 1960 a songwriter named Johnny Lehman brought Nat Tarnopol something he took from a Tchaikovsky piano concerto. It had a big melody. He called it 'Alone at Last,' and it didn't bother me. I did it. And believe it or not, it made R & B charts. I guess that shook up some other songwriters. Now they knew I wasn't just a screamer. Two of them came along with something they took from *Pagliacci,* the opera. 'Night' didn't do as well, but I had no trouble handling it.

"I'm proud that I have been accepted by the white world—but without losing my black audience. That's what counts—not losing your black fans. I'm not going to name names, but many black singers move away from their roots once they get the loot. I'm not a churchgoer, but I've got the gospel in me. Never do a show without 'Amen' as a closer. . . ."

•

In October 1975, while appearing at the Latin Casino near Philadelphia as part of Dick Clark's "Good Ol' Rock 'n' Roll Revue," Jackie Wilson suffered a heart attack, which has incapacitated him. He was then forty-one years of age.

groove 20   DANNY KESSLER
                     AND OKeh RECORDS

OKeh Records, the company that ignited the blues explosion of the 1920s with Mamie Smith and paced the market during the classic blues era, lost its preeminent position during the depression. After Columbia Records acquired its catalogue in the late '30s, it became the company's "cheap" label. Early in the '50s, as the market for R & B opened wide, Columbia reactivated OKeh as an R & B label and put Danny Kessler in charge.

OKeh artists of the '50s included Chuck Willis, who started his recording career on the label; Big Maybelle, who had three chartmakers in '53; and Johnnie Ray, whose color would seem to rule him out as an R & B artist. Yet he was performing in Detroit's leading black club when Kessler signed him, and his record of "Cry" went to the very top of R & B charts, remaining there for fifteen weeks. There was no question that he was a crossover in reverse. Black record buyers may have purchased "Cry" because, to many people, Ray sounded black at first, just as to others he sounded female. This hypothesis may be sound since none of Ray's succeeding disks made R & B charts. After "Cry," they knew he was white.

•

"I began in the record business," Danny Kessler said, as we sat in his Hollywood office, "by working for the Columbia distributor in Philadelphia." Kessler is now associated with the managerial and booking office that handles Gladys Knight as well as B. B. King.

•

"It was a company called Motor Parts that handled vacuum cleaners, air-conditioners, and other appliances. Somewhere up on the fourth floor, they had a Columbia record distributorship. I was a local musician who had to leave school in my senior year when my father passed away. A friend told me about an opening for a record picker. That was somebody who went to the bins and picked out records ordered by number. It might have been a record by Benny Goodman, Gene Krupa or Harry James, but all you knew was a number. After a time, I worked my way up to being a salesman.

"Then one day, a gentleman named Manie Sachs, who headed the A & R department in New York, came in to complain about the promotional procedures of the distributor. I happened to be the youngest guy, probably the most enthusiastic, and very much into records. He offered me the job of promotion manager and I jumped at the opportunity.

"In those days, Philadelphia was what was known as a breakout market. At WIBG we had Doug Arthur; at WPEN there were Eddie Hurst and Joe Grady, 'The 9:50 Club.' If those guys got on a record, they generally could break it and then you could spread it to other big record cities like Detroit, Chicago, etc.

"I was fortunate enough to pick and concentrate on a number of records that Manie was hot about as A & R director. One of the first was a Rosemary Clooney record—'Penny Arcade' might have been the title—and she was probably still singing with the Tony Pastor band. Then I'll never forget his calling me about a Mariners record— they were a mixed group, one of the first, on the Arthur Godfrey show. I listened to the record, loved it, and persuaded Doug Arthur to give me a concentrated play for two weeks. That did the trick. The record became No. 1 in Philadelphia and turned into an enormous seller for Columbia.

"After that Manie invited me to come to New York and sent me to Bridgeport, Connecticut, where Columbia had its main manufacturing plant, there to learn all the aspects of pressing disks. Then I became national promotion manager of Columbia—and I was just nineteen or so. It was an exciting period for me since I set up tours for stars like Doris Day and Frank Sinatra, with whom I went on a promotion trip. Things rolled well for two or three years when Manie Sachs suddenly resigned from Columbia and went to RCA Victor. In his place Mitch Miller came from Mercury to head the A & R department. I had been reporting to a man named Paul Southard, and now the sales manager was Paul Wexler.

"Wexler was a tall, ex-University of Pennsylvania football star whose brother, Elliot Wexler, was the Philadelphia distributor for Musicraft Records. After Paul took over sales, he became slightly involved in A & R. I had always had a great feeling for black records. I promoted the few black artists who were on the Columbia label. When Columbia decided to reactivate OKeh Records as a black label,

Wexler offered me the A & R job. It was a super-thrill, particularly when I was given the green light to go out and sign new black artists.

"Shortly after that, on a promotion tour to Washington, D.C., I heard a group called The Treniers, seven guys led by twin brothers. Their big number was 'Go, Go, Go.' It got standing ovations. So The Treniers became the first black artists I signed, and 'Go, Go, Go' became the first record I produced for OKeh. It became number four or number five in the country. At that time we began to cover stations that Columbia Records had never heard of in the South as well as in the North—you know, stations at the top of the dial. Like WHAT in Philadelphia, basically a gospel station that devoted two hours a day to R & B records.

"I can never forget coming into Atlanta for the first time, looking forward to meeting this phenomenal disk jockey, Daddy Sears. I was sure that Zenas Sears was a black man because I had known for years that he played black records. Listening to him in my hotel, I heard a style of shout-announcing that was typical only of black jockeys. When I arrived at the station, out came this skinny, little, forty-year-old white man, who was the most delightful and charming guy I'd met. He liked me—I was a young, hustling guy—and we became great friends.

"Zenas was unquestionably responsible for breaking some of the black records I produced for OKeh. Once when I was in Atlanta recording some local talent, I had dinner with Zenas, who told me about a young man who was painting his house. He raved so much about the singing of this nineteen-year-old kid that I went out to the house to hear him. His name was Chuck Willis. I signed him to a recording contract, and that was for me the first breakthrough in the national R & B market. Until then, I had had records that broke in different cities at different times—except for the Treniers. But with Willis, I had an artist who commanded a countrywide market. He was also a fine songwriter, producing magnificent songs like 'What a Dream.' He became one of the first black artists that was showcased by Dick Clark on 'American Bandstand.'

"With Chuck Willis, OKeh was on the map. We were making chart disks, and I had an open door to new black artists. Not long after this, I went to Detroit to promote some new releases. There, I met a disk jockey named Robin Seymour at Station WKMH in Dearborn, Michigan, who told me about a young kid singing at the Flame Show Bar. It was the number one black nightclub of Detroit. Obviously, I thought he was talking about a black singer. When I arrived at the Flame to meet Seymour, Maurice King was leading the band and a girl named Little Miss Cornshucks was onstage. I flipped over her, but found that she was unavailable. Then out came a white kid wearing a hearing-aid who played piano. There was no name introduction. I really didn't know that this was the kid Seymour was talking about. But I was probably more overwhelmed with what I heard and saw than by anything I had ever encountered artistically in my life. I was so captivated that, when Johnnie Ray—that was his name—finished his half-hour set, with no applause by the four people then in the club, I rushed up to him and told him that I wanted to record him the next day.

"We actually went into a studio about four days later. It was a little studio in Detroit. Maurice King, the Flame bandleader, scribbled out a few charts. And we recorded two songs that Johnnie had written. One was called 'Whiskey and Gin' and the other was 'Tell the Lady I Said Goodbye.' 'Whiskey and Gin' was the highlight to me. Now at this point, I came back to New York just completely wiped out about this superstar I had found. I play the record for the sales force, and almost in unison they said, 'We don't think *she's* gonna make it!' They all thought that I was pitching a girl who sounded like Dinah Washington. I finally convinced them that "she" was a boy—and then I had to break the news that she was a *white* boy. I know they all felt that I had lost my head completely.

"But we had a convention just about that time. Paul Wexler, who was solidly behind me, asked me to come to the convention and play my new artist. 'We won't give any advance hype,' he said. 'We'll just introduce you as the head of A & R at OKeh, and you play your product.' So I got up, made my little speech, and played this new record. The reaction was overwhelming. They literally stood up and cheered. Then I broke the news about Ray's being a white boy. At that point, they didn't care if he was green or purple. The record came out sometime in '51. Thanks to a number of disk jockeys in Cleveland—Phil McLean and Bill Randle—'Whiskey and Gin' broke open and became number one in Detroit and Buffalo. But that was it. We just couldn't spread the record nationally. But the excitement and the hype were so great that Mitch Miller came to me one day—he was head of A & R for Columbia, the parent company—and said he had found a song for Johnnie Ray to record.

"It was called 'Cry.' With Mitch, I went in and cut it. On the back we put a song that Johnnie had written called 'The Little White Cloud that Cried.' The rest is history. Johnnie became the rage of the world, and I became a young hotshot executive. It was a high point of my life and career. When you're hot, you're hot. And I was lucky enough then to sign artists like Ahmad Jamahl—a local Chicago piano player then known as Fritz Jones—and Joe Williams, who was singing with the Red Saunders Band. I must have been the only white guy who ever walked into the Club De Lisa. When I heard Joe doing 'Every Day I Have the Blues,' that was it. Later, I signed the Dukes of Dixieland and the Four Lads, whom I used as a background group for Johnnie Ray. Then there were the Four Coins, Jay and the Americans, and others.

•

"Promoting R & B records in those days was not easy. Our first step with a new record was to go to the tiny stations in isolated markets, occasionally in big cities. We'd find the black station, which usually played gospel at least half the time. When a record began to draw requests and local R & B sales, I would then approach key jockeys like Bob Clayton in Boston, Doug Arthur in Philadelphia, Bill Randle in Cleveland, Howard Miller in Chicago, Gil Newsome in St. Louis. There were about twelve key cities where, if your record had it and these powerhouse jockeys played it, you immediately felt sales reaction.

"The odds for a black record to crack through were slim. If the black record began to happen, the chances were that a white artist would cover—and then the big stations would play the white record. Many jockeys would pass your record up on the grounds that the black station was playing it. But there were exceptional jockeys like Doug Arthur and Bill Randle who would play a record, black or white, if they liked it. It was not like today when Gladys Knight & the Pips or B. B. King are mass artists. There was a color line, and it wasn't easy to cross. And Gladys Knight is an example—for fourteen years, she had number one records in the R & B field, but she did not get mass radio play until a year or two ago.

"For me, there was no color line. In fact, I got hooked on black singers when I was quite young, even though I came from a white, Jewish, Philadelphia family. Two radio stations performed the magic. One was WHAT and the other was WDAS. I loved the sound, and I started to go to the Earle Theatre when I was just eleven or twelve. That was the local black theater where you could hear the big bands and black artists. I fell in love with Louis Jordan and Jimmie Lunceford. And when I was just fifteen, I went to Duke Ellington and asked him whether I could be his road manager. He laughed, but he took me to his heart, and I became the band's gofer—went to get the guys coffee and cigarettes and whatnot. I don't know how to explain it, but

I was totally moved by artists like Bull Moose Jackson and groups like the Orioles. And then, when I went down South to places like Atlanta and New Orleans, I became so involved and captivated that there was nothing else for me musically. I've always been a bit of a follower of people like B. B. King, Blind Boy Fuller, Sonny Terry, Muddy Waters, Jimmy Reed, and others in the blues idiom. They said things to me musically like what The Beatles years later said to the kids. I got totally hooked on what I regarded as pure music.

"I just happened to be white. But I guess that in those days, if I had been black, I couldn't have gotten a job in a record company. . . ."

groove 21   **AL SILVER
                                        AND HERALD RECORDS**

Al Silver, who built Herald and Ember Records into flourishing R & B companies from a tiny 3-press record plant in a Greenwich Village basement, is a New Englander by birth. He lived in Pittsburgh for a time, but confesses that he cannot get New York out of his system. "That's where the action is," he says, "and the excitement!" In his late fifties, he has occasionally considered settling in Florida. "But that would be hibernating," he says. He thinks young and feels young, despite his years, and wants to remain in action. When I interviewed him in May 1974, he had just taken a sales job with Ray Charles's record company, now run by Larry Newton, an "indie" operator in the R & B years who, as the owner of Derby Records, was one of Silver's competitors.

•

"Herald Records was started in 1953. My brother-in-law and I had organized a small pressing plant in '46 in the basement of a building in Greenwich Village. From the time I was a kid, I always dug music. My grandfather had a store in the black neighborhood of Providence, Rhode Island, and I used to pass the Baptist storefront church. On Sundays when I heard that gospel music, it gave me goose pimples.

"After World War II my brother-in-law and I found that we had several thousand dollars in war savings bonds and decided to go into business together. A friend who had a small record-pressing plant suggested that we go into the field. We were green, but we opened a small outfit at 469 West Broadway, near Houston Street. We shared the basement area with a printer. We found a machinery broker in

Newark who agreed to supply us with free, hand-operated presses. The only thing in our favor was that my brother-in-law was very mechanically inclined. We stole a so-called foreman from a plant uptown by offering him a little more money, and while we waited for our equipment to come in he taught us the business in four months.

"When the equipment finally arrived, we had a steamfitter-plumber hook it up, and then this foreman taught us how to physically press records. It was 1947 by that time. As luck would have it, Jerry Blaine of Jubilee Records had a fast-selling record in 'Essen,' a takeoff in dialect on vacationing in the Catskill Mountains of New York. A friend of ours who was doing Blaine's pressing had trouble with his equipment. When Jerry got frantic, the friend recommended us. That record kept us busy day and night for about four months. We could put out about eight hundred 78-inch shellac records in an eight-hour shift—today they get fifteen hundred 45s—and we worked two ten-hour shifts. Blaine must have sold half a million records.

"That started us. After that, we constantly had new people coming in with stampers and labels, particularly in the R & B field. I would see a guy come in with a thousand labels and return a few weeks later with ten thousand labels. I would listen to the music and feel that I could cut a record as good as any I heard. Slowly, it became an obsession.

"In 1952 a fellow named Fred Mendelsohn, who is now with Savoy Records, formed Herald Records in New Jersey. We had been pressing records for him on a Regent label when he was in business with the Braun brothers. He had no capital when he started Herald. We had little, but we had a pressing plant—so we formed a corporation. He brought us a bunch of Little Walter masters, which we put out. Nothing happened. Since we had no salary to pay, Freddie, who had a family, had to walk away from it.

"We decided to continue Herald on our own. Charlie Singleton, who later was the co-writer of 'Strangers in the Night,' was then working for Fred Fisher. He kept coming to us with songs he had written and offered to bring artists to us to record them. One day when it was pouring, he insisted on taking me to the Hotel America—it was between Fifth and Sixth avenues on Forty-sixth or Forty-eighth Street. There in the ballroom I heard Joe Morris, the black trumpet player, do 'Shake a Hand,' which I eventually recorded. Morris had been trying for a year to get Ahmet Ertegun and Jerry Wexler at Atlantic to record him with the song. But they wouldn't, and, by the time I heard him, his Atlantic option had run out.

"When Joe Morris heard that I had a record company, he became very excited and played a raft of things for us. Many of them were real low-down Southern blues. He had a kid named Stringbean with him who was a country, down-home singer. I didn't hear anything, and I was wet from the rain and getting fed up. When I was about to leave, he called on Al Savage, who sings a thing for me called 'I Had a Notion.' I liked it and thought that was it. But he said, 'No, no,' and calls this little girl, who was sitting in the back of the hall.

"Faye Scruggs—that was her name then—was about seventeen. After he introduced me, she sang 'Shake a Hand' without a mike in front of that big, blasting band—and I got goose pimples. I had contracts in my pocket. I ran across the street, got a bottle of whiskey, went up to Joe Morris's room, pulled out the contract, and signed him up. I never knew that Faye was still signed to Atlantic although Joe Morris's option had run out. I didn't find this out until a week after I had recorded her.

"Charlie Singleton helped me out on the session. I had never been in a recording studio before. We went up to Bell Sound, who were then up on Eighty-seventh Street between Central Park West or Amsterdam Avenue and the next block. Anyway, it was Joe Morris's band. We had no union to contend with. In those days, it didn't matter anyway. We cut eight sides, four with Faye Adams: 'Shake a Hand' and a backup; 'I'll Be True' and a backup; 'I Had a Notion,' with Al Savage, and a backup; and, for a favor, I cut that Stringbean on two blues things.

"The first record we put out was 'Shake a Hand.' Incidentally, I didn't like Faye Scruggs, so I changed her name to Faye Adams. It had a better professional sound. We put the record out and, since it was a few years since my wife and I had taken any vacation, we went up to the Hotel Concord in the Catskills. My brother-in-law and the crew were at the plant. While we were sitting at the pool in the middle of the week, I get paged over the speaker. It was my brother-in-law: 'Al, I don't know what you want to do. That "Shake A Hand" broke wide open. We're getting orders from Cincinnati for ten thousand; from Chicago for twenty thousand. . . . The first three or four days, we were back-ordered three hundred to four hundred thousand.' At that point, we hadn't pressed a record yet. So I packed up and speeded back to New York. A hit record was more important than a vacation. This was the summer of 1953.

"We really had no money to finance the record. We had a little plant with three presses. We could turn out maybe thirty thousand records a week, running full blast. Here we were back-ordered three to four hundred thousand—and the quickest way to lose a hit is not to ship it. So we went to our bank. But we didn't have that much of a track record, and they turned us down. Fortunately the officer we talked to had a friend who made short-term loans at what was then a high interest rate—about 8 percent. So we borrowed fifteen thousand dollars to get out a hundred fifty thousand records, figuring that that would get us over the hump.

"We went over to MGM, who wanted cash to press records. We brought the money along with stampers and labels. In three or four days, they had the hundred fifty thousand records for us. We started to get caught up and got some advance money from our distributors. They wanted the record, and they knew we needed the capital. Now we were in business. That record went on to sell a million. When 'Shake a Hand' was tapering, we put out Al Savage's 'I Had a Notion.' That hit and sold about four hundred thousand. To follow 'Shake A Hand,' we put out Faye Adams doing 'I'll Be True,' and that sold about eight hundred thousand. So out of that one session, we got three hits. They were all head arrangements. Joe Morris played what he had been doing with those things for a year.

"That really started us. But unfortunately my track record on Herald was that our hits came every other year. I had three hits in '53. Couldn't get arrested in '54 at all, and we put out a lot of records. In '55 we hit with 'In the Still of the Night,' with The Five Satins, who came to me through a distributor in Hartford, Connecticut, Gene Gotthelf. He called me up one day and said a local company had a record by a group on which he had sold about eight thousand. He wanted me to take it over for national distribution; otherwise, he'd lose it if he took it to some other company.

"When he sent me the record, I found its quality extremely poor. It was recorded in a church basement with home equipment. But who was I to argue against a local sale of eight thousand copies. We took the record over, making a deal with the people who had it. Standord, with an o, was their label. We put it out on our Ember label. When we were ready to release it, we called the Hartford distributor to ask how many he wanted. He replied that the record had dropped dead and he didn't want any. We released it anyway. And about two weeks later, it started to click in Cincinnati. Then, it began to sell in another area. We had 'The Jones Girl' marked as the 'A' side, which was the way the Standord people marked it, but the disk jockeys and the public thought differently. You can't argue with them. They picked

'In the Still of the Night,' the other side. Freddie Parris wrote it when he was in the army—he hated guard duty and he tried to pass the time at night by writing songs. Eventually, it sold a couple of million. But it was a market-by-market sale, rather than a national smash. And today, it remains *the* all-time oldie in the country. We put out many, many other records by the group, but 'In the Still of the Night' was the one and only hit The Five Satins ever had. We recorded singles, we recorded albums, but nothing ever happened. And today they're a legend.

"Now I recall that we had a second hit with the group, but it wasn't with Fred Parris as lead. When he left, Billy Baker, with a similar voice, took his place. At that time, a small publisher in the Brill Building, George Weiner, brought me a song called 'To the Aisle,' which just seemed to be right for the group. Billy Baker led on it, and it became a hit.

"Some things are hard to explain—and the impact of the Satins, who did not sell that great, is one. Fred Parris' high-pitched voice was not that unusual. But maybe the wailing, gospel background provided by his New Haven pals produced a unique sound that captured teen-age ears. The Satins were popular enough to headline at the Apollo, on Dick Clark and Ted Steele, and they did tour Europe as well as the USA in 1956–57. They did have a strong following—so strong that they're back in action in the 70s.

"This brings us to the Nutmegs, another '55 group for us. Danny Kessler, who had been at Epic Records, and Murray Sporn, a contact man, had a publishing firm together called Rush Music. The Nutmegs came to them with a song called 'Story Untold.' Kessler and Sporn were so excited that they brought them over, and I heard them do it *a cappella*. We got a hold of Leroy Kirkland, the arranger, who spent a couple of nights with the Nutmegs and tightened up their handling. We went in, recorded it, and it was a big hit.

•

"After a cold '56, I had a good year in '57. It was either my biggest, or certainly my second biggest year. I had 'The Joker,' with Billy Myles; 'Walkin' Mr. Lee,' with Lee Allen; 'When You Dance,' by the Turbans—they were all biggies. ['When You Dance' was a hit in '55.] Now, the Turbans, a Philadelphia group, walked into my office when I was in the CBS Building at 1697 Broadway. They walked in cold, wearing turbans. They sang quite a few things for me *a cappella*. I thought they had a good sound, but none of their songs impressed me.

When they had gone through their repertoire. I asked the lead singer, Al Banks, whether they had anything else. He said that they were working on a new song that had to be finished. They were reluctant to do it, but, after urging, they did as much as they had of 'When You Dance.' I said, 'That's it! Finish it, and we'll do it.' He said that they didn't know how. So once again, I got hold of Leroy Kirkland, who took them home, helped them finish it, and coached them. It was a big hit.

"Most of my recording in those days was done at Bell Sound, who had moved to Forty-sixth Street and Eighth Avenue, or at Beltone, down on Thirty-first Street, just west of Fifth Avenue. We also recorded at Bell Sound when they moved to Fifty-fourth Street, between Broadway and Eighth Avenue.

"Billy Myles was just a songwriter when he brought me 'The Joker.' Sat down at the piano and played it for me. When he got through, I said, 'I've got nobody on my roster who can do it. Why don't you do it?' He protested: 'I'm not an artist. I don't wanna record. I'm a writer.' It took several days of talking and pleading before he agreed to try it. It broke for a hit the minute we released it. He went on the Sullivan Show. The record crossed into pop and sold almost a million.

"These are the unexpected and exciting things that make the business. I used to go to New Orleans quite a bit. I had a distributor there, but I also loved that town. Whenever I had new releases, I would make a tour through the South to see my distributors. But when I reached New Orleans, I would stay several extra days. Of course, I was younger and I used to swing a bit. And that town was like an all-night town, especially in the French quarter.

"There was a guy there, Paul Gayten, who had recorded for Chess Records. He was a black guy with a little band whose horn-player was named Lee Allen. Whenever I had nothing to do, I'd go into this Canal Street bar and listen to them. After a time, I befriended this Lee Allen. One day, I got a call in New York from Allen, who told me that he had some fantastic material for recording. The next time I was in New Orleans, I set up some studio time at Cosimo Studio. That's where everybody cut—Fats Domino and everybody—that was *the* studio.

"Well, we go in and, despite what this cat told me, he didn't have a thing prepared. That was a rough town, and the union delegate was right there. I had to pay the musicians for a full session, and I had to pay the studio. But this cat had nothing to record. Fortunately, the piano player was Allen Toussaint—he's a big man today, a big produced for RCA; he was just starting then, but what a talent! Here, I'm frustrated: the clock is running and it's costing me money for nothing.

"In desperation I went over to Toussaint. 'Help me out of this mess,' I pleaded. He fooled around a bit and then he came up with a riff that sounded pretty good. It was simple and melodic. When I told him I liked it, he called over the guitar player and the drummer. After they had the rhythm section set, they brought Lee over and he picked it up. We tried several rough takes and then cut a master. It went along for four sides like that—all from head and all with this one-finger bit.

"The eventual record was 'Walkin' with Mr. Lee.' It was a real, walkin'-type thing. I airmailed the tapes back to New York. I had this kid Doug Moody working for me. His father was Wally Moody, who used to be a bigshot at British Decca. Told Doug to get the record right out. I was still in New Orleans when he called to tell me that he had gotten a fast record to Dick Clark, who flipped over the disk and wanted to talk to me. Right after that I had a call from Clark, who told me he wanted to put the record on the air, but he wanted the group on his show. That meant flying Lee and the other musicians up to Philadelphia. Lee didn't have a band of his own. He was just a sideman with Paul Gayten. But he got together a group that would work with him. And when he came north for the Dick Clark Show, I got him a gig at the Apollo Theatre. Short money, but it paid the plane fare. That was '57.

"Fifty-eight was nothing. But in '59 I was sitting in my office one day when I got a call from Philadelphia distributor, Ed Cohen at Lesco Distributing. He had a record by a group called the Silhouettes on a Junior label owned by Kaye Williams, a disk jockey. Claimed he had sold nine thousand or so in a few weeks and that people were beginning to sniff around for the record. He mentioned Morty Craft at MGM and Larry Newton at ABC Records. He was worried because, if they got it, he would lose it. He indicated that he could get the disk for me for, like, fifteen hundred dollars—and airmailed a copy to me.

"When I heard the record of 'Get A Job,' I was amazed. It was so badly produced—a piece of junk. You couldn't understand one word of the lyric. I called Ed Cohen and told him, 'You gotta be kidding.' He said, 'No, the other companies are really after it. Please take it.' I stalled him for several days. Even Doug Moody hated it. Then, Cohen called me and offered to go partners with me if I would put it out. Finally, I decided I'd go along.

"Unbeknowst to me, the record was lying on Dick Clark's desk for two weeks. Dick wanted to play it in the worst way, but he wouldn't because the Junior label had no national distribution. Dick smelled a smash hit. Anyway, in a few days, I had finished pressings and air-mailed several copies to Dick Clark. As soon as he saw that it was on Ember, a label with national distribution, he programmed it. When I walked into the office the morning after he played it, there were tele-grams with back orders for about five hundred thousand records under-neath the door. Chicago—twenty thousand; Dallas—ten thousand. It was unbelievable. The first record wasn't shipped yet. Eventually, that record sold a couple million. I sold about a million and a half, and I guarantee that the bootleggers—because it was heavy in those days —the bootleggers got me for another million. The reason I know is that in New Orleans the record wasn't selling. We couldn't figure it out. Everywhere else we had tremendous sales. The answer was the bootleggers were shipping it in from Chicago. The Mob had a setup in Chicago—they caught them at the time—in a great, big colonial house. It was stripped from basement to attic and loaded with records, coming in from Cincinnati by bus. It was not just my record, but everybody's label: Andy Williams and The Everly brothers on Archie Bleyer's la-bel; Chess Records; Columbia and Epic; you name it. They were boot-legging everybody. But I had a big record despite them. ['Get A Job' was a hit in '58.]

"In '60 I was dead again. And in '61, another Horatio Alger story. A kid comes into my office with a Southern accent. White kid who says he's a songwriter, and would I listen to some of his songs? I was busy on the phone, so I tell my secretary to have Bill Darnell, who was working for me, audition his material. The kid must have played seventeen or eighteen dubs for Bill. I thought that they were masters. After a while, Bill came out and asked me to listen to one thing. It was 'Stay,' by Maurice Williams & the Zodiacs.

"Thinking it was a master, I offered to put it out. But Williams turned me down: it wasn't a master, it was just an audition disk. I insisted that it was a record. Maurice still argued. So I said, 'Look, you go back home into a studio. I'll take the dub and I'll give you a sheet of paper showing where you have to pull up the group because it's covered. You rerecord it, and I'll pay for the session. Get it back to me and I'll put a record out.' He said, 'That's okay. I've got a studio, and it won't cost you anything.'

"As he was leaving, I reminded him to cut it flat, not to add any echo. He did it, and when the record arrived I thought it was terrific. We went into a studio, added echo and remixed it. We put it out, and

—Boom!—it was a hit. The Zodiacs came from Charlotte, North Carolina. Maurice Williams, the lead, was about twenty–twenty-one. The next record by the group and an album were nothing.

"In '61, too, a guy walks in off the street—a good-looking fellow—and he says, 'My name is William Rose III.' He looked like a Madison Avenue advertising exec or a Wall Street broker. Claimed he worked for Liberty Records for a while and that in Washington he picked up this master which he wanted me to hear. He said that my distributor in Washington, D.C., liked it very much, but that they didn't want to invest in it. He happened to be there while a fellow from Baton Rouge was trying to sell it to them. It was Cajun humor, a mixture of Southern drawl and French, typical of the Bayou region, a kind of pidgin English. We picked up the master for nothing. They were interested simply in getting it released. We made a cover and called it *The Humorous World of Justin Wilson*. He was a big six-foot four-inch white guy, weighed about three hundred pounds, looked like a tackle on a football team. But he was a safety engineer who traveled all through the South, lecturing workers in the oilfields of Texas, Louisiana, etc. He would intersperse his safety talks with humorous stories. The album was a compilation of these stories, which he had taped.

"We shipped the album to our distributors, and it laid an egg. The investment was not big—just the mastering, pressing, and printing the covers. But it was a letdown. Six months later, in December, we had a violent storm here in New York. It was so heavy that I couldn't get to the office from my home in Long Island. I had my nephew working for me then, and he managed to get to the office from his house in the Bronx. It snowed all day, dropping about twenty inches. Sometime during the day, he phoned me all excited. He'd gotten a call from United Record Distributing, my distributor in Houston, and Steve Ponzia told him that the Justin Wilson album had broken wide open. He wanted a thousand immediately. I couldn't believe it, so I called Ponzia, who said that he would need ten thousand, but wanted one thousand shipped at once. Then he told me that a disk jockey named Paul Berlin, who was at Station KNUZ—he's still there—had found the album in the station library. Puzzled because he had never heard it, he listened to it in the library while he was picking records for his show that night. It broke him up. When he went on the air, he made no announcement, but simply let one whole side play through. He went to the next record, still without making an announcement. In about ten minutes, people began calling in to ask where they could get the record. Berlin went and told a fellow disk jockey who was on

KNUZ-FM about the incident, and his associate played the album through the night. In the morning, the station was again flooded with calls. Eventually, we sold sixty thousand albums just in Houston. In the rest of the country, we sold over a hundred fifty thousand. But the bulk of the sales was in Texas, in Houston, and in Louisiana.

"In some markets, the album didn't sell at all. But in Cleveland, Bill Randle on Station WERE tried the trick of just playing one side without any announcement. Elliot Blaine of Cosnat Distributing, my Cleveland distributor, told me about it. The following day, a big department store in Cleveland was flooded with requests. We had to ship several thousand fast. Cleveland was not another Houston, but we disposed of about ten thousand copies in the area. And it all happened through a quirk of fate—a dee jay picking up an unknown album six months after it was put out and laid a *lattke*.

•

"It was a lot of fun until the payola investigation of '59. We got hurt like other independent R & B companies. The Internal Revenue and the Federal Trade Commission started investigating my operation in '59. My lawyers advised me to cooperate. When the IRS got through with me in '62, they disallowed all the payola—all cash payments that they found in my checkbooks if I couldn't account for those payments. They went back to '53—I had to sign a waiver of the statute of limitations. For corporate tax purposes, they went all the way up to '62. They disallowed so much stuff, I got a bill for about a hundred fifty thousand dollars for the three corporations, Herald, Ember, and the Angel publishing company. It was '62, and I was in between hits. And the money just tapped me out. The government wanted it, no ifs, ands, or buts. I limped along for another two years, up to '64. Rather than go bankrupt and hurt creditors that were good to me—it wasn't my nature—I liquidated. My attorney paid off small creditors. Where we couldn't pay in full, we paid in part, and I walked away not owing anybody.

"I leased my catalogue for twenty years. It's due back to me in another ten years. However, I've been in conference with attorneys to get the catalogue back. The contract calls for submission of royalty statements twice a year. In the nine to nine and a half years they've had it, I haven't received a single statement. Music attorneys have told me that I stand a good chance of getting it back.

"As for our pressing plant, it had grown from those three little presses in a Village basement to twenty-seven presses. Situated in River Edge, New Jersey, it had twenty-one presses for 45s and six for LP

albums. It was a compilation of many heartaches. It needed moderni-
zation, and we didn't have the money. Since the firms were all tied in
together, the record company lent the pressing plant money when it
needed it. When Herald and Ember Records got into trouble, the plant
was in even more serious financial trouble. So at this point, we liquidated the whole caboodle—the record companies and the pressing
plant.

"At the same time, I sold my music publishing catalogue, Angel
Music, to Murray Sporn. I think he had just left Eddie Kassner—they
had a breakup—and he needed something to support himself, really.
I actually sold the music publishing company prior to getting rid of
the record business. At the time, my mind was so record oriented that
I made the biggest mistake of my life. I should never have let that
publishing company go. It would have been an annuity for me for life
and for my children. I should have let the record company go and just
continued the music publishing.

"But my track record and the excitement of getting that hit record
—it's like a gambling bug; it's a sickness, really, and once you get that
in your blood, you can't do anything else. That grab for the next hit,
the excitement of latching onto a new hit record! That was what got
me out of the music publishing business. But it's all water under the
bridge, and those R & B years were good years while they lasted."

groove 22   **BOB ROLONTZ
AND GROOVE RECORDS**

As a *Billboard* reporter, Bob Rolontz developed a special interest in
rhythm and blues and accounted for some of the best and most analytical articles on the subject published during the '50s. In the mid-50s,
RCA Victor put him in charge of one of its R & B subsidiaries. In
recent years, he has been associated with the Atlantic label as publicity
director. Today, he functions in a related capacity for Warner Communications, Atlantic's parent company.

•

"I started with the Groove label," he said, as we talked in a plush
corner office, high up in a Rockefeller Center building, "in the spring
or summer of '55.

•

"When I got to the label, they had a few artists that I thought important, The Chuckles and Teddy Randazzo. But their R & B artists,

even though it was supposed to be an R & B label, were unimportant. They had a label called X at the same time and when that got fractured, some artists came over to Groove and some went to the parent company, RCA Victor. Afterward, they founded Vik. I think that was the sequence: X, Groove, then Vik.

"With Groove, they wanted badly to break into the R & B market. They hired Danny Kessler, who had been at Epic, and he ran the label for about two years. Nothing happened, and they let Danny go. It was publisher-songwriter Dave Dreyer who recommended me to them.

"I was then on *Billboard*, had been there for three or four years, and was writing constantly about the whole R & B thing. I guess they thought I had some knowledge of the field. I was hired to revitalize the label and instructed to make it an R & B label. I did hold the Chuckles, and, when they split up, I had Teddy. To the label, I signed Varetta Dillard, who had been on Savoy. We had a backup group that we tried to establish as The Four Students. We had another group called the El Vinos, who have become offbeat famous—like you get six bucks for one of their records if you can find them. Then we signed some jazz people—Jonah Jones, prior to Capitol's having him, and we almost made it with him. We had Sammy Davis, Jr.'s backup bandleader, George Rhodes. We made a couple of pretty good records with him, but nothing happened. And we brought Piano Red back to RCA.

"The first hit we had on Groove was Piano Red, who had a very interesting history. His real name was Willie Perryman, and he was the brother of Speckled Red, whose real name was Rufus Perryman. Speckled Red recorded for both Brunswick and Bluebird in the 1930s. The only recording that Piano Red did at the time was with Blind Willie McTell. The sides were never released, although Blind Willie had releases on both Vocalion and Decca. Around 1950 Victor picked up on Piano Red and recorded him in Atlanta. The first session yielded a back-to-back chart record, 'Rockin' with Red' backed with 'Red's Boogie.' When I heard these and several other titles that sold in 1951, I went down to Atlanta. He was just playing college dates and weekend gigs—private parties at some of the Atlanta mansions. He was also doing beer commercials on one of the local stations.

"I set up a session, which we did in Nashville early in 1955. (Never realized how cold it can get in that town in January or February.) We used a typical R & B combo, including one horn. And out of the session came 'Jump, Man Jump,' our first solid seller. It sold fifty to sixty thousand. Had we been better organized and spent more money on promotion, we might have gone to a hundred thousand. But that was our kickoff.

"As our distributors, we used RCA for the South and our own independent distributors for the North and West. The reason we employed RCA in the South was that their distributors had some idea of how to handle R & B.

"Piano Red cut quite a number of sides for us during '55 and '56. Some of the sessions were held in Nashville and at least one was done in Atlanta at the Magnolia Ballroom. I recall one title, 'Fattenin' Frogs for Snakes,' which Sonny Boy Williamson had done previously for the Chess people. None sold as well as 'Jump, Man, Jump.' But he remained with Victor into '58.

"Another artist we signed was Champion Jack Dupree, who did some records with Teddy McRae, who called himself Mr. Bear. They did moderately well.

"Our first really big seller was by Mickey & Sylvia. Their first record, 'Walkin' in the Rain,' almost kicked off. Within a week of their release, Johnnie Ray came out with a 'Walkin' in the Rain.' It was an entirely different song, but it was enough to confuse buyers. Mickey & Sylvia came back and did 'Love Is Strange,' which by now is probably a million seller. When I left, it was like eight hundred thousand.

"Mickey was a studio musician playing dates all over town. He comes from New Orleans. He did everything: hustled, carried cement bags on his back. He taught himself guitar, came up to New York, and began playing sessions—became a big Atlantic sideman on all their early sessions. His real name is Michouston Baker. Sylvia was a girl who wanted to get into the business, and she went to Mickey's house to ask his help in learning to play guitar. She was known at one point as Little Sylvia and made some records for Herman Lubinsky. He had Little Esther, and she was Little Sylvia. Nothing happened, and that's when she approached Mickey.

"After a time, she got the idea that by working together something might happen for them. They went to Rainbow Records, and Eddie Heller signed them and made six sides with them. Nothing happened, but some of their sides got aired around New York. Disk jockeys got to know them because Eddie did promote and he had a somewhat successful "indie" company. At one point, Bob Astor, who started as a bandleader and then became an agent, approached me about them—and that's how I got them.

"Sylvia's name was Sylvia Vanderpool. Her married name is Robinson. She has her own record label, All Platinum, and she just had a hit, 'Pillow Talk.' I don't regard Mickey & Sylvia as an R & B team; they really made pop records with a touch of blackness that made sense for the time period. They were not rhythm and blues as Shirley & Lee were. They could be, but they weren't. They were one of the big crossover groups. 'Love Is Strange' is today still an up-to-date recording because it was a crossover, and not ethnic.

"At this point, after they had their big smash, RCA decided, in its infinite wisdom, that it had too many labels. They had already gathered up the bones of X, and the new decision was that everybody goes to Vik. They would have been better off closing up Vik and continuing Groove. But there was no way you could change their minds or fight them. The orders came from the corporation, and that was the way it went. So they brought Mickey & Sylvia to Vik and Teddy Randazzo to Vik and a few others. Jonah Jones, I think, left us. Somehow, they expected Jonah's first record to be a smash, which was silly. It made money, and I wanted to keep him. But they refused to spend money on him. And when Dave Cavanaugh wanted him at Capitol, I said that we just couldn't hold him; we had to let him go. And then he happened on his next record.

"Oh, yeah, we also had Brook Benton on the label. And he also almost happened for us. And he happened the moment he left our label and went over to Mercury with Clyde Otis.

"For all of Mickey & Sylvia's sessions, King Curtis handled the band. He arranged, fixed, and did everything with Mickey. I recorded King separately—the first solo recordings he ever made. I got to know King because of Ahmet Ertegun. At one point, I called Ahmet because I needed a horn player. Sam The Man was not available and nobody I wanted was available. Ahmet told me of a kid that was playing in an Eighth Avenue bar. It was a sailor's bar. I went in, told him I was an A & R man, and asked him to come to the studio. He was rather scared on his first date.

"I used quite a number of well-known musicians on my sessions. Panama Francis was frequently the drummer. Kenny Burrell played guitar, backing up Mickey.

"The Vik label was probably the worst collection of talent in the history of the world. On that label, we even had the guy who played Joe Louis in the movies. I did my best to buy out their contracts. Like: 'Here's the money. Take it and run, because we're not going to make any records!' Some, I actually had to record. Diahann Carroll was on the label—a lovely person, but, in my opinion, she couldn't and she can't sing on records. We recorded her, killed ourselves in the process, and, of course, nothing happened. No fault of hers.

"When I got to Vik, it was already in the hole for three hundred thousand dollars. It was a real tough go, trying to make things happen with all those artists. Mickey & Sylvia did a follow-up to their hit. 'Love Will Make You Fail in School' did very well—about four hundred thousand. And they had another one after that. But then they began to have quarrels of their own. Mickey couldn't care less about money or being a star; Sylvia wanted both. The first moment he could get away, the happier he was. Sylvia was the driver. Mickey did whatever he did only because she was on him all the time. There was no love interest. Sylvia was married, and Mickey has had his own troubles with three wives. He dug his privacy and scholastic type of attainment. Like right now, he's working in Europe, playing basic type blues. That's what he likes.

"There was no way we could pull Vik out of that hole. And after about a year, the RCA people decided to discontinue Vik. They tried to switch the artists they wanted to Victor, but some of them didn't want to go to RCA, which was having its own problems. I'm talking about the late fifties.

"I brought Mickey & Sylvia over to Atlantic. They wanted some infinitesimal sum like ten or twenty thousand dollars, and the answer was 'No.' When I brought Brook Benton over, the answer also was 'No.' Teddy Randazzo went his own way and became a songwriter. I left and returned to *Billboard*. King Curtis continued to work as a studio man and finally came into his own in '64 or '65, just about the time that I came to work here. Varetta Dillard never happened, which was a shame.

•

"Of course, I had to promote as well as produce records. I went on the road once I had product to sell. There was a northern tier you covered, which included Philadelphia, Pittsburgh, Cleveland, Detroit, and Chicago. Also Baltimore–Washington, D.C. In Baltimore, you brought your records to Hot Rod Hulbert. You went to see him at midnight with sandwiches and coffee, and you stayed until three and four o'clock in the morning. In New York, you saw Alan Freed, of course, and other guys: Jack Walker at WLIB, big and husky, who was knifed; Tommy Smalls; and the so-called Mayor of Harlem, Willie Bryant. In Cleveland, you saw Bill Randle; you didn't get too much on R & B stuff, but occasionally he'd go for something like Mickey & Sylvia because they were a crossover group.

"In Chicago, there was one R & B station that was not 'owned' by Chess. And there was a big, big jockey who started the first sheet, listing the tunes that you advertised. And we all thought that that was abominable: how could a man do a thing like that? This guy was not on WVON, which had a lineup of guys who have since become well known. But I remember Lou Witch, who is a big man in Chicago today. You see, on account of Alan Freed, sections and segments of R & B went into the pop stations.

"In Pittsburgh, you went to see a guy who was short and limped. You crossed the tracks to get to the station, in the middle of a slum area. In Philadelphia, you had Georgie Woods, who was just coming up then. In Buffalo, the guy who imitated the Freed thing, George 'Hound Dog' Lorenz, became important.

"You'd get on a plane in Pittsburgh to go to Cleveland. And there would be the Epic guy, the Columbia guy, and all your competition. You would all hit the same stations, follow the same routines, go to the same restaurants.

"In the South, Atlanta was very important. You could break records on WAOK because of Zenas Sears, partly because there was a hot distributor in the area. Atlanta was to the South what Cleveland was to the North. Look at the lineup of jockeys you had in Cleveland: Freed, Randle, Don McLaine, and that guy who came to New York. He had two faces: the quiet disk jockey and the wild, shouting dee jay. They couldn't stand him on WNEW. He went to another station where he did well. Then in a fit of depression, he killed himself. Scott Muni, who was big in New York, came out of Dayton, where you went when you couldn't get a record played in Cleveland. Scott would put it on and create movement. Unbelievable that they all came out of one city or area!

"In those days, you had the beginning of the black disk jockey association. It met in some ballroom in Harlem. But everybody went to Harlem then. No problems. You were in the Apollo constantly, listening out front and visiting with the artists backstage. It was not unusual. Then you went to Frank's, the one good restaurant in the area. Again, you'd see everybody who was in the business. Here you'd see the heads of the various record labels. On the planes, you'd see the promotion men.

"In those days, you took a record right to the disk jockey. There was no board, committee, or council. If they liked it, they played it. If they didn't, they threw you out. You waited and sweated your time out to see the jockey. But he was the determining factor. At times, you brought the artist with you.

"If you could happen in one or two of those cities, you could start to cook—because there was the constant phone bit. The jockeys would be talking to each other. It was interesting because there was terrible competition between guys like Randle and Freed. One would grab the record if the other didn't have it. But there were other guys who kept in touch with each other when they weren't monitoring competition. A lot of this changed, of course, after the payola investigations of '59 and '60."

groove 23   SAM WEISS AND OLD TOWN RECORDS

Sam Weiss, a thin, reddish-haired, balding man with sharp eyes, glasses, and a friendly face, is a one-stop operator. For many years, he was located in a large store on Ninth Avenue in New York City. Now he operates out of a warehouse on Long Island. He is basically a distributor; but instead of handling just one record label, he handles many, all of them independents. The service he performs is that a record retailer can get from him almost any new recording on an independent label instead of having to deal with each small manufacturer or many different distributors. We talked in the study of his tree-shaded home, located on the shores of the Long Island Sound in Great Neck.

•

"In 1946 I began working with a company called Runyon Sales. They distributed Exclusive Records and Modern Records, both originating in Los Angeles. Among the first records that I can recall were Joe Liggins's 'The Honey Dripper,' Johnny Moore & The Three Blazers' 'My Silent Love,' and 'Drifting Blues,' by Charles Brown. The first record that I handled, believe it or not, was Ted Fiorito doing 'Kilroy Was There,' on 4 Star Records.

"The René brothers, Leon and Otis, started what was really the first R & B label—Exclusive Records. Saul Bihari, who recently died of a stroke, was also a pioneer in the field. He had the old Sam 'Lightnin' Hopkins records, Smokey Hogg, and he developed Hadda Brooks. Paul Reiner then started Black & White and had the first

'Open the Door, Richard' record. Al Green gave him competition on National, which was distributed by Jerry Blaine.

"Exclusive came into New York about that time and set up their own distribution—again, a first, *the* first true independent distribution. This was unheard-of at that time and the harbinger of later developments in the business. It was, unfortunately, unsuccessful. The Bihari brothers tried the same thing. They located on Forty-second Street and distributed their own Hadda Brooks records, B. B. King and others. After I left Runyon, I became sales manager for both Exclusive and Modern.

"Irving Katz and I got together in the early fifties. He was working for Ikey and Bessie Berman, who had Apollo Records. We found this kid who stuttered, but not when he sang, and we took him up to a studio in Harlem and did 'Butter Beans and Rice.' We got lucky, and that was when Ike and Bess Berman put us into the distribution business, handling Apollo Records. But Ike got a little nervous at one point—he somehow found out that we had money in the bank—and offered to become our partner. We dissolved the business.

"Then I handled Jolly Roger Records, which was probably the first bootleg label that this country has seen. Dante Ballantino took all the old Louis Armstrong, Benny Goodman, and Josephine Baker records, and put them out. The biggest disk we had was by Josephine Baker. We made our own cover, and the weird thing is that Columbia bootlegged our cover! That was in the fifties.

•

"After that, my brother Hy and I started Old Town Records. We took the name from a wholesale stationery company I worked for. Our first big disk was 'The Wedding,' by the Solitaires. They were five kids Hy and I found—a street-corner group that hung out on 142nd Street between Lenox and Seventh avenues. There were Winston 'Buzzy' Willis (who later worked for RCA Victor and now works for Polydor Records), Pat Gaston (who is a cop), and two Bobbys, both tenors. The first lead, if I remember, was a very good singer named Herman Dunham, though I think Milton Love sang lead on 'The Wedding.' Even though we didn't make the big charts with them, the Solitaires became, like, the 'Kings of Sugar Hill' after 'The Wedding' in '55. Fans used to talk of them as a solid New York group. That was high praise. It had something to do with a feeling they seemed to communicate of being lonely and down-hearted in a big city like New York—songs like 'Lonely' and 'I Don't Stand a Ghost of a Chance.' Their 'Wonder Why' was our very first release, Old Town 1000 in

1954, and we put out four or five records before they made it with 'The Wedding.' In '57, they came up with 'Walking Along.' It did well, but not well enough. The Diamonds, who got hot on Mercury with 'The Stroll,' covered us on Mercury and took the play and sales away from The Solitaires.

"We also had Robert & Johnny, a Bronx duo, who stayed with us from '55 until the end of the fifties. They had one biggie in '58, a song they wrote called 'We Belong Together.' It made national R & B charts. And it's come back several times since then by groups you probably never heard of. In '66 two kids named Dee Brown and Lola Grant, on a label you never heard of, Shurfine, made the charts with 'We Belong Together.' And ten years after the Robert & Johnny hit, in 1968, The Webs had a best-seller with the song. They say a good song never dies, and this is proof.

"After a while I left Old Town to concentrate on the distributing business. It was less hazardous. Other people had to worry about making hits; I just sold them. But my brother Hy did quite well with the label. In '59 he had 'So Fine,' with the Fiestas. That was a Johnny Otis song and not the same as 'You're So Fine,' which was a hit at the same time for the Falcons on Unart Records. The Fiestas disk was on national charts for almost six months and went into the Top Three records. Several years later, the group hit with 'Broken Heart.'

"My brother also had Arthur Prysock, a fine singer who could do anything and never achieved the recognition he should have had. He had a great pair of pipes—something like Billy Eckstine—and was on Decca in the fifties. Hy put him on best-seller charts in the sixties with 'The Very Thought of You,' that great Ray Noble ballad of the 1930s, and with 'One More Time' and 'It's Too Late, Baby, Too Late.' Around '66 or '67, Hy sold the label to MGM Records and produced some Prysock records. We now have repossessed the masters and we've begun reissuing Prysock. He still sounds great today.

•

"As a style, I always felt that there were two distinct sounds in R & B. One was a city sound, and the other a country sound. And it was a phenomenon to me that the black people in one area would not buy a record that was popular in another. We had records that were popular in New York that we could not sell in Chicago or California or Detroit. These were called New York hits. 'The Wedding' by the Solitaires is an example. We sold a helluva lot of this record in Harlem and couldn't sell it anywhere else.

"Blues records—I mean the authentic, country variety—would not sell in New York. We couldn't even sell Jimmy Reed in this area, and he's a great blues artist. Same for Smokey Hogg, who sold sparsely compared to what he did in Chicago and the South.

"I recall an experiment I did with Jazzbo Collins when he was on WNEW. I thought that Jimmy Reed was one of the greatest blues artists in the world. After talking with Ewart Abner, who was then president of Vee Jay Records, I asked Jazzbo to program 'Ain't That Lovin' You, Baby?' or 'You've Got Me Dizzy'—they were both R & B hits in the same year, like 1956. It was an unheard-of thing and an unheard-of request. But Jazzbo went for oddball ideas.

"Well, he received a tremendous number of calls. It was really unbelievable that a Jimmy Reed would get that kind of response—in New York, mind you. But it did not really penetrate the NY market, certainly not the white market. And someone on the station called Jazzbo to object to his playing Reed. They didn't think it was his kind of material.

"Reed's label, Vee Jay, came closest to being the number one black-owned pop label. They had the Beatles before Capitol. They had the Four Seasons. They penetrated the white market like a cannonball going through butter. Had they overcome the family and financial problems that ultimately destroyed them, they could have become as big as Motown. They started as a rhythm and blues label, but they had the makings of a big, big major label.

"As for the promotion of records, it has not really changed from the beginning to the present. You have to physically take the record to the disk jockey and incur his favor in some fashion so that he will play it. It takes money—some of it for travel expenses, some of it for romancing jocks at lunch or dinner, and probably some of it for more direct persuasion. The manufacturer and his exclusive distributors worry about that. I just stock every "indie" label that has a record for which there's a demand. Without disk jockey exposure, a record is dead. A buyer has to hear the record to want it. And a dee jay has to play it.

"During the R & B years, as you call them, the powerful black jockeys in New York were Jocko Henderson, Tommy Small (the last of the Dr. Jives—there were others before him), Jack Walker, Hal Jackson, and of course, Willie Bryant and Ray Carroll, who operated out of the window of the Baby Grand club on 125th Street.

"The business has not really changed. It just got bigger. The music has changed and become more sophisticated, but the promotion of a record is still the same. You've got to reach the jockeys. There are a lot more black disk jockeys and more stations today are owned by blacks."

groove *24*   # SOL RABINOWITZ
                          # AND BATON RECORDS

"I started Baton in 1955 with five hundred dollars," said Sol Rabinowitz, now a vice-president of CBS International.

•

"It was the price of a recording session with The Rivileers, the first recording session I had ever done. This was a strange session because my inexperience caused me to use a jazz arranger and jazz musicians with a rhythm-and-blues group. The session was done in the old WOR studios, which had, by that time, deteriorated.

"Nevertheless, out of this session came 'A Thousand Stars,' which was number one in Los Angeles and New York. It also sold in every other territory in which I had a distributor: Detroit, Chicago, Philadelphia, and Boston, becoming somewhat of an R & B standard as the years went by. This group played Alan Freed's first big concert in the St. Nicholas Arena during the time of their second hit, '(I Love You) For Sentimental Reasons.' Just before that they had 'Eternal Love,' which was written by the kid who wrote 'A Thousand Stars.' Eugene Pearson, I think it was.

"During the first few months of operation, Baton also had a hit with The Buddy Tate Band. 'Fatback and Greens' was a big dance instrumental in Philadelphia, primarily due to the Bob Horn TV show.

"Our first truly national hit, and probably the biggest hit Baton had, also came in 1955. It was 'Lonely Nights,' by the Hearts—three Bronx chicks and a cat named Rex Garvin—and it made Top Ten of *Billboard*'s 'Best-Selling R & B Singles.'

"Our next important artist was Ann Cole, whom I tried to find for a year after hearing a record by her on the Apollo label. When I finally caught up with her, we signed a contract, recorded, and had our first record released within a matter of three days. The record was an R & B cover of the Sheb Wooley song, 'Are You Satisfied?' which broke for a hit immediately. It established Ann Cole as an important R & B artist. This was followed by 'In the Chapel,' which made national best-seller charts.

"Ann Cole's third record was the original of 'Got My Mojo Workin',' another best-seller for us. Prior to the release of 'Got My

Mojo Workin',' Ann Cole toured the South with the Muddy Waters Band and sang 'Got My Mojo Workin'.' Muddy Waters liked the song so much that he went back and recorded it on Chess. Not remembering all the lyrics, he concocted his own version. Muddy Waters's version was released, coincidentally, within the same week in 1957 as Ann Cole's record on Baton. Both records competed for chart positions, with Ann's winding up higher; yet because Muddy Waters's recording remained available while Ann Cole's did not, it is common belief to this day that Muddy Waters's record was the original version of the song.

"Noble 'Thin Man' Watts, a fine tenor saxophonist, recorded an instrumental for us, which we named 'The Slop' after the new dance which was just getting started at the time. An acetate was sent to our distributor in Cleveland and one to Jimmy Byrd, then an important disk jockey in Durham, North Carolina. Both felt that we had a smash instrumental. WHK, a major pop station in Cleveland, persuaded us that the title should be changed because they could not play a record entitled 'The Slop.' We made a new run of labels and reserviced the record with the new title, 'Hard Times.' This was the first Baton record which reached the Top Forty on the national pop charts, quite a feat at that time. Only our inability to get this record on the Dick Clark Show, kept this record from reaching the Top Ten.

"Our next hit was 'These Are the Things I Love,' by The Fidelities, a Platters-type group with a strong lead voice. It was a strong pop/ R & B hit in many territories. Ann Cole also did well with 'Easy, Easy, Baby.'

"From this point on, Baton began to have its troubles with the assimilation of R & B music in the pop Top Forty scene. Distributors stopped paying and helping. I saw the handwriting on the wall, and closed up shop in 1960."

•

Chris Kenner, a New Orleans singer-composer born in 1929, had his first release on Baton Records in '55, the year of its formation. The disk sold so poorly that Sol Rabinowitz might well have forgotten him. An Imperial recording in '57 fared little better. But in 1961 Kenner cut a song he had written with noted New Orleans songwriter Alan Toussaint for Instant Records, an offbeat label owned by Joe Banashek. "I Like It Like That" made R & B charts in June '61 and enjoyed a long run that saw it climb to No. 2 nationally. It was later recorded by the Dave Clark Five and Kenner's own Instant disk, along with other titles, appeared as an Atlantic LP. In the late '60s

Kenner ran afoul of the law and was imprisoned in Angola State Penitentiary until 1973. After his release, he suffered fits of depression, which, friends reported, drove him to drink. On January 28, 1976, he was found dead in his Jackson Avenue apartment. The coroner's office attributed death to a heart attack, suffered several days before he was found by neighbors.

I've got a job in a factory
Feedin' a beast that don't like me.
—ANONYMOUS

The Philadelphia Scene

THE CONTRIBUTION of Philadelphia to R & B was minimal by contrast with its role in the rise of rock 'n' roll. In the latter area, through the *American Bandstand* on ABC-TV, the city of brotherly love influenced not only the record-buying habits of teenagers but their dances and even their dress. Imitating the youngsters who danced under the bland scrutiny of host Dick Clark, teen-age boys around the country wore white shirts and dark ties, drape jackets with all the buttons buttoned, and loose-fitting but well-pressed pants. The girls donned heavy rolled socks and sweaters. As the color of pop music changed, the style of dress became blacker: tab shirts and a thin, dark tie; a jacket that buttoned up close to the neck; tight pants that hugged the hips and hung inches above the ankles; and pointed patent leather shoes. But Clark's unstated effort was to give R 'n' R a clean image. The artists lip-syncing their new releases on his program were preponderantly white—and there was no black "regular" to be seen until after the show moved to California in 1964—just as those appearing on Alan Freed's show were black. In this contrast may lie some explanation for the limited number of black artists that emerged from Philadelphia's independent record labels. During Clark's hegemony, a close relationship existed between *American Bandstand* and these "indies." The Congressional investigation into payola in 1959–60 disclosed, in Jerry Hopkins's summary in *The Rock Story*, that Clark's corporate holdings included "financial interests in three record companies, six music publishing houses, a record pressing plant, a record distributing firm and a company that manages singers."

The largest of the Philadelphia "indies" was Cameo Records, a company launched by songwriters Bernie Lowe and Kal Mann in the year (1956) that Dick Clark succeeded Bob Horn as host of radio Station WFIL's *Bandstand* program. (It was renamed *American Bandstand* when it moved onto ABC-TV in 1957.) Lowe and Mann gave their label a flying start with "Butterfly," a rock 'n' roll song they wrote and recorded with a studio musician named Charlie Gracie. Andy Williams's cover on Cadence Records helped develop the song into a '57 best-seller in pop, where his disk went to No. 1. Although Gracie was white, his recording cracked R & B charts, climbing to No. 10 nationally.

Before 1957 was torn off the calendar, Cameo placed another disk on R & B lists. The song was "Silhouettes"; the group was the Rays; and the disk was leased from XYZ, a company owned by the writers of the ballad. Bob Crewe and Frank Slay, Jr., who wrote the interesting tale of an unfaithful lover discovered through silhouettes on a window shade, encountered the Rays after they had had a flop record on Chess. Two of the quartet's members, lead Hal Miller and second tenor Davey Jones, had sung with and previously left the Four Fellows, a group responsible for "Soldier Boy" on Glory Records. (I purchased publishing rights to "Soldier Boy" when I was creative head of Edward B. Marks Music.) The Rays, all of whom were Harlem ghetto youngsters, included tenor Walter Ford and baritone Harry James.

Their record of "Silhouettes" began with the title word, repeated in a series of triplets sounded on the rising notes of a major triad. The impact and appeal were inescapable, partly because the title had a natural triplet rhythm. Hy Lit, an influential disk jockey at WFIL, reacted as the public did. Repeat spins on his turntable led the Cameo execs to solicit a distribution arrangement. "Silhouettes" climbed to No. 3 on R & B charts in the closing weeks of 1957. Unfortunately, it was the only hit scored by the Rays, although XYZ Records released disks by the group into 1961.

Cameo registered its greatest success in 1960–61 when a former chicken-plucker named Ernest Evans covered a King record by Hank Ballard & the Midnighters. Written by Ballard, the original version of "The Twist" appeared on its release in 1959, on the back of "Teardrops on Your Letter." The lachrymose ballad garnered major exposure and sales, climbing nationally to No. 4 on R & B and causing "The Twist" side to linger behind at No. 16. Shortly after King rereleased the Ballard disk in July 1960, Kal Mann heard it on the Dick Clark show. Watching youngsters twisting to the record, he quickly arranged for Ernest Evans to record it.

Chubby Checker—that was the name Evans selected because of his admiration for Fats Domino—had already had one release on Parkway, Cameo's new subsidiary label. But "The Class," in which he impersonated other singers, did not graduate. However, when "The Twist" was rushed out, it rapidly outstripped Ballard's original in sales and popularity, and stirred the biggest dance craze of the '60s. Bouncing onto R & B charts two weeks after Ballard's record, Chubby's platter bounded up to No. 2 in a sixteen-week run. Reissued by Parkway in December '61, the platter performed the unheard-of feat of becoming a best-seller again and ascending nationally to No. 4. By then, the Twist was developing into an older generation dance; crossing national boundaries, it became a worldwide dance craze. It was at least three years before people ceased throwing their pelvises out of whack, a period during which Chubby Checker achieved worldwide renown.

A fantastic dancer, Chubby inevitably became the impresario of many dances, some old and others new. In '60 he recorded "The Hucklebuck" but failed to generate a revival of the black dance of the early '50s. However, in '61 he helped popularize three dances: the Mess Around, the Fly, and the Pony. His recordings of all three were chartclimbers, with "Pony Time" hitting No. 1. In '62 it was the Limbo to which Chubby addressed himself on wax and in person. His success with songs about dances set a pattern which Cameo/Parkway pursued with other artists.

While Chubby was still enjoying the popularity of the reissue of his Twist record in '62, Cameo produced a new No. 1 R & B platter in Dee Dee Sharp's recording of "Mashed Potato Time," based on another current teen-age dance. Dee Dee, whose real name was Dione La Rue and who grew up singing in a church choir, had come to Cameo by answering an advertisement for a pianist who could read music. For a time, before she began recording on her own, she functioned as a studio background singer and vocalized on many disks, including Chubby Checker's "Slow Twistin'."

As a soloist, Dee Dee accounted for R & B best-sellers into 1963. Although only her debut disk, "Mashed Potato Times," went to No. 1, she produced Top Ten platters in "Gravy," "Ride!" and "Do the Bird," the last-mentioned based on another rock 'n' roll dance.

The Orlons burst on the record scene in '62 with another dance-oriented disk, "The Wah Watusi." Formed initially while they were still going to a Philadelphia junior high school, the group consisted of four girls and Steve Caldwell, who sang bass. After they broke up,

Steve and lead Shirley Brickley joined the Cashmeres, later known as the Dovells, and then named their own group after another fabric. The Orlons came to Cameo in 1960 through an audition arranged by the lead singer of the Dovells.

After two years of flop records, the quartet finally made the charts with "The Wah Watusi," written by Cameo co-founder Kal Mann and Dave Appell, a staff arranger-producer. It was the first of four disks that kept the Orlons on R & B charts through '62 and '63. "Don't Hang Up," "South Street," and "Not Me" all made the Top Ten nationally. But like the Rays and Dee Dee Sharp, the Orlons were artists without staying power.

.

Two other Philadelphia companies made minor contributions to R & B. Swan Records, operated by the writers of "Silhouettes," introduced the short-lived team of Billy & Lillie, several of whose disks made R & B charts between '57 and '59. Lillie Bryant, born in Newburgh, New York, and fifteen years younger than her partner, was the youngest member of the Thunderbirds, a vaudeville group of seven, led by Billy Ford of Bloomfield, New Jersey. Billy had sung and played trumpet with the big band of Cootie Williams (for whom Duke Ellington composed *Concerto for Cootie* and Raymond Scott wrote *When Cootie Left the Duke*). Formed in 1957, Billy & Lillie made Top Ten in R & B the following year with the Latin-tinged "La Dee Dah." Again, they were unable to repeat their success with a series of records, released by Swan into 1959.

Swan was able to project another artist onto R & B charts. Freddy Cannon, whose real name is Frederick Anthony Picariello, was a Massachusetts truck driver who recorded a song he wrote and sent to Bob Crewe and Frank Slay, Jr. In remastering the tape, the Swan entrepreneurs apparently made some revisions in the song, for all three names appear as co-writers. Through Arnie Ginsberg, a potent Boston disk jockey on Station WMEX, Cannon secured exposure of "Tallahassee Lassie" and his record took off to become one of the Top 50 pop hits of 1959. But it also made R & B charts (No. 13 nationally), as did some of Cannon's subsequent releases, notably "Way Down Yonder in New Orleans" in '60 and "Palisades Park" in '62. Cannon was not a R & B singer; for that matter, Charlie Gillett feels that "Tallahassee Lassie" "does have some claim to be the worst rock 'n' roll record ever made."

Jamie Records, an offshoot of a Philadelphia record distributing company headed by Harry Finfer, did not develop any black artists.

But it did account for Duane Eddy, a guitar player of Phoenix, Arizona, whose snarling style on "Rebel Rouser" and other guitar hits made a mark on R & B as well as R 'n' R. Eddy developed a howling, loose-stringed style, described by Lester Sill, one of his Phoenix record producers, as *twangy*. That it was, but it also had menace in it, which was doubtless what appealed to young ears. Eddy's major Phoenix mentor was Lee Hazelwood, later songwriter-producer for Nancy Sinatra ("These Boots Are Made for Walkin' "). Hazelwood's knowledge of electronics led to inventive studio sounds that helped develop the guitar as the key instrument of teen-age music.

•

Why Philadelphia, with its large black population, did not make a more substantial contribution to R & B, is not easily explained. Its proximity to New York may account for the movement of accomplished black artists to Gotham. Doubtless *American Bandstand* played a role, since "indie" companies with easy access to national exposure were more interested in the mainstream market than in R & B. And Philadelphia did produce such teen-age idols as Fabian, Frankie Avalon and Bobby Rydell, among others. In the 1970s, however, when the color of pop changed, the city of brotherly love rose to a potent position in black pop through producers Gamble & Huff. (Kenny Gamble, incidentally, is married to Dee Dee Sharp.) In the '50s and '60s, except for Chubby Checker, Philly artists seemed to lack the talent, showmanship and charisma that spell the difference between making occasional hit records and achieving superstardom.

6. Down-South R & B

"You want to make some blues?" Sam Phillips asked,
knowing I'd always been a sucker for that kind of jive. He
mentioned Big Boy Crudup's name and maybe others, too.
All I know is, I hung up and run fifteen blocks to Sun
Records' office before Mr. Phillips had gotten off the line.
We talked about all the Crudup records I knew—"Rock
Me, Mama," "Everything's All Right," "Hey, Mama,"
"Cool Disposition," and others, and settled for "That's All
Right" . . .
                                                    —ELVIS PRESLEY

*I was down in Louisiana, doing as
    I please,
Now I'm in Texas, I got to work or
    leave.*
—RAMBLIN' (WILLARD) THOMAS

The Black-Owned Texas Company

PEACOCK RECORDS of Houston, Texas, was a pioneer black-owned diskery. It was launched in 1949 as the result of an argument. Don Robey, who ran the label until two years before his death in 1975, was the manager of Clarence "Gatemouth" Brown. In '49, Gatemouth was under contract to Aladdin Records. Gatemouth was also the headliner at The Bronze Peacock, the Houston nightclub owned and operated by Robey until his death.

"I wanted him to have a record out," Robey told *Billboard*'s Claude Hall, "because he was playing in my club. But Aladdin waited until the last day of the year before releasing Brown's second record. So I was mad."

Robey was so mad, in fact, that he trundled Gatemouth into a local Houston studio and recorded five sides, using Jack McVea's combo. Until then, Gatemouth Brown, who was born in Vinton, Louisiana, in 1924, had worked with Maxwell Davis's combo. On a contract that called for two records a year, he had had one Aladdin release in '47 and another in '48.

Of the five sides he recorded with Gatemouth, Robey claims that "Mary's Fine" b/w "Time's Expensive" was a hit disk. Probably it was, as a regional seller. In any event, it put Robey into the record business—he named his new label Peacock, after his club—and he continued recording the Louisiana bluesman into 1960, although the statistics do not disclose any national best-sellers.

"In those days," Robey has said, "rhythm and blues was felt to be degrading, low, and not to be heard by respectable people. People thirty-five to forty years old believed that for years."

But they did not feel the same way about gospel records. Early in Peacock's history, Robey recorded The Five Blind Boys of Mississippi singing "Our Father." It became one of the most durable records on the label. Of lead-singer Archie Brownlee, outstanding gospel authority Tony Heilbut has written: "He would demolish huge auditoriums with the bluesest version of the Lord's Prayer. . . . He would interrupt his songs with an unresolved falsetto shriek that conjured up images of witchcraft and bedlam." Brownlee, who died of a perforated ulcer in 1959, is known to have influenced Ray Charles and is sometimes

479

credited with originating the scream that became a staple of soul singing.

In addition to The Five Blind Boys, Robey made "race" charts in the early '50s with the Bells of Joy singing "Let's Talk about Jesus." He acquired The Dixie Hummingbirds, whose lead singer, Ira Tucker, is still regarded as "The Head of the House," in Heilbut's phrase. And with the Nightingales, led by the Rev. Julius Cheeks, Robey scored a series of eight gospel best-sellers.

The first R & B singer with whom he made the charts was Marie Adams, who had a moderate hit in "I'm Gonna Play the Honky-Tonks" in June 1952. The year brought two other acquisitions, one of whom proved to be a major find, and the other a giant of R & B, but not for Robey. The giant was Little Richard, who made four so-so sides for RCA Victor in '52 and cut an equal number of undistin-

Johnny Ace

guished sides for Robey before he went on to Specialty Records in '55 and "Tutti-Frutti."

Robey's major find was John Marshall Alexander, Jr., who recorded as Johnny Ace for Duke Records, a Memphis label founded by WDIA disk jockey James Mattis. Ace played piano in B. B. King's band and, in fact, participated in an unreleased 1953 King session for Peacock produced in Covington, Tennessee. He became a Robey property when Mattis sold the Duke label to him. Ace's style of singing was in the Chuck Willis vein—cool, flat, unemotional, but with a plaintive quality that appealed to teen-age record buyers.

As Willis' first chart-song was "My Story," Johnny Ace's was "My Song";—and the two were released at just about the same time in the fall of 1952. But Ace captured a larger audience, scoring No. 1. During 1953–54, Ace continued building a following with such chart ballads as "Cross My Heart," "The Clock," which reached No. 1, "Saving My Love for You," and "Please Forgive Me." He had an appeal that went beyond the romantic if mundane character of the songs.

His charisma was enhanced by a rather foolish act on Christmas Eve 1954. Sitting in the dressing room of the City Auditorium in Houston, where he was appearing, he occupied himself during the intermission by fooling with a gun. He liked to play with guns. Apparently to impress a girl, he dropped a bullet in the chamber, spun the barrel, clamped the gun to his head, and clicked the trigger. They call it Russian Roulette, but for Johnny Ace, it spelled curtains. The hammer struck the bullet and there was a resounding explosion. Like Hank Williams, who died on New Year's Eve 1954 while a packed house waited to hear him, Johnny Ace never finished his concert on Christmas Eve 1954.

Robey was then about to release a new ballad, "Pledging My Love," that he had co-authored with Ferdinand Washington. It became one of the giant records of 1955, not only in R & B but in pop as well— and the focus of a posthumous Johnny Ace cult. John Marshall Alexander, who was born in Memphis in June 1929, attended the La Rose Grammar School and Booker T. Washington High School, served in the navy during World War II, played piano in Adolph Duncan's Band when Bobby Bland was the vocalist, and was just twenty-five when he shot himself to death.

•

Not long before his senseless demise, Ace went on a tour of nightclubs and theaters with another Robey artist. Willie Mae Thornton, better known as Big Mama Thornton, is a blues singer in the classic vein of the "Empress of the Blues," Bessie Smith. When she was just fourteen, Big Mama went on tour with an Atlanta troupe known as the Hot Harlem Review. For eight years, she wandered around the cities of the Gulf Coast. A self-taught singer, she also learned how to play drums by herself and mastered the harmonica with some coaching from Little Junior Parker, who traveled with the troupe for a time. In 1948 she quit the Review in a disagreement over money and got a job at the Eldorado Club in Houston, where she began making records for Don Robey's Peacock label in 1951.

She worked with an eight-piece R & B combo of horns and rhythm, recording titles like "Mischievous Boogie," "All Fed Up," and "Cotton Picking Blues," and, later, "I Ain't No Fool Either" and "I Smell a Rat." Willie Mae had a sense of humor and a suspicion of men, at least in the songs she recorded.

It was a session in Los Angeles on August 13, 1952, that gave her the only chart-record of a long, distinguished career. The song was by Leiber and Stoller, though the original credits also included Johnny Otis, who played vibes on the date. "Hound Dog" was its name, and though the session included a brass group of four, Big Mama cut "Hound Dog" with only the rhythm section. It made the charts in March 1953 and, during a fourteen-week period, zoomed to No. 1. But it was then just an R & B hit—it took a cover by Elvis Presley in his breakout year (1956) to transform it into a pop smash. When Presley sold several million copies of "Hound Dog," it came as something of a surprise to his fans that his record was a cover and not the original. Presley's version has excitement and drive, but Willie Mae's original has a wallop. And it really makes no sense when a man sings it: The hound dog scratching around the door is a horny and unreliable male—and Big Mama's scorn was sharp and biting.

Willie Mae never made the charts again, but she continued making several sides a year for Peacock into 1957. That relationship ended because, she claims, "Peacock cheated me. I didn't get ma money. After they gypped me, I ups and quit, and stayed quit." After that she made a record or two for Big Tone in Oakland (1961), Sotoplay in Los Angeles (1965), and Kent in Los Angeles (1965). During a trip abroad in 1965, she recut "Hound Dog" in London for an Arhoolie album, *Big Mama Thornton in Europe*. An appearance at the Monterey Jazz Festival with the Muddy Waters Band, including James Cotton on "harp" and Otis Spann on piano, led to her making *Big Mama, the Queen at Monterey* in San Francisco.

Willie Mae (Big Mama) Thornton (Photo by Don Hunstein, courtesy Columbia Records)

"I always kept a smile on my face," Big Mama has said. "They didn't know what was going through my mind. Didn't have nothing to eat. They didn't know. Didn't have nowhere to stay. They didn't know." And she has also said: "I don't use dope, I just stick with my Old Granddaddy one hundred proof and my old moonshine corn liquor. Weeds, pills, needles—I don't need nothing like that jive to get out on the stage and sing. I drink, yeah. It makes me happy. But as for getting drunk—never!" But the weed pushers and the pill pushers and the dope pushers come after her, as they do after most performers.

As late as 1971, she was still the blues shouter par excellence, evoking from critic Craig McGregor the following accolade for a performance at the Apollo:

"When after two choruses, she extracts a mouth harp from her voluminous pink robe and wails tight, beautifully phrased blues into the microphone, that Apollo audience—the toughest in American show business, they say—goes out of its mind. 'Hey!' 'Yeah!' 'Good Gawd Almighty!' 'Play it!' She stops, mumbles something about Janis Joplin and blasts off into 'Ball and Chain.' And as she sings her way majestically through the song, ripping off high falsettos, breaks, swoops and shouts, with the ease of a virtuoso artist, I realize just what Janis was after and never got near, what all that straining and posturing and little-girl-with-a-big-voice melodrama was about: it was about what Big Mama Thornton, with apparently no effort and exquisite control, can achieve on any song at all. Stop. 'Everyone's ripped off this song 'cept me,' says Big Mama bitterly."

Perhaps because of his success in the gospel field, Don Robey's interest was in gospel-oriented R & B singers. In the sides that Little Richard cut for Peacock,—"Fool at the Wheel" (1952), "Rice, Red Beans, and Turnip Greens" (1954), etc.—there is hardly a hint of the emotion-wracked screamer that raced to stardom on the Specialty label.

Bobby Bland

But Bobby "Blue" Bland, having made some sides for Modern Records, exploded on Robey's Duke label. At his birth in Rosemark, Tennessee, in 1930, he was named Robert Calvin Bland. The bluesmen whose influence he acknowledges include Lowell Fulson, Roy Brown, and especially B. B. King. He grew up in the bluesy metropolis of Memphis when B. B. King was a performing disk jockey at Station WDIA and Roscoe Gordon had a four-piece combo that included King and Johnny Ace. Through The Beale Streeters, as they called themselves, Bland came to the attention of the Biharis and made his first recordings in 1952: "Crying All Night Long" and "Drifting from Town to Town." By the following year, he had switched to the Duke label, recording "Army Blues," an expression of his feelings as a Korean War draftee.

It was not until four years later that he cut his first national bestseller. "Farther Up the Road," a ballad with a revenge motif—"someone gonna mistreat you"—anticipated Brook Benton's '59 pop hit, "It's Just a Matter of Time." And then the chart-songs started coming, with Bland accounting for as many as thirty-six R & B best-sellers between 1957 and 1970. He was a giant among rhythm-and-bluesmen, commanding a large, dedicated following. But curiously Bland never attained the renown of giants like Jackie Wilson, Ray Charles or B. B. King, nor was he able to cross over into white clubs, as others did. This was, perhaps, a matter of management, but also a result of Bland's brand of showmanship.

Onstage, Bland has the appearance of an awkward, overgrown boy. He does not resort to the flamboyant costumes of James Brown, the sweating antics of Little Richard, or the intense facial contortions of B. B. King. He is possessed of a good, mellow baritone and works with a well-disciplined band, playing well-made arrangements. He relies on these elements to convey his sincerity, involvement, and emotion.

Not long after he established himself on wax, his style took a decided turn in a gospel direction. "Do I have a witness?" he would ask in personal appearances and sink to one knee like a devotional suppliant. And on disks like "Lead Me On," "Yield Not to Tempation," and "These Hands (Small But Mighty)," he became a preacher leading a congregation. The arrangements were marked by call-and-response patterns, typical of Fundamentalist church services. And Bland himself resorted to all the devices of preachers overwhelmed by feelings too intense for words—extensive *melisma*, stuttering, hoarse cries, and mounting repetition. It is likely that this black gospel style, involving no concessions to pop procedures either in instrumentation or arrangements, limited Bland's audience.

But in the R & B field, his records were sure and consistent winners. In 1959 he had three chart-songs, with "I'll Take Care of You" making No. 2. This was a favorite theme with Bland, reappearing in songs like "Ain't That Loving You?" "Call on Me," and "You're All I Need." It gave him an image of the dependable family man, the father, rather than just the lover.

But he also played the uneasy, the troubled, and the unrequited lover in songs like "I'm Too Far Gone to Turn Around" (1966), "Save Your Love for Me" (1968), and "If You've Got a Heart" (1970). As the pleading lover, his biggest song was "Turn on Your Love Light," a tremulous, gospel-oriented record that led *Cash Box* to name him No. 1 "R & B Artist of the Year" in 1961. At times, Bland waxed cynical, as in "I Pity the Fool" (1961), "Who Will the Next Fool Be" (1962), and "That's the Way Love Is" (1963), another record that went to No. 1. Perhaps his most moving disk in this genre, freighted with a weary but not quite broken-spirited pessimism, was his version of T-Bone Walker's "Stormy Monday Blues." While pop and Latin overtones seep into his work occasionally, he basically remains a rhythm-and-bluesman who records the black experience for black listeners and who has influenced younger bluesmen like guitarist Buddy Guy.

•

Little Junior Parker, born Herman Parker in West Memphis, Arkansas, in 1927, had the good fortune to serve his apprenticeship with Howlin' Wolf when Chester Burnett formed a band in the late '40s. The Wolf was seventeen years Parker's senior; Junior was four years older than another inspired harmonica player in the combo named James Cotton. Playing indigenous country blues, the group backed The Wolf when he served as a performing disk jockey on KWEM of West Memphis—but Parker did not play on the several sides that The Wolf cut for Chess in 1951.

Despite his association with Howlin' Wolf, the initial and major influence in Junior's career was "harpist" Sonny Boy Williamson, to whose King Biscuit Time Show over KFFA of Helena, Arkansas, he constantly listened. When Sonny Boy appeared in Clarksdale, Mississippi, where Junior was working as a cotton field hand in 1948, Junior went to hear his "harp" idol and performed for him. According to legend, Sonny Boy was sufficiently impressed to ask the twenty-one-year-old Parker to appear with him in a show he was giving a few miles away. This accidental collaboration led to an association in which Parker worked with Williamson whenever the older man played in the Clarksdale vicinity. It also led to Herman's being named Little Junior—audiences assumed he and Sonny Boy were kin. From the extremely tall man who walked stoop-shouldered, Little Junior went to Howlin' Wolf's band, where he perfected the shrill, piercing sound that came out of three wailing "harps"—Sonny Boy's, and those of James Cotton and Little Junior.

Junior made his own first recordings in 1952. They were for Modern with a group he called the Blue Flames. Ike Turner, Modern's Memphis talent scout, played piano, as he had done on Howlin' Wolf's first sides. But after one session and two sides ("You're My Angel" and "Bad Woman, Bad Whiskey"), Junior switched to the Sun label, cutting four sides for Sam Phillips late in 1953. They are noteworthy because they included a song entitled "Mystery Train." Co-authored by Junior and Phillips, it was one of the ten Sun sides cut by Presley in '54 and '55 before he became nationally known. In fact, "Mystery Train" became the "A" side of the very first record released by RCA Victor (in November 1955) after it bought Presley's masters from Phillips.

By 1954, Junior was recording in Houston on the Duke label, first with pianist Bill Johnson's Blue Flames, then with his own Blue Flames, and finally with tenorman Bill Harvey's band. It was a session on December 12, 1956, with Harvey's band—included were a typical R & B horn section of trumpet, trombone, and tenor sax—that gave Junior and his "harp" their first chart-song. "Next Time You See Me" climbed into the R & B's Top Ten.

Although he managed to place numbers on the charts in 1958 ("Sweet Home Chicago") and in '59 ("Five Long Years"), Junior did not attain his majority until '61–62, when listeners made five of his records best-sellers. "Driving Wheel" and "In the Dark," recorded after he stopped touring with Bobby Bland and launched his own package show, were the most popular. "Driving Wheel" demonstrated how sex imagery had changed in the blues. Developed at first around country objects like mules, coffee grinders, honey, snakes, etc., sexual connotations began to be attached to mechanized material. Baby no longer "had to work, rob, or steal" because he could make it, but he was also her "driving wheel" in bed.

After "Annie Get Your Yo-Yo" in the spring of 1965, Junior's wailing harp seemed to misfire with the tastes of younger record buyers. By '67, he was on Mercury; by '69, briefly on Blue Rock and Minit; and by '71, on Capitol. After 1962 he was really a bluesman in search of an audience that was buying the Beatles, Rolling Stones, and baroque and psychedelic rock. His material was neither fresh enough nor his style soulful enough to attract listeners on disk.

Yet in 1971, shortly before his death, Parker cut an album for United Artists, *I Tell Stories Sad and True*, which is a rich testimonial to his skill as a songwriter and his unremitting potency as a bluesman. Included is an original song titled, "No One Knows (What Goes On when the Door Is Closed)," obviously the forerunner in thought and even phrasing of a recent country smash, "Behind Closed Doors." Forty-four-year-old Parker died of an eye operation on November 18, 1971.

•

The Robey stable of artists was small but impressive. When you have written about Big Mama, Johnny Ace, Bobby "Blue" Bland, and Little Junior Parker, you have said 'most all of it. Like Little Richard, Johnny Otis paused briefly on Peacock after he left Savoy Records. It was in 1954–5, and he recorded at least four sides, none of which captured the audiences of his Little Esther-Mel Walker recordings of the early '50s or his "Willie and the Hand Jive" hit on Capitol in 1958. As the R & B years lay dying in 1960, Robey scored with a fleeting artist, James Booker, and a number entitled "Gonzo." It was not until the R & B revival after the mid-'60s that Robey was able to interest record buyers again in his new releases. But through the convulsive years of white teen-age music and British rock 'n' roll, Bobby "Blue" Bland kept him and Texas R & B in business with one chartmaker after the other.

Being black, Robey also had to be tough to enter the recording field in 1949 and to remain in it as long as he did. But tough he was—and he was both respected and feared because of his aggressiveness as well as his volcanic temper. Walter Andrus, a recording engineer on many of his sessions, told Joe Nick Patoski for a *Rolling Stone* obituary: "He was just like a character out of *Guys and Dolls*. He'd have a bunch of heavy guards around him all the time, carrying pistols and that kind of stuff, like a czar of the Negro underworld."

Robey remained at the helm of his four labels—Peacock, Duke, Songbird, and Backbeat—until May 1973, when a court decision in a long, drawn-out litigation with Chess Records went against him. It was then that he sold his record and publishing interests to ABC/Dunhill Records, reportedly for $1 million. He remained a consultant until he suffered a fatal heart attack on June 16, 1975. He was seventy-one years old when he died, leaving a wife and seven children.

•

Although the South was basically the source of Blues and Rhythm & Blues, also of its unique and gifted artists, it had limited importance as a record-producing area, at least during the R & B years. (The emergence of studios in Muscle Shoals, Alabama, in Memphis, Tennessee, and Nashville, and the development of Stax as a major record company, came during the so-called soul years after the mid-'60s.) Apart from Peacock/Duke in Houston and Sun Records in Memphis, only two other companies were of consequence during the R & B years. These were Excello/Nashboro of Nashville and Ace Records of Jackson, Mississippi.

I was over in Abderdeen on my way to
New Orleans (repeat)
Them Aberdeen women told me they
will buy my gasoline.
—BUKKA WHITE

From Nashville to New Orleans

EXCELLO RECORDS, out of Nashville, owes its existence to the prosperity of its parent company, a gospel label called Nashboro. According to Tony Heilbut, while Savoy Records rules the gospel market in the East and West, "the South belongs to Nashboro."

The owner of both labels is Ernie Young, proprietor of a Nashville record emporium and, like Randy Wood of Gallatin, Tennessee, of a highly successful mail-order business. In the early '50s, when disk jockey Gene Nobles was host of "Randy's Record Shop" over Station WLAC, his competitor on the same station was John R. [John Richbourg], host of "Ernie's Record Mart." Ernie Young did not do nearly as well with Excello Records, founded in 1953, as his neighbor Randy Wood did with Dot Records. But instead of pursuing a C & W tack, Young went in a blues direction, and was, doubtless, the first to do so in "Jim Crow" Nashville. Excello did not set the world on fire, either with its hits or with its artists, though in the '60s it could boast of Slim Harpo.

The first to score an Excello best-seller—regional rather than national—was Arthur Gunter, a Nashville lad (born in 1926), who hung around Young's record shop. His "Baby, Let's Play House," stirred enough local interest in 1954 so that Elvis immediately covered it. During 1955 Excello scored two R & B hits. "It's Love, Baby," by Louis Brooks & his Hi-Toppers, proved one of the label's all-time biggest sellers, climbing into the Top Three nationally. The second hit, "Rollin' Stone," was by the Marigolds, a quintet, four of whose members recorded for Sam Phillips on Sun as the Prisonaires while they were still in the Tennessee State Prison. Neither Louis Brooks nor the Marigolds were able to repeat their one-time success.

Excello produced two other groups, both of whom made national charts without attaining national renown. In '57, the Gladiolas hit R & B lists with "Little Darlin'," only to have the Maurice Williams song taken away from them by the Diamonds on Mercury. Their "Shoop-Shoop" novelty was a turntable hit without ever attracting a sizable buying audience. The other group was the Crescendos, who were released on a new Ernie Young subsidiary, Nasco, and whose song "Oh, Julie" duplicated the popularity and theme of Paul Anka's "Diana." Both songs were big in 1957, both dealt with the teen-age agonies of a boy in love with an older girl, and both were rock 'n' roll, rather than R & B, hits.

From an R & B standpoint, Excello's important contribution was in waxing three bluesmen who constituted a school, as it were. Call it "swamp blues," as one of the trade papers did; the style emanated from Jimmy Reed, the influential Mississippi bluesman who recorded for Vee Jay. Its characteristics were a steady walking bass, four solid beats to the bar; a cool, rough, slurred, almost detached delivery; and the wedding of electrified instruments to an ethnic, down-home style. A record dealer named J. D. Miller of Crowley, Texas, somewhere along the Gulf highway from New Orleans to Houston, produced recordings of the three men for Excello.

One bluesman went by the colorful name of Lonesome Sundown, the second by the cognomen Lightnin' Slim—and his style was reminiscent of Lightnin' Hopkins—and the third was known as Slim Harpo. All three came from Louisiana, although Otis Hicks (Lightnin' Slim) was born in St. Louis in 1915 and was brought to Baton Rouge when he was a child. Lightnin' touched the charts fleetingly in 1959 with "Rooster Blues," hardly as popular with connoisseurs as are his records of "Bad Luck and Trouble" and the humorous "Hoo-Doo Blues." Lonesome Sundown, born Cornelius Green in Opolousas, Louisiana, in 1925, never proved as attractive as his cognomen, although blues collectors do cherish his record of "My Home Is a Prison."

The most popular of the three was James Moore, of West Baton

Rouge, born around 1925, who became known as Slim Harpo. Playing a wailing amplified harmonica, he was much in demand through the deep South as a performer, and he registered more chart-songs than any other Excello artist. The biggest of these was "Baby, Scratch My Back," a No. 1 disk in 1966. But Harpo's releases went back to 1957, when he cut "I'm a King Bee" on his first session. It made no great buzz in this country, but something of his impact and the appeal of the "swamp school" may be judged from the fact that the Rolling Stones recorded "I'm a King Bee" early in their fantastic career.

Like Savoy Records of Newark, New Jersey, Excello—or, rather, Nashboro, the parent company—continues to flourish through an almost exclusive concentration on gospel.

•

Ace Records was founded in Jackson, Mississippi, in 1955 by Johnny Vincent, a former producer for Specialty Records. A short-lived label, it drew most of its talent from New Orleans, 150 miles due south. Vincent was a more successful producer of rock 'n' roll—mainly with Huey Smith & the Clowns—than he was of R & B. And even Jimmy Clanton, who sounded like Johnny Ace but was white, was a rockabilly balladeer, rather than a rhythm-and-bluesman. His "Just A Dream" went pop, but was a long-lived No. 1 R & B hit in 1958. Managed by Cosimo Matassa, who "discovered" him when he cut a demo at the Cosimo Studio with his band, The Rockets, Clanton had the makings of a teen-age idol, but lacked the charisma to fulfill the potential.

Vincent did not make it either with an R & B singer like Earl King, who hit the charts in '55 on King Records and later in '62 on Imperial, but not on Ace. Another contemporary bluesman, Frankie Ford, enjoyed a brief sail on R & B charts in 1959 with "Sea Cruise," written by Huey "Piano" Smith. When Jimmy Clanton left Ace early in the '60s for an undistinguished career on Vee Jay, Johnny Vincent shuttered Ace Records.

It was not until Stax Records set up shop in a defunct Memphis vaudeville house in 1962 that the South acquired a major record company with a black artist roster. The artists on Dot Records, operating out of Gallatin, Tennessee, were white, although owner/producer Randy Wood built the company into a major label (headquartered in Hollywood) by covering R & B records by blacks. Sun Records never became a major label even though the white artists developed by owner Sam Phillips became national figures and black records produced by him became R & B hits. Just as most of Phillips's artists attained their majority on other labels to which he sold or lost them, so during the R & B years, promising black artists like Muddy Waters, Ray Charles and B. B. King left the South and turned to Northern and Western companies to further their record careers.

·

But at least one artist who might have become a major figure in the history of R & B chose to remain in the South. Although pianist/songwriter/singer Henry Roeland "Roy" Byrd recorded for Northern and Midwest labels (among others), his unwillingness to leave New Orleans or move around the country resulted in his being an influence rather than a star. The rewards were not the same, either in recognition or remuneration; but Professor Longhair, as he is best known, can take pride in knowing that he is the musical father of such New Orleans bluesmen as Allen Toussaint, Dr. John (Mac Rebennack), Huey Smith, and especially Fats Domino. Producer Jerry Wexler, for whose Atlantic label Byrd recorded two sessions, has characterized him as "a seminal force, a guru, an original creator of New Orleans piano style." In *Living Blues*, the Chicago publication, he has been typed "the driving force behind a generation of recorded Rhythm & Blues."

Professor Longhair has described his piano style, on occasion, as a combination of "offbeat Spanish beats and Calypso downbeats"; then again, as "a mixture of rhumba, mambo and Calypso." In a more technical vein, his sound may be defined as the superimposition of fast

triplets (♩♫ ♩♫ ♩♫ ♩♫) on a syncopated rhumba

beat (♫♫♩ ♫♫♩ | ♫♫♩ ♫♫♩). Jelly Roll Morton, a New Orleans jazz predecessor, had spoken of the importance of "the Spanish tinge," like the Habanera rhythm used by W. C. Handy in his famous "St. Louis Blues." Professor Longhair also added Spanish or Cuban rhythms to the blues, playing them with a Calypso or rhumba beat. Perhaps the simplest way to suggest his sound is to say: when you hear Longhair's piano styling, you hear Fats Domino.

Early in his career, the Professor encountered, in fact, Domino's mentor and longtime collaborator, Dave Bartholomew. In a large sense, that encounter marked the beginning of Robert Byrd's career as a pianist. However, Bartholomew's role was that of an unwitting competitor, not a collaborator. The Professor had gone to hear the Bartholomew combo, which was then playing at New Orleans' Caldonia Inn. During a "take five," Byrd managed to take over the keyboard. According to Mike Leadbitter, editor of the British publication *Blues Unlimited*, "the crowd went wild over the 'new sound' " and the owner thereupon "fired Bartholomew and hired Longhair."

Even if Byrd simply succeeded, rather than summarily replaced Bartholomew, it was quite an upward leap, for Bartholomew was then and through the 1950s one of New Orleans' musical kingpins. During the Caldonia Inn booking, Robert Byrd acquired the cognomen under which he became known and made his first featured recording. As the Professor has told it: "We had long hair in those days and it was almost against the law. I was teachin' the fellows—Big Slick on drums, Apeman Black on sax and Papoose Nelson on guitar. Mike Tessitore, owner of the Caldonia Inn, says, 'I'm going to keep this band—we'll call you Professor Longhair and the Four Hairs combo.' "

Professor Longhair's disk debut was on Star Talent, a Texas label owned by Jesse Erickson. Although he recorded four sides in a makeshift studio at Joe Prop's bar on Villere and St. Peter streets, only "She Ain't Got No Hair" and "Bye Bye Baby" were released some time in 1949. Billing on the disk read "Professor Longhair & His Shuffling Hungarians." Apparently, the sideman who most inspired him then was, or claimed to be Hungarian. "He wasn't really white or really black either," the Professor has said. "He played bongos and congas, the sticks, tambourines, combs and Jew's Harp."

Before the record could gain acceptance, Star Talent went out of business, due to problems with the New Orleans Musicians Union. However, the record had caught the ear of, among others, William B. Allen, owner of a local radio store. Acting as the Professor's business representative, Allen brought him to the attention of a Mercury Records representative, who quickly arranged for a session in a Canal Street studio. Recutting "She Ain't Got No Hair" under a new title, "Bald Head," Professor Longhair's combo appeared on the new label as "Roy Byrd & His Blues Jumpers." The Mercury Record made national R & B charts in August 1950, and though it remained for a scant two weeks, it zoomed up to No. 5. By then, incidentally, Fats Domino had just had his first Top Ten R & B record in "Fat Man," which had made national charts five months earlier.

Even before the Mercury disk became a national best-seller, word of Longhair's new sound spread through the record industry. By late '49, Atlantic Records had had its first R & B hit in "Drinkin' Wine, Spo-dee-o-dee" and was veering away from its original orientation as a jazz label. On one of his visits to the Crescent City, co-founder

Ahmet Ertegun went looking for Longhair, who had moved from the Caldonia Inn to the Pepper Pot in Gretna, Louisiana. When he located Longhair, Ertegun offered $100 plus session fees, which, as Longhair told a *Living Blues* interviewer, "was plenty money at that time."

Working in Cosimo's Studio, the Professor cut ten sides for Atlantic. "Mardi Gras in New Orleans," unreleased by Star Talent for whom he had originally recorded it, appeared under the billing of "Roy 'Bald Head' Byrd." On his next Atlantic release—"Walk Your Blues Away" b/w "Professor Longhair Blues"—the credits read "Professor Longhair & His Blues Scholars." The third Atlantic single, "Hey Little Girl" b/w "Willie Mae," was credited simply to Roy Byrd. Although the disks sold well in Louisiana, none made national R & B charts, due apparently to the Professor's unwillingness to give up local bookings and to take time out for promotional appearances around the country.

When he was audible again on disk, Roy Byrd's relaxed vocals and jumping piano were heard on another major R & B label, Federal Records, a subsidiary of King Records of Cincinnati. A session arranged on December 4, 1951, by Joe Assunto of the One-Stop Record Shop on Rampart Street, yielded two singles. They sold in such limited quantities that the following year, Robert Byrd's name was on a Wasco label, a local, black-owned company. The instrumentation was limited to piano, guitar and drums—no horns. The sound was not Professor Longhair's blues with a Latin beat.

Atlantic tried again with Longhair in November 1953. "Tipitina," with horns, became a substantial Southern seller but did not reach out to other areas. Thereafter, Longhair recorded sporadically and invariably on small, local labels: Ebb, owned by the ex-wife of Art Rupe of Specialty Records; Ron, owned by a brother-in-law of Joe Assunto; Rip, owned by Rip Roberts, at whose San Jacinto Club Longhair frequently played with big bands; and finally, on Watch Records, another Joe Assunto undertaking.

Twice in the years between '53 and '65, Professor Longhair seemed on the verge of making it. "Go to the Mardi Gras," recorded by him for the third time, fared so well in '58 on the Ron label that the composition became a regular part of the annual Mardi Gras celebrations. "Big Chief," a two-sided release on Watch Records in 1965, showcased the Professor backed by a nine-piece group, including five horns. It was one of the few recorded selections not composed by Longhair himself. Written by Earl King, who sang and whistled on the disk, it was an ambitious production that even boasted a score by the well-known local arranger, Wardell Quezergue. Nevertheless, it once again failed to attract buyers beyond Louisiana.

During the '70s, the Professor enjoyed the nostalgic excitement of two album releases. In 1972 Atlantic issued all thirteen sides he had cut for it as part of its series of *Blues Originals*, titling the retrospective album *Professor Longhair: New Orleans Piano*. In April 1974, Blue Star Records of France recorded the Professor performing a mixture of his blues as well as old blues and recent R & B hits. Backed by a small combo, he cut traditional blues like "Stag-o-Lee" and "How Long Has This Train Been Gone"; hits of the 1950s like Hank Williams's "Jambalaya (On the Bayou)" and "Rockin' Pneumonia" by Huey "Piano" Smith, one of his disciples; and his own compositions, like "Tipitina" and "Hey Now Baby." The LP captured the Latin-tinged, rhythmic novelty of Longhair's style by its use of a conga drummer as well as a regular drummer.

The Blue Star recording was cut appropriately in Bogalusa, Louisiana, where Henry Roeland "Roy" Byrd was born on December 19, 1918. His parents were both musicians but separated soon after he was born. When he was just two months old, Ella Mae Byrd, his mother, took him to New Orleans where he was raised and still lives. He credits her with teaching him the fundamentals of music and of such instruments as piano, bass, drums, and guitar. Living in the downtown area of New Orleans, in the environs of such clubs as Delpee's at Calliope and Franklin (now Loyola) streets, early on he heard jazz and bluesmen like Louis Armstrong, Champion Jack Dupree and Sonny Boy Williamson, No. 2. In fact, his first professional engagement was at the Cotton Club on Rampart Street with a group that included Jack Dupree. He worked with Sonny Boy at the New York Inn. But his major influences were pianists like Sullivan Rock, Robert Betraud, "Kid Stormy Weather," and Tuts (Isidore Washington); also hony-tonk and barrelhouse pianists whom he heard in all the clubs that were clustered on Rampart Street, between Calliope and Clio, during the late '30s.

Before he became a professional musician, Roy Byrd was an acrobatic and tap dancer, starting at the age of thirteen or fourteen. He recalls dancing later with a trio that included Streamline Isaac and Harrison Hike, the three doing a clog dance like the Nicholas Brothers, at the Cotton Club, Porter's Inn, and the New York Inn. From "playing the bottom of his feet," Byrd turned to drums, practicing on a primitive set of traps consisting of orange crates and metal film cans, or of soapboxes and tin cans.

After he came out of the New Deal's Civilian Conservation Corps in 1937, and later when he was discharged from the service in 1943, he turned each time to gambling. In fact, he supported himself by gambling during the years when music did not pay—and he claims music did not yield a livelihood for most of his life. At various times, he also tried to support himself and his children as a cook, punchboard operator, prize fighter, and as a jitney driver.

•

In 1970 when Mike Leadbitter, who wrote the liner notes for Longhair's Atlantic retrospective LP, flew into New Orleans at Mardi Gras time, he located the Professor through a blues freak who had spotted him sweeping the floors of a record store. "He was down and out," Leadbitter wrote in his liner, "and very sad. Neglect, frustration and poor health had taken their toll."

"He never did get off the ground," said Clarence "Frogman" Henry, the Louisiana singer-pianist who scored R & B hits on Argo Records. "Always was a local guy." And Professor Longhair was a local guy in a city, which despite its jazz orientation really had no blues tradition and little blues recording. In a large sense, he was "destroyed" by the limitations of the very city that nurtured him. Had he settled and grown up in Memphis, his might have been a different story. Certainly, he would not have developed the Latin-inflected blues style that was his unique trademark. New Orleans was a metropolitan musical city; Memphis was a cotton belt town. The explanation may lie in that. As New Orleans nurtured jazz, so Memphis nourished the blues.

Standing at the crossroads, I tried to
   flag a ride (twice)
Ain't nobody seem to know me,
   everybody pass me by.
      —ROBERT JOHNSON

Sun Records

I MET Sam Phillips, the owner of Sun Records, in the fall of 1955 when I was managing the creative department of Edward B. Marks Music Corporation. It was in the period when several major New York recording companies were bidding for the services of Elvis Presley, then under contract to Sun Records. My office was in the RCA Building on Avenue of the Americas, and Phillips came early on a Saturday morning for a breakfast date. The meeting was the climax of several feverish weeks in which the recording world and a portion of the record-buying public suddenly became aware of Elvis's potential as a recording artist. I must accept some share of responsibility for this development.

You see, about a month before Phillips came to my office, I had been down in Nashville and had stayed at the home of Col. Tom Parker in nearby Madison, Tennessee. Parker was then running Hank Snow Jamboree Attractions and, occasionally, helping other managers set up road tours for their artists. As a result of assisting Bob Neal, a disk jockey on Station WMPS of Memphis, Parker became familiar with Presley, whom Neal was then managing.

(At one point, according to Joe Delaney, then sales manager of Victor's Label X, Bob Neal tried to peddle Elvis to the label. All he wanted for his share was $2000, ostensibly money he had laid out in booking and promoting Elvis. The label would have had to make a separate deal with Phillips to buy the recording contract. Manie Sachs, then head of Victor, rejected the deal.)

Before I left Parker's home in the summer of 1955, he asked me to listen to several sides recorded by Presley on Sun. I had not heard of Elvis until then, and I was frankly mystified by his sound. He sounded black, as did the combo behind him. But it was a type of blackness that later came to be known as "rockabilly." It has been described (by me, among other musicologists) as a merging of two regional streams of American music—black rhythm and blues, and white country and western. And it was that, to a degree, though it would probably be more accurate to describe it as the sound of young, white Southerners imitating black bluesmen.

In fact, Elvis's ten Sun sides, released between August 1954 and August 1955, included Arthur "Big Boy" Crudup's "That's All Right, Mama"; Roy Brown's "Good Rockin' Tonight," a Wynonie Harris hit; "Milkcow Blues Boogie," recorded originally by Kokomo Arnold, and later by Joe Williams; "Baby Let's Play House," recorded by Arthur Gunter; and "Mystery Train," written and recorded by Little Junior Parker.

I guess that Colonel Parker sensed that I was both baffled and intrigued by what I heard. He hastened to assure me that while Presley had not really made his mark on wax, he was *dynamite* in personal appearances, affecting Southern girls, white and black—as Sinatra once had. He also indicated that, though he was not then Elvis's manager, he expected to take over when Bob Neal's one-year deal expired.

And that was exactly what he did early in 1956. All of this led to the crux of the colonel's gambit: Did I—big man that I was—think that I could get Presley's Sun Records played in Noo Yahk?

Without committing myself, I put the five records in my attaché case, along with pictures of a sneering youth with long sideburns playing guitar. The fact was that I could not get them played in New York when I approached a friendly disk jockey on CBS. But Bill Randle, who lived and worked in Cleveland and did a Saturday show on CBS, thought he could try them at his home base on Station WERE.

The impact of Randle's spinning of the Sun disks in Cleveland was unforeseen and quite shattering. Teen-age listeners seemed instantly to go beserk and kept calling the station for repeat plays of "Mystery Train," "I Forgot to Remember to Forget," and "Good Rockin' Tonight." The word spread like a contagion from Cleveland record distributors to executive home offices in New York, Chicago, and Los Angeles that there was a *hot* new artist on the record scene. At first, all of the record excitement speared into my office since Randle knew of Presley through me and directed inquiries to me. But then Sam Phillips became the center of a frenzied auction in which Columbia, Mercury, and other majors bid for Presley's contract.

I, too, got in touch with Phillips—as a publisher interested in buying original copyrights recorded by Presley. And it was this that led to our breakfast meeting that Saturday morning in September 1955.

Phillips was a slender, youngish-looking man of medium height, with a large shock of black hair, a gentle mien, and a reserved manner. Although callers from high places in American recording circles had been ringing his Memphis phone for weeks, he displayed no sense of excitement—nor was he boastful or smug. (His accomplishments as a talent scout and record maker might well have led him to be both.) During my phone contact with his office—mainly with a Ms. Marion Keisker—we had reached a tentative understanding that he might sell 50 percent of one of the Presley originals. And that was the deal I set for Edward B. Marks Music that Saturday morning on "I Forgot to Remember to Forget." Presley's explosion on the national record horizon did not occur until four months later, early in 1956.

Of course, Phillips was then in New York on a larger undertaking. Through Col. Tom Parker, RCA Victor had the inside track on the purchase of Presley's recording contract, and Hill & Range Songs was in a similar position with regard to the publishing rights. (The colonel had worked very closely with both during the many years that he managed Eddy Arnold.) And when announcement was finally made

Elvis Presley

in November 1955, Phillips had sold Presley's contract and masters to RCA Victor for $25,000. Hill & Range acquired the publications of Hi-Lo Music, Sun's publishing subsidiary, for the sum of $15,000, all except the 50% share of "I Forgot to Remember to Forget" that Sam Phillips committed at our Saturday breakfast.

When Phillips went into the record business in 1950, he had a rather unusual idea. And if any one company can be credited with initiating the teen-age overturn of Tin Pan Alley, it would be Sam Phillips' Sun Records—and not only because of Elvis.

Born in Florence, Alabama, Sam Phillips was raised on a plantation, where he early heard the blues as sung by black farmhands, among them, an Uncle Silas Payne. In school, he learned to play drums and the sousaphone. After graduating from college, Phillips went into the radio field in Memphis. As an announcer, he also handled "remotes," broadcasts from a local hotel or club where the announcer also served as an engineer, setting up microphones and monitoring a portable control board.

It was not long before Phillips became bored with the music that he announced—both country and western (then known as hillbilly) and society dance-band stuff, to which white, middle-class Southerners waltzed or fox-trotted. When he had accumulated a small cash reserve—by then he was married and had two sons—he decided to go out on his own.

Sun Records started as an adjunct of Memphis Recording Service, a studio where you could record your voice for two dollars a side, order an off-the-air check, or have your wedding ceremony recorded. The service produced regular income to finance Phillips's more hazardous undertaking: recording the bluesmen who came into Memphis from the Mississippi Delta and who performed at the many bars and clubs and on the corners of nearby Beale Street. Phillips's work as a radio announcer had, by contrast, made him all too cognizant of the vitality and gut-freshness of the black music he had heard as an Alabama lad, and this feeling had been confirmed by the music he listened to on Memphis's black station, WDIA. He knew also that the Beale Street bluesmen, flooding into town with the cotton crops that made Memphis the South's leading cotton exchange, could not get themselves commercially recorded unless they went to Chicago or New York.

Yet Phillips, who is a rather conservative businessman, was not ready to go whole hog into the launching of a record label. For the first few years in the early '50s, he functioned as an independent producer, leasing the aluminum masters he cut to two R & B labels, Chess Records in Chicago and Modern/RPM Records in Los Angeles. During these years, he recorded an amazing array of the most important figures in the history of R & B: B. B. King, Bobby Bland, Howlin' Wolf, Walter Horton, Elmore James, and James Cotton, among others.

He was responsible for such giant best-sellers as Jackie Brenston's "Rocket 88," a Top Ten disk of 1951 on Chess; B. B. King's "Three O'clock Blues" on RPM and Little Walter's "Juke" on Checker, both Top Ten of 1952; and B. B. King's "Please Love Me," Top Ten in '53 on RPM. Appearing on labels owned by either the Chess or Bihari brothers, these artists were later signed to their labels.

Whether it was the disconcerting experience of having artists he developed move away from him or the realization that the market for R & B had become tremendous, Phillips established Sun Records as a full-fledged label in 1953. One of its first releases, "Bear Cat," sent the company into orbit, as it climbed national R & B charts to No. 3. An answer to Big Mama Thornton's Peacock disk of "Hound Dog," the recording by WDIA dee jay Rufus Thomas brought a lawsuit for copyright infringement by Peacock Records, garnering additional publicty for the fledgling label.

•

Rufus Thomas, born in the tiny hamlet of Casey, Mississippi, in March 1917, grew up in Memphis, where he was graduated from Booker T. Washington High School in 1936. Nat D. Williams, a history teacher at the school and later the first black dee jay in the South, was M.C. of the amateur hour at the Palace Theatre on Beale Street. Thomas, who began working with him as a comic, succeeded Williams as M.C. in 1940 and later, in 1950, joined WDIA with his help. But before that, Rufus worked with the Rabbit Foot Minstrels as a tap-dancer and scat-singer. He left the amateur show after eleven years in a dispute over money, and when B. B. King left WDIA, he took over the Sepia Swing Club, adding a nightly hoot 'n holler program when the station went on a twenty-four-hour schedule in 1954. From 1941, right after he got married and began raising a family, until 1963, he also held down a steady job in a textile mill, the American Finishing Company.

In 1950, when he was appearing at Johnny Curry's Club, he cut his first record for Star Talent. The following year, Sam Phillips leased six of his sides to Chess. After "Bear Cat" hit in 1953, Thomas cut only one other record for Sun. "When Elvis and Carl Perkins and Johnny Cash come along," he told Peter Guralnick in *Living Blues*, "just like he catered to black, Phillips just cut it off and went to white. No more blacks did he pick up at all." Until Thomas began cutting for Stax (originally Satellite) in the '60s, he made only one other record, and that was for Lester Bihari's Meteor label.

Thomas hit it big on Stax. A disk based on a current dance, "Walking the Dog," which he wrote, shot up to No. 5. Rufus was then forty-six. After that, he had a series of record hits, based on dances like "The Penguin," "The Funky Chicken," "The Breakdown" and "The Push and Pull," the last-mentioned a No. 1 R & B disk in 1970. "The kids create the dances," he has said, "and I write the songs." Today, Rufus Thomas is still dancing in-person, even if he is sixty and not cutting records, and regards himself as an entertainer in the groove of Fats Waller, Louis Armstrong and Gatemouth (Dwight) Moore, all early idols.

•

Initially, Sun was a blues label whose artists included indigenous bluesmen like "harpist" James Cotton, who worked with Sonny Boy Williamson for six years and was a mainstay of Muddy Waters' band for twelve; Little Junior Parker, who had "Feelin' Good" and "Love My Baby" on regional R & B charts; and Dr. Isiah Ross, a one-man band, whose disk of "Chicago Breakdown" was a country dance record replete with washboard and broom. Phillips also recorded a group called the Prisonaires, formed by inmates of the Tennessee State Penitentiary. As Presley covered Little Junior's "Mystery Train," Johnnie Ray made a pop hit of The Prisonaires' "Just Walking in the Rain."

But all through the year or more when he was recording and releasing black artists, Phillips kept saying to Marion Keisker, "If I could only find a white man who had the Negro sound and the Negro feel, I could make a million dollars."

And, of course, he did find that man, or, rather, that young man came to the Memphis Recording Service one day in 1953 and paid four dollars to cut two songs for his mother's birthday. More than a year elapsed before Phillips did his first session with the truck driver, then studying to be an electrician. At first, Sam tried cutting country-and-western material with Elvis, who was imitating Dean Martin, a current best-seller. It did not come off. Then, according to legend, Presley began kidding around in the studio one day and did an exuberant version of Big Boy Crudup's blues ballad, "That's All Right, Mama." That was it! They had a record, and one that was eventually to make pop music history. To Southern white ears, Elvis sounded so black that Phillips had him appear on a local disk jockey show where he identified himself as a student at the local white high school. Both Presley and Phillips felt that without that identification, his record might not be played or sell too well in Memphis.

Phillips did not make a million dollars from launching Presley. But once he sold Elvis to RCA Victor, all roads in the South led to Sun Records. Every white Southern boy with record ambitions felt that Phillips had a magic wand. Jerry Lee Lewis came from Louisiana; Roy Orbison from Texas; Conway Twitty, Charlie Rich, and Johnny Cash from Arkansas; and scores of other young amateurs came charging in, pleading for auditions and taxing the patience of Phillips and his assistants, Jack Clement and Bill Justis. Considering that Sun Records was the springboard for all of these important artists and for Memphis-born Carl Perkins, it is hardly an exaggeration to say that Phillips and his record label were responsible for the rock revolution.

What may be surprising to some readers, perhaps, is that the white absorption of rhythm and blues into mainstream pop should have started in the South and that it was the work of Southern youngsters, most of whom were not devoid of the prejudice against blacks inherent in Southern white culture. But despite social and racial barriers, poor Southern whites were closer psychologically to poor blacks than Northern liberals would like to believe. Patently, there was enough sharing of feeling between alienated white Southerners and segregated black bluesmen to give "hillbilly" handling of blues a vigor, excitement, and rich sense of authenticity.

7. The Disk Jockey Scene

It's the rhythm that gets the kids. They are starved for music they can dance to, after all those years of crooners. They are not bad kids. They are just enthusiastic. When I was a boy in Ohio, I drove twenty-five miles to Youngstown and stood in line three hours to see Benny Goodman.

—ALAN FREED

People, people, I'll tell you the way
it seems (twice)
You can only get a favor when your
money is green.
—ALFRED FIELDS

"King of the Moon Doggers"

I T WAS in 1952 that the country first heard of a white Midwestern disk jockey who called himself Moon Dog. He was just a local dee jay on Station WJW in Cleveland, but he was destined to shake up the entire pop music world. He had a late night show sponsored by a Cleveland record shop; the program was originally known as "Record Rendezvous" after the shop. Not long after Alan Freed—that was his name—took over in June 1951, he changed the program's format and named it "The Moon Dog House Rock 'n' Roll Party," employing the phrase that was soon to become the designation of a new era in pop music. But Freed was programming rhythm and blues. Referring to himself as "King of the Moon Doggers," he used "Blues for Moon Dog," a King recording by Todd Rhodes, as his theme. Rhodes was a Detroit bandleader who had supplied the then all-powerful disk jockey Ed McKenzie—he called himself Jack the Bell Boy—with his theme, "Bell Boy Boogie."

What brought Alan Freed to national notice in 1952 was a show and dance he produced at the Cleveland Arena on the evening of March 21. It was called "The Moon Dog Coronation Ball." On the program were bluesman Charles Brown; Varetta Dillard; the Orioles; the Moonglows, featuring Harvey Fuqua and Bobby Lester; Billy Ward & the Dominoes, featuring Clyde McPhatter; Tiny Grimes & His Orchestra; and Jimmy "Night Train" Forest & His Band.

Station WJW later boasted in a flyer distributed to advertising agencies and potential sponsors: "Radio Alone Pulled 25,000!" And it bolstered its claim with excerpts from the local press: "Police reserves were forced to disperse a crushing mob of 25,000 . . . 30 extra firemen . . . 40 extra police."—Cleveland *Press*; "Doors closed . . . after turnstiles totaled 10,091 admissions and still more ticket holders began to storm the entrance."—Cleveland *News*; "People came from as far as Toledo."—Cleveland *Plain Dealer*; "Radio is not a dead medium when it can singlehandedly draw 25,000 to a dance."—Stan Anderson, Cleveland *Press*.

There were two things that Station WJW did not mention in its flyer. One was that the dance had been promoted solely by Alan Freed on his nightly programs. So potent was his sales pitch and so exciting did he make the dance sound that 18,000 listeners paid *in advance*

507

for admission to an arena that could hold only 10,000. The second unmentioned item was that the gate-crashing riot caused by those who could not get in resulted in a police accusation that the dance had been oversold. Freed and three others, including the sponsor of his nightly shows and his manager, Lew Platt, were brought up on charges. These were later dropped. But the front-page stories attracted attention to Freed.

Whether one focuses on the "Coronation Ball" at the Cleveland Arena or the inception of "The Moon Dog House Rock 'n' Roll Party," 1951–2 was a crucial time in the history of R & B. It was the period that initiated a mushrooming of R & B record labels and an enormous expansion of the market for R & B.

•

Alan Freed was hardly the first white disk jockey to spin R & B disks. In Los Angeles, apparently as early as 1951, there was Dick Hugg, all of nineteen years of age, who was known as Huggie Boy. Hugg came on the air to the wail of tenor saxist Joe Houston playing Johnny Otis's ballad "All Night Long" and his opening announcement went: "Keep alive and listen in! All night long! Hi! Huggie Boy Show! All night long, from Dolphin's in Hollywood! In the studio front window at Vernon and Central, Central and Vernon, Vernon and Central, Central and Vernon . . ." Dolphin's was a record store in the heart of LA's black ghetto, and Huggie Boy played R & B disks over Station KRKD from a small booth in the storefront window until 4:00 A.M. "I was the West Coast Alan Freed," Dick Hugg has said.

So was Hunter Hancock, who is better known and who began playing R & B disks during the mid-'40s. (See Groove 25.) On the West Coast, there were also George Oxford in the Bay Area and Phil McKernan in Berkeley. In the East, black listeners heard their music on the turntables of George Lorenz of Buffalo, Danny "Cat Man" Stiles of Newark, Hal Jackson of New York, and Symphony Sid of Boston and later New York. In the South, Zenas Sears was potent in Atlanta, Ken Elliott and Clarence Hamman in New Orleans, Dewey Phillips and Bill Gordon in Memphis, Gene Nobles and John Richbourgh in Nashville, and Bob Smith, who is known as Wolfman Jack, in Shreveport.

Like Smith and Freed, many of the dee jays adopted colorful cognomens. It was Zenas "Daddy" Sears, Ken "Jack the Cat" Elliott, George "Hound Dog" Lorenz, "Jumpin" George Oxford, and Clarence "Poppa Stoppa" Hamman. They modelled themselves in this sense, after black radio personalities, who went by such oddball names as

Jet Pilot of Jive, Dogface, Fatman Smith, Sweet Chariot Martin, Lord Fauntleroy, Big Saul, Satellite Papa, Professor Bop, Jockey Jack, Dr. Daddy-O, and Daddy-Yo Hot Rod.

John Hardy, a Bay Area disk jockey who was voted 1968's R & B Program Director of the Year at Gavin's Programming Conference, recalled his experience in New Orleans at Station WBOK with patent distaste. He went there back in the '50s as a gospel dee jay named Honey Boy: "Station managers think screaming jocks," he later said, "is the way to reach the Negro. It's a disgrace and antebellum thinking."

But black disk jockeys were a much more colorful group of platter-spinners than their white brethren, whose concern seemed to be with dignity, decorum, and the King's English. Black jockeys tended to take over the manners and mannerisms of black preachers. They were showmen rather than announcers. Their job was to entertain, not just to introduce records. By the early '50s, there were quite a number who had made names for themselves on ghetto stations.

They were mostly to be found in Southern cities: "Jockey Jack" Gibson in Atlanta; Nat D. Williams, "Bugs" Scruggs, Larry Dean, and George White in Memphis; "Sugar Daddy" in Birmingham; "Spider" Burks in St. Louis; Bruce Miller in Winston-Salem; and "Professor Bop" in Shreveport.

But San Francisco had its Willie Mays, about whom Station KSAN bragged: "Man, he moves merchandise!" And New York City had a raucous contingent in Phil "Dr. Jive" Gordon on WLIB; Jack Walker, "The Pear-Shaped Talker," on WOV; Joe Bostic on WBNX; Willie Bryant, who called himself "The Mayor of Harlem" and broadcast from a store window on 125th Street on both WHOM and WOR; and Tommy Smalls, who began his WWRL show: "Sit back and relax and enjoy the wax, from three-oh-five to five-three-oh, it's the Dr. Jive Show!"

While Alan Freed may have been the "King of Rock 'n' Roll," Al Benson was, in the words of author Arnold Passman, "the main man who really epitomized the mush-mouthed spade." Calling himself "The Old Swingmaster," he delivered a bright line of jive in a Jamaican accent. According to dee jay John Hardy, who was in Chicago in the late '40s, "Al Benson was the man." And Marty Faye, an outspoken white dee jay, claimed, "Al Benson made Alan Freed look like peanuts."

A number of rhythm-and-bluesmen were themselves disk jockeys. Before they became recording artists, Howlin' Wolf worked on Station KWEM in West Memphis, Elmore James, on Station WOKI at Jackson, Mississippi, and Muddy Waters on Station WOPA in Chicago. The most notable of these was, of course, B. B. King, whose career began on Station WGUM in Greenville, Mississippi, and who acquired his name as a result of being "the Beale Street Blues Boy" on Station WDIA in Memphis.

By 1951–2 quite a few stations catered to black listeners. Most of them were owned by whites, and most were, again, in the South. "Serving and Selling 328,000 Negroes in the St. Louis area since 1947," was how KXLW advertised itself. "The ONLY way to the 107,000 Negroes of the Jackson, Mississippi metropolitan area," was the slogan of WOKJ, which described itself as the "Nation's Highest Hooper-rated Negro Station." And WOBS of Jacksonville, Florida, boasted that it was first in Pulse's survey of Negro music in an area of which 38 percent of the listeners were Negroes. While WSOK of Nashville had some Negro stockholders, Station WERD of Atlanta claimed in 1951 that it was the first wholly Negro-owned station in the country.

And WDIA of Memphis, advertising itself as "America's Only 50,000 watt NEGRO radio station," offered the following statistics: "Covers the Golden Market of 1,237,686 Negroes—nearly 10% of America's Total Negro Population. 40% of the Memphis Trade Area Is Negro."

During the 1950s, radio was the crucial factor in the growth of R & B, as the Jukebox had been in its early years during the war. Played extensively in one area, a record could be a regional hit. Spun on turntables in many cities, it developed the potential of a national chart disk. But regionally or nationally, disk jockey exposure became the sine qua non of sales for an artist and a record—and, for that matter, for the very existence of a small record company.

•

Thereby hangs a tale. Being the key to the fiscal status of a small independent, the dee jay was in a position to command favors without even asking for them. "The payoff or kickback," Arnold Passman writes in *The Deejays,* "was said to be no different from those in any other business endeavors. It was the distributors in the main who made the temptation difficult to resist. They had the records to sell, and the inventories. Where the reality lay, however, was that the smaller-station jock (and this included some major influencers because they were poorly paid) had a complaint because the diskeries and the distribs never got around to buying commercial time."

And so payola tended to become a way of life with the small dee jay. "The strong groundswell of rhythm & blues," Passman observes, "and the advent of television found more than 500 R & B jocks taking care of business on independent stations in every major city."

Payola made for an unhealthy situation. But it was payola, curiously, that accounted for the rise and growth of the "indie" record companies. When a small label owner, lacking the promotional staffs and regional offices of the majors, felt confident about a record and was willing to pay the tariff, he knew that he could get his record heard.

It was not long before certain cities acquired a reputation as payola (and breakout) towns. *Variety* named Philadelphia, the location of Dick Clark's "American Bandstand," as one, and claimed that without a payoff there was virtually a lockout in Cincinnati, the home of King Records. The situation developed from bad to worse through the '50s and finally, as a spinoff from the investigation of rigged TV quiz shows, the record industry and disk jockeys came in for the scrutiny of local and federal investigatory agencies.

Many motives and situations were at play in the 1959–60 probes of payola. Some payers apparently "blew the whistle" because they felt that the situation was getting out of hand. Station managers, it was reported, were resentful of the tax-free dollars passing into the pockets of their subordinates. Racial prejudice played its part, too. Not the least significant factor was the struggle of older-generation publishers, songwriters, and recording artists to halt the onrushing tide of R & B and R 'n' R that was sweeping them out of the market. It was a question of economics and power, not morality, for these established groups had themselves practiced payoffs as far back as World War I and had, in fact, devised the term *payola* long before it became a commonplace word in the '60s.

The payola scandal toppled a number of influential disk jockeys from their pinnacles of power, brought fines and jail sentences to a few, and foreshadowed the end of the R & B era, though not of the style and sound.

As for Alan Freed, Joe Delaney, then a record executive and now a TV-radio personality, put it well when he said, "Alan took a terrible fall for a lot of guys. It did shorten his life. He deserved better. He was the first major voice on radio, the first breakthrough for black artists. And probably that had something to do with his downfall."

•

By the time he shook up the Midwest scene with his "Coronation Ball," Alan Freed was heard on Cleveland's WJW Monday through Friday from 5:00 to 6:00 P.M. and again from 11:15 P.M. to 2:00

A.M.; and on Saturday night from 11:15 P.M. to 3:00 A.M. Cleveland's "Chief Station" boomed him as the "hottest show in town" and "the nation's Number One Blues and Rhythm Show."

Something of his impact is suggested by a remembrance Clark Whelton wrote for *The New York Times*: "I was driving through Rocky Hill," he recalled, "twisting the dial on my car radio, when suddenly we picked up WINS and Freed, and zap!—we were hooked. . . . In 1954 radio was Gruen Watch commercials, soap operas and Snooky Lanson Hit Parade Music. . . . You heard things you were supposed to think and never the things you thought. Alan Freed jumped into radio like a stripper into Swan Lake. . . . Someone later said that listening to Freed was like having an aisle seat for the San Francisco earthquake. Only it was better than that. Freed knocked down the buildings you hated and turned the rest into dance floors. . . . In 1954 there was no one like him. . . ."

In a more analytical vein, Bob Rolontz, now of Warner Brothers Communications, has said, "Why did Freed become the leader of the R & B revolution? Because he possessed, to a truly extraordinary degree, three qualities that overwhelmed the kids: he was dynamic, he was a showman, and he was sincere. When Freed walked out on the stage, he generated the same kind of electricity as Mickey Mantle or Judy Garland. . . ."

Freed's route to "blues and rhythm," as the music was characterized on the stationery of WJW's "Moondog House," was quite interesting. He moved with the times, as he himself became a shaper of it. Born in Johnstown, Pennsylvania, on December 15, 1921, of Welsh-Lithuanian ancestry, he grew up in Salem, Ohio, where he was a serious student of classical music. Mastering the trombone and music theory, he also studied electrical engineering. His bent is suggested by the name he gave to a daughter of his first marriage. He called her Sieglinde after a character in the Wagnerian *Ring* cycle of operas. His first job in radio was playing classical records over Station WKST in New Castle, Pennsylvania. But as a youth, he had also organized a Dixieland jazz band, naming it the Sultans of Swing after a Harlem band popular on Fifty-second Street.

After settling in Akron in 1946, he became a dee jay on Station WAKR, where his "Request Review," sponsored by a local department store, became so popular that he decided, in 1950, to try his luck in Cleveland. Things did not go well for a time—"Request Review" bombed on WXEL-TV—so he was forced to accept a late-night stint on Station WXEL radio.

June 1951 brought an upturn for him when he landed the Record Rendezvous Shop as sponsor of a late show on Station WJW. It was owner Leo Mintz who played the critical role in setting a new, miraculous direction for him. Mintz kept talking about a strange buying pattern that was developing in his store: white youngsters purchasing records by black artists. It was a pattern that the owner of Mallory's Music in distant New Orleans noted at the same time.

"White people did not shop on New Orleans' Canal Street," Joe Delaney, then manager of the Dukes of Dixieland, told me. "But I was in Mallory's one day and spotted a white woman buying Lloyd Price's recording of 'Lawdy, Miss Clawdy.' When I asked the owner about it, he told me that quite a number of white people were coming in and asking for the record—"for the maid" or "for the handy man or chauffeur." But they were buying it for themselves. It said something to them, and it told me about an impending change in pop music."

At Leo Mintz's urging, Alan Freed finally spent an afternoon at the Record Rendezvous. What he saw not only shook him up, but changed the course of American pop music. Freed returned to the station and tackled the manager, who agreed to have him follow his regular program with a dance program made up of R & B disks.

Using Todd Rhodes's King recording, "Blues for Moon Dog," as a theme—Freed frequently bayed like a hound during its playing—he launched "Moon Dog House," which became "Moon Dog House Rock 'n' Roll Party." Within months, Freed was on the air twenty-three hours a week, six in the daytime and seventeen at night. He adopted not only a colorful name but an announcing style that was characteristically black. His vocal chords had been damaged when he had some polyps cauterized, giving his voice a naturally hoarse and gravelly sound. When he added volume and a fast, excited delivery, he came as close as anyone could to sounding like a blues shouter. In fact, many listeners thought he was black, and for a time he tried to conceal the fact that he was white. Although other white disk jockeys may have devoted full shows to R & B disks, Freed performed the feat of building a large white audience for records that had previously been of interest only to blacks.

The fantastic success of the first "Moon Dog Coronation Ball" led naturally to plans for a second. But Freed, who was a heavy drinker, was in an automobile accident that nearly took his life and left him with maladies that plagued him the rest of his short existence. He suffered severe damage to his liver, spleen, lungs, and circulatory system; his face was so badly scarred that plastic surgery was required. Apart from an almost psychotic fear of automobiles, he was left with lung damage that made him an easy mark for pneumonia whenever he caught cold. (By 1957, at the height of his popularity, he arranged to do his WINS broadcasts from his home in Connecticut so that he wouldn't have to drive to Manhattan or cope with New York's tough winters.)

The WINS association came in 1954 as the result of a rebroadcast of his WJW show that program director Bob Smith caught over Station WNJR in Newark, New Jersey. When Freed came to the NY station, the reaction of Paul Sherman, a WINS disk jockey who later assisted Freed, was typical: "I see this guy sitting in the studio with a big telephone book in front of an open microphone, thumping his hand all the while the record was playing and making gibbering noises in the background, 'Go, man, go' and 'Yeah, yeah! yeah,' and other sounds I can't reproduce. He was accompanying the music, accenting the beat. . . . Lew Fisher and I were working on the night shift and we were next door. . . . We looked at each other, and Fisher said, 'Oh, my God, I give him three months.' I said, 'You're crazy. I give him one week.' "

They were both wrong, of course, as Sherman readily admits: "The kids grabbed him right up," he told Clark Whelton in the *New York Times*. "He was hired for peanuts, but in his first year, he grossed somewhere over seven hundred and fifty thousand dollars. Outside of the alleged payola, the illegal stuff, or the stuff that turned out to be illegal."

When Freed took over WINS's evening hours, 7:00 to 11:00 P.M., New York was definitely not an R & B town. "In fact, the ratings belonged mainly to the 'good music' stations," as Bob Rolontz notes, "and the only kind of records New York stations broke were things like 'Song from Moulin Rouge.' Freed placed a telephone book on the table in the WINS Columbus Circle studios, started beating out the rhythm with his fist, played the tops in R & B releases, and in just a few weeks had turned the town upside down, topping all other stations in ratings. Alan Freed fan clubs sprang up throughout the East. He was the new king, the King of R & B. He forced station after station in the area to program R & B records."

WINS became New York's top pop music station. Freed's program commanded so many phone calls that he quickly announced a policy of accepting requests only by letters or wires. And when he ran his first rock 'n' roll dance at St. Nicholas Arena during the weekend of

January 14–15, 1955—just four months after starting on WINS—the shindig was a complete sellout.

But Freed began having problems almost from the moment of his entry on the New York scene. Louis Hardin, a blind poet-musician, long known to New Yorkers and tourists as Moondog, sued Freed for appropriating his professional name. Wrapped in brown army blankets and wearing Roman sandals, Hardin was a Christlike figure who performed on Sixth Avenue street corners or just stood motionless, hoping for a handout. The courts held with the blind beggar-musician since his use of Moondog antedated Freed's by at least four years. It was then that Freed began using the phrase "The Big Beat" for his show and changed its name to "Alan Freed's Rock and Roll Party," which had much to do with establishing rock 'n' roll as the designation of white R & B, the new teen-age music.

An unexpected bit of trouble developed in Harlem when a heated mass meeting was held to protest Freed's jive-talk style. "The criticism from the Negro community," program director Robert Smith told Arnold Passman, "was that he was an outsider, that he was imitating them and why shouldn't it be a Negro." Smith appeared at the protest meeting, explaining that the station's target was the entire market, black and white. "The auditorium and the stage were full," Smith recalls, "and it was mostly Willie Bryant [former bandleader turned disk jockey] who was complaining. He felt he could do it better than Freed whom we hired without knowing whether he was black or white." Another black bandleader, Lucky Millinder, came to Freed's defense, rejecting the idea that he burlesqued Negroes and praising him for "the fire and excitement of a Rev. Billy Graham."

Nineteen fifty-six was an embattled year for rock 'n' roll and rhythm and blues—and Alan Freed was in the center of the controversy. When the N.Y. *Daily News* ran a series of articles attacking the new music as an inciter of juvenile delinquency, Freed took time on his WINS radio show to plead with mom and dad to recognize the grossly exaggerated accounts of riots in the media. He also appeared on an Eric Sevareid panel show on CBS-TV to state the case for teen-age music. (Of all the networks, incidentally, CBS proved the most receptive to the new sounds. Alan Freed's "Rock and Roll Dance Party" was a feature of CBS radio on Saturday night. And early in '56 Ed Sullivan presented a one-hour R & B show with Dr. Jive—Tommy Smalls—serving as emcee. In April '56 the ABC radio network began airing an R & B program, hosted by Willie Bryant and originating twice a week from Detroit's Flame Show Bar.)

•

Despite lawsuits and protests, Freed's popularity continued to sky-rocket, with his following cutting across color lines. A second dance in St. Nicholas Arena attracted a two-day crowd of over 15,000 in a place ostensibly filled to capacity at 6000; and an Easter Week show at the Brooklyn Paramount in '56 grossed $204,000.

But Washington's Birthday in 1957 yielded an even mightier display of fan adulation at the now defunct NY Paramount. The teen-age crowd was so great that 300 policemen were commandeered for the event. At one point, the second balcony had to be cleared for three hours as building inspectors examined the structure to make certain that it would withstand the crowd's foot-stomping. Freed was then not only onstage with a lineup of the day's record stars, preponderantly black, but also on the screen in a film titled *Don't Knock the Rock*. It was one of several films—*Rock Around the Clock* and *Rock, Rock, Rock* were others—that contributed to Freed's national and international renown.

Dark clouds appeared on the sunlit horizon in May 1958 when Freed was in Boston to produce and emcee a show starring Jerry Lee Lewis. After the performance, a rumble started outside the theater and spread to other parts of the city. Freed was arrested and charged with anarchy and incitement to riot, charges that were later quashed but at great financial and psychological expense to him. The failure of WINS to back him up led the quick-tempered Freed to a hasty resignation. WABC immediately stepped in with a better offer.

The WABC job was only a temporary break in Freed's fall from prominence and power. By the fall of 1959, the payola investigation was in full swing, and Freed was a major target. On November 21, 1959, he was dropped by WABC because he declined "on principle" to sign an affidavit affirming that he had never played records for pay. Two days later, WNEW-TV blacked out his video dance show "by mutual consent."

Through Mel Leeds, WINS's former program director who was also a target of the investigation, Freed secured a job on Station KDAY in Los Angeles, where Leeds had found a berth. But on May 20, 1960, Alan was indicted for accepting $30,650 from six record companies to plug their disks. By 1962 he was associated with WQAM in Miami, at which time he pleaded guilty to part of the charges and received a $400 fine and a suspended sentence. But the end was still not in sight. In 1964 he was indicted for evading income tax payments of $47,920 between 1957 and 1959. Before the case came to trial, he died on

January 20, 1965, the day that Lyndon B. Johnson was inaugurated as president.

Dick Clark of ABC's "American Bandstand" was also a target of the payola investigations. "Clark fell, too," Arnold Passman has written, "but Freed's two hundred thousand dollar billings on WABC as against twelve million dollars for Clark on TV told the story. Going by Clark's Sunset Boulevard headquarters [today a thriving conclave of TV and film production], one can readily see the black and white reality of it all."

Passman's play on words has more truth than metaphor in it. When Freed began using the term *rock 'n' roll* and later *the big beat*, he was really referring to R & B. Initially, it was, perhaps, a device to make black records palatable to white listeners. Between 1954 and 1956, white derivatives or covers became the order of the day, but Freed stuck with the black originals, generally refusing to play copies of Little Richard, Fats Domino, and others. Throughout the days of his greatest popularity, Freed continued to be partial to black artists on his in-person shows and radio-TV program. And the overwhelming number of records he programmed on his turntable came from the presses of the R & B "indies." Chess Records and artists like Chuck Berry, Howlin' Wolf, Bo Diddley, and The Moonglows benefitted tremendously from his support. According to his widow, one of the most disillusioning moments of his life occurred when, after he was dropped by his New York outlets, he found a closed door at the Chess brothers' enclave. (By then, Leonard and Phil owned a number of radio stations in Chicago and the Midwest.)

By his hearty sponsorship of black artists, Freed contributed greatly to breaking down segregation in radio and TV. He also popularized, if he did not introduce into 50,000-watt and big-city platter-spinning, a style of announcing that was typically black. He was exuberant and expansive; he was loud and explosive; his language was jivey and colorful; and he projected a degree of enthusiasm and excitement that brought listeners flocking to his in-person appearances. As a disk jockey, he was, in short, a rhythm-and-bluesman.

Recognizing that he succumbed to the blandishments that all buyers in our society are offered—not merely those in recording and radio-TV—he must, nevertheless, be regarded as a casualty of the establishment war on teen-age manners, mores, and music, and, more specifically, of that discrimination that has been and is still being practiced against the black minority in our society.

groove 25   **HUNTER HANCOCK**

"When I began programming "sepia" or "race" records in the early forties, we were not known as disk jockeys or dee jays. We were just announcers. I started out by playing jazz records, and there weren't very many stations that programmed jazz in the forties. But then, in May 1943—it was the last Sunday in May—I launched a program aimed at average black listeners. The motivation came from Todd Clothes of Los Angeles who sponsored the program every Sunday on Station KFVD. I don't know about the rest of the country. But in the Los Angeles area, I was the first announcer, black or white, to specialize in what later became known as rhythm and blues.

"It was not until June 1948—I can recall the exact day, June 14, 1948—that I started a daily show instead of just a once-a-week Sunday program. I was on six afternoons with recordings addressed primarily to black listeners. Again I began with jazz. But it wasn't more than a few days before a fellow named Jack Allison came in to see me. He was connected with Modern Records, the local record company run by the Bihari brothers. And he told me that if I wanted to reach average Negroes, jazz wouldn't do it. Thank God that I had the good sense to listen to him and switched my shows to an exclusive diet of R & B disks, then still known as 'sepia' or 'race' records. I did keep a jazz program going for quite a number of years, but eventually I turned that to R & B.

"Now, Joe Adams, the black disk jockey who later became Ray Charles's manager, did get on the air a couple of months before me with a daily show. But he was doing more of a pop-type show. I don't think that he was featuring black artists particularly.

"I can't see that there was anything in my Texas background that moved me in this direction. When I was eighteen, I did start playing drums in my brother's band in San Antonio. We played the pop hits of the day and swing. I had another brother who was a musician. He was the best of the three by a long shot. He played with Henry Busse's Band, Herbie Kay, and the Dallas Symphony.

"I managed to get into radio in San Antonio during the war. In 1942, the day after Labor Day, I started on Station KMAC. After four months, I was transferred to a sister station in Laredo, Texas. I stood that for about three months, said 'Phooey,' and headed for California. I was extremely lucky to get connected almost immediately with Station KFVD. Sometime around 1954, they changed their call letters to KPOP because people were constantly associating KFVD with venereal disease. I was on the Sunday shift when Todd Clothes bought an hour in an effort to reach LA's enormous Negro audience. I must confess that I didn't know a damn thing then about Negro music.

"I played the Cecil Gant record of 'I Wonder' on my Sunday show. But I have a much more vivid memory of Nat 'King' Cole in that period. I interviewed Nat quite a number of times. He had a jazz trio and was playing at local LA clubs—The 331 Club, if memory serves me. After he hit the big time on Capitol Records, I did not see very much of him.

"In later years, I did some recording. Roger Davenport and I had a label called Swingin' Records. One of our releases was Big Jay McNeely's 'Something on Your Mind.' We also had a Magnum label. I sold my interest in these to Davenport.

"John Dolphin is the guy who nicknamed me 'Old H.H.' When I'd come into his record store shortly after I got started, he'd always say, 'Here comes old H.H.,' and it stuck. Dolphin's store was on East Vernon near Central Avenue. It was the biggest record shop in the area for many years. He was killed twelve to fifteen years ago by one of the fellows with whom he made some recordings and evidently hadn't paid, or at least the fellow didn't think that he had been paid enough. The story is that John pulled a knife and the fellow put six bullets into his belly. Yeah, I remember old John Dolphin well. Ruth Dolphin, his widow, has been running the business since he was killed. They have another store down on Broadway and, I think, a third. But the original is still at 1065 East Vernon.

"During the late forties and early fifties, the Club Alabam was the biggest on Central Avenue. That was like Harlem's Lenox Avenue. For a period of time, I did an amateur show from there. Before that I produced a talent show with Johnny Otis. That was at the Barrel House, owned by Johnny, Bardu Ali, and Tina de los Santos. I also did a talent show at one point from The Club Alimony. These were all basically black talent shows.

"Station KFVD, on which I did my afternoon R & B shows, was a sundown signoff station. So I managed to get on okay to do a show on a station that functioned at night. Around '52 or '53, I got connected with KGFJ and I did an R & B show for about four years. Then I was talked into switching to KFOX, which was a mistake. I only stayed with them for about a year. I remained with KPOP—KFVD's new call letters—until it was sold around 1959 to the Storer chain, at which time it became KGBF. That was when I became reassociated with KGFJ on a 6:00 to 9:00 P.M. program. I remained until July 27, 1968.

"From about 1952 until 1964, I did my programs from my own office. I had my own equipment—turntables, mikes, etc. But in '64, when Tracy Broadcasting took over KGFJ, they didn't want me doing a show over which they had absolutely no control. I don't blame them. Before that, I used to tape the show. But then I had to do it live. In 1966 I dropped the night show and took on production duties, maintaining only my Saturday night program. However, I was on call when people went on vacation or became ill, so I was on the air quite a bit.

"When I had control of my program, I played records only by Negro artists. During the forties, I guess my listening audience was all black. But as we got into the fifties and teen-agers tired of the stuff their parents were listening to on the fifty-thousand watters, I had more and more white listeners. In 1964, after Tracy Broadcasting took control, they allowed me to stick to my R & B format, though on occasion they'd include a record by a white artist. But in 1966, when they went on a strict playlist, I had to program records by white artists. By then, management was selecting all the records to be played on the air and allowing dee jays no latitude. I can understand that—they were trying to protect their licenses.

"But it was no longer much fun. And that was one of the reasons I quit radio. It used to be a ball playing what you wanted to play and what people wanted to hear—saying what you wanted to say. But those days are long past. As long as I was on the air—to pat myself on the back—I was either the top jockey in R & B in Los Angeles or next to the top man, and that was for a long time: from 1948 to 1968."

Coda.
The End of
an Era

Until the days of rock 'n' roll, a lot of times, a lot of the places just wouldn't accept us. I'm not speaking racially. I'm just talking about where people as a whole just wouldn't accept us. In some of these places, the door's open now for you to go into. Because of people like Mike Bloomfield, Elvis Presley, The Beatles, Fats Domino, and people like that helped us out quite a bit. —B. B. KING

I'm a broken-hearted bachelor, travellin'
through this wide world alone (repeat)
It's the railroad for my pillow, this
jungle for my happy home.
—SON BONDS

The R & B Revival

(T)HROUGHOUT the early '50s, there were rumblings of a youthful uprising on the record and film scene—like the audible, but hidden, cracks in a giant iceberg. Auguries of the threatening tide were evident in James Dean, vulnerable, self-destructive rebel without a cause; Marlon Brando, the wild one in menacing black leather; sad-voiced and reckless Johnny Ace; the ebullient Crew Cuts from Canada, the off-key Orioles, the pleading Penguins, the boastful Dominoes. *Crazy, man, crazy . . . See you later, alligator . . . sh-Boom, sh-Boom . . . rock around the clock . . . rip it up! . . . wop-bop-a-lu bop-a-lop bam-boom . . .*

With the advent of Elvis on the national record scene, pop suddenly became, to use an older critic's epithet, "pimple music," and onto the turntables rolled records by young, white "punks" like Ritchie Valens, Frankie Avalon, Fabian, Ricky Nelson, Bobby Darin, Pat Boone—some hugely talented, others attractive to the female portion of the adolescent buying public as images rather than as potent performers, but all aping the black sound or specific black records.

By 1956, crossovers to pop from the black side were quite frequent, though at first there were also white youngsters on R & B charts. This situation was really bad news for most rhythm-and-bluesmen. The records that crossed invariably had a young, if not amateurish, sound—*Teen-ager* was becoming a revolutionary slogan like *Citizen* had been during the French Revolution. And most rhythm-and-blues artists were men of experience who did not sound young and could not look at the world through the misty eyes of an adolescent. Ironically, at the moment of their greatest impact, at the moment when the sounds they had been creating for a decade were becoming "music" to the ears of a large listening public, at that very moment, they were like over-age ball players or boxers. Retirement was the only course for many. Big Boy Crudup went back into the cotton fields. Wynonie Harris turned to tending bar. Amos Milburn worked as a hotel clerk. Some with the vocal equipment and style, like Jimmy Witherspoon, went into jazz. Others like Muddy Waters and Bo Diddley had to content themselves with the bread-and-butter existence of working long, grinding hours in local bars. John Lee Hooker was able to latch onto the folk revival of the '60s and be rediscovered as a proponent

523

of "folk blues." A small number, like Joe Turner and Little Esther, were able to cross into pop. The day of the rhythm-and-bluesmen was to come again, but not until after the British invasion of the mid-'60s.

•

With its November 30, 1963 issue, *Billboard* ceased publication of its R & B charts. No era ends on a given day, week, month, or for that matter, year. But this date does offer a marker of sorts for the end of the R & B years. *Billboard*'s action was motivated not by the disappearance of R & B, but by its absorption into the mainstream. What had been happening for a period of time was that pop and R & B charts had been largely duplicating each other.

Now, crossovers were to be found all through the '30s, '40s and '50s. The Mills Brothers, Ink Spots, Louis Jordan come quickly to mind. The crossover concept was inherent in R & B from the start. In fact, acceptance by the pop market of an R & B disk (Cecil Gant's "I Wonder") generated the first mushrooming of R & B record companies. While these labels produced disks basically for ghetto consumption, they always hoped that the larger white market might be receptive—as it was with Bill Doggett's "Honky-Tonk," Lloyd Price's "Lawdy, Miss Clawdy," and other R & B disks.

By the mid-'50s, artists like Fats Domino and Chuck Berry were crossing over so regularly that it is difficult to think of them except as teen-age favorites or rock 'n' roll singers. Then, in the late '50s and early '60s, we watched the emergence of artists like Jackie Wilson, Sam Cooke, Jerry Butler, Ben E. King, Gene McDaniels, and Brook Benton, and of groups like the Shirelles and the Crystals—all of whom moved directly into the mainstream instead of traveling by way of the black-ghetto market.

By 1961, the Motown complex out of Detroit was beginning to make its presence felt with the Marvelettes and the Miracles. In '62 it exploded with the Supremes, the Temptations, Marvin Gaye, Mary Wells, and Little Stevie Wonder. Out of Memphis, Stax Records (black-oriented though not black-owned) began hitting pop as well as R & B charts with Carla Thomas, Rufus Thomas, and Booker T & The MGs.

Berry Gordy, as the founder of the Motown complex, was interested in the mainstream. Until he discovered that "Tammy" was a trademarked name, he planned to name his first company Tammy Records after the No. 1 ballad sung by Debbie Reynolds in the film *Tammy and the Bachelor*. Tamla was a second choice. As British historian

David Morse has noted: "Motown was essentially a bridge between gospel and popular music which virtually bypassed traditional rhythm and blues." Stax Records bypassed R & B, too. But it did so not by using the string section of the Detroit Symphony Orchestra or the Memphis Symphony, but by returning to root blues and gospel and building a bridge from them to soul.

The rise of Motown and Stax, and of Scepter, Philles, Cameo, Laurie, and other black-oriented companies of the '60s, as well as the wholesale crossover of black artists, meant that the R & B era was over. The mainstream had taken on a black hue, but R & B had also acquired a white pallor. Call it rockabilly, teen-age music, rock 'n' roll, or soul, it was no longer R & B performed by black or white. This is not a matter of economics or rhetoric, but of esthetics. The sound was different, the backgrounds were different, the vocal accompaniment was different, and the content was different. It all had something to do with big orchestras, big arrangements and big productions, with Phil Spector and Berry Gordy, Jr., acting the supreme impresarios.

During 1964, the year when *Billboard* ran no R & B charts, another remarkable development occurred. The Beatles, whose recordings had been released during '63 on Vee Jay and Swan Records without making any strong impression, suddenly erupted into the kind of fantastic phenomenon that Sinatra had been in '44 and Presley had been in '56. The subsequent inundation of American airwaves by British groups signalled a major shift in taste. Rock in its various manifestations—psychedelic, protest, raga, and baroque—was in the wind.

The '60s were an era of freedom marches ("We Shall Overcome" and "Blowin' in the Wind"), the struggle to enforce school desegregation, and the rise of black nationalism—"Black is Beautiful"; "Say it Loud: I'm Black and I'm Proud." And sometimes the new black mood took the form of riots, violence, and wholesale destruction, as in Newark, Watts, and other black ghettos. Black song inevitably acquired a bitterness—Dinah Washington sang "This Bitter Earth"— a bite, a militancy, and an exacerbated intensity that came to be known as soul. Little Richard anticipated it, Jackie Wilson marked the transition, and with James Brown it flowered.

I have heard black artists as well as white critics claim that soul is R & B and R & B is soul. But these two allied styles, reflecting the moods of two different time zones, are not the same, anymore than R & B is the same as the blues. To be sure, they stem from the same roots, but the expression is different enough to involve a detectable difference of style, the difference between the Isley Brothers' "Twist and Shout" and their "Fight the Power." James Brown is not B. B. King, Aretha Franklin is not Dinah Washington, and Ray Charles is not Muddy Waters.

It is not merely a question of tambourines and the gospel-like call-and-response interplay between vocalist and background group. It is that soul singers are possessed in an almost Holy Roller sense. Their feelings are so intense, their sense of outrage so explosive, their demand for respect so corrosive that they stutter, splutter, scream, howl, and cry out. They are not entertainers, but gospel preachers in song. They are not there to relax or amuse, but to involve. They seek not applause, but witnesses.

•

The British invasion actually had a double effect. Even as it contributed to the end of an era, it prepared the ground for the R & B revival that occurred after 1965. *Billboard* reinstated its R & B charts on January 30, 1965. Muddy Waters explained it in a statement to an American college audience when he said, "I had to come to you behind the Rolling Stones and Beatles. I had to go to England to get here!" The Britishers did three things that contributed to the revival: they recorded songs by the great rhythm-and-bluesmen like Muddy Waters, Howlin' Wolf, Little Richard, et al.; they expressed such a fervent respect and adulation for the black artists on whose records they had been nurtured that they shook up American listeners and record buyers; and they booked some of the R & B men on tours as opening acts, prompting American rock groups to do likewise.

And so the younger generation opened its hearts and bade hearty welcome to men who had been aliens in their own land. "I've been comin' to New York for twenty years," B. B. King said in 1968, "and no one in the press heard of me. But things are lookin' up now." And that year, B. B. was not only a featured performer at the Newport Folk Festival—once too pure for a rhythm-and-bluesman—but Bluesway Records issued two new albums, Kent Records reissued his old RPM albums, and he was in demand on the college circuit where once he could not get booking even at Negro colleges.

Lesser-known Albert King of Indianola, Mississippi, then a Stax artist, surfaced from the ghetto underground to be profiled in *Vogue* and *New York* magazines. "The new boss of R & B," as he was called, had spent most of his years driving a bulldozer or trailer truck, and collecting four to five dollars for a sundown-to-sunup gig. In 1969 he said hopefully, "My days of paying dues are over. Now it's my time to do the collecting."

Chess Records initiated a program, along with Specialty, Atlantic, Modern, and others, of reissuing records cut during the R & B years. That program has developed so that few sides of any consequence are now unavailable. Once confined to what has been described as the "chitlin' circuit," rhythm-and-bluesmen soon found open doors at clubs, theaters, and hotel rooms once closed to them. It was not long before I could walk down the Strip of my present hometown (Las Vegas) and, within blocks of each other, find marquees with the names of Aretha Franklin, Ray Charles, Solomon Burke, Gladys Knight & the Pips, Fats Domino, and Little Richard.

"A few years back," said Berry Gordy, "we couldn't make an ABC pick because they'd say, 'That's a blues sound.' Used to be you had 'good music' or popular music, and you had 'race music.' Then you had rock 'n' roll and rhythm and blues. Now, Motown's bridged the gap between pop and R & B."

But in bridging the gap, Gordy did what the Mills Brothers and Ink Spots and, on occasion, Louis Armstrong had done earlier—tailored the product for the white market, bleached it slightly, resorted to a showmanship that would make the authentic original more palatable to white taste. Self-caricature was always an inherent danger in R & B, and Louis Jordan came perilously close to falling into this trap. The willingness to exploit oneself may have contributed to the economic exploitation practiced by some white record producers and music producers. That royalties were not always paid seems evident from recent lawsuits brought by Arthur "Big Boy" Crudup, Howlin' Wolf, and B. B. King, none of whom altered his style to attract white buyers.

I have never been able to put out of my mind an article titled "Racism: The Acid That Disfigures Black Artists." A *New York Times* review by Craig McGregor of an Apollo show featuring Big Mama Thornton and B. B. King, it observed: "In what is the most bitter irony of all, B. B. seems to be misjudging his own audience; he plays undiluted blues for white kids at the Fillmore, but feeds his own people showbiz corn." And McGregor adds perceptively: "What I didn't understand until the Apollo was the extent to which racism isn't just a barrier but a cruelly destructive acid which disfigures and distorts the black artists who are its victims. It makes them distrust their own music, forces them to conform to acceptable stereotypes, stunts their capacity for growth. By depriving them of the success they need and deserve, it deprives them of the freedom which any artist needs to develop, think and mature."

In destroying barriers, engendering mobility, and opening hitherto shuttered doors, the R & B Revival of the late '60s has, perhaps, helped to neutralize the acid that disfigures. By the '70s, together with Motown's bland R & B and Stax's Memphis Soul, a "neo-classical" form of R & B evolved with groups like the Chi-lites, Main Ingredient, Persuaders, and, notably, the Stylistics. Retaining the toughness, realism, vitality, and artlessness of pristine R & B in its peak years, the new R & B has added polish and, frequently, social relevance.

In the R & B Revival of the '60s and '70s, the records once made for America's black ghettos have become the music of a color-blind younger generation. But their parents, who were growing up when these records were first released and who were, perhaps, mesmerized by Alan Freed and Elvis, are now frequently resisting school desegregation. They seem to be "singing the blues" of a racist society while their kids are dancing to the new rhythms, one hopes, of an integrated world.

discography

This discography contains two sections. The first consists of collections (C), anthologies of more than one artist, arranged alphabetically according to the title of the collection. The second section lists albums of individual artists, arranged alphabetically under artists' surnames, except for artists who are better known under nicknames. The latter are arranged according to the first word in the nickname: e.g., *Big* Mama Thornton, *Little* Anthony, etc. Where no albums are available, rather than omit the artist, I have listed single records, some of which are, unfortunately, collectors' items. The titles of single records appear between quotation marks; album titles are italicized. In a very few instances, I have included albums of foreign origin. (Add to collections a late arrival: *The Roots of Rock 'n' Roll*. Savoy 2221. Includes tracks by Big Jay McNeely, Big Maybelle, Nappy Brown, Varetta Dillard, King Curtis, Little Esther, Johnny Otis, Hal Singer, and Paul Williams.)

Collections

1C. *After Hours Blues*. Biograph 12010.

2C. *All Star Revue*. King 513.

3C. *Angry Tenors*. Savoy 14009.

4C. *Anthology of the Blues*, Vol. 12. Kent KST 9012.

5C. *Anthology of Rhythm and Blues*, Vol. 1. Columbia CS 9802.

6C. *The Birth of Soul*. Decca DL 79245.

7C. *The Blues: A Real Summit Meeting*. Buddah 2BDS 5144.

8C. *Blues Piano—Chicago Plus*. Atlantic SD 7227.

9C. *Blues Piano Orgy*. Delmark 626.

10C. *Original Boogie Woogie Piano Giants*. Columbia KC 32708.

11C. *Boogie Woogie Rarities, 1927–43*. Milestone 2009.

12C. *Bostic, Bradshaw, Dominoes*. King 536.

13C. *Classic Blues, Vols. 1 and 2*. Bluesway BLS 6061/2.

14C. *Coffee House Blues*. Vee Jay VJS 1138.

15C. *Collector's Record of the '50s and '60s*. Laurie SLP 2051.

16C. *Country Blues Classics, Vols. 1, 2, and 3*. Blues Classics 3BC 5–7.

17C. *18 King Size Rhythm & Blues Hits*. Columbia CS 9467.

18C. *14 Golden Recordings from the Historical Vaults of Vee Jay Records*. ABC, ABCX 785.

19C. *Golden Goodies, Vols. 1–19*. Roulette R 25207; 25209–19; 25238–42; 24247/48.

20C. *Graffiti Gold, Vols. 1 and 2*. Vee Jay GG 9000A.

21C. *The Great Bluesmen, Vols. 1 and 2*. Vanguard VSD 25/6.

22C. *Great Groups*. Buddah BDS 7509.

23C. *History of Rhythm & Blues, Vols. 1–4*. Atlantic SD 8161–64.

24C. *The Jug, Jook and Washboard Bands*. Blues Classics BC 2.

529

25C. *Legend of Leadbelly.* Tradition TRD 2093.

26C. *Let the Good Times Roll.* Bell 9002.

27C. *Memphis Blues.* Kent KST 9002.

28C. *Milburn, Hopkins, Gene & Eunice.* Aladdin 710.

29C. *Negro Church Music.* Atlantic 1351.

30C. *Negro Religious Music: The Sanctified Singers, Vols. 1 and 2.* Blues Classics 2BC LP 17/18.

31C. *1950's Rock & Roll Revival.* Kama Sutra KSBS 2015.

32C. *Oldies But Goodies, Vols. 1–10.* Original Sound SR 8850–60.

33C. *The Old Time Song Service, Dr. C. J. Johnson.* Savoy MG 14126.

34C. *Orioles, Dominoes, Four Tunes.* Jubilee 1014.

35C. *Rhythm & Blues, The End of an Era, Vols. 1 and 2.* Imperial LP 94003/5.

36C. *Rhythm & Blues: Best Vocal Groups.* Dootone 204.

37C. *Original Rhythm & Blues Hits.* RCA Camden CAL 740.

38C. *Rock and Roll Festival.* Kent KST 544.

39C. *Rock 'n' Roll Solid Gold, Vols. 1 and 2.* Mercury SR 61371/2.

40C. *Rock 'n' Roll Survival.* Decca DL 75181.

41C. *Rock 'n' Soul, Vols. 1–9.* ABC 9ABCX 1955–63.

42C. *Stars of the Apollo Theatre.* Columbia 2KC 30788.

43C. *Story of the Blues.* Columbia G 20008.

44C. *Teenage Party.* Gee 702.

45C. *Texas Blues.* Kent KST 9005.

46C. *Texas Guitar.* Atlantic SD 7226.

47C. *This Is How It All Began.* Specialty SPS 2117.

48C. *Twenty Original Winners.* Roulette R 25249.

49C. *Underground Blues.* Kent KST 535.

50C. *Versus Rhythm & Blues.* Dootone 223.

51C. *Women of the Blues.* RCA Victor LPV 534.

52C. *Your Old Favorites.* Old Town OT LP 101.

Individual Artists

Johnny Ace: Memorial Album, Duke DLP 71. *See* 32C, Vol. 10; 41C, Vol. 1.

Faye Adams, *Softly He Speaks,* Savoy 14398. *Original Golden Blues Greats, Vol. 5,* Liberty 7525. *See also* 19C, Vols. 8 and 12; 32C, Vol. 2; 41C, Vol. 1.

Ray Agee. *See* 46C.

Arthur Alexander, Warner Bros. BS 2592.

John Marshall Alexander, Jr. *See* Johnny Ace.

Lee Allen. *See* 19C, Vol. 9.

Albert Ammons. *See* 10C.

Gene Ammons, *Soulful Saxophone,* Chess 1440. *Early Visions,* Cadet 2CA 60038.

Gary Anderson. *See* Gary "U.S." Bonds.

Lee Andrews & the Hearts. "Maybe You'll Be There," Rainbow 252. "Long Lonely Nights," Chess 1665. *See also* 19C, Vol. 3.

Sil Austin, *Everything's Shakin',* Mercury 20320; *Slow Walk Rock,* Mercury 20237.

"Baby" Cortez. *See* 19C, Vol. 13.

La Vern Baker, *Her Greatest Record-*

ings, Atco SD 33–372; *Blues Ballads*, Atlantic 8030. *See also* 5C; 23C, Vols. 2, 3 and 4.

Hank Ballard. *See* 5C, 17C.

Jesse Belvin. "Goodnight My Love," Kent 45 MX 17. *See also* 19C, Vol. 8; 32C; 38C.

Chuck Berry's Golden Decade, Vol. 2, Chess 2CH 60023; Vol. 3, Chess 2CH 60028. *See also* 19C, Vols. 8 and 9; 32C, Vol. 10.

Big Bill Broonzy Story, Verve MG 5V 3000–5; *The Young Bill Broonzy*, Yazoo L 1011; *Big Bill Broonzy*, Columbia 30–153; Vocalion 04706; Vanguard VRS 8523–4.

Big Boy Crudup, *The Father of Rock and Roll*, Victor 20–3261. *See also* 7C, 37C.

Big Jay McNeely, *Big Jay in 3-D*, King 530. "Deacon's Hop/Blues in G Minor," Kent 45 MX 32.

Big Joe Williams, 2 Arhoolie 1002/ 1053; *Blues Bash with Lightnin' Hopkins*, Olympia 7115.

Big Maceo Merriweather. *See* 37C.

Big Mama Thornton: She's Back, Backbeat BLP 68; *Sassy Mama,* Vanguard VSD 79354.

Big Maybelle: The Last of, Paramount 2PAS 1011. *Big Maybelle Sings,* Savoy 14005.

Billie & Lillie, *See* 41C, Vol. 4.

Otis Blackwell Singin' the Blues, Davis JD 109.

Billy Bland. *See* 19C, Vol. 12; 48C; 52C.

Bobby Bland: Introspective of the Early Years, ABC/Duke 2BLPD 92. *See also* 27C; 32C, Vol. 9; 41C, Vols. 3, 7, 8, and 9.

Blind Boy Fuller, Blues Classics 11.

Blind Lemon Jefferson, The Classic Folk Blues of, Riverside 2RLP 12–125; 12–136M.

Blind Willie McTell: *Atlanta Twelve String,* Atlantic SD 7224.

Bo Diddley: *16 All Time Greatest*

Hits, Checker 2989. *See also* 19C, Vol. 8; 25C; 32C, Vol. 10.

Bob & Earl. *See* 41C, Vol. 9.

Earl Bostic: Harlem Nocturne, King S1048. *See also* 19C, Vol. 8; 25C; 32C, Vol. 10.

Alex Bradford. *See* 47C.

Hadda Brooks, "Polonaise Boogie," Modern Music 123.

Louis Brooks & His Hi-toppers, "It's Love Baby," Excello 2056.

Buster Brown. *See* 19C, Vol. 17; 20C; 41C, Vol. 6.

Charles Brown: Great R & B Oldies, Blues Spectrum BS 102. *See also* 5C; 13C, Vol. 1.

Clarence Brown. *See* Gatemouth Brown.

James Brown: *The Unbeatable 16 Hits,* King 919. *See also* 5C, 17C.

Maxine Brown. *See* 19C, Vols. 8 and 9.

Mel Brown. *See* 13C, Vol. 1.

Nappy Brown, Savoy 14002.

Robert Brown. *See* Washboard Sam.

Roy Brown: *Hard Times,* Bluesway BLS 6056. *See also* 13C, Vol. 1; 23C, Vols. 1 and 2.

Ruth Brown, Atlantic 8004.

Brownie McGhee & Sonny Terry, Fantasy 3254. *Hootin' and Hollerin',* Olympic 7108. *See* Sonny Terry. *See also* 13C, Vol. 2; 14C; 21C; 25C.

Bukka White, Arhoolie 1019/20. *Parchman Farm,* Columbia C 30036.

Bull Moose Jackson. *See* 5C, 17C.

Bumble Bee Slim, "Ida Red" and "Lonesome Old Feeling," Fidelity 3004.

Carl Burnett. *See* Little Caesar.

Chester Burnett. *See* Howlin' Wolf.

Sam Butera, *The Big Horn,* Capitol T 1098.

Jerry Butler Sings Assorted Songs, Mercury SR 61320. *The Sagittarius Movement,* Mercury SR 61347. *The*

Best of Jerry Butler, Vee Jay VJS 1048. *Jerry Butler Gold*, Vee Jay VJS 2–1003. *Just Beautiful*, Kent KST 536.

Robert Byrd. *See* Bobby Day.

The Cadets, "Stranded in the Jungle," Kent 45s MX 26. *See also* 19C, Vols. 10 and 17; 32C, Vol. 1; 38C.

The Cadillacs, *The Fabulous Cadillacs*, Jubilee 1045. *See also* 19C, Vol. 3; 41C, Vol. 1; 48C.

Cab Calloway: *St. James Infirmary*, Epic LN 3265. *See also* 42C.

The Capris. *See* 31C.

The Cardinals. "Wheel of Fortune," Atlantic 958. "The Door Is Still Open," Atlantic 1054. *See also* 23C, Vol. 1.

Una Mae Carlisle, "Throw It Out Your Mind" and "That's My Man," Savoy 616.

Leroy Carr: Blues Before Sunrise, Columbia C 30496.

Champion Jack Dupree, Atlantic LP 8255; *Cabbage Greens*, OKeh OKM 12103. *See* 5C, 10C.

Gene Chandler, The Best Of, Vee Jay VJS 1199. *The Two Sides of Gene Chandler*, Brunswick BL 754149. *See also* 18C; 19C, Vol. 18; 20C, Vol. 7; 32C, Vol. 6; 41C, Vols. 8 and 9.

The Channels. *See* 19C, Vol. 11; 32C, Vol. 5; 41C, Vol. 2.

The Chantels. *See* 19C, Vols. 2, 3, 6, 10, and 11; 32C, Vol. 4; 41C, Vol. 4; 48C.

Jimmy Charles & the Revillettes. *See* 41C, Vol. 6.

Ray Charles: The Greatest Hits of, Atlantic 7101; *Hallelujah I Love Her So*, Atlantic 8006; *What'd I Say*, Atlantic 8029. *See also* 13C, Vol. 1.

The Charms. *See* Otis Williams & the Charms.

The Charts. *See* 32C, Vol. 2; 41C, Vol. 3.

Peter Chatman. *See* Memphis Slim.

The Checkers, "House with No Windows," King 4710. "White Cliffs of Dover," King 4675.

Clifton Chenier: Louisiana Blues & Zydeco, Arhoolie F 1024.

The Chords, "Sh-Boom," Cat 104. *See also* 23C, Vol. 2.

Chubby Checker, Twist, Cameo P. 7001. *See also* 26C, 48C.

Savannah Churchill, "Daddy Daddy," Manor 1004.

Jimmy Clanton. *See* 20C, Vol. 2; 41C, Vol. 4.

Dee Clark. *See* 18C; 19C, Vol. 9; 20C, Vol. 2; 32C, Vol. 6; 41C, Vols. 5 and 7.

The Cleftones. *See* 19C, Vols. 2, 7, and 19; 20C, Vol. 1; 41C, Vol. 7; 48C.

James Cleveland & the Cleveland Singers: He Leadeth Me, Savoy MG 14131. *James Cleveland & the Angelic Choir, Vol. 7*, Savoy 14171.

The Clovers, Atlantic 8009 and 1248. *Their Greatest Recordings: The Early Years*, Atco SD 33–374. *See also* 23C, Vols. 1, 2, and 3; 32C, Vol. 2.

The Coasters: Their Greatest Recordings: The Early Years, Atco SD 33–371. *Their Greatest Hits*, Atco 33–111. *See also* 19C, Vol. 2; 20C, Vols. 3 and 4; 26C.

Nat "King" Cole: Original Sounds, Up Front UP 151.

Sam Cooke: The Golden Sounds of, Trip 2TLP 8030. *Songs by Sam Cooke*, Keen 2001. *Encore*, Keen 2003.

Eddie Cooley & the Dimples. *See* 41C, Vol. 2; 48C.

Les Cooper & the Soul Rockers. *See* 41C, Vol. 8.

David Cortes Clowney. *See* Baby Cortez.

James Cotton Band, 100% Cotton, Buddah BDS 5620. *The James Cotton Band, High Energy, Buddah BDS 5650. See 21C.

Ida Cox. See 21C, 42C.

The Crescendos, "Oh Julie," Nasco 6005.

The Crows, Oldies But Goodies, Vol. 2, Original Sound OSR 8652. See also 19C, Vols. 2 and 19; 32C, Vol. 2; 48C.

Arthur Crudup. See Big Boy Crudup.

The Crystals. See 19C, Vol. 16; 35C, Vol. 2.

The Cuff Links. See 19C, Vol. 15.

The Danleers. See 39C, Vol. 1.

Eddie "Lockjaw" Davis: The Cookbook of, Prestige P 24039.

Rev. Gary Davis. See 21C.

Maxwell Davis & His Tenor Sax, Aladdin 804.

Bobby Day. See 32C, Vols. 5 and 9.

The Dells: Greatest Hits, Vol. 2, Cadet CA 60036. The Dells in Concert, Vee Jay VJS 7305. See also 18C; 19C, Vols. 5 and 6; 32C, Vol. 3; 41C, Vol. 2.

The Delta Rhythm Boys. See 23C, Vol. 1.

The Del-Vikings: They Sing—They Swing, Mercury 20314; Record Date, Mercury 20353. See also 32C, Vol. 3; 39C, Vols. 1 and 2.

The Diablos, "The Wind," Fortune 511.

The Diamonds. See 23C, Vol. 1.

Varetta Dillard, "Easy, Easy Baby," Savoy 847. "Mercy Mr. Percy," Savoy 897.

Dixie Hummingbirds: The Best Of, Peacock PLP 138.

Floyd Dixon, "Call Operator 210," Aladdin 3135. "Telephone Blues," Aladdin 3075.

Willie Dixon: Catalyst, Ovation OVQD 1433. Memphis Slim & Willie Dixon: Blues Every Which Way, Verve V 3007.

Bill Doggett, King 585. See also 5C, 17C, 32C, Vol. 6.

The Dominoes, King 536. See Billy Ward.

The Dootones, "Teller of Fortunes," Dootone 366.

Lee Dorsey. See 19C, Vol. 17; 20C, Vol. 1; 41C, Vol. 7; 48C.

Thomas A. Dorsey. See Georgia Tom.

K. C. Douglas, Cook LP 5002. "Mercury Boogie," Down Town 2004.

Minnie Douglas. See Memphis Minnie.

The Dreamlovers. See 19C, Vol. 11.

The Drifters: Their Greatest Recordings: Early Years, Atco SD 33–375; Golden Hits, Atlantic SD 8153. See also Vols. 3 and 19; 20C, Vols. 2, 3, and 4; 48C.

The Dubs. See 19C, Vols. 2 and 10; 20C, Vol. 1; 32C, Vol. 4; 41C, Vol. 3.

Amos Easton. See Bumble Bee Slim.

Billy Eckstine: Golden Hits, Mercury 60796.

The Edsels. See 19C, Vol. 10.

Tommy Edwards. See 32C, Vol. 7.

The El Dorados: Crazy Little Mama, Vee Jay 1001. See also 19C, Vols. 3 and 11; 20C, Vol. 2.

The Elegants. See 32C, Vol. 5; 41C, Vol. 4.

The Essex. See 19C, Vol. 18.

Ernest Evans. See Chubby Checker.

Betty Everett. See 18C; 20C, Vol. 2; 41C, Vol. 9.

The Falcons, "You're So Fine," Flick 001/Unart 2013.

Fats Domino: Sings Million Record Hits, Imperial 2103. Rock & Rollin' with Fats Domino, Imperial 9004. This Is Fats Domino, Imperial 9028. Very Best of Fats Domino, United Artists UA LA 233G. See also 26C; 32C Vol. 10.

The Fiestas. See 19C, Vol. 19; 52C.

Five Blind Boys of Mississippi: The Best Of, Peacock PLP 139.

The Five Discs. *See* 15C.

The Five Keys: The Best Of, Aladdin 806; *On Stage!* Capitol T 828. *The Connoisseur Collection of,* Harlem Hitparade HHP 5004. *See also* 35C, Vol. 1.

The Five Red Caps, Davis DA 1. "Atlanta, Ga.," Davis 2102. "You Thrill Me," Joe Davis 7135.

The Five Royales, "Dedicated to You," King 580. *See also* 5C, 17C.

The Five Satins Sing, Ember 100. *See also* 19C, Vols. 6 and 11; 26C; 31C; 32C, Vols. 1 and 4.

The Five Willows, "My Dearest Darling," Allen 1000. "Lay Your Head on My Shoulder," Herald 433. "Church Bells May Ring," Melba 102.

The Flairs, "I Had a Love," Hollywood 185/Flair 1012.

The Flamingos. *See* 16C; 19C, Vols. 2, 3, 6, and 19; 20C, Vol. 1; 32C, Vol. 3; 41C, Vol. 5; 40C.

Frankie Ford. *See* 41C, Vol. 5.

The Four Clefs. *See* 37C.

The Four Fellows, "Soldier Boy," Glory 234.

The Four Flames. *See* 47C.

The Four Tunes, "Marie," Jubilee 5128.

Inez Fox. *See* 32C, Vol. 8.

Alan Freed: Go, Go, Go, Coral 57177; *Rock Around the Clock,* Coral 57213; *Rock 'n Roll,* Coral 57063; *Rock 'n Roll Dance Party,* Vol. 2, Coral 57115; *Rock 'n Roll Show,* Brunswick 54043.

Bobby Freeman. *See* 19C, Vol. 4; 20C, Vol. 1; 41C, Vol. 4.

Ernie Freeman. *See* 32C, Vol. 8.

Jesse Fuller. *See* 21C.

Johnny Fuller: California Blues, Kent KST 9003.

Rocky Fuller. *See* Louisiana Red.

Lowell Fulson: I've Got the Blues, Jewel LPS 5009; *In a Heavy Bag,* Jewel LPS 5003; *Tramp,* Kent KST 520; *Let's Get Started,* Kent KST 558; *The Ol' Blues Singer,* Granite GS 1006.

Furry Lewis: Slide 'Em on Down, Fantasy F 24703.

The G-Clefs. *See* 19C, Vols. 14 and 15.

Cecil Gant, Gilt Edge 501; *Rock Little Baby* (English), Flyright 4710.

Don Gardner & Dee Dee Ford. *See* 41C, Vol. 8.

Gary "U.S." Bonds. *See* 31C; 32C, Vol. 7; 41C, Vols. 6, 7, and 8.

Gatemouth Brown. *See* 7C.

Rev. Gatemouth Moore: After 21 Years, Bluesway BLS 6074.

Bob Geddins, "Irma Jean," Trilon 1058. "Thinkin' and Thinkin'," Cavatone 5/Modern 20–685.

Gene & Eunice. *See* 28C; 32C, Vol. 3.

Barbara George. *See* 32C, Vol. 7.

Georgia Tom & His Friends, Riverside RLP 8803.

The Gladiolas, "Little Darlin'," Excello 2101. "Shoop Shoop," Excello 2136.

Lloyd Glenn: Chica-Boo, Aladdin 808. *See also* 7C.

Roscoe Gordon, "No More Diggin'," Kent 45s MX 31.

Lil Green: Romance in the Night, Vintage RCA Victor. *See also* 37C.

Guitar Slim. *See* 46C.

Arthur Gunter, "Workin' for My Baby," Excello 2204.

Shirley Gunter & the Queens, "Oop Shoop"/"That's the Way I Like It," Kent 45s MX 27. *See also* 38C.

Lionel Hampton, All American Award Concert, Decca 8088; *Golden Favorites,* Decca (7) 4296; *Lionel Hampton,* Glad-Hamp 3050. *See also* 6C.

The Harptones. Harlem Hitparade

HHP 5006. *See* 19C, Vols. 1, 7, and 17; 52C.

Eddie Harris: In Sound, Atlantic 1448. *See also* 18C.

Peppermint Harris, "I Got Loaded," Aladdin 3097.

Thurston Harris, "Little Bitty Pretty One," Aladdin 3398.

Wynonie Harris. *See* 5C, 17C.

Wilbert Harrison. *See* 19C, Vol. 17; 20C, Vol. 2; 41C, Vol. 5; 48C.

Dolores Hawkins: *Dolores,* Epic LN 3250.

Erskine Hawkins, "Tuxedo Junction," RCA Victor. "I've Got a Right to Cry," RCA Victor 20–1902.

Jalacy Hawkins. *See* Screamin' Jay Hawkins.

Ronnie Hawkins. *See* 19C, Vol. 8.

Roy Hawkins. *See* 4C.

Arthur Lee Hays & the Crowns, "Truly," RPM 424. "A Fool's Prayer," Dig 133.

The Heartbeats. *See* 19C, Vols. 1, 2, and 5; 20C, Vol. 1; 32C.

The Hearts, "Lonely Nights," Baton 208.

Joe Henderson. *See* 19C, Vol. 12; 41C, Vol. 8.

Andrew Hogg. *See* Smokey Hogg.

Billie Holiday Sings, Kent KST 600. *The History of the Real Billie Holiday,* Verve 2V6S–8816. *The Golden Years, Vol. 1,* Columbia C3L 21; *Vol. 2,* Columbia C3L 40.

The Hollywood Flames, "Tabarin," Unique 005. "Wheel of Fortune," Specialty 429. "Buzz, Buzz, Buzz," Ebb 119.

Homesick James, *Chicago Blues,* Spivey 1003. *See also* 21C.

John Lee Hooker: The Greatest Hits, Kent KST 559. *Detroit Special,* Atlantic SD 7228. *Boogie Chillun,* Fantasy 24706. *The Best of John Lee Hooker,* Vee Jay VJS 1049. *John Lee Hooker Gold,* Vee Jay

VJS 2–1004. *See also* 13C, Vol. 1; 18C; 21C; 41C, Vol. 8; 47C; 49C.

Sam Hopkins. *See* Lightnin' Hopkins.

Walter Horton. *See* Little Walter.

Eddie House. *See* Son House.

Camille Howard, "Money Blues," Specialty 401. *See also* 47C.

Howlin' Wolf: The Back Door Wolf, Chess CH 50045. *Chester Burnett AKA Howlin' Wolf,* Chess 2CH 60016. *Moaning in the Moonlight,* Chess 1434. "Riding in the Moonlight," Kent 45s MX 12. *Howlin' Wolf,* Chess 2A CMB 201. *See also* 27C, 49C.

Helen Humes: Talk of the Town, Columbia PC 33488.

Ivory Joe Hunter, Atlantic 8008; Everest FS 289. *16 of His Greatest Hits,* King 605. *Ivory Joe Sings the Old & the New,* Atlantic 8015. *I Got That Lonesome Feeling,* MGM 3488. *See also* 17C; 23C, Vol. 3.

J. B. Hutto & His Hawks, *Hawk Squat,* Delmark DS 617. *Slidewinder,* Delmark DS 636. *See also* 21C.

The Impressions: Best of, ABC S 654. *Three the Hard Way,* Curtom CRS 8602. *See also* 41C, Vols. 7 and 9.

Isley Bros.: Soul on the Rocks, Tamla 275; *Greatest Hits,* T Neck 3011. *See also* 32C, Vol. 10.

The Jacks, "Why Don't You Write Me," Kent 45s MX 18. *See also* 19C, Vol. 10; 38C.

Benjamin Jackson. *See* Bull Moose Jackson.

Mahalia Jackson: The World's Greatest Gospel Singer, Columbia CL 644.

Walter Jacobs. *See* Little Walter.

Illinois Jacquet, Epic BA 17033; *Message,* King S 1048; *How High the Moon,* Prestige P 24057.

Elmore James, The Legend of, Kent

KST 9001; *Blues After Hours*, Crown 5168. "Dust My Blues," Kent 45s MX 15. "Standing at the Crossroads," Kent 45s MX 55. *See also* 38C, 49C.

Etta James, Chess CH 50042; Cadet S 4013. *Come A Little Closer*, Chess 60029. *Twist with Etta James*, Crown CLP 5250. "Roll with Me Henry/Good Rockin' Daddy," Kent 45s MX 17. *See also* 19C, Vol. 4; 32C, Vol. 1; 38C.

The Jarmels. *See* 15C.

Jazz Gillum. *See* 37C.

Cathy Jean & the Romantics. *See* 32C, Vol. 9.

The Jesters. *See* 19C, Vol. 17.

The Jewels. *See* 32C, Vol. 5; 35C, Vols. 1 and 2.

Buddy Johnson: Walkin', Mercury 20322. *Rock & Roll with Buddy Johnson*, Mercury 20209.

Lonnie Johnson, Bluebird B 8779; OKeh 8775. *See also* 17C.

Pete Johnson. *See* 10C. *See* Joe Turner.

Robert Johnson: King of the Delta Blues Singers, Vol. 1, Columbia CC 1654; *Vol. 2*, C 30034.

Eddie Jones. *See* Guitar Slim.

Jimmy Jones. *See* 32C, Vol. 7.

Joe Jones. *See* 19C, Vol. 12; 20C, Vol. 1; 41C, Vol. 6.

Louis Jordan, Blues Spectrum BS 101; Decca 8593, 8627, 8638, 23631, 29018. *Let the Good Times Roll*, Decca 8551. *See also* 6C.

Juke Box Bonner, 2 Arhoolie 1036/1045.

Don Julian. *See* Don Julian & the Meadowlarks.

Junior Parker, *I Tell Sad Stories and True*, United Artists UAS 6823.

Junior Walker. *Shotgun*, Soul 701. *Soul Session*, Soul 702. *See also* 4C.

Junior Wells, *South Side Blues Jam with Guy & Spann*, Delmark 628. *See also* 21C.

King Curtis: Everybody's Talkin', Atco SD 33–385. *The Best of King Curtis*, Atco SD 33–266; Prestige S 7709. *See also* 19C, Vol. 13.

B. B. King, Modern RLP 498. *Blues in My Heart*, Crown 5309. *Live at the Regal*, ABC S 509. "Please Love Me," Kent 45s MX 1. "Sweet Sixteen," Kent 45s MX 5. "Every Day I Have the Blues," Kent 45s MX 7. "3 O'Clock Blues," Kent 45s MX 9. *See also* 13C, Vol. 2; 38C; 49C.

Ben E. King: Greatest Hits, Atco SD 33–165. *See also* 19C, Vols. 12 and 18; 23C, Vol. 3.

Gladys Knight & the Pips: Queen of Tears, Vee Jay VJS 1197. *See also* 18C; 32C, Vol. 6; 41C, Vol. 7.

Marie Knight: Songs of the Gospel, Mercury MG 20196. *See also* 6C.

Sonny Knight. *See* 32C, Vol. 1; 41C, Vol. 2.

The Larks: Super Oldies, Capitol T2562.

Annie Laurie. *See* 5C.

Leadbelly Soundtrack, ABC ABDP 939. *Huddie "Leadbelly" Ledbetter Memorial*, Stinson 17/19/48/51. *Huddie Ledbetter*, Fantasy F 24715. *Good Night Irene*, Allegro LEG 9025. *See also* 23C, Vol. 1.

Bobby Lewis. *See* 19C, Vol. 12; 48C.

Meade Lux Lewis, Tops 1533; Atlantic 133; Decca 3387. *See also* 8C, 10C.

Jimmy Liggins. *See* 47C.

Joe Liggins, Blues Spectrum BS 106. *See also* 47C.

Lightnin' Hopkins: And the Blues, Imperial 12211. *The Blues Giant*, Olympic 7110. *Early Recordings*, Arhoolie 2007/2010. *Fast Life Woman*, Verve V 8543. *Double Blues*, Fantasy 24702.

Lightnin' Slim, "Mean Old Lonesome Train," Excello 2106.

Mance Lipscomb: Texas Sharecrop-

per & Songster, Arhoolie 1001. See also 21C.

Little Anthony & the Imperials, The Very Best Of, United Artists UA-LA 382. See also 19C, Vols. 2, 7, and 10; 20C, Vols. 1 and 2; 32C, Vol. 3.

Little Brother Montgomery: Tasty Blues, Bluesville BLP 1012. Roosevelt Sykes/Little Brother Montgomery, Fantasy F 24717. Blues Piano—Chicago, Plus, Atlantic SP 7227. See also 1C, 8C.

Little Caesar & the Romans. See 32C, Vol. 6; 41C, Vol. 7.

Little Esther. See 32C, Vol. 9. See Esther Phillips.

Little Eva. See 19C, Vol. 4; 48C.

Little Junior Parker, Duke 72. You Don't Have to Be Black to Love the Blues, Groove 52.

Little Milton: Grits Ain't Groceries, Checker LPS 3011. Greatest Hits, Chess 50013. Little Milton, Chess 2A CMB 204.

Little Richard: Greatest Hits, OKeh 14121; Vee Jay VJS 1124; Specialty 2103. Here's Little Richard, Specialty 2100. Little Richard Gold, Vee Jay VJS 2–1002. Talkin' 'Bout Soul, Dynasty DYS 7304. Little Richard's Back, Vee Jay VJS 1107. Greatest 17 Original Hits, Specialty 5082–2113 M. "Tutti Frutti," Kent 45s MX 39. "Slippin' and Slidin'," Kent 45s MX 42. "Long Tall Sally," Kent 45s MX 40. See also 20C, Vol. 2; 26C; 32C, Vol. 3; 38C.

Little Son Jackson. See 45C.

Little Walter: The Best Of, Chess 1428. Hate to See You Go, Chess 1535. Little Walter, Chess 2A CMB 202. See also 27C.

Little Willie John: Fever, King 564; Talk to Me, King 596. See also 5C, 17C.

Lonesome Sundown, "My Home Is A Prison," Excello 2102.

Louisiana Red Sings the Blues, Atco SD 33–389.

Albert Luandrew. See Sunnyland Slim.

Lucky Millinder, Tod 1037. See also 6C.

Frankie Lymon & the Teenagers, Gee 701. Rock 'n' Roll, Roulette 25036. See 19C, Vols. 1, 2, 9, and 19; 20C, Vol. 1; 41C, Vol. 2.

Jimmy McCracklin, "Just Got to Know," Art-Tone 825. "Think," Imperial 66129. "The Walk," Checker 885.

Ellas McDaniel. See Bo Diddley.

Gene McDaniels: The Facts of Life, Sunset SUS 5122.

Fred McDowell, Mississippi, Just Sunshine JSS 4. Amazing Grace, Testament 2219. See also 21C.

Ruth McFadden. See 52C.

Edna McGriff. See 19C, Vol. 12; 23C, Vol. 1.

Cecil J. McNeely. See Big Jay McNeely.

Clyde McPhatter: Welcome Home, Decca DL 75231. See also 23C, Vols. 2, 3, and 4. See The Drifters.

Jay McShann. See 6C, 7C.

Jack McVea, "Open the Door, Richard," Black & White 792.

Immortal Ma Rainey, Milestone M 47021.

Willie Mabon, "I Don't Know," Chess 1531. "I'm Mad," Chess 1538.

The Magnificents. See 19C, Vol. 6.

The Majors, "A Wonderful Dream," Imperial 5855.

Gloria Mann. See 19C, Vol. 16.

Bobby Marchan. See 41C, Vol. 6.

The Marigolds, "Rollin' Stone," Excello 2057.

Roberta Martin Singers, Savoy MG 14008.

Sallie Martin: The Living Legend, Savoy MG 14242.

Marvin & Johnny. *See* 38C.

Curtis Mayfield, Curtom 8005. *Roots,* Curtom 8009.

Percy Mayfield, Tangerine S 1505. *See also* 47C.

The Meadowlarks. *See* 19C, Vol. 14; 32C, Vol. 1.

The Medallions. *See* 19C, Vol. 15; 32C, Vol. 1.

The Mello Kings. *See* 31C; 32C, Vol. 1.

Memphis Minnie, Blues Classics BC 1.

Memphis Slim, U.S.A., Candid 8024. *The Real Boogie Woogie, Piano Solos,* Folkways FA 3524. *Favorite Blues Singers,* Folkways FA 2387. *With Roosevelt Sykes: Memphis Blues,* Olympic 7136. *And Willie Dixon: The Blues Every Which Way,* Verve V 3007. *Raining the Blues,* Fantasy F 24705. *Honky Tonk Sound,* Folkways 3535. *Blue Memphis,* Warner Bros. 1899.

Mercy Dee Walton. *See* 4C, 47C.

Mickey & Sylvia: New Sounds, Vik LX 1102. *See also* 32C, Vol. 4; 37C.

The Midnighters: Greatest Jukebox Hits, King 41; *Vol. 2,* King 581.

Amos Milburn. *See* 28C.

William Rice Miller (Sonny Boy Williamson 2d). *'The Original' Sonny Boy Williamson,* Blues Classics BC 9. *One Way Out,* Chess CHV 417.

Lucius Millinder. *See* Lucky Millinder.

The Mills Bros., Best, 2 Decca DXS 7193E.

Roy Milton, Roots of Rock, Vol. 1, Kent KST 554. *Rhythm & Blues,* Dooto 223. *See also* 47C.

The Miracles, "Bad Girl," Chess 1734.

Mississippi John Hurt, Piedmont DLP 13157. *See also* 21C.

Mississippi Sheiks, "A Wonderful Thing," Riverside RLP 403.

The Monotones. *See* 19C, Vols. 5 and 19.

Eurreal Wilford Montgomery. *See* Little Brother Montgomery.

The Moonglows, Look It's, Chess 1430. *Rock, Rock, Rock,* Chess 1425. *See also* 19C, Vols. 3, 6, 7, 10, 11, and 19; 48C.

The Moonlighters, "Shoo Doo Be Doo," Checker 806.

James Moore. *See* Slim Harpo.

Joe Morris. *See* 23C, Vol. 1.

Muddy Waters, The Best Of, Chess 1427. *AKA,* 2 Chess 60006. *Can't Get No Grindin',* Chess CH 50023. *Down on Stovall's Plantation,* Testament 2210. *Muddy Waters,* Chess 2A CMB 203. *See also* 7C, 21C.

Johnny Nash. *See* 41C, Vol. 3.

Jimmy Nelson, "T-99," Kent 45s MX 29. *See also* 4C.

The Nutmegs. *See* 19C, Vol. 6; 32C, Vol. 2.

James Oden. *See* St. Louis Jimmy.

Andrew "Voice" Odom: Further On Down the Road, Bluesway BLS 6055. *See also* 13C, Vol. 1.

The Olympics. *See* 20C, Vols. 1 and 2; 32C, Vol. 10; 41C, Vols. 4, 6, and 9.

The Orioles. *See* Sonny Til & the Orioles.

Johnny Otis, Blues Spectrum BS 103. *Cold Shot,* Kent 534.

The Paradons. *See* 32C, Vol. 5.

The Paragons. *See* 19C, Vols. 14 and 15; 41C, Vol. 3.

Herman Parker. *See* Little Junior Parker.

The Pastels. *See* 19C, Vol. 11.

Charles Patton & the Country Blues, Original Jazz Library 1/7. *Founder of the Delta Blues,* 2 Yazoo 1020.

Pee Wee Crayton, Blues Spectrum BS 105. "Blues After Hours," Kent 45s MX 10. "Texas Hop," Kent 45s MX 22. *See also* 4C.

The Penguins: Decade of Golden Groups, Mercury S 2–602. *See also*

19C, Vols. 14, 15, and 19; 31C; 32C, Vol. 1; 48C.

Richard Penniman. *See* Little Richard.

Rufus Perryman. *See* Speckled Red.

Esther Phillips, Atlantic S 8102. *Black-Eyed Blues*, Kudu KU 14. *From a Whisper to a Scream*, Kudu 005.

Phil Phillips. *See* 39C, Vol. 2.

Piano Red, "Rockin' with Red/Red's Boogie," RCA Victor 0099.

The Pilgrim Travelers: Everytime I Feel the Spirit, Vee Jay VJS 18010.

Pine Top Smith. Vocalion 1245/1256; Brunswick 80008/BL 54014.

The Platters, King 549. *Encore of Golden Hits*, Mercury 60243. *See also* 2C; 17C; 39C, Vol. 2.

Elvis Presley, Victor LPM 1382. *Golden Records*, Victor LPM 1707.

Lloyd Price: Greatest Hits, ABC S 324. *Mr. Personality*, ABC S 297. *See also* 19C, Vol. 14; 41C, Vols. 3, 4, and 5.

Arthur Prysock, Art & Soul, Verve V6 5009.

The Ravens: Write Me A Letter, Regent 6062. *The Ravens*, Harlem Hitparade 5007. *See also* 23C, Vol. 1; 41C, Vol. 1.

The Ray-O-Vacs. *See* 6C.

The Rays. *See* 19C, Vol. 16; 32C, Vol. 4.

Otis Redding: History, Atco S 33–261E. *See also* 17C.

Jimmy Reed, The Best Of, Vee Jay VJS 1039. *The Greatest Hits, Vols. 1 and 2*, Kent KST 553 and 562. *Root of the Blues*, Kent 2KST 537. *Blues Is My Business*, Vee Jay VJS 7303. *See also* 13C, Vol. 2; 18C; 41C, Vols. 1, 6, and 7; 49C.

Della Reese: Amen! Jubilee 1083. *Classic Della*, RCA LSF 2419. *See also* 41C, Vol. 3.

The Rivileers, "A Thousand Stars," Baton 200.

Robert & Johnny. *See* 19C, Vol. 6; 52C.

The Robins, Rock 'n' Roll, Whippet 703. *See also* 23C, Vol. 3; 35C, Vol. 2.

The Ronettes. Philles S 4006.

Rosie & the Originals. *See* 32C, Vol. 5; 41C, Vol. 6.

The Royaltones. *See* 52C.

Otis Rush, Blues Live! (Japanese) Trio PA 3086. *See also* 21C.

Jimmy Rushing, Essential, Vanguard 2VSD 65/66. *Listen to the Blues*, Vanguard Everyman SRV 73007. *Everyday I Have the Blues*, Bluesville BLS 6055. *You and Me*, RCA LSP 4566. *Sent for You Yesterday*, Bluesville BLS 6057. *See also* 13C, Vol. 2; 21C.

St. Louis Jimmy, *Chicago Blues*, Spivey 1003. *See also* 1C.

Screamin' Jay Hawkins, At Home With, Epic LN 3448. *See also* 42C.

Dee Dee Sharp, Biggest Hits, Cameo 1062. *See also* 32C, Vol. 6.

Shep & the Limelites. *See* 31C; 32C, Vol. 5; 41C, Vol. 7.

The Shields. *See* 32C, Vol. 3.

Johnny Shines. *See* 21C.

The Shirelles: Remember When, Scepter 2 SPS 599. *Greatest Hits*, Scepter S 507. *See also* 26C; 32C, Vol. 10; 40C.

Shirley & Lee, Let the Good Times Roll, Aladdin 807. *See also* 19C, Vol. 17; 32C, Vol. 1; 41C, Vol. 2.

The Silhouettes. *See* 19C, Vol. 7; 41C, Vol. 4.

Frankie Lee Sims. *See* 47C.

Sister Rosetta Tharpe: Precious Lord, Savoy 14214 (8 track cartridge). *Gospel Train*, Decca DL 8782; Mercury 20201. *See also* 6C.

The Six Teens. *See* 32C, Vol. 4.

Skip James: Greatest of the Delta Blues Singers, Melodeon MLP 7321. *See also* 21C.

Sleepy John Estes, 1929–40. RBF RF 8. *Legend,* Delmark 603. *See also* 21C.

Slim Harpo. *See* 41C, Vol. 7.

Smiley Lewis, "I Hear You Knocking," Imperial 5356.

Bessie Smith: World's Greatest Blues Singer, Columbia GP 33. *Bessie Smith Story,* 4 Columbia CL 855–8. *See also* 42C.

Huey "Piano" Smith. *See* 41C, Vols. 3 and 4.

Mamie Smith. *See* 42C, 51C.

Smokey Hogg, "Little School Girl," Kent 45s MX 21. *See also* 45C.

The Solitaires. *See* 52C.

Son House with J. D. Short: Delta Blues, Folkways 31028. *See also* 21C.

Sonny Boy Williamson, John (No. 1), Blues Classics BC 3; Bluebird B 8580. *See also* 37C.

Sonny Boy Williamson, (No. 2). *See* William Rice Miller.

Sonny Terry: Blues Is My Companion, Verve V 3008. *See also* 21C. *See* Brownie McGhee.

Sonny Til & the Orioles. *See* 19C, Vol. 2; 20C, Vol. 1; 23C, Vol. 1; 34C; 41C, Vol. 1.

The Soul Stirrers: Tribute to Sam Cooke, Checker LPS 10063. *Best,* Checker S 10015. *Gospel Music,* Vol. 1, Imperial 94007. *Original with Sam Cooke,* Specialty S 2137 E. *See also* 47C.

The Spaniels, "Goodnite, It's Time to Go," Vee Jay 1002. *See also* 19C, Vols. 5, 6, 10, and 11; 20C, Vols. 1 and 2; 21C.

Otis Spann Is the Blues, Barnaby 230246. *Heart Loaded with Trouble,* Bluesway BLS 6063. *See also* 13C, Vol. 2; 21C.

The Sparkletones. *See* 19C, Vol. 16.

Speckled Red: The Dirty Dozens, Delmark DL 601; Brunswick BL 58018/7116/7151. *See also* 9C.

The Spiders. *See* 35C, Vol. 1.

Dakota Station with Strings, United Artists UAL 3355. *Dynamic!* Capitol T 1054.

Arbee Stidham. *See* 37C.

Stick McGee. *See* 23C, Vol. 1.

Barrett Strong. *See* 32C, Vol. 4.

Sunnyland Slim: Sad & Lonesome, Jewel LPS 5010. *Plays the Rag Time Blues,* Bluesway BLS 6068.

The Swallows, "It Ain't the Meat," King 4501. "Besides You," King 4525. "Tell Me Why," King 4515.

Swan Silvertones: Love Lifted Me, Specialty S 2122E. *My Book,* Specialty 2148. *See also* 47C.

Roosevelt Sykes Sings the Blues, Crown CLP 5237. *R.S.,* Bluebird 34–0721. *Hard Drivin' Blues,* Delmark DS 607. *Blues,* Folkways 3827. *And Little Brother Montgomery,* Fantasy F 24717. *Honeydripper,* Prestige 7722.

T-Bone Walker Blues, Atlantic 8020. *Stormy Monday Blues,* Bluesville S 6008. *Dirty Mistreater,* Bluesway BLS 6058. *Want a Little Girl,* Delmark DS 633. *See also* 13C, Vol. 1; 46C.

Tampa Red, The Guitar Wizard 1935–53, Blues Classics BC 25; Bluebird B 34–0711; Bluebird B 9024; Bluesville 1030. *See also* 37C.

The Tams. *See* 41C, Vol. 9.

Laurie Tate. *See* 23C, Vol. 1.

The Teenagers, featuring Frankie Lymon, Gee 701.

The Teen-Queens, "Eddie My Love," Kent 45s MX 14. *See also* 20C, Vol. 2; 32C, Vol. 1; 38C.

Joe Tex. *See* 17C.

Carla Thomas. *See* 23C, Vol. 4; 32C, Vol. 8.

Lafayette Thomas, "Cockroach Run," Jumping 5000. "Please Come Back to Me," Savoy 1574.

Tiny Bradshaw, King 536. *Tiny Plays*, King 501.

The Tune Weavers. *See* 19C, Vols. 10 and 19; 32C, Vol. 10.

The Turbans. *See* 32C, Vol. 2; 41C, Vol. 1.

Ike & Tina Turner: Greatest Hits, United Artists U 8512 (8 track Cartridge). *Please, Please, Please*, Kent 550. *River Deep, Mountain High*, A & M 4178. *From the Beginning*, Kent 2KST 533. "Good Bye, So Long," Kent 45s MX 44. *See also* 38C.

Joe Turner: His Greatest Recordings, Atlantic SD 33–376; *The Best Of*, Atlantic SD 8144; *Sings K.C. Jazz*, Atlantic 1234. *Big Joe Rides Again*, Atlantic 1332. *And Jimmy Nelson*, Crown CST 383. *See also* 13C, Vol. 2; 21C; 23C, Vols. 1, 2, and 3; 32C, Vol. 2.

The Valentines. *See* 19C, Vols. 1 and 11; 52C.

The Vibrations. *See* 19C, Vol. 4.

Eddie "Cleanhead" Vinson, Riverside 3502. *See also* 7C; 13C, Vol. 2; 42C.

The Vocaleers, "Is It a Dream," Red Robin 114.

Mel Walker (with Johnny Otis Congregation), "Rockin' Blues," Savoy 766. "Gee Baby," Savoy 777. "Mistrustin' Blues," Savoy 735.

Billy Ward & the Dominoes, King 536; Decca 8621; Federal 548. *Yours Forever*, Liberty 3083. *See also* 5C; 12C; 17C; 32C, Vol. 5; 34C.

Clara Ward: Gospel's Greatest Hits, 2 Paramount 1028. *Lord Touch Me*, Savoy 14006. *Memorial Album*, Savoy 14308.

Washboard Sam. Blues Classics BC 10; Bluebird 8184. *See also* 37C.

Dinah Washington, What a Diff'rence, Mercury 60158. *Sings the Blues*, Grand Award 318. *The Beat of Bessie's Blues*, Emarcy 36130. *The Best in Blues*, Mercury 20247.

Booker T. Washington White. *See* Bukka White.

Hudson Whittaker. *See* Tampa Red.

Larry Williams, Original Golden Blues Giants, Liberty 7572. *See also* 19C, Vol. 14.

Maurice Williams & the Zodiacs. *See* 19C, Vol. 12; 32C, Vol. 5.

Otis Williams & the Charms, King 570. *See also* 2C, 5C, 17C.

Paul Williams, "The Hucklebuck," Savoy 683.

Robert Pete Williams. *See* 21C.

John Lee Williamson (No. 1). *See* Sonny Boy Williamson.

Chuck Willis: His Greatest Recordings, Atco SD 33–373. *King of the Stroll*, Atlantic 8018. *Wails the Blues*, Epic LN 3425. *See also* 23C, Vol. 3.

The Willows. *See* 19C, Vol. 11; 41C, Vol. 2.

Jackie Wilson: Greatest Hits, Brunswick BL 754185; Brunswick 754140. *Higher and Higher*, Brunswick BL 54130. *Nostalgia*, Brunswick BL 754199.

Jimmy Wilson, "Tin Pan Alley," Big Town 101.

Jimmy Witherspoon, The Best Of, Bluesway BLS 6051. *A Spoonful of Spoon*, Verve V6–5050. "Ain't Nobody's Business," Kent 45s MX 8. "No Rollin' Blues/Big Fine Girl," Kent 45s MX 23. *See also* 13C, Vol. 1.

Jimmy Yancey, Atlantic 525; Bluebird B 8630. *Jimmy & Mama Yancey*, Atlantic SD 7229. *See* 10C.

Jonny Young. *See* 21C.

select bibliography

DIXON, ROBERT M. W., AND GODRICH, JOHN. *Recording the Blues.* New York: Stein and Day, 1970.

GILLETT, CHARLIE. *Making Tracks, Atlantic Records and the Growth of a Multi-Billion-Dollar Industry.* New York: E. P. Dutton, 1975.

GODRICH, JOHN, AND DIXON, ROBERT M. W., compilers. *Blues & Gospel Records, 1902-1942.* London: Storyville Publications and Co., 1969.

GROIA, PHILIP. *They All Sang on the Corner, N.Y. City's R & B Vocal Groups of the 1950s.* Setauket, N. Y.: Edmond Publishing Co., 1974.

GURALNICK, PETER. *Feel Like Going Home, Portraits in Blues & Rock 'n' Roll.* New York: Outerbridge & Dienstfrey, 1971.

HEILBUT, TONY. *The Gospel Sound: Good News and Bad Times.* New York: Simon and Schuster, 1971.

JONES, LE ROI. *Blues People/Negro Music in White America.* New York: William Morrow, 1963.

LEADBITTER, MIKE, AND SLAVEN, NEIL. *Blues Records, January 1943 to December, 1966.* London: Hanover Books, 1968.

LYDON, MICHAEL. *Boogie Lightning.* New York: The Dial Press, 1974.

MILLAR, BILL. *The Drifters, The Rise and Fall of the Black Vocal Group.* New York: The Macmillan Co., 1971.

NEFF, ROBERT, AND CONNOR, ANTHONY. *Blues.* Boston: David R. Godine, 1975.

NITE, NORM N. *Rock On, The Illustrated Encyclopedia of Rock 'n' Roll, The Solid Gold Years.* New York: Thomas Y. Crowell Co., 1974.

OLIVER, PAUL. *The Story of the Blues.* Philadelphia: Chilton Book Co., 1969.

PROPES, STEVE. *Those Oldies But Goodies, A Guide to 50's Record Collecting.* New York: Collier Books, 1973.

SHAPIRO, NAT, Editor. *Popular Music, An Annotated Index of American Popular Songs.* Vol. 1, 1950-1959; Vol. 2, 1940-1949. New York: Adrian Press, 1964, 1965.

SHAW, ARNOLD. *The World of Soul, Black America's Contribution to the Pop Music Scene.* New York: Cowles Book Co., 1970.

————. *The Rockin' '50s, The Decade That Transformed the Pop Music Scene.* New York: Hawthorn Books, 1974.

SHIRLEY, KAY, Editor. Driggs, Frank, Annotator. *The Book of the Blues.* New York: Leeds Music Corp., 1963.

WHITBURN, JOEL. *Top Rhythm & Blues Records, 1949-1971.* Menomonee Falls, Wisconsin: Record Research, 1973.

WILLIAMS, RICHARD. *Out of His Head: The Sound of Phil Spector.* New York: Outerbridge & Lazard, 1972.

542

Index

In the cases where performers are more commonly known by their nicknames, they have been listed alphabetically by nickname.
See the Discography for artists not mentioned in the book.

a

A & M Records, 196, 329
ABC/Dunhill Records, 488
ABC/Paramount Records, 188, 205, 323, 325, 380, 426, 456
ACA Studio (Houston), 140, 205
A.S.C.A.P., 152
Abbey Records, 41
Abco Records, 313, 326
Abner, Ewart G., 316, 322, 329, 335, 337, 340, 469
Abner Records, 322, 324
Abramson, Herb, 133–34, 358, 362, 371, 373, 386, 393–94, 395, 396, 399, 400, 405, 421
Ace, Johnny (John Marshall Alexander), 92, 158, 164, 202, 204, 224, 254, 358, 385, *480–81*, 482, 488, 491, 523
Ace of Clubs Records, 42
Ace Records, 32, 491
Ackerman, Paul, xi, 413
Acorn Records, 320
Adams, Berle, 76–85, 127, 212
Adams, Faye (Faye Scruggs), 452–53
Adams, Joe, 196, 518
Admirals, 232
Agee, Ray, 248, 255, 530
Agorilla Records, 45
"Ain't It a Shame" (Fats Domino), 264, 266, 268
"Ain't Nobody's Business" (Jimmy Witherspoon), xxi, 5, 204
Aladdin Records, 75, 93, 100, 110, 173, 212, 228–35, 252, 254, 263, 269, 343, 428, 479
Alert Records, 41
Alexander, Arthur, 530
Ali, Bardu, 160, 161
Allen, Bill "Hoss," 355
Allen, Ernestine, 403
Allen, Lee, 263, 379, 454, 455–56
Allen Records, 422
Allied Pressing Co. (L.A.), 89, 153, 195
Allman Brothers, 114
Altheimer, Joshua, 8, 9, 43
"American Bandstand," 189, 252, 446, 476
American Guild of Authors & Composers, 34, 405
American Recording Corp. (ARC), 9, 24, 25, 30, 38
Ammons, Albert, 48, 51, 52
Ammons, Gene, xx, 291
Amour Records, 153
Andrea Records, 429
Andrews, Lee, and the Hearts, 383, 427
Andrews Sisters, 54
Anka, Paul, 231, 265, 270, 490

Ann Arbor Blues Festival, 301
Anna Records, 443
Apex Records, 41
Apex Sound Studio (N.Y.C.), 361
Apollo Records, 133, 137–40, 145, 148, 424, 425, 428
Apollo Theatre, xix, xxi, 68–69, 167, 224, 232, 282, 306, 349, 363, 377, 405, 421–22, 425, 428, 430, 436, 456, 483
Appell, Dave, 475
Applebaum, Stan, 377, 389, 398
Arco Records, 132
Argo Records, 496
Arhoolie, 3
Arhoolie Records, 275, 482
Aristocrat Records, 31, 38, 289–91
Armstrong, Louis, 13, 14, 130, 151, 221, 264, 495
Arnold, Kokomo, 27, 497
Around the world theaters, 167
Artistic Records, 313
Art-Tone Records, 248, 252, 326
Asch, Moe, 41, 331–32
Asch Records, 41
Associated Booking Corp., 56, 419–22
Assunto, Joe, 494
Atco Records, 384, 390, 393, 419
Atlantic Records, xvii, xviii, xxii, xxiii, 40, 41, 99, 133, 134, 174, 204, 278, 281, 314, 347, 370–98, 421, 424, 451–52, 464, 493–94
Atlas Records, 95, 179, 182
Audio Video Sound Studio (N.Y.C.), 382
Austin, Sil, 278, 280
Avalon, Frankie, 139, 254, 265, 476, 523
Average White Band, 211

b

Baby Cortez (David Cortez Clowney), 430–31
Baby Dodds, 14
Baby Face Leroy Foster, 297
Baby Grand (N.Y.C.), 239, 362, 367, 368, 469
Backbeat Records, 488
Baker, La Vern, 278, 374–76, *375*, 379, 408, 414, 420
Ballard, Hank, xviii, 164, 169, 209, 241, 244, 285–87, 387, 442, 473
Bang Records, 412
Banner Records, 23
Barbecue Bob (Robert Hicks), 23
Barrelhouse, 3
Barrel House, The (L.A.), 161, 162, 237, 246, 519
Barrett, Richard, 430–33, 435
Bart, Ben, 135, 420

Bartholomew, Dave, 189, 233, 261, 263, 264, 492–93
Basie, Count, xxii, 45, 49, 50, 53, 55, 166, 173, 181, 203, 209, 219, 227, 362
Bass, Ralph, xviii, 115, 137, 162, 226, 228, 235–47, 282, 285, 289, 293, 294, 343, 345–46, 356, 390, 442
Baton Records, xxi, 428, 470–72
Bayou Records, 215, 377
Beachcomber Theatre (Omaha), 68
Beacon Records, xvii, 129, 131, 132, 344, 425
Beale Streeters, 485
Beard, Jimmy, 154–55, 185
Beatles, xix, 155, 193, 207, 299, 325, 339, 347, 396, 469, 521, 526
Be-bop, 229, 315
Bell Sound Studio (N.Y.C.), 244, 452, 455
Bell Studio (N.Y.C.), 435
Bells of Joy, 480
Belters, 50
Beltone Studio (N.Y.C.), 455
Belvederes, 425
Belvin, Jesse, 92, 210, 266
Bennett, Boyd, 101
Benson, Al, 509
Benton, Brook, 383, 409, 463, 464, 485, 524
Berman, Bess, 133, 139–40
Berman, Irving, 132
Bernay, Eric, 145, 329–30
Berns, Bert, 389–90, 395, 411–12
Berry, Charles "Chuck," 64, 215, 266, 290, 293, 307, 309, 320, 425, 524
Besman, Bernard, 199, 320
Big Bill Broonzy, xviii, xxiii, 6, 7, 10, 12, 14, 18, 19–26, 35, 41, 43, 51, 119, 131, 149, 296, 420 425
Big Boy Crudup, xv, xx, xxiii, xxiv, 31–35, 103, 291, 344, 425, 477, 497, 502, 523, 527
Big Jay McNeely, 153, 169, 176, 186, 257, 259, 437, 519
Big Joe Williams, 18, 35, 258, 259, 280, 497
Big Maceo Merriweather, 8, 105, 181, 194, 296, 371
Big Mama Thornton, Willie Mae, xv, 35, 164, 259, 390, 481–84, 483, 501, 527
Big Maybelle Smith, 348–49, 356, 357, 365, 445
Big Tone Records, 482
Big Town Records, 108, 248, 249, 251, 255
Biggs, Howard, 135, 232, 368, 377, 398
Bihari brothers, xviii, xx, 96, 148, 155, 162, 180, 194–211, 223–24, 238, 255, 304, 314, 415, 501, 518; Joe, 195, 197–99, 200–205, 213; Jules, 195, 197, 200, 203, 213; Lester, 201, 202, 203, 502; Saul, 198, 199, 210, 466
Billie (Ford) & Lillie (Bryant), 531
Bird groups, 134, 388
Black, Lewis, 27
Black & White Records, 114, 141, 226, 227–28, 235, 239, 244, 245
Black Bob, 19, 24, 43
Black Patti Records, 4
Black Swan Records, 4
Blaine, Jerry, 136, 358–59, 369, 425, 451, 466
Bland, Bobby "Blue," 37, 94, 97, 114, 202, 204, 262, 270, 365, 484, 485–86, 487, 501

Blenders, 364
Blind Blake, 10, 226, 275, 302, 343
Blind Boy Fuller, 5, 9, 104, 259, 425, 450
Blind John Davis, 8, 43
Blind Lemon Jefferson, xvii, 5, 47, 57, 96, 100, 104, 105, 114, 119, 205, 217, 222, 302
Blind Willie McTell, 461
Bloomfield, Mike, 207, 299, 314, 521
Blow harmony, 425–26
Bluebird Records, 7, 10, 12, 14, 15, 19, 23, 24, 26, 30, 32, 34, 37, 44, 114, 131, 181, 344, 425
Blue Bonnet Records, 198
Blue Flames, 487
Blue Label Records, 31
Blue Rock Records, 488
Blue Star Records, 495
Blues, xvi, 396, 496; classic, 3, 4; country, xvi, 47, 319; down home, 198, 248; party, 9; swamp, 490–91; twelve-bar, 3, 295; urban, xvi, 35, 150
Blues Spectrum Records, 73, 75
Bluesville Records, 11, 37
Bo Diddley (Ellas McDaniel), 26, 48, 159, 215, 273, 290, 306–309, 307, 314, 517, 523
Boogie woogie, 3, 51–57, 65
Booker, James, 488
Booker T. & the MG's, 411
Booker T. Washington Theatre (St. Louis), 13
Boone, Pat, xv, 99, 102, 115, 264, 265, 268, 377, 523
Booze, Bea, 344
Bop Records, 245
Bostic, Earl, 173, 241, 245, 289, 291
Bostic, Joe, 426, 509
Bottleneck guitar, 198, 221
Boyd, Eddie, 326
Bracken, James, 315, 327, 337, 339, 340
Bracken, Vivian Carter, 315, 316, 319, 337, 339
Bradford, Alex, 187
Bradford, Perry, 4
Braun, Jules, 102, 133, 353–55
Brenston, Jackie, 64, 291, 501
Broadcast Music Inc., 80, 129, 410
Bronze Peacock, The (Houston), 479
Brooklyn Crusaders, 426
Brooks, Hadda, 55, 195, 196, 197, 198, 374, 415, 466
Brooks, Louis, and His Hi-Toppers, 490
Brown, Buster, 437
Brown, Charles, xvii, xviii, 36, 92, 93–95, 97, 101, 102, 117, 196, 210, 230, 254, 269, 371, 379, 390, 397, 466, 507
Brown, James, 155, 193, 221, 225, 241–42, 243, 272, 288, 289, 300, 325, 440, 441, 485, 525, 526
Brown, Joseph, 326
Brown, Maxine, 531
Brown, Mel, 531
Brown, Nappy, xxii, 208, 350–52, 356
Brown, Roy, xxiv, 35, 101–102, 485, 497
Brown, Ruth, 81, 209, 232, 363, 372, 373–74, 379, 386, 397, 398–409, 399
Brown, Walter, 203, 211, 212
Brownie McGhee and Sonny Terry, 9, 41, 143, 330–31, 336, 397

Bruce Records, 429
Brunswick Records, 12, 245, 325, 344, 425, 441, 443–44, 461
Bryant, Ray, 293
Bryant, Willie, 56, 58, 239, 277, 362, 365, 465, 469, 509, 515
Buffet flats, 3
Bukka White, xvii, 47, 205, 220–21, 259, 489
Bull Moose Jackson, 48, 59, 65, 222, 276–77, 403, 450
Bullet Records, 37, 91, 217, 281
Bumble Bee Slim (Amos Easton), 8
Bumps Blackwell, 190, 193, 270
Bunk Johnson, 52
Burke, Solomon, 377, 413, 441, 527
Butera, Sam, 531
Butler, Jerry, 268, 321–24, 328, 338, 524
Butterbeans and Susie, 40
Butterfield, Erskine, 61, 69
Butterfield, Paul, 33, 39

C

CTI Records, 347
"Cabbage Greens" (Champion Jack Dupree), 41
Cadence Records, 133, 333, 473
Cadet Records, 210, 289, 317
Cadets, 208
Cadillacs, 423, 425–26
Caldonia Inn (New Orleans), 492–93
Calhoun, Charles, xxiii, 379
Calla Records, 316
Calloway, Blanche, 399, 404–405
Calloway, Cab, 57, 61–62, 69, 124–25, 173, 174
Cameo Records, 437, 472, 473–75, 525
Canned Heat, 33
Capitol Lounge (Chicago), 67, 69, 76, 78
Capitol Records, xxii, 55, 117, 118, 153, 165, 233, 314, 325, 329, 488
Caplan, John, 199
Car groups, 425
Caravans, 426
Cardinals, 385
Carlisle, Una Mae, 131
Carr, Leroy, 6–8, 12, 14, 19, 24, 27, 39, 40, 41, 42, 51, 89, 91, 92, 98, 100, 119, 204, 210, 269, 371, 379
Carroll, Ray, 239, 362, 365, 469
Carter, Benny, 57, 65, 132
Carter, Calvin, 315, 316, 317, 321–22, 327, 328, 337, 338, 339
Case Records, 234
Cash, Johnny, 278, 503
Cashmeres, 475
Cat Records, xxii, 393, 421
Cavanaugh, Dave, 232, 463
Cavatone Records, 248, 251, 255
Central Records, 363, 367
Century Records, 30
"Chains of Love" (Joe Turner), 377
Champagne Records, 293, 310
Champion Jack Dupree, 36, 39–42, 45, 131, 462, 495
Champion Records, 23, 37
Chance Records, 31, 293, 311, 312, 315, 434

Channels, The, 422
Chantels, 431, 432, 433–34
Charioteers, 249, 400
Charles, Ray, xviii, xxv, xxvii, 22, 92, 95, 96, 112, 196, 204, 254, 262, 272, 279, 357, 364, 365, 371, 377, *378*, 379–81, 389, 396, 413–414, 450, 479, 485, 492, 526, 527
Charmers, 363
Chart Records, 199
Chase, Lincoln, 376, 414
Checker Records, 32, 45, 96, 201, 248, 252, 289, 310, 311, 325, 343, 434
Cheers, The, 416
Chenier, Clifton, 194, 259–60
Chess brothers, xviii, 96, 112, 113, 240, 273, 343, 517; Leonard, 289, 291, 293; Marshall (son), 293, 299
Chess Records, xvii, xviii, 19, 31, 199, 210, 235, 245, 255, 289–314, 315, 317, 326, 341, 343, 381, 426, 462, 465, 488, 501, 527
Chessler, Deborah, 135–36
Chief Records, 201
Chips, The, 423
"Choo Choo Ch'Boogie" (Louis Jordan), xvii, 63, 103
Chords, The, xxii, 234, 393, 420
Choreography, 425
Christian, Charlie, 10, 115–16, 121–22, 205, 217, 219
Chubby Checker (Ernest Evans), 266, 473–74
Chudd, Lew, 120, 229, 261, 263, 264–65, 266, 335
Churchill, Savannah, 65, 131, 132–33, 143, 425
Cita, Raoul, 428–29
Clanton, Jimmy, 491
Clapton, Eric, 42
Clark, Dick, 137, 445, 454, 456–57, 472–73, 511, 517
Class Records, 130
Clayton, Peter "Doctor," 31
Cleftones, 431
Cleveland, James, and the Angelic Choir, *355*, 356, 443
Cleveland Arena (Cleveland), 507–508
Clovers, 112, 283, 291, 317, 366, 377, 386–87, 390, 412, 413, 427
Club Alabam (L.A.), 160, 241, 519
Club De Lisa (Chicago), 149, 374, 449
Club 51 Records, 31
Coasters, xx, 197, 270, 346, 390–93, *391*, 412, *417*, 419
Cobra Records, 31, 313, 314
Cohen, Oscar, 419–22
Cole, Ann, 470–71
Cole, Nat "King," 64, 91, 92, 93, 94, 153, 155, 160, 182, 210, 221, 229, 270, 324, 335, 344, 354, 359, 379–80, 383, 519
Collector Records, 44
Collins, Judy, 328
Colonial Records, 377
Colony Records, 215
Columbia Records, 4, 9, 12, 15, 38, 227, 271, 287, 292, 328, 331, 374, 383, 386, 425, 445, 467
Conover, Willis, 399, 404

Constellation Records, 31, 325
Continental Records, 41, 141
Cooke, Sam, xviii, 189, 193, 194, 210, 220, 267, 268–72, 288, 434, 441, 524
Coral Records, 152, 311, 426
Cosimo Studio (New Orleans), 190, 262, 364, 455, 491, 494
Cotillion Records, 314
Cotton, Elizabeth, 51
Cotton, James, 291, 297, 299, 304, 310, 482, 486–87, 501, 502
Cotton Club (Harlem), 54, 61; (Cincinnati) 275; (Indianapolis) 40; (L.A.) 151
Courtney, Alan, 359
Cow Cow Davenport, Charles, 3, 11, 28, 52
Cox, Ida, 4, 23, 114, 422
Craft, Morty, 429, 456
"Crazy Blues" (Mamie Smith), xv, xvii, 4, 47, 89
Cream, The, 39
Creedence Clearwater Revival, 33
Crescendos, 490
Crew Cuts, xxii, xxvii, 234, 266, 350, 421, 430, 523
Cripple Clarence Lofton, 53
Crosby, Bing, 8, 101, 191, 231, 404
Crown Records, 194, 205, 261, 304
Crossover, 366, 524
Crows, xvii, 430
"Crying in the Chapel" (Orioles), 136
Cryin' Sam Collins, 5
Crystals, 395, 423, 433, 524
Cuff Links, 266
Curlicues, flowers, frills, 270, 441
Curtom Records, 323
Cut-in, 432

d

Daddy-Yo Hot Rod, 509
Dances: the Bird, 474; Breakdown, 502; Fly, 474; Funky Chicken, 502; Limbo, 474; Lindy Hop, 345; Mashed Potato, 474; Mess Around, 474; Peckin', 345; Penguin, 502; Pony, 474; Push and Pull, 502; Slop, 471; Stroll, 468; Suzy Q, 345; Truckin', 345; Twist, 286, 474; Wah Watusi, 474; Walk, 252; Walkin' the Dog, 502
Daniels, Billy, 97
Darin, Bobby, 407, 419
Darnel, 353, 354
Davis, Eddie "Lockjaw," 59, 277
Davis, Genevieve, 129
Davis, Joe, 131–32, 425
Davis, Maxwell, 110, 174, 479
Davis, Sammy, Jr., 81, 324, 433
Davis, Walter, 37, 43, 248, 253
Davis Sisters, 356
Dawn Records, 361
Day, Bobby (Robert Byrd), 155, 381
Dean, James, 523
Decca Records, 4, 8, 12, 14, 15, 26, 37, 42, 46, 61, 69, 74, 75, 78, 79, 80, 83, 84, 89, 92, 139, 151, 227, 276, 278, 344, 364, 425, 434, 441, 461
"Dedicated to the One I Love" (Five Royales), 285

Dee Clark, 324–25, 329, 338, 381
Dee Dee Sharp, 474, 476
Deek Watson, 91, 227
Deep River Boys, 249
Delaney, Joe, 497, 511, 513
Dells, 311, 317–18, 318, 423–24
Delmark Records, 37
Delta influence, 414
Delta Rhythm Boys, 134, 425
DeLuxe Records, xvii, 102, 133, 199, 232, 283, 284, 344, 345, 354, 424
Del-Vikings, 268
Derby Records, 363, 426, 450
Desires, 423
Dew Drop Inn (New Orleans), 102, 261, 354
Dexter, Dave, 343
Diamonds, 385, 468, 490
"Diggin' My Potatoes" (Washboard Sam), 41–42, 44
Dillard, Varetta, 349–50, 350, 356, 358, 363–364, 366, 368, 461, 464, 507
"The Dirty Dozens" (Speckled Red), 27
Disk jockey, 128–29, 505–17
Dixie Cups, 436
Dixie Hummingbirds, 442, 480
Dixieland Jazz, 20
Dixon, Floyd, 230–31
Dixon, Willie, 31, 44, 230, 248, 272, 292, 297, 304, 310, 313, 314
Dr. Jive, 469
Doggett, Bill, 59, 79, 130, 173–74, 176, 245, 258, 279–80, 524
Dolphin, John, 196, 258, 508, 519
Dominoes, 241, 245, 373, 381–82, 383, 387–40, 412, 422, 441, 442–43, 523
Don't Knock the Rock (film), 516
Dootone Records, 103, 266
Dootones, 266
Dootsie Williams, 266
Doo-wop groups, xix, 232
Dorsey, Lee, 437–38, 441
Dorsey, Thomas A., 139, 144, 148–49. See also Georgia Tom.
Dorsey, Tommy, 54, 168, 214, 276, 306
Dot Records, 98, 102, 208, 264, 266, 268, 489, 491
"Double Crossing Blues" (Johnny Otis & Little Esther), 162, 236–37, 346
Douglas, K.C., 248
Dovells, 475
Dovers, 423
Dowd, Tommy, 361–62, 382, 395, 411
Down Beat Records, 91, 380
Down Town Records, 248, 250, 251, 252, 253, 259
Drifters, xvii, xix, xxv, 135, 283, 377, 381, 382–83, 384, 412–13, 590
"Drifting Blues" (Charles Brown), 92, 94, 230, 466
"Drinkin' Wine, Spo-Dee-O-Dee" (Stick McGhee), 42, 134, 281, 372
Drive 'em Down, 40
Dubs, The, 431, 435
Duke Records, 114, 202, 314, 383, 481, 485
Duponts, 435
Dupree, Reese, 58

Durham, Eddie, 115–16
"Dust My Broom" (Elmore James), 201

e

E.M.I. Records, 325
Earle Theatre (Philadelphia), 406, 449
"Earth Angel" (Penguins), 210, 266
Ebb Records, 494
Eckstine, Billy, xxiii, 35, 110, 133, 161, 210, 277, 289, 291, 344, 359, 362, 407
Eddy, Duane, 306, 418, 476
81 Theatre (Atlanta), 189
El Dorados, 285, 316–17, 425
El Rays, 317
Electric Flag, 299
Elks Rendezvous (N.Y.C.), 61, 66, 67, 76
Ellington, Duke, 13, 57, 61, 69, 93, 97, 118, 166, 181, 205, 212, 219, 242, 261, 277, 399, 404, 449, 475
Ellis, Ray, 376, 377, 383
Emarcy Records, 141
Ember Records, 450, 453
End Records, 312, 433, 434, 435
Enjoy Records, 175, 201, 436
Epic Records, 445–50, 454, 461
Ertegun, Ahmet, xviii, xxi, 48, 120, 184–85, 314, 343, 361, 362, 370–71, 373–77, 382, 386, 387, 394, 395–99, 400, 405, 408, 410, 411, 412, 413, 419, 420, 421, 451, 463, 494
Ertegun, Nesuhi, 371, 394, 411, 412
Essex Records 429
Everett, Betty, 313, 325, 338
"Every Beat of My Heart" (Gladys Knight and the Pips), 168, 285, 318–19, 439
"Every Day I Have the Blues" (Memphis Slim), 42, 45; Lowell Fulson, 96–97, 108, 112; B.B. King, 96, 223, 253
Excello Records, 148, 208, 320, 489–91
Excelsior Records, 50, 91, 117, 153, 229
Exclusive Records, xxi, 117, 129, 130, 153, 154, 344, 466, 467

f

Fairfield Four, 220
Falcon Records, 324
Falcons, 42, 441, 442, 468
Fame Recording Studio (Muscle Shoals, Ala.), 314, 376
Fantasy Records, 248, 325
Fast Western piano, 52
Fats Domino, 102, 187, 190, 207, 258, 262, 379, 397, 442, 455, 474, 492, 493, 517, 521, 524, 527
Fats Waller, 131, 502
Fats Washington, 97, 291
Feather, Leonard, 58, 116, 143, 170
Feathers, The, 209
Federal Records, 241, 282, 285
"Fever" (Little Willie John), 287–88
Fidelities, 471
Field holler, 3
Fields, Alfred, 507
Fiestas, 425, 428, 468
Fifty-second Street (Swing Street), 42, 54, 55, 57, 58, 67, 131, 153, 345, 362, 373, 439
Fillmore (San Francisco), 209, 527

Fire Records, 33, 201, 436, 437
Fireball Records, 33
Firebird Records, 436
Fishtail, 28
Fitzgerald, Ella, 56, 66, 74, 191, 221, 344, 359, 427
Five Blind Boys of Mississippi, 479–80
Five Crowns, 384, 389, 422, 427
Five Keys, 231–33, 283, 317, 385
Five Red Caps, 131, 222, 344, 425
Five Royales, xxv, 136–37, 285
Five Satins, 453–54
Five Stars, 316
Flair Records, 194, 201
Flame Show Bar (Detroit), 122, 245, 359, 367, 368, 374, 443, 447–48, 515
Flamingos, 312, 315, 317, 430, 431, 434
Flash Records, 208
Fleetwoods, 425
Fletcher, Dusty, xxii, 226, 227, 241, 371
Folkways Records, 17, 29, 41, 44, 331–33
Fontane Sisters, 208, 264
"(I Love You) For Sentimental Reasons" (Deek Watson, Nat "King" Cole), 227, 470
"44 Blues" (Roosevelt Sykes), 30
Four Fellows, xxii, 426–27, 473
Four Seasons, 325, 329, 338
4 Star Records, 89, 91, 98, 255, 413
Four Tunes, 133, 136, 425
Fox Head (Cedar Rapids, Ia.), 67, 78
Franklin, Aretha, 210, 221, 225, 319, 347, 376, 389, 400, 408, 433, 526, 527
Freed, Alan, xix, xxiv, 26, 210, 243, 277, 293, 310, 311, 332, 365, 369, 428, 431, 432, 435, 464, 465, 466, 470, 472, 505, 507, 508, 509, 511–17, 528
Freedom Records, 377
Freeman, Bobby, 137–39
Friday Ford, 29
Frolic Show Bar (Detroit), 403
Fuller, Johnny, 248, 250, 255
Fulson, Lowell, xxi, xxv, 36, 45, 92, 93, 95–97, 102, 104–13, 194, 205, 223, 248, 249–251, 253, 257, 259, 260, 290, 379, 485
Funky, 412
Fuqua, Harvey, 293, 310, 311, 312, 317, 507
Furry Lewis, 42
Fury Records, 201, 319, 436, 438, 439

g

Gabler, Milt, 62, 64, 70, 74, 84
Gaither, Bill, 8
Gale, Moe, 57, 60, 127, 345, 368, 420, 424
Gamble & Huff, 324, 476
Gant, Cecil, xvii, 85, 89–92, *93*, 94, 102, 129, 195, 210, 245, 269, 281, 519, 524
Garner, Erroll, 238, 333, 364, 372
Gatemouth Brown, Clarence, 479
Gatemouth Moore, 134, 149–50, 502
Gaye, Marvin, 336, 524
Gayten, Paul, 353, 354, 455–56
Geddins, Bob, 89, 96, 107, 108, 109, 198, 199, 247–56, *249*, 256, 258, 259, 260, 326
"Gee" (Crows), 135, 430
Gee Records, 384, 429, 430, 433

Gene and Eunice, 234, 312, 434
Gennett Records, 23, 37, 130, 131
Georgia Tom, 8–11, 131
Gibbs, Georgia, 50, 164, 376
Gibson, Andy, 357
Gillespie, Dizzy, 114, 141, 169, 356, 405
Gilt Edge Records, 89–91, 108, 245
Gladiolas, 490
Glaser, Joe, 56, 58, 83, 127, 144, 419–22
Glenn, Lloyd, 95, 96, 111–12, 165
Globe Records, 252
Glory Records, xxii, 426, 473
Glover, Henry, 243, 245, 246, 275–76, 277–79, 286
"Goin' Down Slow" (St. Louis Jimmy), 42
Gold, Steve, 215–16
Gold Star Studio (Houston), 198, 418
Golden Gate Quartet, 220, 249
Golden Peacock (Houston), 164
Goldner, George, 312, 429–36
Gone Records, 320, 433
"Good Rockin' Tonight" (Wynonie Harris), 102, 497
Goodman, Benny, 20, 57, 116, 121, 166, 173, 205, 211, 261, 345, 467, 505
Gordon, Roscoe, 204, 485
Gordy, Berry, 168, 312, 326, 367, 443, 525, 527
Gospel music, xvi, xviii, 3, 9, 10, 137, 139, 144, 146, 147, 148–50, 187, 320, 341, 352, 356–57, 380, 388, 389, 397, 402, 426, 485–486, 489, 491, 524
Gospel Singers' Convention, 10
Gotham Records, 41, 199
Graham, Bill, 164
Grand Terrace (Chicago), 57, 59
Gravenites, Nick, 299, 314
Green, Al (Detroit), 367, 368, 374, 443
Green, Al (National Records), 240, 245, 359–60
Green, Lil, 43, 45
Green, Tuff, 217, 225
Green, Lee "Pork Chops," 15
Groove Records, 33, 41, 425, 460–66
Guitar Slim (Eddie Jones), 42, 110, 258
Gunter, Arthur, 35, 489–90, 497
Gunter, Shirley, and the Queens, 208
Gutshall, Jack, 153, 154, 185, 186
Guy, Buddy, 202, 297, 299, 314, 486

h

Haley, Bill, xxiii, xxvii, 62, 64, 73, 82, 101, 174, 234, 264, 351, 379
Hallway sound, 436
Hamilton, Roy, 272
Hammond, John, 26, 55, 57, 116, 125, 143, 343
Hampton, Lionel, 57–58, 61, 81, 83, 90, 114, 124–25, 143, 144–45, 168, 173, 175, 229, 257, 277, 279, 289, 344, 358
Hamp-Tone Records, 103, 281
Hancock, Hunter, xxvi, 196, 241, 257, 258, 518–22
Handy, W. C., 42, 52, 398
Hansen, Barry, xxiii
Harlem Footwarmers, 13

Harlem Hamfats, 344, 425
"Harlem Hit Parade," 63, 79, 90, 91, 127, 131, 145, 344
Harlem Hotshots, 276
Harps, The, 423
Harptones, xix, 422, 428–29
Harris, Rebert, 269, 271–72
Harris, Thurston, 231
Harris, Wynonie, xxiv, 48, 59, 65, 101, 102, 140, 222–23, 243, 278, 280, 281–82, 497, 523
Harrison, Wilbert, 437
Harvey Records, 312
Hawkins, Erskine, 57, 59–60, 61, 69, 80, 152, 368
Hawkins, Roy, 198, 199, 248, 253
Hayes, Isaac, 114
Hazelwood, Lee, 418, 476
Head arrangement, 292, 376, 415
Headhunters, 297
Hearts, 470
Heller, Eddie, 427, 462
"Hellbound on My Trail" (Robert Johnson), 35, 301
Henderson, Fletcher, 46, 57
Henderson, Jocko, 469
Henry, Clarence "Frogman," 496
Hendrix, Jimi, 193, 441
Herald Records, xxi, 38, 343, 345, 355, 377, 424, 427, 450–60
Herman, Woody, 69, 80, 115
Hi Records, 255
Hibbler, Al, 205, 366, 367, 368, 369
Higginbotham, Irene, 131
Hill, Bertha "Chippie," 3, 53
Hines, Earl "Fatha," 57, 65, 81, 93, 228, 362
Hit Records, 344
Hite, Les, 57, 65, 114, 116, 117, 119, 121, 122, 151
Hokum craze, 9–11
Holiday, Billie, 42, 55–56, 144, 204, 405
Homesick James, 201
"The Honeydripper" (Joe Liggins), 130, 154–55, 420, 466
Honey Hill, 8
"Honey Hush" (Joe Turner), 378
Honkers, 168–76, 277
"Honky Tonk" (Bill Doggett), 130, 173–74, 176, 186, 524
Honky-tonk influence, 414
"Honky Tonk Train Blues" (Meade Lux Lewis), 51, 53
Hooker, Earl, 299
Hooker, John Lee, 194, 199–200, 223, 320–321, 336, 338, 523
Horton, Walter, 297
"Hound Dog" (Big Mama Thornton), 165, 233, 482
House-rent parties, 52
Houston, Joe, 169, 257, 258, 259, 508
"How Long, How Long Blues" (Leroy Carr), 6–7
Howard, Camille, 186, 187
Howard, Rosetta, 5
Howard Theatre (Washington, D.C.), 68, 160, 167, 232, 371, 397, 399, 404, 527
Howlin' Wolf (Chester Arthur Burnett), xx,

26, 39, 201, 203, 207, 230, 273, 290, 291, 293, 297, *300*, 301–306, 314, 486–87, 501, 509, 517, 526, 527
Hub Records, 134, 362
"The Hucklebuck" (Paul Williams), 168–69, 357, 362
Humes, Helen, 203, 229, 371
Hunter, Alberta, 4, 58
Hunter, Ivory Joe, xx, 92, 93, 97–99, 102, 210, 222, 268, 280–81, 397, 409, 414
Huntom Records, 319, 439
Hutto, J.B., 202
Hytone Records, 31, 44, 235

i

"I Almost Lost My Mind" (Ivory Joe Hunter), 99, 268, 281
"I Got a Woman" (Ray Charles), 380, 413
"I Hear You Knocking" (Smiley Lewis), 12, 128
"I Only Have Eyes for You" (Flamingos), 434
"I Put a Spell on You" (Screamin' Jay Hawkins), 440
"I Wonder" (Cecil Grant), xvii, 89–90, 91–92, 195, 245, 524
"I'm Your Hoochie Coochie Man" (Muddy Waters), 296, 298, 313
Impalas, 425
Imperial Records, xvii, 91, 103, 215, 229, 248, 257, 261–65, 335, 336, 377, 426, 471, 491
Imperials, 425
Impressions, 321–22, *323*
"In the Evening When the Sun Goes Down" (Leroy Carr), 7, 91, 119
Ink Spots, xvii, xxiii, 63, 92, 94, 101, 125, 131, 132, 133, 160, 173, 279, 282, 344, 359, 383, 386, 388, 425, 442, 524, 527
Instant Records, 471
Irma Records, 248
"Is You Is or Is You Ain't (Ma Baby)?" (Louis Jordan), 63, 70–71, 80
Isley Brothers, 412, 421, 526
"It's Tight Like That" (Georgia Tom & Tampa Red), 8, 9
"It's Too Soon to Know" (Orioles), 135
Ivory Records, 98, 280

j

J.O.B. Records, 31, 131, 325
Jacks, 208
Jackson, Hal, 365, 469, 508
Jackson, James "Stump," 37
Jackson, Jim, 28
Jackson, Mahalia, 22, 127, *138*, 139–40, 148
Jackson, Willis "Gatortail," 171
Jacquet, Illinois, 58, 140, 173, 277, 281
Jamahl, Ahmad (Fritz Jones), 449
James, Elmore, 194, 200, 201–202, 501, 509
James, Etta, xviii, 158, 164, 195, 209–10, 286, 293–94
James, Ida, 65
Jamie Records, 418, 475–76
Jayhawks, 208

Jazz Gillum, William, 18, 24, 26, 43, 344, 425
Jazzbo Collins, 85, 469
Jefferson Airplane, 193
Jefferson Theatre (Newport News, Va.), 232
Jeffries, 130, 153
Jelly Roll Morton, 29, 52, 398, 492
Jerusalem Stars, 389
Jesters, 423
Jewel Records, 96
Jo, Damita, 352
Jim Crow, 51, 124, 172
Joe Davis Records, 41
John, Elton, 33
Johnson, Budd, 61, 374, 398
Johnson, Buddy, 61, 140, 277
Johnson, Bunk, 37
Johnson, Lonnie, xxvi, 8, 10, 12, 14, 17, 23, 24, 31, 42, 208, 217, 280, 281, 302, 344, 403, 420, 425
Johnson, Marv, 384, 443
Johnson, Pete, 47, 51, 53, 54, 103, 133, 377. *See also* Turner, Joe.
Johnson, Robert, 38–39, 47, 220, 294, 301, 496
Jolson, Al, 442
Jones, Ollie, 364
Jones, Richard M., 23
Joplin, Janis, 97, 483–84
Jordan, Louis, xvii, xviii, xx, xxii, 55, 59, *61*–75, *66*, 76–85, 87, 160, 173, 221, 227, 259, 279, 344, 359, 425, 442, 449, 524, 527
Josephson, Barney, 172
Josie Records, 137–38, 425
Jubilee Records, 133, 136, 283, 369, 424, 425, 451
Jug bands, 3, 9
Jukebox, 128, 510
Juke Box Records, 103, 179, 186
Juke Boy Bonner, Weldon, 248, 256
Junior Records, 456
Junior Wells, 299, 310

k

KRC Records, 188
Kansas City Bill, 11
Kansas Joe (Wilkes "Joe" McCoy), 11, 23, 32, 45
Kapp, Dave, 78–79, 83; Jack, 4, 334
Kapp Records, 334–35
Katy Red's (St. Louis), 14, 37
Keen Records, 193, 268, 270–71
Kenner, Chris, 471–72
Kent Records, 96, 109, 168, 205, 217, 482, 520
Kessler, Danny, 367, 425, 445–50, 454, 461
Keyes, Bert, 398
Keynote Records, xvii, 129, 145, 329, 425
Kid Edwards, 39, 41
Kid Ory, 31, 263
King, Albert, 120, 526–27
King, B.B., xxi, 26, 33, 42, 45, 96, 97, 110, 114, 120–21, 166, 199, 202, 203, 204–08, *206*, 216–25, *218*, 253, *300*, 336, 415, 432, 445, 449, 450, 481, 485, 492, 501, 509, 521, 526, 527
King, Ben E., xviii, 149, 377, 384–85, 389, 524

550   INDEX

King, Earl, 491
King, Martin Luther, Jr., xvi, 11, 316
King, Maurice, 367, 448
King Curtis (Curtis Ousley), *175*–76, 439, 463
King Oliver, 4, 20
King Records, xvii, xviii, xxii, 12, 14, 41, 44, 95, 98, 137, 140, 173, 199, 209, 228, 232, 233, 235, 237, 245, 273, 275–89, 290, 320, 354, 374, 382, 387, 390, 428, 473, 491, 494
King Solomon Records, 356
Kirk, Andy, 56, 69, 94, 116, 354
Kirkland, Leroy, 357, 387, 454, 455
Knight, Gladys, & the Pips, 168, 285, 318–319, 421, *438*–39, 445, 449
Koester, Robert, 28
Kudu Records, 347

l

Label X, 461, 497
Laine, Frankie, 50, 95, 197, 406
Lang, Eddie, 8, 13
Largo Theatre (L.A.), 162
Larks, 137, 428
Lauderdale, Jack, 96, 108, 111, 112, 249, 250, 251
Laurie, Annie, 289, 353, 354
Laurie Records, 525
Law, Don, 38–39
"Lawdy Miss Clawdy" (Lloyd Price), 188, 189, 350, 513, 524
Lazy Lester (Leslie Johnson), 320
Leadbelly (Huddie Leadbetter), 9, 20, 21, 26, 52, 92
Led Zeppelin, 395
Lee, Peggy, 45, 83–84, 287–88, 329
Leiber, Jerry, and Mike Stoller, xviii, 149, 165, 216, 346, 373, 384, 387, 389, 390–92, 394–95, 398, 412, 416–18, 436, 437, 482
Lenoir, J.B., 329, 336
Lenox Records, 347
"Let the Good Times Roll" (Shirley & Lee), xviii, 233
Levy, Lou, xi, 55, 71
Lewis, Jerry Lee, 36, 231, 270, 278, 320, 503, 516
Lewis, Meade Lux, 48, 51, 52, 53, 54, 192
Lewis, Stan, 96, 113
Liberty Records, 283
Liggins, Jimmy, 186
Liggins, Joe, xvii, 130, 153, 155, 420, 466
Lightnin' Hopkins, Sam, 96, 100, 140, 142–43, 194, 198, 200, 223, 230, 258, 259, 466
Lightnin' Slim (Otis Hicks), xx, 320, 490
Lincoln Theatre (L.A.), 80
Lipscomb, Mance, 250, 258
Lip-sync, 472
Litchman Theater chain, 406
Little Anthony and the Imperials, 435–36
Little Brother Montgomery, Eurreal, 5, 15, 25, 29–31, 52, 292
Little Caesar (Carl Burnett) & the Romans, 537
Little Esther, 158, 161, 162–64, 235–37, *346*, 347–48, 356, 358, 364, 374, 488, 524
Little Junior Parker, Herman, 35, 255, 303, 486–88, 497
Little Miss Cornshucks, 365, 374, 400, 448

Little Richard (Richard Penniman), xv, 149, 155, 166, 189–93, *191*, 209, 214, 268, 270, 287, 325, 336, 349, 365, 442, 484, 486, 517, 525, 527
Little Son Jackson, 259
Little Walter (Walter Jacobs), xxiv, 31, 223, 292, 296, 297, 309–10, 356, 501
Little Willie John (John Davenport), 158, 168, 245, 287–89, 442
Little Willie Littlefield, 203, 390
"Lonely Teardrops" (Jackie Wilson), 443
Lonesome Sundown (Cornelius Green), 490
Long Tall Friday, 30
Lorenz, George "Hound Dog," 465, 508
"A Lover's Question" (Clyde McPhatter), 383
Lowe, Bernie, 473
Lubinsky, Herman, xx, xxii, 133, 148, 235–40, 246, *277*, 314, 343–53, 356, 357, 366–67, 437, 462
Lucky Millinder, 58–59, 61, 69, 101, 125, 140, 173, 174, 183, 224, 275, 276, 277, 278, 279, 344, 373, 402, 403–404, 515
Lunceford, Jimmie, 55, 57, 58, 69, 116, 124, 166, 221, 277, 449
Lymon Frankie, & the Teenagers, 234, 347, 423, 430, 431–33

m

McCall, Bill, 89, 245, 255
McClennan, Tommy, 19, 43, 247, 302, 315, 425
McCoy, Rose Marie, xxii, 352, 409
McCracklin, Jimmy, 194, 198, 248, 252–53, 265
McCullum, Ann, 100
McDaniels, Gene, 524
McDonald, Cliff, 89, 245
McDowell, Fred, 259
McFadden, Charlie "Specks," 37
McGuire Sisters, 50, 311, 315–16, 351
McKinney's Cotton Pickers, 9
McMurray Studio (Jackson, Miss.), 33, 201
McPhatter, Clyde, 241, 245, 270, 272, 282–283, 286, 325, 377, 381–84, 385, 387–89, 412, 420, 441, 442, 443, 507
McRae, Teddy, 387
McShann, Jay, 95, 111, 141, 203, 211, 212, 214, 229, 329
McVea, Jack, xxii, 120, 226, 228, 244, 479
MGM Records, 99, 281, 364, 383, 429
Ma Rainey, 3, 4, 10, 23, 48, 51, 66, 114, 148, 376, 385, 400
Mabon, Willie, 290, 291–92
Machismo, 296
The Macomba (Chicago), 289
Magic Sam, 313
Magid, Lee, xviii, 345, 349–50, 356, 358–70
Magnum Records, 519
Majors (Brooklyn), 426
Majors (Philadelphia), 426
Mann, Kal, 473, 475
Manor Records, 132, 133, 142, 143, 148, 425
Marchan, Bobby, 437
Mardin, Arif, 411
Marigolds, 208, 490

Mariners, 446
Martin, Roberta, 139
Martin, Sallie, 10, 139, 144, 148
Martin, Sara, 4
Matthews, Count Otis, 158–59, 161
Matassa, Cosimo, 262, 364, 491
Mayall, John, 42
"Maybellene" (Chuck Berry) 64, 266, 425
Mayfield, Curtis, 321–24
Mayfield, Percy, 92, 193, 210, 213
Meadowlarks, 266
"Mean Old Frisco" (Big Boy Crudup), 425
Medallions, 266
Melba Records, 208, 422
Mellowlarks, 423
Melodisc Records, 25
Melotone Records, 15, 23, 30
Melrose, Lester, 24, 33, 34, 35, 37, 292
Memphis Minnie (Minnie Douglas McCoy), 5, 6, 11, 23, 45, 194, 259, 425
Memphis Recording Service, 500, 502
Memphis Slim (Peter Chatman), 19, 37, 40, 42–45, 202, 207, 292, 302, 420
Mendelsohn, Fred, 277, 343, 345, 353–58, 355, 451
Mercury Records, 25, 31, 81, 140, 145, 146, 152, 164, 174, 212, 266, 268, 324, 325, 329, 373, 383, 421, 463, 488, 490, 493
Mercy Dee (Walton), 215
Mesner brothers (Leo and Edward), 75, 95, 110, 148, 180, 228–35, 238, 343
Meteor Records, 201, 502
Mickey and Sylvia (Michouston Baker and Sylvia Vanderpool Robinson), 462–63, 464, 465
Midnighters, xxv, 158, 168, 209, 241, 285–287, 373, 386, 441, 442
Mighty Clouds of Joy, 426
Mighty Joe Young, 312, 313
Milburn, Amos, 99–101, 102, 223, 229–30, 263, 397, 523
Miller, Dave, 429
Miller, J.D., 490
Miller, William Rice (Second Sonny Boy Williamson), 17, 201, 259, 301, 302, 495
Millionaires, 431
Mills, Irving, 127
Mills Blue Rhythm Band, 59
Mills Brothers, xvii, 63, 67, 76, 77, 131, 132, 135, 359, 386, 388, 425, 442, 524, 527
Milton, Roy, xvii, 103, 168, 184–85, 186, 188, 397
Minit Records, 488
Miracle Records, 44, 292
Mississippi Sheiks, 9, 130–31, 302
"Moanin' at Midnight" (Howlin' Wolf), 304
Modern Records, xvii, xviii, xx, 55, 93, 96, 161, 169, 194–211, 248, 252, 260, 415, 420, 432, 466, 467, 487, 501, 527
Moms Mabley, 246
Money Records, 44
Monterey Jazz Festival, 102, 204, 482
Moonglows, xvii, 137, 310, 311–12, 317, 351, 426, 507, 517
Moonlighters, 311
Moore, Johnny, & the Three Blazers, 93, 94, 95, 130, 153, 161, 196, 205, 230, 387, 466

Morris, Joe, 371, 396, 409, 451–53
Motown Records, 312, 315, 326, 336, 376, 395, 439, 524, 525, 528
Mound City Blue Blowers, 13
Mount Lebanon Singers, 282
Muddy Waters (McKinley Morganfield), 10, 26, 31, 38, 39, 48, 201, 207, 208, 219, 248, 259, 273, 290, 292, 293, 294–301, 295, 309, 310, 313, 314, 388, 450, 470–71, 482, 492, 502, 523, 526
Musicraft Records, 446
Myles, Billy, 455

n

Nasco Records, 490
Nashboror Records, 148, 489, 491
Nathan, Syd, xviii, xxii, 168, 235, 238, 245, 246, 255, 275–89, 277, 314, 354, 442
National Records, xvii, 90, 133–35, 142, 227, 244, 359–61, 397, 425, 466
Navarro, Esther, 426
Neal, Bob, 497
Nelson, Jimmy, 203
Newport Folk Festival, 321, 526
Newport Jazz Festival, 50, 74
Newton, Larry, 363, 367, 426, 450, 456
Nicholson, J.D., 253
Nightingales, 480
Nighthawk, Richard, 207, 217, 219, 220, 292
Nite, Norm, 170
Nobles, Gene, 489, 508
Noone, Jimmie, 9, 25
Norman, Fred, 147
Northern Jubilee Gospel Singers, 321
Nugetre, A., 377, 387
Nutmegs, 454

o

Oberstein, Eli, 130–31
Ode Records, 271
OKeh Records, xv, 4, 9, 12, 13, 14, 15, 41, 89, 192, 324, 357, 424, 425, 440, 445–50
Old Town Records, 384, 428, 430, 467–69
"Only You" (Platters), 287
"Open the Door, Richard" (Jack McVea), 226–27, 228, 244–45
Opera Records, 31
Ora Nelle Records, 309
Oriole Records, 23
Orioles, xvii, 135–36, 282, 315, 386, 388, 425, 430, 450, 507, 523
Orlons, 474–75
Otis, Clyde, 99, 146, 383, 463
Otis, Johnny, xvi, xxi, 72, 73, 75, 102, 119, 153, 158–68, 177, 179, 209, 211, 212, 236–37, 241, 246, 250, 257, 285, 286, 287, 306–307, 318, 343, 346, 347, 356, 364, 415, 442, 468, 488, 508, 519; Shuggie, 75, 162
Oxley, Harold F., 281, 420

p

Pacific Records, 98, 280
Palace Theatre (Memphis), 42

Palitz, Morty, 137, 369
Papa Charlie Jackson, 22
Papa Lord God, 29
Papa Oscar Celestin, 263
Paradise Records, 429
Paradise Theatre (Detroit), 91, 167–68, 403, 442, 443
Paramount Records, 4, 5, 12, 22, 30, 130, 372
Paramount Theatre (Brooklyn, N.Y.), 432, 435, 516
Paramount Theatre (N.Y.C.), 68, 80, 81
Paris, Freddie, 454
Parker, Charlie "Bird," 46, 141–42, 172, 356, 357
Parkway Records, 474
Parrot Records, 312, 434
Patton, Charles, 5, 302, 303
Pauling, Lowman, 137, 285, 286
Payola, 356, 436, 459, 466, 472, 510–11, 516
Peacock Records, xvii, xx, 44, 164, 165, 189, 190, 426, 479–89, 501
Pee Wee Crayton, 110, 194, 198–99, 255
Pee Wee's (Memphis), 42
Peetie Wheatstraw (William Bunch), 5, 26, 105, 248, 425
Pendergast era (Kansas City), 46, 48
Penguins, xix, 210, 266, 315, 523
Peppermint Harris (Harrison Nelson), 140, 231
Pepper's Club (Chicago), 312
Perfect Records, 9, 23
Perkins, Carl, 278
Philles Records, 395, 419, 525
Phillips, Esther, 209, 347–48
Phillips, Sam, xxiii, 33, 35, 203, 278, 304, 477, 487, 490, 491, 496–97, 498, 500–501
Philo Records, 181, 212, 228
Piano Red (William Perryman), 259, 461–62
Pickett, Wilson, 225, 413
Pierce, Don, 245
Pig 'n' Whistle Red, 353
Pigmeat Markham, 142
Pilgrim Travelers, 249, 269
Pinetop Slim, 200, 344
Pine Top Smith, Clarence, 52–53, 310, 425
Piney Brown, 46
Plaid Records, 248
Platt, Lew, 508
Platters, 234, 240–41, 286, 287, 373
"Please, Please, Please" (James Brown), 241–42, 289
"Please Send Me Someone to Love" (Percy Mayfield), 193
"Pledging My Love" (Johnny Ace), 266, 481
Pompanelli, Rudy, 64, 114
Poppa Stoppa, 261, 355
Pops Foster, 13
Portrait Records, 238, 245
Premier Records, 212
Premium Records, 44
Presley, Elvis, xv, xxiii, xxiv, 26, 33, 34, 113, 137, 165, 166, 174, 192, 205, 207, 214, 215, 233, 264, 270, 278, 306, 320, 352, 430, 434, 477, 482, 487, 489, 496–98, *499*, 501, 502–503, 521, 523, 525, 528
Prestige Records, 11

Price, Lloyd, 36, 188–89, 261, 262, 263, 409, 524
Prisonaires, 490, 502
Professor Longhair (Henry Roeland "Roy" Byrd), 492–96
Prysock, Arthur, 468

q

Queen Records, 276
Quezergue, Wardell, 495
Quinn Studio (Houston), 230

r

RCA Victor Records, xxii, xxiv, 10, 15, 18, 19, 33, 34, 35, 37, 41, 61, 80, 133, 189, 227, 249, 271, 278, 326, 329, 335, 368, 369, 425, 427, 460–61, 480, 487, 499, 500, 503
RPM Records, 103, 201, 205, 208, 217, 415
Rabinowitz, Sol, xxi, 428, 470–72
Racial discrimination, 45, 74, 91, 93, 123, 125, 127–28, 171–72, 176, 397, 423, 449, 517, 527
Ragtime, 3
Rainbow Records, 384, 386, 427, 462
Raitt, Bonnie, xx
Rama Records, 14, 377, 429, 430, 433
Randle, Bill, 22, 85, 448, 449, 459, 464–65, 466, 498
Randy's Record Shop, 215, 365, 489
Raven Records, 429
Ravens, 133–35, 136, 232, 359, 360, 362, 366, 368, 371, 388, 397, 430
Ray, Johnnie, 291, 367, 388, 443, 445, 448–49, 502
Rays, 473, 475
Razaf, Andy, 70, 78, 345
Red Bird Records, 412, 436
Red Robin Records, 436
Red Saunders, 37, 449
Redding, Otis, 192, 268, 271, 287, 377, 385
Reed, Jimmy, 256, 258, 270, 319–20, 327, 328, 336–37, 338, 450, 469, 490
Reels, 20
Reese, Della, 368–69, 443
Regal Records, 31, 199, 345, 353, 355
Regal Theatre (Chicago), 68, 144, 155, 167
Regent Records, 199, 320, 345, 356, 451
Regis Records, 132
Reig, Teddy, 345, 356, 362
Reiner, Paul, 115, 181, 228, 239, 244, 245, 343, 466
Reinhardt, Django, 205, 217–18
René brothers (Leon and Otis), xxi, 117, 130, 150–58, 160, 181, 466
Reno Club (Kansas City), 45, 48, 49
Reprise Records, 192
Rhodes, Todd, 245, 277, 278, 280, 365, 507, 513
Rhumboogie Records, 228
Rhythm Records, 248
Rhythm and blues, xv–xx, 166, 315, 421; attitude toward, 479; audience, 335–46; decline, 523–25; humor, 390; origin, 503; revival, 526, 528; rise, 424–25, 508, 510;

sound and style, 169, 273, 290, 349, 397, 468; term, xv–xvi, xvii, 127, 221, 517
Richbourg, John R., 489, 508
Righteous Brothers, 395
Rip Records, 494
Riviera Records, 384
Rivileers, 470
Robert and Johnny, 428, 468
Robert, Dehlco, 30
Robey, Don, xx, 148, 164, 190, 314
Robins, 163, 236, 346, 390, 415
Robinson, Bobby, 201, 319, 436–39
Robinson, Jessie Mae, 70, 95, 100
Robinson, L.C. "Good Rockin'," 320
Robinson, Smokey, & the Miracles, 336, 384, 443, 524
Rocco, Maurice, 67, 76, 77, 344
Rock Around the Clock (film), 516
Rock 'n' roll, 73
Rockabilly, 64, 497, 525
Rock, Rock, Rock (film), 516
Rockin' Records, 284, 380
Rogers, Leo, 429
Rojac Records, 349
Rolling Stones, xix, 39, 155, 193, 207, 299, 300, 395, 396, 488, 491, 526
Rolontz, Bob, 425, 460–66, 512, 514
Ron Records, 494
Ronald & Ruby, xxii
Rondo Records, 359
Ronettes, 395, 433
Roosevelt, Franklin Delano, 56, 124
Rose, Philip, 426
Roulette Records, 147, 276, 347
Royal Theatre (Baltimore), 68
Royals, 168
Rubber Legs Williams, 141
Ruffin, David, 268
Ruler Records, 326
Rupe, Art, xviii, xx, 179–94, 263, 269, 314, 343
Rush, Otis, 312–14
Rushing, Jimmy, 45, 49–50, 53, 55, 65, 96, 109, 153, 203, 204, 212

S

St. Louis Jimmy (James Burke Oden), 11, 15, 24, 37–38, 42, 45, 228, 326, 425
Sainte-Marie, Buffy, 33
St. Nicholas Arena (N.Y.C.), 470, 514, 516
Satellite Records, 502
Savage, Al, 452–53
Savoy Ballroom (N.Y.C.), 50, 57, 60, 345
Savoy Records, xvii, xviii, xxii, 38, 133, 148, 161, 168–69, 173, 199, 208, 228, 245, 320, 327, 343–53, 361–62, 363–64, 366–67, 424, 425, 461, 488
Savoys, 423
Scepter Records, 137, 525
Schiffman, Bobby, 422; Frank, 68–69, 135, 422
Schoolboys, 423
Scott, Clifford, 279–80
Scott, Winfield, 376
Scrapper Blackwell, 7, 41, 310

Screamin' Jay Hawkins (Jalacy Hawkins), 439–41
Sea Ferguson, 39–40
Sears, Zenas, 354, 361, 365, 447, 465
Seeco Records, 361
Selah Jubilee Singers, 282
Sellers Recording Studio (Dallas), 112
Selvin, Joel, 248, 249, 254
Seminole, 28
Sensation Records, 199
708 Club (Chicago), 308, 313
Sepia (as a term), 344
Sepia Tones, 180, 184
Session Records, 53
Shad, Bobby, xviii, 140–44, 164
"Shake, Rattle and Roll" (Joe Turner), 379, 411
Shangri-Las, 436
Shaw, Arnold, xxii, 92, 118, 146, 206–207, 227, 256, 273, 279, 283–84, 306, 350–52, 393, 410, 418, 426–27, 473, 496–98
"Sh-Boom (Life Could Be a Dream)" (The Chords), xvii, xxvi, 135, 234, 421, 430, 523
Shepard, Ollie, 5
Sheridan, Art, 311
"Shimmy, Shimmy, Ko-Ko-Bop" (Little Anthony and the Imperials), 436
Shines, Johnny, 38, 303
Shirelles, 137, 285, 524
Shirley and Lee, 231, 233–34, 463
Sholes, Steve, xi
Shuffle, 64, 65, 73, 74, 103, 414
Siegel, Sid, 361
Sill, Lester, xviii, 114–15, 196, 390, 415–19, 417, 476
Silver, Al, xxi, 356, 427, 450–60
Silverman, Max, 365, 397, 399
Silvertone Singers, 389
Shorty George, 23
Sinatra, Frank, 50, 90, 91, 101, 147, 168, 270, 271, 446, 525
"Sincerely" (Moonglows), 293, 311
Singer, Hal, 169, 257, 356
Singleton, Charlie, 352, 409, 451–52
Sippie Wallace, 4
Sister Rosetta Tharpe, 59, 81, 344
Sittin' In With Records, 140, 142, 231, 380
"Sittin' on Top of the World" (Mississippi Sheiks), 131, 303, 305
"Sixty Minute Man" (Dominoes), 282, 420
Skip James, Nehemiah, 5
Sleepy John Estes, 21, 23, 35
Slim Harpo (James Moore), 320, 489, 490–491
Smalls, Tommy, 431, 464, 469, 509, 515
Smiley Lewis (Overton Lemon), 36, 258, 265
Smith, Arlene, 433
Smith, Bessie, 3, 4, 13, 23, 48, 51, 114, 148, 181, 261, 332, 396, 400
Smith, Clara, 4, 9
Smith, Huey "Piano," 364, 437, 491, 492, 495
Smith, Mamie, xv, xvii, 3, 4, 47, 445
Smitty's Corner (Chicago), 296, 298
"Smokestack Lightning" (Howlin' Wolf), 304
Smokey Hogg, Andrew, 194, 198, 265, 466
"So Long" (Ruth Brown), 400

Solitaires, 428, 467–68
Solo Art Records, 53
Solo Records, 41
Son Bonds, 523
Son Framion, 29
Son House, Eddie, 5, 144, 294, 301
Son Long, 53
Songbird Records, 488
Sonny Boy Williamson (original), 12, 17–18, 26, 43, 205, 219, 223, 290, 296, 310, 425, 462, 486–87, 502
Sonny Boy Williamson, the second. See Miller, William Rice.
Sonny Terry (Saunders Terrell), 9. See also Brownie McGhee.
Sonny Thompson, 279
Sonny Til. See Orioles.
Sotoplay Records, 482
Soul, 166–67, 380, 415, 441, 525–26
Soul Records, 439
Soul Stirrers, 194, 220, 269, 271–72
Spaniels, 315–16, 327
Spann, Otis, 297, 298, 308, 482
Spark Records, 346, 390, 391, 419
Specialty Records, xvii, xviii, xx, 103, 148, 179–94, 248, 260, 263, 269–70, 481, 491, 527
Speckled Red (Rufus Perryman), 27–28, 37, 100, 425
Spector, Phil, 335, 394–95, 412, 418–19, 525
"Speedo" (Cadillacs), 426
Spiders, 265
Spinners, 311
Spire Records, 215
Spirituals, 3, 97
"Spirituals to Swing" concert, 26, 48, 54
Spivey, Victoria, 4, 14
Spivey Records, 37
Staff Records, 320
Staple Singers, 258, 327–28, 332–33, 426
Star Talent Records, 493, 494, 501
Starday Records, 245, 276
Starlight Gospel Singers, 249
Starr Piano Co., 5, 37
Staton, Dakota, 368
Stax Records, 97, 269, 376, 411, 489, 491, 502, 524, 525, 528
Stewart, Rod, 33
Stick McGee, 331, 372
Stokes, Frank, 5
Stoller, Mike. See Leiber, Jerry.
Stone, Jesse, 13, 376, 398, 411
Storm, Gale, 265, 268
"Stormy Monday" (T-Bone Walker), 114–15, 118, 120
Storyville (New Orleans), 3, 20
Storyville Records, 17, 25, 29, 40, 41, 44
Strachwitz, Chris, 256–60
Street-corner groups, 422–38
Stylistics, 528
Sugar Hill (N.Y.C.), 423, 436, 467
Sun Records, xxiii, 33, 203, 487, 490, 491
Sunny Gale, 366, 427
Sunny Records, 31
Sunnyland Slim (Albert Luandrew), 17, 29, 30, 31, 38, 290, 297, 310
Sunset Club (Kansas City), 45, 46, 47, 49

Supreme Records, 81, 204, 212
Supremes, 336, 433, 524
Swallows, 428
Swan Records, 475, 525
Swing Club (L.A.), 67, 80, 94
Swing Time Records, 45, 91, 108, 111, 248, 249, 250, 251, 252
Swingin' Records, 437, 519
Sykes, Roosevelt, xviii, 6, 12, 14–17, 16, 24, 25, 26, 29, 30, 37, 43, 90, 194, 228, 425
Sylvio's (Chicago), 202, 297, 304
Symphony Sid, 32, 508

t

T-Bone Walker, Aaron, xvii, xx, xxvi, 52, 65, 96, 104, 110, 113–23, 118, 205, 208, 212, 216, 228, 249, 250, 265, 341, 486
Taj Mahal, 39
Tamla Records, 524
Tampa Red (Hudson Whittaker), 6, 8–11, 12, 17, 18, 26, 27, 40, 51, 214, 259, 296, 302, 310, 344, 425
Tarnopol, Nat, 245, 443, 444
Tarriers, 427
Tay May Club (Chicago), 201, 296
Taylor, Eddie, 327
Sam "The Man" Taylor, 174
Teacho Wilshire, 398
"Tears on My Pillow" (Little Anthony and the Imperials), 435
"Teardrops from My Eyes" (Ruth Brown), 232, 374, 406
"Tell Me So" (Orioles), 136
Temple, Johnny, 25
Tempo Tone Records, 310
Temptations, 336, 442, 524
Texas Alexander, Alger, 13, 95, 96, 100, 106, 250, 251
Theatre Owners Booking Association (TOBA), 3
"There Is Something on Your Mind" (Big Jay McNeely), 519
Thomas, Carla, 524
Thomas, Lafayette, 253–54
Thomas, Rufus, 501–502, 524
Thrasher Wanderers, 389
331 Club (L.A.), 94, 344, 519
"Three O'Clock Blues" (B.B. King), 42, 96, 110, 121, 203, 223, 250, 251, 253, 501
Thunder Smith, Wilson, 100, 259
Thunderbirds, 475
Tibbs, Andrew, 290
Tico Records, 361
Tiger Haynes, 227
Time Records, 140
Tindley, Dr. C.H., 9, 149
Tiny Bradshaw, 224, 245, 277, 278, 349
Tiny Grimes, 345, 371, 396, 439, 507
Tip Top Records, 429
"Tomorrow Night" (Lonnie Johnson), 42
Toombs, Rudolph, 350, 374, 386, 405–407
Toscano, Eli, 313
Toussaint, Allen, 438, 455–56, 471, 492
Treniers, 447
Tri Phi Records, 312
Trilon Records, 109, 249, 251, 252, 255

Triumph Records, 32, 201, 394
"Trouble Blues" (Charles Brown), 169
Trumpeters, 220
"Try Me" (James Brown), 242
Tupelo Sam, 28
Turbans, 454–55
Turner, Ike and Tina, *202*, 245, 291, 304, 487
Turner, Joe, xviii, xxiii, 45–49, 50, 54, 65, 103, 194, 203, 204, 207, 212, 223, 234, 258, 259, 262, 350, 351, 377, 379, 411, 420, 524
Turner, Sammy, 384
Turpin, Charles, 13
"Tutti Frutti" (Little Richard), 190, 268
"Tweedle Dee" (La Vern Baker), 376
"The Twist" (Hank Ballard and the Midnighters), 286, 473

u

Unart Records, 468
Uni Records, 325

v

Valens, Ritchie, 265, 523
Valentines, 430–31
Vanguard Records, 314
Varsity Records, 129, 130–31, 425
Vee Jay Records, 31, 44, 192, 201, 273, 285, 315–26, 327–29, 335, 336–40, 381, 439, 469, 490, 525
Velvets, 423
Verve Records, 7, 20, 44
Vik Records, 41, 461, 463
Vincent, Johnny, 193, 491
Vincent, Gene, 234
Vinson, Eddie "Cleanhead," 48, 143, 277
Vocaleers, 424, 436–37
Vocalion Records, 4, 6, 7, 9, 12, 14, 19, 23, 24, 25, 26, 28, 38, 47, 181, 372, 461

w

Walker, Jack, 363, 464, 469, 509
Walker, Mel, 161, 162, 345, 364, 488
"The Wallflower" (Etta James), 209, 286
Walls, Henry Van "Piano Man," 377
Wand Records, 412
Wanderers, 422
Ward, Billy, and the Dominoes, xxiv, 112, 168, 282–83, 381, 386, 387, 420, 441, 442–43, 507
Ward, Clara, 356, 361
Warwick, Dionne, 389, 433
Warwick Records, 429
Wasco Records, 494
Washboard bands, 3
Washboard Sam (Robert Brown), 5, 6, 12, 18–19, 24, 26, 43, 44, 51, 259, 344, 371, 397, 425
Washington, Dinah (Ruth Jones), xviii, xxii, 58, 65, 81, 140, 143–50, 164, 209, 221, 269, 346, 347, 350, 354, 358, 363, 403, 525, 526
Washington, Ferdinand, 481
Watch Records, 494
Waterman, Dick, 34
Watts, Dr. Isaac, 8
Watts, Noble "Thin Man," 471

Webb, Chick, 57, 61, 66, 69, 74, 242, 345
Webster, Ben, 46, 164, 215, 345
Weiss brothers (Sam and Hy), 428, 429, 466–69
Wexler, Jerry, xviii, xxi, xxiii, 314, 341, 343, 361, 370, 371, 377, 382, 385, 388, 393, 395, 400, *410–15*, 420, 421, 451, 492
"What a Difference a Day Makes" (Dinah Washington), 147
"What'd I Say" (Ray Charles), 380
Whippet Records, 390
Whirlin' Disc Records, 422
White, Georgia, 25, 51
White, Josh, 20, 26, 172, 330, 336
"Why Do Fools Fall in Love" (Frankie Lymon and the Teenagers), 234, 430, 431–32
Wild Bill Davis, 70, 79, 173
Williams, Clarence, 4
Williams, Hank, 481, 495
Williams, J. Mayo, 4, 9, 12, 22, 23, 78, 297, 372
Williams, Joe, 45, 54, 449
Williams, Larry, 101, 189, 336
Williams, Mary Lou, 46, 47, 116
Williams, Maurice, and the Zodiacs, 457–58, 490
Williams, Mel, 427
Williams, Nat D., 501, 509
Williams, Otis, and The Charms, 232, 283–84
Williams, Paul, 130, 168–69, *170*, 213, 356, 357, 362
Williams, Ralph, xxiv
Williams, Spencer, 14
Williams, Tony, 241
Willis, Chuck, 36, 232, 362, 377, 385, 408, 445, 447, 481
Willows, 208, 422
Wilson, Jackie, xxi, 168, 245, 272, 283, 420, 441–45, 485, 525
Wilson, Jimmy, 248, 255, 258
Wing Records, 266
Wings Over Jordan Choir, 318
Winter, Johnny, 33
Witherspoon, Jimmy, xxi, 195, 203–204, 210–216, 523
Wonder, Stevie, 336, 524
Wood, Randy, xviii, 325, 327–40
Wood, Maceo, 327
"Work with Me Annie" (Midnighters), 164, 209, 243–44, 285
Worry, 388, 485–86
Wyche, Sid, 387

x

XYZ Records, 473

y

"Yakety Yak" (Coasters), 392
Yancey, Jimmy, 53
"You Send Me" (Sam Cooke), 270–71
Young, Ernie, 148, 489
Young, Lester, 46, 229, 344, 356

z

Zion Kings of Harmony, 426